THE 10... OF

BUSI... ORY

THE OXFORD HANDBOOK OF

BUSINESS HISTORY

Edited by
GEOFFREY JONES
and
JONATHAN ZEITLIN

OXFORD
UNIVERSITY PRESS

OXFORD

UNIVERSITY PRESS

Great Clarendon Street, Oxford OX2 6DP

Oxford University Press is a department of the University of Oxford.
It furthers the University's objective of excellence in research, scholarship,
and education by publishing worldwide in

Oxford New York

Auckland Cape Town Dar es Salaam Hong Kong Karachi
Kuala Lumpur Madrid Melbourne Mexico City Nairobi
New Delhi Shanghai Taipei Toronto
With offices in
Argentina Austria Brazil Chile Czech Republic France Greece
Guatemala Hungary Italy Japan South Korea Poland Portugal
Singapore Switzerland Thailand Turkey Ukraine Vietnam

Oxford is a registered trade mark of Oxford University Press
in the UK and in certain other countries

Published in the United States
by Oxford University Press Inc., New York

ISBN 978-0-19-957395-0

Printed in the United Kingdom by
the MPG Books Group Ltd

ACKNOWLEDGEMENTS

The Editors would like to acknowledge the editorial and logistical assistance of Katherine McDonald at Harvard Business School in preparation of this Handbook. Katherine took on the responsibility over two years of monitoring the progress of each chapter manuscript, undertook adroit language and style editing, and engaged in regular, sometimes daily, communications with authors. At Oxford University Press, David Musson initiated the entire project, and subsequently he and Matthew Derbyshire have been unfailingly helpful and supportive as it progressed. The whole project proved rather more lengthy and time-consuming than the Editors had imagined. We would therefore like to thank our respective families, Dylan and Rattana, and Claire, Sam, and Josh.

Geoffrey Jones
Jonathan Zeitlin

Contents

PART III FUNCTIONS OF ENTERPRISE

PART IV ENTERPRISE AND SOCIETY

LIST OF FIGURES

LIST OF TABLES

Notes on the Contributors

Rolv Petter Amdam is Professor of Business History at BI Norwegian School of Management in Norway. He has a Ph.D. in History from the University of Oslo. His research interests include the history of business education, and globalization since the 1980s, with a special focus on emerging economies and cross-cultural management. He is the author of several monographs as well as numerous articles.

Trevor Boyns is Professor of Accounting and Business History at Cardiff Business School at Cardiff University, UK, where he is also Assistant Director of the Accounting and Business History Research Unit and Director of Postgraduate Studies. A former President of the Association of Business Historians, he has a Ph.D. from the University of Wales. His research interests include the economic and business history of Wales and the history of the development of cost and management accounting in Europe (especially France, the UK, Italy, and Spain). He has published widely in journals and was the founding assistant editor and currently the joint editor of *Accounting, Business & Financial History*.

Youssef Cassis is Professor of Economic and Social History at the University of Geneva, Switzerland, and a Visiting Fellow at the London School of Economics and Political Science. His publications include *City Bankers 1890–1914* (Cambridge, 1994), *Big Business: The European Experience in the Twentieth Century* (Oxford, 1997), and *Capitals of Capital: A History of International Financial Centres 1780–2005* (Cambridge, 2006). He was the co-founder, in 1994, of *Financial History Review*, which he co-edited until 2005. He is currently President of the European Business History Association.

Andrea Colli is Associate Professor in Economic History at Bocconi University, Italy, where he is the Director of the undergraduate studies program in International Markets and New Technologies and Deputy Director of EntER, a research center on entrepreneurship and entrepreneurs. He has a Ph.D. in Economic and Social History from the same university. His research interests range from family firms to the history of multinationals. He has published several books and articles on the history of the Italian industrial enterprise, the history of family capitalism, and the dynamics of small and medium-sized enterprises. He is currently a member of the Board of the European Business History Association.

Jeffrey Fear is an Associate Professor at the University of Redlands in the United States. He previously taught at Harvard Business School and the University of Pennsylvania. He has a Ph.D. in history from Stanford University. His research interests include the study of organizational capabilities and learning, German and European history, and specializes in German business history. His book, entitled *Organizing Control: August Thyssen and the Construction of German Management* (Cambridge, Mass., 2005) combines each of these interests. He has published widely in journals.

Robert Fitzgerald is Reader in Business History and International Management at Royal Holloway, University of London, UK. He has a Ph.D. from the University of London. He is the author of books and numerous journal articles on labor management, business organization, and comparative and international business, as well as marketing.

Patrick Fridenson is Professor of International Business History at the Ecole des Hautes Etudes en Sciences Sociales, Paris, France. He previously taught at the University Paris X-Nanterre, and has been Visiting Professor at the University of Tokyo. He is the author, co-author, or editor of several boks, including *The Automobile Revolution* (Chapel Hill, NC, 1982), *The French Home Front, 1914–1918* (Oxford, 1992), *Thomson's First Century* (Jouy-en-Josas, 1995), *Histoire des usines Renault*, vol. I (Paris, 1998), and the author of many articles. He is a former President of the Business History Conference of the United States and a former member of the Executive Committee of the International Economic History Association. He is editor of the journal *Entreprises et Histoire.*

W. Mark Fruin is Professor of Corporate and Global Strategy in the College of Business at San Jose State University in the United States. Currently, he is researching governance, functional and performance differences relating to hierarchical and scale-free network organizations. He is also interested in the emergence of organizational and knowledge management practices in different industry and national environments, including China, Japan, and the United States.

Howard Gospel is Professor of Management at King's College, University of London; a Research Associate at the Centre for Economic Performance, London School of Economics; and a Fellow of the Said Business School, University of Oxford, all in the UK. His research interests include the development of employer labor policy, corporate governance and human resource management, forms of employee representation, and training and development. He has published widely on these topics in historical and contemporary contexts, often with an international and comparative perspective.

Margaret B. W. Graham is Associate Professor of Strategy and Organization at the Desautels Faculty of Management, McGill University, Canada. She holds a Ph.D.

in History and an MBA from Harvard University. She has published *RCA and the VideoDisc: The Business of Research* (1986), *R&D for Industry: A Century of Technical Innovation at Alcoa* (co-authored by Bettye H. Pruitt) (1990), and *Corning and the Craft of Innovation* (co-authored by Alec T. Shuldiner) (2001). She is a founding director of the Winthrop Group, Inc., a group of consulting historians and archivists, and for several years in the 1990s she was an executive at Xerox PARC (The Palo Alto Research Center).

Gary Herrigel is Associate Professor of Political Science at the University of Chicago, United States. He received his Ph.D. from the Political Science Department and the Program in Science Technology and Society, MIT. His research interests include comparative business history, comparative industrial analysis, political economy, economic sociology, and economic geography. Herrigel has published *Industrial Constructions: The Sources of German Industrial Power* (Cambridge, 1996) and co-edited *Americanizaiton and its Limits: Reworking US Technology and Management in Postwar Europe and Japan* (Oxford, 2000) with Jonathan Zeitlin, in addition to many scholarly articles dealing with business and industrial governance matters both historical and contemporary.

Geoffrey Jones is Isidor Straus Professor of Business History, Harvard Business School, United States. He previously taught at the universities of Cambridge and Reading, and at the London School of Economics, in the UK. He is the author and editor of many books and articles on the history of international business, including *British Multinational Banking 1830–1990* (Oxford, 1993), *Merchants to Multinationals* (Oxford, 2000), *Multinationals and Global Capitalism* (Oxford, 2005), and *Renewing Unilever* (Oxford, 2005). He is a former President of both the European Business History Association and the Business History Conference of the United States, and is co-editor of the journal *Business History Review*.

Matthias Kipping is Professor of Strategic Management and Chair in Business History at the Schulich School of Business, York University, Toronto, Canada. He has degrees in history and public administration from Germany, the United States, and France, and held previous appointments at the University of Reading, UK and Universitat Pompeu Fabra, Barcelona, Spain. His main research interest is the international transfer of management knowledge, in particular the evolution and role of management consultants and management education. He has published widely on these topics in business history and management journals. A book on *The Management Consultancy Business in Historical and Comparative Perspective* is forthcoming with Oxford University Press.

Wolfgang König is Professor of the History of Technology at the Technical University of Berlin, Germany. He earned distinctions at the Verein Deutscher Ingenieure and the Verband der Elektrotechnik, Elektronik, Informationstechnik (VDE) for his contributions on the history of technology and electrical engineering and on technology assessment. His interests include the history of education, the engineering profession, and mechanical and electrical engineering, the historiography of technology, technology assessment, and the philosophy of technology. He is currently working on technology in consumer society and is finishing a book on the technical interests of Emperor Wilhelm II.

Naomi R. Lamoreaux is Professor of Economics and History at the University of California, Los Angeles in the United States and a Research Associate of the National Bureau of Economic Research. She received her Ph.D. in 1979 from the Johns Hopkins University. She has written *The Great Merger Movement in American Business, 1895–1904* (Cambridge, 1985) and *Insider Lending: Banks, Personal Connections and Economic Development in Industrial New England* (Cambridge, 1994), as well as a number of articles on various topics in business history, financial history, and the history of technology. Her current research interests include projects on the organization of invention in the late nineteenth and early twentieth century United States, corporate governance and business's choice of organizational form in the United States and France in the same period, and the emergence of the public/private distinction in American history.

Luca Lanzalaco teaches Political Science and Public Policy at the University of Macerata, Italy. He is the author of numerous books and articles in Italian and English on political institutions and the organization of business interests, including *Dall'impresa all'associazione. Le organizzazioni degli imprenditori: La Confindustria in prospettiva comparata* (Milan, 1990); *Le politiche istituzionali* (Bologna, 1995); *Istituzioni, organizzazioni, potere: Introduzione all'analisi istituzionale della politica* (Rome, 1995); and *Istituzioni, amministrazioni, politica: Analisi delle istituzioni e ruolo degli apparati amministrativi* (Naples, 2000).

William Lazonick is University Professor at the University of Massachusetts Lowell, United States, and Distinguished Research Professor at INSEAD, France. His research seeks to understand how institutions and organizations support innovative enterprise, and the implications for income distribution and employment stability.

Michel Lescure is Professor of Economic and Social History at the University of Paris X-Nanterre, France. His publications on business and financial history include *Les banques, l'Etat et le marché immobilier en France à l'époque contemporaine* (Paris, 1982), *PME et croissance économique en France dans les années 1920* (Paris, 1996), *Banques locales et banques régionales en Europe au XXe siècle*, edited with Alain Plessis (Paris, 2004). He is currently the manager of the research center Institutions et Dynamiques Historiques de l'Economie.

Kenneth Lipartito is Professor of History at Florida International University, United States, and editor of *Enterprise & Society: The International Journal of*

Business History. A specialist on technology, business, and culture, he is the author or editor of five books, including *Constructing Corporate America: History, Politics, Culture* (Oxford, 2004), *Investing for Middle America: John Elliott Tappan and the Origins of American Express Financial Advisors* (New York, 2001), and *The Bell System and Regional Business: The Telephone in the South, 1877–1920* (Baltimore, 1989). His articles have appeared in numerous journals.

Robert Millward has been Professor of Economic History at the University of Manchester in the UK since 1989, having previously held the Chair in Economics at the University of Salford. His research interests are in economic organization, including the history and economics of industry and the public sector. He has published widely in journals. His latest book is *Private and Public Enterprise in Europe: Energy, Telecommunications and Transport: c 1830–1990* (Cambridge, 2005).

Daniel M. G. Raff is Associate Professor of Management at the Wharton School and Associate Professor of History in the School of Arts and Sciences at the University of Pennsylvania in the United States. He is also a Research Associate of the National Bureau of Economic Research. He previously held teaching appointments at the business and law schools of Columbia University, the Harvard Business School, and Oxford University. He has published widely in journals such as *American Economic Review, American Historical Review, Business History Review, Journal of Economic History*, and *Journal of Political Economy*.

Mary Rose is Professor of Entrepreneurship in the Institute of Entrepreneurship and Enterprise Development in the Management School at Lancaster University, UK. She specializes in business history, especially international perspectives on family business and also the history of textiles. Throughout, her work has linked business history methodology with the study of entrepreneurship and her most recent work explores these links to the field of innovation. She has published numerous books, edited collections, and journal articles. She is Director of the Pasold Research Fund and was President of the European Business History Association 2003–5.

Peter Temin is Elisha Gray II Professor of Economics at the Massachusetts Institute of Technology (MIT), United States. He was a Junior Fellow at the Harvard Society of Fellows and has a Ph.D. in Economics from MIT. He was Head of the Economics Department and currently is its Director of Graduate Studies. His research interests include the development of American business and industry in the nineteenth and twentieth centuries. He has written books on the iron and steel and pharmaceutical industries, edited books on business history more generally, and written many articles on business and economic history.

Kathleen Thelen is the Payson S. Wild Professor of Political Science at Northwestern University in the United States, and a Permanent External Scientific Member of the Max Planck Institute for the Study of Societies in Cologne, Germany. Her most recent single-authored book, *How Institutions Evolve: The Political Economy of Skills in Germany, Britain, the United States and Japan* (Cambridge, 2004) was selected as winner of the 2006 Mattei Dogan Award of the Society for Comparative Research and co-winner of the 2005 Woodrow Wilson Foundation Award of the American Political Science Association. Other recent publications include *Beyond Continuity: Institutional Change in Advanced Political Economies* (co-edited with Wolfgang Streeck, Oxford, 2005).

Behlül Üsdiken is Professor of Management and Organization at Sabanci University, Istanbul, Turkey. He has previously taught at Bogaziçi University and Koç University. His research has appeared in numerous journals. He was co-editor of *Organization Studies* 1996–2001. His research interests are in organization theory, history of managerial thought, and history of management education.

R. Daniel Wadhwani is Assistant Professor of Management and Fletcher Jones Professor of Entrepreneurship, University of the Pacific in the United States. He previously taught at Harvard Business School and the University of Pennsylvania. His research interests include entrepreneurship and financial system development in historical perspective. His co-authored paper with Geoffrey Jones, "Schumpeter's Plea: Historical Approaches to the Study of Entrepreneurship", won the Best Conceptual Paper Prize from the American Academy of Management's Entrepreneurship Division in 2006.

Jonathan Zeitlin is Professor of Sociology, Public Affairs, Political Science, and History at the University of Wisconsin–Madison in the United States, where he is also Director of the Center for World Affairs and the Global Economy (WAGE), and Founding Director the European Union Center of Excellence. He previously taught at Birkbeck College, London, and was Research Fellow at King's College, Cambridge, in the UK. He is the author and editor of numerous books and articles on the comparative and historical analysis of business organization, employment relations, and socio-economic governance, including *Local Players in Global Games: The Strategic Constitution of a Multinational Corporation* (Oxford, 2005), *Governing Work and Welfare in a New Economy: European and American Experiments* (Oxford, 2003), *Americanization and its Limits: Reworking US Technology and Management in Post-War Europe and Japan* (Oxford, 2000), and *World of Possibilities: Flexibility and Mass Production in Western Industrialization* (Cambridge, 1997). He is co-editor of the journal *Socio-Economic Review*, a member of the editorial board of *Enterprise & Society*, and a former Trustee of the Business History Conference.

CHAPTER 1

···

INTRODUCTION

···

GEOFFREY JONES
JONATHAN ZEITLIN

THIS Handbook provides a state-of-the-art survey of research in business history. Business historians study the historical evolution of business systems, entrepreneurs, and firms, as well as their interaction with their political, economic, and social environment. They address issues of central concern to researchers in management studies and business administration, as well as economics, sociology, and other social sciences, and to historians. They employ a range of qualitative and quantitative methodologies, but all share a belief in the importance of understanding change over time.

As the chapters in this Handbook show, this research domain is wide-ranging, dynamic, and has generated compelling empirical data, which sometimes confirms and sometimes contests widely held views in management and the social sciences. However, much of this research is presented in specialist journals and in books, a form of publication which business historians—like other historians—regard as essential for understanding complex issues, but which most management and social science researchers seldom read. As a result, business history research is often overlooked, even by scholars who assert that "history matters" or emphasize the importance of path dependencies. This Handbook seeks to liberate this research, by presenting it in a form that researchers in other disciplines can discover and access.

For many years by far the most recognized scholar in business history was Alfred D. Chandler Jr. Although business history had been written for several decades before Chandler began publishing in the late 1950s and 1960s, he is rightly regarded as the founder of the modern subject. Chandler was so influential not only because he undertook first-rate historical research, but also because he advanced a number of general propositions which exercised enormous influence on a generation of management researchers. In three major studies, each dealing with the growth of big business in manufacturing since the nineteenth century and its role in the growth of the United States as the world's largest economy, Chandler identified the role of organization building and professional management in the performance of firms. Chandler (1962), in a study which considers the growth of the multidivisional organization during the first half of the twentieth century, argued that new organizational structures result from changes in the strategic direction of firms. Chandler (1977), which examined the rise of large-scale business in the United States before 1940, explored why professional managers replaced markets in co-coordinating goods and services. Chandler (1990), which made a comparison between the United States, Great Britain, and Germany, showed how firms that made a three-pronged investment in production, distribution, and management were able to become first-movers in many industries.

The influence of Chandler's insights and research is acknowledged in many essays in this volume. Some essays are focused on the central themes in Chandler's work, such as the growth of big business (Cassis) and innovation (Graham). However the chapters in the Handbook also demonstrate how far contemporary business history has moved beyond the Chandlerian paradigm, with its focus on large manufacturing firms, mass production, mass distribution, and corporate R&D; its presentation of the US case as a normative, even teleological model of business development; and its explanation of the rise of the modern managerial enterprise as a functional response to the imperatives of markets and technologies.

The chapters in this Handbook demonstrate how research agendas have changed and broadened. There is much more research on forms of business enterprise beyond the large, vertically integrated, horizontally diversified, professionally managed corporation. These include industrial districts and clusters (Zeitlin), family enterprises (Colli and Rose), business groups (Fruin), and entrepreneurial start-ups (Jones and Wadhwani). There is also much more emphasis on the porous and variable boundaries of the firm (many of whose "core" functions such as finance, research, or human resource management may be wholly or partially externalized) in different national, sectoral, and historical contexts, as well as on the reciprocal interactions between business enterprises and their cultural and political environment. There has also been a distinct shift in chronological focus. While the hundred years between 1850 and 1950 were central to Chandler's work, the Handbook essays report extensive research conducted on the business history of the second half of the twentieth century. This was an era during which, for example, large diversified and integrated firms were replaced in part by markets or networks, while the global pre-eminence of US-based firms was challenged in many sectors.

Even where the focus remains Chandlerian, addressing big business, mass distribution, or corporate R&D, the Handbook chapters demonstrate how recent scholarship has greatly qualified if not overturned altogether some of the key claims of the Chandlerian paradigm, concerning the national and sectoral incidence of large managerial enterprises, the origins and effectiveness of the multidivisional form, and the centrality of internal "paths of learning" to technological innovation. Business historians have not converged on a full-fledged alternative to the Chandlerian paradigm, but the field has nonetheless evolved over the past generation in a much more open and pluralistic direction.

The Handbook shows that the growth of comparative research has been an important driver of changing scholarly agendas. While the prevalence of quantitative methodologies and the consequent need for large datasets has contributed to an overwhelming focus on the United States in many areas of management research, the chapters in this Handbook demonstrate how far business history has developed into a truly international and comparative field, and how much it has to gain by embracing a more fully global perspective. Most business historians still work primarily within their own national frameworks. This provides one important obstacle to accessing the literature, which is often written in languages other than English. However, as the following chapters show, the leading scholars in the field are increasingly capable of drawing sophisticated, fine-grained comparisons across different countries and regions, at least among the advanced industrialized economies of North America, Western Europe, and East Asia. A number of the contributors to this Handbook examine the cross-border activities and strategies of firms, states, business associations, cartels, entrepreneurial diaspora, and other transnational actors. Their international and comparative perspective raises new questions about national trajectories of business development, and enables business historians to contribute actively to current debates in adjacent fields such as comparative political economy and global history.

The wide-ranging topics and approaches covered by this Handbook reflect the fact that business history, as both a body of literature and a community of academic researchers, has both a narrow and a broad definition. The narrower definition includes researchers who conduct primary archival research, although using a plurality of sources and methods, on the history of business enterprises, who belong to the professional business history societies now established in many countries, and publish in the "core" business history journals, including *Business History*, *Business History Review*, *Enterprises et Histoire*, *Enterprise & Society*, *Japan Business History Review*, and *Zeitschrift für Unternehmensgeschichte*. The broader definition comprises scholars from a variety of social science disciplines (including management studies) who study the historical development of business (sometimes doing original archival research of their own, and sometimes bringing new theoretical perspectives and conceptual frameworks to bear on existing research).

These two circles interact and enrich the field, which remains open to multiple methodologies and new questions, without falling under the spell of crippling orthodoxies which constrain research agendas. This is evident in the four opening chapters of the Handbook on the relationship between business history and other adjacent disciplines (history, neo-classical economics, evolutionary/institutional economics, and management), as well as in many of the more thematic chapters that explore key issues in contemporary political economy and/or management debates, including corporate governance (Herrigel), entrepreneurship (Jones and Wadhwani), industrial districts (Zeitlin), finance (Lescure), business interest associations (Lanzalaco), and skill formation and training (Thelen).

The "open architecture" of business history as a discipline means that it is unusually well-placed to participate in vigorous two-way exchanges with scholars in adjacent fields. On the one hand, careful empirical research by business historians can effectively challenge or qualify many of the "stylized facts" on which influential theoretical analyses in the social sciences sometimes rest. Corporate governance and financial systems are particularly striking examples, as few if any of the typological frameworks influential in the comparative literature (insiders vs. outsiders, stakeholders vs. stockholders, banks vs. capital markets, common vs. civil law) can account persuasively for the range of variation observed by historians over long time periods within and across countries. On the other hand, comparative social-scientific analyses suggest new questions for business historians, concerning the morphology and explanation of cross-national differences in the organization of business interest associations, the development of vocational education and training systems, and other similar issues which have not hitherto figured prominently in national historiographies.

The organization of this volume reflects and embodies these broad trends in the field. Part I examines the central methodological approaches and theoretical debates within business history, while situating them in terms of its complex, overlapping relationship to other adjacent fields. Part II surveys a variety of forms of business organization and emphasizes the diversity of routes to economic efficiency and business success in different times and contexts. Part III focuses on a series of key functional activities of business enterprise (including some that are often neglected in the narrower business history literature such as design and engineering and accounting systems), analyzing the variety of institutional mechanisms through which these have been performed inside and outside the firm itself. Part IV considers the changing relationship between firms and their wider social, cultural, and political contexts, stressing the reciprocal interactions between enterprise and society.

No single volume can be fully comprehensive. There are topics to which the editors would have liked to devote greater coverage. These include the regulatory role of the state, for example through antitrust/competition, industrial, and environmental policy, which is addressed in the chapters by Millward on business and the state and by Fear on cartels among others, but which merits more extensive comparative analysis.

There are two serious omissions caused by the inability of the commissioned authors to complete chapters due to other obligations. We had hoped to include a chapter on the role of gender in business by Mary Yeager. This is an important research area which is highlighted in a number of chapters, including Fridenson, Colli and Rose, Jones and Wadhwani, and Lipartito, but which deserves a full-scale chapter of its own in which the largely national studies to date could be placed in a systematic comparative context. Kwolek-Folland (1998) provides a pioneering historical overview of women in business in the United States, while Yeager (1999) provides an edited collection of studies from around the world.

The editors had also hoped to include essays on business history in developing countries, but this goal was abandoned after C. K. Lai was unable to complete his essay on the business history of the Chinese-speaking world. The literature on the history of business beyond the United States, Western Europe, and Japan is not extensive, but it is growing. Both Canada and Australia have quite extensive business history literatures which are rarely incorporated into wider narratives (Taylor and Baskerville 1994; Fleming *et al.* 2004). The literature on developing countries is scarcer, and also overlooked. Monolingual English speakers are often simply unaware of the increasingly rich literature in Spanish on Latin America and in Chinese on East Asia. Family firms and business groups feature extensively in much of this literature, as do relations with governments and the historical impact of imperialism. A number of chapters in this Handbook, however, do extend their thematic analyses beyond the industrialized world to cover the colonial, post-colonial, and emerging markets in Asia, Latin America, and Africa. For further information, there are valuable surveys of the business history literature on China by Faure (2006), on India by Tripathi (2004), and on Latin America by Barbero (2003). Tignor (2007) discusses the limited research undertaken as yet on the business history of Africa.

REFERENCES

BARBERO, MARÍA INES (2003). "Business History in Latin America: Issues and Debates", in F. Amatori and G. Jones (eds.), *Business History around the World*. New York: Cambridge University Press.

CHANDLER, A. D. (1962). *Strategy and Structure: Chapters in the History of the American Industrial Enterprise*. Cambridge, Mass.: MIT Press.

—— (1977). *The Visible Hand: The Managerial Revolution in American Business*. Cambridge, Mass.: Harvard University Press.

—— (1990). *Scale and Scope*. Cambridge, Mass.: Harvard University Press.

FAURE, D. (2006). *China and Capitalism: A History of Business Enterprise in Modern China.* Hong Kong: Hong Kong University Press.

FLEMING, G., MERRETT, D., and VILLE, S. (2004). *The Big End of Town: Big Business and Corporate Leadership in Twentieth-Century Australia.* Cambridge: Cambridge University Press.

KWOLEK-FOLLAND, A. (1998). *Incorporating Women: A History of Women and Business in the United States.* New York: Twayne.

TAYLOR, G. D., and BASKERVILLE, P. A. (1994). *A Concise History of Business in Canada.* Toronto: Oxford University Press.

TIGNOR, R. L. (2007). "The Business Firm in Africa". *Business History Review*, 81/ 1, p. 87–110.

TRIPATHI, D. (2004). *The Oxford History of Indian Business.* New Delhi: Oxford University Press.

YEAGER, M. (ed.) (1999). *Women in Business.* Cheltenham: Edward Elgar.

PART I

APPROACHES AND DEBATES

CHAPTER 2

BUSINESS HISTORY AND HISTORY

PATRICK FRIDENSON

2.1 INTRODUCTION

BUSINESS history as a specific field was not born inside the historical profession. It appeared in the United States at Harvard Business School in 1927. N. S. B. Gras held the first chair in business history. There is no doubt that the funding for this position came in reaction to the "muckraking" critiques that had dominated public discourse since the turn of the century in order to promote a positive view of the business world (Tedlow 1985). Very early the new field attracted attention elsewhere. The new and innovative French historical journal the *Annales*, founded by Marc Bloch and Lucien Febvre in 1929, carried an article by Gras as early as January 1931. Marc Bloch had been in contact with Gras in 1929 suggesting the foundation of an "American *Annales*" (Harvey 2004). Under the modest title, "Business and Business History", the American historian suggested that the young subdiscipline should expand globally and enrich historical knowledge. However, these hopes of internationalization would be fulfilled only after World War II. Today business history has indeed become universal. For quite a while, however, and in spite of the initial support from the *Annales*, the value and methods of business history were questioned by many historians—first by economic historians and later by others. At the same time, the fact that business history could be taught in departments other than history, mostly business administration and economics, meant that its practitioners could come from these very disciplines and that research and teaching in business history brought them in contact with the trends at work in the historical profession.

The purpose of this chapter is to assess the results of this double process for a field which is thus steeped in two worlds: inside history and outside history. What has business history brought to historians? What have historians brought to business history? This will lead to a third question: how do business historians fare within the historical profession?

2.2 THE IMPACT OF BUSINESS HISTORY

2.2.1 An Array of New Sources

The growth of business history has enriched the repertory of sources in three significant ways. From the 1950s business history has been one of the pioneering forces for oral history. The 150 life stories of Ford Motor Company managers and employees gathered by the American historian Allan Nevins and his team as one of the foundations for their three-volume history of the firm was a path-breaking event (Nevins with Hill 1954–63). They helped to make oral history credible. Business history never fell into the religious wars that general history fought from the 1970s onward about the validity of such sources (Descamps 2001). Business historians have known from the start that they had to apply the same critical stance to oral evidence as to other sources. They began to think about the role of memory in shaping the recollections they gathered and about the role of the historian in the construction of oral testimony. At the same time they became conscious that the historian when doing oral history is not in the same position as in a library or in an archival depot. He or she is playing a social role and becomes involved in a web of expectations and relationships. Oral history has become a standard practice in business history for the study of the 20th and 21st centuries to an extent that is still unrivaled in most other parts of the historical profession.

Business archives and those of related institutions (like chambers of commerce or trade associations) have gradually been visited by historians in pursuit of more general themes. For example, a French historian has shown that in the first half of the 19th century the Paris Chamber of Commerce was a major site for the elaboration and discussion of economic knowledge and in some cases more important than universities or engineering schools (Lemercier 2003). An American historian was able to analyze the rebuilding of continental "bourgeois Europe" in the aftermath of World War I and in an age of inflation by tapping the resources of leading Italian, German, and French companies' archives to check the actions and representations of business leaders in relation to other leaders and to the masses (Maier 1975). A British historian changed the understanding of the French Popular Front by showing that the surprise expressed by the business and government negotiators after the Matignon Agreement on June 7, 1936 was a pure legend deliberately fabricated in order to justify their respective concessions and that the bargaining had been prepared by secret contacts (Rossiter 1987).

Products, artifacts, machines, buildings—in short material culture—have been used quite early and extensively as sources by business historians. This interest in material culture was also motivated by a growing relationship between business history and history of technology. Gradually business historians have learned to act as antiquarian engineers and to carry out close studies of the three-dimensional objects themselves. In this manner, business historians have been part and parcel of the move that led from industrial archaeology to industrial heritage (Chapman and Chambers 1970). It should immediately be added that they were not the only ones. In Sweden the initiative came in the 1970s from workers, with the movement "Dig where you stand". Ten thousand groups of "barefoot researchers" studied the history of their own jobs and workplaces. It was the starting point for similar activities in other countries like Canada or Germany (Thompson and Burchardt 1982).

2.2.2 The Return of the Actors

After the end of World War II, historical research became dominated by what could be termed anonymous forces. There was the spread of the economic history of prices and, in parallel, of crises, both of which had begun in the 1930s and emphasized the role of the conjuncture. There was Fernand Braudel's flamboyant geohistory, which focused on space, cultural areas, and climate. Marxism, influential not only in Eastern Europe but also in Japan, gave priority to macro-categories like capital, profit, rent, labor, and wages. Economics, fueled by macroeconomics, played a similar part with such concepts as growth, development, and take-off. In Latin America at the time, development and underdevelopment were the only questions raised by historians. On top of this came the impact of theoretical approaches which became influential in the 1960s such as modernization theory versus cliometrics in the US and structuralism in Europe. In this context the works of business historians worldwide, even when they were centered on the firm and not the entrepreneur, helped to provide an alternative to the structuralist or macro approach which grew and came to dominate not only economic history, but most of the social sciences. Here actors never disappeared, even when they were usually limited to three categories: owners, entrepreneurs, and managers. When the structuralist and macro approaches broke down at the end of the 1970s, business historians were ready for the new trend, often termed the return of the actors.

But in fact what they had to offer to other historians was a qualified return of the actors. This can be shown by looking at two of their main concepts: decision and strategy. Decision in business was not a spasm of the free and voluntary actor, as in political, military, or religious history. It was a process—a continuum of reflections, projects, conflicts, and compromises. Such an approach is exemplified in the book of the Japanese business historian Akio Okochi, *Management in Vision. The Entrepreneurs: How they Make Decisions* (approximate translation of the Japanese title; Okochi 1979). A major qualification has been added by the historical alternatives approach jointly introduced 20 years ago by Charles Sabel and Jonathan Zeitlin (Zeitlin, this volume). In particular, it showed that for any given problem in business there was no automatic solution, or no "one best way" as American consultant Frederick W. Taylor would have put it, but always a choice between two or several possibilities. This was a major blow against historical determinism and functionalism. The time was gone when leading economic historians like François Crouzet could explain the First Industrial Revolution in Britain by the exhaustion of British forests as a source of energy. This approach even cautioned business historians against the seductions of the models of irreversibility and path-dependence later successfully devised by economist W. Brian Arthur and economic historian Paul David (Arthur 1994; David 1997). Actors and organizations were not trapped for eternity within their walls. There could be periods and conditions when viable alternatives could be designed and tested. Later, in a second step, business historians showed that, even with the emphasis on the possibility of choice just hinted at, such deliberation about alternatives could not always explain the outcome. There were major cases where a gap could be identified between the available options as presented in written and oral sources and the final decision (Lamoreaux 2001). It is arguable that, in conjunction with the works of political scientists, these approaches have modified to a certain extent the view of decision making in other fields of history.

Even more influential was the concept of strategy. Reinvented in 1962 by the American business historian Alfred D. Chandler (Chandler 1962), a strategy characterized "the determination of fundamental long term goals for an enterprise, the adoption of action goals and the allocation of the necessary resources". The long-term vision was defined by a leading group of entrepreneurs, managers, and owners to select technology, markets, and institutional adaptations in order to improve performance. It was inscribed in organizational structures. Companies were institutions with goals. It meant that companies were not simply opportunistic or adapting to external change. They would be rational actors, behaving functionally in relation to their resources, previous experiences, and competitors, by mobilizing their current or potential assets and assessing their short-term results in connection with their view of the future. In other words, organizations were ruled by inertia and a change in strategy would appear only when the environment modified itself, including the eruption of crises. In European history, the concept of strategy became all the more popular as the French sociologist Pierre Bourdieu defined it in 1972 in rather similar terms for both individuals and social groups, to the point that he lauded Chandler's analyses in one of his last books (Bourdieu 2005). But historical sociology (Freeland 2001) has recently challenged some major bases of this approach, as it mobilized first-hand material on "furious conflicts" between owners and top management of corporations and stressed the dangers of "overlooking the social and nonrational bases of corporate governance", a scholarly result that historians of non-economic types of organizations should bear in mind.

2.2.3 From Economic to Political Crises

The analysis of decision and of strategy by business historians brought nothing new to historians in terms of the different dimensions and scales of time, compared to Braudel's conceptualization ranging from market time to *longue durée*, which has still to be replaced. Nor did it alter historians' established understanding of crises. Accordingly, although regularly confronted with the manifestations of various types of crises in the firms that they research, business historians interpreted them either as accidents or as effects of the conjuncture and the external environment or as consequences of "erroneous strategic choices". Indeed, there is no entry for crisis in the index of the recent survey edited by Amatori and Jones (2003).

Yet it should be immediately observed that in studying one type of crisis—wars—business historians, often after a period of hesitation, finally did remarkably well. Just as a French Prime Minister observed in World War I that war is too serious a business to be left to generals, it is also too serious to be left to military historians. The history of armament firms—such as Putilov in Russia, Vickers in Britain, Krupp in Germany, Schneider in France, and Ansaldo in Italy—has attracted many business historians. One now classical approach deals with how these firms pioneer technologies that then become civilian and thus dual (Fridenson 2004*a*). For the United States, David Hounshell, building on the earlier work of historians of technology (Smith 1977), has argued that the fountainhead of mass production was US government armories, driven by the "technological enthusiasm" of engineers "heedless of cost" (Hounshell 1984). But one of his colleagues, Donald Hoke, has replied that the American system of manufactures had also another origin, via cost-conscious private entrepreneurs (Hoke 1990). A similar argument to Hounshell's has been presented for France: the search for interchangeable parts began there, in the late 18th century, with military engineers (Alder 1997). As the Italian case in particular shows (Segreto 1997), armament companies establish webs of connections with government and public agencies as well as with political parties. Their engineers and workers often enjoy a specific status. They play a specific part in national economic development and in international relations. The taxation of war profits is a highly contentious issue which may take many years to settle.

The regulation of the international arms trade since the end of World War II is of major importance in scientific, economic, and political terms, as recent works on COCOM have begun to show. To quote Luciano Segreto, business historians are tracking the affairs of no less than two Roman gods, Mars and Mercury. Beyond firms specializing in armament, the outbreak of war extends this orientation to formerly civilian firms. This is a particularly complex task for multinationals. Here the work of the American historian of multinationals Mira Wilkins should be mentioned. In her pioneering history of Ford as a multinational (Wilkins and Hill 1964), she was the first to show what could happen in the subsidiaries of the same multinational situated in enemy nations. More generally, business historians were able to show that wars could not be dealt with as simple parentheses in economic growth or as periods of destruction of lives, infrastructures, and capital. They are major episodes in the learning of people and organizations, in the modifications of their representations, in the change of their products, markets, and performances, and in networks and trade associations. They also matter in the renewal of business elites. In Japan and Germany a number of family dynasties were replaced by salaried managers, and this shift influenced the postwar boom (Morikawa 1992; Joly 1996). The reconversion of war industries to peace production is often a source of crises. But it also creates incentives to transfer experts and skilled workers with advanced knowledge, like the Japanese military aircraft engineers whose capabilities have been revealed by business historians to have been key to the modernization of the postwar Japanese automobile industry. On a more dramatic issue, research on the expropriation of Jewish business property during World War II initiated by Swiss historians (Bergier 2002), soon followed by historians of other nations, greatly extended our understanding of the genocide as well as showing the dispersion of the size of such enterprises and also the courage of persecuted Jews.

Similarly, the significance of periods of dictatorship has become much better appreciated since business historians contributed to their approach. This includes China, Japan, Latin America, as well as Germany, Austria, Italy, Portugal, Spain, and Greece. It also includes Eastern Europe and Russia. The old question of financial support of authoritarian regimes by parts of business elites has found new examples, but such studies generally showed that after the seizure of power, tensions and contradictions were inevitable between former partners because of the difference of agendas and horizons. They also indicated that authoritarian regimes nevertheless promoted state-owned enterprises and in some cases welcomed subsidiaries of multinational enterprises (Chick and Lanthier 2004). In the Soviet Union, Eastern Europe, and China, on the contrary, business historians demonstrated the permeability and subordination of state-appointed management to political representatives inside and outside (Cohen 2004).

Another area where business history has illuminated major questions has been its contribution to understanding decolonization. The role of business enterprises in colonial and postcolonial English-speaking Africa has been upgraded, showing competition and conflict between colonial firms and local enterprises (Tignor 1998). In India, indigenous entrepreneurs were able to take over British firms long before the end of the British Empire and rapidly thereafter (Misra 1999). In the French Empire large colonial firms struggled first against independence, but were flexible enough to anticipate decolonization and managed to stage their reconversion, i.e. stay afterwards and integrate the independent economies into the European economic space (Hodeir 2003). But we do not yet have researches on the former French colonies' business people comparable to those already available on India or Nigeria.

2.2.4 The Dynamics of Change

But more generally history is par excellence focused on the interpretation of change. I would like to sketch out various ways in which business historians have attempted to make a contribution to history in that perspective. Of course, this is an oversimplification as business history is never pure, but always impregnated by business administration, economics, sociology, political science, and today tempted by constructivist models.

Business history's input is rich and varied. First, no longer limiting itself to the study of headquarters devising strategies, products, and services top down and experiencing turning points, it highlights firms as organizations within which change takes place (Hounshell 1984; Freeland 2001; Jones 2005b). Second, while of course most enterprises have not persisted, and many have split (as in India during the 20 years after the 1947 independence: Tripathi 2004), business history depicts some enterprises as islands of relative stability on a sea of economic fluctuations and continuous market evolution.

Stability is presented as having two external sources. The first are national cultures, as reflected inside companies and in their relations with the outside world. In India the central role of families in society accounts for the predominance of family businesses and their remarkable durability (Dutta 1997; Lachaier 1999). In the Netherlands there is an emphasis on managers possessing an engineering or technical background and logic of mutual trust (Blanken 1999). German business historians have been busy for 30 years investigating whether their society followed a specific path (*Sonderweg*) leading to a "Rhenish capitalism" connecting business, labor, and government. This approach may have some limitations in hiding intra-national contrasts and the multiple ways in which firms interpret the national culture, as well as obscuring the openness of most national cultures to international influences and collaborations (Herrigel 1996). However, its immediate effects are quite positive. It puts business historians on the path of comparative history. This is no small result. In 1928 the French medieval historian Marc Bloch launched the first major call for comparative history. Its development was much slower than expected. Yet we should recognize that this is one of the areas in history where at least a fraction of business historians have been in the foreground. In Europe, America, and Japan during the past 20 years more and more cross-national comparisons and studies of national differences have been launched by single authors (see for instance Chandler 1990; Welskopp 1994; Cassis 1997; or Jacoby 2005) or by international teams. Binational firms (Jones 2005*b*) or joint ventures have also attracted business historians' attention. A related issue is that of "collaborative capitalism" (Sabel and Zeitlin 2004). Such initiatives also find echoes among political economists, with the Varieties of Capitalism school (Hall and Soskice 2001).

Another source of stability is, since the late 19th century, the growing use of management tools, from accounting ratios to communication systems, from market surveys to motivation studies and from operational research to total quality management (Yates 1989; Shiomi and Wada 1995). These invisible instruments are produced by engineers, accountants, consultants, and even academics. They are on the market. They embody knowledge. They crystallize information, experience, and innovation. They interlock managerial beliefs, technologies, and document types. Their introduction by companies with or without consultants, in their original form or in a modified version, is usually quite lengthy and complex and sometimes difficult (McKenna 2006). Their efficiency has an often unforeseen price: they solidify practices, relations, structures. They are initially loaded with meaning and contribute to motivate executives and employees, but gradually lose some of their significance and hence the institutions have to be recalibrated. Business history adds two caveats. These tools may be used as tricks to win the cooperation of managers to corporate policies (Freeland 2001). Their stability may lead to obsolescence and thus to inaccurate information and misleading targets (Johnson and Kaplan 1987). This approach has received interest on behalf of historians interested in regulation and who are looking to understand how rules come to be adopted and to be abandoned. It also draws the attention of historians of technology who focus more on visible instruments.

Stability is also ascribed by business historians to two types of internal causes. Firms, just like most other human organizations, are at one level physical and technical spaces which ingrain their logic, their architecture and technical solutions, and their procedures and constraints. Historians see the competition between greenfield and brownfield plants. On another, more abstract level, business historians are all sensitive to the inertia of organizational systems. This approach puts them in contact with historians of political parties, bureaucracies, and churches. Together they disagree, however, with the sociology of organizations which believes that in such systems the initiative of the actors is marginal or peripheral.

Also, when business history depicts firms as agents of change, it produces three areas of possible encounters with other historians. One is the relation of tradition and change. Whereas previously business history just extolled innovation, new products, and services, if not new industries, in a quite Schumpeterian way, in recent years it has moved to a much greater consideration of tradition. "Traditional" industries have continued for a relatively long time. They can bring the profits necessary for investments in other fields and broaden markets. They can be carried on side by side with modern production for quite a while. Here Japanese business historians have been highly innovative by describing the potential of such neglected firms producing pottery, soy sauce, or refined sake thanks either to cottage industry or to modern manufacturing (Kasuya 2004). Similarly, Swiss and French historians have rehabilitated the potential of mountain-based traditional industries, like clock-making, founded upon agricultural solidarity and demand (Judet 2004). In the United States between the Civil War and World War I, specialty firms making goods to order or in batches—i.e. not featuring stadardized production—created regional synergies and economies of scope and diversity; they had a crucial impact on the development of the second industrial revolution (Scranton 1997). Tradition in a specific firm may not necessarily be an obstacle to progress, but can be a point of departure for gradual change and for organizational learning. Here the pioneering three-volume work by Japanese historian You Nakanishi, which explores in great detail the shift in Nagasaki shipyards from traditional works to modern, presents a model study (Nakanishi 1982–2003).

A further area where business history has stimulated interest among historians is, by contrast, a negative vision of change—processes leading to the closing (or relocation) of companies, plants, offices and the discontinuation of products and services, even to the destruction of capital or know-how. Social, cultural, and political historians see their impact on employment, welfare, age structures, housing, education, votes, and cultural activities and explore the ways in which local communities in relation to local and national governments struggle between renewal and decay. Business historians who were previously seen by other historians as preaching the stability of the large corporation have become messengers of the importance of uncertainty and risk, hence of flexibility, in human actions. I have therefore recently argued that business failure has become a necessary dimension of the future of business history (Fridenson 2004*b*).

A third area is a positive view of change. This was already true of the picture of proto-industrialization that emerged from the works of economic historians. Business historians analyzing industrialization have either continued it by applying their lens to industrial districts past and present (Zeitlin, this volume) or have qualified it by emphasizing the role of the merchant economy in the first industrial revolution itself (Gervais 2004). Furthermore innovation, usually building on the works of the economists and in particular a neo-Schumpeterian perspective, has been their leitmotiv. Business historians have shown the gaps and processes between projects and achievements and the many pitfalls that separate invention from marketable and profitable innovation, including innovation failures. They have stressed the available options: continuous improvement, repeated innovation, and breakthrough. They have related them to external institutions and to regulation. For instance, Akio Okochi (1992) focused on the invention of activities and connected their development to the patent system. Business historians readily extended the concept of innovation to human resource management, marketing, finance, and now sustainable development (see Graham, this volume). However, a few major points should be emphasized. What business history offers to other historians are patterns of how institutions overcome zones of tensions by questioning prevailing schemes and by reconsidering initial, established knowledge. Change appears neither smooth nor quick nor entirely predictable. Learning is neither uniform nor memorized once for all, and relevant cognitive mechanisms are paramount. But change is more than a process of adaptation or of selection between available methods. When it is fulfilled, it amounts to no less than a process of creation. How much of such creations can be repeated, transferred, imitated, or hybridized remains one of the major topics of discussion in business history. Americanization of companies and nations or their Japanization have given birth to a vast flow of literature (Harp 2001; Kleinschmidt 2002; Zeitlin and Herrigel 2000). Far from the unilateral views of either economists or political historians, business history has avoided the dual pitfalls of an analysis in terms of either progress or hegemony and exploitation. Keeping in mind the theme of unequal exchange, it has stressed the limits of foreign influence, the selectiveness of the transfers, the creativity of the adaptations, and even the existence of "crossings", i.e. transfers from the borrower to the other nation. Fruitful comparisons or connections are thus made possible with history of science and technology or with history of culture.

2.2.5 Society and Politics

Business history has opened research domains which were not really covered by other types of history. For instance, history of education, which has greatly expanded worldwide since World War II, had usually neglected the history of technical and vocational training. In most countries this task was taken up by business historians in search of an understanding of labor markets and human resource management. Their position helped them to avoid two classical pitfalls, which would have been to underestimate the importance of self-taught people and of on the job training or to deduce from the contents taught what was the actual practice at work. By illuminating the schools created by companies or by chambers of commerce at different levels of curricula, business historians showed companies as transmitters of knowledge and could cast new light on the competition or collaboration between the business world and the education system, an alternative of lingering consequences which also helps historians to understand the shifting frontiers between private and public in industrial societies. In addition, business historians have been some of the prominent students in the history of business schools and of engineering schools. Their aim has been to understand the professionalization of managerial activities, thus giving rise to a dialogue with the social historians (and sociologists) interested in the genesis of professions and of professionalization in general. They were able to trace the development of new contents, like the entire field of marketing in business administration, and of new methods, like case studies, which the US exported globally. They shed light on the changes in comparative advantage such as France taking the lead in engineering schools and commerce schools in the early 19th century and then losing ground to German and American universities at the end of the same century. Or, to cite another example, smaller countries like Belgium or Norway pioneering relations between university and industry in the interwar years or after World War II (Bertrams 2006; Thelen, this volume; Amdam, this volume). In this respect business history, partly stimulated by Michael Porter's research on the "competitive advantage of nations" (Porter 1990), has made a distinctive contribution to the growing body of literature written by historians on the growth and decline of national power.

Similarly, the development of the history of medicine and health often ignored the history of work injuries and occupational illnesses. Although a few social historians and historical sociologists ventured into this area, it was mostly explored by a number of business historians. They highlighted the continuing importance of the problem for both individuals and families and even its contemporary recrudescence. They also showed that the very idea of the ability to work was socially constructed between the stakeholders and how people could be excluded. They documented the difficult position of company physicians and the growth of ergonomics. They underlined the spread of intermediate zones between activity and retirement: illness, invalidity, unemployment, and early retirement (Omnès and Bruno 2003). Thus business history stresses the importance of the history of the body, just like gender history or the history of medicine.

Along the same lines, the history of housing and architecture has benefited in recent years from the new interest of business historians who moved from the earlier study of company towns to national assessment of the importance of employers' housing efforts. Such works showed that the resources allocated were much higher than had been thought previously. They also depicted the specificities of migrant workers' housing policies and their consequences on their relationship with host countries' citizens. Finally, they suggested that any attempts by employers to keep workers' stability or even trust by providing housing seduced only a limited proportion of wage-earners. The majority preserved their autonomy.

If we now move from human capital to broader issues, business historians have been instrumental in delineating how companies contribute to the production of society. The work of the German historian Jürgen Kocka on the engineering company Siemens between 1847 and 1914 is particularly relevant here (Kocka 1969). It highlights the interaction of bourgeois society and the creation of the "modern" business organization. Contrary to flexible production systems, the family firm helps economic activity to become a separate sphere of social activity. It transforms social contacts into business contacts. Then paternalistic ties to workers have to be abandoned. The family has to give more autonomy to engineers and workers. New relationships and procedures with all of the firm's employees have to be specified and clarified. In short, because deepening industrialization requires a specialization of tasks, it makes formal rules and procedures more necessary and creates distinctions between professionals and workers, which contributes to class consciousness. German professionals adjusted readily to the new structures because German society and culture had long been familiar with the idea of an efficient bureaucracy, a continuity which, according to recent research (Fear 2005), may have been exaggerated, as German management emerged more collegial, entrepreneurial, and decentralized than is generally believed. Indeed, since the firm's success was the measure of their own competence, they pursued it even more purposefully than family heads who had seen it often as a means to dynastic prestige. Industrialization causes the very definition and composition of the middle class to change, so that it no longer could be equated with "bourgeois". Hence, a fluidity of class structures and boundaries and material productivity erases material differences. The reader should note that this analysis of the creation and diffusion of formal organizations and rule-oriented behavior, of the productivity, durability, and conflicts and by-products of the systems and structures overlooks what is not formally organized, such as gender or symbolic systems and the experience of daily life.

Companies shape society not only in themselves, but also through their products and services (Harp 2001). In postwar Japan the top electrical goods firms thought about America's dynamics and moved into consumer electronics in a deliberate effort to produce an American-style middle class oriented toward purchasing expensive electrical goods (Partner 1999). In many respects firms are also agents of internationalization. Some of them import raw materials, products, services, brands, knowledge, methods, capital, and people (Wilkins 2004). Others or even the same firms export them or invest abroad. Both categories may join international technical organizations or cartels and accept international codes of conduct (Jones 2005a). Such firms thus not only overcome national borders, they combine embeddedness in local and national identities, openness to outside influences and cultures, and promotion of their own model.

Business history illuminates also the shifting boundaries between private and public in society. The creation or development of public enterprise is never only of economic significance. In Spain, for instance, it was supported by the army during the autarkic period of the 20th century (San Román 1999). Business historians have also made major contributions to the history of public governance of the economy at local and national levels, showing how it was fashioned by the very nature of the enterprises and trade associations which it had to supervise and how bargaining with them was a key mission of top civil servants. Economic policies may be the locus of creative adaptation: in postwar Japan exchanges of information took place between the policy-makers and the private sector, leading to the discovery of policy issues and the means to deal with them (Hashimoto 2001).

Business history has decisively contributed to the social history of politics that has been undertaken to renovate political history worldwide. It shows firms to be direct and indirect political actors at local, regional, national, and international levels. For at least two centuries they or their trade associations have not restricted themselves to the defense of "free enterprise" versus regulation or nationalization or to topics such as customs tariffs, prices, economic and financial policy, or industrial relations—all areas where they seek autonomy from pure politics (Plumpe 1999). Resorting simultaneously to the quiet methods of influencing media, of lobbying, and in some cases (as business historians have shown for public works, armament, or oil) corruption, they also openly express their voice on political matters, whether local, national, or international. A number of businessmen apply for political functions. Business supports intermediary bodies (chambers of commerce and trade associations) as necessary relays between citizens and governments. Business historians bring four main conclusions to historians of politics (Tolliday 1987; Dunlavy 1994; Kipping 2002; Laird 2006). Political structures affect the dynamics of business enterprise in ways that are not directly connected to the political nature of government, whereas business may precipitate a transformation of structures. In intervening in the public sphere, businessmen face as many divisions as other social groups (see Lanzalaco, this volume). Their ability to bargain, to compromise, and to build networks or alliances contradicts the common wisdom of a unilateral or even authoritarian government of the economy by politicians and civil servants. And, finally, minority groups within business suggest influential solutions in international relations.

Let us turn now in the opposite direction and consider the sensitivity of business historians to changes in historical reflections.

2.3 THE IMPACT OF HISTORY

Over the past 40 years business history has increasingly opened itself to new trends which came to inspire other historians. This hybridization in turn made business history more reflexive, thus more creative. The following review is by no means exhaustive.

2.3.1 Cultural History

The spectacular boom of cultural history since the 1980s has exerted a growing influence on business history. It came through its methods and concepts, but also through its objects. Cultural history promoted individual and collective representations as meaningful—as "real" as actions and deeds or artifacts. This liberated business history from the tyranny of positivism which had often limited it to facts, results, and performances. It did not estrange it from numbers. On the contrary, it contributed to the growth of accounting history and to its extension to information and control systems. Several types of accounting methods were thus seen not only as "invisible technologies", as mentioned above, but also as attempts to construct or embody new representations of the firm (Boyns, this volume). Cultural history also carefully distinguished the production of representations from their reception. It showed that the reception process is not passive; it is selective, transformative, and creative. Such an analysis contributed to shift the focus of many business histories from the producer to the distributor (Welskopp *et al.* 2003) and to the customer. It gave a new impetus to the history of advertising, public relations, and distribution. Marchand decisively showed how public relations, advertising, and marketing are neither simple manipulations of the minds nor mere technical servants of products and services, but can accumulate knowledge about taste and practices (Marchand 1998). Marie Chessel (1998) has described for France how in advertising such talents were institutionalized as a new profession between 1900 and 1940. Its features were moving from empiricism to science, transmitting knowledge and taking variety into account. Similarly the publication of house organs became a profession in the hands of true journalists and was soon paralleled by customer magazines (Marchand 1998; Malaval 2001). The resulting interest in how firms channel the reception of products, services, and of their representations led business historians to put more emphasis on how the uses of such goods depart from the prescriptions and on how sales specialists cannot succeed without taking into account the interactions between producers, distributors, and customers in local or national markets. Within the history of multinationals, what happened at the local level could no longer be analyzed in terms of faithfulness to headquarters or of exotic variations on a universal corporate theme. Also, most impressive in this direction is the study of the perception and transfer of American and Japanese management and production methods in ten large German firms between 1950 and 1985 (Kleinschmidt 2002). Focusing on the mental horizons of how managers learn and decide about such transfers, Kleinschmidt stresses both that supposedly purely rational decisions are deeply embedded in corporate and national cultures and that transfer processes are dynamic and shape corporate culture. They are not unilateral and involve some element of transfer in the other direction.

Cultural history also induced business historians to look into the study of the cultural investments of businessmen and firms: from art collections to the relations between art and industry, there is a promising field which includes architecture, sculpture, photography, or painting and puts art historians in contact with business historians (Chessel 1998; Harp 2001). There was only one step to a business history of leisure, which emerged in the last decades of the twentieth century. On its agenda came the business history of tourism, itself illuminating such topics as identity, mobility, learning, and cultural transfer (Berghoff *et al.* 2002). It completed earlier investigations of the cultural industries, which previously had often been left to other parts of history or social sciences: the press, books, records, radio, film, and television are no longer just sources, or pastimes (and such a business history now includes entertainments such as theatre or circus or the production and use of musical instruments), but have become respectable topics, although studied by a minority. Furthermore, they push topics such as information and leisure to the foreground of business history.

Paradoxically cultural history led business historians to explore the part played by the past in management and society. Whereas the media always celebrates companies as builders of the future, business historians have illuminated how much they refer to the past and not simply when looking for patents. Memory, as both an individual process and a collective one, became a legitimate goal of analysis. Its constant work of selection and reconstruction—and of oblivion—means that the past in a company is not just like a database. It is a series of explorations and reinterpretations—also fueled by outside actors like the media or academics— which may have far-ranging consequences in decision making, in practices, and in representations. Its relevance for business historians thus goes far beyond corporate legends, but it includes them. It covers a major issue for business historians: brands, as well as perpetual reuse (sometimes misuse) of past products, services, images, and words. It looks at the continuous influence of the past on the present and at the ways in which traditions are constituted and passed on. They always leave some blind spots (Lipartito 2003), which are important too. Meanwhile there is a constant use and abuse of history by management scholars and consultants of which historians should beware. Taking into account the importance of memory may have another effect. Influenced by the success of such different history books as Pierre Nora's *Les lieux de mémoire* (1996–8, 2001, a third of which was translated into English as *Realms of Memory*) and Raphael Samuel's *Theaters of Memory* (1994), some business historians have begun to explore the significance of industrial heritage as a testimony both of what is no more and of what is in continuity with today. They have started to consider how firms are inscribed in various territories and how their corporate culture contributes to and interacts with local, regional, and national cultures.

2.3.2 Gender

In more than one way the recent boom of gender history complements the influence of cultural history on business historians. It too focuses on discourses and representations. Taken up first and foremost by female business historians, it explores the family as a business unit, then the definition and evolution of gender roles among entrepreneurs, managers, employees, and workers. It adds the gendering of labor markets and of human resource management (including family allowances) and the gender segmentation of marketing, distribution, and consumption, including the topic of male domination. It stresses how women and men manage and interpret their lives in relation to one another. Only a few points require mention here.

Such research has completely changed our understanding of internal and external labor markets. It has shown that, barriers to upward mobility and other "glass ceilings" notwithstanding, there is an autonomous and generally dynamic role of women workers in "traditional" industries such as silk weaving in western Japan (Hareven 2002) and in more modern branches like the metalworking industries in interwar Paris despite the world economic depression (Omnès 1997). The same applies to entrepreneurs. The discrimination and dependences experienced by immigrants in interwar Paris did not preclude the emergence of foreign women entrepreneurs in some parts of industry and services (Zalc 2005).

Whereas the pioneering works by Jürgen Kocka on white-collar employees in Germany focused on the growing bureaucratization of society, more recently business historians around the world have emphasized that the growth in size of this occupational group had a major gender component through a change in the sex ratio. Once a male-dominated space, women increasingly began working in offices. Delphine Gardey has shown for France that this shift was facilitated by new technologies, such as the Remington typewriter, and resulted from a deliberate choice by middle-class women who had little vocational training rather than from the promotion of women workers. But employee jobs lost some of their social cachet, while contrasts with the experience of blue-collar workers in terms of the work environment and the use of working time simultaneously increased (Gardey 2001).

Gender history and cultural history have been colonized by enterprising business historians worldwide who want to expand a business history of consumption. A good example of such perspectives is provided by Kathy Peiss' research on cosmetics (Peiss 1998). She argues that women were not oppressed by the beauty industry, but enthusiastically participated in its formation. Social relationships, rituals, and female institutions enabled them to use these products to express themselves. Accordingly, shampoo, created for working-class women, began to be used by middle-class women, who extended the market of the product in quite an unusual way—from the bottom up. Among American business historians two different views have appeared which can be exemplified by comparing two books which typify this approach. Following a far more radical line of interpretation than the late Roland Marchand or Chandler, Regina Blaszczyk argues that "supply did not create demand in home furnishings, but demand determined supply" (Blaszczyk 2000). In other words, in this branch firms succeed not when they try to shape consumers, but when they guess at what they want and endeavor to provide it with the help of "fashion intermediaries". Women as consumers play a distinctive role in a number of industries. First, their tastes support flexible batch production. Then when standardization comes they demand goods that continue to adjust to individuality and personal taste. Pamela Laird accords a lesser degree of sovereignty to the people themselves. She focuses on how professionals hired by business leaders or under contract with them moved from notifying customers to turning them into consumers by changing the form and function of advertising (Laird 1998). Can consumers be created? Or can they manage their desires and to which extent? At this stage of research the question remains open to debate among business historians.

2.3.3 Social History

Social history had its hour of glory much earlier than the other fields we have analyzed and which in many respects are its children. Business historians continue to draw from it central reflections: how does the complex dialogue between enterprise and society evolve? Does the composition of the workforce matter? What is the significance of personnel turnover and labor conflicts? Social historians have had the merit not to limit historical analysis to skilled labor. Thus Raphael Samuel (1977) has stressed the ubiquitous influence of hand labor during the industrial revolution in Britain. Other historians have since shown that unskilled and semi-skilled labor played a major role in most sectors of national economies. In this perspective, human labor can be seen as a linchpin between technological innovations and business structures. In a similar vein Rudolf Boch (1985) has renewed the study of skilled labor in small and medium-sized enterprises in his work on the shock of globalization on cutlery workers in the industrial district of Solingen (Germany) at the end of the 19th century. Globalization paved the way for the influence of unions and Marxist socialists who, like civil servants and engineers, saw no future for flexible production. But the various players were finally able to draw up a new social compact which made a new specialization and the revitalization of Solingen products possible. They could now compete with the English cutlery of Sheffield.

In this perspective business historians usually choose other topics on which to focus than social historians: wage differentiation, work incentives and productivity systems, job classifications, vocational training, internal and external labor markets (Gospel 1992), pensions (Hannah 1986). Also, in keeping with recent sociological research, they put more emphasis on the positions of white-collar employees, middle managers, executives, studying their career routes and the importance of networking in managers' success (Cassis 1997; Laird 2006).

A few historians have undertaken to consider companies as heterogeneous and potentially conflictual communities. This was the perspective of the pioneering book by French social historian Rolande Trempé who, looking at the coal mine of Carmaux in southern France between 1848 and 1914, was able to analyze at the same time its aristocratic owners, its professional managers, and the transformation of its peasant workers into full-time workers (Trempé 1971). Another great work is the late Italian business historian Duccio Bigazzi's book on the first 20 years of the Milan automobile company Alfa Romeo (Bigazzi 1988). The careful analysis of the company's evolving strategies and markets is skillfully combined with insights into the representations and practices of the various internal actors: entrepreneurs, managers, designers, technicians, and workers.

Two American social historians have almost simultaneously stressed that the construction of the modern corporation cannot be explained only top down and by a look at how transaction costs help trace borders between markets and hierarchies. Lenard Berlanstein in a history of the Parisian Gas Company, an early large corporation which with some 10,000 wage earners between 1855 and 1910 was "the city's single largest employer of clerical and factory labor", has shown how both gas workers and gas employees resented the supervision by engineers as arbitrary and struggled to obtain the interposition of work rules and intermediary hierarchies between them and the engineers. They finally resorted to political lobbying and asked the city of Paris, from which the Company held the concession, to regulate its industrial relations, and finally to take over the company itself in 1910 (Berlanstein 1991). This was the blueprint for most French nationalizations after World War II. In a totally different social and political context, Olivier Zunz has shown how the new white-collar employees in American large corporations wanted rules to clarify and try to stabilize the uncertainty of their daily lives and of their careers and that one element of companies' reaction was the provision of gendered welfare programs within individual corporations (Zunz 1990). It can thus be said that much of the private bureaucracies of these corporations did not originate in top management rational strategies but in its responses to demands from below.

Social history, as is well known, has provided numerous histories of conflicts and strike waves. For the 20th century, it has extended the framework of such perspectives to nationwide social contracts. This has led business historians to define authority as a relationship (Cohen 2004) and to take a much more active interest in the management of human resources and of industrial relations, in the relations of firms with public opinion and in their negotiations with political authorities. They have thus devoted more attention than social historians to institutions, to law, and to regulatory processes.

Beyond work, three elements of the relations between business and society have attracted a considerable amount of scholarship in recent years among business historians: welfare, philanthropy, and environment. These are areas where their contribution is threefold: they give full weight to the multiple role of business in society, often underestimated by other historians (for instance employer-provided welfare in the origins of social security), they broaden our understanding of the nature of the firm (Rosen and Sellers 1999), and they take into account both the social costs of business and its current search for sustainable development.

2.3.4 From the Study of Medicine and Science to Business Practice

The influence of the recent body of history of medicine and of public health extends well beyond the history of the pharmaceutical industry and its contribution to a diversified history of innovation. It has enriched the investigations of business historians in the history of the demographic breakdown of the labor force and of aging and in the complex relations between the evolution of working time and health. This kind of approach even includes deviant behaviors (from alcohol to drugs) in a broader view of how in history men and women in business whatever their hierarchical position manage their lives at work. Furthermore, it fuels the growing interest in the history of risk and uncertainty in business. The intense renewal of the history of science and the autonomization of the history of technology have both had prolonged effects on business history.

The emphasis on networks rather than on individuals or firms by the American historian Thomas Hughes has revolutionized the history of innovation. Instead of maintaining the firm as their unit of analysis, business historians following his lead have taken into consideration the management of multi-firm, networked systems (like the electrical power grid). This has been true of students of the network industries in communications, transportation, energy, and finance. The network approach also alters our understanding of the boundaries between business and society.

The theme of the social construction of technology, although criticized by some business historians (Hounshell 1995), has been taken up by many of them. By connecting actors, networks, and systems, it has enabled them to give a deeper significance to innovation which can no longer be reduced to lowering costs and increasing productivity. For instance, many of Du Pont's major innovations, from nylon to the atomic bomb, may be ascribed to the constitution of a new profession: chemical engineering, which was also a key element in the weaving of intense connections between the corporation and government in war and peace (Ndiaye 2001). In recent years, the proponents of this approach have stressed the importance of industrial customers and household consumers as co-constructors of a number of technologies and medical drugs. This new direction found an immediate echo in the business history of information processing (Yates 2005).

Finally, the liveliness and intellectual liveliness of history of science helped spawn a great interest in the multiple uses of science in business. There has been work on how the reference to science was used to legitimize new developments such as "scientific management" of production, how psychology and statistics were applied in marketing, how psychology, ergonomics, information sciences were used in human resource management, or how operational research renewed production management and finance. Economic research by banks or electrical companies and industrial research have become welcome areas for business historians. In a parallel vein, the study of think tanks (with the Rand Corporation in the US as the most prominent example) has been developed, with the goal of understanding how these small groups, interconnecting science, technology, business, and politics, shape a variety of social actors.

2.3.5 Between Micro-history and Global History

As we just mentioned when quoting Thomas Hughes, a key issue for business history has been the proper unit of analysis. This debate is internal to the subdiscipline. It now connects to a broader debate in general history about the relevant scale of analysis.

In continental Europe, micro-history has influenced the rest of history since the end of the 1970s. Born among early modern Italian historians like Carlo Ginzburg and Giovanni Levi, it has insisted that historical observation at the smallest level of analysis (a person, a small group, a local community) was the only way to detect some phenomena and also that this level was the only one left where "total" history may still be attempted after the demise of the various macro-interpretations in the 1970s. A few business historians have ventured such analyses, but many more have used its French derivative of the 1990s, the *jeux d'échelle*, i.e. a combination of micro, meso, and macro analyses (for instance Dessaux 2003). This method of using different, multiple lenses on the same object takes into account the advance of cultural history and the growing necessity of a plurality of approaches in order to seize the significance of a historical object.

More recently, in the 21st century, the opposite approach is being developed from the United States, the "new global history", which targets the multifaceted nature of globalization processes. It has already been applied to topics such as food, migrations, the city, and childhood (see the website <http://www.newglobalhistory.com>). This proliferation of world history in general has spread to other continents, but has still paid too little attention to the business history literature, even though the growing body of research on trading companies, investment banks, free-standing companies, and multinationals is very relevant. It seems possible that business historians aiming at understanding nations like China, India, Indonesia, Japan, or Brazil (Birchal 1999), focusing on colonies and empires, or scrutinizing the inequalities between North and South, or specializing in the history of foreign investment or portfolio investment, will join this new cohort and broaden its approach.

2.4 Conclusions

The growth in numbers of business historians in many countries has had many advantages. The age structure is balanced and the gender ratio has improved over the years. So, the socio-demographic bases for plurality and renewal are present. In a range of countries a national association for business history has been founded so as to structure the group and to formalize intellectual debates, publish journals or newsletters, and later feed websites. Only a few major countries lack national business history societies, either because economic history and business history remain under the same roof or because commissioned business history prevails, as in the Netherlands, or, as in China or Brazil, because the discipline is so recent and small. Some of these national associations pride themselves on being very open to foreign members or to discussions with foreign guests. The Business History Conference in the United States, the Association of Business Historians in Great Britain, the Associazione di Studi e Storia dell'Impresa (ASSI) in Italy, the Fuji Conference organized by the Japanese Business History Society have become dynamic forums for new ideas, new topics, and controversies. A regional association called the European Business History Association appeared in the early 1990s and has continued to develop, but there is no world association. However, all these societies face a permanent dilemma. They cultivate the specificity and the originality of business history, but they thus run the risk of becoming obstacles to greater interaction with other historians. Striving for the latter remains a challenge for their governing bodies.

I am tempted to add that the diversity of intellectual origins and of academic affiliations in each country is not an intellectual drawback. It preserves each national group from uniformity and orthodoxy. However, it is quite often a source of problems for young Ph.D.s who want a job in academia. In a number of countries, it is hard to imagine a history department hiring a business historian per se and many need to repackage themselves as national or international historians, often with uncertain outcomes. The same holds true for young Ph.D.s in departments of business administration for whom maintaining their identity as business historians remains a constant challenge. This rather promising picture leaves aside two difficult topics: the relations with economic history and the position in the field of history.

To be sure, this relationship varies geographically. As Amatori and Jones (2003) point out, considerable differences of emphasis remain. In Scandinavia, business history remains firmly rooted in economic history and centrally concerned with the study of the firm—in other words, wholly different from recent trends in the United States. In Greece and Spain, the links of business history with economic history have been strong, though the subdiscipline has developed a noticeably quantitative dimension in the latter country. In Britain, France, and Italy, business history has shown far more vitality than economic history and to a large extent has superseded it, while business historians have increasingly worked in the fields of management and business studies. Meanwhile, in Japan, the large number of business historians largely work and teach within faculties of management and commerce, and for many years there has been a sharp distinction between business and economic history. In some countries, such as the Netherlands, the lack of academic institutionalization has made business historians dependent on commissions from companies as their main source of employment (Amatori and Jones 2003).

Yet, this relationship increasingly resembles the links between an established older brother and a dynamic younger brother. Economic history has exclusive coverage of the more distant periods in time (ancient, medieval, early modern history), after which there is a quasi-division of labor as modern and contemporary economic history provides far-ranging syntheses and quantitative macro analyses, including assessments of virtual alternative developments by cliometricians, while also assessing national and international public policies. This division is quite visible in the evolving content of the sessions of the Congresses of the International Economic History Association.

A special mention should be made here of banking and financial history. This lies precisely on the border between business and economic history. It was one of the earliest areas of the business world to be studied by business or economic historians in every country because of the general fascination with capital which regularly attracted major historians and has been supported for 15 years by a European Association for Banking History and the *Financial History Review*. Now it generally combines a history of the successes and failures of corporate strategies and structures in individual banking firms with broader analyses of financial centers, national economies, and international developments (Cassis and Bussière 2005).

For the time being, there remains a community of interests between the two family members. It is moreover cemented by a stubborn interest in economic performance, by the complex relationship between business history and economic theory (Lamoreaux *et al.*, this volume), and by common adversaries or common objects (like financial history or maritime history), but it is probably fragile.

On the one hand, the multi-faceted opening of business history to most of the new currents in history outlined previously has made it much more palatable and respectable to most members of the historical profession. However, these developments have inspired more than notes of regrets among some leading business historians. For instance, the American business historian Louis Galambos has deplored the fact that in the United States "the profession's normative ideology has drifted to the left and away from market-related phenomena at about the same pace as the world has drifted to the right and toward the market" and has dubbed the new approaches to knowledge, and the resulting narratives, "postmodernisms". This movement even has a supplementary drawback: "its intellectual origins were in Europe" (Galambos 2003: 26–9). Nevertheless, Galambos ends his assessment on a very positive note: "business history is today more interesting than it has been at any time since the founding of the subdiscipline" (ibid. 29). The case seems strong if one considers the era when business history was "separated by a wide gulf from the strong intellectual currents reshaping the larger discipline of history" (ibid. 11), as in the United States before 1960, or in Germany before 1973 (when the business history journal was still called *Tradition*). Maintaining close links with the historical field seems to be the key to both preserving and renewing the identity of business history.

On the other hand, business history itself has become more and more reflective in recent years. Thus it behaves like any other field, as both history of science and sociology of knowledge have established. In each country journals or conferences have debated "whither business history?" and tried to select the more viable or promising alternatives to the Chandlerian paradigm. But at the same time there are still some general historians who criticize business history for its human or financial links with industry, commerce, and banking or for its connections with the fields of business administration or organization science, at which some historians still gaze suspiciously. Such critics ignore the complex trajectory of the subdiscipline. For example, in France one of its founders after World War II, the banking historian Jean Bouvier, was a Marxist and a true Communist intellectual, while in Italy the second generation of pioneers included a large proportion of not only Communists but also leftists (or ex-members of these parties). They ignore the fact that in every country business history has developed some kind of professional ethic. They do not distinguish between the different trends at work in business administration, whereas everywhere the emergence of small groups of scholars dedicated to what they call a longitudinal approach and working on the bases of multiple sources constitutes a hopeful trend.

In short, business history has good reasons to publicize its achievements better among historians and, despite the fact that business historians may have other bedfellows, history has much to gain from even more intense intellectual exchanges with the turbulent, yet creative, tribe of business historians.

REFERENCES

ALDER, K. (1997). *Engineering the Revolution: Arms and Enlightenment in France, 1763– 1815.* Princeton: Princeton University Press.

AMATORI, F., and JONES, G. (eds.) (2003). *Business History around the World at the End of the Twentieth Century.* Cambridge: Cambridge University Press.

ARTHUR, B. (1994). *Increasing Returns and Path Dependence in the Economy.* Ann Arbor: University of Michigan Press.

BERGHOFF, H., KORTE, B., SCHNEIDER, R., and HARVIE, C. (2002). *The History of International Tourism: The Cultural History of the British Experience, 1600–2000.* Houndmills: Palgrave.

BERGIER, J.-F. (ed.) (2002). *La Suisse, le national-socialisme et la Seconde Guerre mondiale: rapport final.* Zurich: Editions Pendo.

BERLANSTEIN, L. R. (1991). *Big Business and Industrial Conflict in Nineteenth Century France: A Social History of the Paris Gas Company.* Berkeley: University of California Press.

BERTRAMS, K. (2006). *Universités et entreprises: milieux académiques et industriels en Belgique 1880–1970.* Brussels: Le Cri Edition.

BIGAZZI, D. (1988). *Il Portello: operai, tecnici e imprenditori all'Alfa Romeo, 1906–1926.* Milan: Franco Angeli.

BIRCHAL, S. (1999). *Entrepreneurship in Nineteenth-Century Brazil: The Formation of a Business Environment.* New York: St. Martin's Press.

BLANKEN, I. J. (1999). *The History of Philips Electronics N.V.,* vol. 3. Zaltbommel: Europese Bibliotheek.

BLASZCZYK, R. (2000). *Imagining Consumers: Design and Innovation from Wedgwood to Corning.* Baltimore: Johns Hopkins University Press.

BOCH, R. (1985). *Handwerker-Sozialisten gegen Fabrikgesellschaft. Lokale Fachvereine, Massengewerkschaft und industrielle Rationalisierung in Solingen 1870–1914.* Göttingen: Vandenhoeck & Ruprecht.

BOURDIEU, P. (2005). *The Social Structures of the Economy.* Cambridge: Polity Press.

CASSIS, Y. (1997). *Big Business: The European Experience in the Twentieth Century.* Oxford: Oxford University Press, 1997.

——and BUSSIÈRE, E. (eds.) (2005). *London and Paris as International Financial Centres in the Twentieth Century.* Oxford: Oxford University Press.

CHANDLER, A. D. (1962). *Strategy and Structure: Chapters in the History of the Industrial Enterprise.* Cambridge, Mass.: MIT Press.

——(1990). *Scale and Scope: The Dynamics of Industrial Capitalism.* Cambridge, Mass.: Harvard University Press.

CHAPMAN, S. D., and CHAMBERS, J. D. (1970). *The Beginnings of Industrial Britain.* London: University Tutorial Press.

CHESSEL, M. (1998). *La publicité: naissance d'une profession 1900–1940.* Paris: CNRS Editions.

CHICK, M., and LANTHIER, P. (eds.) (2004). "Nationalisations et dénatialisation". *Entreprises et Histoire,* 13, 37.

COHEN, Y. (2004). "Matter Matters to Authority: Some Aspects of Soviet Industrial Management in the 1930s". *Business and Economic History On-Line,* 2.

DAVID, P. A. (1997). *Path Dependence and the Quest for Historical Economics: One More Chorus of the Ballad of Qwerty.* Oxford: Nuffield College.

DESCAMPS, F. (2001). *L'historien, l'archiviste et le magnétophone: de la constitution de la source orale à son exploitation.* Paris: Comité pour l'histoire économique et financière de la France.

DESSAUX, P.-A. (2003). "Des vermicelliers au groupe Danone: consommer, produire et vendre des pâtes alimentaires en France, XVIIᵉ–XXᵉ siècle". Ph.D. thesis. Ecole des Hautes Etudes en Sciences Sociales.

DUNLAVY, C. (1994). *Politics and Industrialization: Early Railroads in the United States and Prussia.* Princeton: Princeton University Press.

DUTTA, S. (1999). *Family Business in India.* Thousand Oaks, Calif.: Sage.

FEAR, J. (2005). *Organizing Control: August Thyssen and the Construction of German Corporate Management.* Cambridge, Mass.: Harvard University Press.

FREELAND, R. S. (2001). *The Struggle for the Control of the Modern Corporation: Organizational Change at General Motors, 1924–1970*. Cambridge: Cambridge University Press.

FRIDENSON, P. (2004*a*). "Le rôle des petites entreprises, des grandes firmes et de l'Etat dans la percée de l'optronique militaire en France", in J.-F. Belhoste, S. Benoit, S. Chassagne, and P. Mioche (eds.), *Autour de l'industrie: Histoire et patrimoine*. Paris: Comité pour l'histoire économique et financière de la France, 603–27.

——(2004*b*). "Business Failure and the Agenda of Business History". *Enterprise and Society*, 5/4: 562–82.

GALAMBOS, L. (2003). "Identity and the Boundaries of Business History: An Essay on Consensus and Creativity", in Amatori and Jones (2003), 11–30.

GARDEY, D. (2001). *La dactylographe et l'expéditionnaire: histoire des employés de bureau 1890–1930*. Paris: Belin.

GERVAIS, P. (2004). *Les origines de la révolution industrielle aux Etats-Unis: entre économie marchande et capitalisme industriel, 1800–1850*. Paris: Editions de l'EHESS.

GOSPEL, H. F. (1992). *Markets, Firms, and the Management of Labour in Britain*. Cambridge: Cambridge University Press.

HALL, P., and SOSKICE, D. (eds.) (2001). *Varieties of Capitalism: Institutional Foundations of Comparative Advantage*. Oxford: Oxford University Press.

HANNAH, L. (1986). *Inventing Retirement. The Development of Occupational Pensions in Britain*. Cambridge: Cambridge University Press.

HAREVEN, T. (2002). *The Silk Weavers of Kyoto: Family and Work in a Changing Traditional Industry*. Berkeley: University of California Press.

HARP, S. (2001). *Marketing Michelin: Advertising and Cultural Identity in Twentieth–Century France*. Baltimore: Johns Hopkins University Press.

HARVEY, J. L. (2004). "An American *Annales*? The AHA and the *Revue internationale d'histoire économique* of Lucien Febvre and Marc Bloch". *Journal of Modern History*, 76: 578–621.

HASHIMOTO, J. (2001). *Sengo nihon keizai no seichou kouzou: kigyou shisutem no bunseki*. Tokyo: Yuuhikaku.

HERRIGEL, G. (1996). *Industrial Constructions: The Sources of German Industrial Power*. Cambridge: Cambridge University Press.

HODEIR, C. (2003). *Stratégies d'Empire: le grand patronat colonial face à la décolonisation*. Paris: Belin.

HOKE, D. R. (1990). *Ingenious Yankees: The Rise of the American System of Manufactures in the Private Sector*. New York, Columbia University Press.

HOUNSHELL, D. A. (1984). *From the American System to Mass Production, 1800–1932*. Baltimore: Johns Hopkins University Press.

——(1995). "Hughesian History of Technology and Chandlerian Business History: Parallels, Departures, and Critics". *History and Technology*, 12: 205–24.

JACOBY, S. M. (2005). *The Embedded Corporation: Corporate Governance and Employment Relations in Japan and the United States*. Princeton: Princeton University Press.

JOLY, H. (1996). *Patrons d'Allemagne: sociologie d'une élite industrielle 1933–1989*. Paris: Presses de la FNSP.

JOHNSON, H. T., and KAPLAN, R. S. (1987). *Relevance Lost: The Rise and Fall of Management Accounting*. Boston: Harvard Business School Press.

JONES, G. (2005a). *Multinationals and Global Capitalism*. Oxford: Oxford University Press.

—— (2005b). *Renewing Unilever: Transformation and Tradition*. Oxford: Oxford University Press.

JUDET, P. (2004). *Horlogerie et horlogers du Faucigny (1849–1934): les métamorphoses d'une identité sociale et politique*. Grenoble: Presses universitaires de Grenoble.

KASUYA, M. (2004). "Foreword". *Japanese Research in Business History*, 21: 5–10.

KIPPING, M. (2002). *La France et les origines de l'Union européenne 1944–1952: intégration économique et compétitivité*. Paris: Comité pour l'histoire économique et financière de la France.

KLEINSCHMIDT, C. (2002). *Der produktive Blick: Wahrnehmung amerikanischer und japanischer Management und Produktionsmethoden durch deutsche Unternehmer, 1950–1985*. Berlin: Akademie Verlag.

KOCKA, J. (1969). *Unternehmensverwaltung und Angestelltenschaft am Beispiel Siemens, 1847–1914*. Stuttgart: Klett Verlag.

LACHAIER, P. (1999). *Firmes et entreprises en Inde: la firme lignagère dans ses réseaux*. Paris: Karthala.

LAIRD, P. W. (1998). *Advertising Progress: American Business and the Rise of Consumer Marketing*. Baltimore: Johns Hopkins University Press.

—— (2006). *Pull: Networking and Success since Benjamin Franklin*. Cambridge, Mass.: Harvard University Press.

LAMOREAUX, N. (2001). "Reframing the Past: Thoughts About Business Leadership and Decision Making Under Uncertainty". *Enterprise and Society*, 1/4: 632–59.

LEMERCIER, C. (2003). *Un si discret pouvoir: aux origines de la chambre de commerce de Paris (1803–1853)*. Paris: La Découverte.

LIPARTITO, K. (2003). "Picturephone and the Information Age: The Social Meaning of Failure". *Technology and Culture*, 44/1: 50–81.

McKENNA, C. D. (2006). *The World's Newest Profession: Management Consulting in the Twentieth Century*. Cambridge: Cambridge University Press.

MAIER, C. S. (1975). *Recasting Bourgeois Europe: Stabilization in France, Germany, and Italy in the Decade after World War I*. Princeton: Princeton University Press.

MALAVAL, C. (2001). *La presse d'entreprise française au XXᵉ siècle: histoire d'un pouvoir*. Paris: Belin.

MARCHAND, R. (1998). *Creating the Corporate Soul: The Rise of Public Relations and Corporate Imagery in American Big Business*. Berkeley: University of California Press.

MISRA, M. (1999). *Business, Race and Politics in British India, c. 1850–1960*. Oxford: Clarendon Press.

MORIKAWA, H. (1992). *Zaibatsu: The Rise and Fall of Family Enterprise Groups in Japan*. Tokyo: University of Tokyo Press.

NAKANISHI, Y. (1982–2003). *Nihon kindaika no kiso katei: Nagasaki zousenjo to sono roushi kankei*. Tokyo: University of Tokyo Press, 3 vols.

NDIAYE, P. (2001). *Du nylon et des bombes: Du Pont de Nemours, le marché et l'Etat américain, 1900–1970*. Paris: Belin.

NEVINS, A. with HILL, F. E. (1954–63). *Ford*. New York: Scribner's, 3 vols.

NORA, P. (ed.) (1996–8). *Realms of Memory: Rethinking the French Past*. New York: Columbia University Press.

—— (2001). *Rethinking France*. Chicago: Chicago University Press.

OKOCHI, A. (1979). *Keiei kosoryoku: kigyosa katsudo no siteki*. Tokyo: University of Tokyo Press.

—— (1992). *Hatumei kai to gijutsu kouso: gijutsu to tokkyo no keieisiteki iso*. Tokyo: University of Tokyo Press.

OMNÈS, C. (1997). *Ouvrières parisiennes: marchés du travail et trajectoires professionnelles au XXe siècle*. Paris: Editions de l'EHESS.

—— and BRUNO, A.-S. (eds.) (2003). *Les mains inutiles. Inaptitude au travail et emploi en Europe*. Paris: Belin.

PARTNER, S. (1999). *Assembled in Japan: Electrical Goods and the Making of the Japanese Consumer*. Berkeley: University of California Press.

PEISS, K. (1998). *Hope in a Jar: The Making of America's Beauty Culture*. New York: Metropolitan Books.

PLUMPE, W. (1999). *Betriebliche Mitbestimmungen in der Weimarer Republik: Fallstudien zum Ruhrbergbau und zur chemischen Industrie*. Munich: Oldenbourg.

PORTER, M. (1990). *The Competitive Advantage of Nations*. New York: Free Press.

ROSEN, C., and SELLERS, C. (1999). "The Nature of the Firm: Towards an Eco-cultural History of Business". *Business History Review*, 73/4: 577–600.

ROSSITER, A. (1987). "Popular Front Economic Policy and the Matignon Negotiations". *The Historical Journal*, 30/3: 663–84.

SABEL, C. F., and ZEITLIN, J. (2004). "Neither Modularity nor Relational Contracting: Interfirm Collaboration in the New Economy". *Enterprise and Society*, 5/3: 388–403.

SAMUEL, R. (1977). "The Workshop of the World: Steam Power and Hand Technology in mid-Victorian Britain". *History Workshop Journal*, 3/1: 6–72.

—— (1994). *Theaters of Memory*. London: Verso.

SAN ROMÁN, E. (1999). *Ejército e industria: el nacimiento del INI*. Barcelone: Critica.

SCRANTON, P. (1997). *Endless Novelty: Specialty Production and American Industrialization, 1865–1925*. Princeton: Princeton University Press.

SEGRETO, L. (1997). *Marte e Mercurio. Industria bellica e sviluppo economico in Italia 1861–1940*. Milan: Franco Angeli.

SHIOMI, H., and WADA, K. (eds.) (1995). *Fordism Transformed*. Oxford: Oxford University Press.

SMITH, M. R. (1977). *Harpers Ferry Armory and the Origins of New Technology: The Challenge of Change*. Ithaca, NY: Cornell University Press.

TEDLOW, R. S. (1985). "Business History in the United States: Past Accomplishments and Future Directions". *Annali di storia dell'impresa*, 1: 387–408.

THOMPSON, P., and BURCHARDT, N. (eds.) (1982). *Our Common History: The Transformation of Europe*. London: Pluto Press.

TIGNOR, R. L. (1998). *Capitalism and Nationalism at the End of the Empire: State and Business in Decolonizing Egypt, Nigeria, and Kenya, 1945–1963*. Princeton: Princeton University Press.

TOLLIDAY, S. (1987). *Business, Banking, and Politics: The Case of British Steel, 1918–1939*. Cambridge, Mass.: Harvard University Press.

TREMPÉ, R. (1971). *Les mineurs de Carmaux, 1848–1914*. Paris: Editions Ouvrières.

TRIPATHI, D. (2004). *The Oxford History of Indian Business*. Oxford: Oxford University Press.

WELSKOPP, T. (1994). *Arbeit und Macht im Hüttenwerk: Arbeits- und industrielle Beziehungen in der deutschen und amerikanischen Eisen- und Stahlindustrie von den 1860er bis zu den 1930er Jahren*. Bonn: J. H. W. Dietz.

WELSKOPP, T., GIRSCHIK, K., and RITSCHL, A. (2003). *Der Migros-Kosmos. Zur Geschichte eines aussergewöhnlichen Schweizer Unternehmens*. Baden: Verlag hier + jetzt.

WILKINS, M. (2004). *The History of Foreign Investment in the United States, 1914–1945*. Cambridge, Mass.: Harvard University Press.

—— and HILL, F. E. (1964). *American Business Abroad: Ford on Six Continents*. Detroit: Wayne State University Press.

YATES, J. (1989). *Control through Communication: The Rise of System in American Management*. Baltimore: Johns Hopkins University Press.

—— (2005). *Structuring the Information Age: Life Insurance and Information Technology in the 20th Century*. Baltimore: Johns Hopkins.

ZALC, C. (2005). "Femmes, entreprises et dépendances: les entrepreneuses étrangères à Paris dans l'entre-deux-guerres". *Travail, genre et sociétés*, 9/13: 47–70.

ZEITLIN, J., and HERRIGEL, G. (eds.) (2000). *Americanization and its Limits: Reworking US Technology and Management in Post-War Europe and Japan*. Oxford: Oxford University Press.

ZUNZ, O. (1990). *Making America Corporate, 1870–1920*. Chicago: University of Chicago Press.

CHAPTER 3

....

ECONOMIC THEORY AND BUSINESS HISTORY

....

NAOMI R. LAMOREAUX

DANIEL M. G. RAFF

PETER TEMIN

3.1 INTRODUCTION

....

BECAUSE work in business history has always consisted largely of studies of individual entrepreneurs, firms, and industries, scholars have continually had to struggle to prevent the field from disintegrating into antiquarianism. From the beginning economic theory has offered a solution—a way of distinguishing important trends from trivial changes and of building general understanding by comparing businesses and business people within and across industries and economies. However, practitioners have long resisted making serious use of economics in their work. Until recently they claimed that neoclassical theory's restrictive assumptions about human behavior and the workings of firms rendered it useless for probing the motives of entrepreneurs or the activities of complex enterprises. This excuse disappeared in the 1970s and 1980s, when economists began to develop new theories based on much more realistic ideas about human behavior and organizations. Some business historians immediately recognized the value of the new theory for their work, but most remained indifferent, skeptical, or even hostile.

The most common objection that business historians have posed to employing economic theory, even in its most recent forms, is that it is founded on a method of analysis that is essentially static and hence cannot account for the development of new business capabilities over time or, more generally, for innovation. This criticism is at best an exaggeration, but for the purposes of this essay we cheerfully acknowledge that there are important tasks for which economic theory, however construed, is not particularly well suited. As with any tool, however, strengths and weaknesses often come bundled together. Indeed, we would argue that aspects of economic theory that critics find terribly limiting can help scholars avoid a major pitfall of business history—its tendency toward Whiggishness. Business historians for the most part study successful enterprises. As a result, they are always in danger of jumping to the conclusion that the enterprises they have been researching are superior in some robust way—that they are the outcomes of historical processes that have produced higher forms of business organization. Judicious deployment of economic theory can help guard against this danger.

In the first section of this essay we explore the use of economic theory in business history during the era when Alfred Chandler's account of the rise of large firms dominated research in the field and neoclassical theory was in its ascendancy in economics. We then discuss the development of new bodies of economic theory and their growing use in business history as the appeal of the Chandlerian paradigm began to wane. We show that the receptivity of business historians in different parts of the world to the new theory was inversely correlated with the extent to which they had embraced Chandler's ideas in the preceding period. In the United States, and to a lesser extent Germany and Japan, many scholars continued to resist using economics in their work. In Britain, by contrast, where Chandler's arguments had long met with considerable skepticism, a number of business historians enthusiastically exploited the new theoretical developments. Even there, however, scholars tended to use economic theory descriptively rather than analytically. In the last section of the essay we argue that by making formal use of economic models to pose and test refutable hypotheses, business historians can both improve the analytical quality of their narratives and avoid Whiggism.

It is useful to begin with a few definitions. We restrict our attention in this chapter to those bodies of theory taught in mainstream economics departments, including standard neoclassical theory, the economics of asymmetric information, transaction cost economics, and game theory. Left out are bodies of theory that are clearly economic in their content but that do not have the same standing in the economics profession. These range from Marxist theory, on the one hand, to the evolutionary economics of Richard Nelson and Sidney Winter, on the other (see Lazonick, this volume). When we discuss work in business history, we refer for the most part to scholars who identify themselves as members of this field.

We take pains to note, however, that especially in the United States, a considerable amount of scholarship whose subject matter is recognizably business history has been written by economists and economic historians who do not identify themselves as members of the field. We argue that the work of these outsiders offers useful models that illustrate the benefits of making more rigorous use of economic theory in business history.

3.2 Business History and Economic Theory in the Era of Chandler

Almost from the moment that business history emerged as a distinct area of scholarship in the late 1920s, its relationship with economics has been fraught with tension.[1] The two founders of the field in the United States, Edwin F. Gay and N. S. B. Gras, had a severe falling out by the early 1930s over their very different visions of the direction research should take. Gay, whose background was in economic history, believed that the goal of business history should be a synthetic understanding of the development of the economy. Precisely because businesses were subject to the discipline of the market, their experiences could provide insight into larger economic processes. Though Gras had been one of Gay's students, he had little use for such abstract theorizing. An inductive thinker, he believed that business behavior should be studied for its own sake and that new generalizations could only be developed after scholars had amassed a large body of case studies.

Although Gras had a significant number of followers, many business historians worried that the growing volume of studies of individual firms and industries was not adding up to significant scholarship. From time to time, as a result, there were attempts to reunite the fields of business and economic history. One of the most significant such efforts, a series of meetings that began at Northwestern University in the 1950s and involved members of both fields, led to the founding of the Business History Conference in 1971.[2] The rapprochement was only partially successful, however. Both fields were then going through major changes, and practitioners were being pulled in different directions.

In business history, scholars got a hint of the deliverance they had been waiting for when Alfred D. Chandler, Jr., published *Strategy and Structure* in 1962. The core of the study consisted of four long chapters devoted respectively to the histories of Du Pont, General Motors, Standard Oil of New Jersey, and Sears Roebuck and

[1] For a more extended discussion of these early years, see Lamoreaux *et al.* (1997).

[2] One of the original members of the group, Harold F. Williamson, worked throughout his career to bring business and economic history closer together. See Williamson (1966). See also Lamoreaux *et al.* (1997); and Hausman (2003).

Company. Each chapter recounted a similar sequence of events: how a change in business strategy during the 1920s led the firm to diversify into new economic activities, causing serious organizational problems that managers were only able to solve by adopting a multidivisional, decentralized managerial structure (the M-form). Chandler used the four case studies to lay out some basic principles of organizational innovation and then generalized his findings to the economy as a whole by tracking patterns in the M-form's subsequent spread. Pointing a way out of the Grasian morass of individual firm and industry studies, Chandler's work was enormously influential and inspired a wave of scholarship in the United States and elsewhere (see Galambos 1970; Kocka 1971; Nakagawa 1975; Hannah 1976*b*).

Chandler's primary theoretical training had been in sociology rather than in economics (McCraw 1988). To the extent that he read economics, his main influences were scholars such as Edith Penrose who worked outside the neoclassical mainstream. Penrose had noticed that more and more economic activity seemed to be occurring inside firms rather than in the market. In *The Theory of the Growth of the Firm* (1959), she explained this trend by positing that firms were more effective sites of learning than markets. When firms took on new economic activities, Penrose observed, their managers had to figure out how to coordinate them efficiently. These lessons could then be relatively easily and valuably applied to new activities, enabling firms to expand the scope of their businesses. Chandler's *Strategy and Structure* can be seen as an extended illustration of Penrose's ideas. For example, when Du Pont first diversified from explosives into paints, it had to learn how to manage these two very different businesses at the same time. Once it hit upon the solution of the M-form of organization, it was able to use its new structure to diversify profitably into a broader range of activities.

At about the same time as Chandler's *Strategy and Structure* was reshaping the practice of business history, a group of economists, variously dubbed the New Economic Historians or Cliometricians, were taking the field of economic history by storm. These scholars advocated a more formally scientific type of scholarship that would make explicit use of economic models to formulate refutable hypotheses (North 1965; Fogel 1965 and 1967). They were strongly neoclassical in their methods, which tended toward comparative-static tests of partial equilibrium models. They were also strongly neoclassical in their belief that changes in technology and in the organization of production were for the most part endogenous responses to market signals. As one participant in this movement later acknowledged, there was not much room in this view of economic history for "good and bad entrepreneurs, leaders and followers"—that is, for what many business historians studied (Parker 1971; see also North 1961).

Robert Fogel's study of American railroads epitomized the New Economic Historians' approach. Challenging the Whiggish claim that railroads were "indispensable" to American economic development, he argued that transportation innovations were a response to economic need and that, if it had been necessary, the canal system could have expanded to provide transportation services almost as efficiently as the railroad. He then proceeded to use historical data on freight shipments to evaluate this road not taken against the road that was. Employing comparative-static methods, Fogel calculated that in the absence of the railroad the Gross National Product (GNP) of the United States in 1890 would not have been much different—at most 5 percent lower—than it actually was (Fogel 1964).

In Chandler's view, Fogel's entire calculation was misguided (Yates 2004). The railroad's most important contribution to economic growth was the greater speed and regularity of transportation it provided compared to canals. As he explained in *The Visible Hand* (1977), this improvement made possible the integration of mass distribution and mass production in large-scale, managerially directed enterprises, which in turn permitted the flow of resources and goods to be coordinated much more efficiently than was possible in the market. Underpinning this essentially Penrosian notion was Parsonian role theory. Chandler believed that managers' new positions of importance encouraged them to adopt professional identities and, unlike owners who were primarily interested in maximizing current profits, pursue policies that enhanced their companies' wealth-creating capabilities over the long term.

Chandler's analysis of the rise and critical importance of the large managerially directed enterprise dominated research in business history in the United States at least through the 1980s (see Cassis, this volume). Given Chandler's orientation toward sociology and his aversion to the New Economic History, it is perhaps not surprising that few practitioners during this period made any use of economic theory in their work. Table 3.1 analyzes articles published in the *Business History Review* for a sample of years beginning in 1960. Virtually none of the articles

Table 3.1 Use of economic theory and methods in articles published in *Business History Review*

Year	Number of articles	Percent that cite economics literature	Percent that use eonomic concepts to frame the analysis	Percent that make use of formal economic models	Percent that use quantitative information to test explicit hypotheses
1960	20	0.0	0.0	0.0	0.0
1965	25	0.0	0.0	0.0	0.0
1970	21	4.8	4.8	0.0	0.0
1975	16	31.2	25.0	6.2	12.5
1980	14	0.0	7.1	0.0	0.0
1985	15	6.7	6.7	0.0	0.0
1990	15	6.7	6.7	0.0	0.0
1995	11	18.2	0.0	0.0	0.0
2000	12	16.7	16.7	0.0	0.0

Table 3.2 Use of economic theory and methods in articles published in *Business and Economic History*

Year	Number of articles	Percent that cite economics literature	Percent that use eonomic concepts to frame the analysis	Percent that make use of formal economic models	Percent that use quantitative information to test explicit hypotheses
1965	12	16.7	16.7	0.0	0.0
1969	15	6.7	6.7	0.0	0.0
1975	9	22.0	0.0	0.0	0.0
1980	17	17.6	11.7	0.0	0.0
1985	16	6.2	12.5	12.5	12.5
1990	28	28.6	17.9	3.6	3.6
1995	35	8.6	11.4	0.0	2.9

Note: There were no issues in 1960 or in either adjacent year. The nearest year to 1970 was 1969. The early publishing history is given in *Proceedings of the Business History Conference* (second series, Vol. 1) (Bloomington, ind.: Indiana University School of Business Division of Research, 1973), first (unnumbered) page. The journal published its final issue in 1999 and the organization commenced a new one, *Enterprise and Society*, in the following year. See the text for further discussion.

surveyed before the 1990s exploited formal economic models or tested hypotheses quantitatively, and very few used economic concepts to frame the analysis. Even in the anomalous year 1975, when one issue included three pieces written by New Economic Historians, less than a third of the articles in the journal cited any economics literature at all. In most years, such references were few and far between.

Business and Economic History, the Business History Conference's annual proceedings journal, was somewhat more receptive to economic theory (see Table 3.2). A small number of economists had maintained their membership in the organization, presenting papers at its annual meetings that subsequently found their way into the journal's pages. Nonetheless, only a small proportion of the articles that it published were organized around economic concepts, and fewer still made any use of formal models. Even in this journal, the vast majority of articles included no references at all to the economics literature.

Chandler's synthesis helped business historians who were working in other countries move from isolated case studies to engagement with questions of broader concern. Although there has been disagreement over the extent to which his ideas applied to the experience of particular nations, his insistence on the importance for economic growth of the creation of large-scale, managerially directed firms provided scholars in many countries with an agenda around which they could organize international discussions and also their own research (see, for example, Yamamura 1970; Daems and van der Wee 1974; Nakagawa 1975; Chandler and Daems 1980; Hannah 1983; Nakagawa and Yui 1983; Kobayashi and Morikawa

1986; Coleman 1987). Chandler's work was particularly influential in Germany and Japan, perhaps because scholarly attention in those countries had already focused on successful, large-scale enterprises (Kudô 2003; Schröter 2003). In neither country did business historians have much ongoing connection with economics, and the spread of the Chandlerian paradigm did little or nothing to change the situation.

In Germany, for example, business historians had mainly come out of political and social history, and they worked to make Chandler's paradigm less abstract— for example, by opening up the "black box" of management and examining the social origins, training, and methods of operation of the professionals who staffed company hierarchies, as well as the role played by large German banks in financing and directing major enterprises (see Kocka 1971, 1978, and 1981; Nakagawa and Yui 1983). They were also preoccupied—understandably given Germany's twentieth-century history—with the relationship between business and the state (see, for example, Horn and Kocka 1979). Richard Tilly, an economic historian who has written extensively on German banking, attempted to stimulate his German colleagues to write a more quantitative, theoretically informed type of business history, but he had little success (see, for example, Tilly 1982).

In 1981 the German Society for Business History established the *German Yearbook on Business History* to translate selected articles published in German periodicals into English in order to gain international recognition for the work (Pohl 1987). None of the articles that appeared in these volumes before the *Yearbook* ceased publication in 1995 used economic models, and only one (authored not surprisingly by Tilly (1993)) employed quantitative tests. One article (Lindenlaub 1984) surveyed different theoretical approaches to research in business history, including some using economic theory, but very few others cited any economics literature at all.

In Japan the situation was very similar. Keiichiro Nakagawa, the scholar behind the formation of the Business History Society of Japan in 1965, envisioned that the new association would foster dialogue between business and economic historians. In practice, however, participants adopted the methods and approaches of those US business historians who had distanced themselves from economic history. Indeed, Chandler was considered one of the "godfathers" of the Japanese branch of the discipline. The first issue of the *Japan Business History Review* in 1966, devoted to a discussion of methodology, focused mainly on the ideas of Chandler and Gras. Although the volume discussed Schumpeter's notions of entrepreneurship, as well as several other approaches, there was no exploration of mainstream theoretical developments in economics (Yamamura 1970). Nor has this orientation shifted over time. The overwhelming majority of the articles published in the *Japanese Yearbook on Business History* (modeled on the German *Yearbook* (Pohl 1987)) contains no references at all to the economics literature. Similarly, very few of the foreign scholars invited to the international conferences that Japanese business historians have hosted annually since 1974 have had any training in economics. Even when the topic of the conference was something about which economic theory clearly had a lot to say (for example, cartels), the organizers made no effort to secure the participation of economists (see, for example, Kudô and Hara 1992).

In Britain, however, business history began to diverge methodologically from that in the United States, Germany, and Japan during this period of Chandlerian dominance. Chandler's approach was less appealing there because the giant managerial enterprises that he thought were the carriers of progress were not as important in Britain as in these other countries. Chandler viewed their relative absence as a cause of the UK's poor performance (Chandler 1980 and 1990), an idea that William Lazonick (1983) among others developed further (see the essays in Elbaum and Lazonick 1986). Although this argument attracted some adherents among British business historians (see, for example, McKinlay 1992), most found it unpersuasive (Church 1990; Harvey and Jones 1990; Supple 1991; Kirby 1992). In response, they amassed evidence pointing to the vibrancy of smaller, less integrated businesses, including family-run enterprises (Jones and Rose 1993; Church 1993; Jeremy 1993; Lloyd-Jones and Lewis 1994).[3]

Perhaps because they were less enamored of Chandler's ideas, a number of British business historians responded with interest to some of the research being produced by New Economic Historians in the United States. Arguing that one should not embrace so sweeping an explanation as entrepreneurial failure unless alternative hypotheses could be falsified, New Economic Historians had re-examined some of the standard examples of failure—for example, British textile firms' reluctance to adopt ring spinning—and were in fact unable to reject the hypothesis that British entrepreneurs had responded rationally to the economic conditions they faced (see Temin 1966; Sandberg 1969; McCloskey and Sandberg 1971; McCloskey 1973; Saxonhouse and Wright 1984). British scholars responded to this work by revisiting the histories of a number of declining industries, including textiles, iron and steel, and automobiles, in some cases developing a new appreciation of the choices British entrepreneurs made (see, for example, Harvey 1979; Foreman-Peck 1981; Fine 1990; Bowden 1991). As Table 3.3 indicates, British scholars' greater interest in and willingness to make use of the insights of the New Economic History is reflected in the higher proportion of articles published in *Business History*, the flagship journal of the British branch of the profession, that cited the economics literature compared to publications in the United States, Germany, and Japan. Though none of the articles we surveyed for the period before 1990 went so far as to use formal models, several did make an effort to test the merits of alternative hypotheses using quantitative data.

---

[3] Some scholars who initially were more positively inclined to Chandler's ideas later changed their minds. For example, Hannah organized a conference in London in 1975 to explore the possibility of applying Chandler's insights to British business history. The papers were published in Hannah (1976*b*). But contrast Hannah (1976*a*) and (1983) with Hannah (1991) and (1999).

Table 3.3 Use of economic theory and methods in articles published in *Business History*

Year	Number of articles	Percent that cite economics literature	Percent that use eonomic concepts to frame the analysis	Percent that make use of formal economic models	Percent that use quantitative information to test explicit hypotheses
1960	7	0.0	0.0	0.0	0.0
1965	6	16.7	16.7	0.0	0.0
1970	7	14.3	14.3	0.0	0.0
1975	8	37.5	12.5	0.0	12.5
1980	11	27.3	0.0	0.0	0.0
1985	15	20.0	0.0	0.0	13.3
1990	25	72.0	32.0	12.0	12.0
1995	23	47.8	26.0	4.3	8.7
2000	26	73.1	34.6	0.0	19.2

3.3 BUSINESS HISTORY AND ECONOMIC THEORY IN THE POST-CHANDLER ERA

Traditional neoclassical theory assumed that economic actors were rational beings who made optimizing decisions on the basis of perfect information and fore-knowledge.[4] This highly stylized view of human behavior was a useful simplification that enabled economists to analyze certain otherwise intractable problems, especially concerning markets (Friedman 1953). But it was not so well suited to understanding the behavior of individual enterprises. Traditional theory treated the firm as a black box—as an equation-solving entity devoted to setting marginal revenue equal to marginal cost. It was not particularly helpful for analyzing how firms would respond strategically (that is, to small-numbers competition) in their product markets and was completely incapable of dealing with firms as complex organizations composed of people with differing experiences and goals. For these reasons its appeal to business historians was understandably limited.

Over the last three decades, however, several new bodies of analysis have emerged that are potentially much more useful to business historians. Agency theory, for example, provides a set of tools appropriate for analyzing organizations whose members have different and often conflicting interests. Take the case of the large-scale managerial enterprises that figure so importantly in Chandler's histories. The owners of these enterprises (the principals) were the stockholders, who might, as in Chandler's account and also in traditional theory, be conceptualized as seeking to

---

[4] The following discussion draws on Lamoreaux *et al.* (1995, 1997, and 1999).

maximize profits. But the managers (their agents) who actually ran the firms were likely to have very different priorities. Perhaps, as Chandler claims, they were interested in the long-run health of the enterprise, but they could also have other goals, such as maximizing their own compensation and perks, guaranteeing themselves job security, or establishing reputations that would enable them to secure more important positions in other firms. In order to ensure that firms operated in their interests, stockholders had to be able to impose their own priorities on managers. But even if they had the power to do so, which was not necessarily the case, they typically had only imperfect information about their agents' activities. Moreover, such information as they had was asymmetric—that is, stockholders knew a lot less about what managers were doing than did the managers themselves.

Because agency theory offers a well-articulated analysis of how principals can use incentives to solve these kinds of problems, it can help business historians evaluate the effect of specific rules and historical contexts on hierarchically structured relationships. We can see the rise of what we might call post-Chandler business history in the application of these new tools. For example, Daniel Raff (1995) has used the theory to show how the kinds of compensation schemes that were best suited to inducing productive effort from workers in automobile factories changed with the kind of technology the firm employed. Plans that rewarded individual achievement made sense where artisanal modes of production prevailed. Firms that used assembly-line methods, however, were better off using group compensation schemes, because it did the company no good to encourage an individual to be more productive than other workers on the line. Finally, firms like Ford, which used both mass-production (interchangeable parts) and assembly-line methods were better off paying flat wages. This particular technology made it easier and cheaper to monitor workers' efforts because it simplified the tasks that individuals had to accomplish and allowed centralized control of the pace of work. All that was necessary was to pay workers a wage that made them want to keep their jobs and fire those that did not keep up. As Raff has shown, other firms abandoned incentive plans in favor of straight-wage compensation schemes when they adopted Ford-style technology.

The top-down models of agency theory are less useful where economic actors interact in ways that affect each others' outcomes. Such situations can often be more fruitfully analyzed using the tools of game theory. Defining a game involves specifying the number of players, the order of play, the choices each player can make at each stage of the game, how each choice affects the other players' choices and payoffs, the information that each has, whether the players can cooperate or not, and the number of periods the game will continue. Perhaps because the game has to be laid out in such detail, business historians have had trouble seeing the value of the exercise. But given adequate definition, game theory offers practitioners a set of tools that can be quite valuable for analyzing the choices of real-world decision makers. Particularly useful is the principle of backward induction, in which players anticipate what will happen at later stages of the game and make their initial choices accordingly. For example, Naomi Lamoreaux and Jean-Laurent Rosenthal use backward induction in a simple three-period game to analyze the decision to organize a business as a partnership or a corporation. Their model yields predictions about the choice of organizational form that are a better fit to the historical evidence than the conventional view that corporations are superior for most types of business enterprises.[5]

Backward induction also plays a role in a third major body of theory—the economics of transaction costs pioneered by Oliver Williamson.[6] Williamson's analysis departed from orthodox economic theory in placing the individual transaction rather than a market equilibrium of supply and demand at the center of the analysis and in rejecting the standard neoclassical assumption of perfect information. In his initial approach (1975), Williamson emphasized the idea that when economic actors enter into transactions, they know more about their own capabilities and circumstances than about those of the parties with whom they are dealing. As a result, they can often take advantage of one another—extract more benefit from the transaction than they could if all parties had the same information. Anticipating such exploitation, economic actors may refuse to enter into such activities unless they are able to find ways of reducing the potential for such ill-gotten gains.

In subsequent work, Williamson (1979, 1981, and 1985) articulated the types of circumstances in which transaction costs tended to be high and also suggested how they could be alleviated. For example, he argued that contracting was likely to be particularly difficult in situations characterized by "asset specificity"—that is, situations in which investments had to be made in assets that were highly specific to the transaction and could not be redeployed at low cost. The best way to deal with this problem, Williamson suggested, was to move the activity inside the firm. Putting both parties to the transaction under common ownership removed the incentive for them to exploit each other. Moreover, any differences that subsequently arose between the parties could be resolved by fiat rather than by costly adjudication.

Williamson himself was one of the first scholars to apply his economic theory of transaction costs to business history. In an important article in 1981, he recast Chandler's account of the rise of big business. As he saw it, the large vertically integrated firm was able, by expanding its boundaries and substituting managerial (hierarchical) coordination for market exchange, to resolve the serious transaction

---

[5] See Lamoreaux and Rosenthal (2006b). For a simpler, more heuristic version of the model, see Lamoreaux and Rosenthal (2006a). Many games have multiple solutions. This theoretical complication may be a boon to business historians, providing an opportunity to explain divergent outcomes to similar problems.

[6] Williamson built on Ronald Coase's classic (1937) but long ignored exploration of the question why some activities were coordinated by the market and others were coordinated within firms. Coase had hypothesized that under certain circumstances internalizing transactions within firms was less expensive than organizing and enforcing them in the market.

problems caused by the asset specificity of its investments. Similarly, the integration of mass distribution and mass production was a consequence of what he called the externality principle, where the failure of one distributor to invest the resources needed to maintain the quality of a good could undermine the reputation of the product more generally.

A small number of other scholars recognized early on the value of transaction-cost theory for the study of business history. Two of the first were Mark Casson and Geoffrey Jones, a British economist and historian respectively, who were both interested in the study of multinational enterprises. Casson, himself a theorist, organized a conference in 1982 that brought together business historians, economists, and scholars in business schools to discuss how to write studies of international business that would be both theoretically and historically informed (Casson 1983). Jones and Peter Hertner organized a conference the next year with a similar agenda (Hertner and Jones 1986). Both Casson and Jones used the new economic theory in their own scholarship, and they continued to work hard to encourage other business historians to do likewise, organizing conferences and publishing collections of essays (Casson 1982; Casson 1984; Buckley and Casson 1985; Casson 1986 and 1987; Jones 1986 and 1990; Jones and Morgan 1994; Jones 2000 and 2005).

Others soon joined Casson and Jones in their call for more theoretically informed work in business history. Australian academics Diane Hutchinson and Stephen Nicholas urged practitioners to use insights from the economics of transaction costs to extract new generalizations from the histories of individual businesses and to improve their understanding of why business organizations evolved in different ways in different countries (Hutchinson and Nicholas 1987 and 1988; Nicholas 1986). The British scholar Clive Lee (1990a and 1990b) published a two-part article in *Business History* in which he similarly argued that recent theoretical developments in the economics of information and organizational design could help scholars extract more powerful generalizations from their case studies. In the United States Naomi Lamoreaux, Daniel Raff, and Peter Temin organized a series of conferences under the auspices of the National Bureau of Economic Research that brought together business historians, economic historians, and economic theorists with the aim of encouraging both more intellectual exchange among these groups and more use of economic theory in business history (see Temin 1991; Lamoreaux and Raff 1995; and Lamoreaux *et al.* 1999).

The response of business historians to these calls has varied around the world. Perhaps not surprisingly, given Casson and Jones's leadership, the British branch of the profession has been most receptive. As Table 3.3 shows, the proportion of articles published in *Business History* that included citations to the economics literature increased, beginning in the mid-1970s and then soared by the 1990s. The same pattern appears, albeit to a lesser extent, in the share of articles that used economic concepts to frame the analysis. No one would mistake *Business History* for an economics journal—explicit economic models and hypothesis testing were still the exception rather than the rule—but the shift in the content of the journal is nonetheless striking.

The change in the type of articles published by *Business History* had much to do with the installation of a new editorial team, one of whose members was Jones, but the rapidity of the transformation suggests that research in the field had already moved substantially in the direction of using more economic theory. This change was encouraged by the location of many British business historians in economic history or even economics departments. Since 1990, however, many economic history departments have been merged into history departments, which may alter future research styles.

This is not to say that the majority of business historians in Britain were part of this movement or that there was no opposition to the trend. The annual surveys of the literature that the journal began to publish in the early 1990s suggest that most scholars continued to work on individual industries and firms in the same way as they had before. Some of the surveys, moreover, were very critical of work by economists. Alan McKinlay (1992: 4), for example, wrote dismissively of "the static sterility of the 'new' economic history". But other writers of the surveys lauded the turn toward economics. Indeed, Martin Chick (1993: 6) went so far as to opine, "Were there an Oscar-style award for 'Journal of the Year' my nomination for 1991 would be *Explorations in Economic History*", which was devoted to publishing research by New Economic Historians.

British scholars have used economic theory to explore topics ranging from ancient Phoenicia (Moore and Lewis 2000) to modern finance (Ross 1996), but their work has focused especially on two areas: multinational enterprises and business networks. British business historians participated vigorously, for example, in a debate stimulated by the economist Jean-François Hennart (1994*a*), who used data on so-called free-standing companies to critique the reigning view (which Casson had done much to promote) that multinational enterprises were devices for the international transfer of firm-specific capabilities. Casson issued a rejoinder, as did T. A. B. Corley, and Hennart responded (Casson 1994; Corley 1994; Hennart 1994*b*). The debate quickly attracted new participants, ultimately giving rise to an edited volume (Wilkins and Schröter 1998) and additional books and articles (for example, Greenhill 1995; C. Jones 1997; G. Jones 2000). Although disagreement persists, what is important for our purposes is the extent to which the debate has focused around the question of what is the most appropriate economic theory for understanding this form of business enterprise.

Initially, the focus on business networks was part of the effort to rescue family enterprises from the Chandlerian scrapheap (see in particular the special issue of *Business History* on "Family Capitalism" in October 1993), but it quickly grew into a broader attempt to understand the dynamics of important regional economies (for example, Casson and Rose 1998), the mechanisms by which capital has been funneled into business enterprises (for example, Cox *et al.* 2003), and the ways in which economic activity is coordinated over long distances (for example, Munro and Slaven 2001). As in the debate over the free-standing company, much of the discussion has revolved around the utility of particular types of theory, including evolutionary and sociological approaches as well as various branches of economic theory (Casson 1997; Westall 1998; Toms and Wilson 2003; Parsons and Rose 2004). Entrepreneurship has also been revived as a topic through the use of new economic tools and explicit tests of hypotheses (Godley 2001; Nicholas 1999 and 2004).

Scholars in Australia played a leading role in showing how economic theory could be applied to business history. Stephen Nicholas followed up his call for this kind of work with studies of multinationals (1983 and 1986), British overseas marketing (1984), and early trading companies (Carlos and Nicholas 1990, 1993, and 1996). Simon Ville joined the debate over early trading companies (Jones and Ville 1996). He also brought the new theory to bear on the agricultural sector, analyzing networks of trade and finance in the pastoral economy (Ville 1996; Ville 2000; Ville and Fleming 2000). Perhaps the most sophisticated applications have been Gordon Boyce's analyses of financial and information networks in the shipping industry (Boyce 1992, 1995, and 2003; Boyce and Lepper 2002). Boyce (2001*a*) expanded his analysis to the study of cooperative ventures in international business more generally, and he and Ville (2002) wrote a business history textbook that aimed to demonstrate the power of what they called "the contracting paradigm".

During the 1990s, as giant managerial enterprises (especially in the US) gave way to more specialized, less vertically integrated competitors, the Chandlerian paradigm lost much of its luster and the new style of economically informed business history attracted increasing attention around the world. A few business historians from Germany and Japan joined this movement (see, for example, Burhop 2004 and Okazaki 1995), but the new style of business history has developed furthest in places that did not already have a business-history establishment founded on the Chandlerian paradigm. Since 1990, for example, *Business History* has published increasing numbers of articles by Dutch and Scandinavian scholars who have made use of insights from the new economics of information. Notable examples include Hugo van Driel's study (2003) of the international coffee trade, Anita Goransson's analysis (1993) of the impact of gendered property rights on the separation of ownership and control in Swedish business, and Hans Sjögren and Sven Jungerhem's discussion (1996) of the venture capital market for small firms in Sweden. Similar publications by Greek, Italian, Spanish, Portuguese, and Eastern European scholars have also found their way into the journal (see, for example, Minoglou 2002; Cuevas 2002; Pérez and Puig 2004; and Stanciu 2000). The several proceedings volumes of papers given at conferences of the newly formed European Business History Association reveal a similar geography. The volumes vary enormously in the extent to which they include papers that reference the economics literature, with Bonin (2002) at the low end and Olsson (1997) at the high end. In the middle (Amatori *et al.* 1999; Kuijlaars *et al.* 2000; Amdam *et al.* 2001) about 20 to 25 percent of the articles cite at least some economics. Virtually all of these are by British, Dutch, or Scandinavian business historians or by scholars from Mediterranean countries.

Scholars in the United States who made use of the new economic theory to tackle problems in business history tended mainly to be trained in economics, to specialize in economic history or one of the other subfields of economics, such as industrial organization, and to publish in the *Journal of Economic History*, the *Rand Journal of Economics*, the *Journal of Law and Economics*, or other similar venues. Many of them belonged to the Business History Conference (BHC), but they typically taught in economics departments. To give just a few examples, Ann Carlos and her various collaborators have used all of the bodies of theory discussed above to analyze early trading companies (see, for example, Carlos 1992; Carlos and Hoffman 1986; Carlos and Nicholas 1990, 1993, and 1996; Carlos and Lewis 1993 and 1999). Charles Calomiris (see Calomiris 1990 and 1995; Calomiris and Gorton 1991), Naomi Lamoreaux (1994), Kenneth Snowden (1995), and Noel Maurer (2002) have employed agency theory to explore the workings of credit markets and the banking system more generally. Avner Greif used game theory with great subtlety to explore the institutions that facilitated trade in the early modern period (the work is synthesized in Greif 2005). Chiaki Moriguchi (2003 and 2005) developed a game-theoretic explanation of what happened when welfare capitalism encountered the shock of the Great Depression, and Knick Harley (1982) and David Genesove and Wallace Mullin (1998, 1999, and 2001) have used ideas from game- theory to explore strategic behavior in the railroad and sugar refining industries respectively. The case of General Motors' acquisition of the Fisher Body has been examined and re-examined from the perspective of transaction-cost economics (see Klein *et al.* 1978; Coase 2000; Klein 2000; Freeland 2000).[7] Concepts from this literature have also been applied to topics as diverse the study of the Cuban sugar industry (Dye 1994 and 1998), the integration of regional and interregional capital markets in the United States (Odell 1989), and the growth of sharecropping in early modern French agriculture (Hoffman 1984).

Very few scholars in the United States who identified themselves primarily as business historians exploited the new theoretical developments in economics. Spurred by the work of Michael Piore, Charles Sabel, Jonathan Zeitlin, and Philip Scranton (see Piore and Sabel 1984; Sabel and Zeitlin 1985 and 1997; Scranton 1983, 1989, and 1997), business historians have willingly abandoned their focus on the large-scale enterprise. But they have not embraced economics as a tool in their explorations. As Table 3.2 shows, the decline of the Chandlerian paradigm resulted in a slight increase in the number of articles in *Business and Economic History* that made use of formal economic models and/or tested hypotheses quantitatively, but there was no similar rise in the *Business History Review*. As late as the 1990s, moreover, less than 20 percent of the articles sampled in the two journals included

---

[7] For an empirical challenge to the transaction-cost view of the acquisition, see Helper *et al.* (2000).

even one citation to the economics literature. The founding by the BHC of a new quarterly, *Enterprise and Society*, did not change the situation. A review of the journal's contents over its first half decade of publication reveals only a few articles that involved economic analysis in a central way (Bakker 2001; Beamer and Lewis 2003; and Boyce 2001*b*), most of them by scholars from other countries. Rather, there seems to have been a shift toward a type of cultural history that is relatively uninformed by any theory, let alone economics (see, for example, the symposia on "Beauty and Business" (2000) and on "Gender and Business History" (2001)).[8]

3.4 TOWARD MORE AND BETTER ECONOMICS IN BUSINESS HISTORY

To the extent that business historians have made use of the new economic theory in their work, they have for the most part employed it descriptively. As the tables show, they have rarely set up formal models or engaged in explicit hypothesis testing. Rather, they have tended to use economics in the same way they have used other types of theory—as a source of ideas and a framework around which to organize their research. They have not been swept up in any social science project of generalization, but have subordinated the theory to what business historians typically do, that is, try to understand the behavior and evolution of specific enterprises, industries, or business practices.

Nonetheless, opposition has arisen even to this modest deployment of economic ideas. Economics, it is objected, is very good at modeling the measures according to which business people decide among alternative courses of action, whether these be price signals in the market, the extent to which incentives can alleviate principal–agent problems, or the effect of different organizational arrangements on transaction costs. But it is not very good at shedding light on where these alternatives come from in the first place. That is, it is not much good at explaining how individuals, firms, and organizations innovate and develop new capabilities over time.

Chandler himself played a role in articulating these criticisms. Although initially he seemed flattered by Williamson's effort to translate his ideas into the language of transaction costs,[9] eventually he came to the conclusion that the framework was

---

[8] The main editor during the early years of the journal was an economist (William Hausman), so the trend was more likely a result of the kind of work then being done by US business historians than the preferences of the editor. We do not mean to imply that no business historians write theoretically informed cultural history—just that much current writing is atheoretical. For a counter-example, see Lipartito and Sicilia (2004).

[9] For example, he and Herman Daems included an essay by Williamson in their volume *Managerial Hierarchies* (1980).

too limiting. From his Penrosian perspective, it was "the specific nature of the firm's facilities and skills"—not its ability to minimize transaction costs—that mattered. For it was these organizational capabilities that "permit[ted] the enterprise to be more than the sum of its parts", that gave "it a life of its own", that made it a site of learning (Chandler 1992: 86–7). Other business historians agreed. S. R. H. Jones (1998) emphasized the limitations of Williamson's comparative static approach for analyzing the development of business capabilities over time. William Lazonick (2003) doubted that the mainstream economics profession could ever develop theoretical tools appropriate to this task. In his view, it would "require an intellectual revolution in economics" that was extremely unlikely to occur. Kenneth Lipartito and David Sicilia (2004) argued that the study of change and development "could never quite be brought under the abstract, generalized models of organization proposed by economic theory".[10]

There is no doubt that these critics are to some extent correct. Mainstream economic theory is not well suited for understanding the sources of innovation or the wellsprings of economic growth. But that does not mean it lacks utility even for these purposes, as the following example drawn from Chandler's own work shows. The use of simple economic models can improve scholars' ability to audit claims about dynamic processes, helping them decide what story they ought to tell.

The Standard Oil Company, according to Chandler, was one of the earliest companies to demonstrate the enormous cost savings that could be reaped by substituting the visible hand of management for the invisible hand of the market. Chandler's account of Standard's rise is a story of efficiency begetting market power begetting efficiency. Frustrated by the failure of their efforts to organize the nation's oil refiners into a cartel, Rockefeller and his associates in the Cleveland refinery decided to obtain the cooperation of their rivals "by relying on the economic power provided by their high-volume, low-cost operation". They approached the manager of one of the two railroads that served Cleveland and asked for a rebate in return for an assured volume of business. The manager agreed because "such high volume meant he could schedule the use of his equipment much more efficiently and so lose nothing by the reduced rate". Standard then used the advantage it derived from these lower costs to cartelize the industry, "invit[ing] the leading refiners first in Cleveland and later in other refining centers to join" in the benefits (Chandler 1977: 321–2).

Elizabeth Granitz and Benjamin Klein (1996) have re-examined Chandler's sources using conventional neoclassical tools and found that his account lacks plausibility. Although Standard operated "the largest refinery in the nation," there

---

[10] Many of these scholars have been attracted to the evolutionary economics of Richard Nelson and Sidney Winter (1982). Other attempts to develop a theory suitable for analyzing the development of capabilities include Langlois and Robertson (1995) and Casson (1998). See also Langlois (2003 and 2004) and Lazonick, this volume.

is no evidence that it had a significant cost advantage.[11] Its share of the US market was only 4 percent, and its share of Cleveland production only about 15 percent. There were no barriers to entry arising from patents or the control of raw material resources. Nor do there seem at that time to have been any significant economies of scale in refining. The minimum efficient scale of operation for a still was only about 500 to 600 barrels, and most of the industry's growth during this early period came from new entrants (Williamson and Daum 1959). For all practical purposes, the petroleum industry was competitively structured. Refineries had U-shaped average cost curves, and bigger did not necessarily mean better.

Given this background, it is unlikely that the railroad's willingness to offer rebates derived from Standard's economic advantages and more plausible that it derived from the dynamics of competition among the small number of railroads that served the major refining regions. In the alternative account offered by Granitz and Klein, it was the railroads' (not Standard's) frustration over failed attempts to form a cartel—a persistent problem for railroads in the period— that set the events of the story in motion. Needing outside parties to police their agreement, the railroads formed the leading refineries in Cleveland, Pittsburgh, and other production centers into an association called the South Improvement Company. The Company allocated each railroad a share of the business of transporting oil and assigned participating refineries the task of ensuring that the railroads did not cheat on one another. In return, the refineries obtained both a rebate on their own shipments of oil and a drawback on their competitors' shipments.

Although the South Improvement agreement was never implemented,[12] there was a several month period (after the company was formed but before it fell apart) when prospects seemed dim for the refineries not included in the scheme. Rockefeller entrepreneurially took advantage of the situation to induce the other firms to sell out. As Granitz and Klein point out, only the competitive advantage that the member refineries stood to gain can explain why so many non-members sold their refineries to Rockefeller during these months, many of them at distress prices.[13] Emerging from this episode with effective control over the Cleveland refining industry, Standard then secretly merged with the original participating refiners in the other production centers. As a result of these acquisitions and mergers, Standard was large enough in and of itself to police the railroads' cartel agreements, and

[11] Indeed, Williamson and Daum's account of advances in refinery operation in the late 1860s and early 1870s focuses on other firms besides Standard, particularly Charles Pratt's "greatly admired refinery" in New York City (1959).

[12] The plan collapsed in the face of determined opposition from producers in the oil fields who threatened to enforce an embargo on shipments to the South Improvement Company with violence (Granitz and Klein 1996).

[13] Under normal conditions, given the petroleum industry's cost structure, refiners would not have been worried by the formation of a cartel for as outsiders they would have been able to "free ride" on Standard's high prices (Granitz and Klein 1996).

they willingly rewarded it for performing this service with the rebates it needed to maintain this position (Granitz and Klein 1996).

Although a full account of this incident would require us to venture into the realm of game theory in order to explain why the railroads needed Standard to monitor their cartels, Granitz and Klein's analysis shows how valuable even the simplest economic theory can be in sorting out the causal elements of an unfolding set of events. Instead of Chandler's simple account of efficiency begetting market power, we end up with a much more realistic story of how Rockefeller exploited the railroads' need for a monitor to "raise rivals' costs" and secure monopoly control over his industry. It is important to underscore, however, that there is nothing in this story that precludes the possibility that monopoly ultimately begot efficiency. It may well be, as Chandler claims, that once Standard secured control of the petroleum industry, Rockefeller used the device of the trust company to reorganize its operations, consolidate production in its most efficient plants, and reduce costs through improved administrative coordination (Chandler 1977 and 1990). But it should also be noted that this part of the narrative has not yet been subjected to similar theoretical scrutiny.

As the Standard Oil example suggests, a judicious use of economic theory not only helps business historians sort out the causal elements of their stories but enables them to avoid a key pitfall to which Chandler, Lazonick, and others who favor a more dynamic approach often succumb: a tendency to write history in the Whig style and portray the achievements of businesses as if they were the end point toward which history has triumphantly been tending.[14] This tendency has not only inflected their histories of individual firms like Standard Oil but has shaped their views of the evolution of business organizations more generally. Hence for Chandler and Lazonick, the managerial hierarchies that large firms created in the early twentieth century were much more than a response to the economic environment of the times, they were a critical stage in the evolution of business—a necessary precondition for ongoing organizational learning and even for innovation itself (Chandler 1992; Lazonick 1991 and 2003).

In our own work (see Lamoreaux *et al.* 2003 and 2004), we have tried to show how recent economic theory could be used to avoid such a tendency toward Whiggism.[15] As we have argued, it is both easy and tempting to write business history as if what happened had to happen. It is much more difficult to write history that focuses on alternatives and choices, acknowledging the significance of possibilities that never took lasting form. But mainstream economics provides a broad arsenal of tools well suited for this purpose. Ranging from the evaluation of counterfactual hypotheses as used by neoclassically oriented New Economic Historians to the techniques of backward induction employed by game theorists, the methods of

---

[14] On this point, see also Hannah (2006).
[15] For criticisms of our arguments, see Langlois (2004) and Sabel and Zeitlin (2004).

modern economics make it possible to consider (and even collect data about) roads that were never taken or alternatives that were never realized. To gain these benefits, however, even those business historians who have been most receptive to economic ideas will have to make fuller use of them. They will have to push beyond the descriptive tasks for which they have hitherto mainly deployed the theory and exploit the greater power that comes from explicitly considering formal models and confronting refutable hypotheses with evidence.

3.5 CONCLUSIONS

This survey has emphasized the uneasy and sometimes tension-filled relationship that has long existed between business history and mainstream economic theorists. Since business history first emerged as a distinct field of research in the early twentieth century, most practitioners have made little use of economics in their work and some have been downright hostile to the idea that economic theory could improve the writing of business history. The development of new bodies of theory in the last several decades, particularly the economics of asymmetric information, transaction cost economics, and game theory, has changed the situation to a considerable extent. Although most business historians in the United States have remained indifferent or even antagonistic, there was a groundswell of interest in the new theory in Britain, Australia, and then increasingly in a number of continental European countries beginning in the 1980s. There was also a flurry of activity in the United States and elsewhere by scholars who do not identify themselves as business historians but who have nevertheless been using the new theory to write what is in effect business history.

It is fitting, therefore, to conclude this essay by emphasizing the positive. Over the last couple of decades, scholars have used economic theory to forge new links between business history and developments in the other social science disciplines. They have revisited in illuminating ways topics ranging from early trading companies to modern financial institutions. They have engaged in lively debate about the sources of advantage held by multinational companies, and they have challenged the idea that the family firm is an outmoded form of enterprise. They have also pioneered the analysis of networks and other economic organizations that fall between the traditional topics of markets, on the one hand, and firms, on the other. In all of these endeavors, they have pushed outwards the frontiers of research in business history.

There is always more to be done, however, and we hope that this essay will encourage scholars to experiment with new types of theory (like game theory) that have been relatively under-utilized for the study of business history. We also hope that our colleagues will be inspired to use theory more formally—that they will make the effort to pose and test refutable hypotheses, not as an end in itself but as a way of enhancing the rigor of their writing and of avoiding the temptations of determinism.

REFERENCES

AMATORI, FRANCO, COLLI, ANDREA, and CREPAS, NICOLA (eds.) (1999). *Deindustrialization and Reindustrialization in 20th Century Europe: Proceedings of the EBHA Conference.* Milan: Franco Angeli.

AMDAM, ROLV P., HAGBERG, ANNE E., and SOGNER, KNUT (eds.) (2001). "Proceedings from the 5th EBHA Conference". Norwegian School of Management. Compact disc.

BAKKER, GERBER (2001). "Stars and Stories: How Films Became Branded Products". *Enterprise and Society*, 2/3, Sept.: 461–502.

BEAMER, GLENN, and LEWIS, DAVID E. (2003). "The Irrational Escalation of Commitment and the Ironic Labor Politics of the Rust Belt". *Enterprise and Society*, 4/4, Dec.: 676–706.

"Beauty and Business" (2000). Special issue of *Enterprise and Society*, 1/3, Sept.

BONIN, HUBERT (ed.) (2002). *Transnational Companies (19th–20th Centuries): European Business History Association.* Paris: PLAGE.

BOWDEN, S. M. (1991). "Demand and Supply Constraints in the Inter-War UK Car Industry: Did the Manufacturers Get It Right?" *Business History*, 33/2, Apr.: 241–67.

BOYCE, GORDON (1992). "64thers, Syndicates, and Stock Promotions: Information Flows and Fundraising Techniques of British Shipowners before 1914". *Journal of Economic History*, 52/1, Mar.: 181–205.

—— (1995). *Information, Mediation, and Institutional Development: The Rise of Large-Scale Enterprise in British Shipping, 1870–1919.* Manchester: Manchester University Press.

—— (2001*a*). *Co-operative Structures in Global Business: Communicating, Transferring Knowledge and Learning across the Corporate Frontier.* London: Routledge.

—— (2001*b*). "Multilateral Contracting in Australian Mining: The Development of Hamersley Iron, 1961–1966". *Enterprise and Society*, 2/3, Sept.: 543–75.

—— (2003). "Network Knowledge and Network Routines: Negotiating Activities between Shipowners and Shipbuilders". *Business History*, 45/2, Apr.: 52–76.

—— and LEPPER, LARRY (2002). "Assessing Information Quality Theories: The USS Co. Joint Venture with William Holyman & Sons and Huddart Parker Ltd, 1904–35". *Business History*, 44/4, Oct.: 85-120.

—— and VILLE, SIMON (2002). *The Development of Modern Business.* Houndmills, Basingstoke, Hampshire: Palgrave.

BUCKLEY, PETER J., and CASSON, MARK (1985). *The Economic Theory of the Multinational Enterprise.* New York: St. Martin's Press.

BURHOP, CARSTEN (2004). "Executive Remuneration and Firm Performance: The Case of Large German Banks, 1854–1910". *Business History*, 46/4, Oct.: 525–43.

CALOMIRIS, CHARLES W. (1990). "Is Deposit Insurance Necessary? A Historical Perspective". *Journal of Economic History*, 50/2, June: 283–95.

CALOMIRIS, CHARLES W. (1995). "The Costs of Rejecting Universal Banking: American Finance in the German Mirror, 1870–1914", in Lamoreaux and Raff (1995).

—— and GORTON, GARY (1991). "The Origins of Banking Panics: Models, Facts, and Bank Regulation", in R. Glenn Hubbard (ed.), *Financial Markets and Financial.* Chicago: University of Chicago Press.

CARLOS, ANN M. (1992). "Principal-Agent Problems in Early Trading Companies: A Tale of Two Firms". *American Economic Review*, 82/2, May: 140–5.

—— and HOFFMAN, ELIZABETH (1986). "The North American Fur Trade: Bargaining to a Joint Profit Maximum under Incomplete Information, 1804–1821". *Journal of Economic History*, 46/4, Dec.: 967–86.

—— and LEWIS, FRANK (1993). "Indians, the Beaver, and the Bay: The Economics of Depletion in the Lands of the Hudson's Bay Company, 1700–1763". *Journal of Economic History*, 53/3, Sept.: 465–94.

—— —— (1999). "Property Rights, Competition, and Depletion in the Eighteenth-Century Canadian Fur Trade: The Role of the European Market". *Canadian Journal of Economics*, 32/3, May: 705–28.

—— and NICHOLAS, STEPHEN (1990). "Agency Problems in Early Chartered Companies: The Case of the Hudson's Bay Company". *Journal of Economic History*, 50/4, Dec.: 853–75.

—— —— (1993). "Managing the Manager: An Application of the Principal Agent Model to the Hudson's Bay Company". *Oxford Economic Papers*, 45/2, Apr.: 243–56.

—— —— (1996). "Theory and History: Seventeenth-Century Joint-Stock Chartered Trading Companies". *Journal of Economic History*, 56/4, Dec.: 916–24.

CASSON, MARK (1982). *The Entrepreneur: An Economic Theory*. Totowa, NJ: Barnes & Noble.

—— (ed.) (1983). *The Growth of International Business*. London: Allen & Unwin.

—— (1984). *Multinationals and World Trade: Vertical Integration and the Division of Labour in World Industries*. London: Allen & Unwin.

—— (1986). "Contractual Arrangements for Technology Transfer: New Evidence From Business History". *Business History*, 28/4, Oct.: 5–35.

—— (1987). *The Firm and the Market: Studies on Multinational Enterprise and the Scope of the Firm*. Cambridge, Mass.: MIT Press.

—— (1994). "Institutional Diversity in Overseas Enterprise: Explaining the Free-Standing Company". *Business History*, 36/4, Oct.: 95–108.

—— (1997). *Information and Organization: A New Perspective on the Theory of the Firm*. New York: Oxford University Press.

—— (1998). "Institutional Economics and Business History: A Way Forward?", in Casson and Rose (1998).

—— and ROSE, MARY B. (eds.) (1998). *Institutions and the Evolution of Modern Business*. London: Frank Cass.

CHANDLER, ALFRED D., JR. (1962). *Strategy and Structure: Chapters in the History of the Industrial Enterprise*. Cambridge, Mass.: MIT Press.

—— (1977). *The Visible Hand: The Managerial Revolution in American Business*. Cambridge, Mass.: Harvard University Press.

—— (1980). "The Growth of the Transnational Industrial Firm in the United States and the United Kingdom: A Comparative Analysis". *Economic History Review*, 33/3, Aug.: 396–410.

—— (1990). *Scale and Scope: The Dynamics of Industrial Capitalism*. Cambridge, Mass.: Harvard University Press.

—— (1992). "Organizational Capabilities and the Economic History of the Industrial Enterprise". *Journal of Economic Perspectives*, 6/3, summer: 79–100.

—— and DAEMS, HERMAN (eds.) (1980). *Managerial Hierarchies: Comparative Perspectives on the Rise of the Modern Industrial Enterprise*. Cambridge, Mass.: Harvard University Press.

CHICK, MARTIN (1993). "British Business History: A Review of the Periodical Literature for 1991". *Business History*, 35/1, Jan.: 1–16.

CHURCH, ROY (1990). "The Limitations of the Personal Capitalism Paradigm". *Business History Review*, 64/4, winter: 703–10.

—— (1993). "The Family Firm in Industrial Capitalism: International Perspectives on Hypotheses and History". *Business History*, 35/4, Oct.: 17–43.

COASE, R. H. (1937). "The Nature of the Firm". *Economica*, 4/16, Nov.: 386–405.

—— (2000). "The Acquisition of Fisher Body by General Motors". *Journal of Law and Economics*, 43/1, Apr.: 15–31.

COLEMAN, DONALD (1987). "The Uses and Abuses of Business History". *Business History*, 29/2, Apr.: 141–56.

CORLEY, T. A. B. (1994). "Free Standing Companies, their Financing, and Internalization Theory". *Business History*, 36/4, Oct.: 109–17.

COX, HOWARD, BIAO, HUANG, and METCALFE, STUART (2003). "Compradors, Firm Architecture and the 'Reinvention' of British Trading Companies: John Swire & Sons' Operations in Early Twentieth-Century China". *Business History*, 45/2, Apr.: 15–34.

CUEVAS, JOAQUIM (2002). "Banking Growth and Industry Financing in Spain during the Nineteenth Century". *Business History*, 44/1, Jan.: 61–94.

DAEMS, HERMAN, and VAN DER WEE, HERMAN (eds.) (1974). *The Rise of Managerial Capitalism*. Louvain and the Hague: Leuven University Press and Martinus Nijhoff.

DYE, ALAN (1994). "Avoiding Holdup: Asset Specificity and Technical Change in the Cuban Sugar Industry, 1899–1929". *Journal of Economic History*, 54/3, Sept.: 628–53.

—— (1998). *Cuban Sugar in the Age of Mass Production: Technology and Economics of the Sugar Central, 1899–1929*. Stanford, Calif.: Stanford University Press.

ELBAUM, BERNARD, and LAZONICK, WILLIAM (eds.) (1986). *The Decline of the British Economy*. New York: Oxford University Press.

"Family Capitalism" (1993). Special issue of *Business History*, 35/4, Oct.

FINE, BEN (1990). "Economies of Scale and a Featherbedding Cartel? A Reconsideration of the Interwar British Coal Industry", *Economic History Review*, 43/3, Aug.: 438–49.

FOGEL, ROBERT WILLIAM (1964). *Railroads and American Economic Growth: Essays in Econometric History*. Baltimore: Johns Hopkins University Press.

—— (1965). "The Reunification of Economic History with Economic Theory". *American Economic Review*, 55/1–2, Mar.: 92–8.

—— (1967). "The Specification Problem in Economic History". *Journal of Economic History*, 27/3, Sept.: 283–308.

FOREMAN-PECK, JAMES (1981). "The Effect of Market Failure on the British Motor Industry before 1939". *Explorations in Economic History*, 18/3, July: 257–89.

FREELAND, R. F. (2000). "Creating Holdup through Vertical Integration: Fisher Body Revisited". *Journal of Law and Economics*, 43/1, Apr.: 33–66.

FRIEDMAN, MILTON (1953). "The Power of Positive Economics", in *Essays in Positive Economics*. Chicago: University of Chicago Press.

GALAMBOS, LOUIS. (1970). "The Emerging Organizational Synthesis in Modern American History". *Business History Review*, 44/3, autumn: 279–90.

"Gender and Business History" (2001). Special issue of *Enterprise and Society*, 2/1, Mar.

GENESOVE, DAVID, and MULLIN, WALLACE P. (1998). "Testing Static Oligopoly Models: Conduct and Cost in the Sugar Industry, 1890–1914". *RAND Journal of Economics*, 29/2, summer: 355–77.

——— (1999). "The Sugar Institute Learns to Organize Information Exchange", in Lamoreaux *et al.* (1999).

——— (2001). "Rules, Communication, and Collusion: Narrative Evidence from the Sugar Institute Case". *American Economic Review*, 91/3, June: 379–98.

GODLEY, ANDREW (2001). *Jewish Immigrant Entrepreneurship in New York and London.* Basingstoke: Palgrave.

GORANSSON, ANITA (1993). "Gender and Property Rights: Capital, Kin, and Owner Influence in Nineteenth- and Twentieth-Century Sweden". *Business History*, 35/2, Apr.: 11–32.

GRANITZ, ELIZABETH, and KLEIN, BENJAMIN (1996). "Monopolization by 'Raising Rivals' Costs': The Standard Oil Case". *Journal of Law and Economics*, 39/1, Apr.: 1–47.

GREENHILL, ROBERT G. (1995). "Investment Group, Free-Standing Company or Multinational? Brazilian Warrant, 1909–52". *Business History*, 37/1, Jan.: 86–111.

GREIF, AVNER (2005). *Institutions and the Path to the Modern Economy: Lessons from Medieval Trade.* New York: Cambridge University Press.

HANNAH, LESLIE (1976a). *The Rise of the Corporate Economy.* London: Methuen.

—— (ed.) (1976b). *Management Strategy and Business Development: An Historical and Comparative Study.* London: Macmillan.

—— (1983). "New Issues in British Business History". *Business History Review*, 57/2, summer: 165–74.

—— (1991). "Scale and Scope: Towards a European Visible Hand?" *Business History*, 33/2, Apr.: 297–309.

—— (1999). "Marshall's 'Trees' and the Global 'Forest': Were 'Giant Redwoods' Different?", in Lamoreaux *et al.* (1999).

—— (2006). "The Whig Fable of American Tobacco, 1895–1913". *Journal of Economic History*, 66/1, Mar.: 42–73.

HARLEY, C. KNICK (1982). "Oligopoly Agreement and the Timing of American Railroad Construction". *Journal of Economic History*, 42/4, Dec.: 797–823.

HARVEY, CHARLES E. (1979). "Business History and the Problem of Entrepreneurship: The Case of the Rio Tinto Company". *Business History*, 21/1, Jan.: 3–22.

—— and JONES, GEOFFREY (1990). "Business History in Britain into the 1990s". *Business History*, 32/1, Jan.: 5–16.

HAUSMAN, WILLIAM J. (2003). "Business History in the United States at the End of the Twentieth Century", in Franco Amatori and Geoffrey Jones (eds.), *Business History around the World.* Cambridge: Cambridge University Press.

HELPER, SUSAN, MACDUFFIE, JOHN PAUL, and SABEL, CHARLES F. (2000). "Pragmatic Collaborations: Advancing Knowledge while controlling Opportunism". *Industrial and Corporate Change*, 9/3, Sept.: 443–88.

HENNART, JEAN-FRANÇOIS (1994a). "International Financial Capital Transfers: A Transaction Cost Framework". *Business History*, 36/1, Jan.: 51–70.

—— (1994b). "Free Standing Companies and the Internalization of Markets for Financial Capital: A Response to Casson". *Business History*, 36/4, Oct.: 118–31.

HERTNER, PETER, and JONES, GEOFFREY (eds.) (1986). *Multinationals: Theory and History*. Aldershot, Hants: Gower.

HOFFMAN, PHILIP T. (1984). "The Economic Theory of Sharecropping in Early Modern France". *Journal of Economic History*, 44/2, June: 309–19.

HORN, NORBERT, and KOCKA, JÜRGEN (eds.) (1979). *Law and the Formation of the Big Enterprises in the 19th and Early 20th Centuries: Studies in the History of Industrialization in Germany, France, Great Britain and the United States*. Göttingen: Vandenhoeck & Ruprecht.

HUTCHINSON, DIANE, and NICOLAS, STEPHEN (1987). "Modelling the Growth Strategies of British Firms". *Business History*, 29/4, Oct.: 46–64.

——— (1988). "Theory and Business History: New Approaches to Institutional Change". *Journal of European Economic History*, 17/2, fall: 411–25.

JEREMY, DAVID J. (ed.) (1993). "Special Issue on Strategies of the Declining Lancashire Textile Industry". *Textile History*, 24/2, autumn.

JONES, CHARLES (1997). "Institutional Forms of British Foreign Direct Investment in South America". *Business History*, 39/2, Apr.: 21–41.

JONES, GEOFFREY (ed.) (1986). *British Multinationals: Origins, Management and Performance*. Aldershot, Hants: Gower.

—— (ed.) (1990). *Banks as Multinationals*. London: Routledge.

—— (2000). *Merchants to Multinationals: British Trading Companies in the Nineteenth and Twentieth Centuries*. Oxford: Oxford University Press.

—— (2005). *Multinationals and Global Capitalism*. Oxford: Oxford University Press.

—— and MORGAN, NICHOLAS J. (eds.) (1994). *Adding Value: Brands and Marketing in Food and Drink*. London: Routledge.

—— and ROSE, MARY (1993). "Family Capitalism". *Business History*, 35/4, Oct.: 1–16.

JONES, S. R. H. (1998). "Transaction Costs and the Theory of the Firm: The Scope and Limitations of the New Institutional Approach", in Mark Casson and Mary B. Rose (eds.), *Institutions and the Evolution of Modern Business*. London: Frank Cass.

—— and VILLE, SIMON P. (1996). "Efficient Transactors or Rent-Seeking Monopolists? The Rationale for Early Chartered Trading Companies". *Journal of Economic History*, 55/4, Dec.: 898–915.

KIRBY, M. W. (1992). "Institutional Rigidities and Economic Decline: Reflections on the British Experience". *Economic History Review*, 45/4, Nov.: 637–60.

KLEIN, BENJAMIN (2000). "Fisher-General Motors and the Nature of the Firm". *Journal of Law and Economics*, 43/1, Apr.: 105–41.

—— CRAWFORD, ROBERT G., and . ALCHIAN, ARMEN A. (1978). "Vertical Integration, Appropriable Rents and the Competitive Contracting Process". *Journal of Law and Economics*, 21/2, Oct.: 297–326.

KOBAYASHI, KESAJI, and MORIKAWA, HIDEMASA (eds.) (1986). *Development of Managerial Enterprise: Proceedings of the Fuji Conference*. Tokyo: Tokyo University Press.

KOCKA, JÜRGEN (1971). "Family and Bureaucracy in German Industrial Management, 1850–1914: Siemens in Comparative Perspective". *Business History Review*, 45/2, summer: 133–56.

—— (1978). "Entrepreneurs and Managers in German Industrialization", in Peter Mathias and M. M. Postan (eds.), *The Cambridge Economic History of Europe, Vol. VII, The Industrial Economies: Capital, Labour, and Enterprise, Part 1, Britain, France, Germany, and Scandinavia*. Cambridge: Cambridge University Press.

KOCKA, JÜRGEN (1981). "Capitalism and Bureaucracy in German Industrialization before 1914". *Economic History Review*, 34/3, Aug.: 453–68.

KUDÔ, AKIRA (2003). "The State of Business History in Japan: Cross-National Comparisons and International Relations", in Franco Amatori and Geoffrey Jones (eds.), *Business History around the World*. Cambridge: Cambridge University Press.

—— and HARA, TERUSHI (eds.) (1992). *International Cartels in Business History: Proceedings of the Fuji Conference*. Tokyo: University of Tokyo Press.

KUIJLAARS, ANNE-MARIE, PRUDON, KIM, and VISSER, JOOP (eds.) (2000). *Business and Society: Entrepreneurs, Politics and Networks in a Historical Perspective: Proceedings of the Third European Business History Association (EBHA) Conference*. Rotterdam: Centre of Business History, Erasmus University.

LAMOREAUX, NAOMI R. (1994). *Insider Lending: Banks, Personal Connections, and Economic Development in Industrial New England*. New York: Cambridge University Press.

—— and RAFF, DANIEL M. G. (eds.) (1995). *Coordination and Information: Historical Perspectives on the Organization of Enterprise*. Chicago: Chicago University Press.

—— —— and TEMIN, PETER (1997). "New Economic Approaches to the Study of Business History". *Business and Economic History*, 26/1, fall: 57–79.

—— —— —— (eds.) (1999). *Learning by Doing in Markets, Firms, and Nations*. Chicago: University of Chicago Press.

—— —— —— (2003). "Beyond Markets and Hierarchies: Toward a New Synthesis of American Business History". *American Historical Review*, 108/2, Apr.: 404–33.

—— —— —— (2004). "Against Whig History". *Enterprise and Society*, 5/3, Sept.: 376-87.

—— and ROSENTHAL, JEAN-LAURENT (2006*a*). "Corporate Governance and the Plight of Minority Shareholders in the United States before the Great Depression", in Edward L. Glaeser and Claudia Goldin (eds.), *Corruption and Reform: Lessons from America's Economic History*. Chicago: University of Chicago Press.

—— —— (2006*b*). "Contractual Tradeoffs and SME's Choice of Organizational Form: A View from U.S. and French History". NBER Working Paper 12455.

LANGLOIS, RICHARD N. (2003). "The Vanishing Hand: The Changing Dynamics of Industrial Capitalism". *Industrial and Corporate Change*, 12/2, Apr.: 351–85.

—— (2004). "Chandler in a Larger Frame: Markets, Transaction Costs, and Organizational Form in History". *Enterprise & Society*, 5/3, Sept.: 355–75.

—— and ROBERTSON, PAUL L. (1995). *Firms, Markets, and Economic Change: A Dynamic Theory of Business Institutions*. New York: Routledge.

LAZONICK, WILLIAM (1983). "Industrial Organization and Technological Change: The Decline of the British Cotton Industry". *Business History Review*, 57/2, summer: 195–236.

—— (1991). *Business Organization and the Myth of the Market Economy*. New York: Cambridge University Press.

—— (2003). "Understanding Innovative Enterprise", in Franco Amatori and Geoffrey Jones (eds.), *Business History around the World*. Cambridge: Cambridge University Press.

LEE, C. H. (1990*a*). "Corporate Behavior in Theory and History: I. The Evolution of Theory". *Business History*, 32/1, Jan.: 17–31.

—— (1990*b*). "Corporate Behavior in Theory and History: II. The Historian's Perspective". *Business History*, 32/2, Apr.: 163–79.

LINDENLAUB, DIETER (1984). "What Can the Businessman Learn from History, Especially Business History?" *German Yearbook on Business History*, 25–53.

Lipartito, Kenneth, and Sicilia, David B. (2004). "Introduction: Crossing Corporate Boundaries", in Lipartito and Sicilia (eds.), *Constructing Corporate America: History, Politics, Culture*. New York: Oxford University Press.

Lloyd-Jones, Roger, and Lewis, Myrddin J. (1994). "Personal Capitalism and British Industrial Decline: The Personally Managed Firm and Business Strategy in Sheffield, 1880–1920". *Business History Review*, 68/4, autumn: 364–411.

McCloskey, D. N. (1973). *Economic Maturity and Entrepreneurial Decline: British Iron and Steel, 1870–1913*. Cambridge, Mass.: Harvard University Press.

—— and Sandberg, Lars (1971). "From Damnation to Redemption: Judgments on the Late Victorian Entrepreneur". *Explorations in Economic History*, 9/1, fall: 89–108.

McCraw, Thomas K. (1988). "Introduction: The Intellectual Odyssey of Alfred D. Chander, Jr.", in *The Essential Alfred Chandler: Essays Toward a Historical Theory of Big Business*. Boston: Harvard Business School Press.

McKinlay, Alan (1992). "British Business History: A Review of the Periodical Literature for 1990". *Business History*, 43/2, Apr.: 1–11.

Maurer, Noel (2002). *The Power and the Money: The Mexican Financial System, 1876–1932*. Stanford, Calif.: Stanford University Press.

Minoglou, Ioanna Pepelasis (2002). "Between Informal Networks and Formal Contracts: International Investment in Greece during the 1920s". *Business History*, 44/2, Apr.: 40–64.

Moore, Karl James, and Lewis, David Charles (2000). "Multinational Enterprise in Ancient Phoenicia". *Business History*, 42/2, Apr.: 17–42.

Moriguchi, Chiaki (2003). "Implicit Contracts, the Great Depression, and Institutional Change: A Comparative Analysis of U.S. and Japanese Employment Relations, 1920–1940". *Journal of Economic History*, 63/1, Jan.: 1–41.

—— (2005). "Did American Welfare Capitalists Breach their Implicit Contracts During the Great Depression? Preliminary Findings from Company-level Data". *Industrial & Labor Relations Review*, 59/1, Oct.: 51–81.

Munro, Forbes, and Slaven, Tony (2001). "Networks and Markets in Clyde Shipping: The Donaldsons and the Hogarths, 1870–1939". *Business History*, 43/2, Apr.: 19–50.

Nakagawa, Keiichiro. (1975). *Strategy and Structure of Big Business: Proceedings of the First Fuji Conference*. Tokyo: University of Tokyo Press.

—— and Yui, Tsunehiko (eds.) (1983). *Organization and Management, 1900–1930: Proceedings of the Japan-Germany Conference on Business History*. Tokyo: Japan Business History Institute.

Nelson, Richard R., and Winter, Sidney G. (1982). *An Evolutionary Theory of Economic Change*. Cambridge, Mass.: Harvard University Press.

Nicholas, Stephen. (1983). "Agency Contracts, Institutional Modes, and the Transition to Foreign Direct Investment by British Manufacturing Multinationals before 1939". *Journal of Economic History*, 43/3, Sept.: 675–86.

—— (1984). "The Overseas Marketing Performance of British Industry, 1870–1914". *Economic History Review*, 37/4, Nov.: 489–506.

—— (1986). "The Theory of Multinational Enterprise as a Transactional Mode", in Peter Hertner and Geoffrey Jones (eds.), *Multinationals*.

Nicholas, Tom (1999). "Wealth-Making in Nineteenth and Early Twentieth Century Britain: Industry v. Commerce and Finance". *Business History*, 41/1, Jan.: 16–36.

NICHOLAS, TOM (2004). "Enterprise and Management", in Roderick Floud and Paul Johnson (eds.), *The Cambridge Economic History of Modern Britain*, vol. 2. Cambridge: Cambridge University Press.

NORTH, DOUGLASS C. (1961). *The Economic Growth of the United States, 1790–1860*. Englewood Cliffs, NJ: Prentice-Hall.

—— (1965). "Economic History: Its Contribution to Economic Education, Research, and Policy". *American Economic Review*, 55/1–2 (Mar.): 86–91.

ODELL, KERRY A. (1989). "The Integration of Regional and Interregional Capital Markets: Evidence from the Pacific Coast, 1883–1913". *Journal of Economic History*, 49/2, June: 297–310.

OKAZAKI, TETSUJI (1995). "The Evolution of the Financial System in Post-War Japan." *Business History*, 37/2, Apr.: 89–106.

OLSSON, ULF (ed.) (1997). *Business and European Integration since 1800: Regional, National and International Perspectives*. Göteborg: Meddelanden Från Ekonomisk-Historiska Institutionen vid Göteborgs Universitet.

PARKER, WILLIAM N. (1971). "From Old to New to Old in Economic History". *Journal of Economic History*, 31, Mar.: 3–14.

PARSONS, MIKE C., and ROSE, MARY B. (2004). "Communities of Knowledge: Entrepreneurship, Innovation and Networks in the British Outdoor Trade, 1960–90", *Business History*, 46/4, Oct.: 609–39.

PENROSE, EDITH TILTON (1959). *The Theory of the Growth of the Firm*. Oxford: Blackwell.

PÉREZ, PALOMA FERNÁNDEZ, and PUIG, NÚRIA (2004). "Knowledge and Training in Family Firms of the European Periphery: Spain in the Eighteenth to Twentieth Centuries". *Business History*, 46/1, Jan.: 79–99.

PIORE, MICHAEL J., and SABEL, CHARLES F. (1984). *The Second Industrial Divide: Possibilities for Prosperity*. New York: Basic Books.

POHL, HANS. (1987). "The Society for Business History: A Decade of Work". *German Yearbook on Business History*.

RAFF, DANIEL M. G. (1995). "The Puzzling Profusion of Compensation Systems in the Interwar Automobile Industry", in Lamoreaux and Raff (1995).

ROSS, DUNCAN M. (1996). "The Unsatisfied Fringe in Britain, 1930s–80s". *Business History*, 38/3 (July): 11–26.

SABEL, CHARLES F., and ZEITLIN, JONATHAN (1985). "Historical Alternatives to Mass Production: Politics, Markets and Technology in Western Industrialization". *Past and Present*, 108, Aug.: 133–76.

—— —— (eds.) (1997). *World of Possibilities: Flexibility and Mass Production in Western Industrialization*. Cambridge: Cambridge University Press.

—— —— (2004). "Neither Modularity nor Relational Contracting: Inter-Firm Collaboration in the New Economic History". *Enterprise and Society*, 5/3, Sept.: 388–403.

SANDBERG, LARS (1969). "American Rings and English Mules. The Role of Economic Rationality". *Quarterly Journal of Economics*, 83/1, Feb.: 25–43.

SAXONHOUSE, GARY R., and WRIGHT, GAVIN (1984). "New Evidence on the Stubborn English Mule and the Cotton Industry, 1878–1920". *Economic History Review*, 37/4, Nov.: 507–19.

SCHRÖTER, HARM G. (2003). "Business History in German-Speaking States at the End of the Century", in Franco Amatori and Geoffrey Jones (eds.), *Business History around the World*. Cambridge: Cambridge University Press.

Scranton, Philip (1983). *Proprietary Capitalism: The Textile Manufacture at Philadelphia, 1800–1885.* New York: Cambridge University Press.

—— (1989). *Figured Tapestry: Production, Markets, and Power in Philadelphia Textiles, 1884–1941.* New York: Cambridge University Press.

—— (1997). *Endless Novelty: Specialty Production and American Industrialization, 1865–1925.* Princeton: Princeton University Press.

Sjögren, Hans, and Jungerhem, Sven (1996). "Small Firm Financing in Sweden, 1960–95". *Business History*, 38/3, July: 27–47.

Snowden, Kenneth A. (1995). "The Evolution of Interregional Mortgage Lending Channels, 1870–1940: The Life Insurance-Mortgage Company Connection", in Lamoreaux and Raff (1995).

Stanciu, Laura (2000). "Free-Standing Companies in the Oil Sector in Romania and Poland before 1948: Typologies and Competencies". *Business History*, 42/4, Oct.: 27–66.

Supple, Barry (1991). "Scale and Scope: Alfred Chandler and the Dynamics of Industrial Capitalism". *Economic History Review*, 44/3, Aug.: 500–14.

Temin, Peter (1966). "The Relative Decline of the British Steel Industry, 1880–1930", in Henry Rosovky (ed.), *Industrialization in Two Systems: Essays in Honor of Alexander Gerschenkron*. New York: Wiley.

—— (ed.) (1991). *Inside the Business Enterprise: Historical Perspectives on the Use of Information.* Chicago: University of Chicago Press.

Tilly, Richard (1982). "Mergers, External Growth, and Finance in the Development of Large-Scale Enterprise in Germany, 1880–1913". *Journal of Economic History*, 42/3 Sept.: 629–58.

—— (1993). "On the Development of German Banks as Universal Banks in the 19th and 20th Centuries: Engine of Growth or Power Block?" *German Yearbook on Business History*, 17–39.

Toms, Steven, and Wilson, John F. (2003). "Scale, Scope, and Accountability: Toward a New Paradigm of British Business History". *Business History*, 45/4, Oct.: 1–23.

van Driel, Hugo (2003). "The Role of Middlemen in the International Coffee Trade since 1870: The Dutch Case". *Business History*, 45/2, Apr.: 77–101.

Ville, Simon (1996). "Networks and Venture Capital in the Australasian Pastoral Sector Before World War Two". *Business History*, 38/3, July: 48–63.

—— (2000). *The Rural Entrepreneurs: A History of the Stock and Station Agent Industry in Australia and New Zealand.* Cambridge: Cambridge University Press.

—— and Fleming, Grant (2000). "The Nature and Structure of Trade Financial Networks: Evidence from the New Zealand Pastoral Sector". *Business History*, 42/1, Jan.: 41–58.

Westall, Oliver M. (1998). "Invisible, Visible, and 'Direct' Hands: An Institutional Interpretation of Organisational Structure and Change in British General Insurance", in Casson and Rose (1998).

Wilkins, Mira, and Schröter, Harm (eds.) (1998). *The Free Standing Company in the World Economy, 1830–1996.* Oxford: Oxford University Press.

Williamson, Harold F. (1966). "Business History and Economic History". *Journal of Economic History*, 26/4, Dec.: 407–17.

—— and Daum, Arnold R. (1959). *The American Petroleum Industry: The Age of Illumination, 1859–1899.* Evanston, Ill.: Northwestern University Press.

WILLIAMSON, OLIVER E. (1975). *Markets and Hierarchies, Analysis and Antitrust Implications: A Study in the Economics of Internal Organization*. New York: Free Press.

—— (1979). "Transaction Cost Economics: The Governance of Contractual Relations". *Journal of Law and Economics*, 22/2: 233–61.

—— (1981). "The Modern Corporation: Origins, Evolution, Attributes". *Journal of Economic Literature*, 19/4, Dec.: 1537–68.

—— (1985). *The Economic Institutions of Capitalism: Firms, Markets, Relational Contracting*. New York: Free Press.

YAMAMURA, KOZO (1970). "A Note on 'Japan Business History Review' and Recent Books". *Business History Review*, 44/1, spring: 126–30.

YATES, JOANNE (2004). "An Interview with Alfred Chandler, Jr.". *Newsletter of the Cliometric Society*, 19/2, summer–fall: 4–9.

CHAPTER 4

BUSINESS HISTORY AND ECONOMIC DEVELOPMENT

WILLIAM LAZONICK

4.1 INTRODUCTION

WRITING at the end of a long and illustrious career, Joseph Schumpeter (1954: 12–13) advised: "Nobody can hope to understand the economic phenomena of any, including the present, epoch who has not an adequate command of the historical *facts* and an adequate amount of historical *sense* or of what may be described as *historical experience*". By "historical experience", Schumpeter meant the ability of the economist to integrate theory and history. For theory to be relevant to real-world phenomena, it must be derived from the rigorous study of historical reality. To develop relevant theory requires an iterative methodology; one derives theoretical postulates from the study of the historical record, and uses the resultant theory to analyze history as an ongoing and, viewing the present as history, unfolding process. Theory, therefore, serves as an abstract explanation of what we already know, and as an analytical framework for identifying and researching what we need to know.

Throughout his own career, Schumpeter sought to integrate the theory and history of economic development, based on the experiences of the advanced economies of the first half of the twentieth century. As a Viennese economics student, Schumpeter was versed in the relatively recent, and increasingly influential,

Austrian and Walrasian theories of how, through the equilibrating mechanism of the market, the economy could achieve an "optimal" allocation of resources across productive uses. Schumpeter's insight was to recognize that such a view of the economic world could not explain economic development. In 1911 Schumpeter wrote *The Theory of Economic Development* (first English translation: Schumpeter 1934) to argue that entrepreneurial activity that results in innovation—what he called the "Fundamental Phenomenon of Economic Development"—can disrupt this "Circular Flow of Economic Life as Conditioned by Given Circumstances" to change the ways in which the economy operates and performs. Without such disruption of equilibrium conditions, the economy would not develop. Over the next four decades Schumpeter sought to elaborate a theory of economic development informed by his own, evolving, understanding of the changing reality of the most advanced sectors and economies.

In particular he sought to understand the role of the business enterprise in advanced capitalist development. By the 1940s he had taken definitive leave of his youthful conceptions of the innovative entrepreneur as an individual actor and innovation as simply "new combinations" of existing resources. Rather, he saw that powerful business organizations both developed and utilized productive resources to create new technologies and access new markets. The creation of new technologies, moreover, destroyed the commercial viability of old technologies. In *Capitalism, Socialism, and Democracy*, first published in 1942, Schumpeter argued that the process of "creative destruction" had become embodied in established corporations as "technological 'progress' tends, through systematization and rationalization of research and of management, to become more effective and sure-footed", being "the business of teams of trained specialists who turn out what is required and make it work in predictable ways" (Schumpeter 1950: 118, 132).

By the end of his life (he died in January 1950 at the age of 66), the study of "business history" had become central to Schumpeter's theory of economic development. As a field of economic inquiry, he probably did not view business history as distinct from economic history, and had he been asked, he probably would have even resisted the notion that business history should be identified as a distinctive subfield, at least as far as the study of economic development is concerned.

In principle, Schumpeter would have been correct. But, in practice, there was a problem. By the 1950s, the economics profession had designated economic theory, not economic history, as the most important field of economic analysis, and the theory that reigned supreme was anything but a theory of economic development. Rather it was the neoclassical theory of the "optimal" allocation of productive resources to alternative uses; that is, the theory of the "Circular Flow of Economic Life as Conditioned by Given Circumstances". For Schumpeter, the theory of the "circular flow" was theory without history; the "firm" played a purely passive role in turning inputs into outputs, according to externally imposed, and hence "given", technological and market constraints. In its obsession with constrained optimization and equilibrium conditions, neoclassical economics systematically excluded the "fundamental phenomenon" of innovation from economic analysis and, with it, the role of business enterprise in transforming technological and market conditions rather than accepting them as "given" constraints (see Lazonick 1991 and 2003).

The economics profession's infatuation with ahistorical theory became more pronounced over the last half of the twentieth century. In this context, from the late 1950s, the "New Economic History" emerged as *the* economic history in the leading US economics departments (and in the process largely drove the study of economic history out of history departments) by taking as its agenda the slavish application of neoclassical economic theory to historical facts. The New Economic History largely ignored business history and with it the study of innovation. In kowtowing to the rule of neoclassical theory, however, by the 1980s and 1990s the "New Economic History" undermined its own *raison d'être* within economics. If economic history was just another field of applied economics in a discipline in which ahistorical thinking dominated, why allocate scarce academic resources to the analysis of old facts rather than new facts? In an essay entitled, "Economics: Is Something Missing?", Robert Solow (1986), whose own claim to fame was in neoclassical growth theory, was highly critical of the failure of prevailing economic theory to learn from the real world—which is what economic historians were supposed to be studying. There was, however, a tendency among current economic historians, Solow (1986: 26) argued, "to give back to the theorist the same routine gruel that the economic theorist gives to the historian. Why should I believe, when it is applied to thin eighteenth-century data, something that carries no conviction when it is done with more ample twentieth-century data?"

While Solow recognized that prevailing economic theory was in part to blame for the failings of neoclassical economic history, he did not propose a methodological approach for correcting the problem. Nor did he inform his audience about why such a sad intellectual state of affairs had come to pass. As a result, the mainstream of the economics profession, which saw no relation between the study of history and the construction of theory, could simply construe his critique as a rationale for ending the misallocation of the profession's scarce resources to the study of history. And that is precisely what in the 1980s and 1990s many graduate economics programs did.

Yet, notwithstanding the dominance of ahistorical, non-developmental theory within the economics profession, the Schumpeterian agenda survived through a combination of "sociological" business history, as exemplified by the work of Alfred Chandler (1962, 1977, and 1990), and "developmental" economic theory, as exemplified by the work of Edith Penrose (1959). Chandler's work is important not because it was Schumpeterian (although Chandler did his early work in the 1950s at the Schumpeter-inspired Harvard Research Center in Entrepreneurial History), but because it focused on the role of the firm in the allocation of resources in the economy and on the relation between strategy and structure in the growth of the firm. Sociological in its orientation (having been influenced by the structural-functionalist approach of Talcott Parsons), Chandler's work made business history relevant and accessible to the social sciences, demonstrating as it did the powerful generalizations and hypotheses that could be derived from a combination of primary research and historical synthesis. At the same time, by focusing on the growth of the major firms in the rise of the world's most powerful economy, Chandler's business history cried out for a theory of innovative enterprise.

Key elements of that theory, rooted in the same history of US managerial enterprise that was the focus of Chandler's studies, can be found in the work of Edith Penrose (Lazonick 2002*a*, 2002*b*). An economist, Penrose did pioneering work on the evolution of the international patent system for her Johns Hopkins Ph.D. thesis, before undertaking the work that led to her 1959 book, *The Theory of the Growth of the Firm*. Like Chandler, Penrose was not overly influenced by the work of Schumpeter. But more than any other economist in the post-Schumpeter generation, Penrose's work elaborated the foundations of a theory of innovative enterprise.

In *The Theory of the Growth of the Firm*, Penrose conceptualized the modern corporate enterprise as an organization that administers a collection of human and physical resources. People contribute labor services to the firm, not merely as individuals, but as members of teams who engage in learning about how to make best use of the firm's productive resources—including their own. This learning is organizational; it cannot be done all alone, and hence is collective, and it cannot be done all at once, and hence is cumulative (see Best 1990). At any point in time, this organizational learning endows the firm with experience that gives it productive opportunities unavailable to other firms, even in the same industry, that have not accumulated the same experience. The accumulation of innovative experience enables the firm to overcome the "managerial limit" that in the neoclassical theory of the optimizing firm causes the onset of increasing costs and constrains the growth of the firm. The innovating firm can transfer and reshape its existing productive resources to take advantage of new market opportunities. Each move into a new product market enables the firm to utilize unused productive services accumulated through the process of organizational learning. These unused productive services can provide a foundation for the growth of the firm, through both in-house complementary investments in new product development and the acquisition of other firms that have already developed complementary productive resources.

Like Chandler's work, Penrose's book reflected a combination of primary research (see Penrose 1960) and the synthesis of the work of others, including a body of research in business history. During the 1960s and 1970s, Penrose became a leading expert on the international oil industry, spending considerable time in Iraq. She also deepened her understanding of the integral relation between theory and history, as is evident in a highly perceptive essay, written in the late 1980s, entitled, "History, the Social Sciences and Economic 'Theory', with Special Reference to Multinational Enterprise" (Penrose 1989). Quoting from Schumpeter's statement on the paramount importance of "historical experience" for economic analysis, Penrose (1989: 11) argued that "universal truths without reference to time and space are unlikely to characterise economic affairs".

The work of Penrose has had minimal impact on economic theory, quite in contrast with the widespread and profound impact of Chandler on business history.[1] For the vast majority of economics graduate students schooled to think in terms of optimization subject to given constraints, the integrated research agenda inherent in *The Theory of the Growth of the Firm* represented, in my view, simply too great a methodological leap. Rather, given their economics training, a younger generation of potential "neo-Schumpeterians" needed as a first step a set of arguments that took deliberate aim at economic orthodoxy, and laid out a preliminary research agenda for moving beyond it. They found this more tractable intellectual path from neoclassical orthodoxy to the Schumpeterian agenda in the 1982 book by Richard Nelson and Sidney Winter, *An Evolutionary Theory of Economic Change*. Labeling their economic theory neo-Schumpeterian, Nelson and Winter focused on the need for a theory of the firm that went beyond the optimization principle of neoclassical orthodoxy, and focused on the interrelated concepts of routines and tacit knowledge as basic explanations of the organizational capabilities of firms.

Especially in subsequent collaborative projects co-directed by Nelson, the evolutionary approach, shed of its original biological crutches (market competition as a "selection process" and organizational routines as "genes"), has fostered considerable work by economists and other social scientists on the organization and dynamics of innovative enterprise (see Nelson 1993; Mowery and Nelson 1999; Fagerberg *et al.* 2004). Best represented in the journals, *Research Policy* and *Industrial and Corporate Change*, this research to varying degrees and in a number of ways recognizes the importance of integrating theory and history. This work has been done, however, almost entirely outside economics departments (including since the last half of the 1980s the teaching and research of Nelson and Winter themselves) as well as mostly in Europe. To this day, the Schumpeterian approach fostered by Nelson and Winter has had virtually no impact on thinking within the mainstream of the economics profession; neoclassical orthodoxy has as tight a hold on the minds of economists as it did when *An Evolutionary Theory of Economic Change* appeared over two decades ago.

---

[1] Penrose's *Theory of the Growth of the Firm* was referenced as a classic in papers on a "resource-based" theory of the firm that developed in business schools from the early 1980s. A "classic" can be defined as a book that everyone cites and no one reads. Resource-based theory did not make use of Penrose's insights into the firm as an innovating organization, and has not fostered an appreciation even among economists working in business schools of the importance of integrating theory and history (see Lazonick 2002*a*).

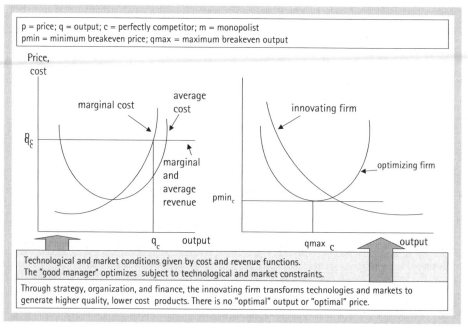

Fig. 4.1 Comparing the optimizing and innovating firm

Those with a vested interest in what I have called "the myth of the market economy" (Lazonick 1991) have good reason to erect and fortify barriers to entry. The Schumpeterian agenda strikes at the very heart of the way neoclassical economists analyze the economy (Lazonick 1991, 2007). The foundation of neoclassical orthodoxy is the theory of the optimizing firm. The Schumpeterian agenda seeks a theory of the innovating firm. In the theory of the optimizing firm, all firms in an industry are constrained to have the same cost structures; that is, they all optimize subject to the same technological and market constraints. As displayed in Figure 4.1, the theory of the innovating firm recognizes that firms can compete in the same industry with different cost structures, and that *if* the innovating firm can transform the high fixed costs of its innovative strategy into low unit costs, it will be able to gain competitive advantage over the optimizing firm, and indeed may be able to dominate its industry.

The right-hand side of Figure 4.1 is Schumpeterian competition. The transformation of high fixed costs into low unit costs depends on "social conditions of innovative enterprise" that characterize the firm's strategy, organization, and finance (Lazonick 1991, 2006c; O'Sullivan 2000b; Lazonick and O'Sullivan 2000). "Strategy" depends on who exercises control over the allocation of the firm's resources, "organization" depends on the skills and efforts of those involved in the firm's hierarchical and functional division of labor that are integrated into the firm's learning process, and "finance" depends on the commitment of resources to the firm's innovation process until it can generate financial returns. The existence and impact of these "social conditions of innovative enterprise" cannot be assumed; they have to be studied historically. A theory of innovative enterprise provides a conceptual framework for engaging in such historical analysis.

In the body of this chapter, under the headings, strategy, organization, and finance, I present a summary of the "historical experience" that I deem to be relevant to a theory of innovative enterprise. Given space constraints, I confine myself, historically and comparatively, to the cases of Japan and the United States. In the conclusion I indicate the importance of a theory of innovative enterprise for understanding the role of the state in economic development.

4.2 STRATEGY

4.2.1 Strategic Control

An innovative enterprise engages in the deliberate allocation of resources to develop superior products and processes. Innovative investment strategies are inherently uncertain; if at the outset, when a company commits resources to an innovative strategy, its decision-makers already knew how to develop higher quality products and processes, then they would not be engaged in innovation.

Any strategic decision-maker who allocates resources to innovative investments faces three types of uncertainty: technological, market, and competitive. Technological uncertainty exists because the firm may be incapable of developing the higher quality processes and products envisaged in its innovative investment strategy. Market uncertainty exists because, even if the firm is successful in its development effort, the innovative enterprise must access a large enough extent of the product market to transform the fixed costs of developing a new technology into low unit costs. Yet, at the time, when resources are committed to an innovative strategy, it is impossible to be certain, even probabilistically, about the extent of the market that will be accessed. Finally, even if a firm overcomes technological and market uncertainty, it still faces competitive uncertainty: the possibility that an innovative competitor will have invested in a strategy that generates an even higher quality, lower cost product.

Who exercises strategic control over the allocation of the firm's resources is, therefore, of paramount consequence to the innovative enterprise. To make innovative investment decisions in the face of uncertainty, strategic decision-makers require deep knowledge of the technological, market, and competitive conditions that characterize their firm and its industry. Strategic decision-makers must also have the incentive to confront uncertainty by allocating resources to innovative investments rather than seeking to "optimize" subject to given technological, market, and competitive conditions (see Fig. 4.1). With the growth of the innovative enterprise, it cannot be assumed that the original owner-entrepreneurs or their descendents will have these abilities and incentives. Hence the importance of the separation of share ownership from strategic control, and the consequent "managerial revolution", in the emergence of large-scale enterprise in the 20th century.

4.2.2 United States[2]

In their 1932 classic, *The Modern Corporation and Private Property*, Adolf Berle and Gardiner Means showed that by the 1920s the separation of ownership from control had become a dominant characteristic of the US corporate economy. During the last decades of the 19th century, a number of owner-entrepreneurs in industries such as steel, oil refining, meatpacking, tobacco, agricultural equipment, telecommunications, and electric power had built innovative firms by investing in managerial organizations. During the Great Merger Movement in the 1890s and early 1900s, industry consolidations and public securities offerings led many owner-entrepreneurs to cash in ownership stakes, and retire from active management. Taking their places in strategic decision-making positions were salaried managers, most of whom had been recruited years or even decades earlier to help build the innovative firms over which they would now exercise strategic control.

By the 1920s, the separation of ownership and control had become a dominant characteristic of companies in industries that entailed large-scale and ongoing investments in new technologies and new markets, and that were driving the rapid growth of the US economy. Shareholding in the major industrial corporations, particularly those listed on the New York Stock Exchange (NYSE), had become sufficiently fragmented, and the collective power of shareholders sufficiently weakened, to enable top executives to control appointments to "their" boards of directors.

The separation of ownership and control served as a powerful inducement for bright young—and typically White, Anglo-Saxon, Protestant—men to consider careers as corporate executives. The fact that nepotism would not block their promotion up and around the company hierarchy induced professional, technical, and administrative personnel to view the growth of the particular corporations that employed them as providing the best opportunities for their own career success. In

---

[2] This section draws on Lazonick (1986, 2005*a*, 2007*a*, and 2007*c*). Key references include Berle and Means (1932); Navin and Sears (1955); Noble (1977); Chandler (1977 and 1990); Brody (1980); Saxenian (1994); Mowery and Rosenberg (1998); Kenney (2000); O'Sullivan (2000*a*).

so far as the rewards of salaried managers depended on the innovative success of the company, the separation of ownership and control promoted innovation.

The transformation of the institutions of higher education supported the separation of ownership and control by preparing the most highly educated Americans for business careers. A four-year undergraduate college degree became important for entry into managerial careers, and in 1908 Harvard University launched the first graduate school in business administration. By the 1920s the top executives of many large industrial corporations had college degrees. As employers of university graduates as well as beneficiaries of university research, big business took an active role in shaping the form and content of higher education to meet its needs for "knowledge assets".

So too the transformation of US financial institutions facilitated the separation of ownership and control. Before the 1890s a national market in industrial (as distinct from government and railroad) securities did not exist in the United States. By issuing stock and bonds to buy out, and typically retire, owner-entrepreneurs, Wall Street helped to create highly liquid markets in industrial securities, with NYSE becoming the market of choice for the best-capitalized and consistently profitable industrial corporations that could meet its stringent listing requirements. Especially during the 1920s, as households gained confidence in holding corporate shares, the fragmentation of share ownership left salaried managers in control.

The productive power and financial resources of these managerial corporations enabled them to survive the Great Crash and the Great Depression. Indeed, during the 1930s they made substantial investments in innovation. In the early 1930s most of these corporations downsized their blue-collar labor forces drastically, even as they sought to maintain dividend payments. As a result, a challenge to managerial control in the 1930s came not from shareholders but from production workers who looked to unions to provide them with employment security. New Deal legislation compelled companies to engage in collective bargaining with the unions. During the late 1930s and 1940s corporate executives defended their "right to manage", and repelled labor's efforts to gain some influence over the allocation of corporate resources. With good employment security, wages, and benefits, unionized "hourly" workers shared in the gains of the growth years of the 1950s and 1960s. But it was top executives, most of them salaried employees, who maintained exclusive control over strategic decision-making.

The breakdown of many US industrial corporations from the 1960s can be understood in terms of a change in the conditions under which top executives exercised strategic control. Through internal growth as well as mergers and acquisitions, many corporations became unwieldy conglomerates as they expanded into scores of unrelated lines of business. As a rationalization of the conglomerate movement, leading business schools propagated the ideology that a well-trained manager could manage any and every kind of business. The business history of the 1970s and 1980s, however, would give the lie to that notion. The conglomerate movement failed to generate innovation because it severed the relation between executives in corporate headquarters who controlled the strategic allocation of the company's resources and the specialists within the organization who had to develop and utilize those resources. Through leveraged buyouts, managers of many corporate divisions regained strategic control by transforming them into independent enterprises. The experience of conglomeration, however, weakened the innovative capabilities of these "new" firms, while the debt incurred in extracting themselves from the conglomerates made it more difficult to reconstruct those capabilities. Meanwhile, US industrial enterprises found that they faced formidable international competitors, particularly the Japanese, who were capable of generating higher quality, lower cost products in precisely those mass-production industries—vehicles, electronics, and machinery—in which US companies had previously been unsurpassed.

Since the 1960s, some of the most innovative sectors in the US economy have been associated more with startups than with established companies or divisions spun off from them. In the 1980s and 1990s, Silicon Valley microelectronics became emblematic of an industry whose sustained growth depended on high-technology startups. While independent entrepreneurship has been important to the development of Silicon Valley, its startups were products of the managerial revolution. The engineers, scientists, and managers who founded these new firms typically left secure salaried positions in established companies. The startups often had the backing of venture capital firms that provided not only financing but also expertise in strategic decision-making. A great strength of the Silicon Valley venture capital model was the fact that many of the leading venture capitalists themselves had had years of experience as specialists and executives in the district's microelectronic firms.

Even in Silicon Valley firms, as relatively new as they are, share ownership has tended to be separated from managerial control. As venture capitalists have provided entrepreneur-founders with the financial resources to develop new products for new markets, they have also played an important role in recruiting professional managers to scale up and commercialize these products. Indeed, when venture capitalists back a company, they seek to dilute the ownership stakes of the original entrepreneurs so that they cannot veto the employment of professional managers or the sale of the company. Venture capitalists also insist that new firms retain large blocks of treasury stock that are available for broad-based stock option plans used to recruit and retain a specialist staff. Moreover, in backing these firms, the objective of venture capitalists and the institutional investors who are their limited partners is to exit their investments within a 5 to 10 year timeframe. They do so either through a private sale of the new firm to an established company with publicly listed shares or by an initial public offering (IPO), typically on the NASDAQ Small Cap Market with listing requirements that are much less stringent than those of NYSE. Either way, ownership tends to become further separated from control, leaving salaried managers in command of the strategic allocation of resources.

4.2.3 Japan[3]

In 1948 the Supreme Commander for the Allied Powers—the occupation authority in Japan—began the dissolution of the *zaibatsu*, the giant holding companies that had dominated the Japanese economy from the Meiji era of the late 19th century to World War II. The dissolution process not only dispossessed the families that owned the *zaibatsu* but also removed from office the top managers. A younger generation, primarily engineers, plucked from the ranks of middle management, took control of strategic decision-making. These managerial personnel were the products of investments in higher education that went back to the Meiji era as well as the widespread employment of university graduates in Japanese industry throughout the first half of the 20th century. In the 1950s the new strategic decision-makers had no alternative but to find new uses for their accumulated capabilities in non-military markets.

To invest in innovative capabilities, executives needed to maintain control over corporate revenues. To defend themselves against outsider demands for "shareholder value", the community of corporate executives engaged in the practice of cross-shareholding. Banks and industrial companies took equities off the market by holding each other's shares. Over time, as business relations among financial and industrial enterprises changed, the web of cross-shareholding became a system of stable shareholding in which bilateral shareholding between any two companies ceased to be important. The institution of stable shareholding is not contractual. Rather, it has been sustained by the acceptance by the entire Japanese business community of the norm that one company does not reap financial gain by selling its shareholdings of another company to public shareholders.[4]

Japanese companies have routinely given their proxy votes to the managers of the companies whose shares they hold. To reduce the possibility for outside shareholders to press their demands on management, virtually all companies listed on the Tokyo Stock Exchange have held their annual general meetings of shareholders at the same time on the same day—the last Friday in June at 2.00 p.m., with the meetings lasting on average, over the course of the 1990s, 28.37 minutes (Hilary and Oshika 2003). Nevertheless, until the government cracked down on the practice in the mid-1990s, *yakuza*, members of Japanese organized crime, routinely extorted bribes from Japanese top managers in return for promises not to ask embarrassing questions at the shareholders' meeting, and, with the bribe having been paid, to intimidate anyone else in attendance who might be thinking of doing so.

---

[3] This section draws on Lazonick (1999 and 2005b). Key English-language references include Hadley (1970); Abegglen and Stalk (1985); Morikawa (1997 and 2001).

[4] When in financial distress, a company might raise cash by selling some of its stable shareholdings to other companies at the going market price but with an understanding that the shares would be repurchased, also at the going market price, if and when its financial condition improved.

In 1955 stable shareholding represented 25 percent of outstanding stocks listed on the Tokyo Stock Exchange, and by 1960 had risen to about 40 percent. It declined slightly in the early 1960s, but after the opening up of Japanese capital markets in 1964, when Japan joined OECD, the business community, fearing foreign takeovers, increased stable shareholding. It surpassed 60 percent in 1975, and remained above that figure until 2000, peaking at over 67 percent in 1988. During the recessionary years of the 1990s, there was a gradual decline of stable shareholdings to 62 percent in 1998 and then a sharp drop to 57 percent in 2000. Financial institutions, burdened by mountains of non-performing loans and compelled to realize the value of their shares to restore capital-adequacy ratios, accounted for the vast majority of the sell-offs. In March 2000 foreigners held 13.2 percent of outstanding shares, up from 4.2 percent in 1990 and 10.0 percent in 1998.

Coming into the twenty-first century, stable shareholding was somewhat weakened but still intact. Contests for corporate control have been limited, while corporate payout ratios remain low. Notwithstanding both the financial instability that followed the bursting of the Bubble Economy and the slow growth of the "Lost Decade" of the 1990s, salaried managers in the electronics and vehicles industries that have been the foundations of Japanese competitive success have continued to allocate corporate revenues to innovative investment strategies.

4.3 ORGANIZATION

4.3.1 Organizational Integration

Strategic control determines the allocation of resources to products and processes. Innovation, however, depends on the generation of higher quality, lower cost products than were previously available at prevailing factor prices. To achieve innovative outcomes, a firm must *develop* as well as *utilize* productive resources. The development of productive resources entails organizational learning, which in turn requires the organizational integration of the skills and efforts of large numbers of people in a functional and hierarchal division of labor.

In and of itself, the development of productive resources entails fixed costs that, unless utilized, place the firm at a competitive *disadvantage* (see the right-hand side of Fig. 4.1). To innovate, the firm must utilize the productive resources that it has developed. It must retain its knowledge base in the face of labor market competition. It must get high rates of throughput from its production processes without sacrificing product quality. It must also access a large extent of the market for its product. The economies of scale that the firm thereby generates are not a *source* of competitive advantage but rather an *outcome* of its organizational capability both to transform technologies into high quality products and to access markets that, by absorbing these products in large quantities, drive down unit costs.

In so far as the firm develops innovative capabilities for use in one product market, it can try to make use of these capabilities in another product market, and thus generate economies of scope. Like economies of scale, economies of scope are an outcome of the development and utilization of productive resources. The move into new markets entails not only more intensive use of existing production, distribution, and R&D capabilities but also new developmental investments, thus increasing the need for economies of scale. The achievement of economies of scale and scope depends on the firm's organizational capabilities.

The development and utilization of productive resources requires the employment of labor with, depending on the markets for which the firm is competing and the technologies with which it chooses to compete, various types of functional capabilities and hierarchical responsibilities. Some types of labor can be employed as if they were an interchangeable commodity that can be easily hired and fired. The "flexible" use of such labor enables the firm to avoid the fixed costs of organization while adjusting employment to fluctuations in demand. But, by definition, commoditized labor does not engage in the organizational learning that is the essence of innovation. Since all firms that compete in an industry have ready access to these flexible labor supplies, the employment of commoditized labor cannot be a source of competitive advantage.

A comparison of nations and industries over time reveals different models of organizational integration characterized by different employment relations for different groups of employees in the functional and hierarchical division of labor. Business history enables us to discover what these organizational models are, why they generate innovation in certain industries in certain eras, and how they change when confronted by new competitive challenges. Of the three activities—strategy, organization, and finance—in which the innovative enterprise must engage, organization is both the most difficult to research and yet the one that most defines the social relations that make "business models" distinctive across nations and industries and over time.

4.3.2 United States[5]

The US business model that evolved during the first half of the twentieth century was characterized by cohesive managerial organization with a well-defined hierarchical segmentation between "salaried" managerial (or more accurately, professional, technical, and administrative) personnel and "hourly" production and

[5] This section draws on Lazonick (1990, 2007a, and 2006). Important references include Whyte (1956); Brody (1980); Jacoby (1985); Lichtenstein and Harris (1993); Saxenian (1994); Hounshell (1996); Kenney (2000).

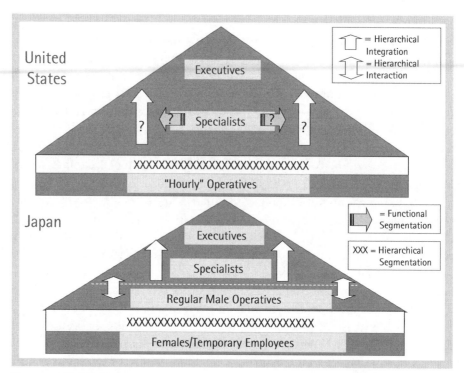

Fig. 4.2 US Old Economy and Japanese business models compared

clerical employees (see Fig. 4.2).[6] The key incentive that fostered organizational integration within the managerial structure was promotion up and around the corporate hierarchy, possibly even to top management positions. In the 1950s the dedicated but largely faceless corporate bureaucrat became known, pejoratively, as "the organization man" (Whyte 1956). He (almost never she) was typically White, Anglo-Saxon, and Protestant with a university education, and had realistic expectations of remaining with one company over the course of his career. So-called hourly employees tended to be more ethnically diverse with at best high school education, and even then not necessarily of the highest quality given local financing of primary and secondary education in the United States. Males predominated as production workers and females as clerical workers. In the post-World War II decades, protected by seniority (last-hired, first-fired) provisions of their union contracts, most of these "hourly" workers, and especially male production workers, also came to expect lifelong employment.

In the immediate post-World War II period the remuneration of top executives reflected the internal salary structures of the managerial organizations over which they presided. The extent of their rewards was largely dependent, therefore,

---

[6] Under US labor law "hourly", or "non-exempt", workers have to be paid 150 percent of their hourly wage if they work "overtime", whereas salaried employees who continue to labor outside normal working hours are exempt from this provision.

on increases in salaries and benefits accruing to members of the managerial organization as a whole. In the early stages of their careers, professional, technical, and administrative personnel would develop expertise in functional specialties, often reflecting their pre-employment higher education. In the middle stages of their careers, however, management development programs rotated them across functions to prepare them for more integrative responsibilities in positions of greater hierarchical authority. As for hourly employees, their only opportunity for entering the salaried ranks was by becoming first-line supervisors or foremen, a hierarchical position that made its occupant a "member of management" and hence, under US labor law, ineligible to compel the employer to engage in collective bargaining.

As a general rule, salaried employees engaged in organizational learning; hourly workers did not. This learning-based segmentation derived from the high levels of interfirm mobility of skilled production workers in the 19th century and the consequent search by employers to displace their skills through the development of machines and materials. The development of these skill-displacing technologies required the employment of technically trained personnel, who were put on annual salaries to gain their commitment to the particular firm. It also placed these salaried personnel in opposition to skilled craft workers, especially as, from the last decades of the 19th century, large numbers of them, confronted by skill-displacing technological change, joined the craft unions of the American Federation of Labor in efforts, largely futile over the long run, to reassert craft control. Indeed, these efforts, combined with the widespread use of shop-floor sabotage as a way for unrepresented workers to exercise their collective voice, furthered the resolve of industrial employers, intent on utilizing skill-displacing technologies and with access to large supplies of unskilled immigrants, to reject collective bargaining during what has become known in US labor history as the "non-union era".

On the shop floor, however, skilled work was not necessarily as a result transformed into unskilled work. In seeking to achieve high rates of throughput in the new mass-production technologies, employers discovered that high rates of turnover of the ostensibly interchangeable workers were very costly in terms of machine downtime and damage as well as materials waste. In the 1920s (the last decade of the non-union era), therefore, mass-production employers instituted job ladders and seniority in order to retain reliable production workers, who were classified as "semi-skilled". With the rise of mass-production unionism out of the crisis of the Great Depression, job ladders and seniority became foundations for collective bargaining over wage rates and benefits.

Since reaching a peak in the immediate post-World War II period, the last half of the 20th century has witnessed a dramatic decline of unionization, especially in the business sector. This decline can be explained by the growth of unorganized sectors but also, especially over the last quarter of the 20th century, by job reductions in unionized sectors as the combined result of automation, loss of international competitive advantage, and the globalization of manufacturing.

In the internationally competitive information and communication technology industries, Silicon Valley companies based on the "New Economy" business model have resisted unionization, except for janitors, and increasingly have outsourced and offshored manufacturing operations.

The rise of the New Economy business model since the 1960s has also served to erode the functional integration of managerial personnel that had characterized the Old Economy industrial corporation, as depicted in the work of Chandler and Penrose. The interfirm mobility of professional, technical, and administrative personnel from Old Economy corporations to New Economy startups led these employees to focus more on specialized learning rather than organizational learning in the pursuit of their careers. The vertical organization of industry on the New Economy model has required industry-wide technology standards that, in turn, have facilitated interfirm labor mobility. Lured by the gains that could be made from participation in broad-based stock option plans, New Economy employees have accepted a high degree of employment insecurity, which in the 2000s had been made much greater by the globalization of the supply of qualified and experienced high-technology labor.

4.3.3 Japan[7]

In the decades after the Meiji Restoration of 1868, the primary and secondary education of the entire Japanese population was raised to a high level. Simultaneously, a transformation of the system of higher education generated a growing supply of university graduates who entered industry. In addition to paying them well, the companies often incurred the considerable expense of sending these employees abroad for varying lengths of time to acquire industrial experience.

As a result of this historical legacy, amidst the post-World War II devastation, Japanese companies could draw on a sizable supply of highly educated and experienced engineers and managers. Many Toyota employees, for example, had accumulated relevant technological experience over the previous decades working for the enterprise group when it was Japan's leading producer of textile machinery. In addition, the automobile industry was able to attract many engineers who had gained experience in Japan's aircraft industry before and during the war.

From the late nineteenth century, a prime objective of US managerial learning had been to develop machine technologies that could dispense with the skills of craft workers. In contrast, with an accumulation of such craft skills lacking in Japan, the problem that had confronted technology-oriented managers from the Meiji era had been to develop skills on the shop floor as part of a strategy of organizational learning that integrated the capabilities of managers and workers. Before the war,

---

[7] This section draws on Lazonick (2001 and 2005b). Key English-language references include Dore (1973); Yonekawa (1984); Cusumano (1985); Gordon (1985); and Aoki and Dore (1994).

moreover, many Japanese companies had integrated foremen into the structure of managerial learning so that they could not only supervise but also train shop-floor workers. In the United States, the foreman, as "the man in the middle", served as a buffer between the managerial organization and the shop floor; in Japan the foreman was an integrator of managerial and shop-floor learning.

The rise of enterprise unions in the early 1950s both reflected and enhanced the social foundations for the hierarchical integration of shop-floor workers. During the last half of the 1940s, dire economic conditions and democratization initiatives gave rise to a militant labor movement of white-collar (technical and administrative) and blue-collar (operative) employees. The goal of the new industrial unions was the takeover of idle factories so that workers could put them into operation and earn a living. As an alternative to these militant industrial unions, leading companies created enterprise unions of white-collar and blue-collar employees. Foremen and supervisors were members of the union, as were all university-educated personnel for at least the first ten years of employment before they made the official transition into "management". Union officials, who were company employees, held regularly scheduled conferences with management at different levels of the enterprise to resolve issues concerning remuneration, work conditions, work organization, transfers, and production. The continued and rapid expansion of the Japanese economy in the high-growth era ensured that enterprise unionism would become an entrenched Japanese institution.

The most important achievement of enterprise unionism was "lifetime employment", a system of permanent employment that, while not contractually guaranteed, gave white-collar and blue-collar workers employment security to the retirement age of, first, 55; from the 1980s, 60; and from the late 1990s at a small but growing number of companies, 65. This employment security won the commitment of the workers to the company and gave the company the incentive to develop the productive capabilities of its workers. Unlike the United States where there was a sharp segmentation between salaried managers and hourly workers, Japanese companies of the post-World War II decades extended permanent employment to both white-collar and blue-collar men, thus providing a foundation for the hierarchical integration of shop-floor workers into a company-wide process of organizational learning (see Fig. 4.2). The hierarchical integration of engineers with shop-floor workers, moreover, fostered functional integration as specialized engineers engaged in teams to solve practical manufacturing problems.

Through their engagement in processes of cost reduction, Japanese shop-floor workers were continuously involved in a more general process of improvement of products and processes that, by the 1970s, enabled Japanese companies to emerge as world leaders in factory automation. Also of great importance was the ability of Japanese manufacturers to eliminate waste in production; by the late 1970s, for example, Japan's competitive advantage in television sets was not in labor costs or even scale economies but in a savings of materials costs. This productive transformation became particularly important in international competition in the 1980s as Japanese wages approached the levels of the advanced industrial economies of North America and Western Europe and, especially from 1985, as the value of the yen dramatically strengthened. During the 1980s and 1990s, influenced by not only Japan's export performance but also the impact of Japanese direct investment in North America and Western Europe, many Western companies sought, with varying degrees of success, to implement Japanese high-quality, low-cost mass-production methods.

By the 1990s, in industries such as automobiles and machine tools, the combination of hierarchical and functional integration enabled Japanese manufacturers to move into higher quality market segments. In producing higher quality goods at lower unit costs, the Japanese challenge shifted from competition with low-cost but (in comparative perspective) low-quality US producers to high-quality but high-cost German producers. By relying on career-long functional specialization as a mode of hierarchical integration, the German business model generated high-quality products but fostered functional segmentation that left its mechanical and electrical engineering companies vulnerable to competitive challenges from the more organizationally integrated Japanese. The result was, in 1993–4, a crisis in these sectors in Germany, with dramatic reductions in employment and concerted attempts, with some success, to learn from the Japanese.

Despite the prolonged recession of the 1990s and many predictions that Japanese "lifetime employment" would disappear in Japan, coming into the 2000s the institution of permanent employment remained intact. At the same time, the institution has shown itself to be flexible. There has been a gradual movement to merit-based pay, but with seniority pay remaining the foundation of the remuneration structure. Besides the apparent increased use of *shukko* and *tenseki*—temporary and permanents transfers of older employees to subsidiaries—to maintain the viability of permanent employment, many Japanese companies began to engage in mid-career hiring when they needed to gain immediate access to people with already developed specialized skills. The practice of mid-career hiring does not, however, spell an end to the institution of permanent employment since, in Japan, the mid-career recruit can still harbor the realistic expectation that he will be able, if he so wishes, to finish his career with the new company.

Alongside the spread of mid-career hiring, there has been a growing tendency for young people known as "freeters" (from "free arbeiters") to job-hop for a while before accepting a regular employment position. The proportion of temporary workers in the labor force has increased steadily since the 1970s, reaching 6.3 percent in 1990 and 9.7 percent in 2003, with the proportion of temporary workers in the male labor force increasing from 2.9 percent in 1990 to 5.1 percent in 2003. Many Japanese companies such as Toyota and Canon that steadfastly adhere to the principle of permanent employment for regular male employees have taken advantage of the growing availability of an uncommitted younger labor force to increase the hiring of temporary blue-collar employees. Considering that since the mid-1980s much blue-collar work has been offshored in a process that the Japanese have called *kudoka* or "hollowing out", the trend to temporary employment among blue-collar workers suggests that Japanese permanent employment is becoming a largely white-collar phenomenon.

4.4 Finance

4.4.1 Financial Commitment

Innovation requires *financial commitment*: a set of relations that, in the face of uncertainty, makes funds available to the innovative enterprise until the productive resources in which it has invested have been sufficiently developed and utilized to generate financial returns. Innovation requires investments in not only physical capital but also human capital. While it is common for a corporate executive to claim that the firm's most valuable assets are its human assets, accounting conventions treat salaries, benefits, and training costs as current expenses. Yet when employees engage in organizational learning, it inevitably takes time before that learning can contribute to the generation of revenues. Accounting conventions aside, in terms of the demands that they place on financial commitment, such investments in human capital are fixed, not variable, costs. Learning is an investment that must be financed until the products made possible by that learning generate sufficient financial returns.

The more collective the learning process, the greater the *size* of the investment that must be made in the innovation process, while the more cumulative the learning process, the greater the *duration* of that investment. Given the physical capital requirements of an industry, therefore, the greater the size and duration of the investment in innovation, the greater the amount of finance that will have to be committed to the innovation process to sustain the development of innovative products that can generate financial returns. The innovation process is, moreover, not only collective and cumulative but also uncertain. Hence there is no guarantee that finance that is committed to the innovation process will be recouped, much less generate positive returns. One should not expect, therefore, all sources of finance to be committed finance.

Internally generated funds represent the most committed form of investment finance because the allocation of these funds is directly under the control of the firm's strategic decision-makers. Depending on the size and duration of the investments in innovation, however, internal funds may be insufficient to sustain those investments until they can generate financial returns. Some form of external finance may be required. Historically, over the course of the twentieth century, different types of financial institutions—venture capital, stock markets, commercial banks, bond markets—have provided committed external finance in different forms that have differed in the size and duration, and uncertainty, of the innovative investments that they were able and willing to support.

4.4.2 United States[8]

During the first half of the twentieth century, the fundamental role of the stock market in the United States was, as we have seen, to separate ownership and control. The most successful of these companies, well capitalized and with years of profitability, were listed on NYSE. When these corporations did new stock issues, as was particularly the case in the stock market boom of the late 1920s, they tended to use these funds to restructure their balance sheets by either paying off debt or augmenting the corporate treasury, rather than to finance new investment. Such financial behavior enabled these companies to better weather downturns, with the Depression of the early 1930s being a dramatic case in point.

These listed companies paid dividends to shareholders and used their retained earnings, conservatively leveraged with bond issues if necessary, to finance the growth of the firm. Indeed, flotation of bond issues, often in conjunction with mergers and acquisitions, was the main corporate-finance role of Wall Street investment houses. By the first decades of the twentieth century, bond-rating agencies such as Standard and Poor's and Moody's had become integral to the US system of industrial finance.

During the last half of the twentieth century, retained earnings continued to be the main source of growth finance for US industrial corporations. Startup companies tended not to pay dividends, conserving all of their earnings for enterprise growth. Venture capitalists encouraged this financial behavior; they wanted to accelerate the growth of the new venture with a view either to listing it on NASDAQ, with less stringent listing requirements than NYSE, within five years or so or selling it to an established corporation in a private sale.

To some extent a New Economy initial public offering (IPO) raised funds to finance the future growth of the firm. But, given the widespread use of broad-based stock option programs by these companies, a prime purpose was often to provide a liquid market on which employees could sell their stock after they exercised their options. Especially during ebullient stock markets, these companies tended to use their stock as a currency to acquire, or merge with, other companies. The dilution of shareholdings as a result of the use of stock as a compensation and combination

---

[8] This section draws on Lazonick (2007c). Key references include Bygrave and Timmons (1992); Baskin and Miranti (1997); Kenney (2000); Gompers and Lerner (2001); Carpenter *et al.* (2003); O'Sullivan (2004, 2006a, and 2006b).

currency placed pressure on companies to do significant stock repurchases to offset dilution and boost their stock prices.

One result was that, unlike the late 1920s when companies took advantage of the stock market boom to restructure their balance sheets, in the speculative boom of the late 1990s US corporations were more likely to be repurchasing rather than selling stock at inflated prices (although the executives of these companies were generally enriching themselves by selling their own stock, mostly secured by means of stock-option compensation). Large-scale stock repurchase programs became very widespread among US industrial corporations from the mid-1980s, resulting in net negative funds raised by US corporations through stock issues in most years. To support their stock prices, companies were in effect providing cash to the stock market rather than vice versa.

4.4.3 Japan[9]

In Japan, the institution of stable shareholding enabled salaried managers to allocate corporate resources to innovative investment strategies, while the institution of permanent employment provided incentives for large numbers of people with different hierarchical responsibilities and functional specialties to engage in the organizational learning that could transform those investments into higher quality, lower cost products than had previously existed. The mutual interaction of these two institutions has been fundamental to the industrial development of Japan over the past half century. In the post-World War II decades, however, the rate of growth of innovative Japanese enterprises would have been severely limited if internal funds had been the only source of committed finance. The Japanese banking system provided a much more expansive form of financial commitment.

The role of the Japanese banking system in providing financial commitment to industrial development goes back to the Meiji era. The major *zaibatsu* were built around banks that channeled funds to constituent firms. Nevertheless much of Japanese industrial development, including cotton spinning, silk weaving, and railroads, occurred outside or with only weak relation to the *zaibatsu*. Many companies were financed by groups of shareholders who typically paid in one-sixth of the value of their shares at the outset, with the remainder being called in as it was needed. The actual source of this finance was often not the shareholders themselves but rather bank loans, backed by the Bank of Japan, that were secured by the shares in the industrial firms. Indirectly, therefore, bank loans made possible the growth of many non-*zaibatsu* industrial enterprises in the first decades of the 20th century.

    [9] This section draws on Lazonick (1999 and 2005*b*). Important English-language references include Hodder and Tschoegel (1993); Aoki and Patrick (1994); and Scher (1997).

The Japanese banking system remained central to industrial finance in the post-World War II decades in the form of "main-bank lending". The role of the banks, supported by the state, is to provide industrial enterprises with the financial resources needed to confront highly uncertain development processes. Backed by "overloans" from the Bank of Japan, the dual purposes of main-bank lending have been to "supercharge" the rate of growth of Japanese firms and to ensure that innovative firms that have accumulated valuable productive capabilities do not fail because of short-term financial exigencies.

As developmental institutions, the banks accepted relatively low returns on their lending activities. A company's "main bank" is the financial institution that takes the lead in providing it with loan finance, even though much if not most of the money that the company borrows is loaned by other financial institutions. By taking responsibility for monitoring the performance of the company and for leading the rescue of the company should it fall into financial distress, the main bank permits other banks to make loans to the company without having to take on these functions themselves. Main-bank lending permitted Japanese industrial enterprises to engage in innovative investment strategies with debt-equity ratios far in excess of those that existed in the advanced economies of the West, and with debt financing that was almost entirely in the form of unsecuritized bank loans as opposed to securitized bonds.

One important implication of the developmental role of main-bank lending is that young firms with uncertain futures have received loans on the same terms as older firms with established market shares. To allocate financial resources on terms that reflected the relative riskiness of firms would have disadvantaged small, young firms. Yet these were precisely the types of firms on which the economic development of the nation depended, and for which the banks had to play a venture capital role. In the 2000s, small firms with growth potential remain important to the Japanese economy, and bank lending remains critical to the growth of these firms.

Until the 1990s, besides the Industrial Bank of Japan—the most important of three long-term credit banks—the most significant main banks were the city banks that were the financial arms of the Big Six enterprise groups (kigyo shudan), Mitsui, Mitsubishi, Sumitomo, Fuyo (Fuji Bank), Dai-Ichi Kangin (Dai-Ichi Kangyo Bank), and Sanwa. These enterprise groups were also called horizontal keiretsu because they linked together a number of powerful companies across an array of distinct industries. In addition, during the postwar decades a number of companies such as Toyota and Matsushita emerged as the core companies of vertical keiretsu. Each of these core companies has provided development finance, in the forms of equity stakes and loans, to large numbers of subsidiaries that supply it with goods and services, either directly or through a chain of suppliers and distributors. Many of the core companies of the vertical keiretsu have relations with the horizontal keiretsu.

Whether the relations among companies are vertical or horizontal, moreover, both stable shareholding and bank lending transcend *keiretsu* relations, and have become inextricable from the dense web of business relations that tie the fates of Japanese companies together.

The role of the main-bank system in supporting Japanese industrial development was critical in the "era of high-speed growth" of the 1950s and 1960s. By the 1970s and 1980s, however, as innovative enterprise transformed Japan into a rich country, the industrial corporations that had underpinned Japan's successful development found themselves much less dependent on the banks. Increasingly they used their abundant retained earnings or substantial funds raised on securities markets at home and abroad to pay off large amounts of their bank debt.

As a result, increasingly during the 1970s and 1980s the Japanese banks lost much of the business of their best borrowers—the manufacturing corporations whose growth they had backed in the postwar decades that had now achieved substantial success. By the mid-1980s the banks, awash with cash, shifted their loan portfolios to more speculative borrowers who invested in real estate or with real estate as collateral. When, along with stock prices, themselves buoyed up by the speculation in real estate, land prices plummeted with the bursting of the Bubble Economy in 1990, Japanese banks were left with a mountain of bad loans that impeded their ability to play their developmental role.

As business enterprises, the banks ultimately did well because the Japanese economy did well. The ongoing problems that Japanese banks experienced in the 1990s were only in part caused by the hangover of bad loans from the Bubble Economy. Small firms in particular needed bank finance, and it continued to be the role of the banks to make loans on terms that did not take into account the high degree of uncertainty that the growth of these firms faced. One reason that, as financial enterprises, banks were willing to participate in such a system is that they expected, as the experience of the early 1990s revealed, that the government would stand behind them should the loans go bad. In the 1990s the banks continued to make loans to finance the growth of firms in the largely no-growth economic environment of the "Lost Decade".

Recently, the financial condition of the banks has improved, in part by selling off a significant portion of their once-stable shareholdings in other companies; stock-price movements had wreaked havoc with the valuation of bank assets and hence with the banks' capital-adequacy ratios. In addition, Japanese banks have been less willing than before to make high-risk, low-yield loans to small and medium enterprises (SMEs), with the government assuming more responsibility for bailing out SMEs in financial difficulty. While bank loans remain important sources of committed finance in Japan, it would appear that in the 2000s the banks are acting less like agents of economic development and more like business enterprises that need to make profits to survive.

4.5 Conclusions

An innovative enterprise develops productive resources to differentiate itself from its rivals, and utilizes the productive resources that it has developed to generate the higher quality, lower cost products that are the source of its competitive advantage. Innovative enterprise makes economic development possible, but not on its own. Government investments in education and research form indispensable foundations for business investments in innovation. Governments sometimes serve as sources of demand for innovative products in their early stages of development when unit costs tend to be high. Governments often subsidize innovative enterprises directly when the returns to innovation remain so uncertain that the business sector would not otherwise make the necessary investments. Governments may protect national markets from foreign competition so that enterprises based in the nation can generate revenues, and stay in business, during the period of time that the cumulative innovation process is taking place. Some governments structure the banking system so that it provides the committed finance to businesses that is needed to sustain the innovation process until it can generate financial returns.

Besides supporting innovative enterprise in these ways, governments may also seek to ensure that the outcome of innovative enterprise is indeed economic development; that is, a process that raises the standards of living for more and more people over time. Left to itself innovative enterprise may generate economic growth, but in an inequitable and unstable manner that undermines its contribution to economic development. A challenge for business history is to analyze whether and how, historically and comparatively, governments have supported innovative enterprise and influenced its outcomes to enhance the contribution of innovative enterprise to stable and equitable economic growth.

A theory of innovative enterprise is essential to the analysis of business–government relations in the development process. Otherwise, one cannot explain why under some conditions government investments and subsidies are transformed into innovative outcomes while under other conditions they are not. One needs to embed such an explanation in an analysis of the "social conditions of innovative enterprise"—strategic control, organizational integration, and financial commitment—as they exist in different nations, in different industries, in different firms, and at different times.

Here too, the Schumpeterian agenda, and with it business history, come to the fore. When, in the first decades of the twentieth century, neoclassical economists were confronted by the reality of the managerial revolution, their theory of the firm led them to depict the "monopoly model" as the analytical basis for assessing the performance of "big business". Indeed, in the post-World War II decades, the monopoly model became the theoretical foundation of the "structure-conduct-performance" school of industrial organization, a neoclassical perspective rooted in the "ideal" of perfect competition. According to the monopoly model, a firm that dominated its industry would raise price and restrict output compared with the price and output under perfectly competitive conditions. But if technological and market conditions make perfect competition a possibility, how can one firm (or even a small number of firms) come to dominate an industry? One would have to assume that the monopolist somehow differentiated itself from its competitors in the industry (see Lazonick 2006c). But, the constrained-optimization comparison that yields the monopoly model argues that both the monopolist firm and perfectly competitive firms *optimize subject to the same cost structures* that derive from given technological and factor-market conditions. So how would monopoly ever emerge under such conditions?

The economics discipline prides itself on its use of logical analysis. The neoclassical comparison between monopoly and perfect competition represents, however, an enormous logical error. It is an error that, in *Capitalism, Socialism, and Democracy*, prompted Schumpeter (1950: 106) to state:

What we have got to accept is that [the large-scale enterprise] has come to be the most powerful engine of [economic] progress and in particular of the long-run expansion of total output not only in spite of, but to a considerable extent through, the strategy that looks so restrictive when viewed in the individual case and from the individual point in time. In this respect, perfect competition is not only impossible but inferior, and has no title to being set up as a model of ideal efficiency.

The Schumpeterian agenda is the construction of a theory of innovative enterprise that provides the microfoundations for a theory of economic development. In effect, the dynamics of the innovating firm that are depicted in Figure 4.1 explain why in the face of established international competition, tariff protection, or some other type of subsidy, may be necessary to transform the high fixed costs of a innovative strategy into low unit costs (see Lazonick 2006c). It also explains why the success or failure of such state subsidies will depend on the social conditions of innovative enterprise. Cost structures are not "given" to the innovating firm; through innovative strategy, organizational learning, and sustained finance, these costs structures must, in the face of uncertainty, be put in place. An analysis of the conditions under which the high fixed costs of an innovative investment strategy are in fact transformed into higher quality, lower cost products requires a rigorous analysis of the roles of strategy, organization, and finance in the evolution of the firm, within the context of specific industrial and institutional conditions. Business history provides the substance for such an analysis of the process of economic development.

References

ABEGGLEN, J., and STALK, JR., G. (1985). *Kaisha: The Japanese Corporation*. New York: Basic Books.

AOKI, M., and DORE, R. (eds.) (1994). *The Japanese Firm: The Sources of Competitive Strength*. Oxford: Oxford University Press.

——and PATRICK, H. (eds.) (1994). *The Japanese Main Bank System: Its Relevance for Developing and Transforming Economies*. Oxford: Oxford University Press.

BASKIN, J., and MIRANTI, P. (1997). *A History of Corporate Finance*. Cambridge: Cambridge University Press.

BERLE, A., and MEANS, G. (1932). *The Modern Corporation and Private Property*. London: Macmillan.

BEST, M. (1990). *The New Competition: Institutions of Industrial Restructuring*. Cambridge, Mass.: Harvard University Press.

BRODY, D. (1980). *Workers in Industrial America*. Oxford: Oxford University Press.

BYGRAVE, W., and TIMMONS, J. (1992). *Venture Capital at the Crossroads*. Cambridge, Mass.: Harvard Business School Press.

CARPENTER, M., LAZONICK, W., and O'SULLIVAN, M. (2003). "The Stock Market and Innovative Capability in the New Economy: The Optical Networking Industry". *Industrial and Corporate Change*, 12/5: 963–1034.

CHANDLER, A. D. (1962). *Strategy and Structure: Chapters in the History of the American Industrial Enterprise*. Cambridge, Mass.: MIT Press.

——(1977). *The Visible Hand: The Managerial Revolution in American Business*. Cambridge, Mass.: Harvard University Press.

——(1990). *Scale and Scope: The Dynamics of Industrial Capitalism*. Cambridge, Mass.: Belknap Press.

CUSUMANO, M. (1985). *The Japanese Automobile Industry*. Cambridge, Mass.: Harvard University Press.

DORE, R. (1973). *British Factory–Japanese Factory: the Origins of Diversity in Industrial Relations*. Berkeley: University of California Press.

FAGERBERG, J., MOWERY, D., and NELSON, R. (eds.) (2004). *The Oxford Handbook of Innovation*. Oxford: Oxford University Press.

GOMPERS, P., and LERNER, J. (2001). "The Venture Capital Revolution". *Journal of Economic Perspectives*, 15/2: 145–68.

GORDON, A. (1985). *The Evolution of Labor Relations in Japan: Heavy Industry, 1853–1955*. Cambridge, Mass.: Harvard University Press.

HADLEY, E. (1970). *Antitrust in Japan*. Princeton: Princeton University Press.

HILARY, G., and OSHIKA, T. (2003). "Shareholder Activism in Japan: Social Pressure, Private Cost, and Organized Crime". Center for Economic Institutions Working Paper Series, 2003-20.

HODDER, J., and TSCHOEGL, A. (1993). "Corporate Finance in Japan", in S. Takagi (ed.), *Japanese Capital Markets: New Developments in Regulations and Institutions*. Oxford: Blackwell.

HOUNSHELL, D. (1996). "The Evolution of Industrial Research in the United States", in R. Rosenbloom and W. Spencer (eds.), *Engines of Innovation: US Industrial Research at the End of an Era*. Boston, Mass.: Harvard Business School Press.

JACOBY, S. (1985). *Employing Bureaucracy: Managers, Unions, and the Transformation of Work in America, 1990–1945*. New York: Columbia University Press.

KENNEY, M. (ed.) (2000). *Understanding Silicon Valley*. Stanford, Calif.: Stanford University Press.

LAZONICK, W. (1986). "Strategy, Structure, and Management Development in the United States and Britain", in K. Kobayashi and H. Morikawa (eds.), *Development of Managerial Enterprise*. Tokyo: University of Tokyo Press, 101–46.

——(1990). *Competitive Advantage on the Shop Floor*. Cambridge, Mass.: Harvard University Press.

——(1991). *Business Organization and the Myth of the Market Economy*. Cambridge: Cambridge University Press.

——(1999). "The Japanese Economy and Corporate Reform: What Path to Sustainable Prosperity?" *Industrial and Corporate Change*, 8/4: 607–33.

——(2001). "Organizational Learning and International Competition", in W. Lazonick and M. O'Sullivan (eds.), *Corporate Governance and Sustainable Prosperity*. London: Palgrave, 37–77.

——(2002*a*). "The US Industrial Corporation and The Theory of the Growth of the Firm", in C. Pitelis (ed.), *The Growth of the Firm: The Legacy of Edith Penrose*. Oxford: Oxford University Press, 249–77.

——(2002*b*). "Innovative Enterprise and Historical Transformation". *Enterprise & Society*, 3/1: 3–27.

——(2003). "The Theory of the Market Economy and the Social Foundations of Innovative Enterprise". *Economic and Industrial Democracy*, 24/1: 9–44.

——(2005*a*). "Corporate Restructuring", in S. Ackroyd, R. Batt, P. Thompson, and P. Tolbert (eds.), *The Oxford Handbook of Work & Organization*. Oxford: Oxford University Press.

——(2005*b*). "The Institutional Triad and Japanese Development" (translated into Japanese), in G. Hook and A. Kudo (eds.), *The Contemporary Japanese Enterprise*, vol. 1. Tokyo: Yukikaku Publishing, 55–82.

——(2006*b*). "Globalization of the ICT Labor Force", in R. Mansell, C. Avgerou, D. Quah, and R. Silverstone (eds.), *The Oxford Handbook on ICTs*. Oxford: Oxford University Press.

——(2007*a*). "Evolution of the New Economy Business Model", in E. Brousseau and N. Curien (eds.), *Internet and Digital Economics*. Cambridge: Cambridge University Press.

——(2007*b*). "Innovative Enterprise and Economic Development", in Y. Cassis and A. Colli (eds.), *Business Performance in the Twentieth Century: A Comparative Perspective*. Cambridge: Cambridge University Press.

——(2007*c*). "The Stock Market in the New Economy Business Model". INSEAD working paper.

——and O'SULLIVAN, M. (2000). "Perspectives on Corporate Governance, Innovation, and Economic Performance", Targeted Socio-Economic Research (TSER) Report to the European Commission (DGXII) under the Fourth Framework Programme.

LICHTENSTEIN, N., and HARRIS, H. (eds.) (1993). *Industrial Democracy in America: The Ambiguous Promise*. Cambridge: Cambridge University Press.

MORIKAWA, H. (1997). "Japan: Increasing Organizational Capabilities of Large Industrial Enterprises, 1880s–1980s," in A. Chandler, Jr., F. Amatori, and T. Hikino (eds.), *Big Business and the Wealth of Nations*. Cambridge: Cambridge University Press, 307–35.

——(2001). *A History of Top Management in Japan*. Oxford: Oxford University Press.

MOWERY, D., and NELSON, R. (eds.) (1999). *Sources of Industrial Leadership*. Cambridge: Cambridge University Press.

——and ROSENBERG, N. (1998). *Paths of Innovation: Technological Change in 20th Century America*. Cambridge: Cambridge University Press.

NAVIN, T., and SEARS, M. (1955). "The Rise of a Market in Industrial Securities, 1887–1902". *Business History Review*, 29, June: 105–38.

NELSON, R. (ed.) (1993). *National Innovation Systems*. Oxford: Oxford University Press.

——and WINTER, S. (1982). *An Evolutionary Theory of Economic Change*. Cambridge, Mass.: Harvard University Press.

NOBLE, D. (1977). *America by Design: Science, Technology, and the Rise of Corporate Capitalism*. Oxford: Oxford University Press.

O'SULLIVAN, M. (2000a). *Contests for Corporate Control: Corporate Governance and Economic Performance in the United States and Germany*. Oxford: Oxford University Press.

——(2000b). "The Innovative Enterprise and Corporate Governance". *Cambridge Journal of Economics*, 24/4: 393–416.

——(2004). "What Drove the Stock Market in the Last Century?" INSEAD Working Paper.

——(2006a). "Celebrating Youth: The US Stock Market & New Industries in Historical Perspective", in N. Lamoreaux and K. Sokoloff (eds.), *Finance and Innovation*. Cambridge, Mass.: MIT Press.

——(2006b). "The Deficiencies, Excesses, and Control of Competition: The Development of the Stock Market from the 1930s to 2001", in L. Galambos and C. Fohlin (eds.), *Balancing Public and Private Control: Germany and the US in the Postwar Era*. Cambridge: Cambridge University Press.

PENROSE, E. (1959). *The Theory of the Growth of the Firm*. Oxford: Blackwell.

——(1960). "The Growth of the Firm—A Case Study: Hercules Powder Company". *Business History Review*, 34, spring: 1–23.

——(1989). "History, the Social Sciences and Economic 'Theory', with Special Reference to Multinational Enterprise", in A. Teichova, M. Lévy-Leboyer, and H. Nussbaum (eds.), *Historical Studies in International Corporate Business*. Cambridge: Cambridge University Press.

SAXENIAN, A. (1994). *Regional Advantage: Culture and Competition in Silicon Valley and Route 128*. Cambridge, Mass.: Harvard University Press.

SCHER, M. (1997). *Japanese Interfirm Networks and their Main Banks*. New York: St. Martin's Press.

SCHUMPETER, J. (1934). *The Theory of Economic Development*. Cambridge, Mass.: Harvard University Press.

——(1950). *Capitalism, Socialism, and Democracy*, 3rd edn. New York: Harper.

—— (1954). *History of Economic Analysis*. Oxford: Oxford University Press.

SOLOW, R. (1986). "Economics: Is Something Missing?", in W. Parker (ed.), *Economic History and the Modern Economist*. Oxford: Blackwell.

WHYTE, W. (1956). *The Organization Man*. New York: Simon & Schuster.

YONEKAWA, S. (1984). "University Graduates in Japanese Enterprises before the Second World War". *Business History*, 26, July: 193–218.

CHAPTER 5

BUSINESS HISTORY AND MANAGEMENT STUDIES

MATTHIAS KIPPING

BEHLÜL ÜSDIKEN

5.1 INTRODUCTION

THE purpose of this chapter is to give an overview of the changing relationship between business history and management studies since the 1950s, with a particular focus on the contributions made by business historians to management research. We also assess the potential for future collaboration among scholars from the two fields. Our main argument is that while both were close at the beginning of the period, they subsequently moved apart. As we will show, it was particularly Chandler's (1962) book *Strategy and Structure* that had a profound and lasting influence on research in management or administration as it was known at the time. But what looked like a promising start never developed into a more fully fledged interaction. Management studies moved in the direction of "scientization",

A draft version of this chapter was presented at the Management History Research Group Workshop at Queen Mary College, University in London on June 13–14, 2005. We would like to thank the participants for their helpful remarks. We are also very grateful to Richard Whittington and Moshe Farjoun for additional suggestions and to the editors for their input and their patience. The usual disclaimer applies.

especially in North America, while much of business history remained rooted in its own legacy of (narrative) history, economic history, and economics. This divergence is mirrored in the current institutional set-up of both fields. Most business historians are working in history or, less frequently, economic history departments rather than business schools or management departments. Business historians have their own academic associations, which are not affiliated with the major learned societies in the management field, such as the Academy of Management. The same is true for publications in academic journals, where there has been little crossover.

Within this framework, there have been some exceptions. Business historians have continued to contribute to research in a few sub-fields outside the core specialties within the broad field of management studies. These sub-fields have primarily been International Business and, perhaps most notably, what might be termed Management History, addressing issues such as the development of production systems from Taylorism and Fordism to flexible specialization, the "Americanization" of European and Japanese businesses after World War II, or the history of management education and management consulting. We will detail these contributions—and their limitations—in the body of this chapter. In terms of institutions, the most prominent exception is the Harvard Business School (HBS), which has had a Chair in Business History since the 1920s. Chandler spent the later part of his career there and since then HBS has continued to attract a number of well-known and well-respected business historians. The phenomenon is somewhat more widespread in Europe, where business historians are affiliated with business schools or management departments at a larger number of institutions.

In general, the last ten years have seen calls from both sides for a closer interaction between business history and management studies and some more pronounced attempts at dialogue and even cooperation. As we will argue in the final section of the chapter, these have yet to reach the central areas of management studies—strategy and organization—which would finally bring business history back to its auspicious beginnings.

5.2 CLOSE ORIGINS: CHANDLER'S CONTRIBUTION TO MANAGEMENT STUDIES

There are few business historians, if any, who left as important a mark on management practitioners and management scholars as Alfred Chandler. His work on the development of the multidivisional form of organization (Chandler 1962) and, to a lesser extent, on the emergence of the large-scale vertically integrated enterprise (Chandler 1977) are still seen as pioneering efforts in the management and in particular the strategy literature (e.g. Whittington 2001; Ghemawat 2002; Jeremy 2002; Micklethwait and Wooldridge 2003). Chandler was not the first to study the large-scale diversified manufacturing enterprises which had become a dominant feature of the American economy at the time—something for which Drucker's (1946) *Concept of the Corporation* probably deserves the credit. Neither did he discover the importance of managers compared to owners and entrepreneurs—a phenomenon already examined by a variety of earlier studies, including Berle and Means (1932), Burnham (1941), Schumpeter (1942), and Penrose (1959).

But in his book on *Strategy and Structure*, he explicitly aimed to make a historical contribution to the study of large-scale firms: "Historians have provided social scientists with little empirical data on which to base generalizations or hypotheses concerning the administration of great enterprises. Nor have the historians formulated many theories or generalizations of their own" (Chandler 1962: 1). Based on a survey of the largest industrial firms in the United States and their organizational structure, Chandler selected four companies that had—independently of each other—pioneered a multidivisional or decentralized form of organization in the 1910s and 1920s (DuPont, General Motors, Standard Oil, and Sears Roebuck) and studied them in detail. He investigated the internal conditions that led to this organizational innovation (prior administrative history and growth patterns) and the context in which the organizational changes took place (changes in the overall market demand for their products and "the state of the administrative art in the United States at the time") (ibid. 3). From the in-depth comparative analysis of the four cases, he deducted his major thesis "that structure follows strategy": companies change their organization to meet the administrative demands created by their different types of—planned—growth, for example an expansion of volume, geographical dispersion, or a diversification of product lines (ibid. 14–15).

For management scholars, *Strategy and Structure* remains one of the "classic" case studies, widely seen as exemplary for comparative, theory-building management research (e.g. Eisenhardt 1991). And it has even earned him the status of a management "guru", as one of the writers who, according to Micklethwait and Wooldridge (1996: 142), "spent the 1950s and 1960s insisting that all companies needed a corporate strategy"—which was actually quite far from being his primary concern, if it was a concern at all. More specifically, in conceptual terms his work on the development of the M-form is still regarded as one of the prime footings in the evolution of the field of strategic management and the pioneer of the processual approach to strategy (Bowman *et al.* 2002). His 1962 book has also been seen as one of the foundational studies in early attempts to develop contingency theories of organization and management (e.g. Kast and Rozenzweig 1970) and has since been regarded as the basis for pointing to the significance of strategy as a contingency factor (e.g. Donaldson 1995). At the same time, his work has also been used as a justification for those perspectives that have questioned the deterministic and overly rationalistic versions of contingency theory and have claimed that the designs of organizations involve an element of choice (e.g. Hall 1987).

Moreover, from an empirical point of view, Chandler's study sparked a research program at the Harvard Business School in the late 1960s and early 1970s, when a group of doctoral students under the supervision of Bruce Scott—and with Chandler as a member of the doctoral committees—examined diversification and divisionalization in the largest 100 industrial firms in the United States (Wrigley 1970; Didrichsen 1972; Rumelt 1986), the United Kingdom (Channon 1973), France and Germany (Dyas and Thanheiser 1976), and Italy (Pavan 1976). Subsequently, Channon (1978) also studied the 100 largest service firms in Britain. Whittington and Mayer (2000: 12), who extended the research on British, French, and German firms into the 1990s, not only call this "the first systematic research program in the strategic management discipline", but also claim that "in its international scope, its historical perspective, and standardization of national data-bases, it still has few peers".

But what looked like a promising, mutually stimulating, and beneficial relationship between historians and other scholars of business and management remained exactly this—a promise. Neither Chandler's later research nor any of the subsequent studies and debates in the business history literature (related or not to his work) have had an influence on management research even mildly comparable to that of *Strategy and Structure*. What happened? Why did what seemed like a fruitful interaction during the 1960s not continue? The answer lies in the evolution of both fields and particularly the introduction of neo-positivist research methodologies in mainstream management studies.

5.3 MOVING APART: SCIENTIZATION IN MANAGEMENT RESEARCH

Flourishing after World War II as a separate discipline housed in business schools, predominantly in North America (Augier *et al.* 2005), the study of management and organizations has in a rather abrupt fashion turned away from history. This has been due to the scientization route that management studies took initially in the United States from the late 1950s onwards and the accompanying early penetration of disciplines such as psychology, social psychology, and sociology. The broad pattern that was set in motion in the field of management in the 1950s was epitomized by the founding of the *Administrative Science Quarterly* (ASQ) in 1956 and of *Management Science* in 1954—though the latter moved and settled on a formalistic and technique-orientated route. Early articles in both of these journals attest to the quest and the aspirations at the time for building a "science of managing" or "administrative science" that would essentially be based upon the emulation of the natural science model. What research should look like in management was clearly spelled out, for example, by Delany (1960: 448–9). It had to meet, as much as possible, the "usual scientific canons of validity, reliability, generality, parsimony, explanatory power and usefulness for purposive control". In stating the means for achieving these aims Delany was also clear about the role of historical research in the emerging science of administration or management (ibid. 449): "An emphasis upon current and immediately observable organizations in the interests of full and rigorous data. Historical research, while not ruled out, is given second-level priority and rigorous comparative studies substituted at the first-priority level."

Scientization did not remain without its critics. Boddewyn (1965: 261), for example, explicitly recognized, as a part of what he saw as the problem of ignoring the international, that in US management studies there was "widespread disinterest in business history". But such views remained a minority and the scientistic orientation clearly triumphed, as Daft (1980) showed in his study of articles in the ASQ between 1959 and 1979. While almost all early contributions were qualitative studies, by the late 1970s the majority of articles employed some kind of quantitative analysis. The field had clearly moved in the direction of scientific precision and rigor—a trend that has increasingly continued since, notably in North America (Augier *et al.* 2005). Moreover, the growing importance of scholarly journals as research outlets for management research to the detriment of the earlier in-depth studies published as books (cf. Dyer and Wilkins 1991) made it increasingly difficult for historians to convey the richness of their material to management scholars.

On the way, the field that was originally defined as "management" or "administration" became divided into what were to develop later as separate disciplines. As a result, "management" or "management studies" increasingly became an umbrella term to include a division between what has broadly been characterized as a "macro" as opposed to a "micro" orientation. The former is often regarded as incorporating strategic management and organization theory as the major sub-fields or disciplines, whereas the latter includes organizational behavior and human resource management. These sub-fields have moved in the way of developing institutional structures providing distinct identities in the way of doctoral training programs, journals, and associations, though companion umbrella structures are also available, such as the American and other academies of management.

There have been some time lags in the pace of scientization, with organizational behavior and organizational theory taking the lead. These developments took somewhat longer to reach the sub-fields of human resource management and business strategy, where until about the mid-1970s the predominant approach in the literature continued to be based on studies of the histories of individual or a small number of firms—Chandler's work constituting the prime example. But from the late 1970s onwards, the sub-field of strategy also turned towards the empirical-quantitative tradition, influenced by the economics of industrial organization (e.g. Porter 1980) and other social sciences (cf. Whittington 2001). The concern with history in management studies itself became confined to the study of early management and organizational practices and the literatures on them. In the United States much of this research has been concentrated around the Academy of Management's Management History Division. The division is based on a model combining professional teachers and business practitioners (prominent in the early years of the business schools). It neither followed the Chandlerian synthesis in business history nor espoused the scientization of management studies and remained rather marginal as a result.

This brief account of the way management studies unfolded in the second half of the twentieth century largely represents the trajectory in North America. There has been a strong American influence on management studies in Europe in the post-World War II period and a considerable transfer of research, content, and institutional models, though the penetration of the latter in particular has been partial. Nevertheless, the dominant research traditions have been different in almost all sub-fields of management, European research leaning more towards inductive, processual, and qualitative case-study methods as opposed to the primacy of the natural science model in North America (Collin *et al.* 1996). Additionally, management research in Europe has sustained stronger ties with social theory at large and more specifically with sociology and anthropology (Üsdiken and Pasadeos 1995). There is in particular a largely European-based literature on comparative/national business systems (with few North American exemplars such as Hamilton and Biggart (1988)), which grew out of organizational and economic sociology, often practiced in the emerging European business schools. It drew explicitly on a long-term perspective—and partially on the historical literature—to explain the differences in institutional contexts in accounting for international variation in dominant forms of big business organization (e.g. Whitley 2002).

Despite these methodological and disciplinary leanings and openness, however, even European management research has not developed until recently a strong engagement with history at large or business history in particular. This is partially due to a lack of institutional overlap—with few business historians located in business schools or management departments. At the same time, it is also due to a lack of interest by many business historians, who preferred to remain closer to their intellectual origins in history, economic history, and economics rather than engaging with management studies.

5.4 STUCK ELSEWHERE: BUSINESS HISTORY BETWEEN HISTORY AND ECONOMICS

Chandler's influence on business history was even more important than his impact in management studies. It is probably no exaggeration to say that his work created business history as a serious field of academic study in the 1960s and 1970s (cf. McCraw 1988). He moved the field decisively away from narrative accounts and from a focus on individual entrepreneurs, which had dominated the earlier business historical literature (cf. Galambos 2003). His work on the emergence and transformation of large-scale managerial enterprise in the United States set the research agenda for several decades to come. Even for those who extended or criticized his findings it became and remains a crucial reference point (cf. John 1997 and the contribution by Cassis in this volume). But while Chandler had suggested that business historians should either provide social scientists with empirical evidence as a basis for generalizations or develop these generalizations themselves, little progress seems to have been made in that direction. There are a number of reasons why the dialogue between business history and management studies stalled.

First of all, despite Chandler, much of business history continued to provide narrative histories of companies, entrepreneurs, and industries. The intention here is not to criticize such an approach per se. Case studies were and continue to be an accepted method of research in the social sciences (Yin 2003)—with some debate about the balance between rich description of a single case (Dyer and Wilkins 1991) and the need for comparison among several cases (Eisenhardt 1989). The point here is that much of the business historical literature insisted on the singularity of the events it described—thus rejecting possible generalizations. Some more recent company histories use existing concepts from the social sciences to provide additional insights into their specific findings or relate them to broader debates (e.g. Jones 2005b; Fear 2005). But the vast majority does not. This is not surprising given that most business historians were trained as historians, worked in history (or economic history) departments, and therefore had little exposure to other social sciences. Moreover, most company histories—whether commissioned or not—are directed at non-academic audiences. In general, these audiences have little knowledge of and interest in the conceptual and theoretical developments in the social sciences, including management studies—where academia has grown increasingly apart from practitioners and practice (cf. Kieser 2002; Whittington 2004).

Second, even if business historians did try to interact with other academic audiences, on the whole they have tended to look at economics, in terms of both their empirical focus and conceptual frameworks. This interest is partially mutual. Chandler's work actually found some echo among the so-called transaction cost economists. In particular Oliver Williamson (e.g. 1985) drew heavily on Chandler's account of the rise and divisionalization of large-scale enterprise to support his argument that the modern corporation in its various manifestations over time was a device to save on transaction costs. Chandler (1992) distanced himself from this approach, as had others before him (Lazonick 1991). Instead, he endorsed the so-called evolutionary economics (Nelson and Winter 1982), since it also had the firm as its basic unit of analysis, and examined organizational capabilities and organizational learning (cf. also Chandler *et al.* 1998). Other business historians in the economic history tradition and economic historians have nevertheless been promoting transaction cost and agency theory, broadly defined as economics of information, which they have recently put forward as an alternative to the Chandlerian framework (Lamoreaux *et al.* 2003, 2004, and this volume).

There is nothing inherently wrong with using concepts from economics, such as information costs, or interacting with evolutionary and institutional economists. Economics has also influenced many important "schools" within the management literature, such as the resource-based view in strategy for example. But it seems to have done business history little good in terms of its relevance outside its own field. First, mainstream economic history at least in the United States and partially in the UK had already moved into different—cliometric—directions from the late 1970s onwards and showed little interest in business historical research. Second, business historians left much of Chandler's original research agenda for others to complete, in particular with respect to the M-form (see above). They did little to participate in the more theoretical debates or provide additional empirical evidence—with a few recent exceptions (e.g. Toms and Wright 2002; Binda 2004). Last not least, the "fixation" of many business historians on market mechanisms and firm performance (cf. Kipping 2003) did little to maintain or generate interest in their work among organizational and economic sociologists as well as neo-institutionalists—in principle more predisposed towards historical approaches. Many of them came to lump together the work of Chandler and others with neo-classical and new institutional economists à la Williamson under the label "efficiency theory", i.e. sharing "the assumption that there is a selection process that ensures that more efficient economic forms will prevail over less efficient forms" (Roy 1997: 7; cf. also Abrahamson 1991).

From the 1980s onwards, many of these scholars carried out their own research on the rise and evolution of the corporation—with interests and power as the major driving forces. Thus, Fligstein (1990) attributed the transformation of corporate control in the US to the legal/political impact of changing anti-trust regulation as well as the shifting educational/functional backgrounds of managers—a view partly accepted by Chandler (1994). Roy (1997) tried to show how the corporate form originated around the turn of the twentieth century in the government-owned utilities and became generalized due to pressures from financial markets rather than as the result of changes in technology and organizational capabilities (cf. also Perrow 2002). Freeland (2001) re-examined the case of General Motors and, based on his own archival research, argued that Chandler's account in *Strategy and Structure* and in Sloan's (1963) autobiography, on which he collaborated, was inaccurate and misleading. He highlighted the role of power struggles and middle managers in the emergence of the M-form, rather than competitive pressures and visionary leadership. But regardless of what appeared like a widening gap between management studies and business history, the latter continued to have some impact on the former—albeit in more marginal areas.

5.5 REMAINING RELEVANCE: INTERNATIONAL BUSINESS AND MANAGEMENT HISTORY

The area where the contribution of business historians is probably most apparent and widely recognized is International Business. This might partially be due to the fact that International Business is a fairly well-delineated field of academic research, with its own conferences (the Academy of International Business and its regional replicas) and scholarly journal (the *Journal of International Business Studies*). Scholars in the field have continuously stressed their interest in history and the importance of the historical dimension—even if much of this seems to have been lip-service (Jones and Khanna 2006). Historians of international business have nevertheless provided extensive empirical evidence, both overviews and specific case studies, many of them internationally comparative in nature. And, while drawing on Chandler, they moved beyond his framework by looking not only at large-scale manufacturing enterprises, but also at natural resources and the service sector as well as small firms. Historians also engaged with part of the prevalent theories in International Business, and even contributed at least one important concept to this literature: the idea of the "free standing" multinational.

This concept was developed by Wilkins (1988) based on a comparison of British and US multinationals. For most of the latter, foreign expansion grew out of a significant domestic business and included subsidiaries in many countries. Instead, many of the pre-1914 British multinationals had only a small head office in the UK, usually in London, where they were registered, but operated exclusively abroad—in general in a single country, where they owned one or more plantations, mines, railroads, or utilities. As subsequent historical research showed, these free-standing companies were confined neither to Britain, nor to the pre-World War I period (Wilkins and Schröter 1998). More importantly, the concept was taken up by other scholars in international business, who discussed the use of the most appropriate economics-based frameworks to explain this particular form of organization (cf. Casson 1994). Jones has also combined conceptual frameworks with historical evidence in his extensive work on multinationals—including his survey text on the historical development of international business and global enterprise (Jones 2005a). Aiming more broadly, in a recent article, he highlighted the reference to an idealized or stylized vision of the past in the current international business literature and tried to promote instead the use of real historical data and cases (Jones and Khanna 2006).

Wilkins and Jones are but the tip of the iceberg. Business historians have made and continue to make important empirical contributions to the study of international business, covering more countries each time, both in the developed and the developing world, and more cases (for a comprehensive overview see Jones 2003 and his contribution in this volume). But it is important to mention at least one major limitation, which is due to the general orientation of business historical research discussed above and might be one of the reasons why historians of international business have not achieved an even wider recognition in the field. Thus, among the available frameworks from the international business history literature, business historians have largely used those broadly based in economics, in particular Dunning's (2003) eclectic paradigm. The same is true when it comes to organizational capabilities and learning or the knowledge-based view of the firm, where the heritage of evolutionary economics is again undeniable. By contrast, concepts closer to management studies have made few inroads into the historical research. Thus, while sometimes mentioning them, business historians have not yet used frameworks such as the internationalization process model, originally proposed by Johanson and Vahlne (1977), which are more dynamic and process oriented and thus should fit their research particularly well. Again, there are some exceptions, like a recent case study of a UK-owned multinational which uses concepts from organizational sociology and the national business systems literature to explain the overall advantages of the company and the local adaptation of its Danish, American, and British subsidiaries (Kristensen and Zeitlin 2005).

This kind of collaboration and mutually beneficial interaction can also be observed in a few other areas, which one might summarize broadly under the heading of Management History. Here, business historians have also made a number of recognizable—and recognized—contributions to broader debates. We will look at three of these areas: the transformation of production systems, which also includes the role of industrial districts; the American influence on the development of European and Japanese companies; and the evolution and role of management education and management consulting.

Since the early 1980s, there has been an important debate in the popular and academic management literature about the future of the scale-intensive Western production system, broadly characterized by the labels "Taylorism" and "Fordism".

This debate was driven in large part by the competitive success of companies originating from Japan and (somewhat later) other Asian countries as well as Italy, which clearly defied the logic of mass production and vertical integration that had been highlighted by Chandler and others as the driving force behind the superior performance of American corporations. Some of the scholars involved in this debate took an explicitly comparative and historical approach suggesting that the previously dominant mass production was giving way to a new system that they characterized as "flexible specialization" (Piore and Sabel 1984). Historians of business and technology also made an important contribution by looking at the origins of the mass production system and its historical alternatives. They also showed that developments of the corporate economy and organizational forms were not teleological, as much of the earlier historical literature had explicitly or implicitly assumed (for a detailed overview, see the chapter by Zeitlin on the "Historical Alternatives" approach in this volume).

A particular focus of the debate about flexible specialization and the contribution by historians was the development of production methods in the automobile industry (cf. Shiomi and Wada 1995), for example about the tiered supplier system in Japan as an alternative to the vertical integration prevalent in the United States. In general, business historians helped elucidate the reasons behind the success of Japanese companies (e.g. Yuzawa 1994). In many cases, their work stressed the role of entrepreneurial initiatives, while downplaying the importance of government intervention and protection. This clearly contradicted widely held views in the United States at the time—some of them fomented by other historical studies (McCraw 1986). The same is true for the Italian case, where scholars from comparative politics, political economy, economic geography, and management had drawn attention to the role of localized trust-based production networks, sometimes referred to as "clusters" or "industrial districts" as the basis for international competitiveness. Business historians played an important part in this research by providing in-depth case studies of the evolution of industries and companies within these districts (e.g. Colli 1998). The historical research on more flexible alternatives to large-scale mass production eventually also reached the homeland of the latter, with Scranton (1997) providing ample evidence for the persistence and success of specialty production even in the United States (see also Zeitlin's chapter on industrial districts in this volume).

Partially following on from the flexible specialization debate was a broader concern among management scholars about the international transfer of management ideas or models. Whereas the previous debate had been driven by comparative politics, political economy, and economic geography, this one mainly involved organizational and economic sociologists. Starting with a focus on Japanese production and management methods (e.g. Kenney and Florida 1993), it soon broadened to encompass the overall evolution of ideas about how to manage (e.g. Guillén 1994), which had so far been left to historians of management thought (e.g. Wren 2005).

Once again, a number of business historians made significant contributions to this debate with their in-depth case study research and some attempts at generalization. This concerned in particular what is now widely known as "Americanization", the transfer and transformation of US technology and management models to other parts of the world. Partially originating in the political history of US hegemony after World War II, this literature originally looked at American efforts to spread its "productivity gospel" (Maier 1977; McGlade 1995) and its labor relations model (Carew 1987).

Subsequent work examined how these ideas were actually received and transformed in particular companies. An important part of the business historical contribution consists in highlighting the active role played by companies, managers, and engineers in the receiving countries (e.g. Kipping and Bjarnar 1998; Kleinschmidt 2002) and the actual reworking of these ideas themselves, often leading to unique hybrid solutions (e.g. Zeitlin and Herrigel 2000). Originally confined to Europe, this research more recently also looked at the Japanese cases in comparison (ibid.; Kudo *et al.* 2004). This work in business history parallels similar work in historical sociology (Djelic 1998), which has drawn attention to the geopolitical dimension and the conformity pressures exercised by the US authorities in post-World War II Europe. Both the historical and sociological research have left their imprint on a growing number of studies on the dissemination of management ideas—sometimes conducted in collaboration between management scholars and business historians (e.g. Engwall and Kipping 2004).

From the dissemination of ideas, it is only a short step to the different ways in which they are disseminated. The role of what was alternatively referred to as the management knowledge industry (Micklethwait and Wooldridge 1996) or management fashion setting communities (Abrahamson 1991) became an important topic in management research during the 1990s. Here, historians have probably left their most important imprint in studying the evolution of management education (for details see the contribution of Amdam in this volume). Important to note, and in many respects exemplary, is the fact that more and more of this work has been done in collaboration between business historians and management scholars. The same is true for historical work on management consulting, where the management literature saw a significant increase in interest and publications from the 1990s onwards (cf. for overviews Clark and Fincham 2002; Kipping and Engwall 2002). On the one hand, business historians provided a long-term perspective to a research that was predominantly focusing on the "explosive" growth of the industry at the end of the twentieth century. Thus, McKenna (2006) has charted the rise of the McKinsey-type strategy and organization consultants since the 1930s, while others have tried to explain the transformation of consultancy services and service providers over time, including scientific management and large-scale IT systems in their studies (e.g. Wright 2000; Kipping 2002). There are also detailed historical accounts of consultancy development for a growing number of countries (e.g. the contributions in Kipping and Engwall 2002) as well as the expansion of US consultancies to Europe (Kipping 1999).

Again, this work was presented not only to the business history community, but also within management studies (e.g. McKenna 1997) and is increasingly conducted jointly by business historians and management scholars. Also, it addressed broader debates such as the development of knowledge-intensive firms (e.g. Kipping and Kirkpatrick 2007). The second strand of historical research on consulting was a growing number of in-depth company case studies looking at the interaction between consultants and their clients (cf. the contributions in Kipping 2000; Kipping and Engwall 2002). These cases provide important insights. On the one hand, they confirm the tendency, stressed in the neo-institutional management literature (DiMaggio and Powell 1983), for companies to imitate their peers and the role consultants played in this process. On the other hand, they highlight the complexity of the consultant–client relationship and its uncertain outcome, which modifies the widespread view about the superficial and even dangerous nature of consulting advice.

There is some hope that this successful model of interaction and collaboration in international business and management history, outlined above, can be extended to other areas of management studies—in particular core areas of strategy and organization. We discuss some of the examples and possibilities for increasing dialogue and interaction in the following section.

5.6 A New Departure: Return to the Centre

It seems that there is now a new chance for business history to reconnect with management studies on a larger scale. There are two powerful reasons: One is necessity because the previous intellectual position of business history between history and economics has become untenable due to the evolution of these fields. The other is opportunity because there have been repeated calls for historical approaches in studies of management and organization (e.g. Kieser 1994; Zald 1996). We will first briefly discuss the former and then more extensively develop the latter.

First of all, history in the United States—and increasingly elsewhere—has taken a post-modern, post-structuralist or culturalist turn (cf. Galambos 2003). Taking such a relativist view is clearly at odds with the truth claims and the efficiency-orientation of most business historians. A move in this direction is not totally out of the question. Fields adjacent to business history, such as the history of technology, have taken it. Some business historians have advocated taking a similar path, and part of business historical research has been developing in this direction (see the contribution of Lipartito in this volume). Incidentally, incorporating culture and a post-modernist stance does not mean that business history would be moving away completely from management studies—at least not all of it. There has actually been a strong post-modernist trend in management studies itself, influenced in particular by the work of Foucault and Derrida. Several management scholars have therefore argued quite forcefully in favor of a historical turn in organization studies (e.g. Clark and Rowlinson 2004).

Mainstream economics has also evolved, moving squarely in a neoclassical direction. Incidentally, this has also led to the marginalization of economic history within economics. As seen above, some business historians together with a minority of economists have sought refuge in transaction cost and more broadly in institutional and evolutionary ("Schumpeterian") economics (cf. Lazonick's chapter in this volume). Taking such a direction does not mean that business history would automatically move away from management, because evolutionary and institutional economics are in many respects closer to management than to neoclassical economics. A recent edited volume on *Constructing Corporate America* has sought to combine several of these trends by incorporating ideas (and authors) from institutional economics, the cultural perspective, and economic sociology (Lipartito and Sicilia 2004).

But one does not need to take the route through the post-modernist history or institutional economics to find a growing appreciation of history and historical approaches—mainly, but not exclusively, outside the United States. As mentioned, the literature on comparative forms of economic organization or national business systems that is based in organizational and economic sociology has already shown an interest in historical approaches and drawn on some historical research. The emphasis in this literature has been on social and political institutions and their development along with histories of industrialization in specific countries and their impact in turn on forms of business organization. Although some of the later work in these traditions considered the histories of individual business firms or specific industries, most approaches focused on trajectories of industrial development at the national level (Whitley 2002). Again, as noted above, they have drawn partially on existing historical research and also inspired some work by business historians. A companion area that has attracted historically oriented studies as well as the interest of business historians has been comparative corporate governance. Among the more recent historical studies in this respect or those that have involved business historians are the work by O'Sullivan (2000) on corporate governance in the United States and Germany and by Maclean *et al.* (2006) on business elites and corporate governance in France and the UK (see also Herrigel's chapter in this volume).

Another possible area for future interaction is studies of entrepreneurship and innovation. Despite the plea to the contrary from one of the pioneers in the field (Schumpeter 1947), there has been little cross-fertilization between the historical research on entrepreneurship and similar work in the other social sciences. Over recent years, attention within the latter has increasingly focused on entrepreneurial behavior and cognition, while less and less importance has been granted to the historical context of entrepreneurial activities (cf. Jones and Wadhwani 2006 and this volume). As a result, the contributions made by business historians in this field have often gone unnoticed. Again, there are some attempts to cross the existing divide. Thus, a recent study on the development of the British outdoor trade draws explicitly on concepts from economics and management to examine the role of entrepreneurs and "communities of practice" in innovation (Parsons and Rose 2004). This study is also worth mentioning, because it is based on close cooperation between an academic and a practitioner.

In addition to these encouraging developments, we would argue that it is now time for business historians to reconnect with the two core macro-orientated sub-fields within management studies: strategy and organization theory—which would help bring business history back to the more central position where it began with Chandler's work half a century ago. This opportunity exists because over the last 10 or 15 years particular streams of research have demonstrated interest in and involvement with history and historical approaches. However, it should be noted that this greater interest has involved a turn towards history more broadly rather than drawing upon business history specifically—though some of the studies have involved investigations of the histories of particular business firms. Moreover, the recourse to history in these theoretical perspectives has been in the form of supplementing the social scientistic enterprise (using history for theory/hypothesis development and/or as testing ground for general theories) or seeking to integrate history in constructing historical theories of organization and/or employing concepts embodying historical effects (Üsdiken and Kieser 2004). Nevertheless, we suggest that business historians can benefit from the concepts developed in this literature and might contribute rich evidence, based on their in-depth, archive-based studies.

There are two particular strands in the strategy literature that have engaged with history. One has been the extension of the processual tradition pioneered by Chandler and later found in the work of Mintzberg and his colleagues (e.g. Mintzberg and McHugh 1985) and that of Pettigrew (1985) on ICI. Rosenbloom (2000), for example, studied the history of NCR over the period 1938–78 to provide a counter-example of how an established firm could successfully cope with and prosper within a context of radical technological changes. Coming closer to treating history as an integral element in a key concept is Coté et al.'s (1999) study where the notion of dominant logic is treated as rooted in the history of the firm and its linkages with the firm's acquisition strategies and business performance are examined over time. Of particular relevance is an article by Farjoun (2002a), where he distinguishes two perspectives in the strategy literature: a dominant mechanistic one, based on planning and design, and an emergent organic one, more evolutionary and process-oriented. Among other things, he shows that, while widely used by the mechanistic tradition, Chandler's *Strategy and Structure* contains a significant number of organic themes.

A second theoretical perspective in the strategy literature that stands out in the role it accords to history is the resource-based view of the firm (e.g. Barney 1991). This view argues that competitive advantage is based on unique resources of companies, finding its more managerialist expression in the idea of core-competencies and dynamic capabilities—concepts some business historians have found appealing. Thus, apart from more recent studies by strategy scholars on the historical development of capabilities (e.g. Tripsas 1997), a good example of how a business historian can participate in these debates and publish in a leading strategy journal is Raff's (2000) study of two book superstores in the United States (Borders and Barnes and Noble) over the period 1975–95, which also draws upon evolutionary ideas.

Within organization theory two perspectives where history does feature are population ecology and neo-institutional theory, which constitute two of the research programs that have gained prominence especially in North America over the last two decades or so (Üsdiken and Pasadeos 1995). Population ecology is an archetypal example of using histories of organizational populations and organizational life histories for testing theoretical arguments. Although some of the studies in this genre cover very long time-frames such as 100 years or more (e.g. Miner *et al.* 1990), the ultimate purpose is to contribute to the testing and refinement of a timeless and spaceless theory of organizational diversity, founding, survival, and change. Little is made therefore of history other than to provide stylized data on organizations that have and do constitute the population. Within this broader framework, however, work on co-evolutionary processes appears particularly promising for more specifically business historical approaches. Thus, Jones' (2001) study of the early history of the American film industry in the period 1895–1920 provides an illustration of co-evolutionary processes involving the external context of the industry, institutional rules, competitive dynamics, and firm practices. Another more recent example is Murmann's dissertation (2003), which has looked at the co-evolution of national institutions—namely those generating and protecting scientific knowledge—and the synthetic dye industry before 1914.

Concern with history has occupied a more prominent role especially in particular strands of institutionalist thinking in organizational analysis. The emphasis on history has had to do with the predominant institutionalist emphasis on stability and the recognition that institutional arrangements are likely to be path dependent and therefore not flexible. Moreover, there has also been the accompanying recognition that organizations are not only influenced by current pressures but also by past circumstances (Scott and Christensen 1995). Likewise, the need for a historical perspective has been acknowledged in studying inter-organizational fields (e.g. Scott 1983). A historical approach has also been necessary in the greater attention devoted to studying the process of institutionalization and the creation and development of

institutions as well as of institutional change. These issues have led to studies with
a historical perspective as well those that have been historically located, though
especially in the latter case, despite incorporating historical narratives, the primary
concern has been with testing more general institutionalist theses. Farjoun (2002*b*),
for example, examined on-line pricing conventions and used historical analysis to
investigate the "motivation and process of building institutions", which are then
used to empirically test the hypotheses that are derived from the historical account.

Narrative historical accounts of institutional development and change are still
relatively rare and perhaps remain more of a European specialty. Notable examples
are Borum and Westenholz's (1995) historical study of the Copenhagen Business
School and the change in institutional models that are adopted and Holm's (1995)
study over the period 1930–94 of the rise and fall of a particular institutional form,
the mandated sales organization in Norwegian fisheries. Leblebici *et al.*'s (1991)
study of changes in institutional practices in the US radio broadcasting industry
over the period 1920–65 is exemplary of the limited work in this tradition coming
out of North America, though very recently US-based work of this genre appears to
be increasing as well. Notable, for example, is Hargadon and Douglas's (2001) study,
which develops the notion of "robust design" to account for the penetration and
acceptance of Edison's electric lighting within an institutional field. Other examples
are studies on the US business incubator industry (Leblebici and Shah 2004) and
the 140-year history of Major League Baseball in the US (Chacar and Hesterly 2004),
which have appeared in a recent special issue of *Business History* on History in
Organization Studies.

As these examples show, there is considerable overlap of interest among certain
areas in strategy and organization theory and parts of business history. But there
are also significant differences, namely in terms of research methodology and ded-
ication to theory building and/or testing. To us, this suggests that in many respects
these perspectives complement each other, which provides ample room for a closer
interaction in the future.

5.7 CONCLUSIONS

Business historians have entertained close, mutually beneficial relationships with
other fields of research, as numerous chapters in this volume show in some detail.
In this respect, the relationship with management studies is somewhat of a paradox.
Having been very close in the formative period of both fields during the 1950s
and 1960s, it subsequently became confined to a few, rather marginal sub-fields,
namely International Business and Management History, where business historians
have been making and continue to make empirical and, albeit to a lesser extent,

theoretical contributions. The lack of a closer interaction in the more central areas of strategy and organization has largely been due, we have argued, to the adoption of a neo-positivist social science methodology in management studies, which has relegated more narrative case studies—typical of (business) historical research—to the margins. But at the same time, a majority of business historians have sought wider recognition and conceptual frameworks elsewhere, in particular within economics—with rather mixed success.

Over the last decade or so, there have been calls from both fields for a renewed dialogue. As we have tried to show, there has already been more interaction in a number of the underlying disciplines of management research, in particular with areas of economics outside the neo-classical mainstream and with organizational and economic sociology. Based on an examination of recent research in strategy and organization theory, we have argued that similar opportunities now exist in these two core areas of management studies. To exploit these opportunities, the first step is a better understanding of what actually constitutes historical research, which— as we have tried to show—is more than the quantitative analysis of longitudinal data sets and, even if closer, also different from process-type studies, where the past remains largely an instrument for present-day concerns. Almost half a century later, Chandler's *Strategy and Structure*, despite its limitations, probably remains the best starting point for both business historians and management scholars to find such a common understanding and a platform for future cooperation.

References

Abrahamson, E. (1991). "Managerial Fads and Fashions: The Diffusion and Rejection of Innovations". *Academy of Management Review,* 16/3: 586–612.

Augier, M., March, J., and Sullivan, B. N. (2005). "Notes on the Evolution of a Research Community: Organization Studies in Anglophone North America, 1945–2000". *Organization Science,* 16: 85–95.

Barney, J. (1991). "Firm Resources and Sustained Competitive Advantage". *Journal of Management,* 17: 99–121

Berle, A. A., and Means, G. C. (1932). *The Modern Corporation and Private Property.* New York: Macmillan.

Binda, V. (2004). "The Strategy of Spanish Industrial Firms in the Late Twentieth Century: A Convergence Failure". Paper presented at the EBHA Conference, Barcelona, Sept. 16–18.

Boddewyn, J. (1965). "The Comparative Approach to the Study of Business Administration". *Academy of Management Journal,* 8: 261–7.

Borum, F., and Westenholz, A. (1995). "The Incorporation of Multiple Institutional Models", in W. R. Scott and S. Christensen (eds.), *The Institutional Construction of Organizations.* Thousand Oaks, Calif.: Sage, 113–31.

Bowman, E.H., Singh, H., and Thomas, H. (2002). "The Domain of Strategic Management: History and Evolution", in A Pettigrew, H. Thomas, and R. Whittington (eds.), *Handbook of Strategy and Management.* London: Sage, 31–51.

BURNHAM, J. (1941). *The Managerial Revolution: What is Happening in the World*. New York: John Day.

CAREW, A. B. (1987). *Labour under the Marshall Plan: The Politics of Productivity and the Marketing of Management Science*. Manchester: Manchester University Press.

CASSON, M. (1994). "Institutional Diversity in Overseas Enterprise: Explaining the Free-Standing Company". *Business History*, 36/4: 95–108.

CHACHAR, A., and HESTERLY, W. (2004). "Innovations and Value Creation in Major League Baseball". *Business History*, 46: 407–38.

CHANDLER, A. D. (1962). *Strategy and Structure. Chapters in the History of the Industrial Enterprise*. Cambridge, Mass.: MIT Press.

—— (1977). *The Visible Hand: The Managerial Revolution in American Business*. Cambridge, Mass: The Belknap Press of Harvard University Press.

—— (1992). "Organizational Capabilities and the Economic History of the Industrial Enterprise". *Journal of Economic Perspectives*, 6/3: 79–100.

—— (1994). "The Competitive Performance of U.S. Industrial Enterprises since the Second World War". *Business History Review*, 68/1: 1–72.

—— HAGSTRÖM, P., and SÖLVELL, Ö. (eds.) (1998). *The Dynamic Firm: The Role of Technology, Strategy, Organization and Regions*. New York: Oxford University Press.

CHANNON, D. F. (1973). *The Strategy and Structure of British Enterprise*. London: Macmillan.

—— (1978). *The Service Industries: Strategy, Structure, and Financial Performance*. London: Macmillan.

CLARK, P., and ROWLINSON, M. (2004). "The Treatment of History in Organization Studies: Towards an 'Historic Turn'". *Business History*, 46: 331–52.

CLARK, T., and FINCHAM, R. (eds.) (2002). *Critical Consulting: New Perspectives on the Management Advice Industry*. Oxford: Blackwell.

COLLI, A. (1998). "Networking the Market: Evidence and Conjectures from the History of the Italian Industrial Districts". *European Yearbook of Business History*, 1: 75–92.

COLLIN, S. O., JOHANSSON, U., SVENSSON, K., AND ULVENBLAD, P. O. (1996). "Market Segmentation in Scientific Publications: Research Patterns in American vs. European Management Journals". *British Journal of Management*, 7: 141–54.

COTÉ, L., LANGLEY, A., and PAQUERO, J. (1999). "Acquisition Strategy and Dominant Logic in an Engineering Firm". *Journal of Management Studies*, 41: 693–723.

DAFT, R. L. (1980). "The Evolution of Organization Analysis in ASQ, 1959–1979". *Administrative Science Quarterly*, 25: 623–36.

DELANY, W. (1960). "Some Field Notes on the Problem of Access in Organizational Research". *Administrative Science Quarterly*, 5: 448–57.

DIDRICHSEN, J. (1972). "The Development of Diversified and Conglomerate Firms in the United States, 1920–1970". *Business History Review*, 46/2: 202–19.

DIMAGGIO, P. J., and POWELL, W. W. (1983). "The Iron Cage Revisited: Institutional Isomorphism and Collective Rationality in Organizational Fields". *American Sociological Review*, 48: 147–60.

DJELIC, M.-L. (1998). *Exporting the American Model: The Postwar Transformation of European Business*. Oxford: Oxford University Press.

DONALDSON, L. (1995). *American Anti-Management Theories of Organization: A Critique of Paradigm Proliferation*. Cambridge: Cambridge University Press.

DRUCKER, P. F. (1946). *Concept of the Corporation*. New York: John Day.

DUNNING, J. (2003). "The Eclectic (OLI) Paradigm of International Production: Past, Present, Future", in J. Cantwell and R. Narula (eds.), *International Business and the Eclectic Paradigm*. London: Routledge, 25–46.

DYAS, G. P., and THANHEISER, H. T. (1976). *The Emerging European Enterprise: Strategy and Structure in French and German Industry*. London: Macmillan.

DYER, W. G., and WILKINS, A. L. (1991). "Better Stories, not Better Constructs, to Generate Better Theory: A Rejoinder to Eisenhardt". *Academy of Management Review*, 16/3: 613–19.

EISENHARDT, K. M. (1989). "Building Theories from Case Study Research". *Academy of Management Review*, 14/4: 532–50.

——(1991). "Better Stories and Better Constructs: The Case for Rigor and Comparative Logic". *Academy of Management Review*, 16/3: 620–7.

ENGWALL, L., and KIPPING, M. (eds.) (2004). *The Dissemination of Management Knowledge*. Special issue of *Management Learning*, 35/3.

FARJOUN, M. (2002a). "Towards an Organic Perspective on Strategy". *Strategic Management Journal*, 23: 561–94.

——(2002b). "The Dialectics of Institutional Development in Emerging and Turbulent Fields: The History of Pricing Conventions in the On-line Database Industry". *Academy of Management Journal*, 45: 848–75.

FEAR, J. (2005). *Organizing Control: August Thyssen and the Construction of German Corporate Management*. Boston, Mass.: Harvard University Press.

FLIGSTEIN, N. (1990). *The Transformation of Corporate Control*. Cambridge, Mass.: Harvard University Press.

FREELAND, R. F. (2001). *The Struggle for Control of the Modern Corporation: Organizational Change at General Motors, 1924–1970*. New York: Cambridge University Press.

GALAMBOS, L. (2003). "Identity and the Boundaries of Business History: An Essay on Consensus and Creativity", in F. Amatori and G. Jones (eds.), *Business History around the World*. New York: Cambridge University Press, 11–30.

GHEMAWAT, P. (2002). "Competition and Business Strategy in Historical Perspective". *Business History Review*, 76/1: 37–74

GUILLÉN, M. F. (1994). *Models of Management*. Chicago: University of Chicago Press.

HALL, R. H. (1987). *Organizations: Structures, Processes and Outcomes*. Englewood Cliffs, NJ: Prentice Hall.

HAMILTON, G. G., and BIGGART, N. W. (1988). "Market, Culture and Authority: A Comparative Analysis of Management and Organization in the Far East". *American Journal of Sociology*, 94: 52–94.

HARGADON, A. B., and DOUGLAS, Y. (2001). "When Innovations Meet Institutions: Edison and the Design of the Electric Light". *Administrative Science Quarterly*, 46: 476–501.

HOLM, P. (1995). "The Dynamics of Institutionalization: Transformation Processes in Norwegian Fisheries". *Administrative Science Quarterly*, 40: 398–422.

JEREMY, D. J. (2002). "Business History and Strategy", in A. Pettigrew, H. Thomas and R. Whittington (eds.), *Handbook of Strategy and Management*. London: Sage, 436–60.

JOHANSON, J., and VAHLNE, J.-E. (1977). "The Internationalisation Process of the Firm— A Model of Knowledge Development and Increasing Foreign Market Commitments". *Journal of International Business Studies*, 8: 23–32.

JOHN, R. R. (1997). "Elaborations, Revisions, Dissents: Alfred D Chandler, Jr.'s, 'The Visible Hand' after Twenty Years". *Business History Review*, 71/2: 151–200.

JONES, C. (2001). "Co-evolution of Entrepreneurial Careers, Institutional Rules and Competitive Dynamics in American Film, 1895–1920". *Organization Studies*, 22: 911–44.

JONES, G. (2003). "Multinationals", in F. Amatori and G. Jones (eds.), *Business History around the World*. New York: Cambridge University Press, 353–71.

—— (2005*a*). *Multinationals and Global Capitalism: From the Nineteenth to the Twenty-First Century*. Oxford: Oxford University Press.

—— (2005*b*). *Renewing Unilever: Transformation and Tradition*. Oxford: Oxford University Press.

—— and KHANNA, T. (2006). "Bringing History (Back) Into International Business". *Journal of International Business Studies*, 37/4: 453–68.

—— and WADHWANI, D. R. (2006). "Schumpeter's Plea: Historical Methods in the Study of Entrepreneurship". HBS Working Paper.

KAST, F. E., and ROSENZWEIG, J. E. (1970). *Organization and Management: A Systems and Contingency Approach*. New York: McGraw-Hill.

KENNEY, M., and FLORIDA, R. (1993). *Beyond Mass Production: The Japanese System and its Transfer to the U.S.* New York: Oxford University Press.

KIESER, A. (1994). "Why Organization Theory Needs Historical Analysis—and How This Should Be Performed". *Organization Science*, 5/4: 608–20.

—— (2002). "On Communication Barriers between Management Science, Consultancies and Business Organizations", in T. Clark and R. Fincham (eds.), *Critical Consulting*. Oxford: Blackwell, 206–27.

KIPPING, M. (1999). "American Management Consulting Companies in Western Europe, 1920 to 1990: Products, Reputation and Relationships". *Business History Review*, 73/2: 190–220.

—— (ed.) (2000). *Les consultants*. Special issue of *Entreprises et Histoire*, 25.

—— (2002). "Trapped in their Wave: The Evolution of Management Consultancies", in T. Clark and R. Fincham (eds.), *Critical Consulting*. Oxford: Blackwell, 28–49.

—— (2003). "Business–Government Relations: Beyond Performance Issues", in F. Amatori and G. Jones (eds.), *Business History around the World*. New York: Cambridge University Press, 372–93.

—— and BJARNAR, O. (1998). *The Americanisation of European Business. The Marshall Plan and the Transfer of US Management Models*. London: Routledge.

—— and ENGWALL, L (eds.) (2002). *Management Consulting: Emergence and Dynamics of a Knowledge Industry*. Oxford: Oxford University Press.

—— and KIRKPATRICK, I. (2007). "From Taylorism as Product to Taylorism as Process: Knowledge Intensive Firms in a Historical Perspective", in D. Muzio, S. Ackroyd, and F. Chalant (eds.), *Redirections in the Study of Expert Labor: Law, Medicine and Management Consultancy*. London: Palgrave, chapter 8.

KLEINSCHMIDT, C. (2002). *Der produktive Blick: Wahrnehmung amerikanischer und japanischer Management- und Produktionsmethoden durch deutsche Unternehmer, 1950–1985*. Berlin: Akademie Verlag.

KRISTENSEN, P. H. and ZEITLIN, J. (2005). *Local Players in Global Games: The Strategic Constitution of a Multinational Corporation*. Oxford: Oxford University Press.

KUDO, A., KIPPING, M., and SCHRÖTER, H. (2004). *German and Japanese Business in the Boom Years: Transforming American Management and Technology Models*. London: Routledge.

LAMOREAUX, N. R., RAFF, D. M. G., and TEMIN, P. (2003). "Beyond Markets and Hierarchies: Toward a New Synthesis of American Business History". *American Historical Review,* 108: 404–33.

————— (2004). "Against Whig History". *Enterprise & Society,* 5/3: 376–87.

LAZONICK, W. (1991). *Business Organization and the Myth of the Market Economy.* Cambridge: Cambridge University Press.

LEBLEBICI, H., SALANCIK, G. R., COPAY, A., and KING, T. (1991). "Institutional Change and the Transformation of Interorganizational Fields: An Organizational History of the U.S. Radio Broadcasting Industry". *Administrative Science Quarterly,* 36: 333–63.

—— and SHAH, N. (2004). "The Birth, Transformation and Regeneration of Business Incubators as New Organizational Forms: Understanding the Interplay between Organizational History and Organizational Theory". *Business History,* 46: 353–80.

LIPARTITO, K., and SICILIA, D. B. (eds.) (2004). *Constructing Corporate America: History, Politics, Culture.* New York: Oxford University Press.

MACLEAN, M., HARVEY, C., and PRESS, J. (2006). *Business Elites and Corporate Governance in France and the UK.* Basingstoke: Palgrave.

McCRAW, T. K. (ed.) (1986). *America versus Japan.* Boston: Harvard Business School Press.

—— (ed.) (1988). *The Essential Alfred Chandler: Essays Toward a Historical Theory of Big Business.* Boston: Harvard Business School Press.

McGLADE, J. (1995). "The Illusion of Consensus: American Business, Cold War Aid and the Reconstruction of Western Europe 1948–1958". Unpublished Ph.D. dissertation. Washington, DC: George Washington University.

McKENNA, C. D. (1997). " 'The American Challenge': McKinsey & Company's Role in the Transfer of Decentralization to Europe, 1957–1975". *Academy of Management Best Paper Proceedings,* 226–31.

—— (2006). *The World's Newest Profession: Management Consulting in the Twentieth Century.* New York: Cambridge University Press.

MAIER, C. S. (1977). "The Politics of Productivity: Foundations of American International Economic Policy after World War II". *International Organization,* 31: 607–33.

MICKLETHWAIT, J., and WOOLDRIDGE, A. (1996). *The Witch Doctors. What the Management Gurus are Saying, Why it Matters and How to Make Sense of It.* London: Heinemann.

————— (2003), *The Company: A Short History of a Revolutionary Idea.* New York: Modern Library.

MINER, A. S., AMBURGEY, T., and STEARNS, T. M. (1990). "Interorganizational Linkages and Population Dynamics: Buffering and Transformational Shields". *Administrative Science Quarterly,* 35: 689–713.

MINTZBERG, H., and McHUGH, A. (1985). "Strategy Formation in an Adhocracy". *Administrative Science Quarterly,* 30/2: 160–97.

MURMANN, J. P (2003). *Knowledge and Competitive Advantage: The Coevolution of Firms, Technology, and National Institutions.* New York: Cambridge University Press.

NELSON, R. R., and WINTER, S. G. (1982). *An Evolutionary Theory of Economic Change.* Cambridge, Mass.: The Belknap Press of Harvard University Press.

O'SULLIVAN, M. (2000). *Contests for Corporate Control: Corporate Governance and Economic Performance in the United States and Germany.* Oxford: Oxford University Press.

PARSONS, M., and ROSE, M. (2004). "Communities of Knowledge: Entrepreneurship, Innovation and Networks in the British Outdoor Trade, 1960–1990". *Business History,* 46/4: 609–39.

PAVAN, R. J. (1976). "Strategy and Structure: The Italian Experience." *Journal of Economics and Business,* 28: 254–60.

PENROSE, E. (1959). *The Theory of the Growth of the Firm.* New York: Oxford University Press.

PERROW, C. (2002). *Organizing America: Wealth, Power, and the Origins of Corporate Capitalism.* Princeton: Princeton University Press.

PETTIGREW, A. M. (1985). *The Awakening Giant: Continuity and Change in ICI.* Oxford: Blackwell.

PIORE, M. J., and SABEL C. F. (1984). *The Second Industrial Divide: Possibilities for Prosperity.* New York: Basic Books.

PORTER, M. E. (1980). *Competitive Strategy.* New York: Free Press.

RAFF, D. M. G. (2000). "Superstores and the Evolution of Firm Capabilities in American Bookselling". *Strategic Management Journal,* 21: 1043–59.

ROSENBLOOM, R. S. (2000). "Leadership, Capabilities, and Technological Change: The Transformation of NCR in the Electronic Era". *Strategic Management Journal,* 21: 1083–102.

ROY, W. G. (1997). *Socializing Capital: The Rise of the Large Industrial Corporation in America.* Princeton, NJ: Princeton University Press.

RUMELT, R. P. (1986). *Strategy, Structure, and Economic Performance,* rev. edn. Boston: Harvard Business School Press.

SCHUMPETER, J. A. (1942). *Capitalism, Socialism and Democracy.* New York: Harper & Brothers.

—— (1947). "The Creative Response in Economic History". *Journal of Economic History,* 7: 149–59.

SCOTT, W. R. (1983). "The Organization of Environments: Network, Cultural, and Historical Elements", in J. W. Meyer and W. R. Scott, *Organizational Environments: Ritual and Rationality.* London: Sage, 155–75.

—— and CHRISTENSEN, S. (1995). "Conclusion: Crafting a Wider Lens", in W. R. Scott and S. Christensen (eds.), *The Institutional Construction of Organizations.* Thousand Oaks, Calif.: Sage, 302–13.

SCRANTON, P. (1997). *Endless Novelty: Specialty Production and American Industrialization, 1865–1925.* Princeton, NJ: Princeton University Press.

SHIOMI, H., and WADA, K. (eds.) (1995). *Fordism Transformed: The Development of Production Methods in the Automobile Industry.* New York: Oxford University Press.

SLOAN, A. P. (1963). *My Years with General Motors.* New York: Doubleday.

TOMS, S., and WRIGHT, M. (2002). "Corporate Governance, Strategy and Structure in British Business History, 1950–2000". *Business History,* 44/3: 91–124.

TRIPSAS, M. (1997). "Unraveling the Process of Creative Destruction: Complementary Assets and Incumbent Survival in the Typesetter Industry". *Strategic Management Journal,* 18: 119–42.

ÜSDIKEN, B., and KIESER, A. (2004). "Introduction: History in Organization Studies". *Business History,* 46: 321–30.

—— and PASADEOS, Y. (1995). "Organizational Analysis in North America and Europe: A Comparison of Co-citation Networks". *Organization Studies,* 16: 503–26.

WHITLEY, R. (ed.) (2002). *Competing Capitalisms: Institutions and Economies.* Cheltenham: Edward Elgar.

WHITTINGTON, R. (2001). *What is Strategy—and Does it Matter,* 2nd edn. London: Thomson Learning.

—— (2004). "Strategy after Modernism: Recovering Practice". *European Management Review*, 1: 62–8.

—— and MAYER, M. (2000). *The European Corporation. Strategy, Structure and Social Science*. Oxford: Oxford University Press.

WILKINS, M. (1988). "The Free-standing Company, 1870–1914: An Important Type of British Foreign Direct Investment". *Economic History Review*, 41/2: 259–82.

—— and SCHRÖTER, H. (eds.) (1998). *The Free-Standing Company in the World Economy, 1830–1996*. Oxford: Oxford University Press.

WILLIAMSON, O. E. (1985). *The Economic Institutions of Capitalism: Firms, Markets, Relational Contracting*. New York: Free Press.

WREN, D. A. (2005). *The Evolution of Management Thought*, 4th edn. New York: Wiley.

WRIGHT C. (2000). "From Shop Floor to Boardroom: The Historical Evolution of Australian Management Consulting, 1940s to 1980s". *Business History*, 42/1: 85–106.

WRIGLEY, L. (1970). *Divisonal Autonomy and Diversification*. Boston: Graduate School of Business Administration, Harvard University.

YIN, R. K. (2003). *Case Study Research: Design and Methods*, 3rd edn. Newbury Park, Calif.: Sage.

YUZAWA, T. (1994). *Japanese Business Success: The Evolution of a Strategy*. London: Routledge.

ZALD, M. N. (1996). "More Fragmentation? Unfinished Business in Linking the Social Sciences and the Humanities". *Administrative Science Quarterly*, 41/2: 251–61.

ZEITLIN, J., and HERRIGEL, G. (ed.) (2000). *Americanization and its Limits: Reworking US Technology and Management in Post-War Europe and Japan*. Oxford: Oxford University Press.

CHAPTER 6

THE HISTORICAL ALTERNATIVES APPROACH

JONATHAN ZEITLIN

6.1 INTRODUCTION

THE aim of this chapter is to present a brief conceptual overview of what has become known as the "historical alternatives" approach to business history. The notion of alternatives is central to this approach in both a historical and a historiographical sense. Historically, the hallmark of this approach is its emphasis on the salience of alternative possibilities, contingency, and strategic choice in the development of modern industry over the past three centuries. Historiographically, this approach represents an alternative to mainstream currents in economic, technological, and business history: an alternative, in particular, to Chandlerian business history focused on the economic and technological efficiency of administrative coordination and learning within large, hierarchically managed enterprises. From its origins in joint work by Charles Sabel and myself in the early 1980s, a substantial body of empirical work on European, American, and Japanese industrial

An earlier and less developed version of this chapter appeared under the title "Productive Alternatives: Flexibility, Governance, and Strategic Choice in Industrial History", in Amatori and Jones (2003), 62–80.

history has since appeared which draws on and extends the historical alternatives approach.[1]

At a more substantive level, the historical alternatives approach opens up theoretical space for the identification of flexibly specialized forms of production in the industrial past. This theoretical possibility, however, should not be confused with empirical claims about the role and importance in particular times and places of flexible specialization as an ideal-typical model of productive efficiency, based on the manufacture of a wide and changing array of customized products in short runs by skilled, adaptable workers using versatile general-purpose machinery. Hence the historical alternatives approach can thus be used to analyze cases in which mass production, understood as the manufacture of standardized goods in high volumes by predominately unskilled labor using special-purpose equipment, overwhelmingly predominated over more flexible forms. At the same time, however, recent research based on this approach has greatly extended the historical scope of flexibly specialized production and identified significant elements of flexibility even within apparently classic cases of mass production.[2]

In the interests of concision, the remainder of this chapter sets out the core elements of the historical alternatives approach in the form of ten positive theses, before going on to respond to five major misconceived objections which have recurrently arisen in the course of the ensuing debate.

6.2 THE HISTORICAL ALTERNATIVES APPROACH: TEN THESES

6.2.1 Against Teleology and Determinism

The point of departure for the historical alternatives approach is the rejection of "narrow track" models of industrialization and economic development in all their forms, from Smith's division of labor and Marx's mechanized factory system through Rostow's stages of growth to Chandler's three-pronged investments in mass production, mass distribution, and professional management. In contrast to

---

[1] Beyond the original formulations in Sabel and Zeitlin (1982, 1985) and Piore and Sabel (1984), historical works explicitly utilizing this approach include: the essays collected in Sabel and Zeitlin (1997a), Zeitlin and Herrigel (2000), and Zeitlin (2000a); as well as Berk (1994), Berk and Schneiberg (2005), Carnevali (2003, 2005), Glimstedt (1993), Herrigel (1996), Kristensen and Zeitlin (2005), Walton (1992), and Zeitlin (1995a, 1995b). From a slightly different theoretical perspective, Philip Scranton (1997) reaches convergent conclusions in his work on specialty production in American industrialization.

[2] For a parallel distinction between the flexible specialization *approach* to industrial change and the flexible specialization *thesis*—i.e. the claim that flexible specialization is becoming the dominant productive model in contemporary industry—see Hirst and Zeitlin (1991).

both classical economists and modern historians alike, the historical alternatives approach thus denies the existence of a unilinear logic of material progress which must be adopted by all those wishing to advance to higher levels of productivity, income, and wealth.[3] Contrary to the claims of orthodox economic historians like David Landes (1987a: 27), for example, the findings of recent historical research on flexible technology and specialty manufacture confirm that neither "the logic of the machine...tireless and repetitive...[which] pushes it in the direction of uniformity and standardization", nor the purportedly inevitable preference for mass production of the majority of the world's "poor consumers whose wants exceed their purse" have prevented firms, regions, and even whole national economies organized along alternative lines from enjoying extensive commercial success over long periods of time.

6.2.2 More than One Way to Skin a Cat: The Plasticity of Technology and Organization

A second core claim of the historical alternatives approach is that technology and organization should not be taken as fixed, given, or even latent parameters to which economic actors must perforce adjust, but rather as objects of strategic reflection and deliberate experimentation in their own right. Technological progress, on this view, should be understood as an endogenous process in which the strategies pursued by economic actors play a key part in shaping developmental trajectories. At any given moment, moreover, multiple efficient combinations of capital equipment, factor supplies, and human resources are typically possible, some more flexible than others. Thus technology and organization may be advanced not only through the pursuit of economies of scale and joint production (Chandler's economies of scope arising from the use of common materials, plant, and managerial capabilities to turn out a related set of final goods), but also through that of economies of variety, understood as the capacity to adjust the volume and/or composition of output flexibly and to introduce new products rapidly in response to shifting demand and business strategy.[4] From this perspective, existing scale bottlenecks or indivisibilities can be overcome through deliberate innovations such as mini-mills and thin slab/strip casting in steel (Balconi 1991, 1993) or "process intensification" and "microreactors" in chemicals (Luesby 1998; Jackson 1998; Ehrfeld *et al.* 2000). Where process interdependencies remain fixed

[3] For an extended critique of narrow-track models of industrialization, including proto-industrialization and Gerschenkron's theory of late development, see Sabel and Zeitlin (1985: 134–41).

[4] For this distinction between "economies of variety" and Chandlerian economies of scope or joint production, compare Storper and Salais (1997: 32, 313), with Chandler (1990: 17, 24–6, 28–31).

in the medium term, similarly, closely related phases of production such as auto body manufacture and final assembly can be combined organizationally in very different ways, as can be seen from the much lower level of vertical integration and greater flourishing of quasi-independent supplier firms in the Japanese motor vehicle industry in comparison to its US counterpart during the post-World War II era (Nishiguchi 1993; Shiomi 1995).[5] Over a longer period, the range of alternative possibilities in productive organization remains bounded only by minimal requirements for internal coherence among interdependent elements and the ability to meet the often loose performance tests of changing competitive environments.

6.2.3 The Mutual Constitution of Actors and Contexts

This malleability of technology and organization is only one example of a larger theoretical point: the mutual constitution of actors and contexts. Unlike most variants of business history, including those which celebrate the creative role of entrepreneurs and managers, the historical alternatives approach does not accept a rigid distinction between maximizing agents and constraining contexts in economic life. Economic actors, in this view, are often at least as concerned with determining, in the double sense of figuring out and shaping, the context they are in—market, technological, institutional—as with pursuing their advantage within any particular context. Self-interested adjustment to conditions taken as given therefore proceeds hand-in-hand with efforts to find or create a more advantageous set of constraints. Strategic action of this type thus moots the standard Schumpeterian distinction between adaptive and creative responses to existing constraints, whose meaning, apart from extreme cases, can rarely be determined except in long historical retrospect.[6] Crucial to this process of strategic reflection is the capacity of economic agents to imagine and weigh up alternative courses of action, connecting the present with both the future and the past through narratives which constitute their identities and interests.[7]

---

[5] For a persuasive historical demonstration that General Motors' purchase of Fisher Body in 1926, long taken as the canonical example of the transactional imperatives of vertical integration under conditions of technological interdependence, was motivated not by any concern to avoid potential hold-up by the possessors of a complementary specific asset, but rather by GM managers' desire to utilize the Fisher Brothers' noted expertise in collaborative product development to reorganize their own relations with outside suppliers, see Helper *et al.* (2000), and the related account in Freeland (2000).

[6] For a restatement of the Schumpeterian view, see Lazonick's chapter in this volume.

[7] For a fuller discussion of the relationship between actors and context in standard economic and business history, together with the role of narrative in strategic action, see Sabel and Zeitlin (1997*b*), 5–20. For a stimulating social-theoretical analysis, which presents the "projective" capacity to imagine alternative possibilities as a central dimension of human agency, see Emirbayer and Mische (1998: especially 983–93).

6.2.4 Uncertainty, Mutability, and Hedging Strategies

Through much of modern history, as once again today, uncertainty, fragility, and mutability have widely been recognized as constitutive features of economic life. Under these conditions, empirical research has found, actors are frequently aware both of the complex dependence of forms of economic organization on multiple background conditions, and of the possibility of sudden, unanticipated shifts in those conditions. Hence, they often seek to avoid definitive choices between polar alternatives and/or to anticipate in their forms of economic organization the need for future reconstruction in the face of changed circumstances. Such self-reflective actors, as historical studies based on this approach show, continuously scanned foreign competitors' practices and debated the merits of alternative models on the basis of well-developed understandings of the relationship between contexts and strategic choices. They could typically see, for example, even when local intellectuals or policy makers could not, the connections between the use of machines and the organization of the firm on the one hand and the structure of the latter's markets and institutional environments on the other. The result was often judicious rejection of apparently successful foreign models, not because they were new or foreign, but because they did not fit local economic and institutional circumstances, matched by an equally aggressive embrace of those elements of foreign practice which served their constantly evolving definition of locally appropriate strategies. At bottom, this selective rejection and acceptance of particular elements from foreign innovations reflected a constant, permanently provisional re-evaluation of local strategy and, more specifically, an anxious effort to avoid entrapment in any given organization of production and its associated markets. Hedging strategies of this sort might appear to observers steeped in Schumpeterian categories as passivity masquerading in the guise of prudence. Yet the historical record shows that they often led to the creation of innovative hybrids that combined indigenous with foreign practices in unforeseen but often remarkably competitive ways, while apparently incremental changes in industrial organization could in the aggregate amount to programs of transformation as radical in their consequences as those directly proclaimed as such.[8]

6.2.5 The Predominance of Hybrid Forms over Pure Types

More generally, the process of strategic reflection and hedging against risk gives rise to a proliferation of hybrid forms of productive organization between mass production and flexible specialization which can be more or less easily reconstructed and recombined in response to changing background circumstances. Hence the

---

[8] For elaboration and illustration of these claims, see Sabel and Zeitlin (1997b: 12–14) and Zeitlin (2000b: 34–41).

predominance of hybrid, mixed, and intermediate forms of productive organization over polar types has proved to be the empirical rule rather than the exception in most times and places.[9] Yet the notion of contrasting strategies and distinct practices remains analytically crucial, since it is economic actors' perception of the advantages and disadvantages of polar possibilities which leads them to hedge their strategies in the first place, and thus appreciation of the full range of possible diversity which provokes the search for ever more varied ways of avoiding risky bets on the extreme positions.

6.2.6 Economic Governance beyond the Firm

Along with much current writing in economic sociology and political economy, the historical alternatives approach denies any ontological or epistemological privilege to the individual business firm as the key unit of analysis and economic governance. The boundaries and internal organization of the firm, on this view, must be treated as empirical variables, both in flexible and in mass production, so that autarky and internalization of activities within the enterprise become phenomena to be explained just as much as decentralization, outsourcing, and networking. While flexible and mass production, at least in their pure form, present distinctive governance problems at both the micro and macro levels, a wide—though by no means infinite—range of institutional frameworks for their solution can be observed in historical practice. Simplifying brutally, the key governance problems for flexible production are how to check opportunism and prevent free riding without stifling fluid cooperation among decentralized economic actors through institutions for the resolution of disputes and the provision of collective services. For mass production, by contrast, the crucial problems are how to balance supply and demand at different levels from individual markets and firms to the national and international economy, though conflict resolution and the reproduction of human resources are also significant. In each case, however, these functions may be performed through a variable mix of governance mechanisms including networks, associations, and states as well as hierarchically managed enterprises.[10] In both flexible and mass

---

[9] See for example the case studies collected in Sabel and Zeitlin (1997a), Zeitlin and Herrigel (2000), Zeitlin (2000a), Boyer et al. (1998), and Crouch et al. (2004), as well as the discussion in Hirst and Zeitlin (1991).

[10] In some of Sabel's recent work on "learning by monitoring" (Sabel 1994; Helper et al. 2000), the "new pragmatic disciplines" of benchmarking, simultaneous engineering, and error detection/correction are presented as an alternative mechanism for governing flexible production based on symmetricizing information and de-specifying assets instead of creating the basis for sustained trust among collaborating firms. For a critical exchange on this question, which concludes that supra-firm governance institutions may be needed to stabilize "pragmatic collaborations" between customers and suppliers for iterative co-design of innovative products, but that these institutions must themselves be co-designed through a second-order application of "learning by monitoring" principles, see Whitford and Zeitlin (2004), Herrigel (2004), and especially Sabel (2004).

production, therefore, together with the vast array of hybrid forms between them, firms' embeddedness in their local institutional contexts reaches far beyond a minimal dependence on clearly defined property rights and enforceable contracts, as the burgeoning literature on national and regional business and innovation systems likewise testifies.[11]

6.2.7 The Historical Construction of Markets

An additional claim shared by the historical alternatives approach with other critical perspectives on the economy in contemporary social science is that there is no such thing as "the market", but only particular markets. Such a conclusion follows directly from the unrealizably demanding conditions for the simultaneous clearing of all markets identified by general equilibrium theory, including perfect competition, a finite set of goods of commonly known quality, constant returns to scale, no externalities, a complete set of contingent markets, and coordination of exchanges by a central auctioneer (Boyer 1997). In the real world of actually existing economies, by contrast, social structures and institutions play a constitutive role in defining the rules and conventions governing particular markets, whether for products, raw materials, capital, or labor. Among the most important of these social and institutional influences on the construction of markets are: taxes, tariffs, and income distribution; family structure and the gender division of labor; product and quality standards; competition and antitrust policies; banking and capital market regulations; and industrial relations systems. "Efficiency", moreover, can only be assessed relative to particular patterns of demand and supply. Thus mass production, as is now well known, depends on the existence of large and stably growing markets for standardized goods. Low unit costs of production are no competitive advantage if consumers reject the product, as the Ford Motor Company painfully discovered in the case of the obsolescent Model T during the mid-1920s; nor do theoretical scale economies yield low costs if capacity cannot be translated into sales, as Ford once again learned with its Dagenham plant, built in 1934 as a one-tenth size model of the River Rouge works, which remained far too large for the British market until the 1950s (Hounshell 1984; Tolliday 1998, 2000). Precisely because managers widely understood the need to ensure a steady and predictable outlet for the amortization of high fixed investments which could not easily be turned to alternative uses, protectionism and market power played a key role in the development of mass production in the United States as well as Western Europe and Japan. Not only mass producers but also their flexible rivals, moreover, have consistently sought to shape as well as respond to market demand through a variety of strategies such as advertising and marketing, forward and

[11] See, for example, Whitley (1999), Whitley and Kristensen (1996), Lundvall (1992), Braczyk *et al.* (1998), and Crouch *et al.* (2001, 2004).

backward integration into distribution and control of raw materials, product differentiation and creation of new niches, cartels and alliances, lobbying and political
struggles.[12]

6.2.8 Neither Frictionless Adjustment nor Path Dependency

Unlike much recent institutionalist and evolutionary work with which it shares
other common ground, the historical alternatives approach rejects both friction-
less adjustment and path dependency as frameworks for the understanding of
economic change. Actors' strategies and decisions really matter in this view and,
whatever their intrinsic merits, often exert a significant influence on the trajectory
of economic development: adjustment to changing market or technological conditions is thus far from automatic. Yet in contrast to the claims of evolutionary
theorists, deliberate adaptation typically predominates over natural selection in
economic adjustment, while actors are rarely so "locked in" by institutions and
history as path-dependency models contend. Hedging strategies, "learning by monitoring", and continuous, provisional re-evaluation of existing practice can thus
be understood as pragmatist mechanisms for "routinely questioning the suitabil-
ity of [firms'] routines...without subverting them as guides to normal activity"
(Helper *et al.* 2000: 14, 17). Similarly, technological hybrids such as converters
and transformers in electric power systems, flexible transfer machinery composed
of standard recombinable units, or programmable automation can likewise be
viewed as conscious devices for avoiding and overcoming potential lock-in. At
a still deeper level, even quite stable institutional arrangements, like technologies and production models, may be reconfigured through apparently marginal
modifications to operate quite differently under new environmental conditions.
Thus continuing relationships or network ties between institutions may belie a
deep transformation in the ways actors conceive of themselves, their mission,
and their strategic possibilities. History, on this view, surely matters, as in the
path-dependency story; but its consequences may often be to facilitate rather
than to obstruct economic adjustment by serving as a cognitive and practical
resource for self-reflective actors in responding to external challenges—without,
however, leading to convergence around a single set of institutions, techniques, or
practices.[13]

---

[12] For an overview and research agenda, see Glimstedt and Zeitlin (1998, 2002). For useful sociological syntheses, see Slater and Tonkiss (2001) and Callon (1998).

[13] For fuller critiques of evolutionary analogies and path-dependency models in economic, business, and technological history, see Sabel and Zeitlin (1997b: 8–11); Sabel (1996); Zeitlin (2000b: 13–14,
19–20); Zeitlin (2003); and Crouch (2005). For recent restatements and defenses of path-dependency
arguments from the perspective of economics and political science respectively, see David (2000) and
Pierson (2004).

6.2.9 Orientations rather than Epochs

The interpenetration of strategies and practices within industries and national economies at any one time resulting from actors' efforts to hedge their organizational and technological bets about future changes in the environment casts inevitable doubt on the possibility of drawing sharp distinctions between epochs or periods such as the "age of Fordism" or the "era of flexibility". From this vantage point, it seems more useful to distinguish historical epochs according to changing orientations towards the ideas of political and economic organization regarded as normal or paradigmatic than to divide history into periods where social life was in fact thoroughly organized according to one or another master principle. This notion of changing orientations towards paradigmatic or normal ideas faithfully conveys both a sense of changing constraints on historical actors and that of continuing scope for localized strategic choice in so far as ideas of normality tend to magnify and thus to increase the importance of dominant conceptions without reflecting or constraining anything like the totality of behavior they purportedly characterize.[14]

6.2.10 Contingency and Strategic Choice as the Mainsprings of Economic Change

Without a teleological and deterministic model of material progress, contingency and strategic choice become the mainsprings of economic change and thus the core theme of industrial history. Nor is the significance of such choices, as Sabel and I originally believed, concentrated at rare moments of historical openness—evolutionary branching points, punctuated equilibria, or industrial divides. Although great events such as wars, revolutions, or radical reforms are undoubtedly critical to economic change, small everyday choices and incremental innovations may cumulatively exert a profound influence on the industrial development of individual firms, regions, and whole national economies.[15] Hence, industrial history should be written in a narrative form attentive to the relationship between economic actors' own self-understanding and strategic calculations on the one hand and the consequences of their decisions, both intended and unintended, on the other, even if the historian need not thereby be confined to the actors' own cognitive horizons. Such narratives will typically involve a variety of devices such as flashbacks, polyphony, and multiple retellings of the same tale as a means of what literary theorists Gary Saul Morson (1994) and Michael André Bernstein (1994) call "sideshadowing": the representation of action as a process of deliberative choice among an open (though not of course infinite) set of alternative possibilities, more

---

[14] For an elaboration of these claims, see Sabel and Zeitlin (1997b: 4–5, 29–33).

[15] Compare Sabel and Zeitlin (1997b), 8–9 with Sabel and Zeitlin (1985).

than one of which might in fact have been realized. At the same time, conversely, they will also seek to avoid narratives based on what Morson and Bernstein term "foreshadowing" and "backshadowing": the abuse of hindsight to recount events as if their outcome were predetermined and could be used to judge the choices of historical actors irrespective of what the latter could realistically have been expected to know at the time.[16]

6.3 FIVE MISCONCEIVED OBJECTIONS

Since the publication of Sabel and Zeitlin (1985), the historical alternatives approach to business history has aroused a storm of critical debate. Some of the objections raised in this debate were of course well-founded, and required a rethinking and reformulation of key assumptions and claims (Sabel and Zeitlin 1997b). But others, by contrast, are based on a series of recurrent misconceptions about the historical alternatives approach, to the most common of which the remainder of this chapter responds.[17]

6.3.1 Size of Firm is not a Determining Variable

Contrary to widespread assumptions, the historical alternatives approach is not a "small is beautiful" argument about the inherent superiority—whether economic, social, or political—of small over large firms. Flexible specialization, in this view, can be pursued both within industrial districts or geographically localized networks of small and medium-sized enterprises, and within large, decentralized, or federated firms, as well as a variety of intermediate forms between the two. Even in mass production, as argued above, the boundaries of the corporation may be fluid and variable, especially when the possibilities of hybrid production strategies are taken into account. Forms of coordination and relationships between economic units, rather than formal ownership or even managerial structure, are thus the key variable in industrial organization. The argument about firm size in the historical alternatives approach is instead really a negative claim: that there are no intrinsic barriers preventing (networks of) small firms from being economically efficient, technologically innovative, and commercially successful, while large size

---

[16] For fuller discussion and examples of narrative practice, see Sabel and Zeitlin (1997b: 15–20), and Zeitlin (2000b: 20–21). For an effort to apply such a "sideshadowing" perspective in reconstructing the historical development of a multinational corporation, see Kristensen and Zeitlin (2005).

[17] For a extended discussion of the closely related debate over the flexible specialization approach to industrial change up to the beginning of the 1990s, see Hirst and Zeitlin (1991).

and vertical integration may have as much to do with struggles for market control as with any efficiency or coordination advantages.[18]

6.3.2 Industrial Sectors are not a Determining Variable

Contrary to another widely held claim, the intrinsic characteristics of industrial sectors (markets, technologies, factor supplies, etc.) do not determine the boundaries between mass production and flexible specialization. In particular, it is not the case that flexible production can only be successfully pursued in light, labor-intensive industries.[19] Although industrial sectors do of course have distinctive economic and technological characteristics at any given time, within each sector there are typically a range of firms pursuing different strategies marked by varying degrees of flexibility and specialization, such as fine versus commodity chemicals, speciality versus basic steels, platform technologies versus therapeutics in biotechnology, or customized information technology services versus standardized software products.[20] Such divergent strategies can in time transform the commercial and technological characteristics of the sector itself by reducing minimum efficient scales of production and/or increasing the fragmentation and specialization of demand, as can be seen from the impact of mini-mills in steel (Herrigel 2002), combined-cycle power plants in electricity supply (Hirsch 1991), and Japanese flexible production and product development techniques in motor vehicles (Clark and Fujimoto 1991). Governance structures and thus the effective boundaries of the firm likewise vary widely within the same sector not only across countries (Hollingsworth *et al.* 1994), but even within different regions of the same country, as in the case of autarkic versus decentralized industrial orders in German mechanical engineering (Herrigel 1996). This point is reinforced by the preceding argument about the size of firm as a non-critical variable, since many large German, Japanese, and even American steel, machinery, and electrical manufacturing companies turn out to have been

---

[18] On the importance of market power as opposed to pure efficiency considerations in the determinants of the great US merger wave at the turn of the twentieth century, see Lamoreaux (1985) and Roy (1997). On the absence of any correlation between the size distribution of industrial firms across national economies and variations in their growth rates, see Dosi (1997).

[19] See, for example, Amatori (1997). The claim that the modern corporation clustered in sectors whose technological characteristics permitted the exploitation of potential scale and scope economies through managerial coordination is a recurrent trope of Chandlerian analysis. For a recent formulation, see Chandler and Hikino (1997).

[20] On software and biotechnology, see Casper *et al.* (1999). Even within a given market segment, "comparisons of closely matched firms in the same country (e.g. Federal Express and UPS or McKinsey and Boston Consulting Group) have shown that there is more than one path to success ... with direct competitors pursuing very different organizational and human-resource strategies": see Cappelli and Crocker-Hefter (1996), cited in Finegold and Wagner (1999: 124), who make a similar point about standardized, assemble-to-order, and customized pump manufacturing in Germany and the United States.

extensively engaged in more or less flexible and specialized forms of production through much of their history (Herrigel 1996, 2000; Fruin 1994; Scranton 1997). Finally, as a variety of critics have noted, the Chandlerian claim that large modern corporations became concentrated in certain industries but not others fails to take adequate account of aggregation problems within sectors, diversity among large firms, and variations in the significance of the top 200 industrial firms and manufacturing itself within individual national economies (Fruin 1994; Cassis 1997).

6.3.3 Strategic Action as Hyper-Rationality?

The emphasis placed in the historical alternatives approach on the role and sophistication of strategizing actors is sometimes accused of representing a form of hyper-rationality, which imposes unrealistic demands on the information-processing and computational powers of actual economic agents, and thereby inadvertently mirrors neoclassical rational actor models, with all their well-known weaknesses (Salais 1999). Whatever its superficial plausibility, such an interpretation constitutes a clear misreading of the historical alternatives approach. Strategic reflection, as Sabel and I explicitly argued, is a necessary but not sufficient condition for competitive success, while well-informed contemplation of alternatives can in extreme cases lead to paralysis through familiar paradoxes such as Hegel's vortex of bad infinity and the dilemma of Buridan's ass (Sabel and Zeitlin 1997b). As in much behavioral and evolutionary economics, the historical alternatives approach recognizes volatility, uncertainty, and incomplete information as fundamental obstacles to economic optimization in the sense of fully "rational" calculation of the best means for achieving predetermined ends in any given situation. But unlike these other non-standard perspectives, the historical alternatives approach regards unreflective dependence on "satisficing" routines such as standard operating procedures, rules of thumb and accounting conventions as myopic and potentially dangerous solutions to the underlying problems of incomplete information and unanticipated change. "Bounded rationality", on this view, is not a "second-best" approximation of rationality *tout court* under adverse conditions, but rather an oxymoron, since no rational means are available to determine the optimal limits of search activity and thus the appropriate scope of any particular set of routines. Hedging strategies, "learning by monitoring", and hybrid, recombinable organizational and productive forms, as argued above, can thus be seen as superior responses to volatility and uncertainty, based on pragmatist mechanisms which enable economic actors to expose their existing beliefs and practices piece-by-piece to possible challenges without thereby plunging into a paralyzing state of complete self-doubt. No assumption of optimality or maximization is entailed by this "practically reasonable" conception of economic action, in which agents are typically capable both of giving provisional reasons for their actions in any given situation, and of reciprocally adjusting ends and means in light of their practical experience with particular courses of action.[21] Economic actors, on this view, do not always make the "right" choices, but their decisions nonetheless are often broadly consequential for others as well as themselves.

6.3.4 Power, Exploitation, Conflict: The Dark Side of Flexibility?

Another frequently raised charge against the historical alternatives approach is that it systematically neglects the "dark side" of power, exploitation, and conflict within industrial districts or flexible regional economies. Thus, critics claim that empirical studies of individual districts and regions such as Birmingham, Sheffield, St Etienne, or Cholet typically find greater evidence of hierarchy and power imbalances than is acknowledged by proponents of the historical alternatives approach, whether in terms of the weight of medium-sized and even large firms in their industrial structure, the role of credit and marketing relations in the subordination of formally independent small producers, or reliance on sweated labor and self or family exploitation to sustain competitiveness. Second, and relatedly, these critics contend, such empirical studies likewise challenge the characterization of these districts or regions in the historical alternatives literature by revealing a greater incidence of overt conflict in the form of strikes and other types of dispute on the one hand, together with that of industrial secrecy and other failures of local cooperation on the other (Berg 1993, 1994; Magnusson 1994; Behagg 1986; White 1997; Aminzade 1986; Liu 1994).[22]

Some of these criticisms are based on confusions about the role of firm size and scale in the historical alternatives approach discussed earlier (e.g. Berg 1993, 1994). Others ignore the explicit analysis in Sabel and Zeitlin (1985; 1997b) of internal cleavages and the scope for conflict within flexible regional economies, arising both from contention for place among individuals and social groups and from the potentially disruptive impact of hybridizing experimentation on the existing institutional order. At issue thus is not the existence or potential for such internal conflicts but rather the institutions and governance mechanisms through which they were handled and resolved. Thus in most successful flexible economies, empirical studies confirm that collective wage-setting institutions, dispute adjudication procedures, and other regulatory mechanisms have played a crucial part in balancing cooperation and competition among decentralized economic actors. When flexible regional economies face difficult adjustments to external shifts in markets

---

[21] For this pragmatist or "practically reasonable" conception of economic action, see Sabel (1994, 2006) and Helper *et al.* (2000).

[22] For the extreme case of an SS garment manufacturing enterprise at the Ravensbruck concentration camp interpreted as an instantiation of the dark side of flexible production, see Allen (1999).

and technology, social stalemate, deregulation, and decline is always a possible outcome, as in Glarus printed textiles, Sheffield cutlery, or Spitalfields silks; but so too is the regeneration of innovative capabilities and competitiveness through collective deliberation and institutional reform, as in Swiss watchmaking, Solingen cutlery, Lyons silks, or Danish agriculture and craft industries more generally.[23] Crucial in each case to these divergent outcomes was whether or not internal conflicts over the challenges posed by economic change could be resolved by reinforcing collaborative governance mechanisms which equitably shared out the burdens and benefits of adjustment among the actors concerned.

What, finally, of the relationship between social power and economic choices? Doesn't the emphasis on the role of power in shaping the outcome of struggles over the evolution of markets, technology, and industrial organization, stressed particularly in Sabel and Zeitlin (1985), undercut the role of contingency and choice by reintroducing an underlying structural logic—based now on social interests rather than efficiency?[24] Here again, this superficially plausible conclusion proves misleading for a number of well-grounded theoretical and empirical reasons. A first such reason concerns the inherent uncertainty surrounding all strategic calculations. In a world in which actions often have unintended consequences, the distribution of power resources does not necessarily determine the outcome of economic and political struggles. Put in the opposite way, in productive competition, as in love and war, it's not so much what you have as how you use it that counts (Hindess 1982; Williams *et al.* 1989). A second reason lies in the structural ambiguity of social interests themselves, together with their frequently observed redefinition through the making and breaking of alliances with other actors in the course of pursuing particular economic or political strategies (Sabel 1982; Helper *et al.* 2000). A final reason for rejecting the idea of an underlying logic of economic and technological development based on the putatively decisive role of social power in determining collective choices at key turning points lies in the ongoing significance highlighted earlier of small, everyday decisions and micro-alternatives as well as large-scale battles and industrial divides in shaping the productive trajectories of firms, regions, and entire national economies.

6.4 CONCLUSIONS: HISTORY IN THE OPTATIVE MOOD?

Nor, finally, can the historical alternatives approach be fairly dismissed as "history in the optative mood", an exhaltation of ideologically desirable but unrealistic

---

[23] For these examples, see Veyrassat (1997), Cottereau (1997), Boch (1997), and Kristensen and Sabel (1997).

[24] See for example the discussion of power-based explanations of industrial change in Roy (1997), and the book review by Levenstein (1998).

alternatives with little empirical relevance (Landes 1987a, 1987b). For as the growing body of research inspired by it testifies, the historical alternatives approach has already yielded a substantial empirical payoff as both a positive and a negative heuristic.[25] As a positive heuristic, the historical alternatives approach has drawn attention to neglected but empirically significant forms of productive organization, both pure and hybrid. The most important such positive finding has been the rediscovery of flexible production as a pervasive feature of industrial history prior to its contemporary resurgence since the 1970s, whether organized through industrial districts dominated by small and medium-sized enterprises, large internally decentralized or federated firms, or some intermediate combination between the two. Some of these flexible production systems have continued to thrive for long periods of time down to the present. Others were large and successful in their day, but eventually declined or were transformed into something different, whether for internal or external reasons. But the same could equally be said of many mass-production firms and regions: the survival of any particular case over a specific time period has no direct bearing on the viability of the broader productive model on which it is based. The key point, by contrast, which emerges from recent research, is that at no stage did flexible production die out altogether, or even fall into a clearly subordinate relationship to mass production, despite the latter's ascendancy as a technological and economic paradigm during the mid-twentieth century (Zeitlin 2000a; Zeitlin and Herrigel 2000; Tolliday and Zeitlin 1992).

At the same time, however, the historical alternatives approach also serves as a negative heuristic, drawing attention to what might have happened but did not, and thereby giving rise to different and richer accounts of the course of business history. For causal explanations in history, as is widely recognized, implicitly depend upon counterfactual arguments; but plausible counterfactual arguments must in turn be grounded in possibilities that were realistically open to historical actors at the time (Elster 1978; Hawthorn 1991; Ricoeur 1984). In this area, too, there is now a growing body of work which traces the role of political struggles, technological paradigms, and strategic choices in shaping trajectories of industrial development. Perhaps the most important findings of this strand of research concern the impact of national institutions and policies on the reproduction or decline of flexible regional economies, such as the degree of administrative centralization as opposed to local government autonomy, the effectiveness of state rationalization and concentration policies, the form and intensity of antitrust regulation, the extent of political tolerance and/or encouragement of associational governance, the territorial structure of banking and finance systems, and the relative concentration of retail distribution.[26] Here, too, however, national cases of flexible production

---

[25] For a similar argument about the flexible specialization approach in the context of contemporary debates about the analysis of industrial change, see Hirst and Zeitlin (1991: 25–6).

[26] For discussions of such national influences on the fate of industrial districts and flexible regional economies, see Zeitlin (1995b) and this volume.

which initially appeared as exceptional deviations from the mainstream of historical development have increasingly come to be understood as the result of variations on a common theme, whereby small differences in the outcome of similar struggles can eventually yield large cumulative divergences in economic governance and productive organization.[27]

But the historical alternatives approach offers a normative as well as an empirical payoff. By expanding our understanding of the range of organizational and productive forms in the past, and enriching our understanding of the reasons for and outcomes of earlier decisions about economic governance, the historical alternatives approach can sharpen awareness and improve the quality of public debate about the range of strategic choices open to us in the present and future. This is arguably not only a legitimate but also a necessary role for business history in the twenty-first century if it is to contribute to public problem-solving in a broad sense rather than to ossify into a purely antiquarian and scholastic activity.

REFERENCES

ALLEN, MICHAEL THAD (1999). "Flexible Production at Concentration Camp Ravensbruck". *Past and Present*, 165: 182–217.

AMATORI, FRANCO (1997). "Reflections on Global Business and Modern Italian Enterprise by a Stubborn 'Chandlerian' ". *Business History Review*, 71/2: 309–18.

——and JONES, GEOFFREY (eds.) (2003). *Business History around the World*. Cambridge: Cambridge University Press.

AMINZADE, RONALD (1986). "Reinterpreting Capitalist Industrialization: A Study of Nineteenth-Century France", in Steven L. Kaplan and Cynthia J. Koepp (eds.), *Work in France: Representations, Meaning, Organization, and Practice*. Ithaca, NY: Cornell University Press, 393–417.

BALCONI, MARGHERITA (1991). *La siderurgia italiana (1945–1990): tra controllo pubblico e incentivi del mercato*. Bologna: Il Mulino.

—— (1993). "The Notion of Industry and Knowledge Bases: The Evidence of Steel and Mini-mills". *Industrial and Corporate Change*, 2/3: 471–507.

BEHAGG, CLIVE (1986). "Myths of Cohesion: Capital and Compromise in the Historiography of Nineteenth-Century Birmingham". *Social History*, 11/3: 375–84.

BERG, MAXINE (1993). "Small Producer Capitalism in Eighteenth-Century England". *Business History*, 35/1: 17–39.

—— (1994). *The Age of Manufactures, 1700–1820*, 2nd edn. London: Routledge.

BERK, GERALD (1994). *Alternative Tracks: The Constitution of Industrial Order in America, 1865–1917*. Baltimore: Johns Hopkins University Press.

——and SCHNEIBERG, MARC (2005). "Varieties *in* Capitalism, Varieties *of* Association: Collaborative Learning in American Industries, 1900 to 1925". *Politics and Society*, 33/1: 46–87.

---

[27] For an eloquent case in point, see Kristensen and Sabel (1997).

BERNSTEIN, MICHAEL ANDRÉ (1994). *Foregone Conclusions: Against Apocalyptic History.* Berkeley: University of California Press.

BOCH, RUDOLF (1997). "The Rise and Decline of Flexible Production: The Cutlery Industry of Solingen since the Eighteenth Century", in Sabel and Zeitlin (1997a), 153–87.

BOYER, ROBERT (1997). "The Variety and Unequal Performance of Really Existing Markets: Farewell to Doctor Pangloss?", in J. Rogers Hollingsworth and Robert Boyer (eds.), *Contemporary Capitalism: The Embeddedness of Institutions.* Cambridge: Cambridge University Press, 55–93.

—— CHARRON, ELSIE, JÜRGENS, ULRICH, and TOLLIDAY, STEVEN (eds.) (1998). *Between Imitation and Innovation: Transfer and Hybridization of Productive Models in the International Automobile Industry.* Oxford: Oxford University Press.

BRACZYK, HANS-JOACHIM, COOKE, PHILIP, and HEIDENREICH, MARTIN (eds.) (1998). *Regional Innovation Systems: The Role of Governance in a Globalizing World.* London: University College London Press.

CALLON, MICHEL (ed.) (1998). *The Laws of the Markets.* Oxford: Blackwell.

CARNEVALI, FRANCESCA (2003). "Golden Opportunities: Jewelry Making in Birmingham between Mass Production and Specialty". *Enterprise and Society,* 4/2: 272–98.

—— (2005). *Europe's Advantage: Banks and Small Firms in Europe and Britain.* Oxford: Oxford University Press.

CAPPELLI, PETER, and CROCKER-HEFTER, ANNE (1996). "Distinctive Human Resources Are Firms' Core Competencies". *Organizational Dynamics,* winter: 7–21.

CASPER, STEVEN, LEHRER, MARK, and SOSKICE, DAVID (1999). "Can High-Technology Industries Prosper in Germany? Institutional Frameworks and the Evolution of the German Software and Biotechnology Industries". *Industry and Innovation,* 6/1: 5–24.

CASSIS, YOUSSEF (1997). *Big Business: The European Experience in the Twentieth Century.* Oxford: Oxford University Press.

CHANDLER, JR., ALFRED D. (1990). *Scale and Scope: The Dynamics of Industrial Capitalism.* Cambridge, Mass.: Harvard University Press.

—— and HIKINO, TAKASHI (1997). "The Large Industrial Enterprise and the Dynamics of Modern Economic Growth", in Chandler *et al.* (1997), 24–57.

—— AMATORI, FRANCO, and HIKINO, TAKASHI (eds.) (1997). *Big Business and the Wealth of Nations.* Cambridge: Cambridge University Press.

CLARK, KIM B., and FUJIMOTO, TAKAHIRO (1991). *Product Development Performance: Strategy, Management, and Organization in the World Auto Industry.* Boston: Harvard Business School Press.

COTTEREAU, ALAIN (1997). "The Fate of Collective Manufactures in the Industrial World: The Silk Industries of Lyons and London, 1800–1850", in Sabel and Zeitlin (1997a), 75–152.

CROUCH, COLIN (2005). *Capitalist Diversity and Change: Recombinant Governance and Institutional Entrepreneurs.* Oxford: Oxford University Press.

—— LE GALÈS, PATRICK, TRIGILIA, CARLO, and VOELZKOW, HELMUT (2001). *Local Production Systems in Europe: Rise or Demise?* Oxford: Oxford University Press.

———————— (2004). *Changing Governance of Local Economies: Responses of European Local Production Systems.* Oxford: Oxford University Press.

DAVID, PAUL (2000). "Path Dependence, its Critics, and the Quest for 'Historical Economics'", in P. Garrouste and S. Ioannides (eds.), *Evolution and Path Dependence in Economic Ideas: Past and Present.* Cheltenham: Edward Elgar, 15–40.

DOSI, GIOVANNI (1997). "Organizational Competences, Firm Size, and the Wealth of Nations: Some Comments from a Comparative Perspective", in Chandler *et al.* (1997), 465–79.

EHRFELD, WOLFGANG, HESSEL, VOLKER, and LÖWE, HOLGER (2000). *Microreactors: New Technology for Modern Chemistry*. New York: John Wiley & Sons.

ELSTER, JON (1978). *Logic and Society: Contradictions and Possible Worlds*. New York: John Wiley & Sons.

EMIRBAYER, MUSTAFA, and MISCHE, ANN (1998). "What is Agency?" *American Journal of Sociology*, 103/4: 962–1023.

FINEGOLD, DAVID, and WAGNER, KARIN (1999). "The German Skill-Creation System and Team-Based Production: Competitive Asset or Liability?", in Pepper D. Culpepper and David Finegold (eds.), *The German Skills Machine: Sustaining Comparative Advantage in a Global Economy*. New York: Berghahn Books, 115–55.

FREELAND, ROBERT F. (2000). "Creating Hold-Up through Vertical Integration: Fisher Body Revisited". *Journal of Law and Economics*, 43/1: 33–66.

FRUIN, W. MARK (1994). *The Japanese Enterprise System: Competitive Strategies and Co-operative Structures*. Oxford: Clarendon Press.

GLIMSTEDT, HENRIK (1993). *Mellan teknik och samhälle: stat, marknad och produktion i svensk bilindustri 1930–1960*. Gothenburg: Historiska istitutionen.

—— and ZEITLIN, JONATHAN (1998). "Constructing Markets, Shaping Production: The Historical Formation of Industrial Markets since 1870", research proposal to the Swedish Council for the Coordination and Initiation of Research (FRN), Stockholm.

———— (2002). "Constructing Markets, Shaping Production: The Historical Construction of Product Markets in Europe and America", introductory presentation to an international conference organized by the Institute of International Business, Stockholm School of Economics, Idöborg, Sweden, July 5–6.

HAWTHORN, GEOFFREY (1991). *Plausible Worlds: Possibility and Understanding in History and the Social Sciences*. Cambridge: Cambridge University Press.

HELPER, SUSAN, MacDUFFIE, JOHN PAUL, and SABEL, CHARLES F. (2000). "Pragmatic Collaborations: Advancing Knowledge while Controlling Opportunism". *Industrial and Corporate Change*, 9/3: 443–88.

HERRIGEL, GARY (1996). *Industrial Constructions: The Sources of German Industrial Power*. Cambridge: Cambridge University Press.

—— (2000). "American Occupation, Market Order, and Democracy: Reconfiguring the Japanese and German Steel Industries after World War II", in Zeitlin and Herrigel (2000), 340–99.

—— (2002). "Varieties of Collective Regeneration: Comparisons of the German, Japanese, and American Steel Industries Since the Mid-1970s", unpublished paper presented to the international conference on "Constructing Markets, Shaping Production: The Historical Construction of Product Markets in Europe and America", Institute of International Business, Stockholm School of Economics, Idöborg, Sweden, July 5–6.

—— (2004). "Emerging Strategies and Forms of Governance in High-Wage Component Manufacturing Regions". *Industry and Innovation*, 11/1–2: 45–80.

HINDESS, BARRY (1982). "Power, Interests, and the Outcome of Struggles". *Sociology*, 16/4: 498–511.

HIRSH, RICHARD F. (1991). *Technology and Transformation in the American Electric Utility Industry*. Cambridge: Cambridge University Press.

HIRST, PAUL and ZEITLIN, JONATHAN (1991). "Flexible Specialization vs. Post-Fordism: Theory, Evidence and Policy Implications". *Economy and Society*, 20/1: 1–55.

HOLLINGSWORTH, J. ROGERS, SCHMITTER, PHILIPPE C., and STREECK, WOLFGANG (eds.) (1994). *Governing Capitalist Economies: Performance and Control of Economic Sectors*. Oxford: Oxford University Press.

HOUNSHELL, DAVID F. (1984). *From the American System to Mass Production, 1800–1932*. Baltimore: Johns Hopkins University Press.

JACKSON, TONY (1998). "How the Mighty are Falling: Many Big, Capital-Intensive Industries are Locked in a Damaging Cycle of Over-Supply—and the Swings May Be Getting Worse". *Financial Times*, Nov. 30.

KRISTENSEN, PEER HULL, and SABEL, CHARLES F. (1997). "The Small-Holder Economy in Denmark: The Exception as Variation", in Sabel and Zeitlin (1997a), 344–78.

——and JONATHAN ZEITLIN (2005). *Local Players in Global Games: The Strategic Constitution of a Multinational Corporation*. Oxford: Oxford University Press.

LAMOREAUX, NAOMI, R. (1985). *The Great Merger Movement in American Business, 1895–1904*. Cambridge: Cambridge University Press.

LANDES, DAVID S. (1987a). "Small is Beautiful. Small is Beautiful?", in Fondazione ASSI/Istituto per la storia dell'Umbria contemporanea, *Piccola e grande impresa: un problema storico*. Milan: Franco Angeli, 15–28.

——(1987b). *A che servono i padroni? Le alternative storiche dell'industrializzazione*. Turin: Bollati Boringhieri.

LEVENSTEIN, MARGARET (1998). Book review of Roy (1997). H-Business, Aug.

LIU, TESSIE P. (1994). *The Weaver's Knot: The Contradictions of Class Struggle and Family Solidarity in Western France, 1750–1914*. Ithaca, NY: Cornell University Press.

LUESBY, JENNY (1998). "Smaller, Cheaper, Safer". *Financial Times*, Sept. 8.

LUNDVALL, BENGT-ÅKE (ed.) (1992). *National Systems of Innovation: Towards a Theory of Innovation and Interactive Learning*. London: Pinter.

MAGNUSSON, LARS (1994). *The Contest for Control: Metal Industries in Sheffield, Solingen, Remscheid and Eskilstuna during Industrialization*. Oxford: Berg.

MORSON, GARY SAUL (1994). *Narrative and Freedom: The Shadows of Time*. New Haven: Yale University Press.

NISHIGUCHI, TOSHIHIRO (1993). *Strategic Industrial Sourcing: The Japanese Advantage*. Oxford: Oxford University Press.

PIERSON, PAUL (2004). *Politics and Time: History, Institutions, and Social Analysis*. Princeton, NJ: Princeton University Press.

PIORE, MICHAEL J., and SABEL, CHARLES F. (1984). *The Second Industrial Divide: Possibilities for Prosperity*. New York: Basic Books.

RICOEUR, PAUL (1984). *Time and Narrative*, vol. 1. Trans. by Kathleen McLaughlin and David Pellauer. Chicago: Chicago University Press.

ROY, WILLIAM G. (1997). *Socializing Capital: The Rise of the Large Industrial Corporation in America*. Princeton, NJ: Princeton University Press.

SABEL, CHARLES F. (1982). *Work and Politics: The Division of Labor in Industry*. Cambridge: Cambridge University Press.

——(1994). "Learning by Monitoring: The Institutions of Economic Development", in Neil J. Smelser and Richard Swedberg (eds.), *The Handbook of Economic Sociology*, 1st edn. Princeton, NJ: Princeton University Press/Russell Sage Foundation, 137–65.

—— (1996). "Intelligible Differences: On Deliberate Strategy and the Exploration of Possibility in Economic Life", *Rivista Italiana degli Economisti* (Journal of the Società Italiana degli Economisti), 1/1: 55–80

—— (2004). "Pragmatic Collaborations in Practice: A Response to Herrigel and Whitford and Zeitlin". *Industry & Innovation*, 11/1–2: 81–88.

—— (2006). "Theory of a Real-Time Revolution", in Charles Heckscher and Paul Adler (eds.), *The Firm as a Collaborative Community*. Oxford: Oxford University Press, 106–36.

—— and ZEITLIN, JONATHAN (1982). "Alternative storiche alla produzione di massa". *Stato e mercato*, 5: 212–58.

—— —— (1985). "Historical Alternatives to Mass Production: Politics, Markets and Technology in Nineteenth-Century Industrialization". *Past and Present*, 108: 133–76.

—— —— (eds.) (1997a). *World of Possibilities: Flexibility and Mass Production in Western Industrialization*. Cambridge: Cambridge University Press.

—— —— (1997b). "Stories, Strategies, and Structures: Rethinking Historical Alternatives to Mass Production", in Sabel and Zeitlin (1997a), 1–33.

SALAIS, ROBERT (1999). "Review of *World of Possiblities*". *American Journal of Sociology*, 104/6: 1857.

SCRANTON, PHILIP (1997). *Endless Novelty: Specialty Production and American Industrialization, 1865–1925*. Princeton, NJ: Princeton University Press.

SHIOMI, HARUHITO (1995). "The Formation of Assembler Networks in the Automobile Industry: The Case of Toyota Motor Company (1955–80)", in Shiomi and Kazuo Wada (eds.), *Fordism Transformed: The Development of Production Methods in the Automobile Industry*. Oxford: Oxford University Press, 28–48.

SLATER, DON, and TONKISS, FRAN (2001). *Market Society: Markets and Modern Social Theory*. Cambridge: Polity Press.

STORPER, MICHAEL, and SALAIS, ROBERT (1997). *Worlds of Production: The Action Frameworks of the Economy*, Cambridge, Mass.: Harvard University Press.

TOLLIDAY, STEVEN (1998). "The Diffusion and Transformation of Fordism: Britain and Japan Compared", in Boyer *et al.* (1998), 57–96.

—— (2000). "Transplanting the American Model? US Automobile Companies and the Transfer of Technology and Management to Britain, France, and Germany, 1928–62", in Zeitlin and Herrigel (2000), 76–119.

—— and JONATHAN ZEITLIN (eds.) (1992). *Between Fordism and Flexibility: The Automobile Industry and its Workers*, 2nd edn. Oxford: Berg. 1st edn. Cambridge: Polity, 1986.

VEYRASSAT, BÉATRICE (1997). "Manufacturing Flexibility in Nineteenth-Century Switzerland: Social and Institutional Foundations of Decline and Revival in Calico-Printing and Watchmaking", in Sabel and Zeitlin (1997a), 188–237.

WALTON, WHITNEY (1992). *France at the Crystal Palace: Bourgeois Taste and Artisan Manufacture in the Nineteenth Century*. Ithaca, NY: Cornell University Press.

WHITE, ALAN (1997). " '…We Never Knew What Price We Were Going to Have Till We Got to the Warehouse': Nineteenth-Century Sheffield and the Industrial District Debate". *Social History*, 22/3: 307–17.

WHITFORD, JOSH, and ZEITLIN, JONATHAN (2004). "Governing Decentralized Production: Institutions, Public Policy, and the Prospects for Inter-Firm Collaboration in the United States". *Industry & Innovation*, 11/1–2: 11–44.

WHITLEY, RICHARD (1999). *Divergent Capitalisms: The Social Structuring and Change of Business Systems.* Oxford: Oxford University Press.

——and PEER HULL KRISTENSEN (eds.) (1996). *The Changing European Firm: Limits to Convergence.* London: Routledge.

WILLIAMS, KAREL, WILLIAMS, JOHN, HASLAM, COLIN, and WARDLOW, ANDREW (1989). "Facing Up to Manufacturing Failure", in Paul Hirst and Jonathan Zeitlin (eds.), *Reversing Industrial Decline? Industrial Structure and Policy in Britain and her Competitors.* Oxford: Berg, 71–94.

ZEITLIN, JONATHAN (1995*a*). "Why are there No Industrial Districts in the United Kingdom?", in Arnaldo Bagnasco and Charles F. Sabel (eds.), *Small and Medium-Size Enterprises.* London: Pinter, 98–114.

——(1995*b*). "Flexibility and Mass Production at War: Aircraft Manufacture in Britain, the United States, and Germany, 1939–1945". *Technology and Culture,* 36/1: 46–79.

——(ed.) (2000*a*). "Flexibility in the 'Age of Fordism': Technology and Production in the International Automobile Industry", special issue of *Enterprise and Society,* 1/1, Mar.

——(2000*b*). "Introduction: Americanization and its Limits: Reworking US Technology and Management in Post-War Europe and Japan", in Zeitlin and Herrigel (2000), 1–50.

——(2003). "Introduction: Governing Work and Welfare in a New Economy: European and American Experiments", in Jonathan Zeitlin and David Trubek (eds.), *Governing Work and Welfare in a New Economy: European and American Experiments.* Oxford: Oxford University Press, 1–30.

——and HERRIGEL, GARY (eds.) (2000). *Americanization and its Limits: Reworking US Technology and Management in Post-War Europe and Japan.* Oxford: Oxford University Press.

CHAPTER 7

GLOBALIZATION

GEOFFREY JONES

7.1 INTRODUCTION

GLOBALIZATION is a central issue, and perhaps the central issue, in business history. The radical shrinking of distance which began in the nineteenth century, but which had a much longer history, transformed the business of firms and entrepreneurs, and transformed the world in which they operated. By the twenty-first century few firms anywhere in the world, even small enterprises, were unaffected by some aspect of globalization, while large corporations were at the heart of the process.

The extensive literature on globalization has attracted scholars from many areas of history and the social sciences. The timing, determinants, and consequences of globalization remain highly contested. Different academic disciplines even differ in their definitions of this phenomenon. Economists have stressed the integration of national markets for capital, commodities, and labor (Bordo *et al.* 2003). Geographers have spoken of the "compression" of space and time (Harvey 1989). Others have described a "process of increasing integration in world civilization" (Kogut 1997).

Historians have been important participants in globalization debates. They have tracked the historical origins of globalization. In the process, they have established both that much that has been assumed to be new is not new and that globalization has been far from being a linear process (Hirst and Thompson 1999). Many sub-fields of history have contributed to this literature. Economic historians have provided quantitative evidence on the integration, or otherwise, of markets, over time (O'Rourke and Williamson 1999). Financial historians have traced the globalization of capital markets back to the seventeenth century (Neal 2000; Flandreau and Zumer 2004). Imperial historians have recast the history of European empires in terms of globalization (Cain and Hopkins 2001; Bayley 2004).

Within this wider context, business historians have made distinctive contributions. They have highlighted the importance of entrepreneurs and firms, rather than markets and technologies, in the history of globalization. They have shown that business enterprises have not simply responded to global markets, but have often created them. It is noteworthy that business historians were interested in the global expansion of business long before globalization as such was identified as an important phenomenon. Mira Wilkins, the doyen of historians of international business, published her first major study in this area—concerning the international expansion of the Ford Motor Company—as early as 1964 (Wilkins and Hill 1964). This was barely four years after the term "multinational" was coined. During the 1970s, she published what have become the classic studies on the historical growth of US multinationals from the nineteenth century (Wilkins 1970, 1974).

Until recently, much of the business history literature on globalization was focused on the history of multinationals. There are literature reviews on this domain in both short essays (Wilkins 2001; Jones 2003) and in a number of anthologies (Wilkins 1991; Jones 1993b). This literature is now being explicitly integrated within the history of globalization (Jones 2005a). This chapter extends this approach by focusing on the contribution of business historians to understanding the history of globalization. The essay suggests that as global perspectives progressively replace national ones, new research agendas and methodologies will need to be employed.

7.2 ORIGINS AND DYNAMICS

7.2.1 Antecedents

When did global business begin? Moore and Lewis (1999) maintain that international trade began to develop in the Near East around 3500 BC. They identify the first multinationals appearing in the Old Assyrian Kingdom shortly after 2000 BC. However, the latter claim raises the issue whether the term multinational can legitimately be used before "nation states" as such existed.

During the following centuries, empires rose and fell, trade routes opened and closed, and international commerce expanded and contracted in response to this shifting environment. The integration of world civilization and the growth of international commerce was never a continuous process. There were constant shocks and discontinuities and periodic backlashes. The Voyages of Discovery of Spanish and Portuguese explorers to the New World and Asia in the fifteenth and sixteenth centuries saw transfers of technology—and disease—across continents. Entire civilizations were decimated in the process. The New World provided large supplies of the silver required by China, in exchange for which European merchants purchased manufactured and other exotic goods from the sophisticated Chinese economy. Some monetary historians, employing a "world history" framework, regard this international silver trade at the center of their contention that "a highly integrated global economy has existed since the sixteenth century" (Flynn and Giráldez 2002). There is little research on the business enterprises which traded the silver and other commodities during this era.

Seventeenth-century Europe saw the creation of state-sponsored trading companies such as the East India Companies in Asia, the Royal Africa Company, and the Hudson's Bay Company to support colonial trading systems. They became the world's first large-scale business organizations, which some see as "proto-multinationals" (Carlos and Nicholas 1988; Carlos and Kruse 1996), and others as "quasi-governments" (Pomeranz 2000). The English East India Company grew as a vertically integrated firm whose activities spanned the procurement of commodities in Asia to their wholesaling in Europe, and which from the 1760s began to acquire political power on the Indian subcontinent (Bowen *et al.* 2002). Smaller firms traded in human beings, transporting ten million Africans to the Americas between the sixteenth and nineteenth centuries.

By the eighteenth century, there was a vibrant Atlantic economy (Hancock 1997). The "great divergence" between Western Europe and East Asia which became apparent in the late eighteenth century may, to a large extent, have been due to European trade with the Americas, which provided new crops that in turn improved nutritional standards, allowed for population growth, and more generally, allowed Europe to grow along resource-intensive, labor-saving paths (Pomeranz 2000). However, geographical distance remained an enormous obstacle to the growth of firms beyond their local regions. It continued to be exceedingly difficult, at least without government charters, to own and control business activities spread over large distances.

7.2.2 The First Global Economy

Globalization intensified greatly during the second half of the nineteenth century. This chapter follows the widespread, if not universally accepted, view that this led to the creation of a "first global economy", while acknowledging the work cited earlier that there is significant evidence of "globalization" in earlier centuries. Quantitative work by economic historians has shown that world capital, commodity, and labor markets had become closely integrated by 1914 (Bordo *et al.* 2003). Beginning in the early nineteenth century, and accelerating from the 1880s, thousands of firms

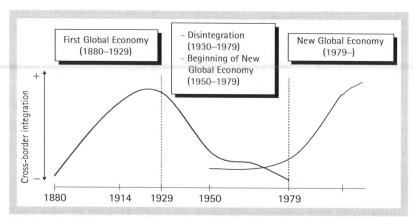

Fig. 7.1 Business enterprises and globalization waves

Source: Jones (2005*a*)

crossed borders, building the sinews of the first global economy. Figure 7.1 provides a figurative illustration of the historical role of firms in worldwide economic integration.

Economists typically count the multinational investment using the measure of foreign direct investment (FDI). FDI, in contrast to portfolio investment, involves a cross-border flow of both capital and management control. The wholly inadequate historical statistics for all types of foreign investment, which reached very large levels during the nineteenth century, mean that estimating the overall size of FDI is problematic. Long believed to have been primarily portfolio, Dunning (1983) has suggested that in 1914 one-third of total international investment, may have taken this form. This amounted to $14.6 billion ($229 billion in 2006 dollars), or the equivalent of 9 percent of world output, a ratio not seen again until the 1990s. However, the variety of corporate forms used to invest across borders in this era make the identification of the relative shares of portfolio and FDI problematic. In her studies of the history of foreign investment in the United States, Wilkins (1989, 2004) considered both types of capital flow.

A number of factors prompted a rapid globalization of business before 1914. First, the advent of modern economic growth, beginning in eighteenth-century England, began a process which saw an accelerating search for markets for manufactured goods, and supplies of foodstuffs and raw materials.

Second, the importance of geographical distance was dramatically reduced by technology. Although global trade networks may have been present since the sixteenth century and functioned as an important driver of change in the world economy, transport costs were very high, and periodic wars further disrupted international commerce. Findlay and O'Rourke (2003) suggest that world trade may only have grown a little over one percent per year between 1500 and 1800. Railroads and steamships shrank distance, opening new markets and making possible the exploitation of natural resources in distant lands more feasible. As or more important was the revolution in communications caused by the telegraph. The first successful trans-Atlantic cable connection was in 1866. Information could now cross continents in minutes. It was now feasible, if still challenging, for entrepreneurs to really manage businesses across borders.

Third, what can be termed the political distance between countries fell dramatically. As the nineteenth century progressed, liberal economic policies took hold in many countries as governments withdrew from economic activities. Most governments treated foreign-owned firms more or less like domestic firms. People could move countries without passports or work visas. The growth of tariffs from mid-century did not obstruct this mobility of capital and people. As important was imperialism, which represented the forcible removal of political barriers to globalization (Cain and Hopkins 2002; Bayley 2004). Even in nominally independent Latin America and elsewhere, the British, and later the Americans, imposed their view of international law which guaranteed property rights. Uncompensated seizure was considered robbery, and the use of unilateral force was considered a legal and legitimate response (Lipson 1985).

Economists and economic historians typically describe the creation of the nineteenth-century global economy without mentioning a single business enterprise (Bordo *et al.* 2003). Business historians have shown why this is misleading. Firms drove globalization by creating trade flows, constructing marketing channels, building infrastructure, and creating markets. By 1914 the production or marketing of most of the world's mineral resources was controlled by US and European firms. A high proportion of world trade in some commodities was intra-firm. In the exploitation of world resources, large corporations co-existed with entrepreneurial firms and other types of business enterprise. German metal trading companies, of which the largest was Metallgesellschaft, used equity and non-equity modes to control the mining, smelting, and sale of many of the world's most important nonferrous metals (Becker 2002). Foreign firms also dominated the production and marketing of many renewable resources including rubber, tropical fruits, and tea. Recent research on commodity chains have stressed their historical role in the process of world economic integration (Topik *et al.* 2006).

Much of the infrastructure of the global economy—the telegraph, ports, and electricity and gas utilities—was put in place by international business enterprises (McDowall 1988; Hills 2002; Ahvenainen 2004). Trading companies both facilitated and created trade flows between developed and developing countries, often investing in plantations, mining, and processing (Jones 1998, 2000; Jonker and Sluyterman 2000; Bonin and Cahen 2001; Yonekawa 1990). International shipping companies carried the world's oceanic trade and moved millions of people (Harlaftis 1993; Harlaftis and Theotokas 2004; Munro 2003). European overseas banks built extensive branch networks throughout the Southern Hemisphere and

Asia, financing the research from manufactured goods for commodities (Jones 1990a, 1993a; Meuleau 1990).

Business historians have also shown how hundreds of manufacturing companies were instrumental in transferring products and brands across borders during the first global economy. The first instances of multinational manufacturing included small Swiss cotton textile firms in the 1830s (Schröter 1993a). The phenomenon intensified from mid-century. Many were small entrepreneurial ventures, but a handful became global giants. By 1914 Singer Sewing Machines, an early pioneer of foreign direct investment, accounted for 90 percent of the sewing machines built in the world. Singer's development of installment plans enabled millions of relatively low income consumers to purchase the machine (Carstensen 1984).

Multinational manufacturing was stimulated by the spread of protectionism from the late nineteenth century. Firms were able to "jump" over the tariff barriers which blocked their exports by establishing local production. This strategy was prominent in industries such as chemicals, machinery, and branded consumer products. Alternative strategies such as licensing and franchising were discouraged because of the complexity of writing contracts for complex technologies and for brand names (Nicholas 1983).

The heterogeneity of business enterprises involved in the first global economy was striking. The firms of different countries varied in their propensity to invest abroad. Britain alone accounted for nearly one half of world FDI in 1914, and the United States and Germany accounted for a further 14 percent each. Firms from a number of small European countries, especially the Netherlands, Sweden, and Switzerland, were very active internationally (Schröter 1993b). Nationality influenced location also. Firms often reduced risks by investing in geographically or culturally proximate regions or in colonial empires. Generally, however, world FDI appears widely dispersed geographically among "rich" and "poor" countries. The United States, Russia, and Canada may have been the world's largest host economies in 1914 (Wilkins 1994).

Large managerial firms co-existed with numerous small and family-owned firms. While much of the theory of the multinational enterprise suggested that firms developed competences or "advantages" before investing abroad, business historians have shown that European firms, especially from smaller economies such as Sweden, made foreign investments at early stages of their corporate lives (Olsson 1993). Thousands of "free-standing" firms were established in Britain and the Netherlands exclusively to operate internationally, without prior domestic businesses (Wilkins 1988; Wilkins and Schröter 1998). "Born global" firms, believed by some management researchers to be a novel feature of the contemporary global economy (Knight and Cavusgil 2004), existed in their thousands before 1914.

Nor was the creation of the first global economy the preserve of US and Western European firms. The commercial networks established by diaspora communities were important drivers of international business in the first global economy. During the late nineteenth century, the Greek diaspora spread over the Mediterranean, and Russia was active in wide-ranging international commercial and shipping business, creating a cosmopolitan business network based on kinship ties extending over Central Europe and even reaching France and Britain (Minoglou and Louri 1997). European empires provided a political and security umbrella for diaspora to flourish. Brown (1994, 2000) examined the history of the Chinese and Indian commercial diaspora, which operated within and between European empires. Another example was Iraqi Jewish firms, especially the Sassoons, which resettled in British India. During the second half of the nineteenth century, they wrested control over the China opium trade from British rivals such as Jardine Matheson and established businesses spanning Europe and South and East Asia (Betta 2004).

7.2.3 The Disintegration of the First Global Economy

The first global economy began to unravel in 1914 and collapsed in 1929. The disintegration of global commodity, capital, and labor markets has been well-documented, again usually without reference to the strategies of business enterprises (Bordo *et al.* 2003). A backlash against the first global economy was under way before the First World War. By 1914 Britain, the Netherlands, and Denmark were the only free trading countries left. The United States started to restrict Asian immigration from the 1880s (James 2001). The First World War intensified these trends. Many countries, including the United States, made the use of passports compulsory for the first time and in 1917 required foreign nationals to have visas. Tight immigration controls based on ethnicity were imposed.

The nationality of firms was identified as an issue during the First World War, as governments sequestrated affiliates of enemy-owned companies. Despite the rhetoric about "stateless firms" in the late twentieth century, if there was ever an era when the nationality of firms was not important it was before 1914, after which capitalism and business enterprises acquired and retained sharper national identities (Jones 2006). The sequestration of German-owned affiliates by US, British, and other Allied governments not only virtually reduced the stock of German FDI to zero, but also signaled the end of the era when foreign companies could operate in most countries on more or less the same terms as domestic ones. The Russian Revolution in 1917 resulted in France and Belgium losing two-thirds of their total foreign investment. Although the United States shifted from being the world's largest debtor nation to being a net creditor over the course of the First World War, this was accompanied by a growing nationalism which resulted in major restrictions on foreign ownership in shipping, telecommunications, resources, and other industries (Wilkins 2004). The world became, and remained, riskier for firms crossing borders.

However, business historians have demonstrated that business enterprises were often more robust than an aggregate view of markets would suggest. During the 1920s, there were still many new multinational investments. Schröter (1990) showed that German chemical and other firms, despite a shortage of capital, rebuilt their international distribution networks and even their foreign production subsidiaries. The Great Depression did result in a meltdown of both cross-border capital flows, and the international trading system. Yet there were entrepreneurial responses. While the global level of FDI may have stagnated, new investments continued to be made (Wilkins 1974; Bostock and Jones 1994). The era saw the creation of numerous international cartels which strove to regulate prices and output on a global scale, though they were rarely able to control them for too long before new competitors appeared (Fear, this volume). In industries such as electrical engineering, they filled the governance gap left by the breakdown of the international economy, while their development was often encouraged by national governments (Glimstedt 2001).

Overall, the interwar wars offered a striking paradox. Technology continued to shrink geographical distances. The advent of cinema and radio provided unprecedented opportunities to see lifestyles real or imagined elsewhere. Telephones and automobiles became items of mass consumption, though largely in the United States. Air travel was expensive, but quite widespread. Yet political distance grew. For diverse reasons, governments sought to block foreign companies, trade, and people.

A global economy was only partially restored after the end of the Second World War. World trade barriers were reduced under the auspices of the General Agreement on Tariffs and Trade (GATT), signed in 1947, but most developing countries became progressively closed to international trade. Even the richest countries retained high levels of protection for agricultural products. Immigration controls remained extensive.

The Second World War also further demonstrated the political risks of FDI. The total loss of all German overseas assets, once again as a result of the war, was followed by an extremely subdued level of German FDI until the 1970s, as German firms opted to export rather than engage in FDI as did Japanese firms (Neebe 1991). These developments left world FDI far from a "global" phenomenon after the Second World War. Between 1945 and the mid-1960s, the United States alone may have accounted for 85 percent of all new FDI outflows.

There was a widespread decline in receptivity to foreign firms after the Second World War, especially in developing and post-colonial countries. They were excluded altogether from Soviet Russia, China, and other Communist countries. During the 1970s, expropriations eliminated virtually all foreign ownership of mining, petroleum, and plantation assets. As a result, vertical integration down to the production level was weakened or eliminated in most commodities (Jones 2005a). Large petroleum corporations responded by switching exploration to the North Sea, Alaska, and other politically "safe" locations (Bamberg 2000).

By 1980 the world stock of US FDI was $500 billion, but this was still only half the size compared to the world economy as a whole than it was in 1914. Two-thirds of all multinational investment was located in Western Europe and North America. The emergent new global economy, unlike the first, was driven by investment, knowledge, and trade flows between rich countries.

7.2.4 The Origins of the Second Global Economy

As suggested in Figure 7.1, a second wave of globalization began during the 1950s and intensified after 1979. In the immediate postwar decades, service firms such as consultants, advertising agencies, hotels, and film distributors were significant conduits for the international diffusion of American management practices, values, and lifestyles. Trading companies developed global networks exploiting information asymmetries. Japan's general trading companies, or *sogo shosha*, survived their dismantling by the Allied occupation after the Second World War to become the central players in both Japan's foreign trade and (until the 1970s) FDI (Yonekawa 1990). World trade in commodities was increasingly handled by giant commodity trading firms such as Cargill, the grain trader and largest private company in the United States (Broehl 1992, 1998).

Multinational banking assumed a new importance. The development of the Eurodollar markets in London from the late 1950s provided a dynamic new source of funding for global capitalism. These unregulated markets captured a rising share of financial intermediation from regulated domestic markets. They were physically located in a small number of financial centers, of which London stood at the apex, and in offshore centers, such as the Cayman Islands, where the primary attraction was not the size of domestic markets, but a combination of regulations and fiscal conditions, and political stability (Jones 1992; Roberts 1994). In one sense, banks escaped from governments, although the new markets flourished with the tacit, and later explicit, support of the British and US governments (Helleiner 1994).

The physical location of international financial markets in a few geographies formed part of a wider pattern of the concentration of business activity in certain cities and regions. Paradoxically, this phenomenon seems to have intensified just as technological advances permitted greater dispersion of economic activity. New economic geography has identified the advantages of proximity and the importance of agglomeration advantages which help to explain such patterns. Sassen (2001) has argued that London, Tokyo, and New York assumed new importance as the "command centers" of the new global economy. Business historians have documented the origins and evolution of such centers, and the nature of the interaction between various actors which lay at the center of their success. Attention has focused especially on financial centers (Michie 1992; Schenk 2001), although research is now exploring the issue more generally. Merlo and Polese (2006) have explained the growth of Milan as an international fashion hub by the 1970s through its accumulation of resources and the ability to harness creative and managerial capabilities.

During the 1950s, the international cartels of the interwar years were dismantled, while US manufacturing companies invested on a large scale in Western Europe, initially in response to the "dollar shortage", which encouraged US firms to establish factories to supply customers in countries that lacked the dollars to buy American products. There was initially little rationalized production, and intra-firm trade was low. However, from the 1960s firms began to seek geographical and functional integration across borders. The process of building integrated production systems was difficult and not linear. European companies such as Unilever were proponents of European economic integration from the 1950s, but struggled over decades to achieve regional integration of their own production and marketing facilities (Jones and Miskell 2005). The history of the corporate role in regional integration strategies over the last forty years remains largely to be written.

7.2.5 The Second Global Economy

From the late 1970s, deregulation and liberalization stimulated increased globalization. China's adoption of market-oriented policies and opening to foreign investors in 1979 was a decisive turning stage in the creation of a second global economy. The collapse of Communism in Russia and Eastern Europe a decade later further re-opened large parts of the globe to foreign firms. By the new century widespread liberalization had re-opened most emerging markets to global capitalism.

Business enterprises were once more the drivers of integration. Multinational investment grew far faster than world exports or world output, and 40 percent of all world trade took place between the subsidiaries of the same firm by 2000. International production systems developed within which firms located different parts of their value chain across the globe, serving as powerful agents of international integration. In some industries international production systems became highly externalized through outsourcing, but large corporations typically continued to control key functions, including brand management and product definition, and setting quality standards. The total stock of world FDI had reached $10.7 trillion by 2005, even though new flows temporarily declined in the early years of the century in response to shocks from terrorism and faltering world equity markets.

In many industries there was consolidation and concentration. The dominant mode of multinational investment became mergers and acquisitions, although this is a mode which business historians have only recently begun to address (Jones and Miskell 2007). During the 1990s, and again during the middle years of the following decade, there were large cross-border merger waves, especially in pharmaceuticals and food, beverages and tobacco, and automobiles. Business historians have started to explore the dynamics of this process at a firm-specific level. Kristensen and Zeitlin (2005) stressed the importance of considering subsidiaries as quasi-independent actors in a case study of how a British engineering multinational grew through mergers to become the world's largest manufacturer of food and drink processing equipment before being acquired itself.

The sustained growth of the Chinese economy after 1979, followed a decade later by accelerating growth in India, resulted in significant geographical shifts in economic power. Foreign firms, initially largely owned by overseas Chinese, drove the initial growth of export-orientated industries in China (Huang 2003). A number of corporate histories have discussed the re-entry of Western firms into China, which involved complex negotiations with the authorities and prospective joint venture partners (Dyer *et al.* 2004; Jones 2005*b*). Indian business remained largely locally owned, although the fast-growing IT services sector relied heavily on outsourcing from global firms.

The global significance of firms based beyond North America, Western Europe, and Japan increased. During the 1960s and 1970s, some manufacturers from South Korea and Taiwan began to invest abroad, typically in other Asian or other emerging markets. They were usually small-scale and used labor-intensive technology (Lall 1983). A second wave of firms, based in both Asia and Latin America, began to expand globally from the 1980s, often after they had built scale and corporate competences in their protected domestic markets. They were prominent in assembly-based and knowledge-based industries including electronics, automobiles, and telecommunications (Hoesel 1999). These investments often originated from firms embedded in the business groups which characterized emerging markets, including the Korean *chaebol* (Amsden 2003) and the *grupos economicos* in Latin America.

A management literature on "emerging giants" has begun to examine how corporations such as Cemex (Mexico), Technit (Argentina), Odebrecht (Brazil), Huawei and Haier (China), and the Tata group (India) grew businesses which were both globally competitive and globally active, despite the challenges of building brands and innovatory capacity, as well as management quality, typically faced by firms based in emerging markets (Khanna and Palepu 2006). A business history literature on such "emerging giants", employing a longer-term perspective, has started to appear (Kosacoff 2002). However business historians face major challenges as many emerging countries lack both the tradition of retaining archives, whether public or private, and enthusiasm for allowing scholars access to them.

The dynamics of the global economy may have lowered the barriers for new entrants compared to earlier decades because of the growing disintegration of production systems and their replacement by networks of interfirm linkages. Firms from emerging markets were sometimes able to piggy-back on incumbent Western or Japanese firms as customers through subcontracting and other linkages

(Mathews 2002). Brazilian-owned Sabó emerged as a multinational automobile supplier through its relations with General Motors and other highly demanding customers, which spurred a concern for quality which enabled successful businesses to be built in developed countries (Sull and Escobari 2005). The spread of management education in the second global economy, and the growing number of international students at leading US business schools, relaxed a further constraint on "emerging giants", as such firms were increasingly able to access well-trained and globally minded managers.

A historical perspective lends support to the view that the second global economy was less "global" than the first in some respects, perhaps being better described as "regionalized" (Rugman 2000) or "semi-globalized" (Ghemawat 2003). The international property rules of the first global economy were not restored. In China, Eastern Europe, Africa, and elsewhere, there remained enormous uncertainties regarding property rights and the enforcement of contracts. Nor had governments withdrawn from the market for capital flows as they had before 1914. Practically every government offered incentives for multinationals to invest. World exchange markets saw massive intervention in efforts to influence exchange rates. International trade in many commodities remained distorted by tariffs and subsidies. Although information could cross borders almost instantaneously, people could not (Chiswick and Hatton 2003). These government-imposed barriers to labor mobility created incentives to the development of cross-national production networks in labor-intensive manufacturing and service industries.

7.3 ORGANIZATION OF GLOBAL FIRMS

Managing a cross-border business has always posed major challenges. In each generation, entrepreneurs and managers struggled to create and sustain organizations which could operate efficiently, find an appropriate balance between centralization direction and local responsiveness, and which were able to transfer knowledge and competencies inside their boundaries but across national borders. Business historians have shown that organizational solutions have been heavily contingent on time, industry, the state of technology, home economy and public policy, as well as the specific competences and routines of each firm (Jones 2005a).

General patterns are apparent. During the first global economy, a broad distinction can be made between "informal" or "network" forms of organization and "formal" or "hierarchical" forms. European, and also later Japanese, firms placed much emphasis on personal relations and socialization, although this did not prevent the development of quite bureaucratic structures in some cases. This built on earlier traditions of international business in past centuries when prevailing technologies left managers with little choice but to rely on trust to control and monitor cross-border operations.

Socialization methods of control remained important in European and Asian companies even as transportation and communication improved. They worked effectively especially in industries such as international trading which involved numerous non-routine transactions and in managing operations in developing countries where political and economic conditions were unpredictable. Inter-firm collaboration provided a means of sharing competencies and spreading risks. As a result, large "business groups" were built around French and Belgium "mixed banks", German electrical companies, and European trading companies (Shiba and Shimotani 1997). In a study of British trading companies in the nineteenth and twentieth centuries, Jones (2000) showed that many ostensibly "free-standing" companies were clustered in business groups linked through equity, debt, cross-directorships, and business flows. A striking feature of these organizational forms was also their persistence, in some cases until the present day. (See also Fruin, this volume.)

In contrast, US-based firms developed an early preference for formal organization and bureaucratic procedures. They expanded within the large domestic market of the United States using hierarchies and rules, creating many of the world's largest corporations by the early twentieth century. When they expanded abroad, they also typically used hierarchies rather than networks to manage complex processes. Rules and standardized reporting procedures were the norm in US firms (Chandler 1990; Wilkins 1970).

There was nothing linear about the development of organizational forms. During the interwar years, many firms which operated in several countries became more national in their organization. Trade barriers and exchange controls made cross-border flows of trade between affiliates more difficult and obliged firms to retain profits in host economies, which were often used to diversify along the value chain. The growing political importance of the nationality of firms encouraged the managers of subsidiaries to emphasize their local nature and autonomy.

However, there remained a wide diversity of practice even among firms of the same nationality and in the same industry. Ford and GM both expanded internationally during the interwar years. With the exception of Canada and the British Empire (outside of Great Britain), during most of the 1920s, Ford was highly centralized, while GM was decentralized. In this decade, Ford expanded in Europe with greenfield operations and GM expanded with acquisition (Bonin *et al.* 2003). Cochran (2000) demonstrated how Japanese, Western, and Chinese-owned firms responded in a variety of organizational forms to the challenges of doing business in China between 1880 and 1937.

In the decades after the Second World War, many large US corporations were organized as coordinated federations in which the parent company exercised quite a close control over overall strategy and sought to transfer knowledge to foreign affiliates. This model contrasted with the preference of European companies for leaving national entities possessing considerable autonomy. All organizational firms encountered problems when transferring knowledge and information within their enterprises. During the 1960s, Ford opened research and development centers in both Germany and Britain, but with little coordination between them as they were embedded in their respective national organizations (Bonin *et al.* 2003). Unilever experienced major problems transferring knowledge between its European operations and its US affiliates between the 1940s and the 1980s (Jones 2002). This research calls into question theories which explain the existence of multinationals by their ability to transfer knowledge that is difficult to understand and codify (Kogut and Zander 1993).

Knowledge diffusion within firms was shaped by organizational context. A study of foreign-owned affiliates active in Canada between the 1880s and the 1950s showed that among the major features affecting decisions involving transfers of technology were the role played by managers in the affiliated firm in negotiating for these transfers and the degree of control exercised by the parent company over the Canadian enterprise (Taylor 1994).

As the process of globalization intensified in the late twentieth century, there was a search for more flexible forms of organization (Nohria and Ghoshal 1997). Business historians could observe that in the periods of fast globalization seen in both the late nineteenth and late twentieth centuries alliances, joint ventures, and other network modes were widely used when crossing borders.

7.4 PUBLIC POLICY AND GLOBAL BUSINESS

The historical growth of global business was heavily shaped by public policy. Business historians have traced the cyclical shifts in policy from the extreme openness seen in the first global economy to the restrictions and controls during much of the twentieth century and the shift toward liberalization from the 1980s.

In retrospect, it was the degree of openness towards foreign firms in the nineteenth century which was striking. The growth of more restrictive policies was evident from the First World War, yet even Nazi regime Germany tolerated the operations of foreign firms, provided they followed government policies, notably the removal of Jews from their employment (Cheape 1988). Business enterprises in turn were often tolerant in their relationships with authoritarian regimes in foreign countries. The complex, but often ethically ambiguous, relationship of foreign firms with the Nazi regime in Germany has been extensively studied by business historians over the last decade (Turner 2005; Kobrak and Hansen 2004; Nicosia and Huener 2004). Aalders and Wiebes (1996) offer a detailed study of the collaboration of leading Swedish firms with Nazi Germany before and during the Second World War. Wubs (2006) shows, in a study of Unilever during the Second World War, that foreign firms could survive without collaboration during the Nazi occupation in part because of the incoherence in Nazi policy towards foreign companies. As Kobrak and Wüstenhagen (2006) show, German firms also faced home country political risk during the Nazi era, and pursued "cloaking" strategies aimed at protecting their international investments.

After the Second World War, sensitivities towards foreign firms grew in most countries. An idiosyncratic example was the uproar in France during the late 1940s caused by the entry of Coca-Cola. Critics of "Coca-Colonization", who spanned a spectrum from the Communist Party to local wine and mineral water producers, regarded the brand as a symbol of US imperialism. There were moves in France's National Assembly to ban the importation, manufacture and sale of the product. Eventually the company was able to overcome its critics, in part through US diplomatic pressures, although per capita consumption of the drink remained subdued in France for decades thereafter (Kuisel 1993).

Both the United States and Western Europe closed entire industries to foreign firms either through regulation or nationalization. In Japan, the government blocked almost all wholly-owned FDI (Mason 1992). In Europe, exchange controls were used to "screen" inward FDI proposals so they met desired policy goals. Some US firms were blocked by such "screening", but the actual number was not great (Jones 1990b; Rooth and Scott 2002). During the 1960s, European policies became more restrictive, as the French and British governments in particular sought to establish "national champions" in high-technology sectors, though rarely with success (Mounier-Kuhn 1987; Campbell-Kelly 1990).

In most developing countries, the end of European colonial empires, the spread of Communism, and growing state intervention resulted in a hostile environment for foreign firms. During the last years of colonial rule in countries such as Nigeria and Kenya, British colonial administrators preferred to promote political tranquillity rather than support British or other foreign firms (Tignor 1998). Decker (2007) has shown how British firms in post-colonial West Africa sought to adjust their strategies, including corporate advertising, to the new local political environment.

Foreign control over resources and utilities aroused the greatest sensitivities. Reactions against foreign firms were particularly strong in countries where a handful of companies dominated natural resources. In Iran the Anglo-Persian Oil Company became a symbol of British imperialism. The nationalization of the company in 1951 and the subsequent Anglo-American overthrow of the Iranian government became key episodes in the tensions between developing hosts and foreign corporations (Ferrier 1982; Bamberg 1994).

Much remains to be learned about the strategies of foreign firms towards public policy. They were sometimes able to assume a local identity even in the most nationalistic environments. In 1947, Sears, the US department store chain, started a successful business in Mexico, a country which had only a decade earlier expelled foreign oil companies and was widely regarded as highly nationalistic. Sears carefully crafted its marketing and strategy to appeal to Mexicans, representing policies such as profit-sharing, pensions, and low-priced meals—some of which it employed in its operations at home—as in the traditions of the Mexican Revolution (Moreno 2003).

Firms survived, and sometimes flourished, by cooperating with governments. In Brazil during the 1950s and 1960s, the German car maker VW responded much more readily than Ford and GM to the government's mixture of threats and incentives designed to encourage foreign firms to create an automobile industry. It began local manufacturing, and by 1980 VW had helped give Brazil an annual production of over one million vehicles a year, making the country the world's tenth largest industry (Shapiro 1994). Western corporations differed in their tolerance of the risks of emerging markets. Unilever built and retained large business in emerging markets such as India, despite numerous government restrictions, and in Brazil, despite high inflation rates. In contrast, Procter & Gamble preferred to stay out of most emerging markets until the 1990s (Jones 2005b; Dyer et al. 2004). Between the 1960s and the 1980s, intensified political risk led many Western firms to reduce their investments in Africa, but much remains to be researched about this process. An emergent literature is exploring the strategies of multinational firms in apartheid-era South Africa, which have some parallels to some of the issues debated in the case of Nazi Germany regarding the strategies and ethical responsibilities of foreign firms in repressive regimes (Kline 1997; Morgan 2006).

7.5 GLOBAL FIRMS AND GLOBAL WELFARE

It is often asserted that the globalization of the world economy has coincided with growing income inequality. While in 1700 the income gaps between people in different parts of the world were small, by 1914 they were substantial. By the early twenty-first century they were even larger. However, such generalizations mask a wide variety of outcomes, and business historians have yet to identify the specific contributions of global business enterprises. Firm strategies interacted with institutional, policy, and cultural factors in multiple ways.

Business historians have yielded important insights on the impact of globalization at the firm and industry level. They have shown how companies transferred capital, technology, organizational capabilities, and employment across national borders. These transfers were significant and positive even in the case of the United States, whose historiography has not emphasized the external contribution to domestic economic growth. Wilkins (1989) shows the contribution of foreign firms to

US industries including chemicals, breweries, mining, and cattle ranching during the nineteenth century. Wilkins (2004) demonstrates the continued importance of foreign firms in some sectors in the United States during the interwar years, despite the faltering of globalization and a growth of government restrictions.

The positive gains from the cross-border transfer of innovation and organizational skills by firms have been identified for other countries. In the case of Britain before the Second World War, foreign—especially American—firms played significant roles in introducing new technologies and marketing methods, creating employment, and improving labor management practices (Jones 1988; Bostock and Jones 1994; Jones and Bostock 1996; Godley 2003). A key issue was the nature of the local response to foreign firms. There was a spectrum of outcomes for local firms, from being forced out of business to being stimulated to become more competitive. Blaich (1984) showed both outcomes in a study of the impact of US machinery firms on German industry before 1914. In sewing machines, some local companies reacted to Singer by reducing their production costs and adopting American manufacturing methods. Others diversified away from sewing machines. Opel became Germany's largest automobile manufacturer.

The positive impact on local firms was lessened if foreign investors were accompanied by suppliers from their own country. This phenomenon was common in the automobile industry. When US automobile companies invested in Europe in the interwar years, they were accompanied by US car body builders, tire companies, manufacturers of wheels, batteries, spark plugs, and window glass (Wilkins 1974). In some cases, their factories were physically located in host countries next to the main automobile assembly plant (Bostock and Jones 1994).

By the interwar years, customer demand for locally adjusted products and rapid service led some manufacturing firms to begin research and development in affiliates. The larger foreign-owned chemical, pharmaceutical, and petroleum firms engaged in R&D in the United States during the interwar years (Wilkins 2004). There is aggregate evidence from patent data that the internationalization of technological activity by large manufacturing firms was quite extensive by the interwar years, but with wide variations between countries, as well as over time (Cantwell 1995). In developing countries, foreign-owned plantation companies often sought to improve crop performance through R&D (Jones 2000; Martin 2003).

The nature of the historical impact of foreign firms on developing countries remains controversial. Multinational investment was widely spread in Asia, Latin America, and Africa during the first global economy. There were income gains to many countries as international firms turned them into major exporters of petroleum, bananas, sugar, rubber, and other commodities. Yet reliance on commodity exports turned out to be risky when prices fell in the interwar years. Corporate strategies also reduced the advantages derived from host economies from their exports. Most minerals and agricultural commodities were exported with only the minimum of processing. This meant that most value was added to the product in the developed economies.

Foreign firms were large employers of labor at that time. However, expatriates were typically employed in handling the newest technologies and installing and managing complex systems. Training was only provided to local employees to enable them to fill unskilled or semiskilled jobs (Headrick 1988). Piquet (2004) explores this issue in the case of the French-controlled Suez Company, which built and operated the Suez Canal in Egypt between 1854 and 1956. The Canal had a major stimulus on the Egyptian economy, yet until 1936 the Egyptian staff was almost exclusively unskilled workers. The gender implications of the employment policies of foreign firms, in this period and later, have hardly begun to be explored.

Global business sometimes transformed entire eco-systems. In Central America, the operations of US-owned United Fruit (subsequently Chiquita) transformed countries into the famous banana republics. The creation of plantations involved cutting down jungle forests. Drainage and water systems were built, and company towns were built in former jungle areas. United Fruit transformed the Central American Atlantic coastline from a sparsely populated location for scattered Indian tribes and exiled American fortune seekers into a well-organized plantation economy. As bananas were highly susceptible to disease and rapidly depleted soils, they could not be cultivated on the same land for more than about ten years. United Fruit moved from the Atlantic to the Pacific coast and back again. When it left disease-infested lands for newer terrain, it removed infrastructure which had any value. There was also a great change in the composition of the population as labor was imported from Jamaica and elsewhere to work the plantations of Costa Rica, Panama, Guatemala, and Honduras (Bucheli 2005).

The establishment and maintenance of mines, oil fields, plantations, shipping depots, and railroad systems involved the transfer of packages of knowledge to developing economies. Given the absence of appropriate infrastructure in developing countries, foreign enterprises frequently not only introduced technologies specific to their activities, but also social technologies such as police, postal, and education systems. The geographical stickiness of knowledge, or more exactly knowledge about how to achieve and sustain modern economic growth, lies at the heart of the development problems of much of the world. Manufacturing firms had—and have—an incentive to minimize technology leakages to competitors. Knowledge spillovers from foreign firms to developing countries were often disappointing. Many investments in natural resources were enclavist, and there were few inputs of local origin. Much of the value added occurred after the product had left the exporting country. In Latin America, US mining operations were often centered on self-sufficient company towns. Yet during the 1950s and 1960s, many enclaves broke down, and foreign companies contributed to the emergence of large middle classes in some countries (Wilkins 1974).

As important, however, was the limited ability of business enterprises in many countries to learn and absorb new technologies. Japan was the primary exception. Although few Western firms invested in Japan in the early twentieth century, Japanese firms showed a remarkable ability to learn from them. There was dissemination of techniques learned from foreign affiliates as companies emulated one another and as workers changed companies. The creation of the Japanese automobile industry was heavily dependent on spillovers from the US automobile companies which established assembly operations in the 1920s (Wilkins 1990; Mason 1992). There are more recent examples in East Asia and elsewhere (Wang 1997; Schmitz 2004).

However, often in Asia Africa, and Latin America, indigenous business systems proved less able to absorb foreign capabilities (Birchal 2001). Some powerful local firms did develop, sometimes working with foreign firms. BAT, which had a huge cigarette business in interwar China, made one-third of its sales through a Chinese-owned firm (Cox 2000). There are intriguing regional and ethnic differences which remain hard to explain. In nineteenth-century India, the first elite group to respond to the British was the tiny Parsee community around Bombay. They were extremely active in developing a modern cotton textile industry by the second half of the nineteenth century. Their entrepreneurial success has been variously described as the result of close relations with the colonial authorities, "outsider" minority status, and a "Protestant" style work ethic. However, during the interwar years, Marwaris, originally a trading community from Rajasthan, began building powerful business groups in Calcutta, which eroded the British commercial presence in the interwar years well before the end of colonialism in 1947. Marwari entrepreneurs were competitors rather than collaborators with British interests, and while the Bengalis might have considered them as "outsiders", the British considered them as "insiders". Meanwhile, the cotton textile industry of Ahmedabad was built by "mainstream" Hindus who had lived in the region for generations and who had little relationship at all with the British (Oonk 2004).

After the Second World War, foreign firms continued to transfer organization and technologies across borders, but the shifting geographical location of multinational investment meant that transfers were largely confined to developed countries. Service providers such as management consultants assumed a new importance. During the 1960s, McKinsey in particular diffused the M-form organization in Europe, although it has been shown the transfer of US management practices was "selective" (Kipping 1999; Zeitlin and Herrigel 2000).

The dispersal of innovative activity was quite limited, at least until the 1980s. There is firm-specific evidence to support the case that the largest US and Swedish industrials lost interest in internationalizing their research after the Second World War (Attman and Olsson 1977). A large share of the foreign R&D undertaken between the 1950s and the 1970s was adaptive or development-oriented (Behrman and Fischer 1980). This was largely confined to the larger markets in Western Europe and

North America. The foreign-owned corporate sector in postwar Australia mainly relied on importing innovation undertaken elsewhere (Fleming *et al.* 2004).

As the subsidiaries of foreign firms grew, adapted to local conditions, and developed specific competences, they became "hybrids". This phenomenon was as old as multinational investment itself, but the term was first used to describe the Japanese transplants built in the US automobile and electronics industries during the 1980s. The Japanese companies transferred parts of their production system, including work teams, limited job classifications, and open plan offices, but other practices, such as consensus decision-making and seniority systems, were not transferred, creating a kind of "hybrid" factory which was neither fully Japanese nor American in its organization (Abo 1994). Studies of the international automobile industry demonstrated how factory management systems were adapted in different contexts (Boyer *et al.* 1998; Freyssenet 1998). Much research remains to be done on the nature and impact of hybridization. There is a need for more research at the level of the subsidiary. One study of the role of the affiliates of Ericsson and ITT in the twentieth-century Norwegian telecom industry shows how corporate strategies were formulated in response to the often conflicting pressures of the corporate parent and the host government (Christensen 2006).

Research on the historical impact of global firms on consumer preferences and choices remains more suggestive than comprehensive. In most consumer and other products, there has been a transition over the last 150 years from local and regional products and brands, to national ones, to—from the 1960s in particular—"global" products and brands. However, this process was not linear and varied greatly between industries. In some respects, globalization can be seen as the imposition of uniformity. In alcoholic beverages, Lopes (2002) identified the demise of thousands of national and regional brands from the 1960s as firms began to identify "global" brands to be promoted worldwide. Yet globalization and hyper-segmentation of consumer markets often proceeded simultaneously. In the 1950s, for example, margarine was a homogeneous product eaten by bread-eating northern Europeans and their descendants. Subsequently, Unilever used branding, packaging, and research capabilities both to segment the product into health and taste categories and to expand consumption into countries with quite different culinary traditions (Jones 2005*b*).

The cosmetics industry has generated studies on the relationship between firm strategies and consumption patterns. Houy (2002) explored the marketing strategies and impact of American cosmetics companies in Nazi Germany, which developed large businesses despite nationalistic and sometimes anti-cosmetic rhetoric. Jones (2008) showed, in a study of the globalization of the beauty industry between 1945 and 1980, how firms employed marketing strategies to diffuse products and brands internationally, despite considerable business, economic, and cultural obstacles to globalization in this industry. The process emerges as difficult and complex, however, and by 1980 there remained strong differences between consumer markets. Although US-based firms, which were pre-eminent, exported American beauty ideals, this study suggests that by 1980 globalization had not resulted in the creation of a stereotyped American blond and blue-eyed beauty female ideal as the world standard, although it may have significantly narrowed the range of variation in beauty and hygiene ideals.

7.6 CONCLUSIONS

Business historians have demonstrated the extraordinary transformation of business as a result of globalization. They have shown how entrepreneurs built markets beyond their national borders, identified and exploited natural resources all over the globe, and figured out ways to control and manage geographically dispersed operations. They have investigated how firms interacted with the governments which at various times promoted and obstructed globalization. They have explored the impact of the globalization of business on countries and social groups. They have demonstrated the lack of linearity in the globalization of business, and provided evidence that the globalization of business has historically resulted in losers as well as winners.

In contrast to much management literature, business historians have demonstrated the heterogeneity of firm strategies, organization, and impact, and shown the frequency and variety of network and other collaborative arrangements in the past. The business history literature provides a caution against easy generalizations, either positive or negative, about the role and impact of global firms. In providing empirical evidence on the complexity of historical outcomes, business history enables debates about globalization to be conducted at a more informed and nuanced level. It also challenges the academic discipline of international business to move beyond the comfort zone offered by datasets on contemporary US business to explore the complexities, ambiguities, and potential learning opportunities offered by the history of global business (Jones and Khanna 2006).

Business history literature has been particularly strong on the historical evolution of corporate strategies. It is now established broadly when, why, and how firms have crossed borders since the nineteenth century, even if many details remain to be discovered. However, many other aspects of the globalization of business require further research. There remains limited evidence on the extent to which globalization has permitted firms to change consumer habits and consumption preferences. The impact of the globalization of business on employment opportunities for women requires far more research. Nor has there been systematic research, leaving aside the specific instance of Nazi Germany, by business historians on the ethical practices of firms as they globalized. Given that corruption has become a major developmental constraint for many developing countries, there is a need for empirical research on the historical role of multinational corporations in facilitating, or resisting, corrupt practices. Far more research is required also on the local entrepreneurial responses to foreign firms in different time periods and countries.

As the study of the business history of globalization intensifies, it will require shifts in methodologies and approaches. The new global business history needs a more clearly defined research agenda within global frameworks. Much of the research reviewed in this chapter has taken the nation state as the starting point. It has examined, for example, the investments of firms from one country into other countries, or the impact of national policy regimes on flows of multinational investment. A global perspective should move beyond such national frameworks to look more closely at the nature of the linkages between geographies, as already seen in the literature on business diaspora and on communication and transport networks. There needs to be more research on the global linkages between financial and business centers, and between regional business systems located in different countries. The history of the environmental impact of global business, as well as the emergence and nature of corporate environmental policies, has hardly begun to be written, yet over a century of plantations, logging, and construction have literally changed the face of the earth. Business historians have unique skills to investigate the nature of global knowledge creation and flows within corporations active in different geographies. The next stage of research on the business history of globalization looks set to be both very exciting and highly rewarding.

References

AALDERS, G., and WIEBES, C. (1996). *The Art of Cloaking Ownership*. Amsterdam: Amsterdam University Press.

ABO, T. (ed.) (1994). *Hybrid Factory. The Japanese Production System in the United States*. New York: Oxford University Press.

AHVENAINEN, J. (2004). *The European Cable Companies in South America before the First World War*. Helsinki: Finnish Academy of Science and Letters.

AMSDEN, A. H. (2003). *The Rise of "the Rest": Challenges to the West from Late-Industrializing Countries*. Oxford: Oxford University Press.

ATTMAN, A., and OLSSON, U. (1977). *LM Ericsson 100 Years*, vol. 2. Orebro: LM Ericsson.

BAMBERG, J. H. (1994). *The History of the British Petroleum Company*, vol. 2. Cambridge: Cambridge University Press.

——— (2000). *British Petroleum and Global Oil 1950–1975*. Cambridge: Cambridge University Press.

BAYLEY, C. A. (2004). *The Birth of the Modern World 1780–1914*. Oxford: Blackwell.

BECKER, S. (2002). *Multinationalität hat verschiedene Gesichter*. Stuttgart: Steiner.

BEHRMAN, J. N., and FISCHER, W. A. (1980). *Overseas R&D Activity of Transnational Companies*. Cambridge, Mass.: Oelgeschanger, Gunn and Hain.

BETTA, C. (2004). "The Trade Diaspora of Baghdadi Jews: From India to China's Treaty Ports, 1842–1937", in I. B. McCabe, G. Harlaftis, and I. P. Minoglou, (eds.), *Diaspora Entrepreneurial Networks*. Oxford: Berg.

BIRCHAL, S. (2001). "The Transfer of Technology to Latecomer Economies in the Nineteenth Century: The Case of Minas Gerais, Brazil". *Business History*, 43/4: 48–67.

BLAICH, F. (1984). *Amerikanische Firmen in Deutschland 1890–1918*. Wiesbaden: Franz Steiner Verlag.

BONIN, H., and CAHEN, M. (2001). *Négoce blanc en Afrique noire*. Saint Denis: Diffusion Allerna.

——LUNG, Y., and TOLLIDAY, S. (eds.) (2003). *Ford: The European History 1903–2003*, 2 vols. Paris: PLAGE.

BORDO, M. D., TAYLOR, A. M., and WILLIAMSON, J. G. (eds.) (2003). *Globalization in Historical Perspective*. Chicago: University of Chicago Press.

BOSTOCK, F., and JONES, G. (1994). "Foreign Multinationals in British Manufacturing, 1850-1962." *Business History*, 36/1.

BOWEN, H. V., LINCOLN, M., and RIGBY, N. (2002). *The Worlds of the East India Company*. Woodbridge: Boydell Press.

BOYER, R., CHARRON, E., JÜRGENS, U., and TOLLIDAY, S. (eds.) (1998). *Between Imitation and Innovation: The Transfer and Hybridization of Productive Models in the International Automobile Industry*. Oxford: Oxford University Press.

BROEHL, W. G. (1992). *Cargill: Trading the World's Grain*. Hanover, NH: University Press of New England.

——(1998). *Cargill: Going Global*. Hanover, NH: University Press of New England.

BROWN, R. A. (1994). *Capital and Entrepreneurship in South East Asia*. London: Macmillan.

——(2000). *Chinese Big Business and the Wealth of Asian Nations*. London: Palgrave.

BUCHELI, M. (2005). *Bananas and Business: The United Fruit Company in Colombia, 1899–2000*. New York: New York University Press.

CAIN, P. J., and HOPKINS, A. G. (2001). *British Imperialism: 1688–2000*. London: Longman.

CAMPBELL-KELLY, M. (1990). *ICL: A Business and Technical History*. Oxford: Oxford University Press.

CANTWELL, J. A. (1995). "The Globalisation of Technology: What Remains of the Product Cycle Model?" *Cambridge Journal of Economics*, 19: 155–74.

CARLOS, A., and KRUSE, J. (1996). "The Decline of the Royal African Company: Fringe Firms and the Role of the Charter". *Economic History Review*, 49: 291–313.

CARSTENSEN, F. V. (1984). *American Enterprise in Foreign Markets: Singer and International Harvester in Imperial Russia*. Chapel Hill, NC: University of North Carolina Press.

CHANDLER, A. D. (1990). *Scale and Scope*. Cambridge, Mass.: Harvard University Press.

CHEAPE, C. (1988). "Not Politicians but Sound Businessmen: Norton Company and the Third Reich". *Business History Review*, 62/3: 444–66.

CHISWICK, B. R., and HATTON, T. J. (2003). "International Migration and the Integration of Labor Models", in Bordo *et al.* (2003).

CHRISTENSEN, S. A. (2006). "Switching Relations. The Rise and Fall of the Norwegian Telecom Industry". Unpublished Ph.d., Norwegian School of Management.

COCHRAN, S. (2000). *Encountering Chinese Networks*. Berkeley: University of California Press.

COX, H. (2000). *The Global Cigarette*. Oxford: Oxford University Press.

DECKER, S. (2007). "Advertising a Brighter Tomorrow: British Companies and the Rhetoric of Development in West Africa, 1950s to 1970s". *Business History Review*, 81/2: 59–86.

DUNNING, J. H. (1983). "Changes in the Level and Structure of International Production: The Last One Hundred Years", in M. Casson (ed.), *The Growth of Global Business*. London: Allen Unwin.

DYER, D., DALZELL, F., and OLEGARIO, R. (2004). *Rising Tide: Lessons from 165 Years of Brand Building at Procter & Gamble*. Boston: Harvard Business School Press.

FERRIER, R. W. (1982). *The History of the British Petroleum Company*, vol. 1. Cambridge: Cambridge University Press.

FINDLAY, R., and O'ROURKE, K. H. (2003). "Commodity Market Integration 1500–2000", in Bordo *et al.* (2003).

FLANDREAU, M., and ZUMER, F. (2004). *The Making of Global Finance 1880–1913*. Paris: OECD.

FLEMING, G., MERRETT, D., and VILLE, S. (2004). *The Big End of Town: Big Business and Corporate Leadership in Twentieth Century Australia*. Cambridge: Cambridge University Press.

FLYNN, D. O., and GIRÁLDEZ, A. (2002). "Cycles of Silver: Global Economic Unity through the Mid-Eighteenth Century". *Journal of World History*, 13/2: 391–427.

FREYSSENET, M., MAIR, A., SHIMIZU, K., and VOLPATO, G. (eds.) (1998). *One Best Way? Trajectories and Industrial Models of the World's Automobile Producers*. Oxford: Oxford University Press.

GHEMAWAT, P. (2003). "Semiglobalization and International Business Strategy". *Journal of International Business Studies*, 34/2: 138–52.

GLIMSTEDT, H. (2001). "Between National and International Governance: Geopolitics, Strategizing Actors, and Sector Coordination in Electrical Engineering in the Interwar Era", in G. Morgan, P. H. Kristensen, and R. Whitley (eds.), *The Multinational Firm*. Oxford: Oxford University Press.

GODLEY, A. (2003). "Foreign Multinationals and Innovation in British Retailing, 1850–1962". *Business History*, 45/1: 80–100.

GUILLÉN, M. F. (2001). "Is Globalisation Civilizing, Destructive or Feeble? A Critique of Five Key Debates in the Social Science Literature". *Annual Review of Sociology*, 27: 235–60.

HANCOCK, D. (1997). *Citizens of the World*. Cambridge: Cambridge University Press.

HARLAFTIS, G. (1993). *A History of Greek-Owned Shipping*. London: Routledge.

—— and THEOTOKAS, J. (2004). "European Family Firms in International Business: British and Greek Tramp-Shipping Firms". *Business History*, 46/2: 219–55.

HARVEY, D. (1989). *The Condition of Postmodernity*. Oxford: Blackwell.

HEADRICK, D. R. (1988). *The Tentacles of Progress: Technology Transfer in the Age of Imperialism, 1850–1940*. Oxford: Oxford University Press.

HELLEINER, E. C. (1994). *States and the Re-emergence of Global Finance*. Ithaca, NY: Cornell University Press.

HILLS, J. C. (2002). *The Struggle for Control of Global Communications. The Formative Century*. Urbana, Ill.: University of Illinois Press.

HIRST, P., and THOMPSON, G. (1999). *Globalization in Question*, 2nd edn. Cambridge: Polity Press.

HOESEL, R. VAN (1999). *New Multinational Enterprises from Korea and Taiwan: Beyond Export-Led Growth*. London: Routledge.

HOUY, Y. B. (2002). " 'Of Course the German Woman Should Be Modern': The Modernization of Women's Appearance during National Socialism". Unpublished Ph.D., Cornell University.

HUANG, Y. (2003). *Selling China: Foreign Direct Investment during the Reform Era*. Cambridge: Cambridge University Press.

JAMES, H. (2001). *The End of Globalization: Lessons from the Great Depression*. Cambridge, Mass.: Harvard University Press.

JONES, G. (1988). "Foreign Multinationals and British Industry before 1945". *Economic History Review*, 41/3: 429–53.

—— (ed.) (1990*a*). *Banks as Multinationals*. London: Routledge.

—— (1990*b*). "The British Government and Foreign Multinationals before 19701", in M. Chick (ed.), *Governments, Industries and Markets*. Aldershot: Edward Elgar, 194–214.

—— (1992). "International Financial Centres in Asia, the Middle East and Australia: A Historical Perspective", in Y. Cassis (ed.), *Finance and Financiers in European History, 1880–1960*. Cambridge: Cambridge University Press.

—— (1993*a*). *British Multinational Banking 1830–1990*. Oxford: Clarendon Press.

—— (ed.) (1993*b*). *Transnational Corporations: A Historical Perspective*. London: Routledge.

—— (ed.) (1998). *The Multinational Traders*. London: Routledge.

—— (2000). *Merchants to Multinationals*. Oxford: Oxford University Press.

—— (2002). "Control, Performance and Knowledge Transfers in Large Multinationals: Unilever in the United States, 1945–1980". *Business History Review*, 76: 435–78.

—— (2003). "Multinationals", in G. Jones and F. Amatori (eds.), *Business History around the World*. Cambridge: Cambridge University Press.

—— (2005*a*). *Multinationals and Global Capitalism: From the Nineteenth to the Twenty-First Century*. Oxford: Oxford University Press.

—— (2005*b*). *Renewing Unilever: Transformation and Tradition*. Oxford: Oxford University Press.

—— (2006). "The End of Nationality? Global Firms and 'Borderless Worlds' ". *Zeitschrift für Unternehmensgeschichte*, 51/2: 149–65.

—— (2008). "Blonde and Blue-Eyed? Globalizing Beauty c1945–c1980". *Economic History Review*, 61.

—— and BOSTOCK, F. (1996). "U.S. Multinationals in British Manufacturing before 1962". *Business History Review*, 70/1: 207–56.

—— and KHANNA, T. (2006). "Bringing History (Back) into International Business". *Journal of International Business Studies*, 37/4: 453–68.

—— and MISKELL, P. (2005). "European Integration and Corporate Restructuring. The Strategy of Unilever c1957–c1990". *Economic History Review*, 58/1: 113–39.

—— —— (2007). "Acquisitions and Firm Growth: Creating Unilever's Ice Cream and Tea Business". *Business History*, 49/1: 8–28.

JONKER, J., and SLUYTERMAN, K. (2000). *At Home on the World Markets*. The Hague: Sdu Uitgevers.

KHANNA, T., and PALEPU, K. G. (2006). "Emerging Giants: Building World-Class Companies in Developing Countries". *Harvard Business Review*, 84/10: 60–9.

KIPPING, M. (1999). "American Management Consulting Companies in Western Europe, 1920–1990: Products, Reputation and Relationships". *Business History Review*, 73/2: 190–220.

KLINE, B. (1997). *Profit, Principle and Apartheid, 1948–1994*. New York: Edwin Mellen Press.

KNIGHT, G. A., and CAVUSGIL, S. T. (2004). "Innovation, Organization Capabilities, and the Born-Global Firm". *Journal of International Business Studies*, 35/2: 124–41.

KOBRAK, C., and HANSEN, P. H. (eds.) (2004). *European Business, Dictatorship and Political Risk 1920–1945*. New York: Berghahn Books.

——and WÜSTENHAGEN, J. (2006). "International Investment and Nazi Politics: The Cloaking of German Assets Abroad, 1936–1945". *Business History*, 48/3: 399–427.

KOGUT, B. (1997). "Globalization", in M. Warner (ed.), *Concise International Encyclopedia of Business and Management*. London: International Thomson Business Press.

——and ZANDER, U. (1993). "Knowledge of the Firm and the Evolutionary Theory of the Multinational Enterprise". *Journal of International Business Studies*, 24: 625–45.

KOSACOFF, B. (2002). *Going Global from Latin America: The ARCOR Case*. Buenos Aires: McGraw-Hill Interamericana.

KRISTENSEN, P. H., and ZEITLIN, J. (2005). *Local Players in Global Games: The Strategic Constitution of a Multinational Corporation*. Oxford: Oxford University Press.

KUISEL, R. F. (1993). *Seducing the French: The Dilemma of Americanization*. Berkeley, Calif.: University of California Press.

LALL, S. (1983). *The New Multinationals: The Spread of Third World Enterprises*. Chichester: John Wiley.

LIPSON, C. (1985). *Standing Guard: Protecting Foreign Capital in the Nineteenth and Twentieth Centuries*. Berkeley: University of California Press.

LOPES, T. (2002). "Brands and the Evolution of Multinationals in Alcoholic Beverages". *Business History*, 44/3: 1–30.

McDOWALL, D. (1988). *The Light: Brazilian Traction, Light and Power Company Limited, 1899–1945*. Toronto: University of Toronto Press.

MARTIN, S. M. (2003). *The UP Saga*. Copenhagen: NIAS Press.

MASON, M. (1992). *American Multinationals and Japan*. Cambridge, Mass.: Harvard University Press.

MATHEWS, J. A. (2002). *Dragon Multinationals: A New Model for Global Growth*. Oxford: Oxford University Press.

MERLO, E., and POLESE, F. (2006). "Turning Fashion into Business: The Emergence of Milan as an International Fashion Hub". *Business History Review*, 80/3: 415–47.

MEULEAU, M. (1990). *Des Pionniers en Extrême-Orient*. Paris: Fayard.

MICHIE, R. (1992). *The City of London: Continuity and Change 1850–1990*. Basingstoke: Macmillan.

MINOGLOU, I. P., and LOURI, H. (1997). "Diaspora Entrepreneurial Networks in the Black Sea and Greece, 1870–1917". *Journal of European Economic History*, 26/1: 69–104.

MOORE, K., and LEWIS, D. (1999). *Birth of the Multinational*. Copenhagen: Copenhagen Business School Press.

MORENO, J. (2003). *Yankee Don't Go Home*. Chapel Hill, NC: University of North Carolina Press.

MORGAN, E. J. (2006). "The World is Shrinking: Polaroid and South Africa". *Enterprise & Society*, 7/3: 520–49.

MOUNIER-KUHN , P. (1989). "Bull, a Worldwide Company Born in Europe". *Annals of the History of Computing*, 41: 279–98.

MUNRO, J. F. (2003). *Maritime Enterprise and Empire*. Woodbridge: Boydell.

NEAL, L. (2000). "How it all Began: The Monetary and Financial Architecture of Europe during the First Global Capital Markets, 1648–1815". *Financial History Review*, 7: 1117–40.

NEEBE, R. (1991). *Überseemärkte und Exportstrategien in der westdeutschen Wirtschaft 1945 bis 1966*. Stuttgart: Franz Steiner Verlag.

NICHOLAS, S. (1983). "Agency Contracts, Institutional Modes, and the Transition to Foreign Direct Investment by British Manufacturing Multinationals before 1939". *Journal of Economic History*, 43: 675 –86.

NICOSIA, F. R., and HUENER, J. (eds.) (2004). *Business and Industry in Nazi Germany*. New York: Berghahn Books.

NOHRIA, N., and GHOSHAL, S. (1997). *The Differentiated Network: Organizing Multinational Corporations for Value Creation*. San Francisco: Jossey-Bass.

OLSSON, U. (1993). "Securing the Markets: Swedish Multinationals in a Historical Perspective", in G. Jones and H. Schröter (eds.), *The Rise of Multinationals in Continental Europe*. Aldershot: Edward Elgar.

OONK, G. (2004). "Industralisation in India, 1850–1947: Three Variations in the Emergence of Indigenous Industrialists". Mimeo: Erasmus University Rotterdam.

O'ROURKE, K. H., and WILLIAMSON, J. G. (1999). *Globalization and History: The Evolution of a Nineteenth Century Atlantic Economy*. Cambridge, Mass.: MIT Press.

PIQUET, C. (2004). "The Suez Company's Concession in Egypt, 1854–1956: Modern Infrastructure and Local Economic Development". *Enterprise & Society*, 5/1: 107–27.

POMERANZ, K. (2002). *The Great Divergence*. Princeton, NJ: Princeton University Press.

ROBERTS, R. (ed.) (1994). *International Financial Centres*, vol. 1. Aldershot: Edward Elgar.

ROOTH, T., and SCOTT, P. (2002). "British Public Policy and Multinationals during the 'Dollar Gap' Era, 1945–1960". *Enterprise & Society*, 3/1: 124–61.

RUGMAN, A. (2000). *The End of Globalization*. London: Random House.

SASSEN, S. (2001). *The Global City*. Princeton, NJ: Princeton University Press.

SCHENK, K. (2001). *Hong Kong as an International Financial Centre: Emergence and Development 1945–65*. London: Routledge.

SCHMITZ, H. (ed.) (2004). *Local Enterprise in the Global Economy*. Cheltenham: Edward Elgar.

SCHRÖTER, H. G. (1990). "Cartels as a Form of Concentration in Industry: The Example of the International Dyestuffs Cartel from 1927 to 1939". *German Yearbook on Business History 1988*. Berlin: Springer-Verlag, 113–44.

——(1993*a*). "Swiss Multinational Enterprise in Historical Perspective", in G. Jones and H. G. Schröter (eds.), *The Rise of Multinationals in Continental Europe*. Aldershot: Edward Elgar.

——(1993*b*). *Aufstieg der Kleinen: Multinationale Unternehmen aus fünf kleinen Staaten vor 1914*. Berlin: Duncker und Humbolt.

SHAPIRO, H. (1994). *Engines of Growth: The State and Transnational Auto Companies in Brazil*. Cambridge: Cambridge University Press.

SHIBA, T., and SHIMOTANI, M. (eds.) (1997). *Beyond the Firm: Business Groups in International and Historical Perspective*. Oxford: Oxford University Press.

SULL, D., and ESCOBARI, M. (2005). *Success against the Odds*. Rio de Janeiro: Elsevier.

TAYLOR, G. D. (1994). "Negotiating Technology Transfer within Multinational Enterprises: Perspectives from Canadian History". *Business History*, 36/1: 127–58.

TIGNOR, R. L. (1998). *Capitalism and Nationalism at the End of Empire*. Princeton: Princeton University Press.

TOPIK, S., MARICHAL, C., and FRANK, Z. (eds.) (2006). *From Silver to Cocaine: Latin American Commodity Chains and the Building of the World Economy, 1500–2000*. Durham, NC: Duke University Press.

TURNER, H. A. (2005). *General Motors and the Nazis*. New Haven: Yale University Press.

WANG, P.-K. (1997). "Creation of a Regional Hub for Flexible Production". *Industry and Innovation*, 4/2: 183–205.

WILKINS, M. (1970). *The Emergence of Multinational Enterprise*. Cambridge, Mass.: Harvard University Press.

——(1974). *The Maturing of Multinational Enterprise*. Cambridge, Mass.: Harvard University Press.

——(1988). "The Free-Standing Company, 1870–1914: An Important Type of British Foreign Direct Investment". *Economic History Review*, 41/2: 259–85.

——(1989). *The History of Foreign Investment in the United States before 1914*. Cambridge, Mass.: Harvard University Press.

——(1990). "The Contributions of Foreign Enterprises to Japanese Economic Development", in T. Yuzawa and M. Udagawa (eds.), *Foreign Business in Japan before World War II*. Tokyo: University of Tokyo Press.

——(eds.) (1991). *The Growth of Multinationals*. Aldershot: Edward Elgar.

——(1994). "Comparative Hosts". *Business History*, 36/1: 18–50.

——(2001). "The History of Multinational and Enterprise", in A. M. Rugman and T. L. Brewer (eds.), *The Oxford Handbook of International Business*. Oxford: Oxford University Press.

——(2004). *The History of Foreign Investment in the United States 1914–1945*. Cambridge, Mass.: Harvard University Press.

——and F. E. HILL (1964). *American Business Abroad: Ford on Six Continents*. Detroit: Wayne State University Press.

——and SCHRÖTER, H. (eds.) (1998). *The Free Standing Company in the World Economy, 1836–1996*. Oxford: Oxford University Press.

WUBS, B. (2006). *Unilever between Reich and Empire 1939–1945*. Rotterdam: Erasmus University Ph.D.

YONEKAWA, S. (1990). *General Trading Companies: A Comparative and Historical Study*. Tokyo: United Nations University Press.

ZEITLIN, J., and HERRIGEL, G. (eds.) (2000). *Americanization and its Limits: Reworking US Technology and Management in Post-War Europe and Japan*. Oxford: Oxford University Press.

PART II

FORMS OF BUSINESS ORGANIZATION

CHAPTER 8

....

BIG BUSINESS

....

YOUSSEF CASSIS

8.1 INTRODUCTION

....

BIG business has been at the heart of business history from its very beginnings whether as a mere literary genre (hagiographic anniversary monographs have usually been devoted to large companies); or, more seriously in the last half century, as an academic discipline (early interest centered on various aspects of large enterprises, in particular the separation between ownership and control). The Chandlerian paradigm, which dominated the field in the last quarter of the twentieth century, has of course considerably reinforced this trend, with other approaches to the subject being largely marginalized. Interest in big business has not waned with the advent of the post-Chandler era and is unlikely to do so, given its crucial role in economic development; but this role has been put in proper perspective and alternative forms of business organization reappraised as part of modern societies rather than mere archaisms.

The fact remains, however, that big business encompasses most aspects of business history, as a glance at the contents of this Handbook will immediately reveal. Several central issues, such as corporate governance, management practices, multinational expansion, innovative capacity, state regulation, sources of financing—to quote but a few—are discussed in greater or lesser detail elsewhere in this volume. This chapter will thus concentrate on defining the notion of big business; on comparing the various stages and the specific context of its development, especially in the United States, the major economies of Western Europe, and Japan; and on briefly discussing the socio-political dimension of the phenomenon.

8.2 Definitions, Concepts, and Issues

The concept of "big business" is one of the most commonly used yet least clearly defined in business history. Big business is most commonly equated with large companies (Newcomer 1964; Nakagawa 1975; Turner 1984; Supple 1992; Schmitz 1993; Chandler *et al.* 1997). Though fairly simple and straightforward, this definition leaves several questions unanswered—relating in particular to what should be considered as a large company and what type of large companies should be considered as part of big business.

Large companies are usually identified on the basis of national rankings rather than actual size. Whatever the country or the period studied, big business is as a rule considered as consisting of the 50, 100, or 200 largest companies (Chandler 1962; Chandler 1977; Chandler 1990; Hannah 1983; Wardley 1991; Kocka and Siegrist 1979; Siegrist 1980; Feldenkirchen 1988; Houssiaux 1958; Kogut 1999; Smith 2006; Fruin 1992). However, the *largest* companies of a given country are not necessarily all *large* companies. One would expect that for large industrialized countries such as the United States, Britain, France, Germany, or Japan, there could be little doubt about the top 100 or at least the top 50. In fact, with the exception of the United States, and to a certain extent Britain, this was not the case during the first half of the twentieth century. Tellingly, Maurice Lévy-Leboyer did not include more than 40 companies for the year 1912 in his study of the French *grand patronat* (Lévy-Leboyer 1979), in other words a lower limit of only $6 million in terms of assets. Japan was even further off the mark as its tenth largest manufacturing company in 1913 would not have ranked among the top 25 in France. In Germany, the assets of the company ranked 101 in 1913, Daimler Motoren, did not reach $6 million, with just over 3,000 workers—a typical *Mittlestand* company. In many respects, big business could be seen primarily as an American phenomenon. In both 1913 and 1929, respectively 17 and 16 German industrial enterprises would have ranked among the United States top 200 measured by total assets (Chandler 1990, appendices A1, A2, C1, and C2), an enormous difference, even if measuring size by total assets probably favors American firms. In terms of market capitalization, 54 of the 100 largest firms in 1912 (and eight of the top ten) were American, as against 15 for the UK, 14 for Germany and six for France (Hannah 1999).

Three questions must be answered before attempting a more precise understanding of the concept of big business. First, should the notion be defined in absolute or in relative terms, and in the latter case, should it be contingent on period, country size, or other factors? Second, should only large *industrial* enterprises be considered as making up the world of big business or should firms from the primary and tertiary sectors also be included? And third, should the frontiers of big business be limited to the unit of the firm or should other forms of organization be taken into account?

Defining big business in absolute terms requires a yardstick with which to measure its level of development. A convenient one is provided by international league tables—the 500 or, better, the 1,000 world's largest companies. However, such lists have only been readily available in the last 30 years or so. Those painstakingly established for earlier periods, especially before 1945 (Schmitz 1993; Hannah 1999) only include the top 50 or top 100 and are thus limited to giant firms, a much narrower concept than that of big business. The choice of another yardstick is inevitably somewhat arbitrary, as regards both the measure of a company's size (using share capital, total assets, turnover, market capitalization, or workforce will produce similar though by no means identical results) and the minimum size required to qualify for big business status.

A few implicit and explicit yardsticks have been put forward to identify large firms. In the *Visible Hand* (Chandler 1977), Alfred Chandler provides a list of American industrial enterprises—280 in total—with assets of $20 million or more, a reasonable lower limit though still too high to include more than a handful of French and Japanese firms, in the latter case *zaibatsu*. From another standpoint, 1,000 employees has been proposed as a possible benchmark for pre-1914 years (Kocka and Horn 1979), a respectable size at the time though more characteristic of the upper reaches of medium-sized enterprises, typical as it were of the French textile industry where 44 firms employed more than 1,000 people in 1906 (Caron 1981). Combining financial and physical measures, I have suggested a yardstick of 10,000 employees and/or a share capital of £2 million before 1914, £3 million in the late 1920s and £5 million in the mid-1950s in a comparison among big business in Britain, France, and Germany (Cassis 1997). Such an approach enables a comparison in both space (in order to assess the respective weight of big business in each of the major European economies) and time (the number of firms in the three countries employing 10,000 people or more increasing from about 50 in 1907 to 325 in 1972).

Big business must thus be defined in absolute terms in order to clearly circumscribe the object of study and make international comparisons meaningful. At the same time, its relative significance should not be entirely disregarded, especially at a national level. Whatever the lack of large firms compared with the United States, the perception of big business by contemporaries has always been strong in European countries, as witnessed by the impact of such groups as the *dynasties bourgeoises* (Beau de Loménie 1977) or the *deux cents familles* (Jeanneney 1984; Sédillot 1988) on French collective imagination or the ongoing debate over *Finanzkapital* in Germany (Hilferding 1981). This is also true of big business in countries with an even smaller proportion of large firms, such as Italy (Amatori 1997), Spain (Carreras 1997), or Australia (Fleming *et al.* 2004), to name but a few of those which it has not been possible to include in this study.

The more so as big business should not be reduced to manufacturing industry. In the Chandlerian perspective, the "modern business enterprise"—synonymous with big business—is a large, diversified, and integrated *industrial* firm, even though its forerunners were the railroad companies. Yet big business is a wider concept. On the one hand, it includes firms from both the tertiary (in particular banking, insurance, and public utility companies) and the primary (especially extractive industries) sectors. On the other hand, it includes large-scale operations undertaken through vehicles other than integrated firms—various types of loosely or tightly knit, ad hoc or permanent business groups (including holding companies, *zaibatsu*, financial syndicates, cartels, and others) as well as independent financiers. In that respect, size, including the scale of financial transactions in certain undertakings, rather than organizational forms (level of integration and diversification, separation of ownership and control, managerial hierarchies) should be seen as the key element in defining big business, even though the latter have been its dominant characteristics.

The main issues and debates regarding big business have mainly centered on large-scale companies and, given the dominance of the Chandlerian paradigm over an entire generation of business historians, on large-scale industrial companies. The principal questions have concerned their origins and the factors that have caused their emergence, their organizational structure, the sectors in which they have held a dominant position, and the countries where they have been most successful. While there has been a relative consensus around the answers provided to these questions, more controversies have surrounded discussions related to the singularity or universality of the Chandlerian model and, at a more general level, to the various aspects of their contribution to economic development.

8.3 BIG BUSINESS AND THE FIRST INDUSTRIAL REVOLUTION

Although big business is primarily a 20th century—and probably also a 21st century—phenomenon, it was not absent from the 19th century economic landscape or, more precisely, in the age of the first industrial revolution, from the 1830s to the 1880s. Significantly, this was probably more the case in Europe, primarily Great Britain, than the United States, but data on large companies remain scarce for this early period.

Large firms, employing 5,000 workers or more, were still uncommon in manufacturing industry. There is no systematic listing of companies of such size whether at national or international level, for say 1850 or 1870. However, anecdotal evidence suggests that, while being the exception rather than the rule, a not insignificant group of large firms towered over the rest. By 1870, this was the case of the Dowlais Iron Company, Bolckow Vaughan, Bell Brothers, or the Consett Iron Co. in Britain;

Schneider, de Wendel, and Saint-Gobain in France; and Krupp in Germany. With the exception of Saint-Gobain, a chemical and glass concern, they were, not surprisingly, all engaged in the coal, iron, and steel industries.

The new joint stock banks, which emerged in the 1830s in Britain and in the 1850s in France and Germany, soon established themselves as big businesses, at any rate the largest among them. The National Provincial Bank of England, for example, established in 1833, had a paid-up capital of £1 million in 1865 and 122 branches throughout England and Wales. In France, the Crédit Mobilier was founded by the brothers Émile and Isaac Pereire in 1852 with a share capital of 60 million francs (£2.4 million) and the ambition to promote industrial growth in France and Continental Europe, but it collapsed in 1863 (Autin 1984). The Banque de Paris et des Pays-Bas, an investment bank, was founded in 1872 with a capital of 125 millions francs (£5 million), half of which was paid-up. Moreover, the leading private banks, all in family ownership and management, were among Europe's largest companies until the 1870s. Baring Brothers & Co., the London merchant bank, had a capital of £1 million in 1854 and £2.5 million in 1872 (Ziegler 1988). And the combined capital of the five Rothschild houses (London, Paris, Frankfurt, Vienna, and Naples), which then formed an integrated multinational group, reached the colossal amount of £22 million, making it Europe's and probably the world's largest firm (Ferguson 1998).

Nevertheless, big business in the third quarter of the 19th century primarily meant the railroad companies. The first rail link, between Stockton and Darlington, in the north of England, was completed in 1825 and several others followed in the 1830s, but the real railroad boom dates from the 1840s. In England, the average annual amount of investment increased from some £6 million in the late 1830s to more than £25 million during the fever of the mid-1840s and remained at this level throughout the boom of the 1860s; in 1875, the British rail network was more than 70 percent complete, having required, over 50 years, capital to the tune of £630 million. In France, where the first speculative fever gripped the public in the mid-1840s, the railroads' accrued expenditure went from a little over a billion francs in 1852 to more than seven billion in 1869. In Germany, net investment increased steadily during the third quarter of the 19th century, going from an annual average of 88 million marks at the beginning of the 1850s to a little over 500 million at the end of the 1870s. In the United States, the railroad network grew from 3,300 miles in 1840 to 30,600 in 1860; by this date, more than $1.2 billion had been invested in the railroads (Gourvish 1980; Ribeill 1993; Fremdling 1977).

Investment on such a large scale gave rise to the first real giant firms of the industrial age, whose organizational structure prefigured that of modern business enterprises. In Britain, 19 railroad companies had capital in excess of £3 million, at a time when only a handful of industrial companies had capital of more than £500,000 (Gourvish 1980). France's five largest businesses in 1881 were all railroad companies, the capital of the leading firm (Paris-Lyon-Méditerranée) reaching

400 million francs (£16 million). Employment also reached huge proportions: in 1891, the Pennsylvania Railroad employed more than 110,000 workers, probably more than any other company, public or private, in the world (Chandler 1977).

The railroad companies were thus the first firms to face the challenges posed by the sheer size of big businesses, in terms of costs, investment, depreciation, internal organization, and the coordination of complex operations. Meeting these challenges required setting up a hierarchy of professional managers in charge of the company's various tasks. Joint stock banks and insurance companies were also increasingly run by salaried managers at the time, though to a lesser degree and with fewer layers than in railroads whose operations were technologically more complex, especially with regard to the coordination of traffic flows. A division between line and staff system of administration was designed for that purpose, with the former being responsible for the movement of trains and the latter for the other functions, such as the movement of freight and passengers, maintenance and finance. As Alfred Chandler put it, "the railroad was...in every way the pioneer of modern business administration" (Chandler 1977), an observation that applies not only to the United States, but also to Europe, above all Britain and France.

8.4 Big Business and the Onset of the Second Industrial Revolution (1880–1914)

The railroad companies remained the world's largest well into the twentieth century. However, by the late nineteenth century, they had become increasingly regulated and assimilated into public services, if they had not been nationalized, as happened in Germany on Bismarck's initiative during the 1880s. In terms of entrepreneurial activity, they tended to be on the fringes of big business, which came to be epitomized by the large firms in the new industries of the second industrial revolution—steel, chemicals, electricity, oil, motor cars, rubber, but also machinery and consumer durables in food, drink, and tobacco.

Large firms came to dominate these industries because of the economies of scale or scope made possible by significant advances in production techniques, in particular continuous-process production and the assembly of interchangeable parts. Continuous production was used from the 1860s in the refining and distilling industries: oil, sugar, beer, whisky, and other drinks. It also came to be used in the transformation of agricultural products into consumer durables (flour, cereals, cigarettes), in the chemical industry (sulphuric acids, matches, dye products, photographic films), and in the metallurgical industries, with the mass production of steel and the integration in a single plant of blast furnaces for the production of iron, of Bessemer converters for the production of steel in large batches, and of rolling mills for the fabrication of rails, girders, and other semi-finished products. The cost reduction induced by mass production was spectacular: from 270 marks per kilo in 1869 to 9 marks in 1886 for a new synthetic dye in the German chemical industry; or by 80 percent for cigarettes made with the machine invented by James Bonsack in 1880, whose patent was acquired by Duke in the United States and W. D. and H. D. Wills in Britain—the respective leading players in American Tobacco and Imperial Tobacco.

The assembly of interchangeable parts was more characteristic of the machine industry, including electrical engineering, and the fabrication of metallurgical products. Here, the cost advantages arose from the possibility of making a number of products in the same plant, using the same raw and semi-finished materials and often the same tools, especially lathes and milling machines, which appeared in the United States in the 1860s. But it also applied to the chemical industry where around 1900 the three leading German firms (BASF, Bayer, and Hoechst) could manufacture dye products in hundreds of different colors, or the same color applied to a different material, such as cotton, wool, silk, or leather.

Achieving such economies of scale and of scope was thus the first factor leading to the emergence of large-scale enterprises in the new industries of the second industrial revolution. However, other concomitant factors were also at work, especially the need for backwards and forwards integration. With their increasingly high fixed costs and level of throughput, firms had to ensure their supply of raw materials and outlets for their products. Backwards integration was more characteristic of European enterprises, particularly in German heavy industry, with the leading iron and steel producers (Krupp, Deutsch-Luxemburg, Phoenix, Thyssen, and others) acquiring collieries (Fear 2005). Conversely, forwards integration, especially in distribution, was a strategy more commonly pursued by American companies. Those engaged in consumer products had at first to compensate for the lack of established distribution networks in the country in the 1880s, while the machinery industry required a more specialized sales force. In addition, backwards or forwards integration, when undertaken, appeared more cost-effective than relying on market mechanisms.

Businesses assumed large, sometimes very large proportions through internal and/or external growth, the combination of the two being the most common occurrence. While a number of firms considerably extended their productive capacities and, especially in the United States, set up their own distributing and/or purchasing capabilities, very large enterprises were more often than not the result of wide horizontal mergers between firms which in some cases were already vertically integrated. In both the United States and the United Kingdom, a wave of mergers took place in the last years of the nineteenth century and the first years of the twentieth century: more than 1,800 companies disappeared in mergers in the US between 1895 and 1904, and more than 650 in the UK between 1898 and 1900, from which emerged several of the two countries' largest companies, including United States Steel, the world's largest company, formed in 1901, I. E. du Pont de Nemours (DuPont), International Harvester, or Eastman Kodak in the US and Imperial Tobacco, or the Fine Cotton Spinners' and Doublers' Association in the UK (Lamoreaux 1985; Hannah 1976). These waves of mergers consolidated into single companies various business combinations already existing between firms, which were aimed at curbing price competition, but whose implementation left much to be desired. In the United States, they were often the result of a quest for market power (Lamoreaux 1985; Roy 1997) and in part triggered by the Sherman Antitrust Act of 1890, which banned combinations but allowed full mergers. In Germany, the takeovers of collieries by iron and steel manufacturers were clearly motivated by the fact that the quotas imposed by the powerful coal cartel did not apply to production and sales within a single firm.

As a result, the large enterprise of the turn of the 20th century, often dubbed the "Chandlerian firm", appears as a centralized and vertically integrated firm, with its own distribution and purchasing facilities, whose various functions, including marketing, were entrusted to a hierarchy of salaried managers, and which tended to cluster around sectors where economies of scale and of scope could be achieved through mass production, especially food (including drink and tobacco), chemicals, oil, rubber, metals, and machinery (including electrical engineering).

However, the reality of big business at the time was more varied than suggested by this "ideal-type". In the first place, there were sharp differences between countries. Not surprisingly, American big business came closest to this model of development, with fully fledged "Chandlerian" companies dominating all sectors of the second industrial revolution—Armour, Swift, American Tobacco, DuPont, Standard Oil (and its successor companies after its dismemberment in 1911), US Rubber, Goodrich, US Steel, Bethlehem Steel, American Can, International Harvester, Singer, General Electric, Westinghouse, to name but the leading enterprises in each of the relevant sectors. In the other major economies, even though the distribution per sector of the 200 largest companies was more or less the same as in the United States (Chandler *et al.* 1997), few companies came close to their American counterparts whether in terms of size or internal organization.

Everywhere, large enterprises emerged in the iron and steel industries, with a particularly high degree of vertical integration in Germany, less so in Britain and France. Otherwise, only in Britain was big business present in all industrial sectors, whether in consumer (especially textiles as well as food, drink, and tobacco) or capital goods, though somewhat timidly in chemical and electric engineering. Hardly any large firm in the consumer industries emerged in France or Germany before the First World War. Mechanical engineering, one of strong points of German industry, was the home of medium-sized firms (Humboldt, Deutz, Demag, and others), with only the largest, MAN, having assets in excess of $20 million in 1913. In addition to iron and steel, German large manufacturing companies were only to be found in chemicals and, especially, electrical engineering, with AEG and Siemens towering above the rest in Europe.

On the other hand, European big business was not confined to manufacturing industry. By the early twentieth century, British, French, and German banks had become giant firms, in contrast to American banks whose expansion was limited as they were legally banned from establishing branches in another state. In 1913, the largest American bank, the National City Bank, of New York, ranked only 13th in the world with total assets ($276 million) about half those of the then number one, the Crédit Lyonnais, of France (Cassis 2006). In Germany, 40 of the 100 largest companies in 1907, measured by share capital, were banks, including four of the top five (Deutsche Bank, Dresdner Bank, Disconto-Gesellschaft, and Darmstädter Bank). Moreover, as a result of their long-term relationships with the major industrial concerns, reinforced by their massive representation on their supervisory boards, the German universal banks held a commanding position within the German economy.

The same was true of the leading American investment banks (J. P. Morgan, Kuhn Loeb, and several others) which, despite a comparatively modest size, were at the very heart of American big business, due to their financing of the railroads and then the large industrial companies, and playing a crucial role in the merger wave at the turn of the century. Their main task was to supply these firms with capital, usually through public issues, but they built lasting links with them, served as their financial adviser, and were usually represented on their board of directors. So much so that a commission was appointed in 1912 to investigate the existence of a "money trust", the substantial involvement of bankers on the boards of directors of manufacturing companies, and the concentration of issues in the hands of a few investment banks, cumulatively giving the impression that Wall Street was controlling the country's business (Carosso 1970).

British merchant banks (N. M. Rothschild, Baring Brothers, Morgan Grenfell, Schroeder, Kleinwort), for their part, were at the heart of international big business, even though they were dwarfed in size by the clearing banks. They succeeded in keeping supreme control over the issuing of foreign loans—on behalf of governments and large corporations—in the City of London, the world's financial center in the age of the first globalization. Big business in the City was different from its traditional embodiment in a large or giant firm, with huge financial transactions being undertaken by medium-sized enterprises organized as partnerships or even by individual financiers. While merchant banks were primarily engaged in the accepting and issuing businesses, merchant houses diversified into non-trading activities, organizing and financing the commercial, financial, and manufacturing operations carried out abroad and in the Empire by their subsidiaries and parent companies and forming in the process investment groups of truly big business dimensions, the capital of the largest among them (James Finlay, John Swire, Balfour Williamson, Ralli Brothers, and others) being in excess of $20 million before 1914 (Chapman 1992; Jones 2000).

The separation between ownership and control, one of the main characteristics of modern big business, proceeded at an uneven pace. It has long been assumed that, in the United States, entrepreneurial firms, whose owners entrusted salaried managers with the day to day running of the firm while retaining overall strategic control, increasingly gave way to managerial firms where, from the early 20th century, salaried managers had become the dominant force on the boards of directors. Recent research, however, suggests that family ownership and control remained very strong in the largest American companies, with 57 of the 100 largest not even publishing their balance sheet in 1899 (Hannah 2006). This was also the case in Europe (Cassis 1997; Colli 2003), including several of the largest and best performing companies, such as Krupp and Siemens in Germany, Schneider and de Wendel in France, Vickers and Barclays Bank in Britain, to give but a few examples. Differences between countries were more a matter of nuance: interestingly, the lowest percentage of inheritors among the chairmen and chief executives of the leading British, French, and German companies in 1907 was in France (17 percent).

8.5 THE MATURING OF BIG BUSINESS (1914–1960)

With the growth of the industries of the second industrial revolution from the First World War to the early 1960s, big business took on a new dimension—in terms of size, forms of organization, and share of national and international business activities. This was the classical age of managerial capitalism, of the integrated "Chandlerian" firm, despite the persistence of other forms of business organization.

The First World War, a total war fought between industrialized countries, gave a strong impetus to the new industries—steel, motor cars, oil, rubber, chemicals (especially explosives), and machinery. In all these sectors, firms grew significantly larger, as a result of internal growth or through mergers, during the 1920s, especially in the motor industry. Measured by assets, the number of American manufacturing companies worth $50 million or more increased by 50 percent (in real terms) between 1917 and 1930—from 84 to 128 (Chandler 1990, appendices A1 and A2). Measured by size of workforce, the number of British companies employing 10,000 people or more increased from 17 in 1907 to 39 in 1929 (Cassis 1997). The largest companies also grew larger: at Siemens, for example, the German giant electrical engineering concern, the workforce grew from 81,795 in 1913 to 138,069 in 1929 (Feldenkirchen 1995). Business concentration likewise intensified, the share of the 100 largest enterprises in manufacturing net output rising from 17 to 26 percent in Britain, 17 to 20 percent in Germany, and 22 to 25 percent in the United States between 1918 and 1929. The Depression put a halt to the growth of big business, though the Second World War boosted the high-tech industries, in particular aerospace and electronics. However, before the 1960s, the forward march of big business was slower than in the 1920s, and in any case proceeded at a different rhythm and in different ways in each of the major countries.

The United States remained in every respect the country of big business, with large firms already established in all sectors before 1914. Moreover, most giant firms were American—34 of the world's 52 largest companies (measured by market capitalization) in 1939 (Schmitz 1993). In the 1920s, the most spectacular growth was in the motor industry, which became, in Alfred Chandler's words, "almost overnight...the largest in the nation" (Chandler 1990). In 1929, 4.6 million cars were produced in the United States, over 20 times more than in France or Britain. Ford Motor Company, the first manufacturer to introduce the assembly line in 1914, took an early lead before being overtaken by General Motors in the late 1920s, the latter better adapting its production and marketing to a changing, more mature demand. General Motors became the country's third largest company by total assets in 1930, up from 29th 13 years earlier, its assets having increased eightfold, in real terms, during this period to reach $1,300 million. Elsewhere, it was a matter of consolidation, with large firms expanding in the capital-intensive industries, especially in those related to the motor industry, in the first place oil, but also rubber, as well as in food, electrical equipment (with General Electric establishing a worldwide dominant position), and chemicals, which really took off in the United States after the First World War.

The structure of German big business remained fairly stable given the political upheavals experienced by the country, with the heavy industries, chemicals, and electrical engineering remaining its backbone. Even though all three industries were weakened as a result of Germany's defeat in the First World War (loss of territory, confiscation of assets abroad), wide-ranging national mergers gave rise to giant firms, with no equivalent elsewhere in Europe: IG Farben (formed in 1925) in chemicals and Vereinigte Stahlwerke (1926) in primary metals. Both had assets in excess of $500 million and employed well over 100,000 people in 1929, though the former held a stronger position within the German chemical industry than the latter within the iron and steel industry, as a few big names, above all Krupp, remained outside the combine. Both the Vereinigte Stahlwerke and IG Farben were dismantled by the Allies after the war, leaving in their wake, in broad outline, the firms which had merged in the mid-1920s, in particular Thyssen in metals and the "big three" (BASF, Bayer, and Hoechst) in chemicals. Fewer institutional changes took place in electrical engineering with the two leading firms (Siemens and AEG) remaining ahead of their European competitors. In motor cars, by contrast, Germany lagged behind Britain and France, while big business remained a rarity in other industrial sectors.

In Britain, on the other hand, the new industries came increasingly to dominate the world of big business, with large firms emerging in chemicals, in particular with the creation of Imperial Chemical Industries (ICI) in 1926, but also with the Anglo-Dutch concern Unilever, formed in 1929, both among Europe's largest companies; in electrical engineering, with several firms, especially General Electric Company (GEC) and Associated Electrical Industries (AEI), reaching big business status; in motor cars, with Austin and Morris (which merged in 1952), as well as Ford, the subsidiary of the American company; and in rubber, with Dunlop. In oil, British firms consolidated the lead they had established in Europe before the First World War, with its two world players: Shell (and its parent company Royal Dutch) and Anglo-Persian Oil (renamed Anglo-Iranian Oil in 1935 and British Petroleum in 1954); and they retained their lead in the consumer industries, especially in food, drink, and tobacco—Imperial Tobacco was the world's second largest firm by market capitalization, behind General Motors, in 1939 (Schmitz 1993). In the 1930s and 1940s, large firms also developed in pharmaceuticals (Boots, Beecham) and aerospace (De Haviland, Hawker Siddeley), making Britain the European country where big business reached its highest level of development.

French big business followed the British example in the new industries, but from a distance. Its main strength lay in motor cars (with Citroën, probably Europe's leading car manufacturer until its collapse in 1935, Renault, and Peugeot), where it maintained its lead throughout the 1920s before falling behind Britain and then Germany, as well as in rubber with Michelin. A certain amount of catching up took place in electrical engineering (CGE, Thompson), chemicals (Kuhlmann, Saint-Gobain, Pechiney, and increasingly from the 1930s Rhône-Poulenc), and oil, with the Compagnie Française des Pétroles. However, big business remained mainly concentrated in the heavy industries, (with no significant mergers in the 1920s, but major consolidations after the Second World War, with the formation of Usinor in 1946 and Sidelor in 1950) and hardly made any inroads into the consumer industries. Though weakened by the Depression and German occupation, French big business grew closer to its British and German counterparts, especially the latter, during this period.

In both Britain and France, the main characteristic of the post-Second World War years was, however, the extent of direct state intervention through the nationalization of a significant chunk of big business. The move was essentially political, with the Labour Party coming to power in 1945 in Britain, and a more general consensus over state control in France, reinforced by the weight of the Communist Party and more generally the Resistance in French politics. In 1945 and 1946, in both countries, coal mining, electricity, gas, air transport, railroad companies (nationalized in France in 1936), and the central bank were transferred to state ownership, in addition to the iron and steel industry in Britain, and the main commercial banks and insurance companies, as well as the car manufacturer Renault, in France (Prost 1986). Privatization would proceed at a very uneven pace, including new nationalizations, during the following 50 years.

The development of Japanese big business followed a different path. In terms of size, the largest industrial companies grew closer to their German and French counterparts, with 14 of them employing 10,000 people or more in 1930 and 25 in 1954 (Fruin 1992)—the figures were respectively 27 and 26 in Germany and 22 and 20 in France (Cassis 1997). In terms of sectors, however, the new industries were far less prominent among the country's largest firms where textiles and food (with shipbuilding) dominated in the 1930s and steel (with textiles and electrical engineering) in the 1950s.

As businesses grew larger, the way they were run had to change, though in varying degrees, in order to adapt to increasingly complex operations—whether technical, financial, logistical, or organizational. Big business became more professional during this period. While managerial control had established itself in large American companies by the 1920s, family ownership (with extensive delegation of power to salaried managers) persisted in Europe, before sharply declining after the Second World War. The level of education also improved, with a particularly high proportion (over 70 percent) of university degrees in France and Germany, though hardly any connected to business studies (Cassis 1997). The power of salaried managers also strengthened considerably in Japan's largest corporations, with managerial control becoming established after World War II (Morikawa 1989).

New organizational structures also emerged as a response to large firms' strategy of diversification into new products, which posed serious problems to the managerial hierarchies set up to deal with the multiple tasks linked with the production and distribution of single products. The solution was found in the multidivisional structure, often known as the M-form, whose emergence and subsequent diffusion has been analyzed in masterly fashion by Alfred Chandler (Chandler 1962, 1990). This new structure, which appeared in the United States in the 1920s in such firms as General Motors or DuPont, was decentralized and consisted of autonomous divisions, each of them corresponding to the firm's main product lines and responsible for the various functions previously found in the multifunctional structure. This new organizational structure enabled top managers to concentrate on the firm's global strategy and the allocation of resources to the various divisions, leaving to general managers the task of running each division. However, practice did not always entirely conform to theory, even at General Motors, one of the originators of the model—it was introduced in order to perpetuate owners' control and operating executives were frequently integrated into strategic planning (Freeland 2001).

The multidivisional structure spread slowly but steadily among the world's largest firms: in 1932, it had only been adopted by eight American, five British, and three French companies. By 1960, this was case for 43 percent of the 100 companies in the United States, 30 percent in Britain, and 21 percent in France, as well as 15 percent in Germany and 29 percent in Japan (Hannah 1999). It was to grow much further. In the meantime, other organizational structures continued to exist or to co-exist with others. In France, for example, holding companies controlling dense networks of crossed ownerships and interlocking directorships proved a flexible structure facilitating cooperation, financing, and technological transfers while saving managerial resources (Lévy-Leboyer 1980). In Japan, the *zaibatsu* were a common, though not unique, form of organization before the Second World War, consisting of diversified business groups, owned and controlled by a single family (Mitsui, Sumitomo, Mitsubishi, and Yasuda being the most prominent among them). They were dissolved by the Americans after the war, but soon came together again in the form of enterprise groups, through meetings of former salaried executives and companies formerly belonging to a *zaibatsu* buying each other's shares (Morikawa 1997).

Manufacturing industry rather than finance and services came to embody big business during this period, as a result of the extraordinary growth of the new industries on the one hand, and the increasingly regulated context within which financial institutions had to operate from the 1930s onwards on the other. Yet the big banks remained an essential part of the world of big business, even in the countries where their position was weakened, such as France, where they lost their position as the country's largest companies after the First World War and were driven to the fringes of big business after their nationalization in 1946; or Germany, where they suffered from the hyperinflation of 1923, the financial crisis of 1931, their marginalization under the Nazi regime, and their dismantling by the Allies after 1945 (though they had been reconstituted by 1956)—yet without losing their key role in the country's "cooperative" type of capitalism.

In Britain, by contrast, the "big five" (Barclays, Lloyds, Midland, National Provincial, and Westminster) which emerged from the 1918 merger wave ranked among the country's top companies (Wardley 1991) and remained the world's largest banks for nearly four decades. Admittedly, the City's international activities were gradually weakened by two world wars and the world's economic depression, yet the persistence of the British Empire and the sterling area enabled the networks of merchants, bankers, and financiers to pursue their large-scale operations (Jones 1993, 2000; Cassis 2006). The same was true of American banks, especially in the 1920s, when New York was vying with London for world financial supremacy, with both investment banks (this was J. P. Morgan & Co.'s apogee) and commercial banks (above all the National City Bank) very much involved in big business operations, whether at national or international level. The Wall Street Crash of 1929, the banking crisis of the 1930s, and the regulations of the New Deal (which among other things enacted the separation between commercial and investment banking) were of course a setback. Yet by the mid-1950s, the country's three leading commercial banks (Bank of America, First National City Bank, and Chase Manhattan Bank) had supplanted their British counterparts as the world's largest banks, despite regulations prohibiting them from opening branches in another state, and were set to expand abroad with the gradual resumption of international capital flows.

8.6 NEW CHALLENGES (1960–1990)

The industries of the second industrial revolution reached full maturity during the 30 years following the Second World War with, as a corollary, a further development of large "Chandlerian" firms. Big business grew in size and number. In the three largest European economies (Britain, France, and Germany), for example, the number of companies employing 10,000 people nearly trebled—from 111 to 325—between 1953 and 1972, of which 22 employed 100,000 people or more (Cassis 1997). While remaining broadly concentrated in the same sectors as in the early 20th century, a higher proportion of large firms were to be found, with national variations, in electrical equipment, chemicals, oil, and motor cars than in iron and steel, food, and mechanical engineering. As in earlier periods, American firms were the largest, by a significant margin: in 1972, the 300 largest US industrial companies all had a turnover of $400 million or more, a size reached by 60 companies in Britain, 38 in Germany, and 29 in France. The world's largest companies were all American. Measured by turnover, General Motors was way ahead, with about $30 billion, followed by Exxon and Ford, with about $20 billion. Only the two Anglo-Dutch concerns Royal Dutch Shell, in fourth position (with $14 billion) and Unilever, in ninth, made it to the top ten alongside General Electric, Chrysler, IBM, Mobil Oil, Texaco, and ITT (*Fortune*, Sept. 1973).

The gap between American and European companies was particularly strongly felt on the Old Continent in the 1960s, as witnessed by the instant success of *The American Challenge*, a book published in 1967 by the French journalist and politician Jean-Jacques Servan-Schreiber, and the following year in English translation. Servan-Schreiber was not only concerned by the extent of American foreign direct investment in Europe or even the much larger size and higher profitability of US companies, but by their dynamism and their superior organizational capabilities (Servan-Schreiber, 1968). And yet Europe was catching up with America, not only in terms of levels of incomes and productivity (Crafts and Toniolo 1996), but also in terms of business organization. In particular, the multidivisional structure was spreading fast among the largest European firms to reach 58 percent in France and Germany and 80 percent in Britain in 1980, as against 81 percent in the United States (Dyas and Thanheiser 1976; Rumelt 1974; Channon 1973). However, the adoption of the M-form and American style of managerial capitalism was no guarantee of success, as can be seen from the mediocre performance of British industry in the 1970s (Jones 1997), where diversification and multi-division appear to have been associated with ineffective governance and poor monitoring (Toms and Wright 2002). For individual firms, including giant multinationals, the tension between the benefits of local knowledge and the disadvantages of excessive decentralization could lead to poor performance, as witnessed by Unilever during this period (Jones 2005).

The "Japanese challenge", which marked the later part of the period, was both a competitive threat to the established positions of American and European firms, in particular in electronics and motor cars, and a new way of coordinating business activities. The growth of Japanese big business was spectacular in the 1960s and 1970s. By 1973, 79 of the 300 largest non-American industrial companies, measured by sales, were Japanese, as against 61 British, 43 German, and 31 French. This could be seen as a reflection of the tremendous growth of the Japanese economy during the three decades following the Second World War. And yet this was only part of the story. In other respects, Japanese industrial companies were smaller than their Western counterparts—for example if measured by workforce. Of the 401 companies employing 20,000 or more in 1973, 211 were American, 50 were British, 29 German, 28 Japanese, and 24 French. The difference was particularly striking in the motor industry: in 1989, Toyota's employment (65,000) was more than ten times less than that of General Motors (750,000), even though it produced more than half as many vehicles (4.5 million as against 7.9 million) (Fruin 1992). Toyota's employment was also substantially smaller than that of all the major Euopean manufacturers.

Such differences reflected the specific organization of Japanese big business, where networks of relationships between companies prevailed over internalization and vertical integration. Japanese companies were less diversified than their Western counterparts, not only American, but also European. They tended to concentrate on core technologies and to entrust the more peripheral ones to outside companies belonging to the enterprise group, the *keiretsu*, organized around a leading company—such as Toyota, Nissan, Honda, Toshiba, Sony, Hitachi, to name but a few. Cross-shareholding linked these companies and a hierarchy existed within the group, depending on the degree of closeness to the parent company. In the motor industry, for example, where a company like Toyota dealt with some 10,000 suppliers, there were several tiers of parts manufacturers: the first directly supplied the car manufacturer, a second tier supplied the first, and so on. (Morikawa 1997). As a result, most Japanese companies remained organized in a functional rather than in a divisional structure; and when adopted, the M-form was only partly implemented, with decisions related to financial matters, personnel, and long-term planning being as a rule outside the scope of the divisions (Fruin 1992).

With the successes of Japan's manufacturing industry in the 1970s and 1980s, this system not only aroused interest and admiration, but was seen by some as a new model of business organization—in particular as far as quality control and innovative capacity were concerned. Yet just as Japanese big business was starting its meteoric rise, the strategy of American large firms was moving in the opposite direction—into far more pronounced diversification. The product range of the 148 companies, out of the 200 largest in 1950, that survived until 1975 increased from an average of 5.22 per company in 1950 to 9.74 in 1975 (O'Sullivan 2000). This strategy was mainly achieved through mergers and acquisitions, whose number rose to 1,951 between 1963 and 1967 and to 3,736 between 1968 and 1972, leading to the widespread forming of conglomerates, largely dominated by a financial strategy of control (Fligstein 1990). Conglomerates were characterized by their diversification into activities that were completely unrelated to each other, with the underlying idea being that such diversification would shield them from the economic ups and downs in a particular sector and thus increase their profitability. Further profit came from selling some of the conglomerate's constituent parts (Baskin and Miranti 1997). In this way, International Telegraph and Telephone (ITT), probably the best known among them, acquired 163 companies in the 1950s and 1960s, becoming the ninth largest American company in 1973, with a turnover of $8.6 billion.

The performance of conglomerates proved disappointing, opening up the way to the wave of mergers and acquisitions which took place in the 1980s. The conviction that the interests of shareholders were not always well served by their salaried managers had become widespread in the United States by the late 1970s. From this viewpoint, a takeover bid, if necessary unfriendly and addressed directly to shareholders, seemed to be the best penalty for poor management and the threat of such an action the best way of compelling management to remain vigilant. A wave of buying and selling businesses and of mergers and de-mergers followed. The latter were often friendly and guided by real strategies aimed, for example, at refocusing a firm's activities on its most profitable trade. At other times, they were hostile and undertaken with the sole aim of taking advantage of out-and-out dealing in companies, notably by using their assets for the benefit of the operation's promoters and shareholders. While hostile takeover bids were few in number, in value they represented nearly a quarter of the total and were by far the most spectacular. It was the era of the great Wall Street raiders, amongst whom were Carl Icahn, Thomas Boone Pickens, and the firm Kohlberg, Kravis, Roberts. They henceforth took on very large enterprises—RJR Nabisco was purchased for $25 billion in 1985—and their acquisitions were financed to a great extent through leveraged buyouts (Baskin and Miranti 1997; O'Sullivan 2000).

The merger and acquisition trend spread to Britain, thus giving rise to the term "Anglo-Saxon capitalism", meaning dominated by market forces. The raiders were also present in London, an extreme example being Lord Hanson, who in 1986 acquired the Imperial Group, one of the ten largest British companies, and in 1989 Consolidated Goldfields, one of the largest mining groups in the world, taking his conglomerate, Hanson Trust, into the top ten British companies before being thwarted in 1991 in the face of his ultimate prey, the chemical giant ICI (Brummer and Cowe 1994). But it was the Thatcher government's privatizations which altered the face of British big business, with public utility companies, in the first place British Telecom (BT) emerging among the country's largest firms by market capitalization—a measure which would prevail in the financially oriented 1990s.

On both sides of the Atlantic, these operations were orchestrated by the main investment banks, which re-emerged at the heart of big business in the 1980s, with the large American firms—Goldman Sachs, Merrill Lynch, and Morgan Stanley—in the lead, followed by Crédit Suisse First Boston, J. P. Morgan, Citigroup, Deutsche Bank, UBS, Nomura, and several others.

8.7 BIG BUSINESS IN POST-INDUSTRIAL SOCIETIES

On January 4, 2000, the distribution of the top 500 global companies, by market capitalization, was as follows: by country, 219 were American, 77 Japanese, 46 British, 26 French, and 20 German—in other words, nearly 80 percent of the total for the five leading economies, with a persisting US dominance (more than 40 percent). And by sector, banks came first in terms of number of companies, though information technology hardware and telecommunications services accounted for a higher aggregate capitalization, with respectively $3,548 billion (55 companies) and $3,480 billion (52 companies), as against $1,978 billion for banks (65 companies). Software and computer services came fourth ($1,906 billion and 41 companies) and pharmaceuticals fifth ($1,467 billion and 21 companies). Media and photography accounted for a larger number of companies (33), but with about only half pharmaceuticals' market capitalization (*Financial Times*, May 4, 2000). Whatever the volatility of market capitalization, the major characteristics of big business in post-industrial societies were clearly taking shape.

First, new sectors have come to hold sway over the world of big business. On the one hand, there is the weight of finance (with not only banks but insurance and other financial services) and services (telecommunication and computer services as well as media, entertainment, and retailing), together making up more than half the total. And on the other hand, within the manufacturing sector (to the extent that it is possible to clearly differentiate it from services), a shift towards the industries of the third industrial revolution, above all information technology, is clearly perceptible. The bursting of the new technology bubble in spring 2000 did not fundamentally alter this trend.

Second, large and giant firms have remained, more than ever, a distinctive feature of the "new economy", with big business continuing to expand, both through internal and external growth. The wave of mergers reached new heights during the 1990s. In the United States, the trend got relentlessly under way again from 1994, with the total volume of mergers and acquisitions reaching more than $1,600 billion in 1998, compared with just over $200 billion in 1989 (O'Sullivan 2000). In early 2000 the purchase of Time Warner by AOL for more than $180 billion surpassed all previous transactions, including the mergers between Citicorp and Travelers, or Exxon and Mobil. Foreign enterprises participated widely in this trend, notably with the buyout of Chrysler by Daimler Benz and that of the Bankers Trust by Deutsche Bank. Hostile takeovers and stock-market battles began to hit Continental Europe: in France, the Banque Nationale de Paris (BNP) acquired Paribas, even though it had been coveted by the Société Générale; in Germany, Mannesmann, the country's second industrial group in the process of reconverting from metallurgy to telecommunications, fell under attack from the British mobile telephone operator Vodafone, after a battle that shook the very foundations of the Rhineland model of capitalism, distinguished by the dominating role of the banks and the pre-eminence of management over shareholders. As in earlier periods, market control played a significant role in this latest phase of cross-border mergers and acquisitions, spurred among other things by a combination of market integration with increasingly severe controls on cartels and inter-firm collusion.

Third, big business has remained as much an American phenomenon as a century earlier. More significantly, at the turn of the 21st century, American dominance was particularly strong in the new technologies, with six of the 10 largest firms in software and computer services, including the top three (Microsoft, IBM, and Oracle); and eight of the ten largest firms in information technology hardware, including the top two (Intel and Cisco Systems)—though in telecommunications services European and Japanese companies were in the lead (*Financial Times*, May 27, 2004).

Fourth, the strategy and structure of big business has not been fundamentally altered with the advent of the new economy. Admittedly, many large firms have divested some of their activities in order to refocus around those in which they are most competitive; while the more recent large firms in the new technologies have tended to be less diversified, with more flexible organizational structures. And yet the "Chandlerian" firm has, if anything, become more widespread in Europe during the 1990s, with an increasing proportion of the largest British, French, and German firms adopting a strategy of related diversification and, especially, a multidivisional structure, though the latter has taken a new, more horizontal form with the adoption of internal networks of coordination (Whittington and Mayer 2000). As for the United States, the reorganizations of Intel and Microsoft in 2005 suggest a persistence of the multidivisional model, in particular with Intel moving to the M-form for the first time.

8.8 Conclusions

If big business expanded tremendously with the advent of the second industrial revolution, it is unlikely to retreat with the transition to the third. Large firms were best suited to the great industries of the twentieth century—electrical equipment, chemicals, motor cars, aircrafts, oil, rubber—and their development and decisive contribution to economic growth would scarcely have been possible with a different type of business organization. Globalization and the third industrial revolution might have led to the emergence of a new institutional framework, with an enhanced role for markets and networks, but global enterprises have remained in force (Galambos 2005). Depending on specific factors, business activities might be better organized through market mechanisms, managerial hierarchies, or network relationships, as has recently been argued in the case of American business history (Lamoreaux *et al.* 2003). The permanence of big business, seen from the perspective of large-scale operations, stems from its capacity to accommodate various forms of internal organization and to adapt to changing external conditions—not least because the roots of its development are not strictly economic, but are also a matter of wealth, status, and power.

References

AMATORI, F. (1997). "Italy: The Tormented Rise of Organizational Capabilities between Government and Families", in A. D. Chandler, F. Amatori, and T. Hikino (eds.), *Big Business and the Wealth of Nations*. Cambridge: Cambridge University Press.

AUTIN, J. (1984). *Les frères Pereire. Le bonheur d'entreprendre*. Paris: Perrin.

BASKIN, J. B., and MIRANTI, P. (1997). *A History of Corporate Finance*. Cambridge: Cambridge University Press.

BEAU DE LOMÉNIE, E. (1977). *Les responsabilités des dynasties bourgeoises*, 5 vols. Paris: Denoël.

BLACKFORD, M. G. (1998). *The Rise of Modern Business in Great Britain, the United States, and Japan*. Chapel Hill, NC and London: The University of North Carolina Press.

BRUMMER, A., and COWE, R. (1994). *Hanson: A Biography*. London: Fourth Estate.

CARON, F. (1981). *Histoire économique de la France, XIXe–XXe siècles*. Paris: Armand Colin.

CARRERAS, A. (1997). "Spain: Big Manufacturing Firms between State and Market, 1917–1990", in A. D. Chandler, F. Amatori, and T. Hikino (eds.), *Big Business and the Wealth of Nations*. Cambridge: Cambridge University Press.

CAROSSO, V. (1970). *Investment Banking in America*. Cambridge, Mass.: Harvard University Press.

CASSIS, Y. (1997). *Big Business: The European Experience in the Twentieth Century*. Oxford: Oxford University Press.

—— (2006). *Capitals of Capital: A History of International Financial Centres, 1780–2005*. Cambridge: Cambridge University Press.

CHANDLER, A. D. (1962). *Strategy and Structure*. Cambridge, Mass.: MIT Press.

—— (1977). *The Visible Hand*. Cambridge, Mass.: Harvard University Press.

—— (1990). *Scale and Scope*. Cambridge, Mass.: Harvard University Press.

—— AMATORI, F., and HIKINO, T. (1997). "Historical and Comparative Contours of Big Business", in Chandler, Amatori, and Hikino (eds.), *Big Business and the Wealth of Nations*. Cambridge: Cambridge University Press.

CHANNON, D. F. (1973). *The Strategy and Structure of British Enterprise*. London: Macmillan.

CHAPMAN, S. (1992). *Merchant Enterprise in Britain*. Cambridge: Cambridge University Press.

COLLI, A. (2003). *The History of Family Business, 1850–2000*. Cambridge: Cambridge University Press.

CRAFTS, N., and TONIOLO, G. (1996). "Postwar Growth: An Overview", in Crafts and Toniolo (eds.), *Economic Growth in Europe since 1945*. Cambridge: Cambridge University Press.

DYAS, G. P., and THANHEISER, H. (1976). *The Emerging European Enterprise*. London: Macmillan.

FEAR, J. (2005). *Organizing Control: August Thyssen and the Construction of German Corporate Management*. Cambridge, Mass.: Harvard University Press.

FELDENKIRCHEN, W. (1988). "Concentration in German Industry 1870–1939", in H. Pohl (ed.), *The Concentration Process in the Entrepreneurial Economy since the Late 19th Century*. Wiesbaden: Franz Steiner.

—— (1995). *Siemens 1918–1945*. Munich: Piper.

FERGUSON, N. (1998). *The World's Banker: The History of the House of Rothschild*. London: Weidenfeld & Nicolson.

FLEMING, G., MERRETT, D., and VILLE, S. (2004). *The Big End of Town*. Cambridge: Cambridge University Press.

FLIGSTEIN, N. (1990). *The Transformation of Corporate Control*. Cambridge, Mass.: Harvard University Press.

FREELAND, R. (2001). *The Struggle for Control of the Modern Corporation: Organizational Change at General Motors, 1924–1970*. Cambridge: Cambridge University Press.

FREMDLING, R. (1977). "Railroads and German Economic Growth: A Leading Sector Analysis with a Comparison to the United States and Great Britain". *Journal of Economic History*, 37/3.

FRUIN, M. (1992). *The Japanese Enterprise System: Competitive Strategies and Cooperative Structures*. Oxford: Oxford University Press.

GALAMBOS, L. (2005). "Recasting the Organizational Synthesis: Structure and Process in the Twentieth and Twenty-First Centuries". *Business History Review*, 79, spring.

GOURVISH, T. (1980). *Railways and the British Economy 1830–1914*. London and Basingstoke: Macmillan.

HANNAH, L. (1983). *The Rise of the Corporate Economy*. 2nd edn. London: Methuen.

—— (1999). "Marshall's 'Trees' and the Global 'Forest': Were 'Giant Redwoods' Different?", in N. Lamoreaux, D. Raff, and P. Temin (eds.), *Learning by Doing in Markets, Firms and Countries*. Chicago: Chicago University Press.

—— (2006). "Why Was New York so Small? An International Comparison of Stock Markets in 1900". Paper presented at the workshop "Divorcing Ownership from Control? New Perspectives on Stock Market History", *Economics Department*, University of Tokyo, January 10, 2006.

HILFERDING, R. (1981). *Finance Capital: A Study of the Latest Phase of Capitalist Development*. London: Routledge & Kegan Paul (trans., 1st edn., Vienna, 1910).

HOUSSIAUX, J. (1958). *Le pouvoir de monopole*. Paris: Sirey.

JEANNENEY, J.-N. (1984). *L'argent caché. Milieux d'affaires et pouvoirs politiques dans la France du XXᵉ siècle*. Paris: Seuil.

JONES, G. (1993). *British Multinational Banking, 1830–1990*. Oxford: Clarendon Press.

JONES, G. (1997). "Great Britain: Big Business, Management, and Competitiveness in Twentieth-Century Britain", in A. D. Chandler, F. Amatori, and T. Hikino (eds.), *Big Business and the Wealth of Nations*. Cambridge: Cambridge University Press.

—— (2000). *Merchants to Multinationals: British Trading Companies in the Nineteenth and Twentieth Centuries*. Oxford: Oxford University Press.

—— (2005). *Renewing Unilever: Transformation and Tradition*. Oxford: Oxford University Press.

KOCKA, J., and HORN, N. (1979). "Introduction", in J. Kocka and N. Horn (eds.), *Recht und Entwicklung der Grossunternehmen im 19. und frühen 20. Jahrhundert*. Göttingen: Vandenhook and Ruprecht.

—— and SIEGRIST, H. (1979). "Die 100 grössten deutschen Industrieunternehmen im 19. und frühen 20. Jahrhundert", in J. Kocka and N. Horn (eds.), *Recht und Entwicklung der Grossunternehmen im 19. und frühen 20. Jahrhundert*. Göttingen: Vandenhook & Ruprecht.

KOGUT, B. (1999). "Evolution of the Large Firm in France in Comparative Perspective". *Entreprises et Histoire*, 19.

LAMOREAUX, N. (1985). *The Great Merger Movement in American Business, 1895–1904*. Cambridge: Cambridge University Press.

—— RAFF, D., and TEMIN, P. (2003). "Beyond Markets and Hierarchies: Towards a New Synthesis of American Business History". *American Historical Review*, 108/2.

LÉVY-LEBOYER, M. (1979). "Le patronat français, 1912–1973", in Lévy-Leboyer (ed.), *Le patronat de la seconde industrialisation*. Paris: Les éditions ouvrières.

—— (1980). "The Large Corporation in Modern France", in A. Chandler and H. Daems (eds.), *Managerial Hierarchies: Comparative Perspectives on the Rise of the Modern Industrial Enterprise*. Cambridge, Mass.: Harvard University Press.

MORIKAWA, H. (1989). "The Increasing Power of Salaried Managers in Japan's Large Corporations", in W. D. Wray (ed.), *Managing Industrial Enterprise: Cases from Japan's Prewar Experience*. Harvard: Harvard University Press.

—— (1997). "Japan: Increasing Organizational Capabilities of Large Industrial Enterprises, 1880s–1980s", in A. D. Chandler, F. Amatori, and T. Hikino (eds.), *Big Business and the Wealth of Nations*. Cambridge: Cambridge University Press.

NAGAKAWA, K. (1975). *Strategy and Structure of Big Business: Proceedings of the First Fuji Conference*. Tokyo: University of Tokyo Press.

NEWCOMER, M. (1964). *The Big Business Executive*. New York: Columbia University Press.

O'SULLIVAN, M. (2000). *Contests for Corporate Control: Corporate Governance and Economic Performance in the United States and Germany*. Oxford: Oxford University Press.

PROST, A. (1986). "Les nationalisations d'après guerre en Europe occidentale". *Le Mouvement social*, 134.

RIBEILL, G. (1993). *La révolution ferroviaire: La formation des compagnies de chemins de fer en France (1823–1870)*. Paris: Belin.

ROY, W. (1997). *Socializing Capital: The Rise of the Large Industrial Corporation in America*. Princeton: Princeton University Press.

RUMELT, R. P. (1974). *Strategy, Structure and Economic Performance*. Cambridge, Mass.: Harvard University Press.

SCHMITZ, C. J. (1993). *The Growth of Big Business in the United States and Western Europe, 1850–1939*. Basingstoke and London: Macmillan.

SÉDILLOT, R. (1988). *Les deux cents familles*. Paris: Perrin.

SERVAN-SCHREIBER, J.-J. (1968). *The American Challenge*. London: Hamish Hamilton.

SIEGRIST, H. (1980). "Deutsche Grossunternehmen vom späten 19. Jahrhundert bis zum Weimarer Republik". *Geschichte und Gesellschaft*, 6.

SMITH, M. S. (2006). *The Emergence of Modern Business Enterprise in France, 1800–1930*. Cambridge, Mass.: Harvard University Press.

SUPPLE, B. A. (1992). "Introduction" in B. A. Supple (ed.), *The Rise of Big Business*. Aldershot: Elgar.

TOMS, S., and WRIGHT, M. (2002). "Corporate Governance, Strategy and Structure in British Business History, 1950–2000". *Business History*, 44/3.

TURNER, H. A. (1984). *German Big Business and the Rise of Hitler*. New York: Oxford University Press.

WARDLEY, P. (1991). "The Anatomy of Big Business: Aspects of Corporate Development in the Twentieth Century". *Business History*, 33/1.

WHITTINGTON, R., and MAYER, M. (2000). *The European Corporation: Strategy, Structure and Social Science*. Oxford: Oxford University Press.

ZIEGLER, P. (1988). *The Sixth Great Power: Barings, 1762–1929*. London: Collins.

CHAPTER 9

....

FAMILY BUSINESS

....

ANDREA COLLI

MARY ROSE

9.1 INTRODUCTION

....

FAMILY firms have been crucial features of the business landscape for centuries and remain important today. They can be small, medium, or large and have appeared in all sectors and in all three industrial revolutions. Throughout they have played an important role in employment, income generation, and wealth accumulation. This makes them remarkably hard to describe as they are multidimensional, and no single definition fully captures their intrinsic diversity. However, a broad general definition of the family firm is one where a family owns enough of the equity to be able to exert control over strategy *and* is involved in top management positions. This definition does transfer through time and space, is one of the most used today, and so can be considered a useful benchmark. However, the international range of institutional, cultural, and governance arrangements means that it must remain a starting point against which to explore variety, rather than an end point on which a rigid taxonomy can be built.

From the 1950s onwards, business historians wrote case studies of family firms (Erickson 1959; Kindleberger 1964). However, from the 1980s the focus was sharpened as a reaction to Chandler's emphasis on the superiority of professionally managed firms (Church 1969; Payne 1984; Morikawa 1992; Broehl 1992; Church 1993; Dritsas and Gourvish 1997; Rose 1999; Colli and Rose 1999, 2003; Colli *et al.* 2003; Colli 2003). Business history anticipated the interest in family business shown by management studies and research. There was a scattering of articles in *Harvard*

Business Review in the 1960s and 1970s, often by consultants, on conflict and inter-generational succession (Donnelley 1964; Levinson 1971). However, the academic study of family business by management, entrepreneurship, and organizational specialists was delayed until the 1980s and the launch of *Family Business Review*, the first scholarly journal devoted to the study of family business, which interestingly had a strong business history bias initially (Hall 1988). Since then the flow of articles has increased considerably leading to several special journal issues in management and entrepreneurship.

Business history is naturally multidisciplinary and this chapter tracks the relationships between history, organizational and network theory, entrepreneurship, and family dynamics which underpin current research on family business. It surveys and assesses the existing historiography and analyses the way understanding of family firms has developed since the 1960s. In this period, growing links with management and sociological research have led to the emergence of different questions and perspectives. By surveying the business history literature alongside management and sociological approaches to family firms, the chapter will highlight the shifting nature of family capitalism and the changes in the economic contribution and management of family firms through time and space. The chapter also identifies potential future developments for the field.

9.2 THE DEFINITION OF THE FAMILY FIRM AND PROBLEMS OF THE GENERIC FAMILY FIRM

A general definition of the family firm has been offered in the introduction and we use it as a starting point. However, historians and management specialists have found definitions remarkably hard to pin down and this is well reflected in the literature. The legal, governance, and financial frameworks of family firms are not universal as indicated by the preface of *Family Business Magazine's* 2004 list of the World's Largest Companies:

Compiling such a list is a stiff challenge by any measure. Between shifting disclosure regulations and varying currency exchange rates, pinning down precise numbers and owners is …challenging. Many Asian and European companies operate behind intricate holding-company structures that make ownership and even management difficult to define.

It is no surprise, therefore, that there is no general consensus among scholars as to what constitutes a family business in quantitative, qualitative terms or historical terms (Handler 1989; Westhead and Cowling 2001; Colli 2003; Colli *et al.* 2003;

Sharma 2004). However, by taking the benchmark definition provided in the introduction, it becomes possible, using history, to explore the subtleties and differences in family business behavior and performance. It can be shown, for example, that although family firms may be efficient, they are not efficient *per se* as much depends on the specific national context and surrounding conditions (Whitley 2000; Church 1993; Poutziouris and Chittenden 1996; Colli and Rose 1999; James and Kobrak 2004).

In the nineteenth century, and indeed well into the twentieth, economic activity was so heavily dominated by family business (Harris 2000) that there was no need to give it a specific name to distinguish it from other legal and organizational forms. It is only since the interwar period (Berle and Means 1932), with growing interest in the divorce of ownership from control, that historians and management specialists have differentiated family firms from other business categories. Differences partly relate to variations in the proportion of family-owned shares and especially to those with voting rights. But they go beyond this, to embrace elements of intergenerational succession and aspects of management.

Definitions have all been developed for analyzing specific issues, i.e. intergenerational transition, financial commitment, strategic control and so on. It is abundantly clear, however, that ownership is only a part of the story (Gallo 1995). In Italy, for instance, the family ownership of large corporations has been maintained during almost all the industrial history of the country through to the present day. This has been achieved through the use of holding companies, agreements, cross-shareholdings, and the issuing of stocks carrying multiple voting powers. This has allowed the founders and their families to raise resources on financial markets, while also controlling the company through ownership of only a small fraction of the share capital. This example is not unique among the industrialized countries in Continental Europe. It shows that the crucial feature is the extent to which a family is able to mold company decisions, through personal influence on leadership succession, often unfettered by any formal institutional regulation of governance. Whilst financial leverage may be critical, power may also be linked to attitudes to family within society as much as to the precise level of a family's stake in a company.

9.3 FAMILY BUSINESS AS A CULTURAL ARTIFACT

Family business is therefore a cultural as well as a purely "ownership-related" concept and understanding the family and its objectives is crucial to the understanding of the family firm (Aldrich and Cliff 2003). Families and firms become so intertwined that the failure of the firm, even where the founding family have no continuing financial stake, can feel like a death in the family. However, the notion of family is as variable as that of the family business, shifting through time and having very specific and distinctive meanings in particular countries and even different regions. The extended family of early industrial Europe has much in common, in terms of both economic and social behavior, with those in India, Africa, and East Asia today and indeed with Italian families in industrial districts. But it has remarkably little in common with the contemporary Western nuclear family. In addition, in the West the breakdown of family stability, with a rising divorce rate, has vastly complicated family dynamics and succession strategies in family firms.

Given such forces and complexity, it is not surprising that defining the family firm is difficult and that a generic definition is unlikely and even undesirable. Very broadly, a family firm has three crucial elements of kin (defined in terms of culture), property (the ownership of a crucial element of capital), ownership, and succession (the ownership of and succession to control of the strategic management of the firm). The power to appoint the chief executive and other board members brings the opportunity to manage the firm according to the family's values and culture. Research has identified seven different types of family business form depending partly on ownership and control and partly on the extent to which family and business objectives coincide (Westhead and Howorth 2004). The definition of the family firm may also shift through the life cycle of the firm and also as the nature of economic activity changes. This discussion confirms that, whilst the definition we offered at the beginning of this chapter is perfectly valid, it could never be anything more than a reference point. Much of the richness of family business research is about refining, or even contesting, the definition in specific cultural, historical, and international contexts.

9.4 FAMILY BUSINESS AS A STAGE IN THE RISE OF MODERN BUSINESS

The importance of family business in early industrialization is relatively uncontroversial. During early industrialization, family business represented a predictable response to instability, uncertainty, and poor property rights and became the central pivot of a network of trust (Casson 1999). As a reaction to market failure, the family can be likened to the interface between market and firm (Ben-Porath 1980; Nafziger 1969). The family represented an internal market for managerial labor, a source of funds for the establishment and expansion of the business and a trusted source of information. As a reaction to uncertainty, family firms were a crucial dimension of industrialization worldwide. During the first industrial revolution business owners derived their managerial knowledge from experience, which tended to evolve within families and communities, rather than from formal training (Pollard, 1965).

9.5 THE RISE OF THE MANAGERIAL CORPORATION

The family firm has sometimes been seen as a hindrance rather than an asset in modern economies. In 1959, the economist Edith Penrose argued that firms in capital-and research-intensive industries transformed themselves from entrepreneurial firms into giant complex corporations (Penrose 1959). Alfred Chandler, on the other hand, in *Visible Hand* (1977) argued that in the United States, the combined impact of technology and market growth transformed the strategy and structure of business.

In 1990, in *Scale and Scope,* Chandler attributed Britain's relative decline, compared to the United States and Germany, to "personal capitalism". The British, he argued, "viewed their businesses in personal rather than organizational terms, as family estates to be nurtured and passed on to their heirs". This dislike of losing personal control over their firms resulted in British entrepreneurs failing to make the required three-pronged investment in production, distribution, and management which was necessary to exploit fully the economies of scale and scope in the industries of the Second Industrial Revolution (Chandler 1990: 286).

Chandler's personal capitalism has been contentious and has stimulated a wide-ranging critique. At the heart of this debate has been the assumption that the resources of the family business are limited. He implied that they lack both the financial and human capital to pursue sustained business growth in capital and technologically intensive industries. It has been the assumption that family business lacks both the financial and human capital to pursue sustained business growth in capital and technologically intensive industries. Changing markets and technologies bring new processes and business demands. In the United States, during the interwar period, the combined pressure of high-income mass markets, new technology, and new, cheap, mass-produced products, like the Model T Ford, transformed capital-intensive business. New patterns of ownership and management seemed to leave little room for the family business. Business was no longer self-financing and the family ceased to be the principal source of human capital (Porter 1993). In addition, the notion that family control was based on nepotism not merit, and that the extended family diverted resources from investment to personal consumption, was applied especially to late nineteenth and twentieth century Britain. Indeed much of the debate initially centered on Anglo-American comparisons and illustrated concern about the relative decline of British competitive performance compared with both the United States and Germany (Church 1993).

9.6 ALTERNATIVE VISIONS

In the last 20 years, there has been growing evidence that Chandler undervalued the resilience and capabilities of the family company, especially in Europe. Indeed, in the Netherlands the long-termism of families stimulated rather than restricted investment (Sluyterman and Winkelman 1993). In addition, family firms, large and small, remained a dynamic element of the Dutch economy in the twentieth century (Arnoldus 2002). Equally there is considerable evidence of the persistence of family capitalism in large firms in Europe generally (Cassis 1997). There are real difficulties in applying Chandler's ideas outside the United States and to sectors where competitive advantage is more reliant on the quality of information flow than simply on technology and capital intensity (Hamilton and Feenstra 1995; Granovetter 1996; Jones and Rose 1993; Scranton 1983). In this respect, part of the problem is that, although Chandler is extremely sensitive to differences in the economic underpinnings of business internationally, both he and Lazonick use the United States as the benchmark for the study of business behavior in other countries. Neither gives much attention to the forces, whether political or developmental, which may have made the culture of business in the United States unusual, rather than being an appropriate blueprint for business worldwide in the twentieth century. In addition, of course, family business remains an important dimension of the United States economy. As McCraw has argued, "American capitalism is extraordinarily significant, but it offers only one among many models of successful development" (McCraw 1997: 302). America's industrial corporations were the product of a specific set of economic, political, social, historical, institutional, and cultural circumstances, rather than necessarily being the model for international convergence (Fruin 1998). It would be foolish to underestimate the role of the American corporation in US political and economic dominance in the twentieth century. However, Chandler's focus on manufacturing industry and especially on capital-intensive sectors excludes vast tracts of business activity, including services and agriculture as well as many manufacturing sectors. These are the very sectors in which historically and contemporaneously family businesses have flourished (Supple 1991: 508). Interestingly, this applies as much to the United States as elsewhere for large family-owned and controlled corporations remain a significant dimension in the twenty-first century.

Networks of interrelated family businesses have proved especially resilient in those sectors where flexibility has been the main source of competitive advantage.

Philip Scranton's work on Philadelphia's specialty family firms in the nineteenth century has shown that the growth of big business and mass production in the United States was accompanied by the emergence of highly creative specialized producers before the First World War. These included furniture makers, hosiery makers, shipbuilders, jewellery, carpets, cutlery and machine-tool makers, and those which lay between specialized and mass production—iron and steel rolling mills, men's clothing, boots and shoes, auto parts, firearms and ammunition, and a wide range of other sectors (Scranton 1997). Like proprietary capitalism in Philadelphia's textile industry in the second half of the nineteenth century, this type of production was widely based upon family business. As in other industrial districts, family firms were embedded in the local community. These firms were reservoirs of skills and gave the entrepreneurs access to the information needed for flexibility in rapidly changing markets (Piore and Sabel 1984). As we will stress later, family firms fulfill the same role in northern Italian industrial districts. Research has shown that since 1945, the highly competitive German *Mittelstand*, with their artisan traditions, have relied heavily on family-based knowledge transfer of both products and processes (Colli 1998; James and Kobrak 2004). However, according to some research (Whitley 2000), the persistence of family ownership (as for instance in the German case) could be associated with a business strategy emphasizing product specialization rather than diversification, as is typical in the managerial enterprise. In this perspective families are more inclined to manage a single-business, specialized firm than a large diversifier.

9.7 THE FAMILY FIRM IN MODERN ECONOMIES

Family dynasties have continued to play a significant role in the United States and worldwide as Table 9.1 illustrates.

Although most family firms are small or medium sized and many are destined to be short-lived, a significant number are large, long-established international businesses, though inclusion in the list depends on the definition used. A third of the companies in the Fortune 500 listing of the largest American firms are family controlled and include Ford, Bechtel, Mars, Estée Lauder, Wal-Mart, W. L. Gore, and Levi Strauss. There is a similar array of prominent names in Europe such as Michelin, the Wallenberg group, IKEA, Lego, Fiat, Benetton, Armani, Ferrero Barilla, C&A, and Heineken. The spectacular importance of large family firms is found across a range of sectors, though it is especially noticeable in retailing and international finance. Half of the largest 20 Swedish multinational manufacturing

Table 9.1 Family business distribution in 1995–2000

Country	Family businesses as a percent of registered companies	percent of GDP
Italy	75–95	na
Spain	70–80	65
UK	75	na
Sweden	90–95	na
Switzerland	85	na
Netherlands	74	54
Belgium	70	55
Germany	60	55
Poland	50–80	35
Portugal	70	60
United States	95	40
Brazil	90	65
India	n/a	65

Source: Neubauer and Lank 1998; Colli 2003; and Colli *et al.* 2003; Anon. 2003.

firms belong to Sweden's biggest industrial group, which has been owned and managed by several generations of the Wallenberg family.

In South and East Asia, family and business remain culturally inseparable. Networks of often small family firms have been characterized as alternatives to Western hierarchical organizations. Examples of large family firms include Tata (India) and Kikkomann (Japan). Thus, whilst family-dominated groups such as the *zaibatsu* in Japan were swept away during the American Occupation, elsewhere family-based business groups remain an important characteristic in many economies. However, while the giant Korean *chaebols* were all family businesses until the 1990s, the Asian financial crisis undermined their position. It saw Daewoo go bankrupt, and Hyundai dismantled (Neubauer and Lank 1998; Kets de Vries 1996; Amsden 1986; Hamilton and Feenstra 1995; Morikawa 1992).

9.8 Synthesis

Historical evidence does not support the notion that family business is a stage in the shift from traditional to corporate capitalism. In the first place, the case that the managerial corporation is more efficient than the family corporation is not proven one way or another. Secondly, it is clear that there is no clear divide between managerial and family firms. Thirdly, family businesses, large and small, are an important dimension of modern economies. Certainly there are examples where family firms have struggled to transform and where the objectives of families to maintain control have conflicted with growth and organizational change.

In Germany, Siemens found competition with managerial AEG difficult until the family-backed modernization at the start of the twentieth century (Kocka 1999). It is clear though that family firms are not a stage en route to modern industrial enterprise nor associated with particular organizational forms. They are shaped by a range of forces which vary through time, by sector and internationally.

9.9 THE FAMILY FIRM AS AN INSTITUTION

Decision making within family firms and their potential for growth is shaped partly by the market mechanism, but also by a formal and informal set of "rules of the game". The formal rules are the legal system—including property rights, company law, taxation, inheritance tax, and bankruptcy law. These are not formed in a legal vacuum and are also the product of interactions between governments and business and other interested parties. The development of laws is shaped by historical forces and is thus path dependent, so there can emerge considerable international differences in the privileges and restrictions faced by family businesses.

The legal status of particular types of company is a significant factor explaining differences in the form family businesses may take. One of the most distinctive features of British company law was the Bubble Act of 1720, which outlawed the joint stock company and also limited liability. The legacy of this legislation has been cited as a long-term explanation for the slowness of British family firms to shift to corporate enterprise in the nineteenth century (Rose 1994: 61–87). Yet this should not be exaggerated since there is ample evidence that in both Spain and Italy, where company law was different, corporate enterprise and limited liability also remained a rarity during the Second Industrial Revolution. The key lay in a combination of financial requirements and attitudes to risk. In the uncertain world of early industrialization, unlimited liability was attractive in all three countries because it could deter speculation (Colli *et al.* 2003). In Germany, corporate law encouraged sustained family involvement in the businesses they founded, even after they went public (James and Kobrak 2004).

Inheritance law is another formal 'rule of the game' which molds the behavior of family businesses. There were considerable variations in inheritance law and its interpretation in Europe in the nineteenth century and into the twentieth, and this undoubtedly influenced the way family firms were controlled. For instance in Italy, the Napoleonic legal code laid down a system of partible inheritance. In practice, however, the norm remained primogeniture, as the legal constraints were adapted for business needs. The technique was to divide the whole assets of the family (adding the value of the shares to other assets and properties) among all their heirs, but to give one of them control over the business, including all the manufacturing or commercial activity (Romano 1985).

Inheritance law and company law change through time and this in turn influences family firm strategy. There is strong evidence, for instance, that a relative decline in family control of business in Britain, after the Second World War, stemmed from the sharp rise in death duties introduced by the Labour Government in 1949. By 1951, 17 percent of firms had taken anticipatory action, many going public (Colli and Rose 1999: 41). Tax law not only varies through time, but contemporary studies show that international discrepancies affect the survival and continued development of family firms today. In twentieth century Germany, where death duties tended to be high, the unquoted company (GmbH) was a way of protecting family wealth. This is because property was assessed significantly below securities and was thus an appropriate way of passing wealth to the next generation (James and Kobrak 2004). The increase in the threshold for inheritance tax in Britain, to £215,000 in 1996 and the availability of business property relief at 100 percent on ordinary shares in unlisted companies were designed to make intergenerational transition easier (Westhead and Cowling 1998).

Women play a crucial role in family business although their formal status, even today, is often hidden. In the nineteenth century in Britain, for instance, women existed only under the protection of their husbands and could not inherit until the second half of the nineteenth century. They were often *de facto* partners in a business, but lacked legal right to the capital of the firm or to other property. This pattern was also fairly common in Europe into the twentieth century. Yet interests of business and family were closely intertwined and women's 'hidden' role extended to finance. Where partible inheritance was being practiced, marriages between cousins could counteract dilution of family wealth. In addition, marriage outside the immediate family group could bring additional sources of finance and contacts (Davidoff and Hall 1987; Colli *et al.* 2003). Intermarriage also played a crucial part in the Netherlands in the nineteenth and twentieth centuries. There, the most important family-owned food multinationals linked their business expansion closely to their marriage strategies (Arnoldus 2002).

9.10 CULTURE AND THE INFORMAL "RULES OF THE GAME"

The institutional and legal environment is the product of a complex historical process, underpinned by cultural forces at both the regional and national level. Geert Hofstede has defined culture "as the interactive aggregate of common characteristics that influence a human group's response to its environment" (Hofstede 1980: 25). His more recent work takes the notion of culture further, describing it as a form of mental programming. Accordingly, he suggests that "culture is learned not inherited. It derives from one's social environment, not from one's genes." As a result of the differing mental programming of societies, there are, therefore, significant variations in behavior and social norms which impact on all forms of business, including family business (Hofstede 1994).

There are striking contrasts in values and attitudes between America and Europe which relate to enterprise, to firms, to innovation, and to technology (Whitley 2000). In US enterprise it has been argued that the company is viewed as a commodity which can be bought or sold, whereas in Europe it is associated with community (Albert 1991; Hau 1995). This approach, however, is rather at odds with the paternalist and community-based strategies which emerged in such American family corporations as Gillette in Boston.

Mary Rose demonstrated that differing histories and values led to sharp contrasts in the behavior of family firms in the British and American cotton industries in the nineteenth and twentieth centuries. The United States' position as a country of recent settlement influenced attitudes towards the family. Since the objectives of families and family firms are inseparable, this also affected business policies. For example, the British desire to found a family dynasty contrasted with the position in the United States. There, high geographical and social mobility are thought to have weakened family ties and certainly ties to specific localities (Rose 2000).

Nor are the long-term ties between family and enterprise confined to Britain, for they are typically European. The enterprise is established for future generations and the result is a type of familialism, where the allocation of power, resources, and responsibilities is strictly on a kinship basis (Colli 2003). This of course amounts to the foundation of dynasties and, whilst attitudes and sources of social prestige vary between America and Europe, there are strong dynastic tendencies in the United States. Examples like the Boston Associates in the eighteenth and nineteenth centuries or the Ford Motor Company or Wal-Mart in the twentieth century illustrate this.

In drawing such distinctions it should be remembered that attitudes and cultures shift through time, as a result of economic and institutional changes. This was especially the case in the UK after 1945 when a range of legal and financial changes, combined with a sharp decline in the role of locality, reduced the position of large family firms in Britain. The 1948 Companies Act made the disclosure of financial information compulsory and provided a springboard for takeovers and especially hostile takeovers in the 1950s and 1960s (Colli and Rose 1999).

Dynastic entrepreneurship has been common in Europe, especially in Italy and Greece with their strong family-based cultures. In Greece, for example, family businesses were both culturally and institutionally embedded (Dritsas 1997). Such familialism has sometimes been particularly associated with Mediterranean societies. However, Colli *et al.* showed that when Spanish and Italian family business behavior was compared there was no conclusive evidence of a Mediterranean style of business. Instead, national cultural and institutional forces created distinct variations in behavior (Colli *et al.* 2003).

In India, the family lies at the very core of culture: "The centre of the Indian social identity is the family. Family businesses are not merely an economic structure, for most...individuals, they are the source of social identity. There is a strong social obligation to continue one's father's work" (Dutta 1997: 91). Japanese and Chinese family firms provide a clear contrast, illustrating the danger of assuming common culture is simply based upon geography. In China, the family is the basic survival unit and people exist only in terms of their immediate family network and exhibit a high level of distrust of outsiders (Redding 1990). Intricate stem-networks of families have emerged, especially where Chinese communities have migrated overseas for example in the ASEAN countries such as Hong Kong, Singapore, Indonesia, Malaysia, the Philippines, and Thailand (Brown 1995). Family ownership and low trust of outsiders leads to an autocratic management style and close family control of diversification. In large East Asian firms, from Indonesian conglomerates to Korean *chaebols*, top and key management positions were and still are reserved for relatives and family members (Lee 1997). In Japan, social values and attitude to the family are different from China and are not defined in biological terms. Instead there is a far stronger influence of Confucian philosophy where family is defined as those who contribute to the economic welfare of the group or "ie". This allowed the *zaibatsu* family groups to expand but employ salaried managers who were seen as "adopted family" (Morikawa 1992). In Japan, therefore, the concept of the family is based on consanguinity and adoption:

The Japanese hardly distinguish between the two meanings. But succession of the property in Japan is often based on the concept of the *ie* according to which the heir of the property is not necessarily a family member by blood. A successor in *ie* can be described as a successor of the role. The main objective of the *ie*, succession, is to protect and expand the wealth of the family led by a capable individual, rather than to bequeath the wealth only to blood-related family members. (Chen 1995: 167)

The divorce of ownership from control in the *zaibatsu* groups meant that the salaried managers were a crucial element of their success and eased the transformation of the old *zaibatsu* into the *keiretsu* after the Second World War. The loss of family power did not mean that the organizational and managerial capabilities were lost. Instead, the pre-war holding company structure was replaced by cross-ownership clustered around a central core or main bank (Morikawa 2001).

Firms are then shaped by the families who own them and by the values and attitudes of the societies of which they are a part. In risky environments the family has provided 'protection against the economic consequences of uncertain adverse events', especially relating to management and choice of successors (Pollak 1985; Granovetter and Swedberg 1992). But cultural forces not only reduce uncertainty. In the Asian case, the interplay between cultural and institutional frameworks helps to explain the evolution of large business groups in Asia and Latin America (Lansberg and Perrow 1991).

For the successful family firm, its boundaries lie beyond the immediate family, within a larger group with a shared culture and values (Casson 1982, 1991, 1993). External family firm networks are frequently associated with the early stages of industrialization, but have remained common to the present day, sometimes dramatically enhancing the power of individual families. In declining markets these arrangements are often horizontal and anti-competitive. However, in rapidly changing markets, loose vertical networks of family firms hold the key to flexibility, innovation, and competitive advantage (Langlois and Robertson 1995).

Networking activity by family businesses typically extends to include relationships with banks and with the state. In most societies economic elites often enjoyed considerable political bargaining power, which in turn benefited and reinforced their businesses. In nineteenth century Britain, for example, City of London financial and commercial families enjoyed unmatched social and economic cohesion (compared say with industrial groups) which brought them strong leverage on government policy, extending, some would argue, into the interwar period (Cain and Hopkins 1993). Similar advantages gave the Boston Associates in nineteenth century Massachusetts sufficient bargaining power to manipulate tariffs to their advantage until the final third of the nineteenth century (Rose 2000).

The picture is every bit as striking in Italy. In the nineteenth century, entrepreneurial families in the so-called 'industrial triangle' around Genoa, Milan, and Turin were closely linked to one another, sharing similar values and culture. During the twentieth century, during the industrial modernization of the country, this cohesion remained the rule, and was underpinned by mutual share exchanges and financial networking among major private groups working as a significant defense against hostile takeovers. This was reinforced by the behavior of financial institutions—namely the universal banks up to the early 1930s, then a powerful merchant bank, Mediobanca, after the Second World War—which acted as 'clearing houses' to maintain family control (Baccini and Vasta 1995; Amatori and Brioschi 1997).

9.11 INDUSTRIAL DISTRICTS, NETWORKS, AND FAMILY FIRMS

Another perspective on the relationship between a locally determined system of values and culture and the persistent efficiency of the family firm is provided by the economics and sociology of the industrial district (ID). This particular form of flexible business organization—*based upon the geographical clustering of small specialized production units enjoying external economies*—diffused in Britain during the First Industrial Revolution as well as on the Continent during the nineteenth century (Sabel and Zeitlin 1985; Zeitlin, this volume).

The relationship between the family firm and the ID can be seen from a number of perspectives. First, in purely demographic terms the family-based production unit has traditionally been the basic building block of the ID. A firm would be managed by the founder, who would depend upon the entire family for skilled and cheap labor. Family members would be employed on the shop floor as well as in managerial positions, depending on the size and the age of the enterprise. As indicated, the family acted as a source of finance, of labor ethics, of skill, and of commitment. Inside the ID itself, the relationships of the members of the family with the surrounding community are important. They meant an increase in the density of the business relationship of the firm itself. This is crucial when the firm is specialized in intermediate production or in a single or a few phases of the production process.

The emphasis on the family dimension is, in this case, confirmed in a number of ways. First, the ID firms have historically been, and are in general, reluctant to grow, given the unwillingness of the founders to abandon control of the firm and to accept the presence of external management. Second, examining the structure of the relationships among the firms in the district, as well as the members of the often informal networks of producers, certain characteristics emerge. It is noteworthy that a single family is able to generate various entrepreneurial initiatives, proportional to the number of its members, which can be connected with the original initiative as well as with the others in the district.

Again, both historians and sociologists interested in the IDs have pointed out the relevance of the family in shaping the entrepreneurial behavior inside the IDs. For instance, early studies of the Italian industrial districts showed a close relationship between the small family firms, the IDs scattered in the northeastern and central regions of the peninsula, and the historical presence of peasant families in the same areas (the Veneto, the Marche, Emilia Romagna, and Tuscany). The most diffused contractual arrangement was sharecropping, stimulating "entrepreneurial" behavior in peasant activities. With the decline of the secondary sector in the Italian economy this attitude easily translated into manufacturing initiatives. This interpretation can appear as too deterministic (because IDs flourish also in regions in which sharecropping was not the main contractual arrangement); however, the idea has some empirical basis. For instance, the "pluriactivity" characteristic of the sharecroppers' families, the idea of labor division and specialization among the extended family's members is undoubtedly a feature of behavior in IDs. Similarly the attitude toward risk and investment does help to explain entrepreneurial effervescence typical of the local systems of production. These were based upon small family firms whose members remained, very often, involved in peasant activities well after the start-up of a new venture in manufacturing (Becattini *et al.* 2001).

What is clear is that this particular form of production organization, based upon the small family firm, was able to show an outstanding level of performance in some economies, for instance in the Italian one. This was thanks to the interaction of positive values at a micro level (i.e. inside the single family firm). This also stemmed from conditions at the macro level. At the macro level the local system of shared values, formal and informal rules of the game, and concrete initiatives sustained local entrepreneurship. The basic features of the relationship between the family firm and a local system of production have, however, also been studied in an international, comparative perspective, showing the similarities occurring in different continental regional cases (Herrigel 1996).

Silicon Valley, with its growing cluster of entrepreneurial ventures in the electronics sector from the 1970s, offers an interesting alternative example. Industrial specialization apart, the situation is not very different from that typical of the European IDs. The ingredients are the same: a geographical cluster of entrepreneurial, specialized firms, the presence of relevant external economies in terms of transport, communications, but, above all, training institutions—universities and colleges. In some cases, it is possible to talk of family business, given that there are often families involved in start-up and early development.

However, this model has some fundamental differences from the discussion of family capitalism provided in this chapter. The two most important are durability and strategic control. In hi-tech clusters such as Silicon Valley, ventures are set up to exploit a temporary competitive advantage based upon technological creativity, rather than as long-term ventures. The rapid entry and exit of firms is confirmed by the birth-death ratio, which has been very high among the Valley's ventures, and by the level of acquisitions by the major companies in the areas of the smaller ones. As far as strategic control is concerned, it is interesting to note that the role of financial institutions in this model is different from the role played by local banks in the ID. Venture capitalists are actors who are highly involved in the management of the initiative. In this context, potential commitment to family control is an obstacle more than an advantage, as it is for a local bank operating on the basis of trust and personal relationships inside an industrial district (Kenney 2000).

9.12 Strength and Weaknesses of the Family Firm in Historical Perspective

Where the objectives of family and firm are united, close networks of trust have the advantage of providing a combination of incentives, including effective monitoring and loyalty, to protect family wealth (Pollak 1985). Loyalty and commitment to family members is assumed to lead to altruism by parents towards their offspring. But if family firms are based on networks of trust, families and their businesses are notoriously conflict-ridden, stretching the bonds of trust to the limit. Family businesses are molded by their external environment, but family members themselves build the culture of their firms. Business culture is closely linked to its leaders and nowhere more so than in a family firm. "For the entrepreneur, the business is essentially an extension of himself...And if he is concerned about what happens to his business after he passes on, that concern usually takes the form of thinking of the kind of monument he will leave behind" (Neubauer and Lank 1997: 145). The founder of a business is a major source of knowledge and expertise and his or her social networks represent important intangible assets for the company. The future prosperity of both family and business depend upon how well understanding and contacts are passed on and how far these are trusted and valued by the next generation (Lee *et al.* 2003).

The relationship between a founder and his family business is often intensely emotional and can be a major source of conflict, especially in Western societies (Corbetta 2001). The intensity and regularity of this conflict and its impact on intergenerational succession has been a major cause of the growing volume of consultancy work on family business since the 1960s. In some companies this encouraged one-time family firms to 'go public'. However, research has shown that management buyouts and buy-ins can be a satisfactory solution to succession failure (Howorth *et al.* 2004).

Social networks are an important dimension of leadership succession in the family business. Both attitudes towards intergenerational succession and its solution are shaped by a combination of the prevailing legal framework and social values. These, of course, vary considerably across the world. In India, for example, the elderly are revered as part of the extended family, making intergenerational succession less problematic. There is certainly rivalry in Indian business families, but apparently lower levels of hostility than in the West. The tendency towards extended, as opposed to nuclear, families is part of the reason, with as many as five generations living under one roof leading to greater conformity (Dutta 1997). The nature of disputes and conflicts is not fixed through time—they have shifted and changed historically, with changing social norms and educational opportunities. In addition, they shift as individual family businesses evolve (Gersick *et al.* 1997).

Conflict surrounding leadership succession in family business is intense, because it involves delicate interpersonal relationships. These include power disputes between parents and children and sibling rivalry, which occur alongside the challenge of managing change (Rose 1993: Cromie *et al.* 1995; Kets de Vries 1996). In some cases generational conflicts, which long predate succession, have had serious repercussions for the future prosperity of the firms and their owners (Donnelly 1964). There is ample evidence of the founders of family firms clinging to power for too long, to the detriment of their successors. Workaholics, suffering from a touch of megalomania, are one type of business leader who can, by undermining their successors or failing to give due credit or responsibility, bequeath a negative legacy to their family. Often, therefore, the very character traits which brought an entrepreneur success, as founder of the business, prevented him from retiring and this was the case for both John Brown the shipbuilder and Lord Lever (Boswell 1973; Jeremy and Shaw 1984–6, vol. 3).

One of the advantages of family firms is their stability. Family owners are far more likely to pursue long-term financial and human capital strategies than those in public companies, constrained as they are by the stock market's obsession from at least the 1960s with quarterly results (Church 1993: 28; Detouze *et al.* 1989). Yet for long-termism to be associated with sustained prosperity there must be a balanced attitude to outsiders. Otherwise the firm will become moribund and inward looking (Wiersema 1992).

In Italy, 'outsiders' may be undermined for failing to give family interests pre-eminence over economic considerations. In addition, family insiders have been preferred to outsiders as a matter of course in several leading Italian businesses. Indeed the concept of family business in Italy should be used in a relatively strict way. Usually—and especially among the largest private groups in the country—families retain a significant proportion (often the majority) of the capital and have their members among the top executives (Colli and Rose 1999). Consequently, in the Italian context, family firms really do mean just that.

Even within Italy, the solution of intergenerational succession problems has typically varied between large and small firms. Part of the dynamism in Italy's industrial districts is because, rather than directly joining their parent's firm, stem firms are spun off for children. These complement existing businesses in the region, facilitating flows of information and skills within vertical networks. If succession is not a problem in Italian industrial districts, it remains an issue both for Italy's 'pocket multinationals' (medium-sized, specialized, and internationalized family businesses) and for large family firms. Partible inheritance is a perennial problem with disputes frequently settled by the employment of consultants (Guerci 1998; Amatori and Colli 1999; Colli and Rose 2003). In Germany, five stages in the evolution of family control can be traced and may take many generations to achieve, but they demonstrate the importance of family in German capitalism. These phases track the family role from financial and managerial dominance in phase 1, through to the symbolic role of the family in the business culture and the brand in phase 5 (Joly 2003, quoted James and Kobrack 2004).

The tension between nepotism and meritocracy surrounds discussion of succession. Yet the division is far less clear-cut than it appears. Leadership by inheritance appears as the antithesis of professional management based on merit. Yet, especially in sectors like merchant banking in the nineteenth century, which relied so heavily on public confidence, a meritocratic approach was the norm—any other approach would have threatened the prosperity of both family and firm (Daunton 1988). A good example of a family business where stable ownership has provided a high level of security and where, until relatively recently, the company has avoided becoming unduly inward looking is the Wallenberg investment group in Sweden. With its origins in the 1850s, the family group has long used the stock market to evaluate its business activities and avoid complacency. This strategy was linked to consistent and growing dominance of the group in corporate Sweden (Lindgren 1979).

Problems do appear to be greatest in older family businesses and may be linked to the life cycle of these firms as illustrated in Italy by Fiat, Pirelli, and Olivetti—which are among the countries most prominent family corporations. At Olivetti, the death of Adriano in the late twentieth century led to considerable conflict, since his son Roberto could not unite the family or persuade them to shift from typewriters, where the market was falling, into computers. The company was finally rescued by a group of investors headed by Mediobanca and sold its computing activities to General Electric (Colli *et al.* 2003).

Portrayed as oases of trust, family businesses are clearly potentially turbulent and some of the major difficulties relate to governance in larger family groups. Corporate governance can be defined as: "the need for boards of directors to balance the interests of shareholders with those of other stakeholders in order to achieve long-term sustained value" (World Bank 1999: 4). This can be especially difficult in large family groups, where managers may be more active on behalf of the owning family than other stakeholders (Morck and Yeung 2003).

The reform of corporate governance in the UK began with the Cadbury Report in 1992. This was followed by reforms elsewhere in Europe and the United States, following the ENRON scandal. But there are many vested interests, often involving powerful family business groups. They oppose greater transparency and disclosure worldwide and have sometimes blocked reform (Colli 2003; Colli *et al.* 2003).

9.13 CONCLUSIONS

This chapter has highlighted that firms are not anachronistic hangovers from a bygone age, but remain a vital part of the business landscape in the twenty-first century. Even a decade ago, those who wrote about family business were assumed to be defending traditional and outdated business methods. Certainly, family firms can, in some circumstances, be inward looking and nepotistic and this may restrict innovation and growth. Family values do not always place business expansion as a primary aim. But being different from publicly owned companies is no longer necessarily taken to imply inferiority. The growing volume of work on contemporary family firms has highlighted how important they are in developed and developing economies. Many prominent large companies can be classed as family firms, while for many others—including the giant DuPont corporation—the family name remained a major symbol of trust, long after the end of any direct family involvement.

One important route forward for family business research involves a continued emphasis on international comparisons. This requires the collection of evidence on family business in different countries through time to allow a thorough analysis of the variations in the institutional and cultural context of family business, its performance, and impact on competitive advantage. Historical research is the ideal framework for exploring the impact of changes in the institutional, financial, and economic environment in differing industries and countries.

The image of the family in brand building is an important area which has received remarkably little attention from business historians. Certainly research into brands and advertising has increased considerably over recent years, but the consideration of the notion of the family brand has often been implicit rather than explicit. Exceptionally Nancy Koehn's *Brand New* does demonstrate how entrepreneurs and their families built consumer trust and how this changed through time. She captures the way in which, in a shifting economic and technological landscape, different entrepreneurs built their brands. She demonstrates that the appreciation of products, processes, and customers, rather than a large advertising budget, were at the heart of successful brand building (Koehn 1999).

This chapter has shown that families and their firms are hard to separate, implying that a family's values, knowledge, and reputation can be counted as the intangible assets of the business. They are, therefore, inseparable from the brand. More research is needed to trace through time the shifting nature of family brands and the realities and myths which lie behind them. A search of family business websites provides fascinating insight into the ways in which families use and abuse their history to build their brand. The Ford Motor Company, for instance, built an interactive family heritage section of its main site to celebrate it centenary (<http://www.ford.com>). On the other hand, some family companies, such as Motorola, downplay the role of family (<http://www.motorola.com>). Far more research is needed, linking visual, cultural, and family images with consumer perceptions, to establish the changing impact of family branding.

New themes and areas of research only emerge when scholars cross boundaries, explore alternative areas of knowledge, and start asking new questions. Gender has become an important issue in business history as a result of interdisciplinary work combining feminist theory, cultural, business, and social history (Kwolek-Folland 2001).

However, even allowing for the exception of books like Davidoff and Hall's *Family Fortunes,* the role of women in family business remains at best supporting, and often invisible. Ongoing work by Eleanor Hamilton, using narrative techniques, places women at the heart of both the family and the business (Hamilton 2006). This chapter has shown that business historians have a proud tradition of recognizing that families and firms are inseparable. Yet this analysis can be taken further by combining historical and postmodern social science methodologies to explore the pivotal and changing role of women in different firms, sectors, and societies.

References

ALBERT, M. (1991). *Capitalisme contre Capitalisme.* Paris: Editions du Seuil.

ALDRICH, H. E., and CLIFF, J. E. (2003). "The Pervasive Effects on Entrepreneurship: Embeddedness Perspective". *Journal of Business Venturing,* 18/5: 573–96.

AMATORI, F., and BRIOSCHI, F. (1997). "Le grandi imprese private: famiglie e coalizioni", in F. Barca (ed.), *Storia del capitalismo italiano.* Roma: Donzelli.

—— and COLLI, A. (1999). *Impresa e industria in Italia dall' Unità ad oggi.* Venice: Marsilio.

AMSDEN, A. (1986). *Asia's Next Giant.* Oxford: Oxford University Press.

ANONYMOUS REPORT (2003). "Family Businesses Dominate: International Family Enterprise Research Academy (IFERA)". *Family Business Review,* 16/4: 233–50.

ARNOLDUS, D. (2002). *Family, Firm and Strategy: Six Dutch Family Firms in the Food Industry, 1880–1970.* Amsterdam: Aksant Akademik Publishers.

ASTRACHAN, J. H., and SHANKER, M. C. (2003). "Family Businesses' Contribution to the US economy: A Closer Look". *Family Business Review,* 16/3: 150–67.

BACCINI, A., and VASTA, M. (1995). "Una tecnica ritrovata: interlocking directorates nei rapporti tra banca e industria in Italia (1911–1936)". *Rivista di storia economica II,* 12/2: 219–51.

BECATTINI, G., BELLANDI, M., DEI OTTATI, G., and SFORZI, F. (eds.) (2001). *Il caleidoscopio dello sviluppo locale: trasformazioni economiche nell'Italia contemporanea.* Turin: Rosenberg & Sellier.

BEN-PORATH, Y. (1980). "The F-Connection: Families, Friends and Firms and the Organization of Exchange". *Population and Development Review,* 6: 1–30.

BERLE, A. A., and MEANS, G. C. (1932). *The Modern Corporation and Private Property.* New York: World Inc.

BOSWELL, J. (1973). *The Rise and Decline of Small Firms.* London: Allen and Unwin.

BROEHL, W. (1992). *Cargill: Trading the World's Grain.* Hanover, NH: University Press of New England.

BROWN, R. A. (ed.) (1995). *Chinese Business Enterprise in Asia.* London: International Thomson Business Printing.

CAIN, P. J., and HOPKINS, A. G. (1993). *British Imperialism: Innovation and Expansion, 1688–1914*. London: Longman.

CASSIS, Y. (1997). *Big Business: The European Experience in the Twentieth Century*. Oxford: Oxford University Press.

CASSON, M. (1982). *The Entrepreneur*. London: Mark Robertson.

—— (1991). *The Economics of Business Culture: Game Theory, Transaction Costs and Economic Performance*. Oxford: Oxford University Press.

—— (1993). "Entrepreneurship and Business Culture", in Jonathan Brown and Mary B. Rose (eds.), *Entrepreneurship, Networks and Modern Business*. Manchester: Manchester University Press.

—— (1999). "The Economics of the Family Firm". *Scandinavian Economic History Review*, 47/1: 10–23.

CHANDLER, A. D. JR. (1977). *The Visible Hand: The Managerial Revolution in American Business*. Cambridge, Mass.: Harvard University Press.

—— (1990). *Scale and Scope*. Cambridge, Mass.: Harvard University Press.

CHANNON, D. F. (1973). *The Strategy and Structure of British Enterprise*. London: Macmillan.

CHEN, M. (1995). *Asian Management Systems: Chinese, Japanese and Korean Styles of Business*. London: Routledge.

CHURCH, R. (1969). *Kenricks in Hardware: A Family Business, 1791–1966*. Newton Abbot: David and Charles.

—— (1993). "The Family Firm in Industrial Capitalism: International Perspectives on Hypotheses and History". *Business History*, 35/4: 17–43.

COLLI, A. (1998). "Networking the Market: Evidence and Conjectures from the History of the Italian Industrial Districts". *European Yearbook of Business History*, 1: 75–92.

—— (2003). *The History of Family Business, 1850–2000*. Cambridge: Cambridge University Press.

—— and ROSE, M. B. (1999). "Families and Firms: The Culture and Evolution of Family Firms in Britain and Italy in the Nineteenth and Twentieth Centuries". *Scandinavian Economic History Review*, 47: 24–47.

————(2003). "Family Firms in Comparative Perspective", in F. Amatori and G. Jones, *Business History around the World*. Cambridge: Cambridge University Press.

—— PEREZ, F. P., and ROSE, M. B. (2003). "National Determinants of Family Firm Development? Family Firms in Britain, Spain and Italy in the Nineteenth and Twentieth Centuries". *Enterprise and Society*, 4/1: 28–64.

CORBETTA, G. (2001). "Family Business", in N. J. Smelser and P. B. Baltes (eds.), *International Encyclopaedia of the Social and Behavioural Sciences*. Oxford: Pergamon Press.

CROMIE, S., STEPHENSON, B., and MOUTEITH, D. (1995). "The Management of Family Firms: An Empirical Investigation". *International Small Business Journal*, 13/1: 11–34.

DAUNTON, M. (1988). "Inheritance and Succession in the City of London in the Nineteenth Century". *Business History*, 30/4: 269–86.

DAVIDOFF, L., and HALL, C. (1987). *Family Fortunes: Men and Women of the English Middle Classes, 1780–1850*. London: Hutchinson.

DETOUZE, M. L., LESTER, R., and SOLOW, R. (1989). *Made in America: Regaining the Productive Edge*. Cambridge, Mass.: MIT Press.

DONNELLY, R. G. (1964). "The Family Business". *Harvard Business Review*, 42/4: 93–105.

DRITSAS, M. (1997). "Family Firms in Greek Industry during the Twentieth Century", in Dritsas and Gourvish (1997).

—— and GOURVISH, T. (1997). *European Enterprise: Strategies of Adaptation and Renewal in the Twentieth Century*. Athens: Trochalia Publications.

DUTTA, S. (1997). *Family Business in India*. New Delhi: Response.

ERICKSON, C. (1959). *British Industrialists, Steel and Hosiery, 1850–1950*. Cambridge: Cambridge University Press.

FRUIN, W. M. (1998). "To Compare or Not to Compare: Two Books that Look at Capitalist Systems Across Centuries, Countries and Industries". *Business History Review*, 72/2: 123–36.

GALLO, M. A. (1995). "Empresa familiar: fortalezas y trampa", in Sindicato Empresarial Alavés (eds.), *Jornadas sobre la Empresa Familiar*, Vitoria: 9–26.

GERSCHENKRON, A. (1966). *Economic Backwardness in Historical Perspective*. Cambridge, Mass.: Harvard University Press.

GERSICK, K. E., DAVIS, J. A., HAMPTON, M. M., and LANSBERG, I. (1997). *Generation to Generation: Life Cycles of the Family Business*. Boston: Harvard Business School Press.

GRANOVETTER, M. (1996). "Coase Revisited: Business Groups in the Modern Economy". *Industrial and Corporate Change*, 4: 93–100.

—— and SWEDBERG, R. (eds.) (1992). *The Sociology of Economic Life*. Boulder, Colo.: Westview Press.

GUERCI, C. M. (1998). *Alle origini del successo: i campioni della media impresa industriale italiana*. Milan: Il Sole 24 Ore.

HALL, P. D. (1988). "A Historical Overview of Family Firms in the US". *Family Business Review*, 1/1: 51–68.

HAMILTON, E. (2006). "Whose Story is it Anyway? Narrative Accounts of the Role of Women in Founding and Establishing Family Businesses". *International Small Business Journal*, 24/3: 253–71.

HAMILTON, G. G., and FEENSTRA, R. C. (1995). "Varieties of Hierarchies and Markets: An Introduction". *Industrial and Corporate Change*, 4: 51–92.

HANDLER, W. C. (1989). "Methodological Issues and Consideration in Studying Family Business". *Family Business Review*, 2/3: 257–76.

HARRIS, R. (2000). *Industrializing English Law: Entrepreneurship and Business Organization*. Cambridge: Cambridge University Press.

HAU, M. (1995). "Traditions comportamentales et capitalisme dynastique: Le cas des 'grandes familles'". *Entreprises et Histoire*, 9: 43–59.

HERRIGEL, G. (1996). "Crisis in German Decentralized Production: Unexpected Rigidity and the Challenge of an Alternative". *European Urban and Regional Studies*, 3/1: 33–52.

HOFSTEDE, G. (1980). *Culture's Consequences: International Differences in Work-Related Values*. Beverly Hills, Calif.: Sage.

—— (1994) *Cultures and Organizations: Intercultural Co-operation and its importance to Survival: Software of the Mind*. London: HarperCollins.

HOWORTH, C., WESTHEAD, P., and WRIGHT, M. (2004). "Buyouts, Information Asymmetry and the Family Management Dyad". *Journal of Business Venturing*, 19/4: 509–34.

JAMES, H., and KOBRAK, C. (2004). "Persistent Traditions: Family Business in German". Working paper quoted with permission of the authors.

JEREMY, D., and SHAW, C. (eds.) (1984–6). *Dictionary of Business Biography: A Biographical Dictionary of Business Leaders in the period, 1860–1980*, 6 vols., London: Butterworths.

JOLY, H. (2003). "Ende des Familienkapitalismus". in *Die deutsche Wirtschaft im 20 Jahrhundert*. Essen: Klartext Verlag.

JONES, G., and ROSE, M. B. (1993). *Family Capitalism*. London: Frank Cass.

KENNEY, M. (2000). *Understanding Silicon Valley: The Anatomy of Understanding an Entrepreneurial Region*. Stanford, Calif.: Stanford University Press.

KETS DE VRIES, M. (1996). *Family Business: Human Dilemmas in the Family Firm: Text and Cases*. London: International Thomson Business Press.

KINDLEBERGER, C. P. (1964). *Economic Growth in France and Britain, 1851–1950*. Cambridge, Mass.: Harvard University Press.

KOCKA, J. (1999). *Industrial Culture and Bourgeois Society: Business Labor and Bureaucracy in Modern Germany*. New York: Berghahn Books.

KOEHN, N. (1999). *Brand New: How Entrepreneurs Earned Consumers' Trust from Wedgwood to Dell*. Cambridge, Mass.: Harvard University Press.

KWOLEK-FOLLAND, A. (2001). "Gender and Business History". *Enterprise and Society*, 2/1: 15–25.

LANGLOIS, R. N., and ROBERTSON, P. L. (1995). *Firms, Markets and Economic Change*. London: Routledge.

LANSBERG, I., and PERROW, E. (1991). "Understanding and Working with Leading Family Businesses in Latin America". *Family Business Review*, 4/2: 65–80.

LEVINSON, H. (1971). "Conflicts that Plague the Family Business". *Harvard Business Review*, Mar.–Apr.: 90–5.

LEE, D. S, LIM, G. H., and LIM, W. S. (2003). "Family Business Succession: Appropriation Risk and Choice of Successor". *Academy of Management Review*, 28/4: 657–66.

LEE, Y. (1997). *The State, Society and Big Business in South Korea*. London: Routledge.

LINDGREN, H. (1979). *Corporate Growth: The Swedish Match Industry in its Global setting*. Stockholm: LiberFörlag.

McCRAW, T. (1997). *Creating Modern Capitalism*. Cambridge, Mass.: Harvard University Press.

MORCK, R., and YEUNG, B. (2003). "Agency Problems in Large Family Business Groups". *Entrepreneurship: Theory and Practice*, 3: 367–82.

MORIKAWA, H. (1992). *Zaibatsu: The Rise and Fall of Family Enterprise Groups in Japan*. Tokyo: University of Tokyo Press.

——(2001). *A History of Top Management in Japan: Managerial Enterprises and Family Enterprises*. Tokyo: University of Tokyo Press.

NAFZIGER, E. W. (1969). "The Effect of the Nigerian Extended Family on Entrepreneurial Activity". *Economic Activity and Cultural Change*, 18: 25–33.

NEUBAUER, F., and LANK, A. G. (1998). *The Family Business: In Governance for Sustainability*. New York: Routledge.

PAYNE, P. (1984). "Family Business in Britain: An Historical and Analytical Surve", in Akio Okochi and Shigeaki Yasuoka (eds.), *Family Business in the Era of Industrial Growth*. Tokyo: University of Tokyo Press.

PENROSE, E. (1959). *The Theory of the Growth of the Firm*. Oxford: Oxford University Press.

PIORE, M. J., and SABEL, C. F. (1985). *The Second Industrial Divide: Possibilities for Prosperity*. New York: Basic Books.

POLLAK, ROBERT A. (1985). "A Transaction Cost Approach to Families and Households". *Journal of Economic Literature*, 23, June: 581–608.

POLLARD, S. (1965). *The Genesis of Modern Management*. London: Penguin.

PORTER, G. (1993). *The Rise of Big Business; 1860–1920*, 2nd edn. Wheeling, Ill.: Harland Davidson.

POUTZIOURIS, P., and CHITTENDEN, F. (1996). *Family Business or Business Families*? Leeds: Institute for Small Business Affairs.

REDDING, S. G. (1993). *The Spirit of Chinese Capitalism*. Berlin: Walter de Gruyter.

ROMANO, R. (1985). *I Crespi: Origini, fortuna e tramonto di una dinastia lombarda*. Milan: Angeli.

ROSE, M. B. (1993). "The Family Firm and the Management of Successio", in Jonathan Brown and Mary B. Rose (eds.), *Entrepreneurship, Networks and Modern Business*. Manchester: Manchester University Press.

—— (1994). "The Family Firm in British Business, 1780–1914", in M. W. Kirby and M. B. Rose (eds.), *Business Enterprise in Modern Britain*. London: Routledge.

—— (ed.) (1996). *Family Business*. Aldershot: Edward Elgar.

—— (1998). "Networks and Leadership Succession in British Business in the 1950s". *European Yearbook of Business History*, 1: 57–74.

—— (1999). "Networks, Values and Business: The Evolution of British Family Firms from the Eighteenth to the Twentieth Century". *Entreprises et histoire*, 22: 16–30.

—— (2000). *Firms, Networks and Business Values: The British and American Cotton Industries since 1750*. Cambridge: Cambridge University Press.

SABEL, C. F., and ZEITLIN, J. (1985). "Historical Alternatives to Mass Production: Politics, Markets, and Technology in Nineteenth-Century Industrialization". *Past and Present*, 108: 133–76.

SCRANTON, P. (1983). *Proprietary Capitalism: The Textile Manufacture of Philadelphia, 1800–1885*. Cambridge: Cambridge University Press.

—— (1997). *Endless Novelty: Specialty Production and American Industrialisation, 1865–1925*. Princeton, NJ: Princeton University Press.

SHARMA, P. (2004). "An Overview of the Field of Family Business Studies: Current Status and Directions for the Future". *Family Business Review*, 17/1: 1–36.

SLUYTERMAN, K. E., and WINKELMAN, H. J. M. (1993). "The Dutch Family Firm Confronted with Chandler's Dynamics of Industrial Capitalism, 1890–1940". *Business History*, 35/4: 152–83.

SUPPLE, B. (1991). "Scale and Scope: Alfred Chandler and the Dynamics of Industrial Capitalism". *Economic History Review*, 44/4: 510–12.

WESTHEAD, P., and COWLING, M. (1998). "Family Firm Research: The Need for a Methodological Rethink". *Entrepreneurship Theory and Practice*, 23, fall: 31–56.

—— and HOWORTH, C. (2004). "Ownership and Management Structure, Company Objectives and Performance: An Empirical Examination of Family Firms". Paper presented at the International Family Enterprise Research Academy, Fourth Annual Research Conference, Sweden: Jonkoping International Business School.

WHITLEY, R. (2000). *Divergent Capitalisms: The Social Structuring and Change of Business Systems*. Oxford: Oxford University Press.

WIERSEMA, M. (1992). "Strategic Consequences of Executive Succession within Diversified Firms". *Journal of Management Studies*, 29: 73–94.

WORLD BANK (1999). *Corporate Governance: A Framework for Implementation*. New York: World Bank.

CHAPTER 10

....

INDUSTRIAL DISTRICTS AND REGIONAL CLUSTERS

....

JONATHAN ZEITLIN

10.1 THE REDISCOVERY OF INDUSTRIAL DISTRICTS: A DISCIPLINARY PARADOX

....

DURING the 1980s, a long-forgotten concept unexpectedly re-emerged at the center of international debates about economic restructuring: the industrial district. Originally coined at the end of the nineteenth century by the British economist Alfred Marshall (1922, 1927, 1975) to describe sectorally specialized agglomerations of small and medium-sized enterprises (SMEs) such as Lancashire cottons, Sheffield cutlery, and South Wales tinplate, the concept was revived nearly a century later by the Italian economists Giacomo Becattini (2004) and Sebastiano Brusco (1982, 1989, 1990) to capture the extraordinary efflorescence of similar decentralized industrial complexes across the central and northeastern regions of

For helpful comments on earlier drafts of this chapter, I am indebted to Luigi Burroni, Francesca Carnevali, Jean-Claude Daumas, Gary Herrigel, Geoffrey Jones, Michel Lescure, Chuck Sabel, and Josh Whitford.

their own country.[1] Economists, geographers, sociologists, political scientists, and business scholars quickly discovered a broad array of analogous local and regional production systems scattered across Western Europe, North America, and East Asia. As in central and northeast Italy, many of these districts specialized in light, labor-intensive industries like clothing, textiles, shoes, jewelry, and furniture, but a substantial proportion could also be found in more technologically demanding and capital-intensive sectors such as metalworking, machine tools, ceramics, plastics, aerospace, electronics, film and other entertainment/communications media.[2]

These industrial districts—sometimes known by other cognate terms such as local production systems, regional economies, or territorial clusters—attracted widespread attention for a number of interrelated reasons. Foremost among these were their impressive economic performance, as measured by new firm formation, employment, and exports; their capacity for endogenous development; and their ability to sustain high relative wages and labor standards in the face of international competition. No less remarkable, however, were the districts' flexibility in adapting to changing markets and demand patterns; their capacity for generating and diffusing technological innovation in products and processes; and their ability to combine competition and cooperation among local actors. Taken together, these accomplishments challenged established models of industrial progress based on mass production by large, vertically integrated corporations, and suggested to many observers that the districts could constitute a new organizational framework for flexible specialization in an increasingly volatile post-Fordist economy.[3]

Such contemporary upheavals in markets, technology, and industrial organization in turn raised new questions about the historical antecedents of industrial districts and flexible production, which Charles Sabel and I among others began to explore (Sabel and Zeitlin 1985, 1997). Few historians at that time were interested in or aware of industrial districts, even if there were points of contact with the burgeoning literature on protoindustrialization, as well as on the origins of mass production and the modern corporation. This disjunction was particularly apparent in the Italian case, where social scientists rather than historians were displaying a keen interest in the origins and development of "diffused industrialization" in the "Third Italy", defined in opposition to the large-firm dominated "industrial triangle" of the northwest and the underdeveloped south (Bagnasco 1988; Trigilia 1986, 1989, 1990; Becattini 1999, 2001, 2003). But the relative disinterest of most historians was equally striking in the case of France, where

---

[1] For early English-language collections of this work, see Goodman *et al.* (1989) and Pyke *et al.* (1990).

[2] For overviews, see Sabel (1989) and Pyke and Sengenberger (1992).

[3] The *locus classicus* for this view is Piore and Sabel (1984); for a review of the ensuing debate, see Hirst and Zeitlin (1991).

"fabriques collectives" closely resembling the Italian industrial districts had played a crucial and dynamic role in nineteenth and early twentieth century manufacturing, as well as in the United States, Germany, and Britain, where the concept itself originated.[4]

It was not until the mid-1990s, some ten to fifteen years after the onset of the original debate, that historians in Italy, France, Britain, Germany, the United States, and Japan really began to produce a significant body of new research on industrial districts and flexible production. This time lag doubtless reflects the long gestation period of historical research projects, as well as the role of generational succession in shifting the balance of historiographical debate. In any case, the results of this shift are extremely impressive: a proliferation of excellent historical articles, monographs, and edited volumes, both national and comparative, documenting an extraordinary range of districts too vast to enumerate individually here.[5]

But therein lies a paradox. At the same time as historians have discovered the attractions of the industrial district as a research subject, regional economies have been changing in ways that are leading contemporary social analysts to question the continued applicability of the concept, at least in its classic form. This is true not only of countries like France and Britain, where claims of a contemporary resurgence of industrial districts met with considerable skepticism from the outset, but also to a growing extent in Italy as well. Is this just the standard "owl of Minerva" syndrome, whereby the serious historical study of a topic can only begin once it is truly past? Or does the contemporary reorganization of the industrial districts and the associated reconfiguration of the relationship between the local and the global open up new questions, both theoretical and empirical, around which historians and contemporary social researchers might conduct a mutually productive dialogue?

I will return to these questions by way of conclusion, after first considering the definition and conceptualization of industrial districts, their origins and

---

[4] For a pioneering historical discussion of the "fabriques collectives" by a French sociologist, see Cottereau (1986); another French sociologist, who participated in the rediscovery of "localized industrial systems" during the 1980s, has referred to them as "invisible objects" (Raveyre and Saglio 1984; Saglio 2005). For parallel critiques of the "blending out" of decentralized regional economies and specialty production in standard narratives of German and American industrial history, see Herrigel (1996) and Scranton (1997) respectively. A major exception to these strictures was Japan, where there was a longstanding historical interest in geographic concentrations of small and medium-sized enterprises known as *sanchi* (production districts) or *jiba sangyo* (community-based industries): see for example Abe (1992, 1999). But even there, as Yonemitsu and Tolliday (2003) point out, much of the most influential work, in both English and Japanese, was produced by social scientists rather than historians.

[5] Any short list is necessarily invidious. But prominent examples of recent historical work in this area include: Sabel and Zeitlin (1997); Scranton (1997); Odaka and Sawai (1999); Amatori and Colli (2001); Eck and Lescure (2002); Alaimo (2002); Colli (2002a); Wilson and Popp (2003); Lescure (2006).

sustainability, governance mechanisms, the influence of national institutions, and the nature of current transformations.

10.2 PROBLEMS OF DEFINITION AND CONCEPTUALIZATION

Part of the problem is one of definition and conceptualization. Those who insist on the limited contemporary relevance of industrial districts typically refer to the "canonical" model of the Marshallian district as a "socio-economic notion" elaborated by Giacomo Becattini and others (Becattini 2004; Becattini *et al.* 2003) on the basis of postwar Italian experience. Like Marshall himself, these Italian authors emphasized the external economies of specialization, information, and skilled labor supply arising from the concentration of large numbers of SMEs engaged in a single industrial sector (including "subsidiary" industries such as machinery manufacture) within a localized geographical area. And they likewise embraced Marshall's account of the dynamic benefits of such districts' "industrial atmosphere" in stimulating the acquisition of specialized skills and the diffusion of innovation through informal socialization and interaction among local actors. But their "canonical" model went on to embellish these elements of Marshall's original concept by adding a series of more explicitly "social" features drawn from a stylized account of the Italian districts, such as a non-metropolitan, small-town environment; a set of shared values like hard work, cooperation, and collective identity; and a local social structure dominated by small entrepreneurs and skilled artisans.[6]

Despite its theoretical coherence and heuristic value, this tightly specified neo-Marshallian model of the "canonical" district had the disadvantage of excluding many apparently similar specialized agglomerations of SMEs that did not share all of the prescribed socio-cultural features, including important Italian cases such as Bologna's packaging machinery cluster, which had to be classified instead as an "urban industrial subsystem" (Capecchi 1997: 381).[7] Hence contemporary scholars like Storper (1997), Porter (1998), Crouch *et al.* (2001, 2004), or Courlet (2005) who argue for the continuing importance of "local production systems" or "regional clusters" typically adopt a looser definition encompassing a wider typology of empirical cases, including not only classic industrial districts like woolen textiles in Prato or metalworking in France's Arve Valley, but also "technological districts"

---

[6] For a fuller discussion of the relationship between Marshall and Becattini's conceptions of the industrial district, see Zeitlin (1992).

[7] A recent careful attempt by Paniccia (2002) to operationalize the quantitative identification of Italian industrial districts found that only a small minority corresponded to the canonical model.

such as Silicon Valley or Cologne's new media complex, "commercial service districts" like Lille–Roubaix–Tourcoing, "financial districts" like the City of London, and "logistics districts" like Duisburg or Venlo on the Dutch-German-Belgian border.[8] Historians, especially those operating outside Italy, have often found the neo-Marshallian model of the industrial district excessively restrictive, and have therefore preferred to develop more variegated typologies of their own. Thus Wilson and Popp (2003), in their recent collection of essays on Britain distinguish between districts, clusters, and regional business networks, mainly in terms of geographical scale and the linkages between firms and industries. More elaborately still, Scranton's grand tour of US specialty production in the late nineteenth and early twentieth centuries not only differentiates firms into "integrated anchors", "networked specialists", "specialist auxiliaries", and "outliers", but also localities into "interactive", "parallel", "derivative", and "narrow focus" sites (Scranton 1997: 81–3).

My own view, formulated originally at the beginning of the 1990s (Zeitlin 1992), is that the industrial districts debate, both contemporary and historical, would benefit by moving away from a "thick", "closed" model based on a stylized account of a particular national experience towards a "thin", "open" model capable of accommodating a variety of empirically observable forms.[9] Such a model might take its point of departure from Marshall's original definition of the district as a geographically localized productive system based on an extended division of labor between small and medium-sized firms specialized in distinct phases or complementary activities within a common industrial sector. Each of these elements in turn could be transformed into empirical scalar variables, yielding a multiplicity of intermediate or hybrid cases defined in terms of their relation to the ideal type: for example, the degree of localization, the size distribution of productive units, and the extent of inter-firm linkages. I also argued for the necessity of separating structure and performance, avoiding the assumption that industrial districts defined in this way are necessarily innovative, flexible, consensual, or otherwise successful. For as comparative and historical research has shown, stagnant or declining districts display many of the same structural features (such as geographical localization and an extended inter-firm division of labor) as their more vibrant counterparts. Nor is there any reason to assume that as industrial districts develop, they will necessarily evolve towards the pure Marshallian model.

At the same time, however, concepts cannot be stretched indefinitely without losing their analytical power, and there is some degree of variation on each of these dimensions (localization, size distribution, linkages) beyond which it becomes no longer useful to speak of a local economy as an industrial district (even if it is

[8] On logistics districts, see also Bologna (1998); on the City of London as a financial district, see Amin and Thrift (1992).

[9] See also the convergent observations in Courault and Romani (1992) and Daumas (2004).

difficult to specify a precise threshold in advance).[10] And it is worth recalling in this context that, as elaborated in Chapter 6 above on the "historical alternatives" approach, industrial districts *per se* are neither necessary nor sufficient conditions for flexible production, but rather one possible organizational framework within which the latter may flourish, alongside large internally decentralized or federated firms and networks of external suppliers.

10.3 ORIGINS AND SUSTAINABILITY

Closely related to the choice between a narrow and an expansive conceptualization of industrial districts is the question of origins. The neo-Marshallian model of the "canonical" district, as we saw, included a series of distinctive socio-cultural characteristics, such as a local collective identity based on cooperation among independent artisans, skilled wage workers, and small-firm owners. And these features of diffused industrialization in the Third Italy were widely interpreted as a product of historical inheritances such as the extended family, sharecropping, and peasant proprietorship, and local political subcultures, both "red" (Socialist/Communist) and "white" (Catholic).

This reinterpretation of the Marshallian district proved fruitful both in focusing attention on the distinctive social and historical features of Italian small-firm development and in stimulating the search for analogous phenomena elsewhere. In certain such cases discovered by social scientists and historians, the social matrix of development bears some affinities to that of the Third Italy. In France, for example, agrarian smallholdings, independent artisans, and a "white" or "red" political subculture also appear to have contributed to the formation of industrial districts in places like Cholet, Oyonnax, and the Arve Valley; and a similar argument could be made for Baden-Württemberg or the Bergisches Land in Germany and West Jutland in Denmark.[11]

But there are many other possible examples which do not fit this model, especially if we are prepared to include technological districts emerging from the decline of large-scale mass production like the automotive and industrial automation complex in and around Turin or contemporary high-tech regions such as Silicon Valley, whose origins turn out, as recent historical research has shown, to owe as much to

---

[10] A logical criterion for defining such a threshold is that a local economy should no longer be considered an industrial district when inter-firm ties *outside* the area become more important than those *within* it. I am indebted to Chuck Sabel for suggesting this formulation.

[11] On Cholet, see Minguet (1992), Courault and Rerat (1992), Lescure (2002). On Oyonnax, see Saglio (1997, 2005). On the Arve Valley, see Courlet (1992) and Judet (2006). On Baden-Württemberg and the Bergisches Land, see Herrigel (1996) and Boch (1997). On West Jutland, see Kristensen (1992) and Kristensen and Sabel (1997).

military procurement, itinerant engineers, and local amateur radio operators as to university science.[12] Even for earlier periods, moreover, Italian historians now place increasing emphasis on the role of medium-sized towns, public technical schools, and large firms themselves as crucial sources of skills and entrepreneurial experience for the emergence of dynamic local productive systems during the course of the twentieth century.[13]

Thus it seems that there is no empirically plausible short list of contextual factors conducive to the formation of industrial districts—any more than for economic development more generally. The deeper researchers dig into the evolution of industrial districts in countries like Italy, France, Germany, Denmark, or the United States, the greater the number of additional factors that need to be integrated into the story, and the more the result comes to look like an irreducibly diverse set of historical descriptions rather than a single overarching theoretical explanation.

This impasse in the search for the origins of industrial districts should have the correlative benefit of redirecting attention towards the more important question of their reproduction and sustainability. For whatever their origins, industrial districts or local productive systems which survive for an extended period of time are typically obliged to surmount a succession of challenges and crises, both internal and external. Most fundamental of these is the need to respond to periodic shifts in markets and technologies, which may involve far-reaching changes in products, materials, and skills, as well as in forms of organization. A capacity for collective innovation, adaptation, and reconversion is thus the hallmark of successful districts over the longer term, whose mechanisms require further exploration.

10.4 Institutions and Governance

This brings us to the question of institutions and governance. Much of the theoretical literature on industrial districts claims that the costs of decentralized transactions are contained by a cultural disposition among local actors towards trust and cooperation resulting from the embeddedness of social relations within a closely knit community. And historians seeking to explain the prevalence of

---

[12] For Turin's evolution from a FIAT company town to an "automotive technology district", see Bianchi *et al.* (2001). For recent historical research on the origins of Silicon Valley, see Lécuyer (2002); Heinrich (2002); Kenney (2000). For discussions of the distinctive properties and developmental trajectories of "high-tech" districts, see Crouch *et al.* (2004: pt. III); Trigilia (2005); Burroni (2004). One could make similar arguments about the evolution of entertainment districts like Hollywood or of financial districts like the City of London, on which there is now a substantial historical literature. For Hollywood, see Storper (1989, 1997); Scott (2005). On the City of London and other international financial centers, see Kynaston (1994–2001); Cassis and Bussière (2005); Cassis (2006).

[13] For a useful synthetic overview, see Alaimo (1999).

opportunistic behavior and conflict within particular industrial districts, such as the North Staffordshire potteries, have often attributed such negative outcomes to a lack of trust and social cohesion within the local business culture (Popp 2001). Explanations of this type are not only intrinsically tautologous, but also run foul of a key finding of comparative research, namely that most successful districts have experienced more or less severe internal tensions and overt conflicts among local actors at various points in their histories. The key issue thus shifts from the assumed role of cooperative business cultures in preventing the emergence of conflicts of economic interest among local actors to the institutional mechanisms through which such conflicts were managed and resolved.[14]

In a recent study of the Birmingham Jewelry Quarter, for example, Francesca Carnevali (2004) argues that trust and cooperation within industrial districts do not arise spontaneously, but depend instead on the conscious efforts of governance institutions such as trade associations. In Birmingham, ease of entry into the trade and the economic incentives for embezzlement of high-value materials meant that control of opportunistic behavior resulted from the ability of the local jewelers' association to assess the character of its members, monitor their activities through credit checks and investigations, and enforce the law against bad actors.

Carnevali's persuasive analysis of the Birmingham case confirms the findings of comparative-historical research on industrial districts more broadly. In order to serve as an effective framework for flexible production, a growing body of empirical studies shows, industrial districts must develop a set of coordination and governance mechanisms capable of checking opportunistic behavior without stifling fluid cooperation among decentralized economic actors. Crucial in this regard are institutions for the resolution of disputes and the provision of collective services beyond the capacity of individual small and medium-sized firms to supply for themselves, such as training, research, market forecasting, credit, and quality control (Sabel and Zeitlin 1985, 1997).

Although the functions performed by such governance mechanisms display many common features across districts, their organizational form varies widely. Examples from the case studies examined in Sabel and Zeitlin (1997) include joint boards of conciliation and arbitration like the French *conseils de prud'hommes*; piece price lists or *tarifs*; standard-setting bodies; collective vocational education and training systems; and cooperative research and technology transfer institutions. There were also institutions which blurred the line between regulation and service provision, such as the rules for apprentice payment, design copyright, and repayment of loans for equipment purchase in the nineteenth-century Lyon silk *fabrique*, which as Alain Cottereau (1997) shows, were designed at one and the same time to ensure equity and encourage collective investments in product and process innovation and training. A recent collection of essays on "intermediate institutions

---

[14] For fuller discussions, see Zeitlin (1992) and Chapter 6 above.

and local development" in Italy (Arrighetti and Seravalli 1999; cf. also Provasi 2002) likewise emphasizes their "variable morphology", with different bodies playing the lead role in organizing the provision of public goods and services in different times and places, from charitable foundations and craft guilds in eighteenth-century Lumezzane, through professional schools in late nineteenth-century Friuli, to municipal governments and rural banks in Modena and Castel Goffredo after 1945.

Neither the range of necessary collective services nor the appropriate organizational framework for their provision can thus be specified precisely in advance. Hence perhaps the most critical, but also the most fragile, institutional requirement for the sustained reproduction of industrial districts is the constitution of a public deliberative forum or policy network open to the full range of relevant local actors within which effective solutions to common problems can be jointly discovered.[15]

10.5 THE IMPACT OF NATIONAL INSTITUTIONS AND PUBLIC POLICIES

If the sustained reproduction of industrial districts depends on the existence of a robust set of governance mechanisms for collective problem-solving, then the differential impact, both positive and negative, of national institutions and public policies must play a major part in any comparative analysis.

I have sought to sketch out elsewhere the key elements of the process whereby the United Kingdom was transformed during the first three-quarters of the twentieth century from a kaleidoscope of Marshallian industrial districts to the most concentrated of all advanced capitalist economies, with few if any dynamic local clusters of small and medium-sized firms (Zeitlin 1995; cf. Crouch and Farrell 2001). Among the critical factors identified in this analysis were the early amalgamation and centralization of the banking system, the promotion of industrial concentration through mergers and acquisitions by the state and the capital markets, and the progressive reduction of local government autonomy within a unitary constitutional polity.[16]

On the more positive side, Gary Herrigel (1996) and others have traced in rich detail how the changing national framework of German federalism influenced the fortunes of decentralized regional economies in different eras from the Kaiserreich through Weimar and Nazism to the postwar *Bundesrepublik*. Among the key elements of this story are the shifting fiscal autonomy of state and local governments,

---

[15] For the concept of an "industrial public sphere", see Hirst and Zeitlin (1991) and Zeitlin (1992).
[16] For a convergent and more fully documented analysis, see Carnevali (2005).

the (re)construction of a multi-tiered regional banking system oriented towards *Mittelstand* finance (cf. also Deeg 1999), and the 1957 compromise on antitrust legislation which permitted the survival of specialization cartels.

The French case presents a number of peculiarities which have begun to attract the attention of historians in recent years. One of these is the flourishing of *fabriques collectives* during the nineteenth and early twentieth centuries[17] despite the absence of a firm legal/political basis for local regulation stemming from what Hirsch and Minard (1998) call "the Le Chaplier effect", the weakness of intermediate institutions between state and citizen resulting from their *de jure* abolition during the Revolution. Another puzzle is the longstanding persistence of numerous local and regional banks despite the rise of a powerful circle of Paris-centric financial institutions, which as Michel Lescure (1995, 2003, 2004) has argued, depended not only on the informational advantages derived from intimate knowledge of their small and medium-sized industrial customers, but also on the favorable discounting policies pursued by the Bank of France from the 1900s to the 1930s. After 1945, conversely, there is a broad consensus on the responsibility of national state industrial, credit, and merger policies for the dramatic destructuration and decline of most of the country's historic industrial districts and flexible regional economies.[18]

Comparatively little attention, by contrast, has been devoted to the impact of national institutions and policies on the development of industrial districts in Italy. Insofar as Italian scholars have seen the national state as a causal factor in the rise of the industrial districts, it is generally in negative terms, emphasizing for example the failure of French-style efforts at rationalization and centralization of industrial policy and labor relations during the 1960s and 70s (Locke 1995). Other forms of state intervention such as the favorable legal regime for artisanal firms or subsidized loan schemes for small business are viewed as too generic to explain much about the territorially differentiated growth of industrial districts in certain regions but not others.[19] Yet some recent research suggests that the national state may have played a larger part in this story. Thus Giovanni Ferri (2006) makes a strong case for the negative impact on Italian industrial districts of the trade, industrial, and financial policies of the Fascist regime, which were largely reversed after 1945. Ferri and Giuseppe Conti (Conti and Ferri 1997) have also underlined the positive contribution of the Bank of Italy's postwar "via svizzera" strategy in supporting through its discount policies local and regional bank lending to small and medium-sized district firms—another sharp point of contrast with the French situation during *les trentes glorieuses*.

In the United States, many features of national institutions and public policy appear to have exerted a negative influence on the long-term prosperity and survival of industrial districts and regional clusters. Thus, for example, as Alfred Chandler

---

[17] For useful surveys, see Cottereau (1986) and Dewerpe (1992).

[18] See for example Ganne (1995), and for the key case of Lyon textiles, Sabel and Zeitlin (1985).

[19] Compare Weiss (1988) with Trigilia (1992).

(1977, 1990) himself has long emphasized, antitrust policy made a major contribution to the growth of mergers and concentration in US industry by prohibiting cartels, pools, and other cooperative arrangements between legally separate firms prevalent in other capitalist economies like Germany during the late nineteenth and early twentieth centuries.[20] But as Gerald Berk (1994) has persuasively demonstrated, judicial actions such as court-ordered receiverships, debt write-downs, and rate regulation decisions played an equally critical part in shaping the outcome of late nineteenth and early twentieth-century struggles between regionalist and transcontinental system-building strategies on the US railroads. During the 1920s and 1930s, similarly, the Justice Department and the Supreme Court repeatedly struck down efforts by firms and public officials (including Federal Trade Commissioners and prominent antitrust jurists like Louis Brandeis) to regulate competition, orchestrate information exchange, and promote collaborative learning within decentralized specialty trades through institutional mechanisms such as "trade conferences", "open price associations", and industry codes. Yet as both Scranton (1997, 1998) and Berk (forthcoming) have also shown, localized specialty producers like Cincinnati machine tool makers and Grand Rapids furniture manufacturers were nonetheless able to organize the provision of collective services, enforce informal rules of trade behavior, and even coordinate effective resistance to price cuts in recessions, while "developmental" trade associations in industries such as printing were permitted by the courts to collect and disseminate detailed information on production costs provided that they refrained from explicitly discussing selling prices. After World War II, moreover, antitrust consent decrees obliging Bell Laboratories and IBM to license their transistor and computer technologies to competing firms provided a vital stimulus to the development of Silicon Valley as a regional electronics complex (Borrus and Zysman 1997). Another important, though still scarcely explored issue, concerns the likely contribution to the continuing emergence of new local industrial clusters of the United States' decentralized commercial banking system, reinforced until the mid-1990s by federal legislation prohibiting cross-state branching (Verdier 2002; Berger et al. 1999).

In the case of Japan, a growing wave of scholarship has documented the largely positive impact of both public and private institutions, especially at the local level, in fostering the development of industrial districts. In the name of freedom of trade, the early Meiji government abolished craft guilds and local trade associations which had played an important role during the Tokugawa era in regulating business transactions, endorsing credit applications, and organizing apprenticeship training. But following widespread discontent among domestic merchants and artisans, the Meiji state legalized the formation of local trade associations (*dōgyō kumiai*) in 1884 and authorized them over the next two decades to perform collective functions such as quality inspection and the creation of trade schools for technical training.

---

[20] See also Keller (1980); Hannah (1979).

These local trade associations rapidly took root not only in historic urban craft centers like Kyoto and Osaka, but also in rural small-firm districts like the silk-reeling and cotton-weaving *sanchi* (producing centers). During the 1920s and 1930s, the national government sought to reinforce cooperation among localized groups of small firms, especially those producing for export, through the formation of industrial or manufacturers' associations (*kōgyō kumiai*) armed with stronger powers of compulsory membership and authorized to engage in collective activities such as joint purchasing, processing, marketing, and credit intermediation, which enabled them to do business on more equal terms with the large-firm sector. Although these compulsory organizations were formally disbanded after World War II, many of their functions were taken over by new trade and cooperative associations, which continue to provide a range of collective services to localized clusters of SMEs such as the urban machining districts of Hishagi-Osaka and Tokyo's Ota Ward (Fujita 1998; Abe 1992, 1999; Morris-Suzuki 1994; Whittaker 1997).

From the late nineteenth century onwards, Japanese small-firm associations of all types collaborated closely with prefectural and municipal administrations in adapting imported technologies, improving indigenous production methods, diffusing innovations, and training skilled personnel through the creation of experimental workshops, research laboratories and institutes, trade schools, and technical schools, whose numbers, scope, and sophistication have continued to expand during the post-World War II era (Morris-Suzuki 1994; Whittaker 1997; Sawai 1999). During the 1950s and 1960s, the Ministry of Trade and Industry (MITI) vigorously attempted to promote rationalization and concentration of fragmented sectors like machine tools and auto parts through a combination of administrative guidance and selective financial incentives. Not only did firms and their associations in these sectors prove largely successful in resisting such bureaucratic pressures for mergers and amalgamations, but local chambers of commerce (*shōkōkai*) were often able to redirect MITI funds towards the contrary purpose of promoting the development of small enterprise clusters through support for technology diffusion, start-up finance, and the provision of collective services, as David Friedman (1988) has shown in detail for the machining district of Sakaki. More generally, small firms in Japanese industrial districts have benefited from a wide range of specialized financial institutions and credit guarantee schemes, both governmental and associational, which have also encouraged commercial lending to approved enterprises by regional and city banks (Whittaker 1997). At the same time, however, recent accounts of declining craft districts like Arita pottery and Nishijin silk weaving suggest that access to credit and provision of collective services have not been matched by the development of institutional mechanisms for regulating competition and resolving conflicts among local actors (Yonemitsu and Tolliday 2003; Hareven 2002).

Synthesizing the results of comparative research on these six countries, as well as on other major cases such as Denmark (Kristensen and Sabel 1997), it seems possible to identify on a *prima facie* basis those institutional and policy conditions which have had the greatest impact on the reproduction and decline of industrial districts. Among the major axes of such cross-national variation are the territorial structure of the banking and financial system, the relative concentration of retail distribution, the effectiveness of state rationalization and merger policies, the form and intensity of antitrust regulation, the extent of political tolerance and/or encouragement of associational governance, and the balance between administrative centralization and local government autonomy.[21]

From this last consideration, it is apparent that the reconfiguration of territorial governance may have a significant impact on the fortunes of industrial districts within different national contexts. Thus the prospects for the emergence and sustainability of dynamic industrial districts and clusters seem to have been enhanced by the widespread trend towards decentralization and devolution of authority from the national state to local and regional governments visible in historically unitary polities like France and the UK as well as in federal systems such as Canada and Belgium.[22] In some respects, too, the development of multi-level governance within the European Union has operated in a similar direction. Thus the construction of collective problem-solving capacities through concertation among local actors has been stimulated in many areas by the partnership requirements imposed by the European structural cohesion funds, as well as by related EU programs such as territorial employment pacts and local/regional action plans for employment and social inclusion.[23] Conversely, however, other dimensions of European economic and political integration may have a more negative impact on the institutional supports for flexible regional economies, such as the European Commission's current efforts to eliminate public guarantees for the non-profit savings and co-operative banks which remain the predominant source of finance for Germany's industrial *Mittelstand* (Deeg 1999; Hommell and Schneider 2003; Grossman 2006).

10.6 CONTEMPORARY TRANSFORMATIONS AND CHALLENGES

But the greatest challenges to today's industrial districts come less from such political shifts than from deeper economic and technological transformations: the

---

[21] For stimulating discussions of the historical relationship between political and financial centralization/decentralization, as well as their implications for the fortunes of industrial districts in different countries and periods, see Verdier (1998, 2002); Forsyth and Verdier (2003).

[22] For an overview of this trend, see Ansell and Gingrich (2003). It is far too early to gauge the economic impact of the recent constitutional movement towards federalization and regional devolution in Italy. See, for example, the discussion in Ferrera and Gualmini (2004) and Vandelli (2002).

[23] See, for example, Sabel (1996); Geddes and Benington (2001); Zeitlin and Trubek (2003); Kristensen and Zeitlin (2005); Zeitlin and Pochet (2005).

dramatic acceleration in the pace and volatility of change in products, markets, and production processes, often subsumed under the ambiguous concept of "globalization". At issue here is not so much competition from suppliers of similar goods and services in lower-wage countries, though that is certainly a problem for some districts. The more fundamental challenges instead are how to combine continuous improvements in cost, quality, design, and service for existing types of products and processes, while simultaneously developing the capacity to respond rapidly to the emergence of alternative technologies and/or abrupt shifts in demand for whole classes of goods.

Schematizing brutally, we can say that successful responses to these challenges have generally required closer, more continuous, and more formalized collaboration among economic actors within the districts on the one hand, and new combinations of knowledge and capabilities from multiple geographical sources on the other. The precise outcomes vary significantly across nations and regions, for example between Tuscany and the Veneto.[24] But three broad trends can nonetheless be delineated: (1) increased differentiation in the size distribution of enterprises within the districts, whether through the emergence of large "leader firms" or through the creation of formal and informal groups of firms (often including equity participations in key suppliers); (2) increased sourcing of products and materials from outside the district, including through direct investment in production facilities in other regions and countries; and (3) increased investment within the districts by foreign multinationals, who have often bought up key local firms.[25]

One major result of these trends towards greater internal differentiation and external openness of the districts has been to place great strains on their traditional governance mechanisms, especially where these have relied primarily on local tacit knowledge and informal social norms. Thus in the case of Prato, often viewed as the closest living example of a "canonical" Marshallian district, asymmetries in information and power among local economic actors resulting from such trends gave rise in the 1990s to a breakdown in the capacity of what Gabi dei Ottati (one of Becattini's close collaborators) has termed the "communitarian market" to contain opportunistic behavior. One particularly striking consequence of this breakdown was the crisis of Prato's Cassa di Risparmio, which was no longer in a position to evaluate authoritatively the financial position of local businesses or the technical and commercial merits of proposed investment projects.[26]

[24] See, for example, the outstanding recent studies by Burroni (2001) and Messina (2001).

[25] For well-documented analyses of recent Italian developments, see Lazerson and Lorenzoni (1999), Brioschi et al. (2002); TeDIS Group (2003). For a parallel interpretation of recent trends in French districts, see Courlet (2005).

[26] For the crisis of communitarian governance mechanisms and local banking in Prato during the 1990s, see Dei Ottati (1996, 2003); and Conti and Ferri (1997). For Prato as a canonical district, see Becattini (2001); Becattini et al. (2003).

But these upheavals and structural changes within the districts should not be taken as evidence for either the end of geography or the triumph of hierarchy.

First, although some historic districts are struggling, others are flourishing. Within Italy, the districts have radiated outwards from their original heartland in the center and northeast to cover much of the northwest "industrial triangle" and even parts of the *mezzogiorno*, especially along the Adriatic coast.[27] And new districts and clusters are constantly being discovered, including in many developing economies.[28] Much of China's recent explosive growth, for example, has been driven by the proliferation of local industrial clusters or "specialized towns", concentrated in the Pearl River and Yangtze delta regions (Bellandi and di Tommaso 2005; Bellandi and Biggeri 2005; Enright *et al.* 2005; Barboza 2004).

Second, a central motivation behind much inward investment by multinational firms in the districts is to tap into the latter's specialized local knowledge and capabilities. In some cases, such as the mechanical engineering cluster of Jæren in southern Norway, foreign acquisitions of key local companies have disrupted the informal collaborative ties among specialists that underpinned these districts' innovative capabilities and historic success in world markets (Asheim and Herstad 2003a, 2003b). In others, however, like the sport shoe district of Montebelluna in northeast Italy (Belussi 2003), the biomedical equipment district of Mirandola in Emilia (Biggiero and Samara 2003) or the Finnish pulp and paper machinery district of Varkaus (Lovio 2003), foreign multinational corporations (MNCs) which purchased key local firms have increased the latter's competences and role both in production and R&D, while also stimulating a parallel movement towards enhanced internationalization and competitiveness among indigenously owned companies and their suppliers.

Third, as these contrasting outcomes suggest, it is far from clear that (MNCs) themselves have worked out fully effective mechanisms for promoting global cooperation and cross-fertilization of knowledge among subsidiaries embedded in local innovation clusters. Recent empirical studies of British and American multinationals and their suppliers support the view that these organizations are also beset by opportunistic behavior at all levels, which they struggle to control through various combinations of hierarchical and non-hierarchical governance mechanisms (Kristensen and Zeitlin 2005; Whitford and Zeitlin 2004; Herrigel 2004; Sabel 2004a).

So what is the upshot of these reflections? Successful industrial districts today are becoming more conscious and more organized, as dei Ottati (1996, 2003) observes in the case of Prato. They are also becoming less self-contained and more integrated into global supply chains and knowledge exchange networks: "windows on the

[27] Among numerous studies, see Signorini (2000), Viesti (2000a, 2000b).

[28] For a state-of-the-art overview of emerging clusters in developing economies, see Schmitz (2004), as well as the special issues of *World Development* edited by Humphrey (1995) and Schmitz and Nadvi (1999).

world" rather than "worlds in a bottle", as Charles Sabel (2004b) puts it. Crucial to both processes are the "new pragmatic disciplines" of "learning by monitoring" which facilitate cooperation in design and production across organizational and geographical boundaries by making tacit knowledge explicit: benchmarking, simultaneous engineering, procedural quality assurance standards, just-in-time logistics, "root cause" error detection and correction analysis, and so forth. It should come as no surprise, therefore, that collective benchmarking and training in quality assurance standards and related techniques have been among the most widely demanded services in Italian industrial districts over the past decade. By increasing transparency and reducing informational asymmetries among transacting partners, the use of these mutual monitoring and evaluation techniques can also contribute to resolving the governance problems of the new-style district. A similar processual approach can likewise be applied to defining the new "public goods" or infrastructural services required to support the district's development. In each case, however, there is wide agreement among external analysts and local actors alike on the need for a public deliberative forum to facilitate collective information exchange and joint problem-solving.[29]

10.7 CONCLUSIONS

What, finally, of the relationship between historians and contemporary social scientists with which this chapter began? Do the contemporary transformations underway within the districts open up an unbridgeable gap with historical analyses of their operations in earlier periods? Are we simply faced with a case of "that was then, this is now"? Or do current changes in the organization of the districts instead suggest new questions about their past around which a mutually productive research agenda can be constructed?

As a scholar whose work has straddled this disciplinary divide, my own intellectual predilections point naturally in the latter direction. So let us conclude by highlighting three major questions such an interdisciplinary research agenda might address, each of which is already of active concern to historians.

The first of these concerns the relationship between the districts and the wider world. Arguably, the self-contained character of the districts has been overstated even for earlier periods. We know, for example, from the work of Becattini (1999, 2003) and others that Anglo-Florentine buyers played an important part in stimulating awareness of foreign markets and consumer tastes among Tuscan artisans and district firms during the nineteenth and early twentieth centuries. Long-distance

---

[29] On the "new pragmatic disciplines" of "learning by monitoring" and the restructuring of Italian industrial districts, see Sabel (2002, 2004a, 2004b, 2004c) and Helper et al. (2000).

collection of specialized raw materials such as rags for Prato's regenerated wool mills and steel scrap for Brescia's electric arc furnaces are likewise reputed to have served both districts as a rich source of foreign commercial and technological intelligence (Avigdor 1961; Instituto Regionale di Ricerca della Lombardia 1985; Balconi 1991). It would also no doubt prove illuminating to investigate more closely the experience of multinational subsidiaries in the districts, as well as local firms' own attempts at internationalization.[30]

A second issue concerns the changing morphology of the districts and the relationship between different sizes and types of firms within them. Italian historians, as mentioned earlier, now place increasing emphasis on the role of large firms as sources of technical skills and entrepreneurial experience for the districts, and comparisons could be explored with similar cases in other countries. It would also be worthwhile to analyze more systematically the shifting and often non-linear evolution of firm size and structure within particular districts, as Jean-Claude Daumas (2002) has done in a fascinating essay on *la draperie elbeuvienne* between 1870 and 1975.[31]

A final issue concerns governance and coordination mechanisms within the districts, which are by no means fully understood. Beyond the role of intermediate institutions, which is attracting increasing attention from historians in Italy and elsewhere, researchers might consider the contribution of product standards and accounting techniques in the coordination of economic activity within and across districts. Here there are already some remarkable surprises. Thus Gerald Berk and Marc Schneiberg have discovered that American trade associations in localized specialty industries like printing developed uniform cost accounting standards during the first third of the twentieth century, which served as open benchmarking systems fueling collaborative learning, productivity growth, and technological innovation within a decentralized framework. So successful was this approach that it had begun to spread outwards to historically more concentrated industries like iron and steel before the outbreak of World War II (Berk 1996, 1997, forthcoming; Berk and Schneiberg 2005).

As this final example suggests, when historians return to the past with new questions inspired by current developments, they often (re)discover important phenomena which were well known to contemporaries, but forgotten or obscured by succeeding generations. The results may serve not only to challenge false or misleading genealogies of current practice (like the frequently repeated accounts of benchmarking which present it as a managerial invention of the 1980s), but also to stimulate new thinking about future possibilities.

---

[30] For a recent survey of Italy's district-based "pocket multinationals", see Colli (2002*b*). For a broader discussion of the role of global buyers in the development of local industrial clusters, see Schmitz and Knorringa (2000).

[31] See also his comparative analysis of the evolution of nineteenth-century French woolen districts in Daumas (2004).

References

ABE, TAKESHI (1992). "The Development of the Producing-Center Cotton Textile Industry in Japan between the Two World Wars". *Japanese Yearbook on Business History*, 9: 4–27.

—— (1999). "The Development of the Putting-Out System in Modern Japan: The Case of the Cotton-Weaving Industry", in Odaka and Sawai (1999), 217–49.

ALAIMO, AURELIO (1999). "Small Manufacturing Firms and Local Productive Systems in Italy", in Odaka and Sawai (1999), 168–93.

—— (2002). *Un altra industria? Distretti e sistemi locali nell'Italia contemporanea*. Milan: FrancoAngeli.

AMATORI, FRANCO, and COLLI, ANDREA (eds.) (2001). *Communità di imprese: Sistemi locali in Italia tra Ottocento e Novecento*. Bologna: Il Mulino.

AMIN, ASH, and THRIFT, NIGEL (1992). "Neo-Marshallian Nodes in a Global Economy". *International Journal of Urban and Regional Research*, 16/4: 571–87.

ANSELL, CHRISTOPHER, and GINGRICH, JANE (2003). "Trends in Decentralization", in Bruce E. Cain, Russell J. Dalton, and Susan E. Scarrow (eds.), *Democracy Transformed? Expanding Political Opportunities in Advanced Industrial Democracies*. Oxford: Oxford University Press, 140–63.

ARRIGHETTI, ALESSANDRO, and SERAVALLI, GILBERTO (eds.) (1999). *Istituzioni intermedie e sviluppo locale*. Rome: Donzelli.

ASHEIM, BJØRN T, and HERSTAD, SVERRE J. (2003a). "Regional Clusters under International Duress: Between Local Learning and Global Corporations", in Asheim and Mariussen (2003), 203–40.

—— —— (2003b). "Regional Innovation Systems, Varieties of Capitalism and Non-Local Relations: Challenges from the Globalising Economy", in Asheim and Mariussen (2003), 241–74.

—— and MARIUSSEN, ÅGE (eds.) (2003). *Innovations, Regions and Projects: Studies in New Forms of Knowledge Governance*, Nordregio Report 2003: 3. Stockholm: Nordregio.

AVIGDOR, EZIO (1961). *L'industria tessile a Prato*. Milan: Feltrinelli.

BAGNASCO, ARNALDO (1988). *La costruzione sociale del mercato*. Bologna: Il Mulino.

—— and SABEL, CHARLES F. (eds.) (1995). *Small and Medium-Size Enterprises*. London: Pinter.

BALCONI, MARGHERITA (1991). *La siderurgia italiana (1945–1990): Tra controllo pubblico e incentivi del mercato*. Bologna: Il Mulino.

BARBOZA, DAVID (2004). "In Roaring China, Sweaters are West of Socks City". *New York Times*, December 24.

BECATTINI, GIACOMO (1999). *L'industrializzazione leggera della Toscana: Ricerca sul campo e confronto delle idée*. Milan: FrancoAngeli.

—— (2001). *The Caterpillar and the Butterfly: An Exemplary Case of Development in the Italy of the Industrial Districts*. Florence: Le Monnier.

—— (2003). "Industrial Districts in the Development of Tuscany", in Becattini *et al.* (2003), 11–28.

—— (2004). *Industrial Districts: A New Approach to Industrial Change*. Cheltenham: Edward Elgar.

—— BELLANDI, MARCO, OTTATI, GABI DEI, and SFORZI, FABIO (2003). *From Industrial Districts to Local Development: An Itinerary of Research*. Cheltenham: Edward Elgar.

BELLANDI, MARCO and MARIO BIGGERI (eds.) (2005). *La sfida industriale cinese vista dalla Toscana distrettuale*. Florence: Toscana Promozione.

—— and DI TOMMASO, MARCO R. (2005). "The Case of Specialized Towns in Guangdong, China". *European Planning Studies*, 13/5: 707–29.

BELUSSI, FIOREUZA (2003). "The Changing Governance of IDs: The Entry of Multinationals in Local Nets", in Asheim and Mariussen (2003), 318–47.

BERGER, A. N., DEMSETZ, R. S., and STRAHAN, P. E. (1999). "The Consolidation of the Financial Services Industry: Causes, Consequences, and Implications for the Future". *Journal of Banking and Finance*, 23/2–4: 135–94.

BERK, GERALD (1994). *Alternative Tracks: The Constitution of Industrial Order in America, 1865–1917*. Baltimore: Johns Hopkins University Press.

—— (1996). "Communities of Competitors: Open Price Associations and the American State, 1911–1929". *Social Science History*, 20/3: 375–400.

—— (1997). "Discursive Cartels: Uniform Cost Accounting among American Manufacturers before the New Deal". *Business and Economic History*, 26/1: 229–51.

—— (forthcoming). *American Possibilities: Brandeis, Associations and Antitrust, 1890–1935*.

—— and SCHNEIBERG, MARC (2005). "Varieties *in* Capitalism, Varieties *of* Association: Collaborative Learning in American Industries, 1900 to 1925". *Politics & Society*, 33/1: 46–87.

BIANCHI, RONNY, ENRIETTI, ALDO, and LANZETTI, R. (2001). "The Technological Car District in Piedmont: Definitions, Dynamic, Policy". *International Journal of Automotive Technology and Management*, 1/4: 397–415.

BIGGIERO, LUCIO, and SAMARA, ALESSIA (2003). "The Biomedical Valley: Structural, Relational, and Cognitive Aspects", in Fiorenza Belussi, Giorgio Gottardi, and Enzo Rullani (eds.), *The Technological Evolution of Industrial Districts*. Boston: Kluwer, 205–32.

BOCH, RUDOLF (1997). "The Rise and Decline of Flexible Production: The Cutlery Industry of Solingen since the Eighteenth Century", in Sabel and Zeitlin (1997), 153–87.

BOLOGNA, SERGIO (1998). "Trasporti e logistica come fattori di competitività di una regione", in Paolo Perulli (ed.), *Neo-regionalismo: L'economia-arcipelago*. Turin: Bollati Boringhieri, 152–86.

BORRUS, MICHAEL, and ZYSMAN, JOHN (1997). "Globalization with Borders: The Rise of Wintelism as the Future of Global Competition". *Industry and Innovation*, 4/2: 141–66.

BRIOSCHI, FRANCESCO, BRIOSCHI, MARIA SOLE, and CAINELLI, GIULIO (2002). "From the Industrial District to the District Group. An Insight into the Evolution of Local Capitalism in Italy". *Regional Studies*, 36/9: 1037–52.

BRUSCO, SEBASTIANO (1982). "The Emilian Model: Productive Decentralization and Social Integration". *Cambridge Journal of Economics*, 6/2: 167–84.

—— (1989). *Piccole imprese e distretti industriali*. Turin: Rosenberg & Sellier.

—— (1990). "The Idea of the Industrial District: Its Genesis", in Pyke *et al.* (1990), 10–19.

BURRONI, LUIGI (2001). *Allontanarsi crescendo: Politica e sviluppo locale in Veneto e Toscana*. Turin: Rosenberg & Sellier.

—— (2004). "Concentrazione territoriale, istituzioni e reti sociali nelle attività del software: il caso italiano", *Economia e politica industriale*, no. 4: 175–89.

CAPECCHI, VITTORIO (1997). "In Search of Flexibility: The Bologna Metalworking Industry, 1900–1992", in Sabel and Zeitlin (1997), 381–418.

CARNEVALI, FRANCESCA (2004). " 'Crooks, Thieves, and Receivers': Transaction Costs in Nineteenth-Century Industrial Birmingham". *Economic History Review*, 62/3: 533–50.

CARNEVALI, FRANCESCA (2005). *Europe's Advantage: The Political Economy of Small Firms and Regions in Britain, France, Germany and Italy since 1918*. Oxford: Oxford University Press.

CASSIS, YOUSSEF (2006). *Capitals of Capital: A History of International Financial Centres, 1780–2005*. Oxford: Oxford University Press.

—— and BUSSIÈRE, ERIC (eds.) (2005). *London and Paris as International Financial Centres in the Twentieth Century*. Oxford: Oxford University Press.

CHANDLER, ALFRED D., JR. (1977). *The Visible Hand: The Managerial Revolution in American Business*. Cambridge, Mass: Harvard University Press.

—— (1990). *Scale and Scope: The Dynamics of Industrial Capitalism*. Cambridge, Mass: Harvard University Press.

COLLI, ANDREA (2002*a*). *I volti di Proteo: Storia della piccola impresa in Italia nel Novecento*. Turin: Bollati Boringhieri.

—— (2002*b*). *Il quarto capitalismo: Un profilo italiano*. Venice: Marsilio.

CONTI, GIUSEPPE, and FERRI, GIOVANNI (1997). "Banche locali e sviluppo economico decentrato", in Fabrizio Barca (ed.), *Storia del capitalismo italiano dal dopoguerra a oggi*. Rome: Donzelli, 429–66.

COTTEREAU, ALAIN (1986). "The Distinctiveness of Working-Class Cultures in France, 1848–1900", in Ira Katznelson and Aristide Zolberg (eds.), *Working-Class Formation: Nineteenth-Century Patterns in Western Europe and the United States*. Princeton: Princeton University Press, 111–55.

—— (1997). "The Fate of Collective Manufactures in the Industrial World: The Silk Industries of Lyons and London, 1800–1850", in Sabel and Zeitlin (1997), 75–152.

COURAULT, BRUNO, and ROMANI, CHRISTINE (1992). "Questions aux modèle italien de la flexibilité", in Ganne (1992), 233–48.

—— and RERAT, FRANÇOISE (1992). "Cholet, un exemple de système local construit par des enterprises", in Ganne (1992), 337–44.

COURLET, CLAUDE (1992). "Du développement spontané an développement construit: l'example du système industriel localisé de la vallée de l'Arve", in Ganne (1992), 287–310.

—— (2005). "Les systèmes productifs localisés en France: Une histoire récente", in Lescure (2005).

CROUCH, COLIN, and FARRELL, HENRY (2001). "Great Britain: Falling through the Holes in the Network Concept?" in Crouch *et al.* (2001), 154–211.

—— LE GALÈS, PATRICK, TRIGILIA, CARLO, and VOELZKOW, HELMUT (2001). *Local Production Systems in Europe: Rise or Demise?* Oxford: Oxford University Press.

—— —— —— —— (2004). *Changing Governance of Local Economies: Responses of European Local Production Systems*. Oxford: Oxford University Press.

DAUMAS, JEAN-CLAUDE (2002). "La draperie elbeuvienne à l'époque contemporaine (1870–1975): Territoire, structures d'entreprise et coordination de la production", in Eck and Lescure (2002), 307–20.

—— (2004). *Les territoires de la laine: Histoire de l'industrie lainière en France au XIXème siècle*. Villeneuve d'Ascq: Presses Universitaires du Septentrion.

DEEG, RICHARD (1999). *Finance Capitalism Unveiled: Banks and the German Political Economy*. Ann Arbor: University of Michigan Press.

DEI OTTATI, GABI (1996). "Economic Changes in the District of Prato in the 1980s: Towards a More Conscious and Organized Industrial District". *European Planning Studies*, 4/1: 35–52.

—— (2003). "Exit, Voice and the Evolution of Industrial Districts: The Case of the Post-World War II Economic Development of Prato". *Cambridge Journal of Economics*, 27: 501–22.

DEWERPE, ALAIN (1992). "Les systèmes industriels localisés dans l'industrie française", in Ganne (1992), 17–60.

ECK, JEAN-FRANÇOIS, and LESCURE, MICHEL (eds.) (2002). *Villes et districts industriels en Europe occidentale XVIIIe–XXe siècles*. Tours: Université François Rabelais de Tours.

ENRIGHT, MICHAEL J., SCOTT, EDITH E., and CHANG, CHA-MUN, (2005). *Regional Power-house: The Greater Pearl River Delta and the Rise of China*. New York: John Wiley & Sons.

FERRERA, MAURIZIO, and GUALMINI, ELISABETTA (2004). *Rescued by Europe? Social and Labour Market Reforms in Italy from Maastricht to Berlusconi*. Amsterdam: Amsterdam University Press.

FERRI, GIOVANNI (2006). "Centralisation fasciste e institutions de district: Le cas de l'Italie pendant la crise des années trente", in Lescure (2006), 317–42.

FORSYTH, DOUGLAS J., and VERDIER, DANIEL (eds.) (2003). *The Origins of National Financial Systems: Alexander Gerschenkron Reconsidered*. London: Routledge.

FRIEDMAN, DAVID (1988). *The Misunderstood Miracle: Industrial Development and Political Change in Japan*. Ithaca, NY: Cornell University Press.

FUJITA, TEIICHIRO (1998). "Local Trade Associations (*Dôgyô Kumiai*) in Prewar Japan", in Hiroaki Yamazaki and Matao Miyamoto (eds.), *Trade Associations in Business History*. Tokyo: University of Tokyo Press, 87–113.

GANNE, BERNARD (ed.) (1992). *Développement locale et ensembles de PME*. Lyon: GLYSI.

—— (1995). "France: Behind Small and Medium-Size Enterprises Lies the State", in Bagnasco and Sabel (1995), 115–33.

GEDDES, MIKE, and BENINGTON, JOHN (eds.) (2001). *Local Partnerships and Social Exclusion in the EU: New Forms of Social Governance*. London: Routledge.

GOODMAN, EDWARD, and BAMFORD, JULIA, WITH SAYNOR, PETER (eds.) (1989). *Small Firms and Industrial Districts in Italy*. London: Routledge.

GROSSMAN, EMILIANO (2006). "Europeanization as an Interactive Process: German Public Banks Meet EU State Aid Policy". *Journal of Common Market Studies*, 44/2: 325–48.

HANNAH, LESLIE (1979). "Mergers, Cartels, and Concentration: Legal Factors in the U.S. and European Experience", in Norbert Horn and Jürgen Kocka (eds.), *Law and the Formation of the Big Enterprises in the 19th and Early 20th Centuries*. Göttingen: Vandenhoeck & Ruprecht, 306–15.

HAREVEN, TAMARA (2002). *The Silk Weavers of Kyoto: Family and Work in a Changing Traditional Industry*. Berkeley: University of California Press.

HEINRICH, THOMAS (2002). "Cold War Armory: Military Contracting in Silicon Valley". *Enterprise & Society*, 3/2: 247–84.

HELPER, SUSAN, MACDUFFIE, JOHN PAUL, and SABEL, CHARLES (2000). "Pragmatic Collaborations: Advancing Knowledge while Controlling Opportunism". *Industrial and Corporate Change*, 9/3: 443–83.

HERRIGEL, GARY (1996). *Industrial Constructions: The Sources of German Industrial Power*. Cambridge: Cambridge University Press.

—— (2004). "Emerging Strategies and Forms of Governance in High-Wage Component Manufacturing Regions". *Industry & Innovation*, 11/1–2: 45–80.

HIRSCH, JEAN-PIERRE, and MINARD, PHILIPPE (1998). "'Laissez-nous faire et protégez-nous beaucoup': Pour une histoire des pratiques institutionelles dans l'industrie française

(XVIIIe–XIXe siècle)", in Louis Bergeron and Patrice Bourdelais (eds.), *La France n'est-elle pas douée pour l'industrie?* Paris: Belin, 113–34.

HIRST, PAUL, and ZEITLIN, JONATHAN (1991). "Flexible Specialization vs. Post-Fordism: Theory, Evidence and Policy Implications". *Economy and Society*, 20/1: 1–55.

HOMMELL, ULRICH, and SCHNEIDER, HILMAR (2003). "Financing the German Mittelstand". *EIB Papers*, 7/2: 52–90.

HUMPHREY, JOHN (ed.) (1995). "Industrial Organization and Manufacturing Competitiveness in Developing Countries", *World Development*, 23/1, special issue.

Istituto Regionale di Ricerca della Lombardia (1985). *Siderurgia lombarda: Problemi e prospettive.* Milan: FrancoAngeli.

JUDET, PIERCE (2005). "Patrons et ouvries dans le monde de l'horlogierie—décolletage de la vallée de l'Arve (milieu du XIXe siècle–milieu. du XXe siècle)", in Lescure (2006), 197–210.

KELLER, MORTON (1980). "Regulation of Large Enterprise: The United States in Comparative Perspective", in Alfred D. Chandler, Jr. and Herman Daems (eds.), *Managerial Hierarchies: Comparative Perspectives on the Rise of the Modern Industrial Enterprise.* Cambridge, Mass.: Harvard University Press, 161–81.

KENNEY, MARTIN (ed.) (2000). *Understanding Silicon Valley: The Anatomy of an Entrepreneurial Region.* Palo Alto, Calif.: Stanford University Press.

KRISTENSEN, PEER HULL (1992). "Industrial Districts in West Jutland, Denmark", in Pyke and Sengenberger (1992), 122–73.

—— and SABEL, CHARLES F. (1997). "The Small-Holder Economy in Denmark: The Exception as Variation", in Sabel and Zeitlin (1997), 344–78.

—— and ZEITLIN, JONATHAN (2005). *Local Players in Global Games: The Strategic Constitution of a Multinational Corporation.* Oxford: Oxford University Press.

KYNASTON, DAVID (1994–2001). *The City of London: A History*, 4 vols. London: Chatto & Windus.

LAZERSON, MARK H., and LORENZONI, GIANNI (1999). "The Firms that Feed Industrial Districts: A Return to the Italian Source", *Industrial and Corporate Change*, 8/2: 235–66.

LÉCUYER, CHRISTOPHE (2002). "Electronic Component Manufacturing and the Rise of Silicon Valley". *Journal of Industrial History*, 5/1: 89–111.

LESCURE, MICHEL (1995). "Banks and Small Enterprises in France", in Youssef Cassis, Gerald D. Feldman, and Ulf Olsson (eds.), *The Evolution of Financial Institutions and Markets in Twentieth-Century Europe.* London: Scolar Press, 315–28.

—— (2002). "Entre ville et campagne: L'organisation bancaire des districts industriels. L'exemple du Choletais (1900–1950)", in Eck and Lescure (2002), 81–104.

—— (2003). "The Origins of Universal Banks in France during the Nineteenth Century", in Forsyth and Verdier (2003), 117–25.

—— (2004). "La crise bancaire des années 1930: La crise des banques locales et régionales en France?" in Michel Lescure and André Plessis (eds.), *Banques locales et banques régionales en Europe au XXe siècle.* Paris: Albin Michel, 162–205.

—— (ed.) (2006). *La mobilization du territoire: Les districts industriels en Europe occidentale, du XVIIe au XXe siècle.* Paris: Comité pour l'Histoire Économique et Social de la France.

LOCKE, RICHARD M. (1995). *Remaking the Italian Economy.* Ithaca, NY: Cornell University Press.

Lovio, Raimo (2003). "Multinational Corporations in a Local Perspective—The Case of Varkaus in Finland", unpublished paper for the 17th Conference on Business Studies, Reykjavik, August 14–16.

Marshall, Alfred (1922). *Principles of Economics*, 8th edn. London: Macmillan (1st edn., 1890).

——(1927). *Industry and Trade*, 4th edn. London: Macmillan (1st edn., 1919).

——(1975). *The Early Economic Writings of Alfred Marshall, 1867–1890*, vol. 2, ed. J. K. Whitaker. London: Macmillan.

Messina, Patrizia (2001). *Regolazione politica dello sviluppo locale: Veneto ed Emilia-Romagna a confronto*. Turin: UTET.

Minguet, Guy (1992). "La petite république du Choletais: Bilan de la recherché, prospectives", in Ganne (1992), 345–57.

Morris-Suzuki, Tessa (1994). *The Technological Transformation of Japan*. Cambridge: Cambridge University Press.

Odaka, Konosuke, and Sawai, Minoru (eds.) (1999). *Small Firms, Large Concerns: The Development of Small Business in Comparative Perspective*. Oxford: Oxford University Press.

Paniccia, Ivana (2002). *Industrial Districts: Evolution and Competitiveness in Italian Firms*. Cheltenham: Edward Elgar.

Piore, Michael J., and Sabel, Charles F. (1984). *The Second Industrial Divide: Possibilities for Prosperity*. New York: Basic Books.

Popp, Andrew (2001). *Business Structure, Business Culture and the Industrial District: The Potteries, c. 1850–1914*. Aldershot: Ashgate.

Porter, Michael E. (1998). *On Competition*. Boston: Harvard Business School Press.

Provasi, Giancarlo (ed.) (2002). *Le istituzioni dello sviluppo: I distretti industriali tra storia, sociologia ed economia*. Rome: Donzelli.

Pyke, Frank, Becattini, Giacomo, and Sengenberger, Werner (eds.) (1990). *Industrial Districts and Inter-Firm Co-operation in Italy*. Geneva: International Institute for Labour Studies.

——and Sengenberger, Werner (eds.) (1992). *Industrial Districts and Local Economic Regeneration*. Geneva: International Institute for Labour Studies.

Raveyre, Marie-Francoise, and Saglio, Jean (1984). "Les systèmes industrielles localisés, éléments pour une analyse sociologique des ensembles de PMEs industriels". *Sociologie du Travail*, 2: 157–76.

Sabel, Charles F. (1989). "Flexible Specialization and the Re-emergence of Regional Economies", in Paul Hirst and Jonathan Zeitlin (eds.), *Reversing Industrial Decline? Industrial Structure and Policy in Britain and her Competitors*. New York: St. Martin's Press, 17–70.

——(1996). *Ireland: Local Partnerships and Social Innovation*. Paris: OECD.

——(2002). "Diversity, Not Specialization: The Ties that Bind the (New) Industrial District", in Alberto Quadro Curzio and Marco Fortis (eds.), *Complexity and Industrial Clusters—Dynamics, Models, National Cases*. Heidelberg: Physica-Verlag.

——(2004*a*). "Pragmatic Collaborations in Practice: A Response to Herrigel and Whitford and Zeitlin". *Industry and Innovation*, 11/1–2: 81–8.

——(2004*b*). "Mondo in bottiglia o finestra sul mondo? Domande aperte sul distretto industriale nel spirito di Sebastiano Brusco", *Stato e Mercato*, no. 1: 143–58.

SABEL, CHARLES F. (2004c). "Districts on the Move: Note on the Tedis Survey of the Internationalization of District Firm", unpublished paper presented at the conference on "Local Governance and Production". Turin, December.

——and ZEITLIN, JONATHAN (1985). "Historical Alternatives to Mass Production: Politics, Markets and Technology in Nineteenth-Century Industrialization". *Past and Present*, 108: 133–76.

————(1997). *World of Possibilities: Flexibility and Mass Production in Western Industrialization*. Cambridge: Cambridge University Press.

SAGLIO, JEAN (1997). "Local Industry and Actors' Strategies: From Combs to Plastics in Oyonnax", in Sabel and Zeitlin (1997), 419–60.

——(2005). "Des objets invisibles", in Lescure (2005).

SAWAI, MINORU (1999). "The Role of Technical Education and Public Research Institutes in the Development of Small and Medium Enterprises: The Case of Osaka between the Wars", in Odaka and Sawai (1999), 250–89.

SCHMITZ, HUBERT (ed.) (2004). *Local Enterprises in the Global Economy: Issues of Governance and Upgrading*. Cheltenham: Edward Elgar.

——and KNORRINGA, PETER (2000). "Learning from Global Buyers". *Journal of Development Studies*, 37/2: 177–205.

——and NADVI, KHALID (eds.) (1999). Special Issue on "Clustering and Industrialization". *World Development*, 27/9.

SCOTT, ALLEN J. (2005). *On Hollywood: The Place, the Industry*. Princeton, NJ: Princeton University Press.

SCRANTON, PHILIP (1997). *Endless Novelty: Specialty Production and American Industrialization, 1865–1925*. Princeton, NJ: Princeton University Press.

——(1998). "Webs of Productive Association in American Industrialization: Patterns of Institution Formation and their Limits, 1880–1930". *Journal of Industrial History*, 1/1: 9–34.

SIGNORINI, L. FEDERICO (ed.) (2001). *Lo sviluppo locale: Un indagine della Banca d'Italia sui distretti industriali*. Rome: Donzetti.

STORPER, MICHAEL (1989). "The Transition to Flexible Specialization in the US Film Industry: External Economies, the Division of Labour, and the Crossing of Industrial Divides", *Cambridge Journal of Economics*, 13: 273–305.

——(1997). *The Regional World*. New York: Guilford Press.

TeDIS Group (ed.) (2003). *Internazionalizzazione dei sistemi locali di sviluppo*. Center for Studies on Technologies in Distributed Intelligence Systems (TeDIS), Venice International University.

TRIGILIA, CARLO (1986). *Grandi partiti e piccole imprese*. Bologna: Il Mulino.

——(1989). "Small-Firm Development and Political Sub-Cultures in Italy", in Goodman and Bamford (1989), 174–97.

——(1990). "Work and Politics in the Third Italy", in Pyke *et al.* (1990), 160–84.

——(1992). *Sviluppo senza autonomia: Effeti perversi delle politiche nel Mezzogiorno*. Bologna: Il Mulino.

——(2005). "Distretti industriali e distretti high tech", in Trigilia, *Sviluppo locale: Un progetto per l'Italia*. Rome: Laterza, 49–73.

VANDELLI, LUCIANO (2002). *Devoluzione e altre storie: Paradossi, ambiguità e rischi di un progetto politico*. Bologna: Il Mulino.

VERDIER, DANIEL (1998). "Domestic Responses to Capital Market Internationalization under the Gold Standard, 1870–1914". *International Organization*, 52/1: 1–34.

——(2002). *Moving Money: Banking and Finance in the Industrialized World*. Cambridge: Cambridge University Press.

VIESTI, GIANFRANCO (2000a). *Come nascono i distretti industriali*. Rome: Laterza.

——(ed.) (2000b). *Mezzogiorno dei distretti*. Rome: Donzelli.

WEISS, LINDA (1988). *Creating Capitalism: The State and Small Business since 1945*. Oxford: Blackwell.

WHITFORD, JOSH, AND ZEITLIN, JONATHAN (2004). "Governing Decentralized Production: Institutions, Public Policy, and the Prospects for Inter-Firm Cooperation in the United States". *Industry and Innovation*, 11/1–2: 11–44.

WHITTAKER, D. H. (1997). *Small Firms in the Japanese Economy*. Cambridge: Cambridge University Press.

WILSON, JOHN F., and POPP, ANDREW (eds.) (2003). *Industrial Clusters and Regional Business Networks in England, 1750–1970*. Aldershot: Ashgate.

YONEMITSU, YASUSHI, and TOLLIDAY, STEVEN (2003). "Micro-Firms and Industrial Districts in Japan: The Dynamics of the Arita Ceramic-Ware Industry in the Twentieth Century". Unpublished paper presented to the Business History Conference, Lowell, Mass., June 26–8.

ZEITLIN, JONATHAN (1992). "Industrial Districts and Local Economic Regeneration: Overview and Comment", in Pyke and Sengenberger (1992), 179–94.

——(1995). "Why are there No Industrial Districts in the United Kingdom?", in Bagnasco and Sabel (1995), 98–114.

——and POCHET, PHILIPPE WITH MAGNUSSON, LARS (eds.) (2005). *The Open Method of Co-ordination in Action: The European Employment and Social Inclusion Strategies*. Brussels: PIE-Peter Lang.

——and TRUBEK, DAVID M. (eds.) (2003). *Governing Work and Welfare in a New Economy: European and American Experiments*. Oxford: Oxford University Press.

CHAPTER 11

BUSINESS GROUPS AND INTERFIRM NETWORKS

W. MARK FRUIN

11.1 INTRODUCTION

BUSINESS groups and interfirm networks, the subjects of this chapter, along with cartels, consortia, industrial districts, innovation clusters, joint ventures, strategic alliances, unions, industry and professional associations, are significant examples of organized cooperation in business. Cooperation has been and continues to be a primary force for change in business and in nature.

What distinguishes business groups and interfirm networks from other examples of organized cooperation are, first, they are composed of legally distinct firms and, second, they persist for long periods of time (Granovetter 2005). Thus, unions and professional associations differ on the first dimension, strategic alliances and joint ventures on the second. Business groups and interfirm networks are long-lasting federations of firms. They have been relatively unsung until lately. Economists conventionally recognize only two forms of organization, markets and "hierarchies" (firms and bureaucracies), and competition, not cooperation, is deemed the driving force of business.[1] Interest has grown of late because business groups are identified

---

[1] In neoclassical economics, firms are not very different than markets. Alchian and Demsetz argued that employment relations did not differ "in the slightest degree from ordinary market contracting between two people" (1972). Williamson's transaction cost model asserted that firms differ from markets

as playing crucial roles in economic development and interfirm networks in innovation, especially when complex coordination problems overwhelm firms (Arrow 1974; Kauffman 1993; Barabasi 2003).

11.2 CONCEPTS AND DEFINITIONS

"Business group" and "interfirm network" are often and confusingly used interchangeably. Conceptually, both are social networks wherein economic action is embedded in systems of actors and relationships linking actors. An extensive literature on social networks exists, focusing on interpersonal, not interorganizational, networks (Granovetter 1973, 1985, 2005).[2] It does not accept economists' faith in markets (Roberts 2004; Granovetter 1985), characterize firms as markets or nexuses of contracts (Alchian and Demsetz 1972; Powell 1990), and portray firms as responding effectively, in terms of internal processes and capabilities, to environmental complexities (Williamson 1994; Scott 2001, 2003). Association, trust, goodwill (Dore 1986), and interaction fields (Bourdieu 2005; Davis 2005) are seen to function above and beyond markets and hierarchies.

Business groups and interfirm networks differ in important ways. When ownership and control are more centralized and organizational subunits enjoy limited autonomy, the commonly used term is business groups. When subunits enjoy more autonomy with respect to ownership, control, and operations, interfirm network is the correct term. In other words, business groups are more centralized and closely held, while interfirm networks are more decentralized and loosely held.

Beyond this, specificity can be added on the basis of three elements—ownership, control, and levels of transactions—recognizing that the legally bounded nature of firms affects behavior and governance in both business groups and interfirm networks (Bethel and Liebeskind 1998; Dine 2000; Ruef 2000; Kobayashi and Ribstein 1996). These elements are juxtaposed in a two by two matrix (see Fig. 11.1).

Until the mid- to late nineteenth century, few firms separated ownership and control or carried out national and international operations. Firms were simple, family-based, functional organizations with limited resources and capabilities. In

---

only insofar as their governance structures to control opportunistic behavior differ (Williamson 1975, 1985).

[2] The advantage of strong versus weak ties (cohesion versus structural equivalence) is the major issue in the study of social networks. The weak ties model works well when wide circulation of data and incremental innovation (contagion models) are desirable (Granovetter 1973; Piore and Sabel 1984). Burt and others argued that strong ties are better when highly useful knowledge is sought (Burt 1992), when complex knowledge is communicated (Bureth et al. 1997; Gulati 1999), when social control is paramount (Kogut 1988; Coleman 1988), and radical innovation is desired (Walker et al. 1997).

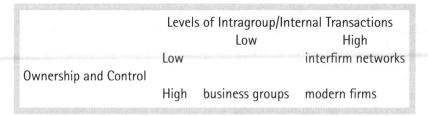

Fig. 11.1 Complex organizational forms and levels of ownership, control, and intragroup/internal transactions

such firms, shareholders were few, ownership and control (management) were unified. Later, as investors became more numerous, as when railroad and steamship line companies sold shares on the London and New York stock exchanges, for example, preferred shares—those without management participation rights—were sold. Common shares—often with management participation rights—were closely held among family and friends of company founders.

Even when business activities were not so localized, ownership and control remained unified. British trading companies offer many examples of this. Ownership and control were only disaggregated during the mid- to late twentieth century, according to Jones (Jones 2000). Even then, when ownership was diluted, often control remained intact. This was possible for several reasons.

Trading firms in extraction and plantation industries hired a few mining, engineering, and agricultural specialists to ensure local operations. They had little or no voice in how firms ran. Where agents represented trading or manufacturing interests, they worked on commission and had no voice in management. As a result, trading firms prospered without raising a lot of capital, hiring many employees, diluting ownership, and giving up control (Jones 2000). The same could be said of railroad, steamship, mining, brewing, and textile firms.

As Alfred D. Chandler, Jr. documents, however, entirely new sorts of firms appeared in the late nineteenth and early twentieth centuries to harness the possibilities of high-throughput, scale, and scope economies linked to transportation and communication advances (Chandler 1962, 1977, 1990). So-called "modern firms" hired large numbers of managers to schedule massive resource flows and to coordinate prodigious product outputs. Such firms differed in terms of size, scope, complexity, and velocity of throughput as compared with firms and groups of firms that previously populated the landscape.

Once modern firms appeared, the ways to compete on the basis of scale, scope, and speed were few, essentially limited to four organizational models:

(1) Modern firms: firms internalize needed resources and capabilities.
(2) Business groups: firms work together on the basis of common ownership and control.
(3) Industrial districts: firms work together on the basis of location, shared resources, governance, and political economic agenda.

(4) Interfirm networks: firms of various sizes and specialties work together on the basis of shared information, frequent interactions, and mutual benefit.

In every case, the organizations in question marshal sufficient resources and capabilities to participate in industries characterized by scale, scope and speed. Each model is considered below.

11.3 SCALE, SCOPE, SPEED, AND ORGANIZATIONAL FORM

Large firms can specialize in a single line of business, but truly large firms—the Fortune 500—are multibusiness firms. To make apt comparisons with business groups and interfirm networks, multibusiness firms are considered analogues of Chandler's modern firms.

11.3.1 Modern Firms

US firms began to offer multiple lines of business for reasons of market demand, government policy, and technological and market relatedness in the early twentieth century (Chandler 1962, 1977, 1990). Diversification in the United States generally came after horizontal integration and industry consolidation. A new organizational form, the multidivisional or M-form firm, appeared to handle issues of organization, coordination, and control in multibusiness firms.

Multibusiness firms are located in the southeast quadrant of Figure 11.1. They typically enjoy high levels of relatedness in their business activities and, accordingly, display high levels of intrafirm transactions. A shift to firms characterized by size, scope, and speed heralded a separation of ownership and control; ownership was diluted by massive sales of equity shares; management ranks swelled with eager and increasingly well educated junior executives and engineers.

In Western Europe and Asia, M-form firms came later, generally after World War II and assumed varying forms in different institutional environments (Chandler 1990, 2001; Fruin 1992). After the war, some multibusiness firms moved to the southwest quadrant. Control and sometimes ownership were high in such firms, sometimes called conglomerates, but levels of interdivisional (or interbusiness) transactions were lower.

11.3.2 Business Groups

Business groups occupy the same southwest quadrant as conglomerates, but they differ notably in organization and management. As single legal entities, the component businesses of conglomerates typically enjoy high levels of ownership and control. If ownership is dispersed, control remains intact. Control allows conglomerates to take advantages of certain resources and capabilities, like management skills, transport facilities, plant and equipment, that can be spread across many businesses. Without that, reasons for combining businesses in a single firm are not apparent. Even with firm-wide abilities, analysts typically levy a sizeable diversification discount against them (Bettis 1981; Lang and Stulz 1994; Montgomery 1994).

In business groups, businesses are separate legal entities. They may be separate for many reasons but two often stand out. They share little in common, and they cannot be related meaningfully. In addition, managers may not have the requisite information, tools, and experience to administer and direct multiple businesses as a single entity. Combining businesses requires management capabilities of a much higher order.

Business groups combine strong ownership and weak control over numerous firms, contrary to multibusiness firms with their weak owners and strong managers (Roe 1994). Corporate law in America generally focuses on the multibusiness model, treating multibusiness firms as single units regardless of the diversity and number of their businesses. Because of this, in America, business group formation is pictured as a transitional process of incubation with parent firms spinning-in, nurturing, and then spinning-out businesses.

Business groups in emerging economies are seen differently. They are not considered good at combining businesses. New business formation is seen as opportunistic, without apparent rhyme or reason. Business groups grow by taking over but not necessarily consolidating their competitors. Absent a market need and the managerial means to integrate businesses, group performance is inconsistent. Such differences suggest dissimilar roles, capabilities, and strategies for business groups in advanced and emerging economies (Khanna and Palepu 1997, 2000).

11.3.3 Location/Industrial Districts

Industrial districts are discussed elsewhere in this volume (see Chapter 10) and little need be said here, except to situate them in the same northwest cell as interfirm networks. In industrial districts, location organizes cooperation; relevant actors and resources are geographically defined. Research has focused on Europe although both Toyota and Chrysler could be categorized as industrial districts at various times in their past. Recently, the informal contracting relations characterizing industrial districts in Europe are giving way to more formalized relationships permitting increased scale and scope advantages, inward investment, crossfertilization of knowledge, and international marketing campaigns (Brioschi et al. 2002).

11.3.4 Interfirm Networks

Internalized/intragroup transactions are high but levels of ownership and control low in interfirm networks. Such a configuration occurs in two possible ways. Either frequently needed resources and capabilities, such as financial, logistical, and information services, are sourced from within a group of firms, or the outputs of many firms are the inputs of others in a group.

Japan and Silicon Valley offer examples of both types. As for the first, in Japan, interindustry federations, called enterprise groups (*kigyo shudan/kigyo gurupu*),[3] are composed of firms offering banking, trading, logistical, engineering, information technology, and other specialized services, to related firms. In Silicon Valley, accounting, headhunting, legal, financial, and consulting companies group together around venture capital firms. Groupings coalesce for numerous reasons, including a desire to economize on limited resources (Fruin 1992), preferential attachment (Barabasi 2003), and government policy (Hamilton 1998). They remain vital, when they do, because there are costs and benefits to learning each other's businesses. Law firms, for example, cannot be "of counsel" until they master their clients' needs. Thereafter, high switching costs keep firms working together.

Postwar enterprise groups in Japan have low levels of ownership and control in comparison with prewar enterprise groups (*zaibatsu*), which might be considered closer to business groups than interfirm networks although the so-called "new zaibatsu" were clusters of techically related businesses. During the postwar Occupation, the assets of *zaibatsu* families were confiscated and their scions banned from management (Hadley 1970). Ownership and control were irrevocably alienated. Business groups were restructured around banks and other firms providing core resources, like capital and import–export capabilities.

Two enterprise groups appeared in the postwar era: legacy or namesake groups, like Mitsubishi, Mitsui, and Sumitomo, and city bank-based groups, like DKB, Fuyo (Fuji), and Sanwa. The former have higher levels of intragroup lending, trade, shareholding, and dispatch of directors (Lincoln and Gerlach 2004) but, overall, differences are small, and it is not clear how meaningful they are (Odagiri 1992; Ramseyer and Miwa 2002). In 1990, for example, internal buying and selling among Mitsubishi group companies amounted to 16–18 percent of total sales (Fruin 1992). Within groups of 200 to 300 firms, with less than 20 percent cross-shareholding and 16–18 percent intragroup sales, group effects at the level of individual firms are mild, except perhaps when single firms fall into difficulty (Lincoln and Gerlach 2004).[4]

---

[3] Literally, an enterprise group, *kigyo shudan* or *kigyo gurupu*, the Japanese word for enterprise and English word "group" written in *katakana*, the Japanese script for foreign words. The term applies to inter-industry federations of firms of which there are two well-known types: those related to prewar *zaibatsu* groupings or namesake groups, including Mitsui, Mitsubishi, and Sumitomo, and those affiliated with the large city banks, DKB, Fuyo, and Sanwa.

[4] Methodological issues vex comparisons. All else being equal, the more diversified the group, the lower and more stable its average profits and more likely intragroup lending. Business groups may

A second type of interfirm network is a vertical integration model. In Silicon Valley, clusters of software design, development, testing, deployment and maintenance firms are linked to software end users. Suppliers of auto parts and components working with final assemblers are other examples. In these cases, the costs and benefits of learning to work together are considerable (von Hippel 1998; Fruin 1992; Shiba and Shimotani 1997). Vertically linked interfirm networks are called *keiretsu*[5] in Japan, and typically they display high levels of intragroup transactions and low levels of intragroup ownership and control. Toyota and its suppliers, Toshiba and its affiliates are well-known examples (Fruin 1992, 1997). Vertically linked production and distribution networks were widely found in prewar Japan and, not surprisingly, they remain institutional norms after the war.

Both sorts of interfirm networks, interindustry (*kigyo shudan*) and vertically oriented (*keiretsu*), are substantially different than prewar *zaibatsu* with their high levels of family-based ownership and control (Kanno 1966; Hadley 1970). Interindustry groups, especially loosely linked, city bank-based ones, are weak interfirm networks while vertically oriented groups, like Toyota, are stronger with high levels of intragroup transactions and low levels of ownership and control.[6]

11.4 BUSINESS GROUPS IN THE PAST AND TODAY

In the next section, two examples of business groups are explored. First, the British Trading Company, John Swire & Sons, is considered and, next, Kikkoman is examined. Thereafter, a brief appraisal of business groups in emerging economies is undertaken.

---

also define market boundaries and, hence, affect diversification activities differently. Also, analyzing surviving and departing resources associated with single firms in groups of several hundred firms should be controlled for.

[5] Literally, a lineage succession or ordering of a group. *Keiretsu* are firm groupings, organized according to size or function, so that the actions of one affect the next in line. Eighty to 90 percent of small- and medium-sized firms in Japan are linked to larger firms in production and distribution chains. *Keiretsu* groupings are very different in character, structure, strategy, and behavior from *kigyo shudan* groupings.

[6] Scale-free versus hierarchical networks: when whole systems can be broken down into discrete subsystems, modularity or substituting subsystems becomes possible. In scale-free networks, nodes with critical resources (routines) are more central than others and they cannot be easily substituted for; in hierarchical networks, nested (time-sensitive) functions are built into the design and this allows subsystems to function independently.

11.4.1 A British Trading Company

Business groups are a large and varied lot. Among them, John Swire & Sons is an excellent example of British trading companies (Jones 2000). John Swire & Sons, along with Alfred Holt & Co., began in 1816 as Liverpool-based merchants importing cotton from New Orleans and exporting finished Lancashire cotton goods. The next generation of Swires moved the company's headquarters to London, helped to found the Ocean Steamship Company, the Blue Funnel Line, set up Butterfield & Swire in 1867 to sell manufactures in China, established a China coastal and river shipping firm in 1872, and opened a New York office in 1873.

In the 1870s, the Holts and Swires were joined by a family of shipbuilders, the Scotts, based on the Clyde River. Swire purchased ships from Scott's, and Scott's invested in Swire. During a fifty-two year period, 1868 to 1920, 28 percent of Scott's shipbuilding business came from the Holts and Swires (Jones 2000). Like other British traders, John Swire & Sons raised funds for separate 'free-standing' firms on British capital markets. These were operating subsidiaries of holding companies. They allowed capital to be raised to finance operations while parent holding companies were closely held (ibid.).

Like other trading firms, John Swire & Sons focused on particular host regions where local knowledge was acquired and exploited (Jones). John Swire & Sons husbanded knowledge of coastal China. Only when China was consolidated under communist rule in 1949 and the Cultural Revolution made China's future unpredictable did John Swire & Sons begin to diversify their business interests. In 1948, John Swire & Sons took a controlling interest in Cathay Pacific Airways, lining up additional investment from the Borneo Co. and P&O. In doing so, John Swire & Sons was behaving like other British trading firms for which the distinction between trading and banking was often blurred. In 1952, John Swire & Sons, through the China Navigation Co., opened a shipping service between Brisbane and Papua New Guinea, and acquired a small haulage firm; in 1956, a freezer trucking company; and, in 1970, a cold storage company in Australia.

These moves, especially the acquisition of Cathay Pacific, are examples of linked or technology-related diversification. Using their China-based transportation know-how, John Swire & Sons expanded into related air and regional-based transportation services. Diversification was based on acquisitions. Newly purchased businesses put minimal demands on previously held properties because, often, they were located far from China. After 1948–9, John Swire & Son's diversification efforts did not seek to leverage its knowledge of China and maritime/coastal transportation there.

For more than a century, John Swire & Sons remained a family-controlled firm, a private, limited liability company controlled by the Swire and Scott families. In 1974, as part of a reorganization of the company that had been continuing since

1949, ownership of a majority of its Far Eastern businesses was placed in a public company, Swire Pacific. John Swire & Sons initially held 27 percent of Swire Pacific's shares.

Ten years later, in 1983, John Swire & Sons (China) Ltd. was incorporated. Four years later, John Swire & Sons sold 12.5 percent of Cathay Pacific to China International Trust & Investment (Citic). In 1990, together with Citic, John Swire & Sons took control of Dragonair, Hong Kong's entrepreneurial air carrier. This left John Swire & Sons with less than 50 percent of the shares of Cathay Pacific but with management control. At the same time, John Swire & Sons made a number of other investments in China, again with Citic, most notably a Coca-Cola bottling plant.

With the exception of Coca-Cola bottling, John Swire & Son's diversification efforts were not especially scale-based, and they took little advantage of John Swire & Son's China knowledge. As already noted, John Swire & Sons expanded via acquisitions rather than through internal development. Acquisitions were safe, relatively minor purchases in shipping, trucking, and cold storage in Brisbane, Australia and Papua, New Guinea.

Throughout the nineteenth and twentieth centuries, the Swire group was closely held by John Swire & Sons. The parent company, in turn, was two-thirds owned by the Swires and one-third by the Scotts. All senior managers of Swire companies were employed by John Swire & Sons. Swire Pacific, a publicly listed firm, was controlled by the family through minority equity stakes purchased on the Hong Kong stock exchange.

Parent company ownership and control of Swire businesses remained high while levels of intragroup transactions were low. John Swire & Sons was clearly a business group, far from an interfirm network. Ownership and control are (and were) closely held; intragroup transactions are (were) notably low. As Swire's senior management emphasized in a late twentieth century interview, they had successfully insulated the group from capital market pressures; they had ensured the continued existence of John Swire & Sons as a diversified, business group (Jones 2000).

While the details of other British trading companies and, indeed, of other family-based business groups differ, certain regularities stand out across business groups. Ownership and control, often family-based, are closely held. Diversifications typically come via acquisition rather than internal development. Managerial hierarchies of size to consolidate control are eschewed in favor of decentralized operations. Preserving family wealth and power are common preoccupations, as seen in Japan as well.

11.4.2 Kikkoman

Kikkoman began as a collection of individual families that became, in time, a family-based business group and firm. This progression preserved ownership and control of key assets and provided strategic continuity. Ultimately, Kikkoman became the world's largest producer of soy foods and the oldest continuously operating enterprise among the largest industrial firms in Japan (Fruin 1983).

Kikkoman traces its soy sauce-making history in the city of Noda back to 1661. From then until 1887, production of soy sauce was carried out by Mogi or Takanashi stem family (*ie*) households. Wealthy households decided how their resources should be invested and managed over time, and a number of them invested in handicraft manufactures, including soy sauce brewing, which was fermented in large vats on six-month production cycles.

A dozen Mogi and Takanashi families, each with its own production facilities, decided to form a manufacturing cartel (see Fear's chapter on cartels in this volume) in 1887 (Fruin 1983). Nineteen different breweries (but only a dozen families) combined to purchase raw materials, control wages, ship and market soy sauce, *miso*, and *sake*, but not to standardize production and control output. Production facilities were owned and controlled by single families, while purchasing, shipping, and marketing functions were co-owned and managed.

In 1918, nine of the cartel families, all from the Mogi–Takanashi households, formed a single joint-stock company, the Noda Shoyu Company (later renamed Kikkoman). For the first time in 250 years, owners became managers. Before 1918, owners were indirectly involved in running household breweries, relying instead on *banto* (front office managers) and *toji* (brew masters). After 1918, owners became officers of the Noda Shoyu Company and responsible for managing company assets. Family members constituted 85 percent of the first board of directors, and 63 percent of the first eighty managers hired were previously employed in Mogi–Takanashi family enterprises (Fruin). Owners, their *banto,* and *toji* became employees.

Although the percentage of family members as managers declined as Kikkoman grew larger and other opportunities claimed ambitious Mogi–Takanashi scions, control of Kikkoman and affiliated commercial and non-commercial endeavors, a bank, railroad line, and hospital, remained in the hands of Mogi–Takanashi kinsmen. A family-based holding company was formed and it controlled investments in the soy and non-soy businesses.

A preference for debt rather than equity financing preserved family interests. Like many emerging economies today, equity markets were undeveloped in Japan. When firms sought outside funds, they turned to banks. Accordingly, Mogi–Takanashi family ownership and control of Kikkoman were easily maintained because capital resources for funding growth were obtained privately.

Late in the twentieth century, a shift toward diluted ownership and professional management occurred. Family ownership of Kikkoman shares slipped to less than 20 percent by the 1970s. But in spite of the growth in equity funding, internationalization of Kikkoman's operations, anti-trust troubles, and diversification of company interests, top executives of Kikkoman still come from the Mogi–Takanashi families for the most part.

Kikkoman is the most efficient producer of naturally brewed soy sauce in the world. Yet, for all its success, Kikkoman's ranking among Japan's largest industrial enterprises has steadily fallen. Decline, in my opinion, can be partially attributed to the family-based management of the Kikkoman group of companies. As with most family firms, there is an almost irresistible urge to preserve, maintain, and pass down family ownership and control at the expense of finding the best use for and the best managers of the company's resources (for an alternative view, see the chapter by Rose and Colli in this volume). The stories of Kikkoman and John Swire & Sons are echoed in many business groups found in today's emerging economies (Khanna and Palepu 2000).

11.4.3 Business Groups in Emerging Economies

Studies of business groups in emerging economies are increasing. Business groups appear to prosper when markets and bureaucracies fail by leveraging ties that bind. Trust and cooperation enable them to survive. Studies suggest that business groups facilitate economic development (Fisman and Khanna 2004), enhance market intermediation and reduce transaction costs (Khanna and Palepu 1998), affect economic performance and boost profitability for average members (Khanna and Rivkin 2001). In India, affiliates of diversified business groups outperform unaffiliated firms (Khanna and Palepu 1999). It is thought that business groups offset capital, labor, and product-market imperfections and substitute for the need for property rights enforcement (Jones 2000). Apparently, they burgeon in countries with foreign trade and investment asymmetries (Guillen 2000), reduce risk by income smoothing but without reducing operating profitability (Khanna and Yafeh 2005), and, they appear to foster trust, and trust may be ascendant in a global economy racked by uncertainty and risk (Casadesus-Masanell and Khanna 2003).

In short, business groups are well regarded in emerging economies because they appear to reduce risk, share resources, and contribute positively to infrastructure-building. However, because business groups and extended kinship networks are connected in many cases, conflicts between family solidarity and profit maximization may arise. Also, new communication, transportation, and information-processing technologies are transforming the calculus of ownership, control, and localization in business groups, as are new sources and types of financing. Recent writings suggest that business groups have to be understood within particular contexts, be they local/national, environmental, or institutional (DiMaggio and Powell 1983; Kobayashi and Ribstein 1996; Scott 2003).

11.5 Interfirm Networks

Interfirm networks and business groups differ with respect to levels of ownership, control, and intragroup transactions. The magnitude of the differences suggests that interfirm networks and business groups do not necessarily follow upon or replace one another. Until the twentieth century, interfirm networks were less common than business groups because communication and transportation technologies limited the possibilities of high velocity interactions among firms not connected by ownership and control.

Today, a heady mix of better information, IT, communication, and transportation technologies, rising competitive pressures, and changing ideas with respect to finance, risk management, and corporate governance help promote interfirm network-based cooperation, especially among firms seeking solutions to complex organizational problems. Japan's *kigyo shudan* and *keiretsu* and South Korea's *chaebol* (Hamilton 1998) are post-World War II examples. Silicon Valley's interfirm networks are no more than fifteen to twenty-five years old.

In some ways, interfirm networks resemble multibusiness firms pursuing constrained and related diversification strategies (Rumelt 1974). Internal transactions are high because component businesses are connected. Unlike multibusiness firms, ownership levels are typically low. Control is exerted indirectly through contractual agreements, training, and standardization, and command of downstream, value-adding resources, like distribution and sales. Indirect control also occurs when dedicated resources (asset-specific investments) have few alternative uses. Symbolic power, words, signs, and behaviors with network-wide meanings, such as campaigns to promote Just-in-Time or productivity-enhancing capabilities may also buttress control (Fruin 1997). When ownership levels are (atypically) high, control is exerted through the selection, promotion, and compensation of top executives and company officers.

11.5.1 Working Definition

Interfirm networks are hard to characterize because many different kinds of networks exist and social science research has focused on interpersonal, not interorganizational, networks. Nevertheless, a working definition can be stated: "Network organizations are composed of sets of independent actors who cooperate frequently for mutual advantage and, in the process, create communities of practice" (Fruin 1998: 4; see also, Podolny and Page 1998; Barnes 1979).

Several words or phrases stand out: sets, independent actors, frequent cooperation, mutual advantage, and communities of practice. In most networks, many arrangements of nodes and nodal connections are possible. Actors join networks freely and control is not based on ownership/property rights. Instead, mutual advantage drives interactions, and frequent interactions lead to dynamic, evolving networks, replete with possibilities (Nelson and Winter 1982).

Various kinds of networks are depicted in the literature: regular, scale-free, hierarchical/ nested, and random (chaotic) networks.[7] Various models of global firms, Toyota Motor and its suppliers, Sun Microsystems and its Java programmers are discussed below in order to illustrate the nature and variety of interfirm networks.

11.5.2 Interfirm Networks and Uncertainty

In turbulent environments, *ex ante* strategizing by top executives is practically pointless (Roberts 2004). Firms are unsure what to do, especially in the most turbulent environments, like Silicon Valley (Saxenian 1994; Castells 1996; Kenney 2000). In these circumstances, network organizations are likely to appear, seemingly as substitutes for the market and bureaucratic failures of lesser organizations. Global competition creates the greatest turbulence and most uncertainty.

11.5.3 Global Firm Models

A growing literature on globalization and firms picks up where Chandler's studies of organizations characterized by scale, scope, and speed left off. Porter's Home Base model (1990), an early global firm model, asserted that superior performance accrues to firms when key resources and capabilities are physically and organizationally centralized and governance mechanisms closely controlled. Porter's model adheres to a common belief of economists: firms can respond effectively, in terms of their internal structure and organizational design, to environmental complexity (1980).

Because of agglomeration benefits, global firms not headquartered in the West or in places of advanced resource accumulation are unlikely to realize the competitive

[7] In regular networks, the average path length connecting nodes is about the same. A telephone circle is an example. Everyone is directly connected to a few persons—generally, two others—and indirectly to everyone else. Because every node is connected to two others, redundancy is built into the system, but as a whole, the system is not very complex. Classical network studies assume that nodal ties occur at random and there is a characteristic, average connectivity for the network as a whole. However, recent studies question if there is "an average connectivity". Instead, a few nodes are linked to many, but most are linked to a few (Barabasi 2003; Barabasi and Oltvai 2004). Such hub-based networks are called scale-free networks. Chaotic/random networks display extreme variability in which nodes are linked and average pathway lengths; perturbations in initial conditions prevent them from settling down. However, the number of alternative states is not limitless; chaos/randomness is the regular alteration between steady states.

advantages of location (nation), according to Porter. Yet, rapidly adapting Chinese, Indian, South Korean, and Taiwanese firms appear to integrate disparate, cross-border learning and organizational capabilities among numerous, tightly coupled but distinct actors. Emergent interfirm networks are driven by distributed intelligence and periphery-inward, not center-outward, innovation.

To catch up with the West, Asian firms have seemingly moved faster and more flexibly than Western firms. The late development effect[8] may help to explain their willingness to eschew ownership in favor of relational ties for mobilizing core resources and accessing key markets (Dore 1986; Fruin 1998). While such strategies may be available to stand-alone firms, issues of ownership and control often stand in the way.

Interfirm networks composed of homogeneous actors may suffer in terms of adaptive speed and flexibility. Larger networks of more heterogeneous actors may facilitate self-organization, as in Adler's notion of learning bureaucracies (1993), and more frequent innovations, as seen in von Hippel (1998, 2005) and Rodan and Galunic's (2004) research. The large number (20,000) of national product standards that China's high-tech producers have developed, in comparison with 8,000 international product standards, may also illustrate the advantages of network size for accelerated learning (Lohr 2004; Fruin 1997).

Bartlett and Ghoshal (1989) analyzed global firms from Asia, Europe, and North America. The transnational firms they studied were highly decentralized organizations composed of national branches/subsidiaries of multinational firms with high cohesion and low coordination costs. Extensive networks of overseas subsidiaries may benefit from the redundancy of interactions that many networks seem to enjoy, but many multinationals are hard-pressed to capitalize on this, given information, coordination, and transaction costs when they try to compete globally (Arrow 1974; Rugman and Verbeke 2004).

The metanational firm (Doz *et al.* 2001) recognized the heterogeneity of tasks in globally decentralized firms, but did not address the diminishing importance of firm boundaries and need for adopting genuine network-based strategies among disparate actors that arise as a result. Firms, even highly decentralized ones, are not truly network-like in function. The self-organization of actors (autonomy of decision-makers and actions) and multiplicity and redundancy of mutually beneficial roles in interfirm networks are not at all firm-like (Barabasi 2003; Podolny and Page 1998). To illustrate the structures, strategies, and behaviors of interfirm networks in more detail, Toyota Motor's supplier network and Sun Microsystem's Java developer network are described below.

---

[8] To minimize the gap between advanced and emerging economies, firms and governments attempt to accelerate development through better informed, more centralized and "rational" policies. Japan, South Korea, and Taiwan are countries where late development has been used to explain the efficacy of coordinated market development.

11.5.4 Toyota Motor Company

Toyota Motor Company and its suppliers offer an outstanding example of what is called a *keiretsu* or vertically-linked, interfirm network.[9] Given its multi-tiered structure, Toyota's supplier network is a prime example of a nested, hierarchical interfirm network.[10] *Keiretsu* should not be confused with business groups, *zaibatsu*, that were common during Japan's emergence as an economic power before the Pacific War. *Zaibatsu* were widespread for the same reasons that business groups are commonly found in emerging economies today.

Toyota Motor started off as one of a prewar group of Toyota companies. Postwar occupation reforms and economic necessity triggered a transition to an interfirm network form of organization, as described below. From its founding in 1937, Toyota Motor leveraged the name and resources of its parent company, Toyoda Automatic Loom Works, which constituted the core of a business group centered on the manufacture of textile machinery, fabricated metals and equipment, and engineering skills.

Production at Toyota Motor, founded by Kiichiro Toyoda, expanded rapidly with the coming of the Sino-Japanese War. Demand outstripped even the ambitious building program that Kiichiro had envisioned. To keep pace, Kiichiro broke away from the loosely coupled group model of his father's Toyoda Automatic Loom and founded two highly specialized firms: Toyoda Steel and Toyoda Machine Works (later Toyota Engineering); their outputs were wholly dedicated inputs to Toyota Motor. This laid a basis for a new model of organization with high levels of intragroup transactions among firms.[11]

At the end of World War II, nearly 10,000 persons were working for Toyota Motor, not including those employed at Toyoda Steel, Toyoda Engineering, and other suppliers affiliated with Toyota. The postwar era was tough for Toyota. Production was down, the payroll could not be met, and Kiichiro resigned as president of Toyota Motor in 1950. In an effort to lower costs, simplify management, and reduce risk, seven key departments and divisions were separated from Toyota Motor and established as independent companies: Toyota Auto Body, Aichi Industries, Toyoda Trading, Nippondenso, Aichi Horo, Toyoda Spinning and Weaving, and Toyota Motor Sales. Survival, not diversification or growth, was the impetus for doing so.

---

[9] The better known, interindustry, sometimes called intermarket, combinations are known as *kigyo shudan* or *kigyo gurupu* (business groups) as compared with vertically oriented *keiretsu*. Besides these terms, Japanese use *oyagaisha* and *kogaisha* (parent and offspring) as well as *noren wake* (separated/parceled out enterprises) *kanren kigyo* (affiliated enterprises), and other terms to distinguish parent, offspring, and related firms.

[10] Hierarchical networks have nodes and subsystems that are specialized by task and function, resulting in multiplexing and nesting. Multiplexing uses nodal connections for multiple purposes. Nesting limits the number of needed connections because nested nodes/subsystems may act autonomously and their interactions are integrated at appropriate times.

[11] Chrysler before World War II offers a similar set of circumstances involving catch-up with more advanced and internalized motor vehicle production systems (Schwartz 2000).

The Korean War broke out and demand began to pick up in June 1950. Instead of internalizing the resources of previously spun-out departments and divisions, Toyota responded by strengthening its own internal production and managerial capabilities. Toyota began to develop the information and operations control methodologies that we have come to know as Just-in-Time production and supply. Toyota Motor was able to realize economies of scale and scope without internalizing the capabilities needed to coordinate product and process flows and absorbing the inevitable transaction costs.

Coordination and transactions costs cannot be wished away, however. In Toyota's case, a network of suppliers, dozens at first, and eventually hundreds and thousands strong, minimize and absorb those costs. If Toyota's network of suppliers were merely alternatives to or substitutes for vertically integrated firms, Toyota would have to own major shares in them or lock them up contractually to cover for those costs. Ownership is the essence of control in markets where contract law is poorly developed, as in prewar and early postwar Japan.

In fact, Toyota was and is a major shareholder in the first dozen or so firms that coalesced around it. They were the spin-outs from Toyota and Toyoda group of firms. As more and more firms huddled under Toyota's umbrella, however, Toyota eschewed ownership in them. In all likelihood, Toyota had better uses for its capital and revenue than taking minority and majority stakes in literally dozens of firms. Other modes of control, like Just-in-Time process controls, are second-best to well-enforced property rights. But with limited investment resources and rapid expansion of output, Toyota chose indirect over direct methods of control.

At Toyota and anywhere, for that matter, ownership facilitates desired actions. But once asset-specific investments are put in place by suppliers and patterns of supplier–assembler interaction established, ownership rights are not needed to sustain high levels of intraorganizational transactions and performance. Toyota owns shares in less than 10 percent of its 200 first-tier companies and no shares in the thousands of lower-tier firms in its auto parts supplier network (Fruin 1992). In fact, after interaction routines are in place, an absence of ownership rights may actually encourage initiative on the part of suppliers, ultimately leading to higher returns and more mutually beneficial relations (Fruin and Nishiguchi 1993; Gulati 1999; von Hippel 1988).

Toyota's supplier network did not emerge overnight as a solution to problems of ownership, control, and management. A historical process defines which firms were recruited and how they were socialized into Toyota's way of doing things (Fruin and Nishiguchi 1993). Indeed, the history of interactions between Toyota and its many suppliers offers a classic example of the co-evolution of organizations and their environments. Toyota encouraged a nested, multi-tiered network of suppliers, suppliers remained autonomous enough to remain profit- and innovation-oriented, and civic institutions, like local banks and town governments, buttressed a process of mutual adaptation. Single-mindedly and selectively, Toyota recruited, educated, and evaluated suppliers on how well they followed the Toyota way without losing their own way. An interfirm network began to emerge:

Toyota's financial interests in its suppliers never exceed a minority share. Unlike American divisions of a large multidivisional firm, Japanese affiliates do not simply move cash (profits) back to parent firms. Toyota does own between 11 and 49 percent of fifteen key, first-tier firms (about 200 in number) that along with Toyota Motor are known as the Toyota Group. Outside this group, however, Toyota's financial ties with affiliates are not substantial, generally less than 10 percent. And, even this figure extends only to first-tier firms.

More generally, the front-rank of Toyota affiliates and suppliers raise much of their own capital, hire their own people, prepare, organize, and execute their own production plans and budgets, and design and make their own parts. In these ways and others, they are independent. (Fruin 1992)

Nurturing and encouraging suppliers transformed Toyota's internal production system into an externalized, network-based production system. That, in turn, required the development of a governance system, the Toyota Supplier Associa-tion, that works well with hundreds of autonomous suppliers. After decades of experimentation and trial-and-error learning, an interfirm network appeared that promotes not only a specialization of function and purpose, but also encourages a sense of camaraderie and community binding together suppliers.

11.5.5 Sun Microsystems

Sun's organizational model and strategy are quite different from Toyota's. Sun was founded in 1982 as a maker of engineering workstations. From the beginning, Sun included TCP/IP or what is now known as the Internet protocol suite in its products. Sun wanted to bring the power of the network to PC users. Its motto, "The network is the computer", incorporated that vision.

Sun shipped a million systems in its first ten years. The company was growing faster than any computer company had ever grown before, even though it was one of the few firms designing, building, and selling both hardware and software solutions. Sun introduced the Java programming language in 1995. Until Java, the computing universe was a Tower of Babel. Hardware and software systems were proprietary; users could only interact with the same or similar systems. The power of computers and computing dissipated in drips and drabs. Java changed all that.

Programs written in Java run on almost any computer and operating system. Hence, Java technology allows programmers to write applications only once. From the start, Java was designed for corporate intranets and the Internet. Java was going to bring down the Tower of Babel. Sun licensed Java technology inexpensively for as little as several thousand dollars. Before long, the price dropped to several hundred dollars, and by 2000, it could be downloaded for free via the Internet.

In 1998, Sun introduced Jini technology, enabling all kinds of devices to be easily connected to networks. In the same year, Sun launched Java 2: software that offered more speed and flexibility than the 1995 version and was backed by a set of foundation and application classes. Java and Jini transformed the computing scene, powering the growth of the worldwide web, tying together millions of previously incompatible, mutually unintelligible computers, operating systems, and databases.

Surprisingly, given their power and appeal, Sun gave away its Java and Jini technologies. Sun was pursuing a new model of how firms create value and profit. Instead of chipping away at the market shares of deeply entrenched rivals and absorbing the cost-cutting and penetration pricing strategies that accompany such an approach, Sun did something else. Java was priced low, eventually given away, to steal market share from Microsoft Windows, the dominant operating system in the desktop computing environment. Sun was banking on the power of network effects.

Network effects are gains realized by joining with large numbers of fellow users. Network effects occur when the benefits of becoming a subscriber increase exponentially, while costs merely increase linearly. For network effects to occur, large numbers of users are necessary. In fact, the larger the number of subscribers, the greater the benefits of subscription because subscribers can be connected in many different ways.

Sun tries to capitalize on network effects by doing everything via the Internet, using universal languages like Java and Jini. Sun encourages Java and Jini programming for any and all applications. Sun stands behind Java and Jini programmers, providing them with worldwide service and support, offering quarterly upgrades, and guaranteeing the interoperability of Java and Jini within a worldwide computer environment.

By making Java and Jini freely available and standing behind them, Sun created an interfirm network of software users that is even larger than Toyota's network of auto parts suppliers. By offering software with universal application and appeal, by standing behind it, upgrading it, and offering service and support at little or no cost to users, Sun has forged a worldwide network of enterprise and program users where applications are quickly and inexpensively shared, refined, and reborn (Lessig 2002; von Hippel 2005). Software bugs are caught early, increasing reliability and the number of applications. The more users, the better. With Java and Jini, software developers can concentrate on adding value rather than making efforts to lock up markets with proprietary standards.

In 2004, Sun Microsystems decided that its flagship operating system, Solaris, should also be given away. This puts Solaris in the same ring with Linux, the popular Open Source operating system that is competing with Windows to be the *de facto* standard in the network computing marketplace. Linux is free and continually improved by the voluntary efforts of thousands of programmers worldwide who rewrite its source code and openly share the fruits of their labors. Solaris goes one better than Linux. Sun provides Solaris users with the open-source benefits of Linux and the industry strength and corporate resources of Sun (Menn 2004). Sun's Java, Jini, and Solaris programming and user networks offer prime examples of (scale-free) interfirm networks.

Toyota versus Sun   Comparing Toyota's supplier network to Sun's network of Java, Jini, and Solaris users illustrates not only different forms of network organization, but also very different network strategies. Briefly put, Toyota's supplier network operates on a Toyota-specific, proprietary technology, namely, the Toyota Production System. That technology is only disclosed to firms that show they are willing, worthy, and able to operate in the Toyota way. Toyota continuously monitors their performance, and rewards them according to their contributions to the network.

Sun's model is quite different. Instead of keeping its proprietary technologies close to its chest, Sun gives them away and believes that the more users, the better (Lessig 2002). Sun does not monitor or control how its Java, Jini, and Solaris products are used. The more idiosyncratic and novel the use, the better, because if uses have any value, they will be shared and refined by a worldwide, self-interested, self-organizing network of Sun software users. Without Toyota-style, hands-on management, Sun benefits from the positive interactions (network effects) of large numbers of users.

11.6 CONCLUSIONS

Cooperation and competition share a short history as countervailing business concepts. They became so in the late nineteenth and early twentieth centuries, as ideas of natural selection, competitive selection, survival of the fittest, fair and unfair competition were popularized with the promulgation of the Sherman and Clayton Anti-Trust Acts. Until then, there was relatively little effort to distinguish between them when characterizing business activities.

Business groups reflect the absence of a stark contrast between cooperation and competition. In such groups, kinship and property rights are the basis of cooperation. They lead to communities of similar interests that, in turn, may beget contentiousness in balancing those interests. Whether in emerging or advanced economies, therefore, business groups reflect the tension between cooperation and competition. Cartels and professional associations, on the other hand, cooperate for reasons of efficiency, quality, and safety.

Alfred D. Chandler, Jr. describes how modern, complex, multibusiness firms appeared, first in the United States and later around the world. They are amazing examples of how far an internal division of labor can be advanced in the interest of cooperation. Hundreds, thousands, and tens of thousands of employees cooperate in the interest of planning, scheduling, coordinating, and offering firm-specific goods and services.

Such firms changed the nature of business groups. In order for business groups to compete with modern firms, they had to adapt in similar ways: develop organizational capabilities to manage scale and scope economies, create managerial hierarchies to coordinate, command, and control. In the United States, many business groups evolved into conglomerate forms of organization, while in Western Europe, others became holding companies with operating subsidiaries.

Interfirm networks are still different. High levels of information exchange and transactions reflect frequent interactions among network nodes; these facilitate complex problem-solving, like designing, developing, making, and assembling the 15–20,000 components and sub-assemblies that producing full-sized automobiles require. In this way, interfirm networks and modern firms arose as adaptive responses to the complexities of organizing and managing high-throughput operations. One is based on voluntarism and self-organization while the other depends on command-and-control hierarchies to promote property rights.

Notions of cooperation and competition reflect cultural assumptions as to the costs and benefits of organization. In view of the dramatic changes sweeping across the United States in the late nineteenth and early twentieth centuries, the benefits of competition over cooperation in terms of operational efficiency and social welfare were strongly reflected in the Sherman and Clayton Anti-Trust Acts. Such laws were and are less well accepted and enforced elsewhere.

Models of acceptable behavior—at individual, community, organizational, and societal levels—compete and vie for support. The new standards of corporate behavior embodied in the Sherman and Clayton Anti-Trust Acts required years of education and enforcement before they were widely followed because, in part, alternative models of acceptable (cooperative/competitive) behavior existed. *Shane* and *Dirty Harry* reveal the ambiguity. Decisive individuals who act alone, often without remorse and reference to others, are idealized in popular American culture. In most of Asia, on the other hand, *Shane* and *Dirty Harry* are both considered highly antisocial.

The reality is that businesses everywhere are cooperating more. Given the increasing costs and complexities of developing new technologies, time-to-market pressures, turbulent markets, uncertain policies, and heightening difficulties of doing business globally, cooperation is growing apace. It is impossible, for example, to describe the business activities of any major Silicon Valley firm without employing a cooperative network model of organization.[12]

---

[12] Silicon Valley partnerships are often described as strategic alliances although strategic alliances and interfirm networks differ notably. Strategic alliances do not last long, generally no more than two to four years. Also, the density, intensity, and duration of relations in strategic alliances pale in comparison with those in Toyota or Sun's interfirm network. A combination of strategic alliances of less enduring and nested networks of more enduring ties may be an important feature of how Silicon Valley is organized.

Looking ahead, business success will require firms to cooperate and compete, and, as we have seen, this is nothing new. History and emerging economies are replete with examples. Augmenting these with what we are learning about complex systems in the natural sciences (Barabasi and Oltvai 2004; Kauffman 1993, 1996) and cooperation in the social sciences (for example, Axelrod 1997; Holland 1998; von Hippel 1998) will advance our knowledge of cooperation and competition and how they interact. Companies with global reach and fast-to-market, scale and scope ambitions will need to combine internal, resource-based and external, relationship-based capabilities and to deploy and manage both enthusiastically and well. Cooperation and competition will co-evolve.

References

ADLER, PAUL S. (1993). "The New 'Learning Bureaucracy': New United Motors Manufacturing, Inc.", in Barry Staw and Larry Cummings (eds.), *Research in Organizational Behavior.* Greenwich, Conn.: JAI Press.

ALCHIAN, A. A., and DEMSETZ, H. (1972). "Production, Information Costs and Economic Organization", *American Economic Review*, 82: 777–95.

ARROW, KENNETH (1974). *The Limits of Organization.* New York: W. W. Norton.

AXELROD, ROBERT (1997). *The Complexity of Cooperation.* Princeton, NJ: Princeton University Press.

BARABASI, ALBERT-LASZLO (2003). *Linked.* London: Plume.

—— and OLTVAI, ZOLTIN N. (2004). "Network Biology: Understanding the Cell's Functional Organization", *Nature Reviews*, 5, Feb.: 101–14.

BARNES, J. A. (1979). "Network Analysis: Orienting Notion, Rigorous Technique or Substantive Field of Study?" in P. W. Holland and S. Leinhardt (eds.), *Perspectives on Social Network Research.* New York: Academic Press.

BARTLETT, CHRISTOPHER, and GHOSHAL, SUMANTRA (1989). *Managing across Borders—The Transnational Solution.* Boston: Harvard Business School Press.

BETHEL, JENNIFER, and LIEBESKIND, JULIA (1998). "Diversification and the Legal Organization of the Firm". *Organization Science*, 9/1: 49–67.

BETTIS, R. A. (1981). "Performance Differences in Related and Unrelated Diversified Firms". *Strategic Management Journal*: 379–94.

BOURDIEU, PIERRE (2005). "Principles of an Economic Anthropology", in Neil J. Smelser and Richard Swedberg (eds.), *Handbook of Economic Sociology.* Princeton, NJ: Princeton University Press, 75–89.

BURETH, A., WOLFF, S., and ZANDER, A. (1997). "The Two Faces of Learning by Cooperating: The Evolution and Stability of Inter-firm Agreements in the European Electronics Industry". *Journal of Economic Behavior and Organization*, 32: 519–37.

BRIOSCHI, FRANCESCO, BRIOSCHI, MARIA SOLE, and CAINELLI, GIULIO (2002). "From the Industrial District to the Industrial Group: An Insight into the Evolution of Local Capitalism in Italy." *Regional Studies*, 36/9: 1037–52.

BURT, RONALD (1992). *Structural Holes.* Cambridge, Mass.: Harvard University Press.

CASADESUS-MASANELL, RAMON, and KHANNA, TARUN (2003). "Globalization and Trust: Theory and Evidence from Cooperatives". William Davidson Institute Working Paper No. 592, June, p. 30.

CASTELLS, MANUEL (1966). *The Rise of the Network Society*. Cambridge, Mass.: Blackwell Publishers.

CHANDLER, ALFRED D. (1962). *Strategy and Structure*. Cambridge, Mass.: MIT Press.

—— (1977). *The Visible Hand*. Cambridge, Mass.: Harvard University Press.

—— (1990). *Scale and Scope*. Cambridge, Mass.: Harvard University Press.

—— (2001). *Inventing the Electronic Century*. New York: Free Press.

COLEMAN, J. S. (1988). "Social Capital in the Creation of Human Capital". *American Journal of Sociology*, 94: 95–120.

DAVIS, GERALD F. (2005). "Firms and Environments", in Neil J. Smelser and Richard Swedberg (eds.), *Handbook of Economic Sociology*. Princeton, NJ: Princeton University Press, pp. 478–502.

DIMAGGIO, PAUL, and POWELL, WALTER W. (1983). "The Iron Cage Revisited: Institutional Isomorphism and Collective Rationality in Organizational Fields". *American Sociological Review*, 48/2: 509–603.

DINE, JANET (2000). *The Governance of Corporate Groups*. Cambridge: Cambridge University Press.

DORE, RONALD (1986). *Flexible Rigidities*. Stanford, Calif.: Stanford University Press.

DOZ, YVES, SANTOS, JOSE, and WILLIAMSON, PETER (2001). *From Global To Metanational*. Boston, Mass.: Harvard Business School Press.

FISMAN, RAYMOND J., and KHANNA, TARUN (2004). "Facilitating Development: The Role of Business Groups". *World Development*, 32/4, Apr.: 609–28.

FRUIN, W. MARK (1983). *Kikkoman—Company, Clan, and Community*. Cambridge, Mass.: Harvard University Press.

—— (1992). *The Japanese Enterprise System*. Oxford: Oxford University Press.

—— (1997). *Knowledge Works—Managing Intellectual Capital at Toshiba*. New York: Oxford University Press.

—— (1998). *Networks, Markets, and the Pacific Rim*. New York: Oxford University Press.

—— and NISHIGUCHI, TOSHIHIRO (1993). "Supplying the Toyota Production System", in Bruce Kogut (ed.), *Country Competitiveness*. New York: Oxford University Press.

GRANOVETTER, MARK (1973). "The Strength of Weak Ties". *American Journal of Sociology*, 78/6, May: 1360–80.

—— (1985). "Economic Action and Social Embeddedness: The Problem of Embeddedness". *American Journal of Sociology*, 91: 481–510.

—— (2005). "Business Groups and Social Organization", in N. Smelser and R. Swedberg (eds.), *Handbook of Economic Sociology*, 2nd edn. Princeton, NJ: Princeton University Press.

GUILLEN, MAURO F. (2000). "Business Groups in Emerging Economies: A Resource-Based View". *Academy of Management Journal*, 43/3: 362–80.

GULATI, RANJAY (1999). "Network Location and Learning: The Influence of Network Resources and Firm Capabilities on Alliance Formation". *Strategic Management Journal*, 15: 291–309.

HADLEY, ELEANOR (1970). *Anti-trust in Japan*, Princeton, NJ: Princeton University Press.

HAMILTON, GARY (1998). "Patterns of Asian Network Capitalism: The Cases of Taiwan and South Korea", in Fruin (1998), 181–99.

HOLLAND, JOHN H. (1998). *Emergence*. Reading, Mass.: Addison-Wesley.

JONES, GEOFFREY (2000). *Merchants to Multinationals. British Trading Companies in the Nineteenth and Twentieth Centuries*. Oxford: Oxford University Press.

KAUFFMAN, STUART (1993). *The Origins of Order*. New York: Oxford University Press.

—— (1996). *At Home in the Universe*. New York: Oxford University Press.

KANNO, WATARO (1966). *Nihon Kaisha Kigyo Hasseishi no Kenkyu (Research on the Origins of Japan's Joint Stock Companies)*. Tokyo: Keizai Hyoronsha.

KENNEY, MARTIN (ed.) (2000). *Understanding Silicon Valley*. Stanford, Calif.: Stanford University Press, 2000.

KHANNA, T. (2000). "Business Groups and Social Welfare in Emerging Markets: Existing Evidence and Unanswered Questions". *European Economic Review*, 44/4–6: 748–61.

—— and PALEPU, KRISHNA (1997). "Why Focused Strategies may be Wrong for Emerging Markets". *Harvard Business Review*, 75/4: 41–51.

—— —— (1998). "Emerging Market Business Groups, Foreign Investors, and Corporate Governance". Harvard Business School Working Paper No. 99-017.

—— —— (1999). "Policy Shocks, Market Intermediaries, and Corporate Strategy: Evidence from Chile and India". *Journal of Economics and Management Strategy*, 8/2: 271–310.

—— —— (2000). "Is Group Affiliation Profitable in Emerging Markets? An Analysis of Diversified Indian Business Groups". *Journal of Finance*, 55/2: 867–91.

—— and RIVKIN, JAN W. (2001). "Estimating the Performance Effects of Networks in Emerging Markets". *Strategic Management Journal*, 22: 45–74.

—— and YAFEH, YISHAY (2005). "Business Groups and Risk Sharing around the World". *Journal of Business*, 78/1; Jan.: 301–40.

KOBAYASHI, B., and RIBSTEIN, L. (1996). "Evolution and Spontaneous Uniformity: Evidence from the Evolution of the Limited Liability Company". *Economic Inquiry*, 34: 464–83.

KOGUT, B. (1988). "Joint Ventures: Theoretical and Empirical Perspectives". *Strategic Management Journal*, 9: 319–32.

LANG, LARRY H. P., and STULZ, RENE M. (1994). "Tobin's q, Corporate Diversification, and Firm Performance". *Journal of Political Economy*, 102/6: 1248–80.

LESSIG, LAWRENCE (2002). *The Future of Ideas: The Fate of the Commons in a Connected World*. New York: Vintage Books.

LIKER, JEFFREY, FRUIN, W. MARK, and ADLER, PAUL (eds.) (1999). *Remade in America—Transplanting and Transforming Japanese Management Systems*. New York: Oxford University Press.

LINCOLN, JAMES, and GERLACH, MICHAEL (2004). *Japan's Network Economy*. Cambridge: Cambridge University Press.

LOHR, STEVE (2004). "China Poses Trade Worry as it Gains in Technology". *New York Times*, Jan. 13.

MENN, JOSEPH (2004). "Sun Micro's Answer to the Linux Invasion: Give Away Solaris 10". *Los Angeles Times*, Nov. 15, C1–2.

MONTGOMERY, C. A. (1994). "Corporate Diversification". *Journal of Economic Perspectives*, summer: 163–78.

NELSON, RICHARD, and WINTER, SIDNEY (1982). *An Evolutionary Theory of Economic Change*. Cambridge, Mass.: Harvard University Press.

ODAGIRI, HIROYUKI (1992). *Growth through Competition, Competition through Growth*. Oxford: Oxford University Press.

PIORE, MICHAEL, and SABEL, CHARLES F. (1984). *The Second Industrial Divide: Possibilities for Prosperity.* New York: Basic Books.

PODOLNY, J. M. and PAGE, K. L. (1998). "Network Forms of Organization". *Annual Review of Sociology*, 24: 57–76.

PORTER, MICHAEL (1980). *Competitive Strategy.* New York: Free Press.

—— (1990). *The Competitive Advantage of Nations.* New York: Free Press.

POWELL, WALTER W. (1990). "Neither Market nor Hierarchy: Network Forms of Organization". *Research in Organizational Behavior*, 12: 295–336.

RAMSEYER, J. MARK, and MIWA, YOSHIRO (2002). "The Fable of the Keiretsu." *Journal of Economics and Management Strategy*, 11/2: 169–224.

ROBERTS, JOHN (2004). *The Modern Firm.* Oxford: Oxford University Press.

RODAN, SIMON, and GALUNIC, D. C. (2004). "More than Network Structure: How Knowledge Heterogeneity Influences Managerial Performance and Innovativeness". *Strategic Management Journal*, 25: 541–56.

ROE, MARK (1994). *Strong Managers, Weak Owners.* Princeton, NJ: Princeton University Press.

RUEF, MARTIN (2000). "The Emergence of Organizational Forms: A Community Ecology Approach", *American Journal of Sociology*, 106/3: 658–714.

RUGMAN, ALAN, and VERBEKE, ALAIN (2004). "Towards a Theory of Regional Multinationals: A Transaction Cost Economics Approach". *Management International Review*, 44/4, special issue: 3–15.

RUMELT, RICHARD (1974). *Strategy, Structure, and Economic Performance.* Cambridge, Mass.: Harvard University Press.

SAXENIAN, ANNA LEE (1994). *Regional Advantage.* Cambridge, Mass.: Harvard University Press.

SCOTT, W. RICHARD (2001). *Institutions and Organizations*, 2nd edn. Thousand Oaks, Calif.: Sage Publications.

SHIBA, TAKAO, and MASAHIRO SHIMOTANI (1997). *Beyond the Firm.* Oxford: Oxford University Press.

—— (2003). *Organizations: Rational, Natural and Open Systems*, 5th edn. Englewood Cliffs, NJ: Prentice Hall.

SCHWARTZ, MICHAEL (2000). "Markets, Networks, and the Rise of Chrysler in Old Detroit, 1920–40". *Enterprise and Society*, 1/1: 63–99.

VON HIPPEL, ERIC (1998). *The Sources of Innovation.* Oxford: Oxford University Press.

—— (2005). *Democratizing Innovation.* Cambridge, Mass.: MIT Press.

WALKER, G., KOGUT, B., and SHAN, W. (1997). "Social Capital, Structural Holes, and the Formation of an Industry Network". *Organization Science*, 8: 109–12.

WILLIAMSON, OLIVER E. (1975). *Markets and Hierarchies: Analysis and Antitrust Implications.* New York: Free Press.

—— (1985). *The Economic Institutions of Capitalism.* New York: Free Press.

—— (1994). "Transaction Cost Economics and Organizational Theory", in N. Smelser and R. Swedberg (eds.), *Handbook of Organizational Sociology.* Princeton, NJ: Princeton University Press, 77–107.

CHAPTER 12

....

CARTELS

....

JEFFREY FEAR

12.1 INTRODUCTION

....

BEFORE 1945 most of the world thought that cartels brought widespread benefits. Backed by US economic might, after 1945 antitrust ideas spread across the world so that now Adam Smith's devastating verdict on them as "conspiracies against the public" has become the prevailing interpretation. Business historians have shown, however, that this consensus about cartels as conspiracy is historically the exception to the rule, a product of a post-1945 constellation of ideas and events. Cartels are not necessarily the opposite of liberalism and competition, but a variation on them. For better or for worse, they shaped economic and business history from the late 19th century. From the company perspective, joining, managing, or combating cartels was a major entrepreneurial act. Finally, business historians have shown the varied effects and services provided by cartels (quality standards, technology transfers, or risk management) that extend beyond the conspiratorial motivation to raise prices.

In short, studying cartels through the lens of conspiracy does a severe injustice to their empirical reality and short-circuits many important theoretical questions. Section 12.2 offers an array of different cartel types that blur the distinction between legitimate cooperation and illegitimate collusion. It is actually difficult to decide when a cartel is a cartel, what cartel success means, let alone if it acts inefficiently or destructively. Section 12.3 argues that the voluminous scale and scope of cartels before 1939, together with lingering cartelization after 1945 in Europe and Japan, means that any analysis of entrepreneurship, corporate strategy, and organization, as well as national economic development, must incorporate the impact of cartels. Yet the most neglected area of research is the most important one for business historians. What impact did cartels have on economic and corporate development (Section 12.4)?

This chapter makes a few broad points. First, cartels do not abolish competition, but regulate it. The question is not cartels *or* competition, but cartels *and* competition. Historically, cartels provided participating firms with a range of market-ordering options that antitrust has since foreclosed. Economic analysis works with a stark dichotomy of markets (cartels as distortions) or hierarchies (cartels as incomplete, inefficient internalization). This conceptual straitjacket leads to one of the largest misconceptions about cartels that they halt competition and innovation. Instead they reshape the rules of the game on which competition rests (similarly Wurm 1993).

Second, to fully understand company development and behavior in a cartel-laced world—that is, most of the 20th century—business historians need to recover those strategic options in between markets and hierarchies. If one takes the perspective that joining cartels is a form of *competitive* strategy, or at least a cooperative waystation on the road towards future competition, one can explain why cartels have not damaged economic growth as much as some might expect.

Third, if one reframes cartels as private self-management of an industry, cartel research can fruitfully intersect with studies of government regulation and the burgeoning discussion about business self-regulation. Rightly or wrongly, people conceived cartels for over a century as a legitimate form of market governance and national industrial policy. Cartels represented at least one way in which contemporaries debated capitalism and attempted to manage its excesses. The cartel question raised important issues about the benefits and risks of competition—and for whom.

To be clear, these cooperative arrangements were by no means benign, mostly second-best forms of competition, and were largely but not exclusively in producers' interests. They were, however, sometimes more congruent with the public interest than Smith's claim that they were only an "absurd tax" created by an "order of men ... who have generally an interest to deceive and even to oppress the public" (Smith 1776/1976: 278). We need to broaden the discussion of cartels beyond conspiracy.

12.2 A TYPOLOGY OF INTERFIRM COOPERATION

The classic cartel study by Great Britain's Board of Trade (1944: p. vi) noted that "the variety of arrangements is very striking and attests to the ingenuity of industrialists, or at least that of the accountants and lawyers who advise them".

It is difficult to generalize about cartels because they come in such a variety of forms, objectives, and effectiveness. What constitutes a cartel is by no means an easy question.

Economists have established a plausible but stylized baseline of theories where cartels are most likely to appear and endure. George Stigler (1964) famously argued that the acute desire to limit competition was not sufficient to explain when and why collusion occurs; collusion was more difficult than many assumed. Since cartels created an incentive to cheat, they were inherently instable. The great virtue of this economics literature, reviewed by Levenstein and Suslow (2004, 2006) and Levenstein and Salant (2007) more fully, is that it frames questions about inner-cartel behavior more precisely unlike the older literature that relied on individual case studies.

This literature tends to find all sorts of ways in which cartels fail, which, when pushed to the extreme, ironically obviates the need for antitrust policy and cannot explain how or why many cartels succeed. Levenstein and Suslow found it difficult to generalize about cartel sustainability at all. In their sample, a good number of cartels lasted longer than ten years; others collapsed quickly. One wheat cartel lasted just one year, but another wheat cartel managed to last 29 years. Japan's cartel movement practically begins with the cotton textile industry after 1880, where the great number of players should have destroyed it; Europeans never developed stable ones. Considering that most capital-intensive firms attempted to form cartels, the automobile industry never generated one. Innumerable "idiosyncratic and history-dependent determinants" on top of well-understood structural factors contributed to cartel success, defined as durability.

External shocks or demand instability destabilized cartels as much as cheating. Debora Spar's (1994) analysis of diamond, gold, uranium, and silver cartels concluded that: "At best, structural variables are the necessary but still insufficient precursors of cooperation" (p. 218). Although the term cooperation connotes a warm and fuzzy comportment, durable cartels depended upon constant bargaining, the ability to react flexibly over time, and harsh retaliation. Having a robust collective organization or a dominant player acting as a "hegemon" (Spar) enhanced cartels' effectiveness, such as in aluminum (Alcoa), electric lamps (General Electric), diamonds (De Beers), or oil (Saudi Arabia). The perils of price wars often helped cartels cohere.

Siegfried Tschierschky (1903), the long-time editor of Germany's leading cartel journal and a cartel director himself, differentiated firms' desire to form cartels (motivation), industry conditions (structure), from their capacity to do so (competence), but "practical cartel policies have found numerous ways to confront these difficulties in one or another manner" (p. 68). He stressed the "psychological willingness", or the "ethnological" and "personal moment". Cartel sustainability depended on their ability to regard customers, not disregard them, and their ability to lower prices at times to secure higher, long-run profitability (pp. 58–68). German coal, iron, and steel prices actually fell relative to British domestic prices after the formation of cartels around the turn of the 20th century (Kinghorn and Nielsen 2004).

Given that "idiosyncratic" elements are so important and that some cartels were major business organizations in their own right, business historians informed by economic theory would excel here. The model German cartel, the Rhenisch-Westphalian Coal Syndicate, formed in 1893, employed over 500 people, consisted of over 67 firms in 1912, was an independent joint-stock company with its own headquarters, and managed about 1,400 different prices for varying coal qualities (Peters 1989). Since cartels had to act like businesses to maintain their effectiveness and participants had to learn to work with one another to build more sophisticated structures over time, the lens of organizational capabilities or theories of organizational learning, rather than just analyzing the dynamics of cheating, would prove useful (Levenstein and Suslow 2006). Harm Schröter (1996) has argued that Germany's first-mover advantages in forming cartels provided a crucial learning experience that they leveraged when building international cartels. Rather than viewing cartels as inherently dysfunctional, researchers might examine how some cartels provide valuable services. DeBeers invented an ingenious marketing and distribution strategy to associate diamonds with weddings. American fire insurers learned how to develop stable local cartels to prevent rate-cutting that permitted them to build up reserves that staved off disaster after the San Francisco earthquake of 1906 and the Baltimore fire of 1904, unlike the disastrous municipal fires of the 1870s (Baranoff 2003).

Figure 12.1 classifies cartels along their objectives, rather than industry, which might promote more systematic comparisons.

Cartels are a subset of inter-firm cooperation, which ranges from highly, fluid spot markets with no individual market power to fully integrated enterprise hierarchies. The range describes the degree to which a formal organization wields authority over market transactions, but one cannot judge actual market power from the graphic. Long-term contracts between businesses or tacit oligopolistic collusion might wield more market power than a cartel if it has important outside competitors or is wracked by internal competition.

In general, cartels were voluntary, private contractual arrangements among independent enterprises to regulate the market. State-managed cartels or forced cartelization during wartime are important exceptions to this rule. Both Robert Liefmann (1932) and Harm Schröter (1988) stressed cartels' fundamental orientation toward security and stabilization, a sort of risk management strategy. Some definitions of cartels include the *intent* to monopolize markets, but the motivations to form cartels were so varied, so few cartels actually achieved monopolies, and many were established with the implicit aim to *preserve* competitors rather than competition, that this assumption is unnecessary (Barjot 1994). Early German cartel theorists viewed cartels as an anti-merger policy, contrasting dangerous

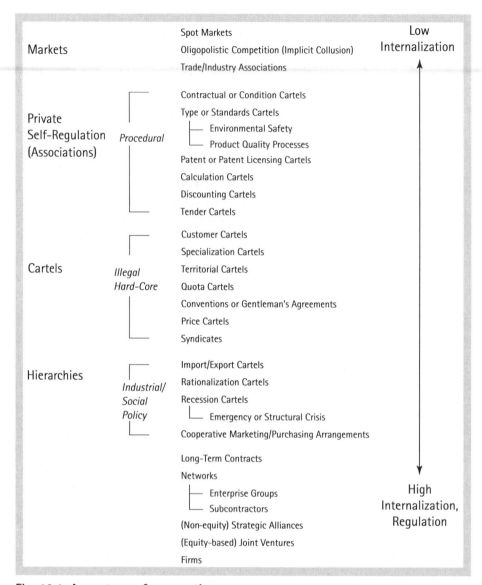

Fig. 12.1 A spectrum of cooperation

Source: Adapted from Korndörfer (1988: 128–32); Feldenkirchen (1988).

American-style trusts with responsible cartels (Fear 2005). Empirical studies have confirmed that prohibiting cartels speeded up concentration (Freyer 1992; Symeonidis 2002). Antitrust policy is a misnomer; it is more accurately an anti-cartel policy.

For the most part, cartels oriented themselves to controlling *similar* product markets in *horizontal* fashion, classically to avoid ruinous competition. While long-term contracts with suppliers, subcontractors, wholesalers, or retailers or enterprise groups might be anticompetitive, they are not cartels. One might conceive such arrangements as "vertical cartels", but they are better described as networks of firms, strategic alliances, enterprise groups, or joint ventures.

A fine line exists between legitimate associations and cartels. In Figure 12.1, the types of *procedural* cartels shade into the realm of desirable private self-regulation and associational life. Regulators have made *hard-core* types of cartels illegal. Antitrust regulations often exempt four types of *industrial or social policy* cartels because of their alleged benefits. The most problematic types of cartels occur at either end of this spectrum.

Contractual condition cartels might establish desirable procedures for transacting on markets. Standards cartels can set quality standards, or codes of behavior, or minimum environmental, labor, or safety regulations. The vast majority of industry standards originated as voluntary standards, which later became public regulations (Salter 1999; Spar 1999). Such arrangements might not be cartels at all, but one firm's standard might be another firm's barrier to entry.

Patent or patent-licensing cartels might clarify patent rights and often did lead to technological diffusion. Popular in the 1920s, patent cartels commonly guaranteed spheres of interest (territorial cartels) or restricted the use of related, unpatented articles or processes (for instance, GE and Krupp, or ICI and DuPont, or Standard Oil and IG Farben in Reader 1975 and Mason 1946). Highly specialized, startup companies in technology and knowledge-based sectors today frequently pool patent rights.

Customer cartels allocate customers or suppliers to certain producers; they often acted as incentives for firms to join broader cartels. Specialization cartels assign lines of commerce, product lines, or production techniques to firms—a non-price-oriented strategy, which clarified the division of labor to promote the industry. In contrast with other cartels, which tended to manage common products, specialization cartels divided the market differently. Gary Herrigel (1996) found these types of cartels critical throughout the 20th century as a mechanism for governing German small and medium-sized manufacturing businesses; Germany's 1957 anti-cartel law therefore exempted them from its proscriptions.

The middle four types of "hard-core" cartels are the most familiar (OECD 2000), yet the distinctions have great implications for understanding cartel behavior and durability. For instance, quota cartels limited the output of members, but they often could not control price fluctuations and suffered greatly from cheating because they often had few monitoring or enforcement measures. Price cartels usually created an independent agency to monitor production to hold members accountable. For these reasons, many industrialists preferred syndicates because they restricted access to customers. Syndicates could also pose a more united front against outsiders and punish wayward firms.

Export cartels played crucial roles in national economic development and continue to be one of the most popular types of cartels, exempted even in a cartel-hostile United States after 1918 (Dick 1996, 2004). Rather than raising prices, they often lowered them through common marketing arrangements or by cooperating at home, while competing abroad as with the Japanese television cartel (Schwartzman 1993). Export cartels blend into the last set of industrial or social policy cartels, which are frequently condoned. Such cartels' social benefits allegedly outweigh price increases or permit long-term production efficiencies to form that will offset short-term allocation losses. Here national interest is not necessarily congruent with the consuming public; this distinction underlies Japanese competition policy (Matsushita 1997: 170–3).

Finally, cooperative marketing, purchasing, R&D, or credit arrangements blur the lines between legitimate cooperation and collusion. The Japanese Association of Cotton Spinners, for instance, acted as a collective bargaining agent in negotiations with shipping companies for freight-rate rebates. Allied with the main Japanese shipping company, the NYK, it paved the way to establish a service to India and acted as a countervailing power to Japan's powerful *zaibatsu* trading companies (Wray 1984).

Such cooperative forms also proved immensely attractive to small and medium-sized businesses because they provided crucial services (rather than rate hikes). Such small business cartels are severely understudied; antitrust regulation often exempts them. The Tsukiji Market in Tokyo is the world's largest marketplace for seafood, yet cartelized, family businesses run it (Bestor 1998). It appears that hairdressers, fishmongers, and innkeepers are among the most prone to cartelization (Liefmann 1932).

This spectrum of possibilities raises a number of issues. First, cartels did not only aim to fix prices or restrain trade. Alice Teichova (1974, 1988) stressed the need to discover what exactly cartels agree upon. Second, the most problematic areas are those cooperative arrangements that fall in the grey zone of desirable associational freedom versus attempts to restrain trade (collusion). Yet free association and liberty of contract, on which cartels rest, is an integral part of a liberal market economy. The cartel question proved a conundrum for British, French, German, American, and Japanese courts. They always involved particular assumptions about appropriate business behavior, reputation, credibility, trust, and social order. Finally, economists wrestled with the implications of industries weighed down by fixed costs and new forms of competitive behavior by debating cartels and trusts, whose formation raised central corporate governance issues such as the separation of ownership and control, risk, as well as the social impact of big business. We need richer comparative studies of contemporaries' judgments about cartels, which would necessarily connect politics, culture, and law with business history (Blaich 1973; Freyer 1992; Peritz 1996; Iyori *et al.* 1994).

12.3 SCALE AND SCOPE OF CARTELS (PERIODIZATION)

Business historians have generated a broad narrative pattern about the rise and fall of cartels over the last century. However, the reasons for this pattern are still debatable, the exact scale and scope of cartels is still surprisingly fuzzy, and major exceptions to the rule exist. Some "pools" appeared early in the nineteenth century, but the first modern cartels materialized after the 1870s as a reaction to the downturn (Fischer and Wagenführ 1929; Schröter 1996: 132). Cartels appeared most strongly in those industries defined by scale and scope economies in industries saddled with high fixed costs (Mirow and Maurer 1982). Therefore, their weight lay in wealthy countries with big businesses. Cartels also tended to appear among domestic firms first, before going international (excepting early zinc, rail, and shipping cartels) (see Table 12.1). Cartels boomed in the 1920s, peaked in the 1930s, reappeared strongly after 1945 before they gradually faded away, especially after the 1970s. This broad periodization, however, disguises fascinating subcurrents.

Surprisingly, we have few systematic, comparative studies about cartels, although the general trend is clear.

Certain industries (steel, aluminum, chemicals, potash, explosives, salt, cement, paper, fertilizer) and certain economies (Germany, Austria, Czechoslovakia, Switzerland) appeared near synonymous with cartelization. Even the more wary British saw a burgeoning cartel movement before World War I, but their cartels remained looser and not contractually enforceable. Once British courts became more accepting of their "reasonable" provisions, their number exploded after 1920 (Freyer 1992).

Table 12.1 Number of domestic cartels

Year	Germany	Austria	Czech.	Hungary	Switzerland	France	Britain	Japan
1865	4							
1887	70							
1890/1	117			8				
1900/2	300	50						
1905/6	385	100		50			40 [93]	
1911/2	550–660	120						
1921							446	8
1929/30	2100	40–50, 70–80	100+		90+	80+		30+

Source: Fischer and Wagenführ (1929); Wagenführ (1931); Hadley (1970).

Japan's cartels emerged in 1880 with the formation of the Japan Paper Manufacturers Federation and in 1882 with the Japanese Cotton Spinning Federation. The cotton-spinning cartel endured as a national cartel for over 50 years although it assembled over 80 producers. Government ministries encouraged both of them as quality control cartels and to limit excessive competition. Unlike many European businesses, Japanese business tended to welcome government involvement. Yet, given its cooperative reputation Japan had a small cartel movement until the 1920s. Horizontal agreements remained rare (only three before 1920), although it created other forms of cooperation (Tilton 1996; Hadley 1970).

After World War I, the nature, number, and aims of cartels shifted dramatically. Based in part on the experience of managing war economies, governments increasingly found cartels useful instruments of public policy. The Japanese government passed two export promotion laws, which sanctioned privately initiated cartels in bleaching powder, wool, cement, coal, copper, and canned crabmeat. Trading companies' and commodity producers' cartels received legal protection. In 1931, another Japanese law empowered the government to forcibly cartelize critical industries as Japan prepared for war (Hadley 1970).

In Europe, between 1926 and 1929 Spain required cartelization of coal, lead mines, paper, resin, sugar, rice, and wine industries as a form of industry promotion (Fischer and Wagenführ 1929). During the Depression, most European countries followed suit with their own cartel enforcement laws. Germany, which had entertained few state-sponsored cartels (potash, certain coal agreements), forced outsiders into existing cartels as a means of extending direct control over prices and production (Schröter 1997). The French government tightened its administrative connections to national cartels and the British government encouraged industry to join major international cartels. Even the United States permitted Webb-Pomerene export cartels after 1918 and established the National Industrial Recovery Act in the early 1930s (Pohl 1985; Wurm 1993).

The 1920s and 1930s were the heyday of international cartels. A few international cartels appeared by the 1880s and 1890s in steel rails, aluminum, zinc, electric lamp, explosives, synthetic alkali, and shipping sectors. The conferences in liner (but not tramp) shipping were among the most robust cartels. Shipping conferences helped spawn other forms of countervailing cooperation as well as competition. Tea growers, for instance, established the Indian Tea Association to negotiate collectively with shipowners. Having failed, they sponsored a rival independent line and encouraged defectors (Davies 1985; Sjostrom 2004). Despite major challenges from American, German, and Japanese companies, these conferences proved surprisingly "resilient" until 1939 and were by no means "highly monopolistic, inflexible institutions" (Deakin and Seward 1973: 43). The conference system actually helped to restore German shipping after World War I (Scholl 1985). Shipping conferences demonstrated the paramount importance of government backing behind these national champions (Miwa 1985).

For industrial manufacturing, George Stocking and Myron Watkins (1946) marked the beginning of a robust international cartel movement with the 1896 bilateral agreement between the Aluminium Industrie AG (Swiss-German) and Alcoa (US). By 1905, General Electric created a world-spanning cartel through equity holdings, the exchange of patent rights, and territorial agreements (Reich 1992*a*). That American firms helped kick off the international cartel movement in manufacturing indicates that the propensity to form cartels knew few national boundaries. Research has demonstrated that it was generally easier to form stable international agreements if the global industry was highly concentrated among a few key players or if national producers formed a coherent national cartel to represent their joint interests. The International Steel Cartel (Hexner 1943; Barbezat 1989; Nocken 1989), the nitrogen cartel of 1929 (Chadeau in Kudō and Hara 1992), the world oil cartel (Yergin 1992; Sampson 1991), the International Potash Syndicate (Schröter 1994), and the British cotton and steel cartels in relation to its foreign policy (Wurm 1993) provide some of the best-researched examples of this complicated interplay among domestic interest group politics, manufacturers' objectives, international industrial rivalry, and geopolitical diplomacy during the interwar period.

Then and now, such international cartels were crucial sites of transnational interaction in the global economy, even during the hypernationalist 1930s. Raw materials and foodstuffs cartels also involved complicated economic diplomacy, but colonial relations mediated their formation. Here poorer countries participated in the international cartel movement (United Nations 1947, table 1). World-spanning cartels could be found in copper, lead, zinc, tin, aluminum, mercury, potash, petroleum, rubber, and diamonds. With over an 80 percent market share in mercury, for instance, Spain and Italy (with Mexico receiving a cut) ran an especially robust cartel between 1928 and 1972 (MacKie-Mason and Pindyck 1987). Foodstuffs cartels could also be found in products such as cocoa, coffee, sugar, tea, bananas, or wheat (Hexner 1946). The rubber cartel is an especially good example of the complex bargaining relations among national states, between empire and colonies, between home government and multinational corporations, among corporations involving automobile, chemical, and rubber tire manufacturers, and among plantation owners (Stocking and Watkins 1946).

Governments turned international cartels into steering wheels of domestic government policy navigating highly protected, tense global markets. A number of historians have highlighted the inverse relationship between multinationalization prior to 1914, which presumes relatively welcoming (even if risky) home country operations, and international cartelization between 1918 and 1945, which closed off home markets to foreign competition. The British and German examples offer contrasting perspectives. While the British, the leading foreign direct investor and home base for multinationals, reluctantly entered cartel agreements until there was little other choice, the Germans willingly entered into international agreements to protect against potential expropriation as had occurred after World War I, to secure access to raw materials or markets, and to influence host country domestic policy. In both cases, defense and security rather than expansion proved the overriding objective (Schröter 1988; Casson 1985; Glimstedt 2001). Although regrettable, international cartels helped ease national fears by avoiding trade wars that might have fed national rivalries even more. Clemens Wurm (1993: 291) called them an "exercise in damage limitation", a second-best solution to the end of globalization.

Although it is tempting to conclude that the rise of international cartels was *directly* related to hypernationalized geopolitics, the relationship between business and national interests was often oblique. The International Steel Cartel or the International Potash Syndicate also represented the seeds of Franco-German cooperation; the signatories of the International Steel Cartel formed the core of the future European Coal and Steel Community (Kipping 1996). The International Potash Syndicate with its French-German axis milked the rest of the world (Herbert Hoover's words) in spite of poor relations between the two countries.

The big three major European industrial powers formed the core of the international cartel movement with the United States and Japan acting as outliers (Kudō and Hara 1992). American firms had to watch their backs for fear of homegrown anti-trust actions; if they participated they did so through cover organizations or by abiding informally by others' agreement and shadowing prices (Devos 1994). Japan's participation in international cartels involved a complicated balancing act among different objectives. Japan essentially traded access to her home market for technological know-how or protection of market share for infant domestic industries (Hasegawa 1994). Japanese dyestuffs firms, for instance, gained leverage through cartels against more powerful intruders such as the IG Farben-led, international dyestuffs cartel, or against ICI in soda ash (Kudō 1994; Miyajima 1994).

Schröter (1996) differentiated four groups of countries: those with overwhelmingly positive assessments of cartels (Austria, Belgium, Czechoslovakia, Finland, France, Germany, the Netherlands, Norway, Sweden, and Switzerland); those with largely positive views but which developed supervisory agencies (Hungary, Italy, Japan, Poland, and Spain); those with ambivalent stances (Bulgaria, Canada, Denmark, South Africa, and the UK); and those with outright negative stances (Argentina, Australia, New Zealand, the United States, and Yugoslavia). We have no synthetic, scholarly work that can explain this pattern. In spite of greatly different legal traditions and political attitudes toward cartels, British, German, and French firms involved themselves in cartel formation in roughly equal numbers. For example, the French had legislation that could punish restraint of trade in theory, yet the French were more than equal in practice to the Germans, the most notorious colluders. Both British (common law) and French cartel legislation (civil law) stressed the primacy of freedom of competition, but their acceptance of cartels at home differed greatly (Fischer and Wagenführ 1929). We need a study that tackles the intellectual, legal, and economic issues raised by cartels in a comparative fashion; literature on finance and capital markets has begun to analyze these differences.

By the advent of World War II, cartels governed about 40 percent of world trade at the apex of the cartel movement (United Nations 1947; Great Britain Board of Trade 1944). Cartelization became equated with defending domestic economic security, as an instrument of economic warfare, and then war planning. Not surprisingly, our knowledge about international cartels stems from a dramatic sea change in thinking around 1945 when the classic works on international cartels appeared. By the 1940s and 1950s cartels appeared to be exactly the *opposite* of competition and liberalism, let alone part and parcel of the German war effort: "The cartels made Hitler and Hitler made war" (quoted in Mason 1946: 280). Hexner (1946: p. vii) claimed, "cartels are by nature enemies of democracy". The earlier meaning of cartels as an expression of private industrial self-regulation through voluntary associations became lost. American cartel-busters portrayed the shocking extent of cartel-controlled world markets, setting the agenda for postwar liberalization.

However, as Harm Schröter (1996: 153) states: "It took 60 years and two generations to thoroughly cartelize Europe up to the 1930s, and another 60 years for a complete change in policy in favor of intense decartelization". In 1957, Germany went furthest by prohibiting most cartels. In Britain, a good portion of businesses actually welcomed the 1956 Restrictive Trade Practices Act in the hope that judicial reviews would provide more clarity about the limits of cartel-building. As they eagerly registered their collusive agreements rather than dropped them, the Act unexpectedly provided a legal sword that cut down most cartels there (Symeonidis 2002). In France, legislation outlawed abuse and price-fixing, but not necessarily cartels until the mid-1980s; the state registered cartels and monitored prices to prevent abuse. Most of Europe tended to follow the French example to varying degrees and varying degrees of speed. Switzerland trailed everyone, favoring cartels as a "school for consideration of the big for the small" (quoted in Schröter 1996: p. 149). The European Economic Community officially prohibited cartels, but did not receive strong antitrust powers until the 1980s (Graham and Richardson 1997).

In contrast to this European pattern of gradual retreat, the heyday for cartels in Japan came after 1945 and before the oil shocks of the 1970s. Industries enthusiastically rejoined cartels sanctioned by the Ministry of International Trade and Industry (MITI). At its peak in the mid-1960s, about one thousand authorized cartels existed, most of which (*c*.60%) consisted of small and medium-sized businesses. In 1962 about 42 percent of Japan's export trade was cartelized. Japanese cartels appeared in almost every major industry, especially in textiles, apparel, publishing, ceramics, steel, non-ferrous metals, and shipping (Hadley 1970; Iyori *et al.* 1994).

Only inflation stoked by rising oil prices delegitimized cartels. In 1973 the Fair Trade Commission launched its first criminal investigation against Japanese oil companies (Schwartzman 1993). Thereafter, the number of cartels declined steadily. However, recession or rationalization cartels remained a significant tool of industrial policy in sectors such as in steel, shipbuilding, glass, ceramics, cement, petrochemicals, and aluminum (Tilton 1996). Political connections in the construction industry kept cement cartels strong. At the beginning of the 1990s, the government still explicitly exempted small and medium-sized businesses in textiles, to improve sanitary conditions in hairdressing salons, to support restructuring initiatives for fisheries or canned fish industries, and in general to promote exports.

Major international cartels reasserted themselves after 1945 in key strategic sectors, the most visible of which was OPEC, the first time developing countries found significant leverage over wealthy countries. The 1973 oil crisis sparked a plethora of studies about cartels to assess their threat and potential longevity (Eckbo 1976). But even before OPEC, raw materials cartels found a subtle revalorization in the developing world. Since the 1960s G-77 developing nations had argued for stronger commodity cartels to improve the terms of trade for bananas, coffee, cocoa, rubber, tin, or sugar. Cartels became part of the decolonization and development process. Many developing countries began working through the United Nations Conference on Trade and Development (UNCTAD). Unlike OPEC, which managed to maintain some forms of price control into the mid-1980s, most of these cartels "accomplish[ed] far less than their signatories set out to achieve" (LeClair 2000: 81). After a wave of nationalizations, a complicated geopolitical interplay between the economics of the industry, multinationals, and national governments reconstructed commodity cartels. Such cartels needed tacit approval of major multinationals in the developed world and tacit acquiescence by former colonial states. Collusion among aluminum MNCs and governments in a "profit-sharing cartel" created a fairly solid cartel for bauxite (Holloway 1988). Mix in the Cold War, populist-democratic revolts against neo-colonial rule, and control over key strategic minerals such as uranium or copper or titanium, and one quickly found more than enough room for controversy.

Commodity cartels had to overcome slightly different challenges. Potential colluders had to find a way to collectively manage buffer stocks, more difficult for perishable goods such as bananas. Most agricultural commodities that could be stored such as cocoa, coffee, sugar, or natural rubber had easy substitutes. Minerals proved easier to control, but still did not ensure success as natural resource commodities could not usually be branded. Finally, most commodity cartels had to manage the great disparity of interests across the North–South divide, let alone neo-colonial discord.

Excepting OPEC, international cartels largely remained a prerogative of wealthier countries and their big businesses, although evidence has become scantier as they have been driven underground. Kurt Mirow and Harry Maurer (1982: 33) argued that cartels were hardly "endangered species" and accused the International Electrical Association (IEA), consisting of 55 members from 12 countries in 1977, of arranging predatory price wars against new Brazilian competitors. Developing countries then had to pay higher prices than customers in wealthy countries. In one remarkable case of the pot calling the kettle black, the Saudis accused eight IEA members of rigging "bids to share in illegal profit" (p. 53).

Backed by the notion of national champions, international cartels reasserted themselves strongly in shipping and airline industries. Deakin and Seward (1973) estimated that at the beginning of the 1970s about 360 shipping conferences still existed. The resiliency of shipping cartels is astonishing, especially after the advent of new competitors and the challenge of container services. Until the 1970s, a "sky club", better known as the International Air Transport Association (IATA), comprehensively managed the world airline industry. Not surprisingly, it had its home base in cartel-friendly Geneva, Switzerland. The IATA acted not only as a "fare-fixer", but also as a standards and conditions cartel that "provided the central machinery" of global coordination (Sampson 1984).

Today, information about cartels increasingly derives from prosecution data, which depends entirely on whether firms get caught. The OECD (2003) found 16 international cartels harmed trade by an estimated $55 billion. Competition authorities exposed important international cartels in graphite electrodes (for mini-mills), lysine (an additive for chemical feed), vitamins, and carbonless paper. They fined domestic German power cable and road-marking firms, Danish electric wiring contractors, Slovakian breweries, Japanese ductile iron pipe-making firms, Spanish and British sugar enterprises, to name just a few. No country managed to avoid sugar, cement, or asphalt cartels.

Thus in spite of the strong antitrust winds blowing from the United States since 1945, business historians cannot discount the continuing, even if declining, role of cartels in rich countries (except Japan) at least into the 1970s. Most of the cartel literature focuses on the pre-1945 period, rather than the post-1945 period. The general narrative about cartels may not be a story of rise and fall, but rise, boom, collapse, revitalization, gradual decline, and then criminalization.

The most significant dilemma is that cartels appeared in the most dynamic sectors and played a significant role during the fastest period of European and Japanese economic growth, which begs the question of what economic effects they actually had. The Japanese have tended to view cartels as contributing to capitalist growth rather than corrupting it (Tilton 1996; Matsushita 1997). Would growth have been still faster without cartels? Why did they not lead to stagnation? Business historians must narrate a century of economic and business development in conjunction with cartels rather than without them.

12.4 CARTELS, STRATEGY, AND CORPORATE ORGANIZATION

The strategy of most major business firms had to take into consideration cartels. We have many excellent discussions of how firms can expect to behave inside cartels (firms as unitary actors), but we have far fewer discussions about how cartels altered corporate strategy and organizational development (decision-making and internal processes). What difference did it make to permit or prohibit cartels, or to join or not to join one? Deciding to join a cartel, negotiating the specifics of the cartel contract and its quotas, was a major entrepreneurial act. Alfred D. Chandler made Germany the home of cooperative managerial capitalism, but did not theorize the relationship between cartels and German corporate development. Tony Freyer (1992), on the other hand, claimed that British tolerance of cartels permitted family capitalism to survive longer at the cost of national competitiveness. Yet German industrial firms worked within a much denser web of cartels than did British firms and often remained in the family, yet became highly competitive. A few contrasts highlight the need to understand the relationship between cartels and firms more closely.

Neil Fligstein (1990) created a sort of unified field theory of corporate development constructed around antitrust. He argued that changes in US antitrust legislation were the main driver behind shifts in corporate strategy. After prohibiting pools, antitrust legislation forced the leading firm to become a price-setter in the industry based on its large market share or a small number of large firms (oligopolies) tacitly cooperated to set prices in the interests of avoiding a full-scale price war. In both cases, vertical integration in unitary functional organizations became the accepted form for large-scale enterprises. Once the "manufacturing conception of control" or strategy had played itself out by the 1920s and 1930s, a "sales conception of control" spread that was predicated upon product and marketing segmentation. Diversification of products in turn placed new pressures on internal organization that led to the multidivisional structure.

However, if we examine the development of the German coal and steel industries, we would expect little drive toward a "manufacturing conception of control" (that is: vertical and horizontal integration, unitary functional organizations, plus a dominant price-setting firm or set of firms) because German firms could collude. Cartels have "the effect of providing a market for everyone and made even the smallest firms viable" (Fligstein 1990: 23). Indeed, German heavy industry had three of Germany's strongest cartels in coal, pig iron, steel and steel products. By 1925, they managed to control over 100 percent of coal production, and roughly 90 percent of crude steel production. Yet Germany managed to field some of the premier steel firms in the world with a high degree of vertical integration (cartels encouraged it) and diversification (coal to machine engineering), which also led to differentiated organizational structures—sometimes quite close to multidivisional structures, so-called *Konzerne*. After the 1926 formation of the Vereinigte Stahlwerke, modeled on US Steel, German steel had a remarkably similar market structure to the US although it simultaneously strengthened its cartels. It even developed a multidivisional form without being sales-oriented at all.

Where German and American steel firms did differ was in the speed of the concentration process, their development trajectories, their strategy, and their organizational forms. Cartels helped drive these differences. As desired, cartels slowed but did not halt mergers and acquisitions. (German firms often purchased smaller firms just for their quotas.) German heavy industrial firms integrated vertically to avoid cartel distortions, while American steel firms extended horizontally first, then vertically. Because of cartels, German industrialists had to learn how to manage a firm with a high degree of vertical integration, highly diversified product lines, and small-batch production in capital-intensive industries. They initially faced different organizational dilemmas than those faced by most American firms (Fear 2005).

This contrast calls into question some commonsense notions about cartels. Why did these cartels not lead to stagnation or a lack of innovation? Cartels did not eliminate competition, but rechanneled it. *Competition* remained within the cartels through a number of mechanisms which go beyond the standard story that cartels attract new competitors or encourage chiseling. Since participants knew that they would renegotiate quotas in the near future (every two to five years), industrialists put themselves in the best possible position for the next round. Cartels encouraged capacity growth for negotiating leverage rather than estimated market demand, which made next-round negotiations more difficult and eventually created dysfunctional market competition; in turn this dysfunction might lead to collapse but also to possible reconstitution. Executives might be content to let the cartel work for them, but this was not an effective long-term strategy.

Horizontal cartelization encouraged vertical integration. Not only did industrialists feel the necessity to control input prices upstream, but also they could sell excess production downstream to permit intermediate materials to maintain steady volume. Integrated combines then had a cost advantage over independents because they had a cheaper supply of input materials. Cartels might even speed the drive to find cost efficiencies. Inside cartels, firms could still increase the differential between the cartel-set price and the production cost through greater scale or scope economies, or higher technical efficiencies, or vertical integration, or all three. Cartels could subsidize a type of niche strategy into new or higher value-added product lines exempted from cartel jurisdiction or encourage exports by dumping excess production (Webb 1980). The post-World War II Japanese television industry competed at home through product differentiation or new models, rather than price, but abroad they competed viciously on price, which kept them on their innovative toes (Schwartzman 1993).

Because of vertical integration and product differentiation (scope), industrialists competed across a broad array of cartelized and non-cartelized goods. On the surface, the Steel Works Association was one of Germany's most impressive cartels, but vicious price wars broke out in finished steel products such as pipes at the same time they successfully syndicated intermediate products (Peters 1984). International chemical cartels or domestic agreements between AEG or Siemens provide other examples of such complicated cooperative competition in scope economies (Reader 1975; Feldenkirchen 1999). Expansion into other products or greater geographical expansion into unregulated territories could enhance bargaining clout in cartels.

In short, all these examples imply that a powerful incentive to innovate, reinvest profits, or engage in R&D still existed even under highly cartelized regimes. How and whether individual firms take advantage of cartels and how competitive market conditions might change firm strategy is an empirical question.

Arguably the most important but most inconclusive area of cartel research is the link between cartels and investment, technological innovation/diffusion, and productivity (Levenstein 2006). Edward Mason (1946: 114) dramatically reminded Americans that one secret cartel between Germans and Americans brought plexiglass to the United States, which enhanced its ability to fight World War II. Harm Schröter (1988) identified the importance of sharing patents and know-how through cartels. After examining the IG Farben-Standard Oil cartel, Rolf Petri (1994) found that the cartel actually "speeded up geographical diffusion of new technologies [among cartel members], while it slowed down diffusion of know-how among external actors". Gary Saxonhouse (1976) argued that the Japanese Cotton Spinners Association speeded up the adoption of best practices throughout the industry. Another group of historians, however, concluded more ambivalently about whether international cartels promoted technology transfers and economic development for Japan (Kudō and Hara 1992).

A number of authors have shown how cartels positively contributed to technological innovation by stabilizing volatile markets, permitting firms to invest and engage in R&D. In the 1920s, radio and telephone manufacturers formed associations to limit excess capacity, encourage large-scale production, pool research costs, set standard prices, and design interchangeable product standards. Despite such collusion, British telephone density and automation accelerated greatly during the war. However, with the advent of antitrust laws and competitive pricing in the 1950s, which hindered industry coordination but promoted mergers and squeezed profit margins through price competition, the industry lost the incentive to expand capacity, enhance product quality, and fund crucial innovations that moved telephony into the electronic age (Lipartito 2000). George Symeonidis (2002) also found that intensified price competition and greater concentration had no significant effect on firms' innovative output. Others have shown the devastating effect of decartelization on innovation and market share for the postwar British electrical engineering industry (excepting the cable industry where a dominant firm could create price lists) relative to the prewar cooperative regime (compare Reindl 1997; Glimstedt 2001; Zeitlin 2002). Another study using quantitative methods found that cartels did not particularly encourage or discourage patenting, which appeared dependent on other variables (Cantwell and Barrera 1994). Recent debates reproduce another inconclusive debate in the 1920s about cartels and productivity (compare Hoppmann 1971; Reich 1992b). Many held Japan as a model for managing sunset industries using cartels, but Mark Tilton (1996) views this claim more skeptically. Whether cartels can positively rationalize industries and enhance productivity remains an open question.

The bottom line paradox is that competition may stimulate innovation but effectively hinder firms from carrying it out, while cartels may stabilize markets to permit firms to engage in innovation but may effectively discourage it through complacency. Whether firms use cartel rents to innovate or become complacent is a question of firm strategy and entrepreneurship. Cartels altered strategic incentives, but hardly ensured tranquillity. Setting quotas or market shares involved highly mysterious rounds of negotiations, more equivalent to late-night poker games than rational worksheet calculations. Somewhat appropriately, the "conspirators" in the Japanese television cartel used Igo (English: Go) stones to vote on quotas (Schwartzman 1993). In practice, cartels were a motley collection of compromises that fundamentally restructured the nature of competition depending on the provisions of the individual cartel agreement. They undoubtedly caused perverse results. In the US salt industry, some contracts provided "lease-back" arrangements to firms, paying them not to mine their salt (Levenstein 1995: 583). The 1893 German coal contract stipulated that sinking new shafts would raise the production quota of any company. Suddenly a boom of new shafts occurred, many with no intention of ever mining a single piece of coal. Determining these dysfunctions depends on the specifics of the cartel and the agency of its members—in short: history.

Yet they also enabled breakthroughs. William Wray's study of Mitsubishi and the NYK (1984) offers one of the more comprehensive views of the interaction between the government, cartels, and corporate strategy, which also demonstrates how cartels collaborated and competed with one another. NYK gained entry into the lucrative Indian shipping business through alliances with the Cotton Spinners Association and the Indian firm of Tata & Sons. After entering the new conference, the NYK helped redefine the division of labor and new rate setting. The NYK then managed to "tap discontent" with another conference to break into British ports *before* the Japanese government guaranteed its additional subsidies, which only strengthened its negotiating position. A strong relationship between Mitsui Bussan and NYK, which generated rebates for Mitsui imports of crucial machinery such as locomotive machinery, rails, and spinning equipment, then helped load NYK's ships, lower Mitsui's costs, and spur Japanese industrialization. Wray demonstrates how company strategy formed out of the vagaries of specific cartel agreements, alliances with cartels and firms, and then how NYK's strategy altered subsequent cartel agreements. Cartels and alliances *enabled* greater competition and NYK's strategic breakthrough.

Such strategic considerations have major implications for understanding organizational structure and capabilities. The bromine syndicate offered its "superior distribution services" and brand name to Dow Chemical. Acting as a sort of incubator, the cartel taught Dow how to build and sell with a reputation (Levenstein 1998). It also affected its managerial and accounting system. As long as Dow and Midland operated within the pool, they had less incentive to know their costs precisely. Once they broke with the pool, they had to change their organization and accounting system to track technical efficiency, product costs, quality, and the cost of capital so as to effectively innovate. Yet in the cooperative capitalism of German steel, cartel quotas made it that more important to utilize capacity and know one's costs. Cartels sometimes decided where certain products could be produced internal to the firm, if factories in one place could be shut down, with what firm one could trade, or where new plants would be located (Fear 2005).

In short, because cartels regulated industry, they redesigned incentives, barriers, and sanctions for firms—in principle no differently than public policy regulations shaping competitive practices. Multinationals operating in poor countries with weak state regulatory capacity or bridging a world with few global governance mechanisms have frequently developed inter-firm institutional practices of self-regulation. Liberal political theory and neoclassical economics have had a difficult time theorizing such forms of cooperation (Cutler *et al.* 1999; Haufler 2001). If one reconceptualizes the study of cartels as (self) regulation, then one shifts attention away from cartel success or failure to how enterprises competitively react within given industry constraints over time. Instead of cartels halting competition, cartels recast competition.

This perspective begins to explain why cartels did not damage growth more. Inside this cooperative framework, they still *competed*, especially for quota share. As Sir Harry McGowan of Imperial Chemical Industry argued, "the purpose of these agreements is, in the main, to regulate but not to abolish competition" (Reader 1975: 425). How far can we view cartels as cooperative ventures and not competitive constellations? Given the constant renegotiation and temporary breakdowns even in durable cartels, are we dealing with a single cartel or a series of consecutive ones? What exactly is cartel "success"? (Grossman 2004; Levenstein and Suslow 2006). What sorts of services, efficiencies, or innovations can cartels and other such forms of cooperation create? Can cartels, like networks, act as an incentive to innovate even if consumers lose in the short run?

Cartels and networks are interrelated phenomena. In reality and in concept they reinforce one another. If one conceives of cartels as a subset of networks, a richer set of motivations than just the desire to raise prices would come to the fore. Broader studies of social and professional webs that embed specific cartels would enhance our understanding of the critical organizational and "idiosyncratic" factors that help cartels endure. Horizontal networks among hundreds of small businesses, laced by a web of kinship, upstream and downstream trading relationships, and mutual interests, created the institutions that made the (literal) marketplace work in the Tsukiji seafood market (Bestor in Fruin 1998). Entrepreneurs and managers commonly came from similar professional, geographic, or cultural milieus, which helped overcome gaming inside cartels. Informal norms are crucial variables. A mutual love of hunting and fishing over two decades enhanced cooperation in the international petroleum cartel of 1928–38 (Yergin 1992). The US Department of Justice (2000) concluded that golf courses facilitated collusion. Also the constant negotiations and monitoring that allow cartels to work created new social networks. Once one learns to cooperate over time, the socialization process might strengthen further cooperation/collusion. The more one moves from markets to networks, the more social history approaches would prove invaluable and the less effective price considerations alone can gauge the value of such relationships.

12.5 CONCLUSIONS

Cartels are a surprisingly slippery subject. There is no mystery as to cartel dynamics, yet those dynamics are not sufficient to explain any given cartel. So far, the weight of research has stressed why cartels fail, rather than why they endure. The internal organizational dynamics of cartels needs more research, embedding it in economic, organizational, and political theory.

Cartel research can provide a portal into questions such as the nature and speed of concentration, strategic behavior, differing ideas about legitimate and illegitimate market behavior (competition policy and regulation), economic thought, comparative law, social policy, economic development, the boundaries between the state and civil society, business diplomacy, and international relations. Cartels stand obliquely in the liberal tradition (rather than in direct opposition to it). Moreover, if contemporaries truly believed that cartels were useful instruments of economic and business policy, this alone would contribute to cartel stabilization, unlike the criminalization of cartels today.

We need better comparative studies about cartels' relationship to politics, political culture, and law for "clearly cartels, directly or indirectly, served different national objectives" (Great Britain Board of Trade 1944). They provided a form of social policy (employment, sunset industries, regional industrial policy), risk management (an attempt to manage macroeconomic fluctuations during downturns, limit volatility), and development policy (export promotion, technology transfers, knowledge dissemination, infant industry protection). Today, governments or hedge funds have usurped many of these functions, but historically—or in poorer countries with limited state capacity—cartels have provided one (biased) means of addressing these issues.

We should place the cartel question into a wider framework of regulation rather than conspiracy. Such self-regulation had major effects on the strategy and structure of firms. As networks, they may help scholars understand more legitimate, softer, more positive forms of cooperation (Mariti and Smiley 1983). Depending on their objectives, cartels often provided joint services rather than just rate hikes; the more non-price objectives, the more durable they appear to be.

The rise and fall of cartels remind us that a fluid, international division of labor based on comparative advantage and competition is entirely dependent upon peace and cooperation among nations. This is not a trivial consideration given the history of the 20th century as rising nationalism disfigured world markets, often forcing firms to cooperate to survive. Given the world of intense rivalry that limited the extent of the market, cartels formed a disappointing but perhaps appropriate second-best strategy. International cooperation helped dispel economic cooperation among firms after 1945—slowly.

Finally, studying cartels opens the intriguing question: when is competition essential to efficiency and innovation? The cartel question highlights the tradeoffs between costs of stop-go, boom-and-bust volatility under capitalism and the benefits of moderate stability and risk management, between price and quality, between consumer and producers—tradeoffs not easily addressed. Graham and Richardson (1997: 6) noted that, "while competition is familiar to most, few reflect deeply on cooperation. Almost all market competitors are firms—business organizations (social groupings) that are, for the most part, internally cooperative, not competitive." Cartels provide one forum for reflecting on how and when cooperation can be efficient and innovative.

REFERENCES

BARANOFF, DALIT (2003). "A Policy of Cooperation: The Cartelisation of American Fire Insurance, 1873–1906". *Financial History Review*, 10: 119–30.

BARBEZAT, DANIEL (1989). "Competition and Rivalry in the International Steel Cartel 1926–1932". *Journal of Economic History*, 49/2: 435–47.

BARJOT, DOMINIQUE (ed.) (1994). *International Cartels Revisited 1880–1980*. Caen: Editions-Diffusion du Lys.

BESTOR, THEODORE C. (1998). "Making Things Clique: Cartels, Coalitions and Institutional Structure in the Tsukiji Wholesale Seafood Market", in Fruin (1998), 154–80.

BLAICH, FRITZ (1973). *Kartell- und Monopolpolitik im kaiserlichen Deutschland: Das Problem der Marktmacht im deutschen Reichstag zwischen 1879 und 1914*. Düsseldorf: Droste.

CANTWELL, JOHN, and BARRERA, PILAR (1994). "The Influence of International Cartels on Technological Development in Large Firms", in Barjot (1994), 301–24.

CASSON, MARK (1985). "Multinational Monopolies and International Cartels", in Peter Buckley and Mark Casson (eds.), *The Economic Theory of the Multinational Enterprise: Selected Papers*. London: Macmillan, 60–97.

CUTLER, A. CLAIRE, HAUFLER, VIRGINIA, and PORTER, TONY (eds.) (1999). *Private Authority and International Affairs*. Albany, NY: State University of New York Press.

DEAKIN, B.M., and SEWARD, T. (1973). *Shipping Conferences: A Study of their Origins, Development and Economic Practices*. Cambridge: Cambridge University Press.

DAVIES, P. N. (1985). "British Shipping and World Trade: Rise and Decline, 1820–1939", in Yui and Nakagawa (1985), 39–85.

DEVOS, GRETA (1994). "International Cartel Agreements in the Zinc Industry, 19th–20th Centuries", in Barjot (1994), 143–51.

DICK, ANDREW (1996). "When are Cartels Stable Contracts?" *Journal of Law and Economics*, 39: 241–83.

—— (2004). "If Cartels were Legal, When would Firms Fix Prices?" in Grossman, 144–73.

ECKBO, PAUL L. (1976). *The Future of World Oil*. Cambridge: Ballinger Publishing.

FEAR, JEFFREY R. (2005). *Organizing Control: August Thyssen and the Construction of German Corporate Management*. Cambridge, Mass.: Harvard University Press.

FELDENKIRCHEN, W. (1998). "Concentration in German Industry, 1870–1939", in Hans Pohl (ed.), *The Concentration Process in the Entrepreneurial Economy since the Nineteenth Century*. Stuttgart: Frauz Steiner, 113–46.

—— (1999). *Siemens 1918–1945*. Columbus: Ohio State University Press.

FISCHER, PAUL THOMAS, and WAGENFÜHR, HORST (1929). *Kartelle in Europa (Ohne Deutschland)*. Nuremberg: Hochschulbuchhandlung Krische & Co.

FLIGSTEIN, NEIL (1990). *The Transformation of Corporate Control*. Cambridge, Mass.: Harvard University Press.

FREYER, TONY (1992). *Regulating Big Business: Antitrust in Great Britain and America 1880–1990*. Cambridge: Cambridge University Press.

FRUIN, W. MARK (ed.) (1998). *Networks, Markets, and the Pacific Rim*. Oxford: Oxford University Press.

GLIMSTEDT, HENRIK (2001). "Between National and International Governance: Geopolitics, Strategizing Actors, and Sector Coordination in Electrical Engineering in the Interwar Era", in G. Morgan, P. H. Kristensen, and R. Whitley (eds.), *The Multinational Firm: Organizing across Institutional and National Divides*. Oxford: Oxford University Press, 125–52.

GRAHAM, EDWARD M., and RICHARDSON, J. DAVID (eds.) (1997). *Global Competition Policy*. Washington: Institute for International Economics.

Great Britain Board of Trade (1944). *Survey of International Cartels*. London: Board of Trade.

GROSSMAN, PETER Z. (2004). *How Cartels Endure and How They Fail: Studies of Industrial Collusion*. Cheltenham, UK: Edward Elgar.

HADLEY, ELEANOR M. (1970). *Antitrust in Japan*. Princeton, NJ: Princeton University Press.

HASEGAWA, SHIN (1994). "International Cartels and the Japanese Electrical Machinery Industry in the Interwar Period", in Barjot (1994), 243–52.

HAUFLER, VIRGINIA (2001). *A Public Role for the Private Sector: Industry Self-Regulation in a Global Economy*. Washington: Carnegie Endowment for International Peace.

HERRIGEL, GARY (1996). *Industrial Constructions: The Foundations of German Industrial Power*. Cambridge: Cambridge University Press.

HEXNER, ERVIN (1943). *The International Steel Cartel*. Chapel Hill, NC: University of North Carolina Press.

—— (1946). *International Cartels*. London: Sir Isaac Pitman & Sons.

HOLLOWAY, STEVEN KENDALL (1988). *The Aluminium Multinationals and the Bauxite Cartel*. New York: St. Martin's Press.

HOPPMANN, ERICH (ed.) (1971). *Rationalisierung durch Kartelle?* Berlin: Duncker & Humblot.

IYORI, HIROSHI, UESUGI, AKINORI, and HEATH, CHRISTOPHER (1994). *Das Japanische Kartellrecht*, 2nd rev. edn. Cologne: Carl Heymanns Verlag.

KINGHORN, JANICE RYE, and NIELSON, RANDALL (2004). "A Practice without Defenders: The Price Effects of Cartelization", in Grossman (2004), 130–43.

KIPPING, MATTHIAS (1996). *Zwischen Kartellen und Konkurrenz: Der Schuman-Plan und die Ursprünge der europäischen Einigung 1944–1952*. Berlin: Duncker & Humblot.

KORNDÖRFER, WOLFGANG (1988). *Allgemeine Betriebswirtschaftslehre*. Wiesbaden: Gabler.

KUDŌ, AKIRA (1994). "The Japan Strategy of the International Dyestuffs Cartels", in Barjot (1994), 215–22.

——and HARA, TERUSHI (eds.) (1992). *International Cartels in Business History*. Tokyo: University of Tokyo Press.

LECLAIR, MARK S. (2000). *International Commodity Markets and the Role of Cartels*. Armonk, NY: M. E. Sharpe.

LEVENSTEIN, MARGARET C. (1995). "Mass Production Conquers the Pool: Firm Organization and the Nature of Competition in the Nineteenth Century". *Journal of Economic History*, 55/3: 575–611.

——(1998). *Accounting for Growth: Information Systems and the Creation of the Large Corporation*. Stanford, Calif.: Stanford University Press.

LEVENSTEIN, MARGARET C. and SALANT, STEPHEN W. (eds.) (2007). *Cartels*. Cheltenham: Edward Elgar.

——and SUSLOW, VALERIE Y. (2004). "A Comparison of Methodological Approaches", in Grossman (2004), 9–52.

————(2006). "What Determines Cartel Success?" in *Journal of Economic Literature*, 54: 43–95.

LIEFMANN, ROBERT (1932). *Cartels, Concerns and Trusts*. New York: E. P. Dutton and Co.

LIPARTITO, KENNETH (2000). "Failure to Communicate: British Telecommunications and the American Model", in Jonathan Zeitlin and Gary Herrigel (eds.), *Americanization and its Limits: Reworking US Technology and Management in Post-War Europe and Japan*. Oxford: Oxford University Press.

MACKIE-MASON, JEFFREY K., and PINDYCK, ROBERT S. (1987). "Cartel Theory and Cartel Experience in International Minerals Markets", in Richard L. Gordon, Henry D. Jacoby, and Martin B. Zimmerman (eds.), *Energy: Markets and Regulation*. Cambridge, Mass.: MIT Press, 187–214.

MARITI, P., and SMILEY, R. H. (1983). "Cooperative Agreements and the Organization of Industry". *Journal of Industrial Economics*, 31/4: 437–51.

MASON, EDWARD S. (1946). "Cartels and American Security", in *Controlling World Trade: Cartels and Commodity Agreements*. New York: McGraw-Hill, 96–132.

MATSUSHITA, MITSUO (1998). "The Antimonopoly Law of Japan", in Graham and Richardson (1998), 151–98.

MIROW, KURT RUDOLF, and MAURER, HARRY (1982). *Webs of Power: International Cartels and the World Economy*. Boston: Houghton Mifflin Company.

MIWA, R. (1985). "Maritime Policy in Japan: 1868–1939; Structure and Strategy", in Yui and Nakagawa (1985), 123–52.

MIYAJIMA, HIDEAKI (1994). "Strategic Intervention against International Cartels: The Case of the Japanese Chemical Industries in the Interwar Period", in Barjot (1994), 223–32.

NOCKEN, ULRICH (1989). "International Cartels and Foreign Policy: The Formation of the International Steel Cartel 1924–1926", in Clemens A. Wurm (ed.), *International Cartels and Foreign Policy: Studies on the Interwar Period*. Stuttgart: Franz Steiner Verlag, 33–82.

OECD (2003). *Hard Core Cartels: Recent Progress and Challenges Ahead*. Paris: OECD.

PERITZ, RUDOLPH J. R. (1996). *Competition Policy in America, 1888–1992: History, Rhetoric, Law*. New York: Oxford University Press.

PETRI, ROLF (1994). "Cartels and the Diffusion of Technologies: The Case of Hydrogenation and Catalytic Refining", in Barjot (1994), 287–300.

PETERS, LON LEROY (1984). "Are Cartels Unstable?: The German Steel Works Association before World War I", in Gary Saxonhouse and Gavin Wright (eds.), *Technique, Spirit and Form in the Making of the Modern Economies.* Greenwich, Conn.: JAI, 61–85.

—— (1989). "Managing Competition in German Coal, 1893–1913". *Journal of Economic History*, 49/2: 419–33.

POHL, HANS (ed.) (1985). *Kartelle und Kartellgesetzgebung in Praxis und Rechtsprechung vom 19. Jahrhundert bis zur Gegenwart.* Stuttgart: F. Steiner.

READER, W. J. (1975). *Imperial Chemical Industries: A History, Vol. II.* London: Oxford University Press.

REICH, L. S. (1992a). "General Electric and the World Cartelization of Electric Lamps", in Kudō and Hara (1992), 213–28.

—— (1992b). "Lighting the Path to Profit: GE's Control of the Electric Light Industry 1892–1941". *Business History Review*, 66/2: 305–34.

REINDL, J. (1997). "Competition and Collusion: The Electrical Engineering Industry in the United Kingdom and West Germany between 1945 and the late 1960s". *Business and Economic History*, 26/2: 738–50.

SALTER, LIORA (1999). "The Standards Regime for Communication and Information Technologies", in Cutler *et al.* (1999), 97–127.

SAMPSON, ANTHONY (1984). *Empires of the Sky: The Politics, Contests and Cartels of World Airlines.* New York: Random House.

—— (1991). *The Seven Sisters: The Great Oil Companies and the World They Shaped.* New York: Bantam.

SAXONHOUSE, GARY (1976). "Country Girls and Communication among Competitors in the Japanese Cotton-Spinning Industry", in H. Patrick (ed.), *Japanese Industrialization and its Social Consequences.* Berkeley: California University Press.

SCHOLL, LARS U. (1985). "Shipping Business in Germany in the Nineteenth and Twentieth Centuries", in Yui and Nakagawa (1985).

SCHRÖTER, HARM (1988). "Risk and Control in Multinational Enterprise: German Businesses in Scandinavia, 1918–1939". *Business History Review*, 62/3: 420–43.

—— (1994). "The International *Potash* Syndicate", in Barjot (1994).

—— (1996). "Cartelization and Decartelization in Europe, 1870–1995: Rise and Decline of an Economic Institution". *Journal of European Economic History*, 25/1: 129–53.

—— (1997). "Small European States and Cooperative Capitalism, 1920–1960", in A. D. Chandler, Jr., F. Amatori, and T. Hikino (eds.), *Big Business and the Wealth of Nations.* Cambridge: Cambridge University Press, 176–204.

SCHWARTZMAN, DAVID (1993). *The Japanese Television Cartel: A Study Based on Matsushita v. Zenith.* Ann Arbor: University of Michigan Press.

SJOSTROM, WILLIAM (2004). "The Stability of Ocean Shipping Cartels", in Grossman, 82–110.

SMITH, A. (1776/1976). *The Wealth of Nations.* Chicago: Chicago University Press (1st pub. 1776).

SPAR, DEBORA L. (1994). *The Cooperative Edge: The Internal Politics of International Cartels.* Ithaca, NY: Cornell University Press.

—— (1999). "Lost in (Cyber)space: The Private Rules of Online Commerce", in Cutler *et al.* (1999), 31–51.

STIGLER, GEORGE J. (1964). "A Theory of Oligopoly". *Journal of Political Economy*, 72/1: 44–61.

STOCKING, GEORGE W., and WATKINS, MYRON W. (1946). *Cartels in Action: Case Studies in International Business Diplomacy.* New York: Twentieth Century Fund.

SYMEONIDIS, GEORGE (2002). *The Effects of Competition: Cartel Policy and the Evolution of Strategy and Structure in British Industry*. Cambridge, Mass.: The MIT Press.

TEICHOVA, ALICE (1974). *An Economic Background to Munich: International Business and Czechoslovakia 1918–1938*. London: Cambridge University Press.

——(1988). *Internationale Grossunternehmen: Kartelle und das Versailler Staatensystem in Mitteleuropa*. Stuttgart: F. Steiner Verlag Wiesbaden.

TILTON, MARK (1996). *Restrained Trade: Cartels in Japan's Basic Materials Industries*. Ithaca, NY: Cornell University Press.

TSCHIERSCHKY, SIEGFRIED (1903). *Kartell und Trust: Vergleichende Untersuchungen über deren Wesen und Bedeutung*. Göttingen: Vandenhoeck & Ruprecht.

United Nations Department of Economic Affairs (1947). *International Cartels: A League of Nations Memorandum*. New York: Lake Success.

US Department of Justice (2000). "An Inside Look at a Cartel at Work: Common Characteristics of International Cartels". Presentation by James M. Griffin, available at <http://www.oecd.org/dataoecd/19/2/2080696.pdf>, accessed September 1, 2007.

WAGENFÜHR, HORST (1931). *Kartelle in Deutschland*. Nuremberg: Verlag der Hochschulbuchhandlung Krische & Co.

WEBB, STEVEN B. (1980). "Tariffs, Cartels, Technology, and Growth in the German Steel Industry, 1879 to 1914". *Journal of Economic History*, 40/2: 309–29.

WRAY, WILLIAM D. (1984). *Mitsubishi and the N.Y.K., 1870–1914: Business Strategy in the Japanese Shipping Industry*. Cambridge, Mass.: Harvard University Press.

WURM, CLEMENS (1993). *Business, Politics and International Relations: Steel, Cotton and International Cartels in British Politics, 1924–1939*. Cambridge: Cambridge University Press.

YERGIN, DANIEL (1992). *The Prize: The Epic Quest for Oil, Money, and Power*. New York: Free Press.

YUI, TSUNEHIKO, and NAKAGAWA, KEIICHIRO (eds.) (1985). *Business History of Shipping: Strategy and Structure*. Tokyo: University of Tokyo Press.

ZEITLIN, JONATHAN (2002). "Reconstructing and Deconstructing Product Markets in Postwar Britain: The Case of Electrical Engineering". Unpublished Conference Paper, *Constructing Markets, Shaping Production*, Idöborg, Sweden.

CHAPTER 13

....

BUSINESS INTEREST ASSOCIATIONS

....

LUCA LANZALACO

13.1 INTRODUCTION

....

THROUGH much of the twentieth century, business interest associations (hereafter BIAs) were neglected as the object of academic study and systematic research. Although the topic attracted considerable interest among institutional economists and social reformers on both sides of the Atlantic during the late nineteenth and early twentieth centuries, it is only from the late 1970s that modern scholars have once again begun to delve seriously into BIAs' organization and strategies. The ensuing debate has involved both social scientists and historians, who have frequently dealt with similar topics, even if usually separately.[1] This disciplinary divide has negatively affected the study of business history since the structural and functional properties of BIAs have had a significant impact on the evolution of capitalism. So, explanations for the different historical evolution of capitalism in national political

---

[1] Major exceptions to this periodization include the work of Clarence Bonnet (1922, 1956), the Japanese business history school (Yamazaki 1988; Kikkawa 1988: 54–8), early and policy oriented (antitrust legislation, regulative effectiveness of BIAs, etc.) literature about BIAs in the USA (Lynn and McKeown 1988: pp. XIII–XV, especially footnotes), and recent historical literature on the role of employers and their associations in the development of the welfare state (Pedersen 1993; Ebbinghaus and Manow 2001a; Swenson 2002; Mares 2003).

Table 13.1 Forms of capitalist action

Capitalists may act as	Capitalists may act	
	Individually	Collectively
Employers	Collective bargaining at firm level human resource management	Employers' associations
Businessmen	Firm strategies and choices	Trade associations trusts

economies cannot omit a careful comparative analysis of BIAs' institutional role (Hall and Soskice 2001; Ebbinghaus and Manow 2001*b*).

The introductory section of this chapter presents the main theoretical issues at stake, synthesizes the outcomes of historical research, and analyzes the interrelations between them. The second section sketches a comparative-historical framework to explain the development of BIAs, while the third section outlines the long-term historical development of BIAs since the Middle Ages. The final section proposes an agenda for future research.

The role of BIAs can best be understood by analyzing the various forms of action by capitalists. First, they may act either *individually*, as managers of firms, or *collectively*, as members of coalitions and organizations such as trusts, associations, joint ventures, clubs, etc. (Martinelli *et al.* 1981). Second, they may act either as *employers*, when they interact with workers and trade unions in the labor market, or as *producers* (or *businessmen*) in their relationships with customers, suppliers, politicians, and other firm managers in product and capital markets (Sisson 1979; Streeck 1991). By crossing these two orthogonal dimensions, we obtain a simple typology of the various forms of capitalist action (Table 13.1).

A first point to stress is that there are two different types of BIAs: trade associations and employers' associations (hereafter TAs and EAs respectively). This distinction is quite relevant since these two types of associations are characterized by different political functions, organizational structures, and patterns of historical development. Very briefly, from an organizational point of view TAs tend to privilege the "vertical" dimension (in which associational domains and identities are delimited by sector, category, or product), since they have to bring out the peculiar interests of specific groups of producers and firms, while EAs are more prone to a non-sector-specific or "horizontal" mode of organizing (namely, on a local or regional basis, regardless of firms' productive specialization), since they have to reflect the territorial configuration of the labor market. From a functional point of view, trade associations not only provide all those services needed by firms, such as marketing, fiscal and financial advice, research and innovation, regulation of competition, etc., but they also act as pressure groups (or lobbies) for defining, promoting, and defending the interests of their membership in the political arena *vis-à-vis* government authorities, public administrations, and state agencies. Employers' associations, on the other hand, specialize in industrial relations issues and deal with all issues concerning not only collective bargaining and strikes, but also labor and social policies.[2] This four-cell typology makes clear that the study of capitalists' action must not be seen as a field of inquiry which is fragmented into a variety of circumscribed topics (the content of the individual cells), but should be seen as an integrated area of research in which market trends, technological innovations, entrepreneurial strategies, industrial relations and political concerns are all interrelated (the links among the various cells). In other words, when explaining the evolution of a specific form of action, what is happening—or what has happened—in the other forms cannot be ignored. In the case of BIAs, for example, the choice of combining and acting with other capitalists, the way in which this collective action is organized, the goals pursued in both the political and industrial relations arenas, and the services that are provided to firms all depend on their individual strategies, which are influenced in turn by associational choices (Tolliday and Zeitlin 1991*b*).

From a theoretical point of view, two linked core issues stand at the center of the debate about BIAs. The first concerns the reasons why capitalists decide to combine and to form associations. The second focuses on the relationship between the collective action of capitalists and that of workers.

The simplest answer to these problems has been given by the pluralist school in Political Science. According to the group theory of politics, BIAs emerge spontaneously as an effort to defend capitalists' collective interests, for the same reason that trade unions are founded by workers.

The pluralist approach was questioned by Mancur Olson (1965) in his seminal work on the logic of collective action. He assumes, as do the pluralists, that capitalists and workers act according to the same logic, that is, as rational actors. But he shows that precisely because both sets of actors rationally pursue their *individual* interests, they will *not combine spontaneously* to defend their *collective* interests, unless (a) the group is small and provides some selective incentives (services, rewards, offices) to those who contribute to collective action or (b) some coercive mechanism (compulsory membership, control over monopolistic goods, etc.) is deployed. Hence Olson identifies no substantive difference between the logic of collective action of capitalists and that of workers. He only suggests that employers

---

[2] This distinction is not empirical but analytical, since it does not necessarily give rise to distinct organizations. In some countries, the same organization acts both as an employers' and as a trade association, whereas in some others there are distinct associations which have specialized in each of the two functions. As Streeck *et al.* (2005) argue, this functional distinction appears to be diminishing in recent years because of the declining relevance of unions and class conflict.

are likely to overcome the "free rider" problem more easily than workers, since they are fewer in number and better endowed with resources.[3]

These theses have been radically criticized by Offe and Wiesenthal (1980) in an important and theoretically subtle article. Taking off from a rigorous Marxist position, they contend that—contrary to the claims of both the pluralist school and Olson's rational-choice approach—the logic of collective action is not single, but *double*. Workers' logic of action is essentially (even if not exclusively) *dialogic* since they have to discover and define their collective interests together by means of complex organizational processes (e.g. identity building, communication, decisions, etc.) whose costs tend to increase with the number of participants. Capitalists' logic of action is, on the contrary, *monologic* since capital is "dead labor" which is already organized and whose interests and preferences can be taken for granted. The crucial conclusion of the authors is that the collective action of capitalists is less demanding, less resource consuming, and less divisive than that of workers' and that this structural asymmetry reproduces in the political arena the class inequality of capitalism and thereby distorts the mechanisms of pluralist representation in democratic regimes. Offe and Wiesenthal's contribution is quite interesting since they emphasize that the costs of collective action, and hence of political representation, vary for different types of actors and, above all, they underline the consequences of this variation for democratic theory. Where they fail is in their attempt to root these differences between capitalists and workers in their logics of action, overlooking that what BIAs organize are not *quotas of capital* (namely firms), but *social actors*, namely capitalists, just as trade unions (and other interest groups) do. So, the issue of the *logic* of collective action must be kept distinct from that of its *organization*: even if different social actors surely have to cope with different organizational dynamics, dilemmas, and costs, they share a common logic of action.

This approach has been adopted by Schmitter and Streeck (1981). In very simple terms, according to their framework, the structural and operative properties of BIAs, like those of every interest representation organization, may be conceptualized and explained, from both a comparative and an historical perspective, as a compromise between the logic of *membership*, leading to associative structures reflecting the fragmented and specialized demands and characteristics of firms, and the logic of *influence*, which tends to produce more unitary and encompassing structures in response to the demands and characteristics of capitalists' interlocutors such as state agencies and trade unions.

---

[3] The "free rider" problem emerges whenever a public good must be provided. Once a public good has been produced nobody can be excluded from its consumption, including those who did not contribute to its production. So, a rational actor will not participate in a collective effort but will try to exploit freely the public goods created by the other members of the group. Olson's crucial point is that the outcomes of pressure group activities (e.g. regulations, collective agreements, etc.) can be seen as public goods for their actual and potential membership, thereby obliging these groups to cope with the "free rider" problem.

The main challenge for BIAs comes from the logic of membership, since capitalists are always in conflict with one another. If they operate in the same sector they struggle as competitors in product and labor market, whereas if they act in different sectors, they have conflicting interests in raw material and capital markets as sellers and buyers. Furthermore, these differences are reinforced by the fact that firms come in different sizes, often operate in different markets (internal vs. international), have different forms of ownership (private, public, cooperative, or mixed), and use different technologies. So, BIAs have to cope with a challenge that trade unions do not have, namely the *management of diversity* of the interests they organize and represent (Martinelli *et al.* 1981). This makes the collective action of capitalists not *easier*—as Offe and Wiesenthal, and partially Olson, claim—but more *difficult* and *divisive* than that of workers, because of the heterogeneity of their interests and their unwillingness to accept associational discipline (Streeck 1991). This is why state intervention (e.g. incorporation in decisional processes and bodies, privileged relationships with public administration, devolution of public functions, and recognition of public status) is so important for the birth, development, and consolidation of BIAs. This point has been stressed not only in the literature about corporatism (Berger 1981). Bowman (1982, 1985, 1989), for example, adopting a sophisticated game-theoretical approach, demonstrates on the one hand that *intra*class conflicts among capitalists create collective action problems that "are distinct from and logically prior to those that are generated by antagonism of capitalists and workers" (Bowman 1985: 36), while claiming on the other hand that the state may play an important role in helping capitalists to solve these conflicts by supporting BIAs. This thesis has also been empirically corroborated by Schmitter and Brand (1979) in an impressive quantitative-diachronic analysis of the development of BIAs in the United States and the UK from 1871 to 1970. They show that *intra*sectoral conflicts, economic crises, and market trends are much more salient explanatory factors than unionization, strikes, and wars in accounting for BIAs' birth and development. So, in order to understand the logic of capitalists' collective action they propose to substitute what they call the "orthodox" or "defensive" model, based on the assumption that BIAs emerge as a reaction to *inter*class conflict, with a "revised" model in which *intra*class conflicts between and within sectors give rise to TAs that then play a "pivotal" role in founding EAs when the challenge of trade unions emerges (Schmitter and Brand 1979: 5). This means that, contrary to the practice of many scholars, EAs and TAs must be jointly studied, especially in their historical evolution.

Many of these topics at the center of the social science debate have also been addressed by historians (or rather by historically oriented scholars), even if they adopt an approach which is much less prone to wide generalizations and much more careful about national, regional, and sector contexts and specificities. Another peculiar trait of historical studies is the absence of those sharp contrapositions among different research traditions that, as we have seen, characterize the social science debate. The rare divergences are often due to the characteristics of the specific national system studied, and not to the approaches adopted, as is demonstrated by the debate about the impact of the industrial infrastructure upon the birth and development of TAs (Cochran and Miller 1961; Feldman and Nocken 1975; Pierenkemper 1988) and EAs (Jackson and Sisson 1981).

To sum up, the overlapping, if not convergence, of interests between the historical and social scientific traditions of research on BIAs is evident, which makes cross-fertilization between them plausible and promising, even if so far explored by relatively few scholars.[4] For example, many social scientists emphasize the historical reconstruction of the origins, development, and evolution of BIAs (Schmitter and Brand 1979; Sisson 1979, 1987; Jackson and Sisson 1981; Windmuller and Gladstone 1984; Lanzalaco 1990; Grant, Nekkers, and van Waarden 1991), just as Tolliday and Zeitlin (1991a: 18–22) link the historical study of business strategies to the theoretical debate about BIAs. Historical reconstruction and theoretical speculation need one another.

At first glance, we may distinguish those topics where historical research substantially confirms the suggestions of theoretical models from those where they add new, original, and promising themes of inquiry.

More specifically, historical analysis undoubtedly confirms the point at the core of the theoretical debate, namely the centrality of the "management of diversity" of business interests in explaining BIAs' organization, strategies and functions. For example, the "diversification" of capitalists' interests—namely, the emergence of new industrial sectors alongside handicrafts and traditional industries and the conflicting objectives among firms of different sizes, mainly in international markets—played a central role in Japan and Germany, first in separating BIAs from chambers of commerce, and then in promoting differentiation among themselves, at the beginning of the twentieth century (Gellately 1974; Miyamoto 1988; Pierenkemper 1988). In similar terms, the internal politics of the British Engineering Employers' Federation before World War II cannot be understood without taking into consideration the heterogeneity of the sector and the regional cleavages within it (Zeitlin 1991). Similarly, the failure of the four attempts to unite French employers into a single encompassing national peak association can be explained only by the divisions among different sectors (Ehrmann 1957: 17; Lefranc 1976: 31–2). Historical evidence also shows that, because of the intrinsically divisive nature of business interests, the state played a crucial role in fostering the birth and consolidation of BIAs as a tool for policy making in many countries, such as France (Ehrmann 1957/1981), Germany (Bunn 1984; Ullmann 1988), Italy (Lanzalaco 1990), and Japan (Miyamoto 1988; Gao 2001).

---

[4] Among the common research interests should be recalled: the causes of BIAs' birth and consolidation, the relationships between economic and political action (trusts vs. associations), the functions performed by BIAs in the political and industrial relations arenas, and the origins of the different structural properties of BIAs at the national level (Yamazaki and Miyamoto 1988).

Historical studies provide not only confirmation, but also new hints for theoretical speculation and empirical research. Four themes of great interest are highlighted by this literature.

The first is the competition between BIAs and political parties as channels of representation of business interests in the political arena (Kocka 1981; Davenport-Hines 1988; Pierenkemper 1988). The second concerns the peculiarities of the "national context"—namely the specific milieux within which BIAs emerged and operated—and the ways in which these historical legacies molded BIAs' organizational properties (Feldman and Nocken 1975; Tolliday and Zeitlin 1991a). The third is the effectiveness of EAs vis-à-vis their interlocutors and membership. The differences between those nations (e.g. Germany or Sweden) where BIAs are strong and influential organizations and those where they are weak (e.g. the UK) has been explained in various ways. Some authors stress the relevance of long-term explanatory factors, such as the existence, in the early phase of development of BIAs, of legislation forbidding the regulation of competition or the founding of associations, as in France (Daviet 1988). Others emphasize instead more structural elements, such as the position of the country in international markets, its technological and managerial endowments, the strength of national trade unions and the structure of collective bargaining, or the different relationships between that state and BIAs during war mobilization (Jackson and Sisson 1981; Harris 1982; Sisson 1987, 1991; Grant et al. 1991).

The fourth theme, largely neglected by political scientists, concerns the substantive content of *policies* pursued by BIAs, in relation to managerial strategies at the firm level. Some authors have focused on economic policies and industrial relations (Braunthal 1965; Lynn and McKeown 1988; Tolliday and Zeitlin 1991b), while more recent work has analyzed comparatively and historically the role played by employers and their associations in the origins and development of the welfare state (Pedersen 1993; Ebbinghaus 2001; Swenson 2002; Mares 2003). Three elements emerge from these contributions. The first is the existence of sharp disagreements among employers in different sectors when a new social policy has to be introduced. Since employers are exposed to different levels of uncertainty and risk—which they share with workers to some extent—their strategies vary in relation to the trade-off between risk distribution and labor-force control (Mares 2003). Employers are not a monolithic group, hence *intra*class conflicts are salient explanatory factors for understanding their strategies and logic of collective action. Second, these researches reconstruct the emergence in different countries of cross-class strategic alliances between capital and labor in order to foster the adoption of social insurance schemes against sickness, disability, andn unemployment (Swenson 2002; Mares 2003). The third finding of these studies is that the success of "cross-class alliance building" depends not only on interactions between employers and workers at the firm or micro level, but also on BIAs' properties and capabilities at the macro level where they negotiate with trade unions and the state. So, specific attention has been devoted to the analysis of the processes of associative centralization in various countries (Swenson 2002). These findings have some noteworthy theoretical implications, which go far beyond the analysis of the development of the welfare state. First of all, this historical literature emphasizes that the interests of employers— even when they act in the *political arena*—are shaped both by *market constraints* and by *firm strategies* adopted to cope with them. And this assumption—firmly rooted in the political economy approach—could be generalized to other fields of inquiry. Second, these authors' emphasis on the role of *inter*class conflicts and *intra*class alliances forces us to rethink the usefulness of class-oriented explanations of social and political processes.

13.2 THE STRUCTURING OF BUSINESS INTEREST REPRESENTATION: A COMPARATIVE-HISTORICAL FRAMEWORK

In sum, even if scholarly interest in BIAs has developed relatively recently, there is now a substantial body of historical and comparative research that needs to be situated in a more general explanatory framework.

In the historical process of structuring systems of business interest representation, the founding of national peak associations is a *critical juncture*, namely an event which determines the specific way in which capitalists' interests will be defined not only in a given country, but also in the international arena (Lanzalaco 1992). Hence, this has to be the starting point for any attempt at systematization.

In very general terms, BIAs—like all political organizations—may emerge at a national level in two ways (Eliassen and Svaasand 1975): either by *diffusion* (namely the spontaneous germination of small associations and, then, their progressive integration into broader federations), or by *penetration* (when a previously founded national federation or confederation "conquers" new domains by generating new associations).[5] These two processes may develop along both territorial and sectoral dimensions. So we may have four types of genetic models of BIAs (Table 13.2). There may be a process of *sectoral diffusion* (e.g. the CBI in the UK), in which spontaneously sprouted sector-specific associations combine in a national federation or confederation. Alternatively, there may be a process of *territorial diffusion*, whereby

---

[5] Both these processes are usually present. What matters is their *timing* and *length*, namely whether the phase of diffusion or that of penetration is predominant in the birth of a peak association. This is the reason why the detailed reconstruction of the historical development of an association, or of an associative system, is so important in the study of BIAs. Different modes of identifying the phases of BIAs development may be found in Alemann (1987) and Pierenkemper (1988: 236).

Table 13.2 Historical processes of peak association formation: a typology

Dimension along which the process of formation occurs	Modes of formation	
	Diffusion	Penetration
Territory	Formation by territorial diffusion (e.g. SGV and Vorort in Switzerland)	Formation by territorial penetration (e.g. VNF in Netherlands and Confindustria in Italy)
Sector	Formation by sectoral diffusion (e.g. CBI in the UK and CNPF in France)	Formation by sectoral penetration (e.g. SAF in Sweden)

the original units that form the national peak association are non-sector-specific associations organized on a local or regional basis (e.g. the Vorort and SGV in Switzerland). In a process of *territorial penetration* (e.g. the VNF in the Netherlands and Confindustria in Italy), a strong local association extends its domain over the whole national territory by creating or incorporating other associations, while in a process of *sectoral penetration* (e.g. the SAF in Sweden), a rather strong sector-specific national association plays this role of federation or confederation builder.[6]

Another important historical factor in the development of associative systems is the role played by exogenous actors in "sponsoring" the formation of the peak associations, leading us to distinguish between *internally* and *externally* legitimized associations. The first type owes its formation to the autonomous and spontaneous action of capitalists, so the association is endogenously legitimized by its representative action. In other cases, less infrequent than one might suppose, the source of legitimization is exogenous to the organization itself. This external "legitimizer" may be the Church, as for example occurred in some Dutch BIAs, a political party, as in the case of many peak associations of retailers, artisans, farmers, and cooperatives in Italy, or often the state itself, as happened in France.

Although more empirical and historical research is needed, in general terms we may infer that the way in which a peak association is formed determines its

---

[6] There are also two intermediate modalities. A national peak association may be formed through a *fusion* of two pre-existing federations or confederations, which we may assimilate to a process of diffusion (as in the British case), or through *structural differentiation*, when as a consequence of a process of functional specialization a peak trade association generates a peak employers' association, or vice versa, which is a kind of penetration process (as in the Japanese, German, and US cases).

Table 13.3 Formation, legitimation, and institutionalization of peak associations

Formation Process	Legitimation	Institutionalization
Penetration	Internal	Strong
Penetration	External	Weak
Diffusion	Internal	Weak
Diffusion	External	Weak

structural properties, in particular its degree of institutionalization.[7] BIAs generated and developed by diffusion, regardless of the source of their legitimization, tend to be weakly institutionalized. In fact, when the national peak association emerges, the territorial and sectoral associations adhering to it are already consolidated and reluctant to devolve their power and authority to a new central organization, as in the cases of the French CNPF or the British CBI. In the case of BIAs born as a result of penetration, their degree of institutionalization will be dependent on their form of legitimization. If the source of legitimization is internal they will be strongly institutionalized (e.g. the Swedish SAF), whereas if the legitimizing source is external, they will be weakly institutionalized (e.g. the Italian Confindustria whose consolidation was fostered by the Fascist regime), since the control over organizational resources and the linkages of loyalty depend on the external "sponsoring" organization (see Table 13.3).

13.3 THE LONG-TERM EVOLUTION OF BUSINESS ASSOCIATIONS

Since the eighteenth century, capitalists, and before them, artisans, have been experimenting with the scale of their collective action, exploring new associative forms, and exploiting those still available. In very general terms we may distinguish four phases of development of BIAs.

---

[7] A strongly institutionalized association is characterized by a high level of *intra*associative homogeneity, integration, and centralization. It is also able to control the behavior of its members (both firms and associations). Conversely a weakly institutionalized peak association is a polycentric organization which is dependent on subunits that are heterogeneous and poorly integrated with one another. So, according to the neocorporatist approach, a relationship exists between the degree of institutionalization of an association and the function (representation of interests vs. control of the membership) it performs within the political system and the industrial relations arena.

The "Primitive" Phase (tenth to eighteenth centuries) The first forms of organization of business interests were the merchant and craft guilds (*corporations* in French; *corporazioni* in Italian), which developed mainly in Germany, Great Britain, France, the Netherlands, Spain, Japan, and Italy. In each country they assumed specific characteristics, but there are some common general traits (Farr 2000: ch. 1). They were compulsory associations, whose membership was composed of merchants and, starting from the twelfth century, craftsmen operating in the same business, profession, or sector (weavers, bookbinders, fullers, painters, etc.). Their formation was due to several historical factors (Kieser 1989). First, the legacy of the first voluntary religious guilds of the seventh century, which provided the organizational "technology" on which they were based, namely the idea of an *autonomous self-regulative associative order*, that even today represents the core rationale of BIAs.[8] Second, this inherited "technology" was used to cope with new emerging challenges: the process of urbanization and the early formation of towns, as a new type of spatial organization of social, economic, and political life, on the one hand; and the need for reciprocal defense against the risks created by the growth of new economic activities on the other (security for the members of merchant guilds, and uncertainties deriving from the market for those of the crafts guilds, respectively). Finally, another factor that must be kept in mind to explain the birth and growth of guilds is the increasing number and differentiation of craftsmen's activities.

The guilds performed very important social and economic functions. In the first place, they erected robust entry barriers to the main professions against external competition: in each town only those belonging to a guild were allowed to exercise the corresponding business activity. This has often led scholars to emphasize the guilds' monopolistic character and, hence, their negative effects. In fact, they also had a positive impact. By controlling many important aspects of jobs—the level of prices, the quality of production, and the training of craftsmen—they prevented the risks of unfair competition, acting as a self-regulating order and as tools for controlling economic activity. Furthermore, the guilds established a sort of "welfare policy" for their members, providing forms of insurance or aid in the case of sickness, death, or economic disaster. Hence the birth and consolidation of these organizations was fostered, with various fluctuations, by public authorities because of their capacity for producing collective goods (Farr 2000: ch. 4). In a few decades, they established robust relationships with the political and religious powers, becoming the main actors in the municipalities, since their leaders often occupied important political positions.

To accomplish this complex set of regulative and distributive functions, the guilds were organized into a rigid system of rules and a pyramidal structure of

---

[8] According to Schmitter and Streeck (1985), BIAs may act as *private interest governments* (PIGs), primarily if they are highly institutionalized and if they are part of a corporatist system of interest intermediation. These are the prerequisites needed to control and discipline their membership.

authority that—in spite of differences from country to country, and within the same country—was always based on the overlapping between the hierarchy of internal authority on the one hand and professional mastery and seniority on the other. Sometimes they also established cooperative relationships with their counterparts in other towns and nations. Between the end of the eighteenth century and the beginning of the nineteenth, the strength of guilds declined. In some cases they were abolished because of state intervention (e.g. France: Minard 2004), in other cases through the expansion of new industrial activities, the prevalence of a liberal conception of the free market, and the strengthening of their "heirs", namely the chambers of commerce.

The analysis of these "primitive forms" of association is important for two reasons. First, they represent the germs of contemporary BIAs. Already a thousand years ago, at the very beginning of the process of industrialization and capitalist development, the need to (self) regulate the market and economic activity by means of an associative order was felt. Second, the decline of guilds created a sort of "regulatory gap" that was filled by the chambers of commerce (e.g. in France, Germany, and Austria) or by modern forms of association (e.g. in Japan).[9] It would be interesting to analyze comparatively the ways the different historical backgrounds of guilds affected the subsequent developments of BIAs in various countries.

The Phase of Diffusion and Integration (Nineteenth Century) This phase stands in-between the birth of the first associations and the founding of national peak associations. Its duration is a very important explanatory variable, since it determines the genetic model of the associations and, hence, their subsequent history and development (see the previous section). A long process of diffusion and integration is usually associated with the diffusive model, while a rapid process of diffusion leads to the penetrative model.

While the founding dates of peak associations are well known (see Table 13.4), much more uncertainty exists about the beginning of the diffusion phase. When did the "very first" BIA spring up in a given country? In some cases, it is possible to establish with a certain accuracy this moment of genesis, while in others it is much more difficult to establish a clear starting point. On the one hand, the first associations were very volatile structures. Often they were really professional lawyers' practices and we can speak of associations only when these associations acquired their own office and a small bureaucratic staff. On the other hand, there is a substantial continuity between the premodern forms of association and the modern ones, often due to the presence of chambers of commerce—an object of inquiry whose interest and relevance has often been undervalued and neglected—which played a crucial role in the development of BIAs as, for example, in USA

[9] For a very exhaustive analysis of this need for self-regulation see, for the French case, the recent volume edited by Kaplan and Minard (2004).

Table 13.4 Foundation date of the first peak associations in certain industrialized countries

Country	Trade Associations	Employers' Associations	Mixed function (TAs and EAs)
Austria			
Germany	1876 Zentralverband der Deutschen Industriallen	1904 Haupstelle Deuscher Arbeitgeberverbande	
	1895 Bund der Industriellen	1904 Verein Deutscher Arbeitbgeberverbande	
France			1919 Conseil Française de la Production
Japan	1922 Japan Economic Federation	1931 National Federation of Industrial Organizations	1917 Industry Club of Japan
Italy			1919 Confindustria
Netherlands	1899 Vereininging van Nederlandse Werkgevers	1920 Centraal Overleg	1917 Verbond van Nederlandse Fabrikan-tenvreiningingen
	1920 Centraal Industrieel Verbond		
UK		1919 National Confederation of Employers' Organizations	1916 Federation of British Industries
United States[1]			1895 National Association of Manufacturers
			1908 National Industrial Council
			1912 Chamber of Commerce of the United States
Sweden	1910 Sveriges Industriforbund	1902 Svenska Arbitsgivareföreningen	
Switzerland	1870 Schweizerische Handerls und Industrie Verein	1908 Zentralverband Schweizerischer Arbeigeber-Organizationen	
	1879 Schweizerische gevernbevernband		

Note: [1]US peak associations, even if they deal with industrial relations, do not have a direct role in collective bargaining, given the predominance of firm and sectoral bargainning levels.

(Lynn and McKeown 1988), Germany (Weber 1991), Japan (Miyamoto 1988), and France (Daviet 1988: 270; Lemercier 2003).

If we jointly consider the suggestions provided both by the "defensive" or "orthodox" model and by the "revised" one (see above), we may say that the first transformations of associative action and integration into more inclusive sectoral and territorial federation emerged—*depending on the country in question*—in reaction to two different stimuli (Lanzalaco 1990): either as an attempt to regulate conflicts within the capitalist class, or in response to the need to cope with the challenge of the working class.

In general, where capitalism started early and developed gradually, the first forms of associationalism were not aimed at coping with the challenge of the labor movement, but were "attempts to avoid cut-throat price competition on the market, efforts to limit or prevent altogether the access of foreign competitors to the domestic market, endeavors to form a common front vis-à-vis the sellers of basic raw materials and other supplies, and the like" (Schmitter and Streeck 1981: 16). The main problem was not to organize against an external enemy, represented by the labor movement, but against an enemy internal to the capitalist class itself, namely producers from other sectors and countries. In such cases *trade associations* and *sectoral* forms of aggregation prevailed. Within this group of countries, it makes sense to distinguish those countries where the processes of organizational centralization, with the formation of the first peak associations, occurred before World War I (e.g. Switzerland and Germany) from those where they occurred afterwards (the UK, France, the Netherlands). Where capitalist development started late and proceeded rapidly, capitalists got organized predominantly as a response to the labor movement. Initial forms of associationalism and early processes of organizational centralization were led by class conflict. In such cases, where unity and cohesion were required against a common external enemy, *employers' associations* and *territorial* modes of organization prevailed. Also in this group of countries, we must distinguish between those countries where the challenge of the labor movement came mainly in the political arena (e.g. Sweden), from those characterized by late democratization, where the challenge of the labor movement occurred mainly in the labor market (e.g. Italy). Typically, peak associations are much more institutionalized and centralized in the former countries than in the latter ones, as is demonstrated by the case of the Swedish SAF.

The Phase of Penetration, Centralization, and Consolidation (Beginning of the Twentieth Century to the End of World War II) More or less quickly, depending on the length of the diffusion phase, on the one hand, the number of associations progressively increased and on the other, they combined with one another to bring about more inclusive federations and confederations (Windmuller 1984). These processes of associative integration, which have been only sporadically studied, gave rise in all industrialized countries to the first national peak associations, beginning from 1870 to 1920, and accelerating in the first years of the twentieth century (see Table 13.4).[10] In the subsequent decades, up to the end of World War II, these BIAs

[10] BIAs tend to integrate their action in more and more complex associative systems that are "pyramid shaped". Peak associations are the highest organization level, in the sense that they are at the top of the system, they are sector unspecific, their domain is national, and their membership is composed of associations or federations of associations, so they are associations of the second or third

strengthened their structures and assumed their present form. So, it is precisely in this period that "national models" of business interest representation emerged with their peculiarities. National trajectories became more clearly defined and, once these associations were fully institutionalized and consolidated, their structural and operative properties remained relatively impermeable, with the exception of some minor adaptive transformations, to the changes that occurred in the productive systems (decline of the primary sector and of traditional industries such as steel and manufacturing, the emergence of high technology sectors, definitive affirmation of the tertiary sector), in the collective bargaining arena (decline of trade unions and labor unionization, reduction of industrial conflict, strengthening of firm and sometimes individual level agreements), and in the institutional context (European integration, globalization and liberalization of market transactions, etc.). And this is why, when a comparative approach is adopted, the historical and diachronic perspective may explain *inter*country differences much better than a structural approach which focuses mainly on industrial infrastructure or collective bargaining arrangements in order to explain national differences and similarities. What happened during this crucial period, and its outcomes, cannot be explained without taking into consideration two key historical events: the involvement of many countries in World War II and the divide between those countries which experienced authoritarian rule and those in which liberal democracies persisted.

As regards the first element, World War II imposed on all states a more or less extensive intervention in the economy in order to plan production, assure the supply of raw materials, control inflation, and finance the conflict. Even if all states had to cope with these challenges, the way in which they organized wartime mobilization varied (Grant *et al.* 1991; Table 13.5). In some cases BIAs were directly involved, in other cases individual businessmen, in some cases corporatism was imposed by the state, while in others it was almost spontaneously organized by trade associations and industries.[11] In general, with the exception of the United States, wartime mobilization had the effect of widening the functions performed by BIAs and reinforcing their role in relation to state agencies and public administration. In other words, it is precisely during World War II, although the first signs of this trend can be

order. Needless to say, the associations that do not have direct relationships with firms and employers have to accomplish functions which are different from those of first-order associations which have to provide services, assistance, and solidaristic goods directly to the membership.

[11] *Corporatism* and *pluralism* are two different ways of organizing and representing functional (e.g. economic) interests. A *corporatist* order is characterized by two traits: a limited number of noncompetitive and hierarchically ordered organizations recognized by the state, and the concertation of major social and economic policies between them and the executive. Conversely, a pluralist order is characterized by a large number of competitive organizations, whose aim is to exert pressure (often called lobbying) on public authorities (mainly parliament) in order to affect the content of collective decisions. So, the difference between corporatism and pluralism deal with both the mode of *interest organization* (monopoly vs. competition) and the mode of *political representation* (concertation vs. pressure). Regarding the difference between these two systems of interest intermediation, see the seminal contributions of Schmitter (1979) and Lehmbruch (1979).

Table 13.5 Modes of interest intermediation during World War II

	Macro level	Meso level
State corporatism	Germany	
	Italy	
	Japan	
	France[1]	
	Belgium[1]	
	Netherlands[1]	
Societal corporatism	Sweden	
	Denmark	UK
Captured étatisme[2]	USA	Canada

Notes: [1]Occupied countries in which state corporatism was imposed.
[2]Captured étatisme" is defined by Grant *et al.* (1991: 275) as "the intervention by a—temporarily—relatively strong but not autonomous state (...) captured by businessmen-cum-civil-servants, who also acted as interest intermediators", where "captured" means that "to man the economic emergency administration most countries had to enlist prominent businessmen (...) since there was neither time nor capacity to train professional civil servants for economic policy".
Source: My elaboration and update from Grant *et al.* (1991).

traced back to World War I, that BIAs acquired a real public status and the sharp distinction between public and private regulation of the economy became blurred.

As far as the second element is concerned, authoritarian regimes tended to influence, both at home and in occupied countries, the structure of business interest representation, and that of labor as well, transforming them into mere organs of the state (state corporatism). In particular, four lines of intervention were adopted: the creation of more inclusive peak associations which were able to represent monopolistically all businesses, their incorporation in corporatist institutions where trade unions were also present, the institution of compulsory membership, and, last but not least, centralized and politically controlled selection of the leadership (Alemann 1987). The legacies of these policies have not been as strong as one might expect. With the return to democratic rule, many associative systems, such as the German and the Italian, reassumed their original configuration, which were often more fragmented and pluralistic that those imposed by authoritarian regimes. The legacy of authoritarian rule led to organizational consolidation of these associations, their expansion over the whole national territory, and the establishment of ongoing relationships with the state and, in particular, with the public administration.

In sum, the events of the 1930s and 1940s not only did not change the original and specific traits of national systems of business representation, but even to a certain extent reinforced these differences.

The "Transnational" Phase (since World War II) The national level was the highest level of business interest association only for some years. At the end of World War I, the International Chamber of Commerce (ICC) and the (International

Organization of Employers (IOE) were founded (in 1919 and 1920 respectively). After World War II, important confederations such as the Conseil des federations industrielles (1949, from 1958 UNICE, Union of Industrial and Employers', Confederations of Europe) and the COPA (Confederation of Professional Agricultural Associations, 1958) were founded at the European level. This process of "transnationalization" of BIAs, and in particular of their "Europeanization", has proceeded rapidly, mainly at the sectoral level and in the economic policy area, with the emergence of a thick and fragmented network of associations and federations which are very active in lobbying and regulatory activities, while non-sector-specific and employers' associations are less developed (Lanzalaco 1995). The relative weakness of this last type of association may be explained both by the absence of a strong trade union movement at the transnational level and by the strict link between capitalism and the nation-state. So, national BIAs (both sector-specific and general) are not declining but are restructuring their organization and strategies. The "transnationalization" of capitalist collective action may be explained on the basis of two distinct factors. The first "wave" of transnational BIAs, those founded after World Wars I and II, can be interpreted as the attempt to create peaceful cross-border relationships among national capitalists, in order to avoid further military conflicts. The second "wave", during the last twenty-five years, is mainly due to the increasing process of regionalization, in some cases, and globalization, of the economy, in others.

In general terms, no clear trend is easily identifiable: globalization and regionalization breed transnational associative structures, but they also involve national and local associative levels; they require the development of new functions (e.g. to support the processes of productive outsourcing and commercial internationalization) but they do not render the older ones obsolete (e.g. services and assistance to firms). These processes originally concerned multinational corporations and large firms but have recently begun to involve small and medium-sized firms in a dramatic way as well. They call for collective action but they also stimulate conflict and associational competition. The main question is whether these inconsistent effects of globalization and regionalization are only temporary processes in the restructuring of BIAs, or are going to became permanent traits of capitalists' collective action (Streeck *et al.* 2005).

13.4 CONCLUSIONS

As has been extensively shown, the historical perspective has almost always been present in the study of BIAs, even if many topics require further empirical research. On the basis of the literature examined, at least five fields of inquiry seem promising.

As we saw at the beginning of this chapter, the first broad area of research concerns the relationship between BIAs and the development of capitalism. If it is true that different modes of development of national "capitalisms" have created different systems of capitalist representation, it is also true that BIAs, once consolidated and frozen, can operate as an independent variable as well. Their strategies and policies may influence the evolution of national, sectoral, or local systems of firms by promoting specific types of industrial and economic policy, providing different types of services and assistance, and influencing the distribution of public financial aid (Hall and Soskice 2001). For example, BIAs may adopt different policies when faced by the crisis of declining economic sectors, such as agriculture, small-scale retailing, or traditional manufacture: they may seek to protect firms in these sectors or, conversely, may foster economic choices and policies aimed at rationalizing these economic activities, even if this implies the closure of many inefficient productive units. In sum, BIAs are able to make strategic choices not only in the industrial relations arena (Tolliday and Zeitlin 1991*a*), but also in that of public policy (Swenson 2002; Mares 2003). These choices in turn may have dramatic implications that should be the object of careful research in a variety of policy areas. Such research should not only consider different levels of policy making (national, local, and sectoral) and different historical periods, but also compare phases of economic growth with those of decline in the face of national or international competition.

The second major area of research concerns the causes of the different degrees of fragmentation of business interest representation systems. In some countries these are highly inclusive and there are a few peak associations representing firms of different sectors (industry, agriculture, and commerce), size (large, small, and medium-sized) and type of ownership (private, public, cooperative). In other countries, on the contrary, the system of representation is highly fragmented into many peak associations that not only represent different types of firms, but often compete with one another. What factors explain this cross-national variation? Why, in some countries, has the industrial bourgeoisie achieved a hegemonic position vis-à-vis farmers, traders, craftsmen, and other sectors of the business class, while in other countries it has remained relatively insulated from an associative point of view? What role, in particular, did the financial sector play in the historical birth and development of BIAs? In order to tackle these core issues a comparative-historical perspective is needed, which can identify the different national trajectories and explain the similarities and differences between them.

The third area of inquiry concerns, in very broad terms, the relationships between BIAs and the political system. As Isabella Mares (2003: 8) has noted, recent literature has rediscovered the political role of capitalists, but this topic needs further investigation. In political science and sociology it is normal to distinguish two forms of political representation: territorial (political parties) and functional (interest groups such as trade unions, BIAs, etc.). Many studies on the relationship between these two channels of political representation exist for the working class, while they are almost absent in the case of capitalists. What is the relationship between political parties and BIAs? What type of functions do these two channels of representation perform? In some countries certain associative expressions of business interests exist that are characterized by marked ideological radicalism, mainly involving small and medium-sized firms (e.g. France, Spain, and to some extent Italy). In certain other countries this peculiarity is almost completely absent. How can these differences be explained? Studies of political parties and trade unions teach us that the answers to these questions may be found only in a historical perspective, since path dependence has a crucial role in structuring the systems of working-class representation. The same holds true for capitalists.

A fourth area of research deals with the relationships between BIAs and public administrations. We know, from the seminal contribution of La Palombara (1964) and others, that bureaucrats are the main interlocutors of interest groups. The weight of public administration in policy making has grown increasingly and it would be interesting to analyze how changes in the organization and policies of public administrations have affected—or conversely, have been affected by—BIAs' influence and strategies. This topic has been studied with particular attention to the critical juncture of World War II. The scope of the analysis should be broadened in two directions. On the one hand, comparative research is urgently needed—concerning the impact of World War I similar to that of Grant *et al.* (1991) on World War II. On the other hand, these relationships should be studied also in peacetime, when business cooperation is needed—even if in probably less dramatic forms than during war mobilization—to cope with economic cycles and depressions, market uncertainty, and economic and technological transformations.

Continuing with the question of bureaucracy, there is a fifth almost unexplored theme, to which business history could make a great contribution, namely the relationship *within* BIAs between elective leaders and paid officials. It is well known that political leaders and bureaucrats have different time horizons, aims, and logics of action. In particular paid officials are not simply passive executors of the directives of elected leaders. Hence, it would be interesting to analyze how, as a result of the institutionalization process, associational bureaucracies have grown and affected the policies of BIAs. Who is the actual leader: the president or the director? How has the mode of recruitment and training of associational officials changed over time? How has their role in shaping associative strategies and policies changed? And how are these changes linked to the transformation of entrepreneurial capitalism into managerial capitalism? Is there a symmetry between organizational change within firms and within associations, or were they autonomous processes?

BIAs are not only major actors in the political system and the industrial relations arena, but also play an important role for businesses in both providing them with services, and guiding them toward specific policies of development. Managerial choices and associational strategies are closely linked, a fact that has often been undervalued in the past. This is a gap that business history has contributed—and can contribute more in the future—to filling.

REFERENCES

ALEMANN, U. VON (1987). *Organisierte Interessen in der Bundesrepublik*. Opladen: Leske und Budrich.

BERGER, S. (ed.) (1981). *Organizing Interests in Western Europe*. Cambridge: Cambridge University Press.

BONNET, E. C. (1922). *Employers' Associations in the United States: Studies of Typical Associations*. New York: Macmillan.

——(1956). *History of Employers' Associations in the United States*. New York: Vantage Press.

BOWMAN, J. R. (1982). "The Logic of Capitalist Collective Action". *Social Science Information*, 21/4–5: 35–88.

——(1985). "The Politics of the Market: Economic Competition and the Organization of Capitalists". *Political Power and Social Theory*, 5: 35–88.

——(1989). *Capitalist Collective Action: Competition, Cooperation and Conflict in the Coal Industry*. Cambridge: Cambridge University Press.

BRAUNTHAL, G. (1965). *The Federation of German Industry in Politics*. Ithaca, NY: Cornell University Press.

BUNN, R. F. (1984). "Employers' Associations in the Federal Republic of Germany", in Windmuller and Gladstone (1984), 232–63.

COCHRAN T. C., and MILLER, W. (1961). *The Age of Enterprise: A Social History of Industrial America*. New York: Harper.

DAVENPORT-HINES, R. P. T. (1988). "Trade Associations and the Modernization Crisis of British Industry", in Yamazaki and Miyamoto (1988), 205–26.

DAVIET, J.-P. (1988). "Trade Associations or Agreements and Controlled Competition in France 1830–1939", in Yamazaki and Miyamoto (1998), 269–95.

EBBINGHAUS, B. (2001), "When Labor and Capital Collude: The Political Economy of Early Retirement in Europe, Japan and the USA", in Ebbinghaus and Manow (2001*a*), 77–101.

——and MANOW, P. (eds.) (2001*a*). *Comparing Welfare Capitalism: Social Policy and Political Economy in Europe, Japan and the USA*. London and New York: Routledge.

————(2001*b*). "Introduction: Studying Varieties of Capitalism", in Ebbinghaus and Manow (2001*a*), 1–24.

EHRMANN, H. W. (1957/1981). *Organized Business in France*. Westport, Conn.: Greenwood Press, 1981; 1st pub. 1957.

ELIASSEN, K., and SVAASAND, L. (1975). "The Formation of Mass Political Organizations: An Analytical Framework". *Scandinavian Political Studies*, 1: 95–120.

FARR, J. R. (2000). *Artisans in Europe, 1300–1914*. Cambridge: Cambridge University Press.

FELDMAN, G. D., and NOCKEN, U. (1975). "Trade Associations and Economic Power: Interest Group Development in the German Iron and Steel and Machine Building Industries 1900–1933". *Business History Review*, 4: 413–45.

GAO, B. (2001). "The State and the Associational Order of the Japanese Economy: The Institutionalization of Cartels and Trade Associations in Japan (1931–1945)". *Sociological Forum*, 16/3: 409–43.

GELLATELY, R. (1974). *The Politics of Economic Despair: Shopkeepers and German Politics 1890–1914*. London: Sage.

GRANT, W., NEKKERS, J., and van WAARDEN, F. (eds.) (1991). *Organising Business for War: Corporatist Economic Organization during the Second World War*. New York and Oxford: Berg.

HALL, P., and SOSKICE, D. (eds.) (2001). *Varieties of Capitalism: The Institutional Foundations of Comparative Advantage*. Oxford: Oxford University Press.

HARRIS, H. (1982). *The Right to Manage: Industrial Relations Policies of American Business in the 1940s*. Madison: University of Wisconsin Press.

JACKSON, P., and SISSON, K. (1981). "Employers' Confederations in Sweden and the U.K. and the Significance of Industrial Infrastructure". *British Journal of Industrial Relations*, 14/3: 306–23.

KAPLAN, S. L., and MINARD, P. (eds.) (2004). *La France, malade du corporatisme?* Paris: Belin.

KIESER, A. (1989). "Organizational, Institutional, and Societal Evolution: Medieval Crafts Guild and the Genesis of Formal Organizations". *Administrative Science Quarterly*, 34: 540–64.

KIKKAWA, T. (1988). "Functions of Japanese Trade Associations before World War II: The Case of Cartel Organizations", in Yamazaki and Miyamoto (1988), *Trade Associations in Business History*. Tokyo: University of Tokyo Press, 58–83.

KOCKA, J. (1981). "Class Formation, Interest Association, and Public Policy: The Origins of German White-Collar Class in the Late Nineteenth and Early Twentieth Century", in S. Berger (ed.), *Organizing Interests in Western Europe*. Cambridge: Cambridge University Press, 63–81.

LANZALACO, L. (1990). *Dall'impresa all'associazione*. Milano: FrancoAngeli.

—— (1992). "Coping with Heterogeneity: Peak Associations of Business within and across Western European nations", in J. Greenwood, J. R. Grote, and K. Ronit (eds.), *Organized Interests and the European Community*. London: Sage, 173–205.

—— (1995). "Constructing Political Unity by Combining Organizations: UNICE as a European Peak Associations", in J. Greenwood (ed.), *European Casebook on Business Alliances*. London: Prentice Hall, 259–70.

LA PALOMBARA, JOSEPH (1964). *Interest Groups in Italian Politics*. Princeton, NJ: Princeton University Press.

LEFRANC, G. (1976). *Les organizations patronales en France du passé au present*. Paris: Payot.

LEHMBRUCH, G. (1979). "Liberal Corporatism and Party Government", in P. C. Schmitter and G. Lehmbruch (eds.), *Trends toward Corporatism Intermediation*. London: Sage, 147–83.

LEMERCIER, C. (2003). *Un si discret pouvoir. Aux origines de la chambre de commerce de Paris (1803–1853)*. Paris: La Découverte.

LYNN, L. H., and McKEOWN, T. J. (eds.) (1988). *Organizing Business: Trade Associations in America and Japan*. Washington, DC: American Enterprise Institute.

MARES, I. (2003). *The Politics of Social Risk: Business and Welfare State Development*. New York: Cambridge University Press; Paris: Presses Universitaires de France.

MARTINELLI, A., SCHMITTER, P., and STREECK, W. (1981). "L'organizzazione degli interessi imprenditoriali". *Stato e mercato*, 1/3: 423–45.

MINARD, P. (2004). "Le métier sans institution: les lois d'Allard-Le Chapelier de 1971 et leur impact au début du XIXe siècle", in Kaplan and Minard (2004), 81–95.

MIYAMOTO, M. (1988). "The Development of Business Associations in Prewar Japan", in Yamazaki and Miyamoto (1988), 1–46.

OFFE, C., and WIESENTHAL, H. (1980). "Two Logics of Collective Action: Theoretical Notes on Social Class and Organizational Form". *Political Power and Social Theory*, 1: 67–115.

OLSON, M. (1965). *The Logic of Collective Action: Public Goods and the Theory of Groups.* Cambridge, Mass.: Harvard University Press.

PEDERSEN, S. (1993). *Family, Dependence, and the Origins of the Welfare State: Britain and France, 1914–1945.* New York: Cambridge University Press.

PIERENKEMPER, T. (1988). "Trade Associations in Germany in the Late Nineteenth and Early Twentieth Centuries", in Yamazaki and Miyamoto (1988), 233–61.

SCHMITTER, P. C. (1979). "Still the Century of Corporatism?" in P. C. Schmitter and G. Lehmbruch (eds.), *Trends toward Corporatism Intermediation.* London: Sage, 7–52.

—— and BRAND, D. (1979). "Organizing Capitalists in the United States: The Advantages and Disadvantages of Exceptionalism". Paper presented at the American Political Science Association meetings.

—— and STREECK, W. (1981). "The Organization of Business Interests". Discussion paper, IIM/LMP 1981/13, Berlin, WZB. (Reprinted as *Discussion Paper,* 99/1, Max Planck Institute for the Study of Societies, Cologne.)

———— (eds.) (1985). *Private Interest Government: Beyond Market and State.* London: Sage.

SISSON, K. (1979). "The Organization of Employers' Associations in Five European Countries: Some Comments on their Origins and Development". Paper prepared for the International Institute of Management Workshop on "Employers' Associations as Organizations". Berlin: IMM.

—— (1987). *The Management of Collective Bargaining: An International Comparison.* Oxford and New York: Basil Blackwell.

—— (1991). "Employers and the Structure of Collective Bargaining: Distinguishing Cause and Effect", in Tolliday and Zeitlin (1991*a*), 256–72.

STREECK, W. (1991). "Interest Homogeneity and Organizing Capacity: Two Class Logics of Collective Action?" in Roland Czada and Adrienne Windhoff-Héretier (eds.), *Political Choices: Institutions, Rules, and the Limits of Rationality.* Frankfurt: Campus, 161–98.

—— GROTE, J. VISSER, and SCHNEIDER, V. (2005). *Governing Interests: Business Associations Facing Internationalization.* London: Routledge.

SWENSON, P. A. (2002). *Capitalists against Markets: The Making of Labor Markets and Welfare States in the United States and Sweden.* Oxford and New York: Oxford University Press.

TOLLIDAY, S., and ZEITLIN, J. (eds.) (1991*a*). *The Power to Manage? Employers and Industrial Relations in Comparative-Historical Perspective.* London and New York: Routledge.

———— (1991*b*). "National Models and International Variations in Labor Management and Employer Organization", in S. Tolliday and J. Zeitlin (eds.), *The Power to Manage? Employers and Industrial Relations in Comparative-Historical Perspective.* London and New York: Routledge, 273–343.

Ullmann, H. P. (1988). *Interessenverbände in Deutschland*. Frankfurt am Main: Suhrkamp Verlag.

Weber, H. (1991). "Political Design and System of Interest Intermediation: Germany between the 1930s and the 1950s", in W. Grant, J. Nekkers, and F. van Waarden (eds.), *Organising Business for War: Corporatist Economic Organisation during the Second World War*. New York and Oxford: Berg, 107–34.

Windmuller, J. P. (1984). "A Comparative Analysis of Employers' Associations: Organization, Structure, Administration", in Windmuller and Gladstone (1984), 1–23.

——— and Gladstone, A. (eds.) (1984). *Employers' Associations and Industrial Relations*. Oxford: Clarendon Press.

Yamazaki, H. (1988). "Introduction", in Yamazaki and Miyamoto (1988), pp. ix–xxiii.

——— and Miyamoto, M. (eds.) (1988). *Trade Associations in Business History*. Tokyo: University of Tokyo Press.

Zeitlin, J. (1991). "The Internal Politics of Employer Organization: The Engineering Employers' Federation 1896–1939", in Tolliday and Zeitlin (1991*a*), 52–80.

PART III

FUNCTIONS OF ENTERPRISE

CHAPTER 14

BANKING AND
FINANCE

MICHEL LESCURE

14.1 INTRODUCTION

THIS chapter examines the contributions of business historians to the analysis of comparative financial systems. Beginning with the responses of historical research to questions raised by economists, it then goes on to highlight new questions raised by the work of business historians themselves. After a short presentation of the debates among economists (Section 14.2), five topics will be discussed in an historical perspective: the role of firms' self-financing (Section 14.3), the role of external finance and the structure of its components (Section 14.4), the systemic character of cross-national variations (Section 14.5), the historical origins of national financial systems (Section 14.6), and the consequences of these differences for economic performances (Section 14.7). A short concluding section considers the problem of convergence.

14.2 ECONOMISTS' QUESTIONS

Four main questions are debated among economists about banking and finance: does finance affect economic growth? Do financial systems differ from each other? What are the reasons for these differences? What are their consequences?

Concerning the first question, economists have recently reappraised their assessment. Whereas, following Joan Robinson's views, most economists (Schumpeter excepted) have long considered financial structures as passive factors, they tend now to believe that financial development does in fact affect the development of the real economy. This shift was initiated by historians interested in the economic development of continental Europe and Japan (Cameron 1967; Gerschenkron 1962). But thereafter the paths followed by historians and economists diverged. Even though many recent historical works are sympathetic to the supply-side thesis that finance leads economic development (Sylla 1998), debates on the origins of the industrial revolution or on the decline of leading nations show that this question has not yet found a clear solution among historians. During the same period, the finance-led growth school has become increasingly influential in the economics literature.

Since the seminal work by Goldsmith (1969) first established a positive correlation between economic development and financial wealth or growth, important progress has been recorded in this field. Rigorous theoretical works have highlighted some of the channels through which the emergence of financial systems affects economic growth. The contribution of financial contracts, markets, and institutions to reducing transaction and financial costs has been broken down into a series of more basic functions (diversifying and pooling risk, producing information about possible investments and allocating resources, monitoring firms and exercising corporate control, mobilizing savings, facilitating the exchange of goods and services), each of whose influence on economic growth has been analyzed (Levine 1997). In addition, a growing body of empirical studies has investigated the problem of causality more deeply. Most of these works clearly demonstrate that efficient financial systems facilitate long-run economic growth (Rajan and Zingales 1996).

The existence or not of different kinds of financial systems is the second subject of debate. Corporate finance patterns and the structure of the financial sector vary across countries. The very nature of the financial intermediaries also differs: specialized banks are restricted either to deposit and lending activities (deposit or commercial banks) or to underwriting activities, securities trading, fund management, merger and take-over advice (investment banks); universal banks, by contrast, combine the business activities of commercial and investment banks. In addition some universal banks (ordinary universal banks) engage in commercial and investment banking but do not exercise control over non-banks while some others (privileged ones) add to these activities the exercise of non-default control over non-banks through a closer formalized relationship such as equity holding, proxy voting, and board representation. Are these differences systematic? For the period from 1950 to 1980, an abundant literature describes financial systems as either bank-based, universal, and relational or as market-based, specialized, and arm's length. Germany and Japan head up the first group, while the United States and UK head up the second. Is this classification suitable for other countries? For a number of scholars, the answer is negative. Using net flow-of-funds data instead of balance-sheet data,

Table 14.1 Financing patterns and financial systems around 1990

Country	Debt/equity (1980–1991)	Structure aggregate	Type of Bank
Switzerland	1.75	1.58	UB
USA	1.79	1.34	SB
UK	1.48	1.24	SB
Japan	3.69	0.86	SB
Canada	1.6	0.82	
Sweden	5.5	0.8	UB
Netherlands	2.16	0.33	UB
Germany	2.7	0.17	UB
Denmark		0.17	UB
Belgium	2.02	−0.17	UB
France	3.6	−0.17	UB
Norway	5.37	−0.23	SB
Spain	2.75	−0.31	UB
Italy	3.07	−0.55	UB
Grece		−0.66	UB
Finland	4.9	−0.76	UB
Austria	2.7	−1.27	UB

Notes: Col. 1 gives the ratio of total debt/total equity (source: Demirgücs-Kunt and Maksimovic 1996). Structure aggregate (col. 2) measures the size, activity, and efficiency of stock markets relative to banks (Levine 2002); the higher the ratio, the more market-oriented the financial system. UB and SB (col. 3) designate the predominance of universal banks and specialized banks during the 1990s (Fohlin 2000).

Colin Mayer, for instance, concludes that self-financing is dominant everywhere, that financing patterns do not differ very much between countries, and that those differences which can be observed are inconsistent with the classical distinction between bank-based and market-based systems (Mayer 1988).

In fact the most plausible hypothesis is that, even though the distinction between the two systems is overstylized and oversimplified, firms' financing patterns do really differ and these differences are not unrelated to those observed in national financial systems. This is evident when the financing pattern is measured through gross financial flows or through debt-equity ratios of domestic corporations (Table 14.1). While according to the revisionist account, Germany, for instance, has the lowest leverage among the G-7 countries (along with the UK), on these measures, it clearly has a higher debt-equity ratio than the United States. Because of their dependence on bank finance, German firms figure among the most highly leveraged in the developed world; in spite of the role of bonds in their finance, US corporations, which rely more heavily on self-financing and equity issues, display the opposite pattern. More generally, where capital markets dominate the financial system, firms' debt-equity ratio is low (as in the Anglo-Saxon countries); where bank lending prevails the debt-equity ratio is high (as in Continental Europe). Thus, with the exception of Japan, we can conclude that the distinction between US-style market-based finance and the German-style bank-based pattern is not "inaccurate" (Hacketal and Schmidt 2004).

These differences are also consistent with the prevailing pattern of banking organization. Table 14.1 validates for 1990 the identification of universality with bank domination and specialization with market domination. The reason for this association may be that specialized banks and financial markets are unlikely to develop where universal banks prevail. Since the information acquired in the credit and deposit business is of significant value to the investment business and vice versa, universal banks enjoy important information economies of scope that lead to the crowding out of the other kinds of banks. Without the support of investment banks, financial markets are unable to develop. Financial markets will also be affected by the growing tendency for universal banks to concentrate their business on lending; not only is this activity more profitable than the provision of underwriting services, but it also generates a stream of information rents, while the information generated by underwriting business is often firm-specific and loses its value after each transaction (Dietl 1998).

In this schema, Japan is a special case since it benefits from both a well-developed financial market and a strong banking sector. The key explanatory factor is the very specific organization of its banking sector. For historical reasons, universal banks did not develop in Japan during the second half of the twentieth century. Although Japanese commercial and trust banks did not engage in investment banking activities, they did massively acquire minority equity stakes in non-banks. On the one hand, the separation of commercial and investment banking allowed the growth of an important investment banking sector and a well-developed equity market. On the other hand, banks' holding of company shares opened the door to profitable long-term investment and governance relationships with non-financial firms (Dietl 1998). Thus even though institutions and systems are often difficult to categorize crisply, strong connections can nonetheless be identified between firms' financing patterns, the predominance of financial markets versus bank lending, and the organization of the banking sector itself.

The explanation for these differences constitutes the third major area of debate. Many monocausal hypotheses have been suggested. Given the current obvious role of state policies, a number of scholars consider that the driving force behind them is the role of incumbent interest groups. Thus, for Mark Roe, it is the relative strength of political support for stakeholders that determines the respective importance of banks and markets. In Rajan and Zingales' account (2001) the incumbent interests (the landed gentry in the nineteenth century, industrialists and financiers in the mid-twentieth century) oppose financial development because it aids the entry of new classes or new firms. An increasingly influential stream of research contends that legal factors above all influence the present shape of financial systems. For La Porta *et al.* (1998), the legal rules governing protection of corporate shareholders and creditors explain the organization of financial systems. The basic idea is that securities are not only defined by their cash flows as in the traditional finance model of Modigliani–Miller, but are also defined by the rights they confer on their owners. Where the legal rules protecting investors and the quality of their enforcement are strong (i.e. in common law countries), financial markets are likely to develop; where the legal system is weak (i.e. in civil law countries), powerful financial institutions are needed to force firms to reveal information and to repay their debts. In a closely related approach, Helmut Dietl (1998) distinguishes between the highly stylized poles of neoclassical (US) versus relational (Germany) regulation. Neoclassical regulation is based on the theoretical assumption that perfect markets efficiently allocate capital and is driven by the objective of eliminating market imperfections (such as ownership concentration, insider trading, market manipulations, etc.). Relational regulation focuses primarily on governance efficiency rather than allocative efficiency and is based on the idea that most neoclassical market imperfections far from being harmful should be considered as a means of economizing on governance costs. In this perspective, Japan is a "hybrid" model, with both relational elements (going back to the Meiji era), and neoclassical elements (introduced after World War II), which may account for both the size of its financial markets and the development of its banking system.

The relationship between financial structure and economic performance is the fourth area of debate among economists, which focuses mainly on the relative merits of bank-based versus market-based financial systems. Several competing theses have been advanced (Levine 2002). The bank-based view emphasizes the advantages of such systems in mobilizing savings, identifying good investment projects, and exerting corporate control. In contrast, the market-based view holds that such systems are better for promoting long-run economic growth because markets do a better job than banks at allocating capital and providing "key financial services that stimulate innovation". In addition, the former thesis stresses the shortcomings of market-oriented systems and the myopic investor climate generated by liquid markets, while the latter suggests that banks can inhibit innovation (by extracting internal informational rents and protecting established firms) and impede efficient corporate governance. National economic growth patterns around 1990 allow no clear conclusion, since the best economic performances can be associated with each financial system. A third thesis, which may be termed the financial services view, minimizes the relevance of the previous debate, by emphasizing the quality of services produced by the entire financial system. A fourth thesis contends that the relative merits of each financial system vary according to the context in which it operates. Since banks and markets do not always provide the same kind of services, the relative position of each type of financial institution depends on its ability to adapt to the environment. For a number of scholars, banks outperform markets at low levels of economic development or when the financial sector is underdeveloped, while countries would benefit from finance becoming more market-based at higher levels of wealth. According to Dietl (1998), "neoclassical capital markets are an efficient form of allocating scarce capital within immature industries" (those which need common and scattered knowledge), while relational financial systems based on universal banking would "efficiently allocate scarce capital within mature industries" (those which need common and insider knowledge).

What is the contribution of business history to these debates?

14.3 SELF-FINANCING

Since the early observations by Gurley and Shaw (1955) and Goldsmith (1969), it is usual to consider that with economic development traditional sources of finance (self-financing, trade credit, credits from family, goldsmiths, scriveners, and attorneys) tend to give way first to bank-intermediated debt finance (by commercial banks, then by specialized financial institutions) and later to the emergence of equity markets as additional intruments for raising funds. In this perspective, self-financing has long been considered as a residual source (what firms can use when other sources of finance are lacking), which leads to a misallocation of capital. Self-financing is supposed to characterize situations with poorly functioning financial systems (the early stage of industrialization or periods of economic crisis) and it is expected to diminish once the development of efficient financial institutions and markets enables firms to finance their investments from external sources. New developments in microeconomic theory since the 1980s have modified this point of view. Given market imperfections (resulting in high transaction costs), self-financing is now seen as one among a series of alternative methods, the choice between which depends on a comparison of their total costs and benefits. This perspective invites us to consider self-financing as a permanent source of finance for firms, as well as to evaluate its relative efficiency (Hautcoeur 1999).

This point of view is supported by historical evidence. A diachronic approach shows that in all developed countries at any given time self-financing from retained earnings has been the main source of finance for firms. This was true for early industrializing countries during the initial stage of their development: in Britain, for instance, easy and relatively cheap entry to manufacturing production, coupled with its high profitability, allowed innovative entrepreneurs to finance the first steps of their growth from internal sources of capital. This remained the rule both in those countries that industrialized later without enduring acute conditions of economic backwardness (continental Europe and North America) and for the later stages of development in the early industrializers. A diachronic approach also shows that there were wide cyclical variations in self-financing. These variations reflect either shifts in business income (such as the contraction of gross profits in interwar Britain, aggravated by the rising level of taxation) or the intensity of the investment cycle and the ensuing gap between the level of investment and firms' savings rate. In the United States, for example, during the conglomerate movement of the 1960s and 1970s, financing shifted from cash to stock and then to debt. Firms' saving rates themselves vary according to their productivity and according to the distribution of value-added between different stakeholders. If shareholders long tolerated high rates of self-financing, this has no longer been true in many developed countries since the last decade of the twentieth century. In the United States, for instance, the replacement of organizational by market control that occurred in the 1980s resulted in an increased level of payouts to shareholders of non-financial corporations (Lazonick and O'Sullivan 1997).

Whether the rate of self-financing is declining in the long run is more difficult to assess. High-quality, consistent quantitative data on self-financing are unavailable for the period before World War II. The availability of homogenous macroeconomic data does not allow us to give a correct account of its evolution. In France, for instance, the rate of self-financing declined from the early twentieth century, and in spite of a sharp revival in the 1930s and 1940s, it fell again from 1950 to 1980. Does this evolution reflect a sound tendency imputable to the diversification of financing sources, or is it rather the consequence of the shifting structure of the economy (such as the rise of sectors with massive external capital requirements) or of the changing social organization of the corporate sector (such as the development of state-owned firms with low levels of profitability and unlimited ability to borrow)? What is widely agreed is that during the last decades of the twentieth century internal financing remained the dominant source of finance in all developed countries (based mainly on depreciation and capital transfers rather than retained earnings) so that it is difficult to consider it as a residual factor.

But a synchronic approach shows that, even when we exclude the case of emerging countries where self-financing is less developed, a wide diversity of situations can be observed. During the period from 1960 to 1985, three groups of countries can be distinguished. In the first group, which includes countries with high rates of investment (United States) as well as some with lower rates (UK), self-financing is very high (equal to or higher than 100% as a percentage of fixed investment). The second group including Japan, Italy, and France is characterized by low rates of self-financing. In the third group positions are less stable. In Germany, for instance, the immediate postwar years were marked by exceptionally high rates of self-financing, compared to the pre-war era; in the succeeding period (mid-1950s–late 1960s), the strength of investment, coupled with a contraction of profits resulting from a sharp increase in wages, resulted in a decline of self-financing. Conversely, the years 1970–5 saw a revival of these rates which left German firms among the most self-financed in the world (Straus 1988).

14.4 EXTERNAL FINANCE AND THE ORGANIZATION OF FINANCIAL INTERMEDIARIES

External finance constitutes the symmetrical counterpart to self-financing. Its composition gives rise to multiple axes of differentiation among financial systems. The first is the respective share of financial markets and intermediaries. During the years 1950 to 1980 this axis matches up relatively well with the previous one: countries where firms resort more to financial markets than to intermediaries are those where rates of self-financing are high (United States, UK) while those which resort more to intermediation than to markets are those where the share of external finance is high (Japan, France, Italy). These parallels can be explained by the fact that the creation of banks active in the field of industrial finance, which is the answer to the lack of efficient financial markets, made firms less reluctant to link the level of their investment to that of their earnings.

Although these differences among countries were already visible at the beginning of the twentieth century, the two sources of external finance have evolved in parallel. Both markets and financial intermediaries expanded rapidly from 1850 to 1913–29. However this growth ended in the interwar period. During the "great reversal" of 1930–70 (Rajan and Zingales 2001) the ratio of financial activity to GDP decreased sharply in all developed countries. For financial intermediaries, it reached its trough around 1950 in most countries of Continental Europe and Japan, around 1980 in the United States, UK, and the Netherlands. In several countries of the first group (France, Japan) the ensuing jump recorded in the activity of financial intermediaries was driven by the development of an "overdraft economy" around the years 1950–80 (Aoki *et al.* 1994; Straus 1988). However, by 1999, in many countries (Austria, Germany, Switzerland, Anglo-Saxon countries) financial intermediaries exhibited lower levels of activity than in the interwar period. After the "great reversal", which they too experienced, financial markets recorded a slight recovery around 1960, but difficulties recurred so that it was not until the years 1980–2000 that these markets really boomed, exceeding the level of 1913–38 everywhere. Under the assumption that this evolution reflects the pattern of corporate financing, it is consistent with the general account of financial development as moving first to financial intermediaries and second to financial markets. But this evolution appears to be both recent and somewhat chaotic, not linear and ineluctable.

The internal composition of financial markets and financial intermediaries introduces further axes of differentiation. In spite of their early development in several countries (Netherlands, UK, France), financial markets long played no significant role in the financing pattern of firms. Until 1914, most securities quoted on the stock exchanges were bonds issued by states and railway companies; in 1913, bonds and stocks issued by urban utilities, mines, and industrial or commercial companies represented less than 20 percent of the securities traded on the London Stock Exchange (LSE), the largest and most international market (Michie 1999).

However the years 1880 to 1930 saw the take-off of several financial markets. The emergence of new industries, coupled with the transformation of family firms into public companies and the proliferation of mergers in developed countries, brought about a sharp increase in equity issues that reached its apogee in the 1920s. In addition, turn-of-the-century decades witnessed several financial innovations (lower denominated securities, issuance of preference shares and bonds) designed to spread the use of all kind of securities. No later than 1880–1914 these innovations allowed British manufacturing firms to diversify their sources of finance and to move away from reliance on equity to debenture capital, which increased their gearing ratio (Watson 1999), though preference capital also grew rapidly and equity remained the most important item in the capital structure of firms. The true role played by stock markets varied from one place to another: while the LSE was used to finance investments in new assets, the New York stock exchange was used mainly to transfer ownership of existing assets.

The "great reversal" stopped the switch from a market based largely on public securities to a more privately based market, but this shift recurred in the second half of the twentieth century. The stock market boom of the final decades of the century was supported by various changes among participants; in the UK, for instance, institutional investors started to participate in the market for corporate control from the late 1950s. The diffusion of stock ownership differed among countries: while in the United States the fragmention of ownership among domestic house-holds prevailed by 1990, in Germany and in Japan more concentrated ownership (dominated by non-financial enterprises in the first case, by financial institutions in the second) accounted for nearly one-third of total shareholdings. In spite of these developments, the role of new equity issues in firms' financing pattern should not be overestimated. Even in the United States, new equities represent only a small part of non-financial firms' financing (less than 10% of their gross finance between 1970 and 1990). The role of the stock market today is still less finance of corporate investment than liquidity creation; it is this liquidity that allows short-term savings to be transformed into long-term commitments and enables the capital market to play a significant role in corporate control.

The proportion of bonds in the financing pattern of firms also varies consistently among countries. From the 1950s onwards, bonds were important only in a small number of countries (as in the United States where their share in corporate finance exceeds that of stocks). This is not to say that bond markets are underdeveloped elsewhere; in developed countries the ratio of the nominal value of outstanding bonds to GDP usually exceeds that of market capitalization; but the bond markets either remain state-oriented as in Japan or are dominated by financial institutions as in Germany (where non-financial enterprises do not directly access primary debt markets). Because the US bond market combines an intermediate level of state finance with a low level of finance by financial institutions, it is more oriented towards private non-financial enterprises (Dietl 1998).

The type of financial intermediary generates a number of axes of differentiation. The first is the distinction between public or semi-public banks and commercial banks.

In most countries, public banks coexist with commercial intermediaries but not in a similar proportion. Public banks include two kinds of institutions: special government banks such as mortgage institutions or industrial banks, designed to serve specific sectors; local non-profit institutions (saving and cooperative banks) designed to serve special classes of customers (small firms, craftmen) and to collect savings neglected by commercial banks. The first group has played an important part in certain phases of financial history, especially during periods of financial distress: in Japan, for instance, the Industrial Bank of Japan (1902) was mobilized to support the stock exchanges of Tokyo and Osaka (1916), to provide assistance to a wide range of troubled industries, and to finance firms engaged in foreign investment (1918) and military production (1941) (Lazonick and O'Sullivan 1997). In France, the public institutions that channeled funds (Crédit Foncier de France, Crédit Agricole, Crédit National) have shaped the financial system in an original segmentation pattern where each institution was designed to provide privileged credits to a specific sector of the economy (Baubeau 2003).

Since the mid-nineteenth century, non-profit local financial institutions played a particularly important role in those continental European countries where

Table 14.2 Banking systems and thrift institutions (% of total assets)

Country	1913		1938		1963	
	Banking system	Thrift institutions	Banking system	Thrift institutions	Banking system	Thrift institutions
USA	81.34	18.66	81.94	18.06	69.29	30.71
UK	83.43	16.57	81.41	18.59	82.04	17.96
Germany	52.27	47.73	46.68	53.32	44.18	55.82
France	63.31	36.69	56.50	43.50	58.93	41.07
Italy	48.57	51.43	43.23	56.77	47.30	52.70
Belgium	64.00	36.00	64.03	35.97	65.87	34.13
Switzerland			90.05	9.95	91.65	8.35
Japan			74.79	25.21	67.63	32.37

Note: Thrift institutions include savings banks (private and public) and cooperative banks. In Switzerland, cantonal banks are included in the banking system. Data concerning private and public specialized credit institutions (such as mortgage banks, building societies, investment companies, insurance companies, and pension funds) are not included.
Source: Goldsmith (1969).

intermediaries dominated the financial system (Germany, Italy) (see Table 14.2). In fact it is these banks, not the large private universal banks in these countries, that explain why the financial system is dominated by intermediaries. The reasons why non-profit institutions dominated the banking sector are various. In most continental Europe countries, savings banks had been launched before commercial banks so that they benefited from a first-mover advantage. In some other regions (like Catalonia), savings banks developed in response to the difficulties encountered by commercial banks (Sudria 2006). Everywhere the basic reasons were the support of the state and local authorities, the commitment of these banks to local economies, and in some cases (like Germany) the development of cooperative associations (Conti and Ferri 2004; Hardach 2004). The support of the state and local authorities was originally motivated by the goals of poverty relief (savings banks) and protection of artisans and small firms from unrestricted competition and proletarization (cooperative banks). Their effective role varied. If rural cooperatives for instance were an efficient answer to information asymmetry in the socio-economic environment of nineteenth-century Germany, they fared less well in different contexts like Ireland and southern Italy (Guinnane 1994). More generally Germany, where savings and cooperative banks operated more and more as universal banks, is a model of their good functioning. France is an opposite example since the savings collected by the savings banks have long been captured by the state for unproductive purposes, while cooperative banks after a long period of stagnation until the 1930s experienced a rapid development but to the exclusive advantage of the agricultural sector and at the expense of commercial banking (Gueslin and Lescure 1995).

Even limiting the scope of analysis to commercial banks, many axes of differentiation can be observed. The first opposes banks operating in domestic markets to those operating abroad. The development of multinational banking occurred in two historical waves (Jones 1993). The nineteenth-century wave was led by British banks, followed in steps by some other western banks (especially French, German, and Belgian). While in continental Europe foreign branches were founded by pre-existing domestic banks, British overseas banks (like the Hong Kong and Shanghai Banking Corporation) were launched first by merchant houses conducting no domestic banking; overseas banks were designed to facilitate the financing of the international business of their founders through foreign exchange and acceptance services. Except during the years 1850 to 1870, when a lot of Anglo-European banks came (ephemerally) into being, the large domestic clearing banks stood aside from overseas branching. It is not until 1911 that they actively joined this movement, and with unequal results (successful in South Africa, for instance, but not in continental Europe). Multinational banking formed a part of the large European multinational investment wave of that period; it emerged separately from more traditional international banking (i.e. foreign trade finance and cross-border lending) mainly carried out by merchant bankers (such as Rothschild or Baring in London). Although the role of multinational banks in the conduct of international investment was very important, it "was relatively much greater in short-term trade finance and in foreign portfolio investment of a passive nature than in the active entrepreneurial financing of industry accross national borders" (Cameron and Bovykin 1991). Banks' role in the economy to which capital was channeled (40% in the Western Hemisphere) varied according to their own geographical origin, the host economy's stage of development (colonial empire, developing countries, and sometimes developed countries), and the opportunities offered by the latter. As Fishlow (1985) suggests, it may be that the efficacy of the investments was greater in "developmental borrowers" (the United States, Japan, Scandinavia, British dominions) than in "revenue borrowers" (Russia, Ottoman Empire). Foreign banks' influence on the shaping of national banking systems was particularly strong in those countries where the requirements for the development of banking were lacking (Brazil, China, Middle East) (Cameron and Bovykin 1991).

Following a phase of stabilization during the interwar period, the expansion of multinational banking revived after World War II. This second wave was now led by American banks (in the 1960s and 1970s) and Japanese banks (in the 1980s). By creating foreign branches, US banks initially intended to accompany the growth of American multinational firms in Europe, but they rapidly extended the scope of their operations to local customers and other businesses. They were pushed in this direction by the tight regulation of financial activity in the United States. By tapping the Eurodollar and Eurobond markets, they could alleviate the short-term financing problems generated by US monetary policy and escape prohibitions on universal banking of the 1934 Glass–Steagall Act (Sylla 2002). The greater openness of British policy to internationl finance, coupled with the knowledge advantage of the City in international financial services, explains why London, after a half century of relative decline, reasserted its pre-1913 leadership.

We can also distinguish the domestic behavior of commercial banks along a number of dimensions. At an early stage of banking development, the scarcity of information obliged banks to operate within narrow networks. This led to the creation of two kinds of banks: banks founded by industrialists based on the principle of "insider lending" (with bank directors as their main borrowers), as in antebellum New England (Lamoreaux 1994), and those created by credit professionals and designed to finance bank outsiders, as in England and Wales (Newton 2001). At a subsequent stage of development, legal and organizational axes of differentiation became increasingly crucial. These oppose first unincorporated credit houses and private bankers (such as the Rothschilds in Europe) to new joint-stock banks working with a higher proportion of external resources and operating under limited liability, such as the National Provincial Bank of England (1833), the Crédit Suisse (1856), the Crédit Lyonnais (1863), or the Deutsche Bank (1870). The main difference between the two groups was less qualitative in nature (most of the techniques used by the new banks were well known by the older ones and in continental Europe several joint-stock banks were founded by private bankers) than quantitative and organizational (Lévy-Leboyer 1976). It was reflected in the growing activity of the new banks and the constitution of the first managerial hierarchies.

A second axis of differentiation opposes unit banks and branch networks. These two types of banks coexist in many countries but the evidence is that while the creation of national branch networks prevailed almost everywhere by 1913, a small group of countries including Portugal, Denmark, Norway, and the United States had failed to develop them. This division appeared during the last third of the nineteenth century when, following the British example, new joint-stock banks in continental Europe extended their branch networks. This extension, which went "hand-in-hand" with the take-off of their deposit business, was the answer to both the increased benefits of scale in finance and the need for bank diversification revealed by the widespread financial crises of the period (Fohlin 2000). In the post-World War II era, only the United States maintained its unit banking system in many parts of the country. At the end of the twentieth century branch banking systems prevail everywhere.

A third axis of differentiation opposes specialized and universal banks. The fact that where one type of bank prevails the other can play only a limited role allows us to extend this distinction between banks to a distinction between banking systems. Universality was the predominant form of banking organization during the nineteenth century in both developed and developing countries. At the beginning of the nineteenth century, many private unit banks operated as universal banks, and many new joint-stock banks launched subsequently, whether they were unit banks or not, followed this model. The first experiences of modern universal banking took place in Belgium and in France (Société Générale de Belgique, Crédit Mobilier), but the main successful universal banking laboratories were Germany, Switzerland, and Austria. From these laboratories, universal banking spread over most parts of the world during the nineteenth century including continental Europe, parts of Latin America, and to a lesser extent even New Zealand, Australia, and the United States. In the latter country, a number of banks as in New England had moved from a universal (insider lending) pattern to a specialized one, but others such as the National City Bank of New York had followed the opposite path. By 1913 the most eminent exception to universal banking was the UK.

Most universal banks were in fact ordinary banks. In continental Europe, privileged universal banks only flourished at two moments: first, during the period from 1840 to 1870, when railroadization, coupled with the growing incorporation of companies, multiplied the opportunities for more intimate connections between industrial firms and Crédit Mobilier-type banks; and second, at the turn of the twentieth century, when the start of the second industrialization allowed German-type universal banks to accompany the growth of public utilities and new industrial sectors. But few countries were concerned by these connections (Germany, Austria,

Belgium, France, Italy) and even there, direct equity stakes and board representation were limited to a small proportion of firms. It must be added that if German universal banks wielded greater control than British banks over firms they financed, it was more through proxy voting and supervisory board positions than equity stakes; German banks did not take greater long-term equity stakes than British ones (Fohlin 2000).

In spite of some shifts in the opposite direction (such as Paribas in France), universal banking declined in the ensuing period (1913–50). Some European banks, like the Crédit Lyonnais, had started to move in this direction during the great depression of the late nineteenth century. The disappointing economic circumstances of the interwar period increased the number of banks moving towards specialization (Belgium, Italy, Greece, the United States, Japan). However this shift lasted only a few decades and the second half of the century witnessed a renewal of universal banking; "by the 1990s, most systems had reverted to something ressembling their pre-World War I state" (Fohlin 2000). Even the UK moved away from its steadfastly specialized system. By putting financial institutions of different types under the control of a bank holding company, the movement of concentration and conglomeration that has occurred in most developed countries since the 1970s created quasi-universal banking everywhere.

A final axis of differentiation arises from the way commercial banks matched the two sides of their balance sheet. If this axis is closely linked with the two previous ones, it is not an automatic consequence of them. At the outbreak of World War I, continental European banks operated with more own capital liabilities relative to deposits than those of the English-speaking world (Table 14.3). Although the gap began to diminish at the end of the nineteenth century, it was still visible in 1913. This enabled or forced the former to keep a smaller proportion of their assets in cash or money on call and to lend out a higher proportion of their funds. On this view, continental European banks can be called low-geared in terms of the ratio of deposits to own capital and high-geared in terms of the ratio of loans and investments to cash; the opposite pattern emerges for banks in the English-speaking world (Michie 2003). But if the lending policy followed by each type of bank reflects the nature of the funds on which it relies, the correspondance is not total so that liquidity differs across countries. Continental European banks maintain lower liquidity positions than their counterparts in English-speaking countries; this is consistent with the presence or absence of a dependable lender of last resort (Feiertag and Margairaz 2003). The example of the German and British banks suggests however that these differences should not be overestimated; using short-term coverage ratios rather than cash-deposit or cash-liabilities ratios, Fohlin (2001) finds that German banks were more "conservative" since they covered short-term liabilities with short-term or liquid assets at higher rates than British banks throughout the years 1883–1913, while the policy of the Reichsbank allowed them to reduce this ratio.

Table 14.3 Banking ratios of commercial banks (1913–14)

	Gearing		Liquidity	
	Deposits/capital	Loans+invts/cash	Deposits/cash	Loans+invts/capital
Austria	3.31	40.17	31.33	4.25
Denmark	3.30	32.93	26.03	4.17
Finland	4.55	39.42	33.54	5.34
France	4.46	11.79	10.43	5.04
Germany	3.17	21.32	16.98	3.97
Hungary	5.32	56.71	48.82	6.18
Italy	3.48	16.85	13.91	4.21
Netherlands	2.34	23.68	17.13	3.23
Norway	5.45	51.05	44.47	6.26
Sweden	3.13	35.89	28.07	4.00
Switzerland	4.99	64.93	55.53	5.83
UK-E/W	10.71	2.99	3.71	8.62
Canada	5.73	5.24	5.40	5.56
USA	5.06	6.21	6.04	5.21
Argentina	2.56	2.94	2.87	2.62
South Africa	6.19	5.36	5.63	5.90
Australia/NZ	5.13	2.39	2.93	4.19

Source: Michie (2003).

14.5 FROM THE FINANCING PATTERN OF FIRMS TO NATIONAL FINANCIAL SYSTEMS

Do these different sources of finance create distinct national financial systems as they appeared to do between 1950 and 1980? An answer is difficult to provide because of the lack of data concerning firms' financing patterns and the low quality of data concerning the structure of the financial sector in each country.

Let us first consider the structure of the financial sector. For Rajan and Zingales (2001), who collected data on the financial sector going back to 1913, the distinction between continental European and Anglo-American countries does not hold for the nineteenth century. In 1913 the market capitalization of firms in Belgium, Austria, and France was close to that of the UK and far ahead of the United States; the distinction between the two groups of countries would thus be a post-World War II phenomenon. However this conclusion is in line neither with the strong opposition visible in 1913 between continental Europe and Anglo-American countries in terms of the level of banking development, as measured by Rajan and Zingales themselves, nor with the data collected by Goldsmith (1985): when measured as a proportion of financial assets, the market value of US and British stocks is double that observed in most European countries. The share of financial institutions in total financial assets shows the reverse position, so that it is a legitimate assumption that banks played a more important part in continental Europe and in Japan than they did in the United States and UK. "The conclusion from this evidence is that there (are) long-standing and fundamental differences between the financial systems in place in different countries" (Michie 2003).

Second, if we look at the banking system, we observe that in spite of considerable changes, such as in the level of concentration (Pohl *et al.* 2001), the prevailing pattern of universality versus specialization was in 1913 exactly the same as in 1990. In spite of the major shifts that occurred during the "great reversal", all banking systems had reverted to their original path.

But, third, the connection between the two previous factors seems to be less strong before World War I than in the 1980s. In 1913, the rule that identifies universality with bank domination and specialization with market domination suffers from some exceptions. In many countries (Belgium, Germany, Austria, and even in France where the process of bank specialization was not completed) large universal banks are associated with active capital markets. This undermines the alleged identification of universality with bank domination. The association between universal banking and financial market maturity can be explained by the fact that, at a certain stage of development, as during the years 1850 to 1913, financial intermediaries and markets are complementary rather than competitive with one another. On the one hand, markets add a dimension that banks are not able to provide (as in the financing of railways). On the other hand, the role of the securities markets is not confined to raising capital. The fact that securities were easily transferable made them money-market instruments so that they became an essential component of the global financial system. They were used by the banks themselves. Where banks were highly geared in term of deposits (UK, United States), banks were attracted to the securities markets, since they obtained a return and maintained liquidity; in addition they provided loans to money-market participants. Where banks were less highly geared (Germany, Japan), banks had a vested interest in building up a market for the securities that they received as collateral from their customers (Michie 2003). The financial crises of the middle decades of the nineteenth century highlight the advantages that banks could draw from the existence of well-developed financial markets.

More precise assessments of the existence of distinct national financial systems require us to broaden the scope of analysis. At the first level of the financial systems, local and fragmented markets have long captured a predominant share of the total business. During the eighteenth century, France's lending system was organized around notaries, not around banks and public markets as in other countries (Hoffmann *et al.* 2001); although this system was declining after the Revolution it remained very active, especially in periods of financial difficulties. Taking local banks into account also reveals unexpected segmentations. While in

Britain the disappearance of local banks resulted in a functional segmentation of the banking system between large specialized banks, and in Germany or Italy the segmentation was between large universal for-profit banks and non-profit local universal institutions, in France by 1913 the segmentation was between large for-profit banks on the path to specialization (the British model) and local universal banks (the German model) belonging (in contrast with Germany) to the for-profit sector (Lescure and Plessis 1999). The role of trade credit is another *terra incognita*. Yet, in some countries as in France, this still represented a major component of the firms' financing pattern, related in this case to the important part played by bill discounting services (Plessis 2002).

At the upper level of the financial system, the role of the state as a direct or indirect source of finance should be more deeply scrutinized especially for the central period of the twentieth century when other sources were lacking. In 1949, the state financed 60 percent of the gross formation of fixed capital in France, compared with 50 percent in Belgium, 40 percent in Italy, and 30 percent in the UK. Even after the withdrawal of direct financing, the French state effectively controlled 50 percent of the financing of investments between 1948 and 1965 through the "Treasury circuit", credit policy, and banking regulation (Quennouëlle-Corre 2005). This unorthodox system was the consequence of a political consensus that a strong intervention of the state was needed to assure the country's modernization (Margairaz 1991).

14.6 Determinants of Variations in National Financial Systems

Previous analyses show how inappropriate are some of the monocausal explanations currently proposed to account for cross-national differences in financial systems. Why for instance in 1913, with similar levels of wealth, did certain civil law countries like Belgium and France have better-developed financial markets than some common-law ones like the United States? Obviously the low quality of legal protection provided to small shareholders in the former did not prevent financial markets from developing. Why did countries like the United States and UK with the same legal tradition and well-developed financial markets have such different banking systems during the second half of the twentieth century? Financial history suggests the influence of a lot of other determining factors.

Some of these are historical in nature and emphasize either the conditions of economic development or of state formation. According to Gerschenkron (1962) it was the relative backwardness of those countries which developed after the UK that called universal banks into existence as compensatory institutions. Not only did these countries need to base their development on more capital-intensive technologies than early-industrialized nations, but they also had to compensate for the scarcity of capital, the unreliability of information, and the weakness of entreneurship. In this unfavourable environment, the role of universal banks was to channel resources into industrial investment through processes of transformation, and to provide client firms with valuable information and strategic advice. In this perspective, it is the demand-side variables (the asset side of the banks) that determine the structure of the banking system. The strong relationship between financial institutions' structure and growth during the period 1880–1913 and previous economic development supports Gerschenkron's view that the moderately industrial economies of the time relied more heavily on banks to mobilize capital than more or less developed countries while more developed countries were more market-oriented (Fohlin 2000).

In Forsyth and Verdier's account (2003), by contrast, it is supply-side variables (the banks' liabilities side) that shape the banking system and the historical determining factors are not economic but political in nature. Where the state encouraged the fragmentation of the capital market (by promoting saving and cooperative banks) and hence prevented commercial for-profit banks from capturing a substantial share of the national deposit market, the latter were obliged to combine investment with deposit banking activities; as banks were forced to rely on their own costly resources they could not abandon the field of investment banking. Where the capital market was unified and centralized, commercial banks were able to capture a large part of the national deposit base and thus to concentrate on short-term lending. These differences are claimed to reflect two lines of political cleavage, a socio-economic one (large firms versus farmers, *Mittelstand*) and a territorial one (center-periphery). Although quantifiable factors (such as government centralization during the years 1880–1913) provide greater power in explaining (negatively) the later development of national capital markets than the structure of banking systems (Fohlin 2000), several individual country histories (e.g. Germany and Italy: see Deeg 2003; Polsi 2003) support the view that the existence of a strong agricultural periphery and the presence of powerful local non-profit institutions created the right conditions for the development of universal banks.

The major interest of these theses, whose effects on financial systems may complement each other, is to shed some light on the initial conditions of financial development. However they explain only a part of comparative financial history. A broader explanation must take into account the multiform role played by the state. The overall influence of the state is first visible during the decades that witnessed the formation of the financial system (the end of the eighteenth and the nineteenth centuries), since the conditions required for an early well-functioning capital market also depended on the process of state formation. The development of financial markets in the Netherlands, Britain, and France was the result of an early financial revolution establishing widespread confidence in the public debt and the principle of free capital markets; conversely in Germany the failure to deeply reform public finance resulted in a stunted financial market that encouraged the development of universal banks (Jonker 2002). Second, the role of the state was also visible through the regulations established during the domination of *laissez-faire* financial regimes. The Bubble Act of 1720 and the monopoly of the Bank of England over limited liability banking may have kept English banks small and conservative until 1825, while after its removal, the absence of a reliable lender of last resort may have increased banks' reluctance to engage in risky transformation of short-term deposits into potentially illiquid assets. Similarly US legislation, by prohibiting banks from branching across state lines (a legislation that became federal in 1927) and prohibiting interlocking boards of directors (the Clayton Act of 1914), prevented banks from accompanying the growth of the non-financial sector and restricted their ability to operate as universal banks.

Third, the role of regulatory factors increased in the following period (1930–60); given the tendency of *laissez-faire* financial regimes toward instability, new financial regulations were elaborated that explain, along with the interwar economic crisis, the shifts in financial developments during the "great reversal" (the weakening of the financial system and the withdrawal from universal banking). In many countries (Belgium, Greece, Italy, Japan, the United States, and later France), the state enacted legislation designed to prohibit full-scale universal banking. In addition, several countries passed legislation aimed at imposing restrictive rules on the development of commercial banks. In United States, the restrictive Banking Acts of 1933 and 1935 aimed at limiting the scope of banking by discouraging mergers and branching. In France, the legislation passed in 1941–8 (including the nationalization of the main commercial banks in 1945) imposed severely restrictive rules on the development of these banks. Germany followed an opposite path since the regulations established in 1931 and 1933 introduced corporatist organization into the banking system, while the US occupying authorities failed to impose a US-style financial system. By contrast with the variety of state actions undertaken in the United States to improve the efficiency of financial markets, the German tax system stunted the development of equity markets while a corporatist bond committee controlled access to bond markets. Through restrictions on banking activity initiated in the 1920s and state control of all securities issues and lending decisions above a certain amount from 1937, Japan moved from an economy enjoying both a competitive banking system and a developed financial market to an economy with a dynamic but concentrated banking system and a small financial market. The Japanese state believed that it could better control capital allocation if funds were channeled through banks; not only did the main bank system by which each munitions company was assigned a major bank give them a prominent role, but, through their control of the Bond Committee, financial institutions stifled the flourishing bond market and replaced it by banking loans. In spite of the US efforts to break up this system, it was to continue until the breakdown of the Bretton Woods Agreement gave a new impetus to international capital flows.

Fourth, it is a new shift in regulatory regimes that explains the revival of universal banks in the final decades of the twentieth century. The US Gramm–Leach–Bliley

Act of 1999 that abolished the separation of banking and securities industries put the finishing touches to a legal evolution that began in other countries during the 1950s and 1960s.

Fifth, from the interwar period onwards, the state's influence was not limited to its policies for promoting financial stability. It came also through the way the welfare state organized labor regulation, including welfare regimes. The fact that Germany and Japan have bank-based financial systems is related to their choice of solidaristic retirement systems: the absence of funded pensions, coupled with the relative high income equality (one consequence of the industrial relations in these countries), limits the demand for marketable securities. If the United States is market-oriented, it is also because it has a higher level of income inequality and has opted for an individualized retirement system, which has stimulated in turn the development of a large-scale capitalized private pension system (Vitols 2001).

Financial systems are the result of a lot of different forces and the way these forces interact vary according to the context in which they operate. No historical process that occurs in a given country can be directly reproduced elsewhere. But given the observable strength of path dependency one must be very attentive to the early conditions of financial development itself. Whatever the origins of such precedence (state formation or the timing of industrialization), some countries were early in developing fully-fledged financial markets, while others with small and imperfect markets experienced first the emergence of large (universal) banks (Jonker 2003). In the first case, markets stood from the start at the core of the financial system and it is their development that determined the role played by the banks; in the second case it is the banks which were the driving force (Michie 2003). In Britain the competition of active financial markets forced banks to concentrate on facilitating payments and short-term credits and to specialize more and more; in Germany the advance of the Berlin universal banks and the internalization of the securities market through their control over underwriting, trading, brokerage, and stock-exchange supervision hindered the development of the capital market (Deeg 2003). Once the hierarchy between banks and markets has been established, only exceptional events, such as war or economic and social crises, could modify the evolutionary path.

14.7 FINANCIAL SYSTEMS AND ECONOMIC PERFORMANCE

By contrast with the economics literature, historical research has focused more on the real effects of the various types of banks than on the differences between banks and markets in the allocation of capital. Among historians the debate has long been conducted within a strict comparison between universal banks of the German type and specialized banks of the British type, centered on the period 1880–1913. While German banks were said to have been actively involved in the financing and the conduct of their clients' businesses, British banks were blamed for their reluctance to commit themselves to their clients and on their obsession with liquidity and security in the lending process. From this perspective, it seemed logical to impute the success of German industry to its active universal banks (Gerschenkron 1966) and the relative decline in the British economic performance to its passive clearing banks (Elbaum and Lazonick 1986; Kennedy 1991). Even though it could be objected that the limited industrial involvement of British banks in these years may have been due to demand-side rather than supply-side factors (Capie and Collins 1992), some authors argued that the failure of British banks after World War I to adapt their lending practices to the changing financial needs of the corporate sector was indicative of institutional sclerosis.

This negative appraisal of specialized banks has received a new impetus through its application to a fast-growing economy, the United States in the gilded age (1880–1913). According to Calomiris (1995), US banks suffered from two handicaps that resulted in a high cost of capital for American industry which curbed the large-scale industrial investment needed at that time. Not only did the fragmented structure of American banks prevent them from benefiting from economies of scale and accompanying their clients' growth (unlike British banks), but US banks (unlike German banks) were also specialized so that they could not benefit from economies of scope. Only powerful universal banks would have been able to vary the form of financing as the firm matured (direct lending then underwriting and holding of securities) and consequently would have been likely to create a long-term relationship with their customers leading to a reduction in information and monitoring costs. Even in states like Illinois, where banks played a significant role in financing industrial expansion, this role was limited to the "adolescent" stage of the firm's life cycle. It was not until the 1920s, when US banks strove to operate branches and to combine, through affiliates, commercial banking, investment banking, and trust activities, that these banks were to converge (for a short time) on the universal banking pattern. These handicaps were all the more damaging, according to this author, insofar as the standard criticisms of universal banking (including that these banks might encourage a lack of competition among banks and firms or that they are a factor of destabilization of the financial system and a source of conflict of interest) either lack supporting empirical evidence or are not confined to this type of bank.

However, the recent tendency of historical work has been to reassess the advantages of each kind of bank, thereby smoothing the opposition between German and British banks. As far as universal banks are concerned, the early criticisms pointed out that the main clientele of the large German universal banks were large, old, publicity-traded enterprises so that they were not actively involved in risky and innovative investment (Tilly 1986, 1998) and that by giving priority to the financing of heavy industries "the industrial financing of the Kreditbanken...hampered the growth of non-agricultural output" (Neuberger and Stokes 1974). More recent criticisms have proceeded along two fronts (Edwards and Olgivie 1996). In opposition to Gerschenkron's thesis of universal-bank-led industrialization, the first underlines the limited part played by the large *Kreditbanks*. Holding less than 10 percent of total financial assets in 1913, large Berlin banks were only one part of the German financial system alongside the Reichsbank, which provided the economy with means of payment and short-term trade credits, and local savings and cooperative banks, which granted credits to craftsmen, small firms, and farmers (Ziegler 1997). If we consider that many regions and sectors followed a decentralized industrial development pattern (based on small firms and Marshallian industrial districts), the role played by local banks may have been more crucial than that of large banks (Herrigel 1996; Deeg 2003). Moreover, in the corporate sector of economy where large banks were disproportionately involved, self-financing dominated, which allowed most of the large industrial firms to avoid dependence on banks. The growing replacement by 1900 of exclusive relationships with a *Hausbank* by multi-bank links suggests that industrial firms dominated banks rather than the reverse; the high profitability of the leading firms led to sharp competition among banks to service them. In addition, when large firms turned more to external finance, as after 1895, bank loans generally did not serve as a source of long-term finance (Edwards and Ogilvie 1996).

The second front of criticism opposes the idea that large universal banks were efficient institutions for overcoming problems of informational asymmetry and firm monitoring. During the years 1880 to 1913, the presence of bank representatives on the supervisory board of large firms is claimed to have had no persistent, significant effects on investment, performance, and financial structure. Rather than a response to economic backwardness, the proliferation of formalized bank relationships on this view should be seen as a result of structural changes in the German economy (such as the increasing complexity of the financial system or the growing prevalence of proxy voting) (Fohlin 1998, 1999). In addition, nineteenth-century German bankers seem to have been poorly informed despite their intimacy with industry. Most of these assessments would also apply to the interwar period when the power of the great banks declined and their ability to monitor their customers weakened (Wixforth 1995).

While the image of the German universal banks was revised downward, the assessment of British banks' performance became more favourable. Improved access to banking and industrial firms' archives allowed a more accurate approach to banking practices. At the same time, British banks' role has been placed in the broader context of a financial system in which banks are confined to short-term credit provision supplementing long-term funds raised on large markets (Ross 1996). In various ways, several studies (Cottrell 1980; Watson 1996) highlight evidence of the British banks' supporting business firms during the late nineteenth and early twentieth centuries. Extensive research by Capie and Collins (1999) confirms this view, while emphasizing that this support was achieved through rather conservative prudential criteria. On the one hand, the bulk of commercial bank support for industry came in the form of short-term loans and overdrafts designed to meet cash-flow and working-capital requirements; in addition, as a result of firms' wider adoption of corporate structures and limited liability for shareholdings, the proportion of unsecured loans decreased. On the other hand, thanks to the repeated renewal of overdrafts, the actual duration of loans averaged 19 months, and even though they persisted with an arm's-length approach, banks continued to support their industrial clients during periods of distress.

This approach to business finance was to continue during the whole of the twentieth century. Indeed, on various occasions as in the interwar years, banks were exhorted to intervene more deeply to finance the regeneration of British industry and there is some evidence of their closer involvement in clients' business affairs. But this was largely out of necessity (to protect their own interests) and they withdrew from any such involvement as soon as possible; clearly banks did not use their positions as creditors to implement a coordinated program of rationalization (Elbaum and Lazonick 1986). Similarly, in the post-World War II period, banks developed greater installment credit and leasing facilities and expanded medium-term lending to the corporate sector. But for the core of their business large clearing banks remained associated with a short-term and an arm's-length approach to the business sector (Collins and Baker 2005).

Thus, although the traditional image of British banks providing short-term secured loans is proved true, this view can no longer be considered as a sign of institutional weakness coming from the rigidity created by the growing centralization of the banking system. Instead it can be seen as a source of flexibility and stability since the risks of banking failure were exceptionally low (Baker and Collins 2002). The durability of the British banking model suggests also that it was a rational system. It may be an alternative solution to the problem of asymmetric information, adverse selection, and moral hazard. In relationship banking, as practiced by the Japanese *keiretsu* or most continental Europe banks, banks invest a lot of resources in gathering detailed privileged information on the would-be borrower, in monitoring debtors, and maintaining long-term relationships with their clients. In transaction banking, as practiced by British banks, banks economize on this type of investment and do not become deeply involved in their clients' affairs. Rather they treat each loan as a separate transaction and emphasize the enforcement of rules aimed at minimizing losses from client default: they carefully screen each project, prefer short-term credits subject to frequent review, and impose collateral requirements that guarantee the recovery of the debt in case of client default (Baker and Collins 2005).

The unresolved question is the respective efficiency of these two systems in the allocation of finance. Because relationship banking relies on good information and strong client monitoring, it results in committed finance that may lead to a long-term perspective and to higher levels of investment.[1] By contrast, transaction banking, because it relies on anonymous relationships, results in liquid finance (in both banks and markets) that may limit the investment horizon of firms and lead to short-term strategies. These differences may also play some part in the innovation process since financial commitment is said to be "a social condition permitting collective and cumulative learning to take place" (Lazonick and O'Sullivan 1997). On these points most empirical studies are inconclusive: we need more comparative regional, industry, and firm-level research. The efficiency of each kind of bank depends on the way they are managed (Carnevali 1995). But as shown by the Italian case, where relationship banking operated by local banks was efficient in the "Third Italy" of the center and northeast but not in the *Mezzogiorno* (Conti and Ferri 2004), the efficiency of each kind of bank also depends on the context, including the cultural context (Eichengreen 1998) in which they operate. This pushes historians to engage more deeply in the study of banks and markets as organizations and institutions. Oppositions between universality and specialization, relationship and transaction banking, non-profit and for-profit banks do not allow us to fully understand how banks and markets function, how they coordinate economic activity, how they handle information, how they shape their own processes of organizational learning, how they reflect and manage the various social forces they incorporate (Lamoreaux and Raff 1995).

In addition to the study of firms and markets as organizations and institutions, the question of financial efficiency should lead us to avoid limiting the scope of analysis to separate institutions. Banks' efficiency has to be assessed at the level of the whole financial system. Much recent progress has been achieved by studying banks and markets "in tandem" but other institutions also have to be integrated in a complete appraisal. The example of small and medium-sized enterprise (SME) financing illustrates this point. Small firms are more likely to depend on bank finance than large ones because market costs are too heavy for them. But neither relationship banks nor transaction banks are able to provide small firms with finance on the same terms as larger firms. In both cases new SMEs, the seed-corn of any industrial development, are the most affected. However, the consequences of this financial gap for industrial development and economic growth vary according to the presence or absence of compensatory institutions. The fact that, unlike the UK, Germany has avoided the process of deindustrialization may be attributed to the dense network of non-profit financial institutions active in the field of SME finance (Carnevali 2005). How the different parts of the financial systems

---

[1] Fohlin herself recognizes that for the period post-1901 high debt-equity ratios are associated with provincial bank representation, so that the debt-monitoring hypothesis can not be completely rejected; similarly, for the same period, higher profit margins are positively related to both provincial-bank and great-bank representation, so that the hypothesis that banks provide useful consultancy services can not be completely neglected.

complement one another and how this complementarity has been produced may be one of the most fruitful lines of research for the coming decades.

14.8 CONCLUSIONS

Do national financial systems converge? The question has been raised for several periods of financial history. It has been hypothesized that after having converged during the years 1890 to 1914 financial systems diverged during the major part of the twentieth century: this divergence was a result of the different regulatory solutions developed by national states. Since the 1980s, it was widely expected that shifts in the international context (such as the implementation of the European Single Market) would lead to a relative convergence of financial systems. In spite of some conspicuous common changes (such as the revival of universal banking and the replacement of banks as mobilizers of funds from economic units with surplus capital) the answer seems negative. At least in the period prior to the creation of the common currency no convergence can be observed between the main European financial systems. The single apparent exception is constituted by the French case and it is imputable to state policy, which consciously sought to reshape the financial system on an Anglo-Saxon model. This lack of global convergence has been "attributed to the effects of strong path dependencies, which are in turn an outgrowth of the relationship of complementarity between the individual system components" (Schmidt *et al.* 2001: 1).

REFERENCES

AOKI, M., PATRICK, H., and SHEARD, P. (1994). "The Japanese Main Bank System", in M. Aoki and H. Patrick (eds.), *The Japanese Main Bank System*. Oxford: Oxford University Press.

BAKER, M., and COLLINS, M. (2005). "Engish Commercial Bank Stability, 1860–1914". *Journal of European Economic History*, 31/3: 493–512.

BAUBEAU, P. (2003). "La Caisse des dépôts et consignations et le Crédit national, un essai comparatif: lignes de force et concurrences au sein du secteur financier public français", in Alya Aglan, Michel Margairaz, and Philippe Verheyde (eds.), *La Caisse des dépôts et consignations la Seconde Guerre mondiale et le XXe siècle*. Paris: Albin Michel.

CALOMIRIS, C. W. (1995). "The Costs of Rejecting Universal Banking: American Finance in the German Mirror, 1870–1914", in Lamoreaux and Raff (1995).

CAMERON, R. (ed). (1967). *Banking at the Early Stages of Industrialization*. New York: Oxford University Press.

CAMERON, R. and BOVYKIN, V. I. (eds.) (1991). *International Banking 1870–1914*. Oxford: Oxford University Press.

CAPIE, F., and COLLINS, M. (1992). *Have the Banks Failed British Industry?* London: IEA Hobart Paper.

———— (1999). "Banks, Industry and Finance 1880–1914". *Business History*, 41/1: 37–62.

CARNEVALI, F. (1995). "Finance in the Regions", in Y. Cassis, G. D. Feldman, and U. Olsson (eds.), *The Evolution of Financial Institutions and Markets in Twentieth-Century Europe*. Aldershot: Scolar Press.

——— (2005). *Europe's Advantage*. Oxford: Oxford University Press.

COLLINS, M., and BAKER, M. (2005). "English Bank Loans 1920–1968". *Financial History Review*, 12: 135–72.

CONTI, G., and FERRI, G. (2004). "Banques locales et soutien au développement décentralisé de PME en Italie", in M. Lescure and A. Plessis (eds.), *Banques locales et banques régionales en Europe au XXe siècle*. Paris: Albin Michel.

COTTRELL, P. L. (1980). *Industrial Finance 1830–1914*. London: Methuen.

DEEG, R. (2003). "On the Development of Universal Banking in Germany", in Forsyth and Verdier (2003).

DEMIRGÜÇS-KUNT, A., and MAKSIMOVIC, V. (1996). "Stock Market Development and Financing Choices of Firms". *World Bank Economic Review*, 10/2: 341–70.

DIETL, H. M. (1998). *Capital Markets and Corporate Governance in Japan, Germany and United States*. London: Routledge.

EDWARDS, J., and OGILVIE, S. (1996). "Universal Banks and German Industrialization: A Reappraisal". *Economic History Review*, 49/3: 427–46.

EICHENGREEN, B. (1998). "Economics and Culture in the Writing of Financial History", in Nunez (1998).

ELBAUM, B., and LAZONICK, W. (1986). *The Decline of the British Economy*. Oxford: Oxford University Press.

FEIERTAG, O., and MARGAIRAZ, M. (eds.) (2003). *Politiques et pratiques des banques d'émission en Europe (XVIIe–XXe siècle)*. Paris: Albin Michel.

FISHLOW, A. (1985). "Lessons from the Past: Capital Markets during the 19th Century and the Interwar Period". *International Organization*, 39/3: 383–439.

FOHLIN, C. (1998). "Relationship Banking, Liquidity, and Investment in the German Industrialization". *Journal of Finance*, 53: 1737–58.

——— (1999). "The Rise of Interlocking Directorates in Imperial Germany". *Economic History Review*, 52/2: 307–33.

——— (2000). "Economic, Political and Legal Factors in Financial System Development: International Patterns in Historical Perspective". Social Science Working Paper No. 1089, California Institute of Technology.

——— (2001). "The Balancing Act of German Universal Banks and English Deposit Banks, 1880–1913". *Business History*, 43: 1–24.

FORSYTH, D. J., and VERDIER, D. (eds.) (2003). *The Origins of National Financial Systems*. London: Routledge.

GERSCHENKRON, A. (1962). *Economic Backwardness in Historical Perpective*. Cambridge, Mass.: Harvard University Press.

GOLDSMITH, R. W. (1969). *Financial Structure and Development*. New Haven: Yale University Press.

——— (1985). *Comparative National Balance Sheets*, Chicago: University of Chicago Press.

GUESLIN, A., and LESCURE, M. (1995). "Les banques publiques et coopératives françaises (1920–1960)", in M. Lévy-Leboyer (ed.), *Les banques en Europe de l'Ouest de 1920 à nos jours*. Paris: CHEFF.

GUINNANE, T. (1994). "A Failed Institutional Transplant: Raiffeisen's Credit Cooperatives in Ireland, 1894–1914". *Explorations in Economic History*, 31: 38–61.

GURLEY, J. G., and SHAW, E. S. (1955). "Financial Aspects of Economic Development". *American Economic Review*, 45: 515–38.

HACKETAL, A., and SCHMIDT, R. H. (2004). "Financing patterns: Measurement Concepts and Empirical Results". Goethe-University Working Paper No. 125.

HARDACH, G. (2004). "Banques régionales et banques locales en Allemagne: un système bancaire polarize", in M. Lescure and A. Plessis (eds.), *Banques locales et banques régionales en Europe au XXe siècle*. Paris: Albin Michel.

HAUTCOEUR, P. C. (1999). "L'autofinancement". *Entreprises et Histoire*, 22: 55–77.

HERRIGEL, G. (1996). *Industrial Constructions: The Foundations of German Industrial Power*. Cambridge: Cambridge University Press.

HOFFMAN, P. T., POSTEL-VINAY, G., and ROSENTHAL, J.-L. (2001). *Des marchés sans prix*. Paris: EHESS.

JONES, G. (1993). *British Multinational Banking 1830–1990*. Oxford: Oxford University Press.

JONKER, J. (2003)."Competing in Tandem", in Forsyth and Verdier (2003).

KENNEDY, W. P. (1991). "Portfolio Behaviour and Economic Development in Late Nineteenth-Century Great Britain and Germany". *Research in Economic History Supplement*, 6: 93–130.

LAMOREAUX, N. R. (1994). *Insider Lending: Banks, Personal Connections and Economic Development in Industrial New England*. New York: Cambridge University Press.

——and RAFF, D. M. G. (1995). *Coordination and Information*. Chicago: University of Chicago Press.

LA PORTA, R., LOPEZ-DE-SILANE, A., SHLEIFER, R., and VISHNY, W. (1998). "Law and Finance". *Journal of Political Economy*, 106/6: 1113–55.

LAZONICK, W., and O'SULLIVAN, M. (1997). "Finance and Industrial Development". *Financial History Review*, 4: 7–29, 117–38.

LESCURE, M., and PLESSIS, A. (eds.) (1999). *Banques locales et banques régionales en France au XIXe siècle*. Paris: Albin Michel.

LEVINE, R. (1997). "Financial Development and Economic Growth: Views and Agenda". *Journal of Economic Literature*, 2: 688–726.

——(2002). "Bank-Based or Market-Based Financial Systems: Which is Better?". *Journal of Financial Intermediation*, 11: 398–428.

LÉVY-LEBOYER, M. (1976). "Le crédit et la monnaie", in F. Braudel and E. Labrousse (eds.), *Histoire économique et sociale de la France*, vol. 1. Paris: P.U.F., T. 3.

MARGAIRAZ, M. (1991). *L'Etat, les finances et l'économie: Histoire d'une conversion*. Paris: CHEFF.

MAYER, C. (1988). "New Issues in Corporate Finance". *European Economic Review*, 32: 1167–88.

MICHIE, R. C. (1999). *The London Stock Exchange: A History*. Oxford: Oxford University Press.

——(2003). "Banks and Securities Markets, 1870–1914", in Forsyth and Verdier (2003).

NEUBERGER, H., and STOKES, H. (1974). "German Banks and German Growth, 1883–1913: An Empirical View". *Journal of Economic History*, 39/3: 710–30.

NEWTON, L. (2001). "Assessment of Information, Uncertainty and Risk: The Strategies of English and Welsh Joint-stock Bank Managements, 1826–1860", University of Reading Business School, Discussion Paper No. 431.

NUNEZ, C. E. (ed.) (1998). *Finance and the Making of the Modern Capitalist World, 1750–1931*. Seville: Secretariado de Publicaciones de la Universidad de Sevilla.

PLESSIS, A. (2002). "La révolution de l'escompte dans la France du 19e siècle". *Revue d'histoire du XIXe siècle*, 23: 143–64.

POHL, M., TORTELLA, T., and VAN DER WEE, H. (eds.) (2001). *A Century of Banking Consolidation in Europe*. Aldershot: Ashgate.

POLSI, A. (2003). "The Early Development of Universal Banking in Italy in an Adverse Institutional Context, 1850–1914", in Forsyth and Verdier (2003).

QUENNOUËLLE-CORRE, L. (2005). "The State, Banks and Financing of Investments in France from WW II to the 1970s". *Financial History Review*, 12/1: 63–86.

RAJAN, R., and ZINGALES, L. (1996). "Financial Dependence and Growth". NBER Working Paper No. 5758.

——— (2001). "The Great Reversals: The Politics of Financial Development in the Twentieth Century". NBER Working Paper No. 8178.

ROSS, D. M. (1996). "Commercial Banking in a Market-Oriented Financial System: Britain between the Wars". *Economic History Review*, 49/2: 314–35.

SCHMIDT, R. H., HACKETAL, A., and TYRELL, M. (2001). "The Convergence of Financial Systems in Europe". Goethe-University, Frankfurt, Working Paper No. 75.

STRAUS, A. (1988). "Evolution comparée des systèmes de financement: RFA, Royaume Uni et Japon". *Revue d'économie financière*, 5/6: 44–66.

SUDRIA, C. (2006). "Le modèle catalan de banque de proximité", in H. Bonin and C. Lastécouères (eds.), *Les banques du grand Sud-Ouest*. Paris: PLAGE.

SYLLA, R. (1998). "Finance and Economic Growth", in Nunez (1998).

—— (2002). "United States Banks and Europe: Strategy and Attitudes", in S. Battilosi and Y. Cassis (eds.), *Europeans Banks and American Challenge: Competition and Cooperation in International Banking under Bretton Woods*. Oxford: Oxford University Press.

TILLY, R. (1986). "German Banking 1850–1914: Development Assistance for the Strong". *Journal of European Economic History*, 15/1: 113–52.

—— (1998). "Universal Banking in Historical Perspective". *Journal of Institutional and Theoretical Economics*, 54: 7–32.

VITOLS, S. (2001)."The Origins of Bank-Based and Market-Based Financial Systems", in W. Streeck and K. Yamamura (eds.), *The Origins of Nonliberal Capitalism*. London: Cornell University Press.

WATSON, K. (1996). "Banks and Industrial Finance: The Experience of Brewers, 1880–1913". *Economic History Review*, 49: 58–81.

—— (1999). "Funding Enterprise: The Finance of British Industry during the Nineteenth Century". *Entreprises et Histoire*, 22: 31–54.

WIXFORTH, H. (1995). *Banken und Schwerindustrie in der Weimar Republik*. Cologne: Boehlau.

ZIEGLER, D. (1997). "The Influence of Banking on the Rise and Expansion of Industrial Capitalism in Germany", in A. Teichova, G. Kurgan, and D. Ziegler (eds.), *Banking, Trade and Industry*. Cambridge: Cambridge University Press.

....

CHAPTER 15

TECHNOLOGY AND INNOVATION

....

MARGARET B. W. GRAHAM

15.1 INTRODUCTION

....

SINCE World War II, historians and economists have differed profoundly in their interpretation of technological change and economic development. While economists devoted much of the last half of the 20th century to treating technology as exogenous to the working economy, emphasizing equilibrium and optimization over innovation, historians have considered technology to be the internally generated driving force in economic growth (Warsh 2006; Nelson and Rosenberg 1998). Historians do not agree among themselves, however, on how technology has served as the driving force. Some have emphasized the power of technique; others have emphasized social need; and still others have advanced cultural and philosophical reasons for rapid industrialization (Landes 1969, 1998; Mokyr 1990).

Business historians and historians of technology who have opened the "black boxes" of organization and technology to investigate the processes of technological change have found them to be both complex and situated, with needs and users providing the impetus in some arenas and system builders and developers in others (Rosenberg 1982; Mowery and Rosenberg 1998). Regardless of the impetus for change, according to business historians the enterprise has consistently played a mediating role. Firms may not always have been instigators, but large and small, privately owned or government sponsored, firms have been principal actors in innovation since invention and research became tools of the firm in the nineteenth century (Hagstrom 1998). In the twentieth century, both innovation and R&D were institutionalized, shaping the rate and direction of technological change throughout the industrial and industrializing worlds.

The twentieth century history of technology and innovation has revolved around four basic themes: the dynamics of technological systems, the co-evolution of systems and institutions, technology and corporate strategy, and the internal workings of the R&D laboratory. As a new generation revisits and revises the interpretation of the twentieth century, other themes are emerging that go beyond technology and organization to explore a broader and more global context, more socially driven innovation, the nature of technological networks, and new theoretical frameworks.

This is the chapter in this Handbook that explicitly covers technology, but interested readers may also want to consult other chapters for bibliographical references on the following topics: institutions, economic development, and the theory of innovation (Lazonick), R&D and entrepreneurship (Jones and Wadhwani), government funding of R&D (Millward), international technology transfer (Jones), and industrial districts (Zeitlin).

15.2 Vital Distinctions

Invention and research were both familiar terms in the 19th century, but innovation when used for economic purposes, and R&D (standing for industrial research and development), are twentieth century terms. The *Oxford English Dictionary* attributes the modern usage of "innovation" to Joseph Schumpeter in *Business Cycles* (1939). Schumpeter insisted on a distinction that is often overlooked in historical scholarship, the difference between invention and innovation. Invention, the process of making a novel idea useful, may be deliberate or accidental. Innovation, on the other hand, is the purposeful work of the entrepreneur, or entrepreneurial organization, to bring into widespread practice a new idea or technique, or a recombination of old ideas or techniques, employed in a new setting. A particular innovation may incorporate one or more inventions, but it may contain no new inventions at all. Though both terms came to be popularly identified with formal science during the twentieth century, neither invention nor innovation necessarily involves formal science. Further, although inventor-entrepreneurs like Thomas Edison and George Westinghouse or scientist-entrepreneurs like Elmer Sperry and Robert Noyce have figured prominently in business, as have entrepreneurial firms, the inventor and the innovator have usually been different actors.

For business historians the "organizational synthesis" extending the Chandlerian hypothesis has been the central conceptual framework for the firm's involvement in innovation (Galambos 1983). This framework identified technology, political economy, and professionalization as key components of a unique US innovation system, while holding that some of the most important innovations have not been technical but organizational. It also implied that certain technologies mandated certain organizational forms. As business history has shifted to more social and cultural themes in the past decade it has become evident that, given the risks involved, and the long time to success, even the most self-contained and profit-oriented innovators have been motivated by personal or social forces beyond training, organizational position, or commercial gain (Baumol 2002).

Historians often represent innovation as a generic process, but it is essential for business historians to distinguish between types of innovation because different types of innovation succeed in different conditions (Lazonick, this volume). The irreducible distinction—reflecting both the nature of the source, and the level of uncertainty as to outcome—is the difference between incremental and radical innovation. Incremental innovation occurs in small steps which can cumulate to major outcomes, but involves relatively little uncertainty in execution or impact. Radical innovation refers to a major change based on an original concept, facing great uncertainty in both execution and outcome. In Clayton Christensen's useful terminology, incremental innovation tends to be *sustaining* of existing industrial structures and practices, while radical innovation is *disruptive*, generally undermining or threatening industrial structures and practices (Christensen 1997).

Adopted as an acronym during World War II to designate a set of funding categories, the term R&D has been subject to quantitative distortion and misinterpretation. Like patents, R&D investment numbers are among the few things associated with innovation that can be measured. The use and misuse of such numbers poses a challenge to historians who are obligated to test the underlying assumptions involved.

It is, for instance, a perennial error to equate R&D with innovation. Whatever the numbers seem to suggest, research and development, when present, are only two stages in the involved and often unpredictable process that leads to successful commercialization or widespread use of a truly novel product or service (Graham 2007). Though scientific research is supposed to have replaced craft as the source of inventive ideas, at least after World War II, there were losses as well as gains in this transition and the transition was far from complete. Many companies have had expensive failures in innovation because some of the important elements of craft—local knowledge, tacit knowledge, and learning by doing—were undervalued or eliminated by the scientific community when it was given the responsibility to coordinate the innovation process via institutionalized R&D.

15.3 INNOVATION HISTORY

Historians of technology and business have approached technological change differently, the first focusing on system dynamics and the second on managerial decision-making within the individual firm and industry. For the business historian, the firm has played a primary and largely positive role by tying investment in technology to corporate strategy, with all that implies for resources and power. For historians of technology, and of labor, by contrast, the large corporation has been an inescapable, frequently repressive force, locking up the market for invention, eliminating craft, co-opting the engineering profession, and generally stifling the creativity of inventive individuals in its employ (Hughes 1989; Noble 1984).

Adherents of Thomas Hughes, in particular, have concerned themselves with systems technologies—electrification, railroads, the telephone system and its telecommunications successors—both at the level of the industry or shared across industries. For historians of these systems the technologists—whether independent inventors, technological entrepreneurs, or in-house researchers—have collectively moved their technology forward by identifying problems and fixing "reverse salients". According to the systems interpretation many large-scale innovations have been completed less because of their commercial impact, than because they had what Hughes calls "momentum". Both interpretations find broad support in the scholarly record, but for different industries and strategies. The most interesting scholarly work on these subjects in the twentieth century has been found where business history and history of technology have overlapped (Hounshell 1996).

Although many US firms chose to secure their technology base in the 20th century by internalizing innovation in pursuit of rationalization and efficiency, and this is the dominant narrative in the business history, alternative organizational approaches to innovation never disappeared, and have recently proliferated. The other main alternative, the innovating firm in the Schumpeterian sense, is the firm that innovates in search of a brand-new product or process, or to pursue strategic diversification. The term "novelty" which historians of technology have used to characterize this form of innovation represents a high risk, and important, phenomenon that became riskier but potentially more lucrative when technology, and then science, were institutionalized. Ordinary start-ups mature, stabilize, and rationalize, but to plan to survive from business cycle to business cycle by means of innovation is a very different matter, requiring process flexibility, sensitivity to customer needs and the environment, and a high degree of motivation and autonomy among decision-makers (Scranton 1997).

Firms that have chosen to compete on the basis of novelty rather than scale and cost include consumer product firms like consumer electronics, specialty materials firms supplying profitable niches, and many other high value, high profit goods and services. These firms anticipated market saturation and lived by rapid and significant innovation. What would later be known as a knowledge strategy could substitute expertise for deficits in size and tangible resources. A small specialty-glass company like Corning Glass Works, for instance, could control the rate and direction of innovation in glass technology by sharing its knowledge with other firms through licensing and cross-licensing, and by forming "associations" with other firms to develop new businesses (Graham and Shuldiner 2001). Such examples of simultaneous competition and cooperation are reminders that the standard historical narratives concerning institutionalized innovation and industrialized R&D discussed in this chapter are only partial and stylized accounts of more complicated phenomena. There have been many pathways to innovation, and business historians need to explore more of them in detail.

15.4 INSTITUTIONALIZING INNOVATION IN FIRMS AND INDUSTRIES

Institutionalization of innovation has two meanings in the historical literature: first, the internal ordering inside a firm or industry, and second, co-evolution between the firm's internal innovation process and other institutions beyond the firm such as universities, antitrust and other forms of government regulation, venture capital, labor-management relations, or patent systems. Both forms of institutionalized innovation appeared in the latter part of the nineteenth century. Historians with an interest in the first form of institutionalization have employed as units of analysis particular innovations and innovators, innovating firms, and industries. Historians with an interest in co-evolution have looked at industries, geographical regions—especially creative regions—and nations.

For individual firms, innovation was typically institutionalized long before research was included in the innovation process. In the prototypical German dye firms, generally credited with originating the systematic exploitation of natural science for product development, innovation had been institutionalized for decades before research found a strategic role (Murmann 2003). At Eastman Kodak, George Eastman delegated first the operating function, later invention and new product design, to departmental surrogates, but waited more than a decade before setting up a research laboratory. For Eastman, institutionalization was complete when Kodak could carry out the inventive mechanical work of camera device and process development without his direct intervention. He set up a research laboratory in 1912 when the advanced chemical expertise Kodak needed could only be had among European-trained scientists. Even then Kodak's need for research may have been as much a matter of symbolism and public duty as a requirement for the making of film (Jenkins 1975; Sturchio 1985).

Much the same sequence occurred at Alcoa. Charles Martin Hall, a classic scientist-entrepreneur, willingly provided for operations and a professional engineering department, but opposed the investment when his professional engineers wanted the support of a corporate laboratory. Hall's successors invested in research after World War I partly to demonstrate a "politically correct" commitment to the value of "pure research" (Graham and Pruitt 1990). The matter of including research, especially fundamental research, in the innovation process for externally motivated reasons arose again for US firms after World War II in response to national concerns about the need for US scientific independence (Graham 1985).

Certain exceptional US companies, usually government-sanctioned monopolies, elected to go beyond internalizing the innovation process to integrate vertically and horizontally a complete system of innovation, as Bell did for telephone and Alcoa did for aluminum. Their ambition was to control the long-term rate and direction of technological change for their entire industry in their own interest (Galambos 1992; Reich 1985). Some self-reliant companies, like RCA for television, were able to perpetrate radical, sometimes disruptive, innovation in a relatively short period of time because they dared to risk self-obsolescence. But such instances were hardly the industrial norm. More commonly, an internalized innovation system supported by some fundamental research was intended for commercial self-defense, and the pattern of innovation was sustaining and largely incremental in nature. Eventually, as William Abernathy showed for Fordism in the US car industry, such defensive purposes, and the patterns of management that went with them, led to diminishing returns for both the firm and the industry (Abernathy 1978).

Institutionalization of innovation occurred at the level of the industry rather than the firm when firms shared a technology which did not figure in their competition, when the whole industry feared product substitutes, or when it was providing a service rather than selling a product. This was the case both for American railroads and the American telegraph system (Usselman 2002; Israel 1992). It was also the case for the insurance industry where users played an important role in shaping information technologies from tabulators through computer systems (Yates 2005). In earlier cases this sort of innovation was institutionalized in an open system involving entrepreneurial inventors, with networks of technical personnel and industry associations and standards-setting bodies governing the shared technology. A few in-house laboratories, such as the one established by the Pennsylvania Railroad, worked on trouble-shooting and issues of control rather than significant performance enhancements. In later cases, like business information systems, suppliers such as IBM certainly did develop sophisticated in-house laboratories, but it was the customer interface that sold the technology rather than the performance characteristics of the technology itself (Chandler 2001). With the glaring exception of the IBM 360, this form of innovation was usually incremental and rarely disruptive, but there were times when significant inventions from independent inventors had to be adopted for reasons other than efficiency or the companies' preferred requirements, such as passengers' insistence on reduced accidents in the case of the railroads, or environmental regulation in the case of catalytic converters (Coopey 2004; Usselman 1993; Graham and Shuldiner 2001).

15.5 OPEN VERSUS CLOSED INNOVATION SYSTEMS

The open form of innovation practiced by the railroad industry was common to most US industries until the new electrochemical industries began incorporating science into their innovation systems after the turn of the twentieth century (Mowery and Rosenberg 1998). When a system was open, an innovation was assembled and negotiated in the marketplace, as it was in the early days of the "new" industries—radio and automobiles—in the 1920s. Inventors often grouped together at workshops or machine shops; and independent invention factories, of which Thomas Edison's was the most famous, were businesses (Millard 1990). Radio and automobiles both incorporated ideas and inventions from many independent sources into what only gradually emerged in the 1930s as dominant designs.

When the system was closed, the innovation process was contained inside the boundaries of a corporation or a defined industry, or directed by another "visible hand"—a set of institutions or government agencies, and information was shared only with designated participants. For at least 30 years business historians maintained that the closed innovation system—either integrated within large corporations, or encased in a patterned set of relationships within a particular industry, or in long-term cooperation between an industry and a branch of the military—was associated with a superior form of managerial capitalism in the United States. Great Britain's lagging economic performance in the early 20th century was attributed to national underinvestment by firms in industrial research and the failure of firms to advance to a US-style integrated bureaucracy that incorporated research. This conclusion has since been disputed, leaving the merits of open systems involving a free flow of information between companies, versus closed systems, where Not Invented Here (NIH) signifies inferiority, still open to debate (Mowery 1984; Divall 2006).

Revisiting the "organizational synthesis" Louis Galambos still sees the large integrated firms occupying what he terms the industrial or economic center, as having excelled both in economies of scale and in innovation, though he acknowledges the importance of global forces, and that information technology can mandate networks as coordinating mechanisms in place of bureaucracies (Galambos 2005).

But other historians have discerned more contingent patterns among technology-based companies in many industries.

Center companies that remained innovative past the initial phase of institution-alization, such as General Electric, pursued a serious form of novelty as strategy, and were not self-contained innovators, even though they had distinguished laboratories. Other large and innovative firms like the fabled Minnesota Mining and Manufacturing, or the more recently founded Hewlett Packard, or even the ill-starred Xerox employed quite different forms of organization. RCA under David Sarnoff was an "M-form" in structure but not in management style. When his entrepreneurial functions had been delegated to the corporate laboratory that bore his name, the laboratory soon pursued its own interests, helping to destroy the company in less than a generation (Graham 1986). When closed systems met technological transitions, such as the electronics transition from vacuum tubes to transistors, or the pharmaceutical transition to molecular biology, the centralized industrial research structure could became a powerful source of inertia with the corporate laboratory representing the old technology (Choi 2004; Graham 1986; Galambos and Sturchio 1998). Comparisons between similar technologies in different countries, such as the contrasting interwar experience with the aluminum dirigible in the United Kingdom and the United States, suggest that the more open system of innovation was much better at adopting and incorporating new technologies such as aircraft alloys (Graham 1988).

15.6 INDUSTRIALIZING RESEARCH

The form of institutionalization involving co-evolution with other institutions occurred primarily after research and development was industrialized. Although this happened to some degree in Great Britain and France in the mid-19th century, industrial research was thoroughly institutionalized only later in Germany, the United States, and Japan, meaning that it co-evolved with a set of other institutions in such a way as to standardize the way industrial research operated in all firms. The limits to institutionalization can be seen in all these cases. As industrial R&D became more institutionalized in the United States after World War II, firms that had in-house research, but chose to organize and manage it differently from other firms, paid a price for their deviations from established norms.

The standard narrative concerning industrialization of research is based on laboratories established after 1900 at GE, AT&T, DuPont, and Kodak. Born of the electrochemical revolution, these companies discovered a need for expert knowledge in advanced chemistry and electricity in a way that other large US companies like the railroads, steel, and telegraph companies did not. They had the special problem of attracting university scientists who, unlike most professional engineers, regarded a career in industry as inferior to one in a university. Following in the footsteps of the German dye and pharmaceutical companies, these pioneering research-performing companies in the United States, hired university-trained, often Ph.D. scientists, put them in separate dedicated laboratories equipped to focus on research, not daily operations, and reporting directly to senior executives in the corporate office. Given the academic values of the time, and the persistent inferiority complex of the US scientific community relative to the German scientific community, firms that wanted good scientists had to offer them the chance to do good science (Reich 1985, 1992). This version of the industrial research laboratory, which came to be called the corporate research laboratory, constitutes the final extension of the "organizational synthesis", its strategic intent to control and rationalize, but also to renew, manufacturing companies already well along in developing their manufacturing processes and approaches to distribution (Hounshell 1995; Smith 1990).

The new science-based companies faced a threatening environment at the turn of the 19th century, and established their central research laboratories as their defense. Menaced by antitrust prosecution and competing technologies for expiring patents, they were no longer satisfied with the old arrangement of engineering departments, testing and works laboratories, contract science provided by university professors through sponsored programs, and numerous private research institutes (Reich 1985; Servos 1990). With the new research laboratory at the center of a coordinated, specialized, and eventually rationalized research organization, GE and AT&T positioned themselves to acquire, or invent around, any threatening inventions that appeared in the market. AT&T gave its corporate laboratory the further complicated task of coordinating its developing technological system (Galambos 1992).

Only a few of the early industrial research laboratories were organized according to the standard narrative of the pioneering laboratories. Materials companies like Alcoa and Corning also hired German-educated Ph.D.s, but they attracted scientists with the intrinsic fascination of the scientific problems raised by working out many combinations of materials formulation and physical properties, and the process steps it took to achieve them. Rather than perform fundamental research related to their fields, the challenge for these scientists was to create hybrid disciplines that met the developing needs of their particular materials, and increased the value and use of their material compared to others. Process technologies were so important to these companies that they gave equal weight and standing within their technical networks to their process laboratories and their product laboratories (Graham and Pruitt 1990; Graham and Shuldiner 2001). Even within the electrical and chemical industries not all large firms chose to set up advanced research laboratories performing fundamental research as GE and DuPont did. Westinghouse, for instance, preferred to maintain an engineering research department at the top of its technical hierarchy until the 1930s when it hired physicist Edward U. Condon (Brittain 1992; Lassman 2003; Kline and Lassman 2005).

15.7 THE CHANGING RESEARCH CLIMATE

During the interwar period in the United States, corporate laboratories tested the extremes of innovation strategy. In the 1920s many newly founded laboratories were directed at the objective of rationalizing and optimizing production, implementing in effect the final stage of scientific management. Unfortunately, collective success, and the lack of any aggregate tracking mechanism, resulted in overproduction and a major loss of jobs for which industrial technology was blamed (Pursell 1995; Szostak 1995). In the 1930s America's scientific community—many having lost jobs themselves in the Depression—launched a campaign to convince industry and the public that "science meant jobs" (Kluznick 1987). For firms that took this seriously, the foundation was laid for postwar recovery and more. Whereas previously engineering departments had been almost universally in charge, in many companies the corporate laboratory run by scientists became the lead innovator and new products became the highest priority. A myriad of science-based innovations from artificial fibers to television, from aircraft alloys to artificial rubber, emerged from corporate laboratories, most already under way when the scientists took over (Hounshell and Smith 1988).

Though it has often been said that the lead story of technological change in the 20th century United States was the harnessing of science by industry, it may be more accurate to say that after World War II the scientific community actually shanghaied industry, aided by massive increases in military funding for research (Hounshell 1995; Mowery and Rosenberg 1998). Histories of laboratories staffed by university researchers, especially physicists with no business experience, chronicle decisions that undermined the companies' previous capacity to innovate (Kevles 1987; Graham 1985). Communications inside the technical community, and between the technical community and managements, became difficult, and capabilities shifted to match federal funding priorities. When electronics drove out the mechanical arts, and process technologies were separated from product technologies to protect intellectual property, process technology suffered (Graham 1986; Graham and Pruitt 1990).

For several decades the "linear model" of innovation—which depicted successful innovation as originating in a scientific breakthrough akin to the atom bomb, or the proximity fuse, as well as promoting the idea that patriotic companies performed research—had a powerful hold on the public consciousness. For that era even business historians gauge the return on R&D investment not by financial returns to R&D, but by how much "good science" was done (Hounshell 1995). In the 1960s, the costs of research rose dramatically, bolstered by expensive research equipment, escalating salaries, and huge annual increases in funding, while productivity became harder to measure. For the time being, the demand created by the need to rebuild the industrialized world, and the lack of serious competition, made optimizing output and improving systems performance, not productivity or innovation, the primary target.

So important has this government-funded R&D story been for companies in the high-tech sector of the economy—computers, electronics, aviation, and communications—that historians have paid scant attention to sectors of the economy that either refused or lacked access to the government's largesse. The historical literature contains less about the work performed with the privately funded half of the postwar industrial research budget, massive though that also was (Rosenberg 1994). Many companies, having learned through experience the negative aspects of government research funding, chose to fund R&D themselves rather than submit to bureaucratic controls and technology sharing. Secrecy, lack of flexibility, separation between classified and non-classified projects and personnel, lack of communication between cleared and non-cleared personnel, strings attached to free use, and protection of intellectual property, all raised troubling internal issues for companies that wished to pursue non-military business after World War II (Hounshell 1992; Leslie 1993; Wang 1992).

The Big Science model of research, nirvana to the physics community, reshaped the US innovation system (Leslie 1993). A wedge was inserted between "high-tech" military business and civilian business. Because the military emphasized performance over productivity, and cost-plus contracts were the norm, firms supplying military goods and systems failed to develop the manufacturing disciplines that were needed to compete with emerging foreign products. In formerly dominant US businesses like machine tools, the advanced tools fitted with numerical control for military uses were too expensive, and too complex from an operating standpoint, for regular civilian customers (Noble 1984). The entire US economy suffered the consequences. In the 1980s, for example, the US machine tool industry lost its civilian market to Japanese and European companies that had converted from military goods to civilian goods after World War II and not the other way round. The collapse of the machine tool industry did serious collateral damage to the US car industry just then beginning an overdue phase of investment in its process technology (Best 1990; Cusumano 1985; Fruin 1992).

Problems surfaced for the corporate laboratory, immune to criticism for decades, when the large firms that had performed the leading-edge research in solid-state electronics and computers found it difficult to manufacture the follow-on devices and products. The physicists in control of the technical agenda of many high-tech companies had demoted traditional skills like mechanical engineering. The operating divisions lacked both the skills and the easy relationships with the research laboratory to produce the new electronic products (Choi 2004). It became evident in many sectors that the modern innovation system incorporating research was having more difficulty carrying out the latter stages of innovation than it had previously. It also turned out that the expectations of major new science-based products had been overblown, that "home runs" were hard to achieve, that invention on demand could not be routinized the way incremental innovation had been (Graham and Shuldiner 2001). Having accepted the funding for this mission, laboratories now had to take the blame for the disappointments; and there were many—failures so colossal that they undercut the credibility of corporate research generally, and caused directors to question R&D investment levels (Florida and Kenney 1986).

Even in the favored military contracting business, diminished returns to research were commonplace. Defense contractors found the need to employ organizational workarounds like the infamous Skunkworks at Lockheed to get projects done on time. Valuable entrepreneurial employees left large companies to pursue their own ideas in the relatively creative environment of their own garages. Silicon Valley companies—Varian, Hewlett Packard, and Fairchild—felt compelled to meet these motivational problems head-on. In search of more effective conditions for innovation these companies adopted non-hierarchical organizational innovations, some explicitly influenced by the visionary philosophies of the German optical glass company, Schott and Genossen. Their new practices ranged from employee ownership to profit-sharing plans based on stock options. Hewlett Packard, founded in a garage in Palo Alto, chose to keep its operating units small, dividing and subdividing as the units and their markets grew. Silicon Valley companies doubted the effectiveness of the corporate research laboratory model. Intel, arguably the most successful company formed in Silicon Valley, did not set up a research laboratory, though it employed many Ph.D. researchers. Instead of hiding away in laboratories, its scientists worked directly on the operating floor, supporting its operating personnel (Lecuyer 2003; Bassett 2002).

The last advanced research laboratory set up by an old-style Eastern firm in Silicon Valley, Xerox Palo Alto Research Center (PARC), confirmed that the standard industrial laboratory model had outlived its usefulness for many US companies. The laboratory adopted a number of novel approaches to research, and its spin-offs both official and unofficial helped populate Silicon Valley (Pake 1986). Set up in 1970 to produce the next big product to succeed the Xerox copier ten years hence, the laboratory produced many usable inventions for the digital revolution well before Xerox was ready to attempt the analog to digital transition. PARC's performance, highly productive from an R&D standpoint, but a failure as an innovation strategy for Xerox, epitomized the problem of the standard industrial research model when directed at transformative innovation (Smith and Alexander 1988).

Ironically, at just about the time that the corporate research laboratory declined in the United States, several Japanese electronics companies set up research laboratories in US R&D centers, near major universities or company laboratories. Having run out of further technology to acquire, these famously adept "imitators" judged certain aspects of the US corporate research model to be worthy of adaptation, if not direct imitation.

Faced with humiliating Japanese competition in cars, electronic devices, and consumer electronics, the US innovation system did an about-face in the 1980s. The Reagan government relaxed anti-monopoly regulations and enforcement, and funded Sematech, a cooperative research venture among a group of US electronics and computer companies. This experiment followed congressional legislation mandating cooperative industry arrangements with US government laboratories and agencies. At least some of these government-coordinated and funded efforts were highly successful (Thornberry 2002).

Recent studies of industrial research at Pechiney in France, Philips in Holland, and Unilever in Great Britain and Holland, suggest that World War II was also a turning point for research in the rest of the industrial world, though the turning point took different forms from the United States. In Germany many scientists—especially leading chemists and physicists who were in demand elsewhere—fled the Nazi regime's attacks on universities and Jewish businessmen and resettled abroad. This expertise was gone for good, but ample numbers of German designers and engineers remained in West Germany to carry out the immediate postwar reconstruction effort. Germany's economy recovered with surprising speed, but it lost much of the advanced knowledge, especially in biotech research, that it had generated before the war (Wengenroth 2006).

Meanwhile, large French and British companies set up new research laboratories, or promoted others to corporate laboratories (Le Roux 2003; Grinberg *et al.* 1997). Industrial research in Europe, though more recently established than in the United States, shared the same difficulties with research productivity (Jones 2005). Many European scientists, especially British Ph.D.s, found US research environments and salaries attractive and emigrated to the United States. In Great Britain and France the negative effects of "lock-in" were not offset by opportunities to rebuild defeated opponents, Germany and Japan. In the Netherlands and Great Britain the values of the scientific communities clashed with the business models of European companies even more than they did in the United States (Jones and Sluyterman 2003; Davids and Verbong 2007; Arns 1997). In France the shift away from the dominant engineering model was more contested, and more incomplete, the state remaining the prime mover in Big Science for civilian purposes (Hecht 1998).

Strangely missing from the business history literature of the twentieth century is the small innovative firm, though for economists the relative merits of large versus small-firm innovators was a burning debate. The history of Ampex, a small firm that introduced the video-recorder only to be out-maneuvered by Sony, is a happy exception (Rosenbloom and Freeze 1985). Other scholars have challenged historians of R&D to pay more attention to research in small companies, and proposed new ways of locating the data (Morris 2002). But in general the experience of small-company innovators remains to be addressed. The places where small firms clustered, which might also be called creative regions, have received some attention as historians have studied industrial districts and the geography of innovation (Fields 2005; Scott 1998).

15.8 CREATIVE REGIONS

Explaining the uniqueness of Silicon Valley as a hotbed of innovation has been a cottage industry among business historians and geographers since the 1980s. Silicon Valley achieved entrepreneurial prominence during World War II, with the rapid growth of electronics firms like Varian and Hewlett Packard. While some Silicon Valley enterprises started as outposts of eastern firms, the place was never home to Eastern-style managerial hierarchies. Some attribute this difference to the skilled and free-thinking component of its workforce, some to the influence of utopian socialist ideas on its founders, some to the proximity of Stanford University and local boosterism, some to the need for professional employment on the West Coast (Adams 2003; Bassett 2002; Cohen and Fields 2000; Kenney 2000; Lecuyer 2006).

Although Silicon Valley might appear as a classic example of an open innovation system, it might better be described as an alternative form to the managerial hierarchy, where government contracting took the place of the civilian coordinating hierarchy (Kenney 2000; Leslie 2000). The Valley and many of its companies proved to be resilient, successfully enduring technical transitions from transistors to integrated circuits, military contracting to civilian business, and information technology to biotech and internet start-ups. In the 1970s and 1980s, the region became a prime example of positive institutional co-evolution, when local entrepreneurs found flexible financial backing in a newly constituted venture capital system (Kenney 2000).

But Silicon Valley was hardly the first creative region in the United States. Industrial incubators and invention collectives existed much earlier in the textile, gun, and shoe machinery hubs of industrial New England, the fashion, jewelry, and invention centers of New York, New Jersey, and Philadelphia (Scranton 1997; Lamoreaux and Sokoloff 2000), the electrochemical centers of Niagara Falls, Cleveland, and Pittsburgh (Trescott 1981), and the ceramic and plumbing fixture centers of Wisconsin (Blaszcyzk 2000). Creative regions have manifested similar interrelationships and co-evolutionary patterns in many other parts of the world (Zeitlin, this volume). Such innovation centers were unsuitable for the typical corporate laboratory: information was too leaky, the workforces too mobile. Creative regions were more likely, however, to develop the complementary services that sustained entrepreneurship. Above all creative regions are good places to study networks in innovation, for networking relationships between large and small enterprises were at the heart of successful economic development in all industrialized countries.

15.9 NEW DIRECTIONS

So far, this discussion of technology and innovation has covered the twentieth century, themes that preoccupied Business History and History of Technology. Two common themes—the dynamics of technological systems, and technology and strategy—emerged out of the post-World War II interest in high tech as an engine of development, while two others—R&D's role in innovation, and the workings of the industrial laboratory—were responsive to problems with R&D productivity and intensifying international competition in technology (Le Roux 2003). During the last decade of the 20th century, historians' interest in globalization and cultural studies energized a new and different interest in innovation, changing the way R&D has been interpreted, both cognitively and from the inside out.

15.10 INTERNATIONAL PERSPECTIVES

As globalization became a more prominent force in all economies, even US historians and economists have looked to explain the dynamics of national economies in terms of systematic differences between countries as "national innovation systems" (Nelson 1993). Interpretation of econometric data at highly aggregated levels rests on certain assumptions concerning the interrelationships between patent systems, research universities, government, and industry laboratories that are not always corroborated by the historical record. Nevertheless, it has stimulated historians in various countries to do more empirical work on the specifics of their own innovation systems, and the firms and other institutions they comprise. Second looks at the standard accounts of several countries have yielded fresh insights of the kind that have also arisen out of scholarship on alternative scenarios and industrial districts (Zeitlin, this volume).

Early comparative studies of different countries and their innovative capabilities focused mainly on the original industrial powers—Great Britain, Germany, and the United States. As the leading industrial economies in the world, the problem was to explain the role of innovation, especially science-based innovation, in determining their success, or in Britain's case after World War II, their lagging performance despite substantial investment (Hughes 1962; Mowery 1984). Most studies in the 1970s and 1980s came to the conclusion that there was one best way for economies to develop, and that the success of the contemporary leaders proved it. When the recovered economies of Japan and West Germany challenged US economic leadership after the 1970s, the emphasis shifted to explaining Japan's success vis-à-vis the lagging performance of the United States. Such comparative efforts tended toward the stereotypical and the ideological, using cases of individual companies as illustrations of macroeconomic phenomena, rather than illuminating the range and variety of innovation experience to be found in each country, and between regions.

Studies that were motivated by the Chandlerian paradigm assigned outsized importance to the large, managerial hierarchies in the countries compared, assumed that twentieth century innovation required in-house R&D, and ignored the smaller enterprises and regional groupings on the active periphery where economic novelty has often flourished. As a consequence the business history literature on economic development has developed the innovation and rationalization theme for most industrialized countries, while ignoring the innovation for economic transformation theme. It has been left to economic sociologists to remind historians that historical circumstances matter, that there is no simple formula equating innovation success with economic and social conditions (Dobbin 1994).

15.11 GERMANY, GREAT BRITAIN, AND JAPAN REVISITED

As we have seen, it was the German model of innovation, incorporating research into its innovation system for the purpose of rationalization and competition, that the US scientific community envied and the industrial community emulated. But Germany actually maintained a far more complex and balanced set of institutions to achieve economic recovery after World War I than this one innovation model represents. It was, after all, the only European country to give equal support and equivalent respect to both the research institutions (institutes and universities) that trained industrial researchers and the polytechnics that trained technical people for operations.

A side of the German experience during the 1930s that was largely eclipsed by World War II was the civilian economic program, a story of state-coordinated innovation that ultimately laid the groundwork for the postwar economic recovery. Hitler's economic recovery plan during the 1930s was not just about military production: it featured a radical innovation program sponsored by the government that strove to extend and push Germany's existing infrastructure and civilian manufacturing base along many dimensions simultaneously. The famous "people's car" project, the Volkswagen, designed by Ferdinand Porsche in close collaboration with Adolf Hitler, was intended to develop new manufacturing techniques, new light metal materials and structures, new design concepts, as well as to stimulate road building and other infrastructural improvements, and even new modes of buyer financing (Tolliday 1995). This approach to innovation was coordinated by the design function, not the research function, and implemented by the engineering community. Though disrupted by the war it created favorable circumstances for the postwar recovery by laying the groundwork not only for Volkswagen itself, but also by creating attractive conditions for foreign direct investment in Germany. Such enduring historical continuities are also featured in Japan's postwar business history.

The second chief international contender in the technology-based innovation race after World War II was Japan. Japanese historians have shown that its innovation model, stereotyped as Japan, Inc., was actually rooted in longstanding institutional development dating from before the Meiji Restoration. Japan laid the foundations of its technology policy in the Tokagawa period, when it was recognized that education and technology would be important to Japanese modernization. Japan's approach to modernization flouted the theory of comparative advantage. First, in textiles and later in the heavier manufacturing industries, Japan followed an important principle: to obtain the best process technology that could be found anywhere in the world, not simply for transfer, but for re-engineering and re-invention. Second, it took as a process innovation goal not just cost reduction, but quality and performance. Third, it accepted the notion that research and development were important as activities of the firm, and split the costs of building the national research infrastructure in institutes and universities evenly between government and the private sector (Morris-Suzuki 1994; Odagiri and Goto 1996).

Despite the recognition that research mattered, Japanese companies explicitly rejected the idea of segregated research departments, never performed fundamental research, and rarely did advanced research leading to new products, preferring to acquire the product technology from abroad and develop it in the open competitive market system of Japan where information flowed freely. Research was conducted on the factory floor, involving workers at all levels, and eliminating far fewer of the sources of new ideas, local and craft knowledge than were eliminated in US factories under scientific management. Fourth, especially after World War II when Japanese industry had to make its transition out of producing war materiel into civilian products, it chose to coordinate its longer-term efforts through the Ministry of Trade and Industry, or MITI.

Historians of the Japanese economy point to certain myths concerning MITI and Japanese innovation (Fruin 1992; Odagiri and Goto 1996). After World War II, MITI's role evolved, from directing reconstruction to taking the long-term view, guiding the economy into good relations with its foreign customers, assuring economic security, and predicting which new technologies would have development potential. Recognizing the tendency among companies competing for survival to neglect necessary investments in R&D and social capital, MITI also subsidized and encouraged R&D expenditures among Japanese firms.

While earlier phases of postwar coordination and investment under MITI were effective in Japan, during the 1990s the tables were turned in the high-tech competition between Japan and the United States. The US government openly encouraged the kind of industrial collaboration in high technology that it had previously actively prohibited outside the military sponsored contractors, and backed the collaborative Sematech project headed first by Robert Noyce. MITI's effort to coordinate large high-tech research projects among fierce competitors in the Japanese VLSI project in the late 1990s was less successful (Thornberry 2002).

Finally, a few collective historical works have taken on the daunting task of looking at technological development around the world, often with a focus on particular industries, such as petrochemicals, and information technology. Here we are beginning to see historical accounts of phenomena that traditional business history would have considered unlikely, innovation in mixed or socialist systems, successful examples of government-stimulated or government-coordinated technology policies (Coopey 2004). Such studies should lead not only to a broader consideration of what is possible, but to a re-examination and revision of established interpretations of 20th century history in the traditional industrial countries. Re-examination of the British innovation experience, for instance, has shifted attention from explaining the British lag, attributed to a supposed underinvestment in industrial R&D, to a possible misallocation or overconcentration of significant R&D resources in military projects.

As the emphasis has shifted to a global arena, numerous historical studies have been motivated by the need to explain competitive outcomes in particular industries, most notably the global battle between the Japanese, German, and US steel and auto industries. Related comparisons have explained the relative success of the Dutch innovation system over the British after World War II in co-evolutionary terms of superior Dutch professional education in management, languages, and engineering (Tolliday 1998; Jones and Sluyterman 2003).

Studies of international R&D have reopened the debate between closed and open innovation systems, questioning whether the closed system, integrating research inside large companies, was really as superior to open systems of research as earlier comparisons of British and US economic performance maintained they were. A recent account of R&D at the London, Midland and Scottish Railway finds it to be the best of both the open and closed systems of innovation, combining high-level in-house capability with a network of technological experts in such a way as to minimize transaction costs and create a high level of technology absorption (Divall 2006).

For some the reconsideration of open innovation systems in history is prompted by the success of global companies in organizing communities of designers and manufacturers to supply their needs on a project by project basis, quickly, flexibly, and efficiently (Mowery 2006). Seen from this vantage point, the centralized laboratory of the 20th century, with its lengthy project cycles, its enormous overheads, and its internecine rivalries, looks very much like an organizational dinosaur.

Since the mid-1990s, multiple sources for learning about innovation have opened up. Countries with mixed economies like France, Italy, and the Nordic group, have initiated self-studies of innovation and its role in their own development. These studies, sometimes pair-wise comparisons, point to a more global understanding of the conditions that promote or retard innovation not only internationally but also in domestic settings. The role of small countries like Israel, Taiwan, and Ireland, once thought to be peripheral in a negative sense, can now be seen to be punching above their weight when the state gets involved in coordinating national knowledge strategies towards particular innovative ends (Breznitz 2005). The Dutch self-study program, which emphasizes a holistic approach to all aspects of innovation in its multiple social contexts, charts a direction that business historians in other countries must be inclined to follow also (Jones and Sluyterman 2003).

15.12 SOCIAL CONTEXT OF INNOVATION

Economic sociologists who have emphasized the importance of context have spelled out more clearly than historians have recently the parameters of interest in historical work: institutions, networks, power, and cognition (Dobbin 2004). We have already seen that institutions and networks have come to occupy a prominent place in the thinking of business historians, the former for those most interested in innovation, the latter for those most interested in research. Questions of power have been inherent in the assumptions on which the organizational synthesis is based: there is now a clear historical basis from which to question the assumption that the link between the corporate laboratory and the executive office was the determining link in the design and deployment of any technology. Customers and users, who have often been left out of innovation accounts, are being reintroduced as powerful actors in determining the reality of systems in operation and at work, as opposed to their original, strategic, intent (Kline 2000; Yates 2005). Historians are reminded to consider outcomes over plans, and to evaluate outcomes not measured against their original intent, but according to the cumulative effects they have on firms, economies, and societies. Studies that examine innovations at multiple points in time can be important windows into the social value of failure, and the process of organizational learning (Girschik 2006; Graham 1986, 1988). Indeed, past president of the Business History Conference, Patrick Fridenson, has urged business historians to pay more attention to innovation failure both in firms and in industries: for studies of failure can reveal much about where power has actually rested in the mutual shaping that occurs between technologies and organizations, technologies and societies.

15.13 COGNITIVE ASPECTS OF INDUSTRIAL RESEARCH

Historians of technology and sociologists of science have for decades been studying the many cultures of research and development, the nature of actual work, emphasizing the social and cognitive processes of science and technology as the real stuff of innovation (Carlson 1991; Latour and Woolgar 1986; Lipartito 2003). Some have compared the different research models that governed work in the laboratory and where they came from, including the persistent disputes between engineering research and scientific research, and the differences in cognitive styles between scientists, technicians, and inventors (Kline and Lassman 2005). Others have examined the intellectual and social networks that form around long waves in technology, and the problems pharmaceutical companies and others have experienced trying to make technological transitions from one wave to the next (Galambos and Sewall 1995; Graham and Shuldiner 2001). Whether the shift has been between mechanics and electronics, wood and metal, high performance machines to lower cost machines, organic chemistry and biotech, historians have discovered that technological transitions have involved shifts in meaning and cultural values that have had little to do with the effectiveness of the technology involved for the purpose intended and much to do with the motivation of the technical personnel doing the research and designing the new products (Schatzberg 1994). Extensions of this work have looked at forms of meaning expressed in laboratory architecture, at the influence of physical spaces on research, and at the consequences for an emerging technology of distance and proximity, co-location and separation (Knowles and Leslie 2001; Choi 2004).

Some forms of industrial research have never inhabited a laboratory but have surely qualified as research nonetheless. One example of research *en plein air* was the carefully documented fieldwork of the oil field services company Schlumberger (Bowker 1995). Unable to take refuge behind laboratory walls and exposed more than most to customers and users, Schlumberger's technologists had to rely on the documentation of processes alone to turn their electrical sensing practices into a coherent service customers would trust, license, and use. Likewise in other organizations that had continuous customer contact—designers and market researchers, licensing laboratories and sales laboratories—researchers had similar experiences of developing their shared practices in the open (Blaszczyk 2000).

In cognitive terms as well, Schlumberger's "science on the run" mirrored a myriad of interdisciplinary activities that took place in industrial research settings when disciplines were in their formative stages, as scientists, engineers, inventors, and technicians drawn out of different universities and backgrounds had to create their own cultures of science—becoming no longer chemists or physicists, but "metallurgists", or "glass technologists". Histories of materials innovators show that the days when industrial scientists were constructing their own sciences, often writing the textbooks and educating university departments in them, were times of extraordinary motivation and high returns to research investment (Graham and Pruitt 1990; Graham and Shuldiner 2001).

15.14 Conclusions

The business history of technology and innovation has come a long way from the days when economists had to be persuaded that firms had a role to play, and when the main debate focused on whether small firms or large firms were the true innovators. Organizational networks leading to successful innovation have usually contained both large and small enterprises exchanging mutually valuable information and expertise. It has become all too clear that innovation thrives on variety and open circulation of information, and that access to appropriate knowledge networks has been far more important than physical conditions or even access to boardrooms and executive offices. International comparisons are no longer pursued to explain leads and lags, but to point to different possible models for success, and our limited literature on innovation failures suggests that there is a lot more digging to be done.

Recognizing that research is first of all a mental and social activity that can take place in many physical settings, historians have a professional obligation to record more carefully what types of people and skills have actually been contributing innovators, and not to feed the persistent myth that funding professional researchers alone buys a one-way ticket to effective economic development. There is an obligation to fill out a picture which currently has only one well-defined path, a few faint byways, and many holes in it. It is still necessary to find better explanations for the intricate dynamics of innovation which must always involve exploration and experimentation. Recent studies suggest that the industrialized research model promoted by business historians has been prone to lock-in by a constricting set of institutions, and often closed to new ideas.

Brainwashed by misleading postwar interpretations of large interdisciplinary projects like the atom bomb and radar, many American managements in the 1950s and 1960s harbored the illusion that investing in R&D was all that was needed for significant commercial innovation. This myth was reinforced by the other—the "linear model" of innovation—which held that the innovation process invariably began with a scientifically generated concept, followed by orderly stages of development (Hounshell 1995). When innovation was based on science, so the myth held, a large pay-off could be anticipated as new markets opened and new jobs were created. Disillusionment with these twin myths set in for US industry in the 1970s, and shortly after that in Europe. As Philip Scranton has recently observed, however, public policy at the regional and national level, especially in industrial countries anxious to renew their flagging economies, still misconceives research and development as both necessary and sufficient for innovation (Scranton 2006). Historians of business and technology could do more to set this record straight.

References

ABERNATHY, WILLIAM J. (1978). *The Productivity Dilemma: Roadblock to Innovation in the Automobile Industry.* Baltimore: Johns Hopkins University Press.

ADAMS, B. (2003). "Regionalism in Stanford's Contribution to the Rise of Silicon Valley". *Enterprise and Society*, 4/3, Sept.: 528.

ARNS, ROBERT G. (1997). "The High-Vacuum X-Ray Tube: Technological Change in Social Context". *Technology and Culture*, 38/4: 852–90.

BASSETT, ROSS KNOX (2002). *To the Digital Age: Research Labs, Start-up Companies, and the Rise of MOS Technology.* Baltimore: Johns Hopkins University Press.

BAUMOL, WILLIAM (2002). *The Free-Market Innovation Machine: Analyzing the Growth Miracle of Capitalism.* Princeton: Princeton University Press.

BEST, MICHAEL (1990). *The New Competition: Institutions of Industrial Restructuring.* Cambridge, Mass.: Harvard University Press.

BLASZCZYK, REGINA (2000). *Imagining Consumers: Design and Innovation from Wedgwood to Corning.* Baltimore: Johns Hopkins University Press.

BOWKER, GEOFFREY C. (1994). *Science on the Run: Information Management and Industrial Geophysics at Schlumberger, 1920–1940.* Cambridge, Mass.: MIT Press.

BREZNITZ, DAN (2005). "Innovation and the State: Development Strategies for High Technology Industries in a World of Fragmented Production: Israel, Ireland, and Taiwan". *Enterprise & Society*: 675–86.

BRITTAIN, JAMES E. (1992). *Alexanderson: Pioneer in American Electrical Engineering.* Baltimore: Johns Hopkins University Press.

CARLSON, W. BERNARD (1991). *Innovation as a Social Process: Elihu Thomson and the Rise of General Electric, 1879–1900.* New York: Cambridge University Press.

CHANDLER, ALFRED D. JR. (2001). *Inventing the Electronic Century: The Epic Story of the Consumer Electronics and Computer Industries.* New York: Free Press.

CHOI, HYUNGSUB (2004). "Between Research and Production: Making Transistors at RCA, 1948–1960". Paper presented at the Business History Conference. Le Creusot, France.

CHRISTENSEN, CLAYTON (1997). *The Innovator's Dilemma.* Cambridge, Mass.: Harvard Business School Press.

COHEN, STEPHEN S., and FIELDS, GARY (2000). "Social Capital and Capital Gains: An Examination of Social Capital in Silicon Valley", in Kenney (2000), 190–217.

COOPEY, RICHARD (ed.) (2004). *Information Technology Policy: An International History.* Oxford: Oxford University Press.

Cusumano, Michael A. (1985). *The Japanese Automobile Industry: Technology and Management at Nissan and Toyota.* Cambridge, Mass.: Harvard University Press.

Davids, Mila, and Verbong, Geert (2007). "Intra-organizational Alignment and Innovation Processes: Philips and Transistor Technology". *Business History Review,* 80/4: 657–88.

deVries, Marc (2006). *Eighty Years of Research at the Philips Naturkundig Laboratorium, 1914–1994.* Amsterdam: Amsterdam University Press.

Divall, Colin (2006). "Technological Networks and Industrial Research in Britain: The London, Midland and Scottish Railway, 1926-47". *Business History,* 48/1: 43–68.

Dobbin, Frank (1994). *Forging Industrial Policy: The United States, Britain, and France in the Railway Age.* New York: Cambridge University Press.

—— (2004). *The New Economic Sociology.* Princeton, NJ: Princeton University Press.

Fields, Gary S. (2005). *Territories of Profit.* Stanford, Calif.: Stanford University Press.

Florida, Richard, and Kenney, Martin (1986). *The Breakthrough Illusion: Corporate America's Failure to Move from Innovation to Mass Production.* New York: Basic Books.

Fruin, W. Mark. (1992). *The Japanese Enterprise System: Competitive Strategies and Cooperative Structures.* Oxford: Oxford University Press.

Galambos, Louis (1983). "Technology, Political Economy, and Professionalization: Central Themes of the Organizational Synthesis". *Business History Review,* 57: 471–93.

—— (1992). "Theodore N. Vail and the Role of Innovation in the Modern Bell System". *Business History Review,* 66/1: 95–126.

—— (2005). "Recasting the Organizational Synthesis: Structure and Process in the Twentieth and Twenty-first Centuries". *Business History Review,* 79, spring: 1–38.

—— and Sewall, Jane Eliot (1995). *Networks of Innovation: Vaccine Development at Merck, Sharp & Dohme, and Mulford, 1895–1995.* New York: Cambridge University Press.

—— and Sturchio, Jeffrey (1998). "Pharmaceutical Firms and the Transition to Biotechnology: A Study in Strategic Innovation". *Business History Review,* 72/2: 250–78.

Girschik, Katja (2006). "Machine-Readable Codes". *Entreprise et Histoire,* autumn: 1–14.

Graham, Margaret B. W (1985). "Industrial Research in the Age of Big Science", in Richard S. Rosenbloom (ed.), *Research on Technological Innovation, Management and Policy.* New York: JAI Press, 47–79.

—— (1986). *RCA and the VideoDisc: The Business of Research.* New York: Cambridge University Press.

—— (1988). "R&D and Competition in England and the United States: The Case of the Aluminum Dirigible". *Business History Review,* 62/2: 261–85.

—— (2007). "Financing Fiber: Corning Enters the Telecommunications Industry", in Naomi Lamoreaux and Kenneth Sokoloff (eds.), *Financing Innovation.* Cambridge, Mass.: MIT Press, 326–69.

—— and Pruitt, Bettye H. (1990). *R&D for Industry: A Century of Technical Innovation at Alcoa.* New York: Cambridge University Press.

—— and Shuldiner, Alec T. (2001). *Corning and the Craft of Innovation.* New York: Oxford University Press.

Grinberg, Ivan, Griset, Pascal, and LeRoux, Muriel (eds.) (1997). *Cent ans d'innovation dans l'industrie de l'aluminium.* Paris: L'Harmattan, Inc.

Griset, Pascal (ed.) (1996). *Histoire de l'innovation et entreprise.* Paris: l'Harmattan.

Hagstrom, Peter (1998). "Perspectives on Firm Dynamics", in Alfred D. Chandler, Jr., Peter Hagstrom, and Orjan Solvell (eds.), *The Dynamic Firm.* Oxford: Oxford University Press.

HECHT, GABRIELLE (1998). *The Radiance of France*. Cambridge, Mass.: The MIT Press.

HOUNSHELL, DAVID A. (1992). "DuPont and the Management of Large-Scale Research and Development". in Peter Galison and Bruce Hevly (eds.), *Big Science*. Stanford, Calif.: Stanford University Press.

——(1995). "Hughesian History of Technology and Chandlerian Business History: Parallels, Departures and Critics". *History and Technology*, 12: 205–24.

——(1996). "The Evolution of Industrial Research in the United States", in Richard S. Rosenbloom and William Spencer (eds.), *Engines of Innovation U.S. Industrial Research at the End of an Era*. Boston: Harvard Business School Press, 13–85.

HOUNSHELL, DAVID A., and SMITH, JOHN KENLY (1988). *Science and Corporate Strategy: Du Pont R&D, 1902–1980*. Cambridge: Cambridge University Press.

HUGHES, THOMAS (1962). "British Electrical Industry Lag: 1882–1888". *Technology and Culture*, 3: 27–44.

——(1989). "The Evolution of Large Technological Systems", in Wiebe Bijker (ed.), *The Social Construction of Technological Systems: New Directions in the Sociology and History of Technology*. Cambridge, Mass.: MIT Press, 51–82.

ISRAEL, PAUL (1992). *From Machine Shop to Industrial Laboratory: Telegraphy and the Changing Context of American Invention, 1830–1920*. Baltimore: Johns Hopkins University Press.

JENKINS, REESE V. (1975). *Images and Enterprise: Technology and the American Photographic Industry, 1839–1925*. Baltimore: Johns Hopkins University Press.

JONES, GEOFFREY (2005). *Renewing Unilever: Transformation and Tradition*. Oxford: Oxford University Press.

——and SLUYTERMAN, KEETIE E. (2003). "British and Dutch Business History", in Franco Amatori and Geoffrey Jones (eds.), *Business History around the World*. Cambridge: Cambridge University Press.

KENNEY, MARTIN (ed.) (2000). *Understanding Silicon Valley: The Anatomy of an Entrepreneurial Region*. Stanford, Calif.: Stanford University Press.

KEVLES, DANIEL J. (1987). *The Physicists*. New York: Knopf.

KLINE, RONALD R. (1992). *Steinmetz: Engineer and Socialist*. Baltimore: Johns Hopkins University Press.

——(2000). *Consumers in the Country: Technology and Social Change in Rural America*. Baltimore: Johns Hopkins University Press.

——and LASSMAN, THOMAS C. (2005). "Competing Research Traditions in American Industry: Uncertain Alliances between Engineering and Science at Westinghouse Electric, 1886–1935". *Enterprise and Society*, 6/4: 601–45.

KLUZNICK, PETER J. (1987). *Beyond the Laboratory: Scientists as Political Activists in 1930s America*. Chicago and London: University of Chicago Press.

KNOWLES, SCOTT G., and LESLIE, STUART W. (2001). "Industrial Versailles: Eero Saarinen's Corporate Campuses for GM, IBM, and AT&T". *ISIS*, 92, Mar.: 1–33.

LAMOREAUX, NAOMI R., and SOKOLOFF, KENNETH L. (2000). "The Geography of Invention in the American Glass Industry, 1870–1925". *Journal of Economic History*, 60/3: 700–29.

LANDES, DAVID (1969). *The Unbound Prometheus: Technological Change and Industrial Development in Western Europe from 1750 to the Present*. New York: Cambridge University Press.

—— (1998). *The Wealth and Poverty of Nations: Why Some are so Rich and Some are so Poor.* New York: W. W. Norton and Co.

LASSMAN, THOMAS C. (2003). "Industrial Research Transformed: Edward Condon at the Westinghouse Electric and Manufacturing Company, 1935–1942". *Technology and Culture,* 44: 306–39.

LATOUR, BRUNO, and WOOLGAR, STEVE (1986). *Laboratory Life: The Construction of Scientific Facts.* Princeton, NJ: Princeton University Press.

LECUYER, CHRISTOPHE (2003). "High Tech Corporatism: Management–Employee Relations in U.S. Electronics Firms, 1920s–1960s". *Enterprise and Society,* 4/3: 502–20.

—— (2006). *Making Silicon Valley: Innovation and the Growth of High Tech, 1930–1970,* Stanford, Calif.: Stanford University Press.

LE ROUX, MURIEL (2003). *L'entreprise et le recherche: un siecle de recherche industrielle a Pechiney.* Paris: l'Harmattan.

LESLIE, STUART W. (1993). *The Cold War and American Science.* New York: Columbia University Press.

—— (2000). "The Biggest 'Angel' of them All: The Military and the Making of Silicon Valley", in Martin Kenney (ed.), *Understanding Silicon Valley: The Anatomy of an Entrepreneurial Region.* Stanford, Calif.: Stanford Business School Press.

LIPARTITO, KENNETH (2003). "Picturephone and the Information Age". *Technology and Culture,* 44/11: 50–81.

MILLARD, ANDRE (1990). *Edison and the Business of Innovation.* Baltimore: Johns Hopkins University Press.

MOKYR, JOEL (1990). *The Lever of Riches: Technological Creativity and Economic Progress.* New York and Oxford: Oxford University Press.

MORRIS, SUSAN (2002). "Mirror or Myth: Our Historiographic Picture of American Industrial Research". Paper presented at the Business History Conference, Wilmington, Del.

MORRIS-SUZUKI, TESSA (1994). *The Technological Transformation of Japan: From the 17th to the 21st Century.* Cambridge: Cambridge University Press.

MOWERY, DAVID C. (1984). "Firm Structure, Government Policy, and the Organization of Industrial Research: Great Britain and the United States, 1900–1950". *Business History Review,* 58/4: 504–30.

—— (2006). "Plus ça change: Industrial R&D in the 'Third Industrial Revolution' ". Paper presented at the Conference on the Third Industrial Revolution, Bocconi, Italy.

—— and ROSENBERG, NATHAN (1998). *Paths of Innovation.* New York: Cambridge University Press.

MURMANN, JOHANN PETER (2003). *Knowledge and Competitive Advantage: The Coevolution of Firms, Technology, and National Institutions.* Cambridge: Cambridge University Press.

NELSON, RICHARD (ed.) (1993). *National Innovation Systems.* Oxford: Oxford University Press.

—— and ROSENBERG, NATHAN (1998). "Science, Technological Advance, and Economic Growth", in Alfred D. Chandler, Jr., Peter Hagstrom, and Orjan Solvell (eds.), *The Dynamic Firm: The Role of Technology, Strategy, Organization, and Regions.* Oxford: Oxford University Press.

NOBLE, D. F. (1984). *Forces of Production: A Social History of Automation.* New York: Knopf.

ODAGIRI, HIROYUKI, and GOTO, AKIRA (1996). *Technology and Industrial Development in Japan*. Oxford: Oxford University Press.

PAKE, G. E. (1986). "From Research to Innovation at Xerox: A Manager's Principles and Some Examples", in Richard S. Rosenbloom (ed.), *Research on Innovation, Management and Policy*. New York: JAI Press.

PURSELL, CARROLL (1995). *The Machine in America*. Baltimore: Johns Hopkins University Press.

REICH, LEONARD (1985). *The Making of American Industrial Research: Science and Business at GE and Bell, 1876–1926*. New York: Cambridge University Press.

—— (1992). "Lighting the Path to Profit: GE's Control of the Electric Lamp Industry, 1892–1941". *Business History Review*, 66: 305–34.

ROSENBERG, NATHAN (1982). *Inside the Black Box*. New York: Cambridge University Press.

—— (1994). *Exploring the Black Box: Technology, Economics and History*. New York: Cambridge University Press.

—— and FRISCHTAK, CLAUDIO (eds.) (1985), *International Technology Transfer: Concepts, Measures, and Comparisons*. New York: Praeger.

ROSENBLOOM, RICHARD S., and FREEZE, KAREN J. (1985). "Ampex Corporation and Video Innovation", in Richard S. Rosenbloom (ed.), *Research on Technological Innovation, Management, and Policy*. New York: JAI Press, 113–86.

SCHATZBERG, ERIC (1994). "Ideology and Technical Choice: The Decline of the Wooden Airplane in the United States, 1920–1945". *Technology and Culture*, 35/1: 34–69.

SCHUMPETER, JOSEPH (1939). *Business Cycles: A Theoretical, Historical, and Statistical Analysis of the Capitalist Process*. New York: McGraw-Hill.

SCOTT, ALLEN J. (1998). "The Geographic Foundations of Industrial Performance", in Alfred D. Chandler, Peter Hagstrom, and Orjan Solvell (eds.), *The Dynamic Firm*. Oxford: Oxford University Press.

SCRANTON, PHILIP (1997). *Endless Novelty: Specialty Production and American Industrialization, 1865–1925*. Princeton: Princeton University Press.

—— (2006). "Technology, Science and American Innovation". *Business History*, 48/3: 311–31.

SERVOS, JOHN W. (1990). *Physical Chemistry from Ostwald to Pauling: The Making of a Science in America*. Princeton: Princeton University Press.

SMITH, DOUGLAS K., and ALEXANDER, ROBERT C. (1988). *Fumbling the Future: How Xerox Invented, then Ignored, the First Personal Computer*. New York: Morrow.

SMITH, JOHN KENLY (1990). "The Scientific Tradition in American Industrial Research". *Technology and Culture*, 31/1: 121–31.

STURCHIO, JEFFREY L. (1985). "Experimenting with Research: Kenneth Mees, Eastman Kodak and the Challenges of Diversification". Paper presented at the R&D Pioneers Conference, Wilmington, Del.

SZOSTAK, RICK (1995). *Technological Innovation and the Great Depression*. Boulder, Colo.: Westview Press (Harper Collins).

THORNBERRY, JON B. (2002). "Competition and Cooperation: A Comparative Analysis of SEMATECH and the VLSI Research Project". *Enterprise & Society*, 3: 657–86.

TOLLIDAY, STEVEN (1995). "Enterprise and State in the West German Wirtschaftswunder: Volkswagen and the Automobile Industry, 1939–1962". *Business History Review*, 69/3, autumn: 279–350.

—— (1998). "The Diffusion and Transformation of Fordism: Britain and Japan Compared", in Robert Boyer Elsie Charron, Ulrich Jürgens, and Steven Tolliday (eds.), *Between*

Imitation and Innovation: The Transfer and Hybridization of Productive Models in the International Automobile Industry. Oxford: Oxford University Press.

TRESCOTT, MARTHA MOORE (1981). *The Rise of the American Electrochemical Industry, 1880–1910: Studies in the American Technological Environment*. Westport, Conn.: Greenwood Press.

USSELMAN, STEVEN W. (1993). "IBM and its Imitators: Organizational Capabilities and the Emergence of the International Computer Industry". *Business and Economic History*, 22/2: 1–35.

—— (2002). *Regulating Railroad Innovation: Business, Technology, and Politics in America, 1840–1920*. New York: Cambridge University Press.

WANG, JESSICA (1992). "Science, Security and the Cold War: The Case of E.U. Condon". *ISIS*, 83/2: 238–69.

WARSH, DAVID (2006). *Knowledge and the Wealth of Nations*. New York: Norton.

WENGENROTH, ULRICH (2006). "The German Chemical Industry after World War Two", in Louis Galambos, Takashi Hikino, and Vera Zamagni (eds.), *The Global Chemical Industry in the Age of the Petrochemical Revolution*. Cambridge: Cambridge University Press.

YATES, J. (2005). *Structuring the Information Age: Life Insurance and Technology in the Twentieth Century*. Baltimore: Johns Hopkins University Press.

CHAPTER 16

DESIGN AND ENGINEERING

WOLFGANG KÖNIG

16.1 INTRODUCTION

In presenting a sketch of the development of design and engineering since the Industrial Revolution one has to struggle with a set of difficulties. One is the meaning of engineering design. Design can be interpreted broadly as the whole process resulting in a marketable product. It can also be understood more narrowly as the linking of product planning with production. In this sense, designers and draftsmen transform a concept into drawings which function as production plans. Design theories (e.g. Pahl and Beitz 1996) distinguish three stages of (1) conceptual design, that is elaborating the concept of a solution, (2) embodiment design, the functional and geometrical working out of the concept, and (3) detail design, usually in the form of drawings and other information which can be used directly in production.

It seems that the semantics of "design" differ across cultural contexts. Taking the United States and Germany as two extremes: in the United States "design" is interpreted more as the finished product resulting from the development process, which takes place in the laboratory and the workshop. In Germany and other European countries, "design" (in German: *Konstruktion*) is understood rather as the result of office work—that is, design drawings. "Design" in this chapter deals with engineering design and not with industrial design in the artistic sense. Therefore, the focus is more on technical functions than on aesthetic forms.

In yet another sense, "engineering design" is a department in the industrial company. A difficulty for historical research is that the design departments' positions and tasks within the company have changed significantly over time. The borderlines and interfaces between design and other departments have shifted steadily, influencing their respective interpretations of design. Design may include or exclude other tasks like research, development, planning, calculation, cost accounting, drafting, testing, and production. One crucial point for companies' success was whether they managed to organize the interfaces and communication between the various tasks and departments in an effective way.

Engineering design developed differently within national engineering cultures. Nevertheless, I contend that a general pattern can be observed across industrialized countries. (1) At the onset of industrialization, design and manufacturing were highly integrated. (2) During the nineteenth century, design was separated from production and became the center of the company. (3) During the twentieth century, the design function became more differentiated: in some cases more and more tasks were outsourced from the design office to independent departments; in others design became a part of a larger unit; while in still other cases, it became the task of the company as a whole. Within this general pattern, there were many national variants concerning design function's position in the firm, its internal hierarchies and qualifications, the types of equipment used, and the goals pursued. In the final section of this chapter, I will outline these national design styles and cultures, differentiating in particular between a German (and European) culture of design and an American (and Japanese) culture of production.

Besides such national differences, there were also sectoral differences within each country. The role of design in the customized products sector was much greater than in mass production firms. In the latter, design work was limited and drawing-board work could be replaced by experimental development leading directly to prototypes. In contrast, particularly in the capital equipment industries, much design work had to be performed in order to adapt machines and systems to customers' special requirements. Another relevant criterion for design was the degree of integration. Firms with a lot of suppliers used design drawings as a means of communication, while highly integrated companies could communicate through other means. Within the trade, design developed differently in time, scale, and scope. The origins of modern design lay in heavy machinery. The machine-building industry, in a broad sense, including electrical machinery, cars, aircraft, and shipbuilding, was at the forefront of design development. Other industries, like architecture and civil engineering, came second. All in all, the spectrum of design practices within national industries was larger than between countries. This makes it obvious that no precise dates can be assigned to the three phases of design development in the nineteenth and twentieth centuries, which will be examined in the following sections. These phases should be interpreted as historical types which were more or less widespread and started or ended at different times, depending on the country, the industrial sector, the company's product palette, etc.

The state of research on the history of design is rather lean. It is no contradiction that the term "design", in particular in the United States, plays a prominent role in the modern history of technology. This goes back to the 1970s, when historians of technology tried to find an intermediate path between the internalist "nuts and bolts" approach and the externalist approach, which completely ignored technological content (Staudenmaier 1985). Instead, they recommended contextual approaches linking design and environment. However, in this third approach, design is understood primarily as a set of technological products and systems, rather than as the process whereby goods were produced within companies. Particularly in the American literature, the design of large technological systems (Hughes 1998) was treated more extensively than that of traditional machinery.

Another prominent site of design history is located within the "visual thinking" approach (Hindle 1981; Ferguson 1992; Henderson 1999; critical: Lubar 1995; McGee 1999). Its proponents emphasize that engineers think in pictures, that the "mind's eye" needs the support of drawings. Behind this claim is a polemic against the increasing role of theory, mathematics, and computers in design. Whether or not that concern is legitimate, the visual thinking approach has not contributed much to our historical understanding of design. The authors have illustrated their arguments with historical examples but, because of the limited sources, were not really able to reconstruct the designers' way of thinking. The questions treated in this chapter have largely been ignored within the visual thinking approach.

Business historians have rarely dealt substantially with companies' design and drafting departments (with a few conspicuous exceptions: Edmondson 1987; Brown 1995, 1999). There is only one study which considers design in detail, namely at the Brown-Boveri Company in Switzerland, Germany, and France after World War II (Niemitz 1993). Two works advance comparative approaches covering several countries, but on the basis of limited data, and thus present preliminary results (König 1999; Brown 2000). Berner (2007) confirms these results for Sweden between 1880 and 1940. Moritz (1996) has produced an excellent survey of design in the Japanese machine-tool industry which, however, presents a snapshot of the situation around 1990. Several authors have paid attention to the development of engineering drawings without elaborating on the fundamental changes in practice during the nineteenth century (Feldhaus 1959; Nedoluha 1960; Booker 1963; Deforge 1976; Baynes and Pugh 1981). Since the 1980s, Computer-Aided Design (CAD) became the focus of a large body of sociological and psychological research. Nevertheless, it is difficult to summarize the results, both because the technology and its use is still developing rapidly, and because the perspective of most of this research is quite narrow (Reintjes 1991; Arnold 1984; Poitou 1989; Mackensen 1997).

The rest of this chapter focuses on a series of key questions, trying to provide preliminary answers, or at least to formulate theses to orient subsequent research. A central problem is the position of the design function within company organization and communication between design and other departments, especially production. Another theme is the internal organization of the design department and the hierarchies and qualifications of its working staff. These will form the basis for cautious reflections on changing patterns of creativity and routine in design practice. The design function's products are mainly drawings and other information used in the subsequent steps of production. The designers' and draftsmen's work is supported by a lot of tangible and intangible aids: earlier drawings, printed material, oral hints from colleagues, and so on. Drafting and calculating equipment changed over time. It seems that the greatest transformations took place with the introduction of the drafting machine after 1900 and that of CAD since the 1970s. The designer's task can be formulated as searching for solutions, while taking into consideration a complex web of sometimes contradictory requirements. In the nineteenth and twentieth centuries, design aimed at functionality, economy, and environmental protection, essential design goals which can easily be broken down into many more subgoals.

16.2 DESIGN IN THE WORKSHOP: COMBINATION AND INTEGRATION OF DESIGN AND MANUFACTURE

In early industrialization, small machine shops were often organized according to craft traditions. Owners, foremen, and workers knew each other and communicated directly at the workplace. The workforce's competences and experiences were the shops' most important resources. Usually, the technical personnel acquired its knowledge while working in other companies. The design of machines originated in other shops and was only transformed incrementally. Sometimes, companies learned manufacturing by repairing machines produced by others. This design method can be characterized as designing in the material. Machines were made completely on the shop floor by integrating new features into existing products.

This kind of design predominated until the middle of the nineteenth century, but persisted in smaller shops well into the twentieth. Which persons initiated new designs and design changes depended on the distribution of competences. These could belong to the owner but also to the foremen or craftsmen. Often, these figures cooperated, bringing together their respective competences. Take, for instance, Siemens & Halske, founded in 1847, which manufactured telegraph apparatus and other electrical equipment (Kocka 1969). When the company began, design initiatives reportedly came from Werner Siemens, who was a largely self-educated scientist and engineer, from Siemens' partner, the mechanic Johann Georg Halske, and from the shop workers as well. Early industrialists had to combine many functions. In 1867, Friedrich Voith founded a machine shop in Württemberg, which manufactured water turbines. In the beginning, he had to integrate the tasks of "chief, engineer, accountant, cashier, and foreman" (Pflieger-Haertel 1929: 65).

In that very informal system, oral instructions were the most important means of communication. These could be supported by paper sketches and very rough drawings, sometimes literally on the shop floor, or on wooden boards, cloth, and slates (Brown 2000: 201–5). Wooden models were also widespread, and some companies possessed thousands of them. For instance, National Cash Register (NCR) still used wooden models in production around 1900 (Crowther 1926). It is obvious that in such an environment the workshop had a lot of freedom to work out a detailed design. It is also clear that each construction was unique and could not be copied exactly. The system's advantage was that the technological personnel at each level had the opportunity to bring in their competences.

16.3 THE DESIGN OFFICE AS THE CENTER OF THE COMPANY

During the nineteenth century, design became separated from the workshop. This might begin with a production staff position which extended its scope over time. Sometimes the outcome was a "technological bureau" which combined functions of research, development, planning, design, testing, and calculation. Within this bureau, design could be more or less independent.

The first design offices are documented in the machine-building industry. George and Robert Stephenson's locomotive factory had one at their disposal from the late 1820s, which was perhaps the first in English industry. In other countries, reports on design offices point to later founding dates: the 1840s in the United States and France, the early 1850s in Germany. In countries like France and the United States, the establishment of a design office in mechanical engineering originated from the railways' specifications to the locomotive builders. In Germany we find the first documented design offices at two predecessors of MAN, namely the Sander'sche machine building company in Augsburg and that of Cramer-Klett in Nuremberg. The electrical industry followed later. Siemens & Halske established a design office with numerous functions in 1867–8. Its supervisor was Friedrich von Hefner-Alteneck, who became a prominent figure in electrical engineering. The company was changing at that time from a mechanical workshop into a factory.

In this way, design departments were established between the 1820s and the 1880s in most early industrialized countries. Developing countries adopted the system later. In Japan, which industrialized during the late nineteenth century, design offices were already operating in the machine-building industry before World War I (Sawai 1989).

During the second half of the nineteenth century, the design office became the central department of the company. Control over production shifted from the workshop to the design office. The idea was that the design department prescribed everything in detail and the shop had only to execute it. The foremen and craft workers in the shops regarded this as a kind of de-skilling (König 1999). At Siemens & Halske around 1870, on the one hand, a foreman complained that Hefner's design office would stifle all differing opinions. On the other hand, Werner Siemens accused the foremen of continuing to invent and design informally. In any case, with the design office's strict separation from the shop it became more difficult to integrate the company's accumulated manufacturing knowledge.

Contemporaries interpreted this fundamental change of control in the company by saying that the "governance of the shop" was replaced by the "governance of the (design) office". No longer was the product adapted to manufacture, but instead manufacture was adapted to the product. And the designers who were better qualified than the shop workers integrated more and more knowledge into the product. John Brown (1999) emphasizes that the design offices were the companies' centers of innovation before they established specialized departments for research and development after 1900.

In the multidivisional company which grew considerably in size, informal oral communication no longer worked. Communication had to be formalized as did the responsibilities of the respective departments. The big companies developed into large bureaucracies with numerous departments and a huge workforce which was controlled by a set of orders and rules. Oral instructions were replaced or complemented by written orders. The number of white-collar design personnel increased. So the Baldwin Locomotive Works in Philadelphia employed three designers and draftsmen in 1860, compared to some 450 in 1913 (Brown 1995).

The new communication methods between design and manufacture were the engineering drawings of machine parts, which functioned as production-control plans. They should not be confused with the traditional shadowed perspective drawings of whole machines which can be found in large numbers in prints. Such drawings continued to be used in marketing and advertising until they were replaced by photographs. The new production plans were in orthogonal projection with sections and views from the sides and the top. In contrast to the perspective drawings, the measures and angles were equal to those the workers had to materialize. One can distinguish two phases of engineering drawings. In the first stage, from about 1850, drawings were full-scale and had no dimensions. The foremen or workers took the measures from the drawings with a pair of compasses or a yardstick and transferred them to the material. These imprecise methods left much freedom to the workshop. The rationale behind this system was that, at the time, it was not possible to manufacture with great precision using machine tools. And it made no sense to draft more precisely than could be manufactured. Beyond that, drawings were often colored to indicate materials.

In the second stage from the 1870s, designers worked out dimensional-scale drawings in black and white. Best-practice drawings even contained the tolerances for manufacture. Colors became outdated because of the increasing number of materials. The new mode of drafting was connected with interchangeability like the new mode of production (Hounshell 1984). Interchangeability was achieved first with a mixed system of machine work and hand fitting and afterwards with better machine tools and fixtures which were able to make ready-to-use parts. The system began in the United States and rapidly diffused to other countries. Drawings had to be multiplied in order to instruct the different work stations in the shop or the suppliers. This began with hand-made copies. Around 1850, copying was facilitated by the use of special transparent paper. From the 1870s, blueprinting first with sunlight and later with artificial light allowed easy preparation of as many copies as necessary.

The new dimensional drawings augmented control over production. Management was able to prescribe in detail what workers had to do. In that way, work control by design was established before the advent of Taylorism. In addition, designers now possessed the means of incorporating and transferring increased knowledge into production. From the late nineteenth century, design offices developed into larger units divided horizontally and vertically. Horizontally, the design department could have sections responsible for groups of products, machines, or even machine parts. Vertically, it became a hierarchical organization related to the responsibilities and competences of the staff. At the top was a chief engineer who managed the whole design program. Below him were the senior staff of high-class designers responsible for the conceptual and practical design of complete facilities and machines. Using sketches, they instructed the "run-of-the-mill" designers responsible for the detailed design of machine parts. The draftsmen's job was to work out the whole set of drawings properly. Tracers supported designers and draftsmen, preparing in addition to other work the copies and blueprints.

All in all, designers performed more creative work, draftsmen more repetitive tasks. However, we should keep in mind that the boundary between designers and draftsmen was loose and the terms changed over time. Those employees who were called draftsmen in the nineteenth century were later called designers. There were two main groups of personnel entering the design departments. The first came from the primary and secondary schools, where they had acquired general drafting techniques. They started as apprentices but in principle could move up to design positions if they successfully enlarged their competences within the firm or by self-training or attending evening and Sunday classes. Such bottom-up careers were common in the nineteenth century but became exceptional during the twentieth century. The second group came from the engineering schools and colleges. Engineers possessing no practical experience had to start as draftsmen but could move up more easily. Engineers with shop experience could step in directly as designers.

So, in principle, the career system in the design office was permeable and flexible. Nevertheless, there was a sharp distinction between the professional engineers and the draftsmen. Normally, draftsmen could not become members of the engineering institutions and societies. Hence from the mid-nineteenth century, draftsmen organized in independent associations. The English started in 1852 with a London Association of Foremen Engineers and Draughtsmen. In 1885, in the United States an Association of American Draftsmen and in Germany the *Deutsche Techniker-Verband* were founded. Membership of these draftsmen associations fluctuated widely and depended first of all on the labor market.

There were differences between national engineering cultures in the recruitment and the careers of designers and draftsmen. In German design departments, the level of formal engineering education was rather high. Most design and drafting personnel came from the two- or three-year technical intermediate schools (*Technische Mittelschulen*) which were characteristic of the German dual system of engineering education (König 1993). But the percentage of college-educated designers (*Technische Hochschulen*) and draftsmen was also considerable. The design office was the most important occupational branch for German engineers. Additionally, in 1939, engineering drafting became an officially recognized vocation within the German state-controlled apprenticeship system. The context was that the Nazi policy of autarky and rearmament had resulted in a lack of skilled drafting personnel. Furthermore, the boundary between designers and draftsmen had become stricter. In France, the *Écoles des Arts et Métiers* were the main suppliers of the design department (Edmondson 1987). The graduates possessed a broad technical training, including workshop experience and the making and reading of engineering drawings. Normally, they worked for five or six years as draftsmen, with the prospect of moving to design and management positions or becoming independent industrialists.

The German and French school culture system differed markedly from the American and British shop culture (Calvert 1967; Buchanan 1989). Most of the beginners in the British and American design departments came from the shop. They were trained in drafting on the job and could acquire additional competences by attending evening courses. Over time, they could move up to higher positions. In the twentieth century, alongside the shop draftsmen, more and more school draftsmen entered the design offices. Nevertheless, bottom-up careers were still possible, for an even longer period in Britain than in the United States.

At the beginning of industrialization, the machine-building companies' focus was on functional design. Their main goal was to fulfill the customers' functional requirements, while costs came second. That changed with increasing national and international competition during the nineteenth century. Cost considerations became increasingly important. The fundamental goal of functional design was supplemented by economical design and design for manufacture. Contemporaries believed that cost reductions in production were hampered by design departments which did not design for manufacture. This was hardly surprising, however, since with the separation of design from production, manufacturing experience had been largely excluded from the design process.

Complaints were ubiquitious, but most pronounced in Germany from the late nineteenth century. In the developing discussion on "the American menace", German manager-engineers admitted that US machinery producers designed faster and cheaper, even if it was claimed that German machines used less energy and were more durable. Internationally, "too Dutch" became the catchword for overcomplicated and expensive design. Germans attributed the deficiencies at least partially to the neglect of manufacturing in engineering education. After 1900, this discussion resulted in the founding of chairs for manufacturing at the *Technische Hochschulen*. Thereafter, the new production engineering community engaged itself in formulating manufacturing criteria for designers to bear in mind. Although this initiative was not without results, complaints about manufacturing deficiencies in design nevertheless persisted during the twentieth century. It seems as if the problems could not be solved solely by college reforms and that, in this respect, the British and American way of enriching the design departments with personnel possessing shop experience was more successful.

Another means of making design more economical was standardization. In the machine-building industry, standardization acquired momentum from the late nineteenth century. One approach was to reduce the number of machine types, the other to reduce the number of machine parts. Standardization started within companies and extended later to trade and national standards. For instance, under the special conditions of World War I, German machinery builders founded a national standards institution in 1917, which expanded rapidly in peacetime. Among its first standards were some for engineering drafting. The United States was the forerunner and model of standardization, while France and Britain lagged far behind (Moutet 1997; Zeitlin 2000). The focus of American standardization was on reducing types, with Henry Ford's Model T as the much admired extreme example. This was very appropriate for the American mass market with customers who were content with a limited supply of product variants. On the contrary, the German custom producers focused on standardization of parts, which was more appropriate for its differentiated national and international markets. During the interwar period, German companies used the "meccano-set" principle in order to combine standardization with customer orientation.

In France and Germany, standardization efforts had to overcome difficulties with managers as well as with designers. Managers were sometimes skeptical about the promised economic results. Designers admitted that standards diminished routine drafting work on the one hand, but complained that they restricted creativity on the other. There was a debate among contemporaries, which is continued by historians, whether standardization and other means of rationalization deskilled design work.

One possible conclusion is that design became more limited in scope but more sophisticated in depth (König 1999).

16.4 Design as a Distributed Process within the Company

A fundamental change in the design function began during the late nineteenth century in the context of the efficiency movement ("rationalization movement", *Rationalisierungsbewegung*). Efficiency in the sense of improving the relation between inputs and outputs was an old and basic principle of economic thinking and engineering work. What was new was that such initiatives became more pronounced and systematized. The main focus of the efficiency movement, with Taylorism as its most prominent variant, was to establish control over the workforce. It should be recalled that this was also the goal of the dimensional black-and-white production plans which had been introduced earlier. Taylorism went further by transforming the drawings into production orders on cards, which made competences in reading and interpreting drawings superfluous. Hence new departments for production planning (*Betriebsbüros, Arbeitsvorbereitung*) were established as intermediaries between design and production.

At least in Germany, management assigned an additional task to the production planning departments. Their responsibility was now to examine whether the designers' work was appropriate for manufacturing. Behind that lay the enduring complaints that design did not sufficiently respect manufacturing requirements. In some cases, this control responsibility was given to a senior designer in the office. In this way, the new departments and positions created by the rationalization movement established a two-pronged apparatus of control: one aimed at the workers, and the other at the designers.

The efficiency movement likewise increased the importance of cost control (Garner 1954). Previously, costs were estimated in relation to the weight of the machines. Now, prime cost at least for the main parts, that is the cost of materials and direct labor, was calculated more precisely. Design and manufacture had to deliver data to the accounting department, which in turn prescribed cost limits. Later on, complete cost arrangements followed. Cost thinking became a central issue within the engineering community. That development went furthest in the United States where an engineering instructor coined the phrase: "The dollar is the final term in every engineering equation" (Calvert 1967: 225).

In Germany, these more divided responsibilities led to reflections about whether the design department could still be regarded as the center of the company. For instance the *Dubbel*, one of the most important German engineering handbooks, stated in 1923: "The age of design has been replaced by an age of manufacture" (Buchheim and Sonnemann 1990: 351). In some French firms, the design function was incorporated into larger units which integrated issues like research, development, design, drafting, planning, and cost accounting. This was the case with the *Bureaux d'Études* or *bureaux techniques* which emerged after 1900 (Poitou 1988). In Japan, design was subordinated to product planning departments, which took on a central position within the companies (Moritz 1996). Normally, the chief designer participated in the department's work, but the lead was taken by the marketing and manufacturing representatives.

At the turn of the century, a debate took place about whether and how far design work could be rationalized. An article reported on such efforts in the Westinghouse company (König 1999). It stated that Westinghouse had succeeded in reducing the throughput time of design orders from 34 days in 1903 to 6.3 days in 1907. During the same time period the number of drawings per employee doubled. It could be assumed that this success story resulted from a reorganization of routine work. Another example referring to the construction of skyscrapers pointed to a flow production of drawings (König 1999).

A controversial theme was whether creative design work could be rationalized as well. Behind the 1963 British Feilden Report's statement that design had not been rationalized at all lay an interpretation of design as creative work. Against the Feilden Report and its supporters, German historians held that design was rationalized in a particular way (Niemitz and Paulsen 1992; Niemitz 1993). Their interpretation is that everything that could be formalized was removed from the design office, leaving what could not be rationalized, that is, creative design work. Their main example was the Swiss-German steam turbine manufacturer Brown-Boveri. From the company's foundation in the early twentieth century, thermal calculation was separated from design, followed by the calculation of shaft vibrations in the mid-1950s, and the whole mechanical calculation in the late 1960s. In 1912, Brown-Boveri established a standardization department, and in 1918, one for materials testing. The development department was founded in 1952, turbine control became independent in 1953–54, and so on.

One approach to overcoming the problems of the multidivisional company was to establish development teams with members from the various departments. The development teams' composition and hierarchies depended on national engineering cultures' priorities. In the German teams, for instance, design had a much stronger position than in their Japanese counterparts. Normally, the development teams' focus was on new products but sometimes also on elaborating general design and manufacturing principles for the whole company.

Development teams gained momentum after World War II though their beginnings could be found much earlier. The same is true of simultaneous or concurrent engineering, as an approach to speed up development work. Its origins lay in the large technological projects of World War II, such as radar development and the

Manhattan Project for building an atomic bomb (Hughes 1998). In the postwar period systems approaches were worked out in military projects, like Semiautomatic Ground Environment (SAGE), an anti-bomber radar system, the Atlas intercontinental missile, and spaceflight programs. For instance, nearly 300,000 people and more than 200 companies were involved in the development of the Atlas missile.

The basis of this project management was systems thinking, based on the division of work into subsystems and components, and the definition of interrelations and interfaces between them. Variants of this systems thinking were cybernetics, operations research, systems analysis, and systems dynamics. Their common goal was to deal with complexity. From the 1960s, systems engineering was taught at the universities. During that time it spread from the military to civilian use in government and industry.

During the 1980s concurrent engineering reached the design and development departments under the name of simultaneous engineering. The goal of speeding up design was to be reached by parallel work by the various functional departments coordinated in manifold ways. Another goal was to make design and development more flexible. In addition, the division of labor, the number of departmental interfaces, and difficulties of communication should be reduced.

These new approaches notwithstanding, design remained the most important activity for engineers. Concerning designers' work, it must be admitted that it remains unclear which parts of design were creative and which repetitive. From the interwar period, complaints became ubiquitous that creative elements in design had diminished and more repetitive ones increased. Perhaps as a result, in many countries industry suffered from a lack of designers, while positions in the design department were not in great demand. There are precise figures for Germany stemming from the machinery industry's surveys on the situation of the engineering profession between 1938 and 1995 (Ströer 1957; Kalkowski *et al.* 1995). During that period, half of German engineers worked in the design departments. Until the 1950s, about 10 percent were college educated, 65 percent came from the intermediate technical schools (*Ingenieurschulen*), and 25 percent possessed lower qualifications. The 1955 survey documented that for each designer seeking a position, 48 vacancies were advertised in the newspapers. The founding of a design and drafting school in 1957 by the Swiss company Brown-Boveri in order to overcome the lack of designers demonstrates that Germany was not unique in this respect. Even today, about one-third of German engineers work in design offices.

Design work was not only changed by corporate restructuring but also by new information tools and drafting equipment. For a long time, the most important company resource was its staff's design and manufacturing competences. These resulted from training and experience and encompassed a body of tacit knowledge. Difficulties arose when a leading designer died or left the company. From the late nineteenth century, companies tried to establish an organizational memory from the respective individuals. The solution was a record office which collected and preserved all drawings. For instance, it is reported that after 1900 Westinghouse's record office held about 200,000 drawings. Engineering journals presented numerous proposals on how to systemize drawings and make them accessible through catalogues. As often as possible, designers were encouraged to rely on previous designs in order to save time and money. In the postwar period, companies' record offices combined punched card documentation and microfilm representation of drawings (Niemitz 1993). This made it easier to distribute drawing copies among the company's departments and to use them for communication with suppliers and customers.

Working conditions improved with design's separation from manufacture. The greater the distance between the drawing board and the workshop's dirt and noise, the better. However, even in the twentieth century, the number of designers and draftsmen crowded together in a single room was enormous. Reports and photographs show that dozens or hundreds in one room was no exception. Thus, supervisors ensured that designers did not perform private work. Internationally, the American design office was held up as a model for its use of natural lighting and lamps, as well as for its use of communication methods, such as bells, telephones, talking tubes, and pneumatic dispatches.

US industry was also the leader in introducing the drafting machine from about 1900. Before that designers and draftsmen worked with horizontal or slightly inclined boards. The drafting machine consisted of a vertical board with the rulers and angles fixed such that they could easily be moved. This was a more efficient device which increased productivity but also had ergonomic advantages. We do not know much about its international diffusion, but it seems that the pace at which it spread was rather slow. One piece of evidence is that a German machinery manufacturer had to build his own drafting machines, and then began to market them himself from around 1905. Specialty production started first in the interwar period. From the 1980s, the drafting machine had been replaced by the computer as the central design instrument.

The computer is a multifunctional tool. It began to influence design separately as a calculator, a planning and controlling machine, and a drafting system, before the three applications were brought together. Before the electronic computer, designers worked with numerous calculation tools. Depending on the tasks, they used slide rules, logarithmic tables, and ready reckoners for special calculations in mechanics, fluid dynamics, thermodynamics, etc. Well-distributed graphics allowed a clearer idea of the system and its data. From the 1950s, the digital electronic computer replaced these earlier means of calculation. Beyond that, with the computer it became possible to use calculation methods such as finite element analysis, which had been known before, but could not be applied in many cases because of the immense calculation work necessary.

Using computers for planning and control began in process engineering, such as oil refineries. From there, it was transferred to other industries and to other tasks.

In mechanical engineering, numerical control of machine tools was introduced, particularly in custom production. Over time, computers were envisaged as universal control mechanisms for all company activities, from customer orders, through design and production, to product testing and delivery.

Design work, above all, was transformed by the introduction of Computer-Aided Design (CAD). CAD emerged from research using the Whirlwind computer at the Massachusetts Institute of Technology (MIT) after World War II (Reintjes 1991). Its fundamentals emerged from specific programs for the graphical representation of ballistic trajectories and for the numerical control of machine tools. In the early 1960s, MIT researchers developed systems for generating drawings and stress analyzing geometries. Two-dimensional computer graphics became the first marketable product. Later on, CAD systems became more elaborate. They made it possible to generate three-dimensional geometries, and to use the design data for manufacturing, or for experimental simulations. In the long run, the goal was to create a database for the company as a whole, linking research and development, planning, design, manufacturing, and other departments.

In the mid-1960s, former MIT researchers started commercializing CAD software (Arnold 1984). So too did big companies from the microelectronics, computer, and machinery industries. American companies like Computervision and IBM with CATIA (originally a French program) led the market with turnkey systems. Early customers in the 1970s and 1980s were big automobile and aircraft companies. A survey among German designers in 1988 demonstrated that at least half of them worked with CAD systems (Pfaff and Badura 1991). At first, different CAD systems were introduced by individual departments, which tried to find solutions for their special problems. Later on, the companies opted for a common system in order to link several databases. Often, the first stage was a CAD pool, before cheaper systems and programs allowed designers to be supplied with personal work stations.

It is difficult to give an authorative assessment of CAD's impact (Wolf *et al.* 1992; Kalkowski *et al.* 1995; Mackensen 1997). CAD is still developing and its integration into the company organization is multidimensional. On the one hand, it seems as if CAD saves time in design and drafting work, at least with the design of product variants. On the other hand, however, more work is needed for software development and maintenance, for which some firms established specific departments. It seems that CAD does not completely replace traditional drawings. In "mixed-use practices" (Henderson 1999), drawings and sketches still fulfill special purposes in engineering communication.

Design work can be interpreted as transforming numerous demands into a solution. Often, this solution is a compromise between competing and sometimes contradictory criteria. Traditional goals were design for function and economy with specifications like manufacture, assembly, maintenance, repair, and so on. Over time, the number of design requirements increased considerably. The system of design requirements and its hierarchies depended on economy, culture, and politics, that is on the overall context of designers' work. This became particularly obvious in Nazi Germany with its policies of autarky and rearmament. The most important requirements for design now became substituting domestic for imported materials (*deutsche Werkstoffe*) and using materials as economically as possible (*Sparkonstruktionen*) (Niemitz and Paulsen 1992). Furthermore, it was debated how far quality and durability of products could be reduced. With special tables of materials and training courses for designers, the engineering community tried to establish and disseminate the new thinking.

It is interesting that some of these requirements reappeared in a completely different political context, namely the environmental protection movement. In the Western world from about 1970, environment protection became a prominent political goal. Meadows *et al.*'s *The Limits to Growth* (1972) made it clear that natural resources could restrict economic development. The new agenda also had an impact on the design community (Hellige 1995). Since the 1970s, concepts like design for material saving and design for recycling were developed, which were later extended to "life cycle design and engineering".

16.5 NATIONAL ENGINEERING DESIGN STYLES AND CULTURES

On economic and technological development, historians agree that there are increasing cross-national similarities but also persisting differences. The concept of economic or technological styles and cultures (Hughes 1983; König 1999) focuses on the differences. These differences are interpreted as a result of cultural factors which generate "cultural artefacts". In these approaches, culture is understood very broadly: "Among the cultural factors are geographical, economic, organizational, legislative, contingent historical, and entrepreneurial conditions" (Hughes 1983: 405). In the context of engineering and design, historians mostly use the concept of style to characterize a national product line. For instance, nineteenth-century railway historians distinguish the British style of locomotive building with inside cylinders from the American style with outside cylinders and a bogie. In this section, I will focus instead on design as a department within the company and as the process of moving from functional requirements to solutions in the form of drawings or other databases. Important elements of national design styles or cultures in this sense are economic, political, and cultural goals, designers' competences, the organization of design in the company, and especially the relative position of design and manufacture. I emphasize that there were two extreme models, namely an American culture of production and a German culture of design (König 1999; Brown 2000). Other industrial countries fell between the two. Britain and France were closer to the German model, while Japan was closer to the American.

In German industry, especially machinery construction, design considerations were central (Kalkowski *et al.* 1995; Moritz 1996; König 1999). Companies had to supply extremely differentiated markets consisting of domestic regions and of foreign countries. The often small and medium-sized firms were adapted to fulfilling the differing demands of their fastidious German customers as well those of customers in heterogeneous export markets. Germany was strong in meeting demand for heavy industries' large one-off products and other capital equipment industries' custom products and small series. These premium high-quality goods required a lot of design work, above all, variant design adapting known machinery to particular demands.

German designers and craft workers were educated and trained according to the requirements of such diversified quality production. Craft workers had passed through the formalized German system of apprenticeship which in the late 1930s was extended to drafting personnel. But even earlier, German draftsmen possessed strong competences in generating and reading engineering drawings. During the nineteenth century, they were held in high esteem abroad, for instance in British and American companies (Brown 2000). Design competences were the central objectives in college education, that is in the *Technische Hochschulen*, and as well at the intermediate schools (*Ingenieurschulen*). The majority of designers came from those two types of engineering schools, which both raised their standards over time. These schools' and their graduates' orientation focused on innovation and development. In particular, the *Technische Hochschulen* taught a larger proportion of theory than engineering colleges in other countries.

The designers' orientation and education enabled them to incorporate considerable knowledge into their design concepts. In 1929, the American Society for the Promotion of Engineering Education's Wickenden Report characterized German design work as of high quality, but often uneconomic (Wickenden 1929: 214). This resulted from a gap between academic design culture and hands-on manufacturing. In extreme cases, such as those reported in a 1938 issue of the Bosch Company house journal, this tension was characterized as a "war situation" (*Der Bosch-Zünder* 1938). From the late nineteenth century onwards, the rationalization movement did much to bring design and production together. But complaints did not disappear, indicating that the results were limited. The rationalization movement succeeded in establishing the new professional group of production engineers which was a new specialization rather than a reconciliation of design and manufacture. The German design tradition was not easy to overcome even under extreme conditions. So, during World War II, aircraft manufacturers showed more interest in new design than in mass production (Zeitlin 1995; Budraß 1998). Even today, there is a discussion whether German products are over-engineered (Herrigel and Sabel 1999).

The German design culture contrasts with the American culture of production. In the US industry, design work was interpreted as a means and not as an end. The goal was design for production and economy. American industry sought to supply the domestic market with products which could be afforded by the broad masses. On the other hand, American customers were more inclined to accept standardized products. In the United States, materials and energy were cheap whereas labor—and especially qualified labor—was expensive. This was the background for the American system of manufacturing which had developed since the mid-nineteenth century (Hounshell 1984). The American system meant mass production by machines, standardization, and interchangeability. It is true that the spectrum of American manufacturing stretched from mass to specialty production (Scranton 1997). However, that does not reduce the importance of mass production (e.g. Kranakis 2004). In comparison to Europe, mass production was more widely diffused in the United States. The dominant industrial mentality arose from mass production. And it must be pointed out that specialty goods were manufactured with mass-produced parts and materials. Mass production structures and mentalities, originating during the nineteenth century, had an enduring influence even in the twentieth century. So, after World War II, American automobile "manufacturers pursued productivity gains at the expense of product innovation" (Zeitlin 1995: 75).

Within American production culture, the design function focused on economy and manufacture. Cost considerations and cost accounting played a greater role than in Europe. One principle was that design should not be more durable than necessary for the product's estimated lifetime. Engineers' competence in design for production was high because the design personnel had more workshop experience than in Germany.

In the American system of mass production, less design work was performed than in Europe and engineering drawings played a minor role. Variant and adaptive design, which constituted the great bulk of design work in German custom production, was less important. At the extreme, integrated mass manufacturers and even custom producers could do without design altogether. Research and development could lead directly to prototypes and marketable products. In this way, design was displaced by engineering. Nonetheless, drawings were often necessary for communicating with suppliers. Reports on difficulties in cooperation between firms and their suppliers might indicate deficiencies in American design culture.

Even in American custom production, dimensional black and white drawings came late (Brown 1995, 1999). In the 1870s, drawings at the Baldwin Locomotive Works in Philadelphia had no dimensional tolerances but indicated only the go/no-go gauges to be used in manufacturing. In the early twentieth century, one author reporting on the diversity of drafting systems in American industry, doubted the importance of engineering drawings on the whole: "A free use of good Anglo-Saxon is better understood than a pretty cobweb of fanciful lines" (König 1999: 182–3). In the United States, drafting only became standardized in the mid-1930s. Even after World War II, German designers sneered at the American (and Japanese) "simplified drafting practice". This referred to a special US variant of orthogonal projection: three-angle instead of the European first-angle method (Belofsky 1991). There were no fundamental differences between the two, but the three-angle-method made drafting easier to learn and perform.

One prominent example of these differing American design mentalities and practices is that of Henry Ford and the Ford company (Ford and Crowther 1922; Hounshell 1984; Brinkley 2003). With its Model T, Ford pushed the principle of standardization to the extreme. Henry Ford boasted that in his company paperwork had been totally eliminated. This was not true but threw light on his personal opinion of design. Contemporaries reported that: "Mr. Ford ... didn't seem to have the idea that things could be designed. He seemed to have the idea that you had to make them by manual methods rather than by sitting down and putting it on a piece of paper." "He couldn't read blueprints ..." (Brinkley 2003: 63–4). In fact, Ford's engineers practiced a mixture of designing in the material and designing at the blackboard and on paper. Furthermore, the Ford company used drawings for documentation and communication with suppliers. However, drawings were not employed for shop instruction. It seems that, in 1927, the deficiencies of drafting practice contributed to the difficulties when Ford replaced the Model T by the Model A. In World War II, when Ford started building aircraft, it became necessary to redraw the plans passed on by the original designers because of the limited blueprint-reading skills of Ford's personnel (Zeitlin 1995). Something similar happened in shipbuilding during the war (Brown 2000). British plans had to be redrawn for the American manufacturers. In the end, the number of drawings tripled.

There can be no doubt that in the American culture of production, design played a minor role in engineering education and as well within the engineering profession. When a prominent German professor of design visited American engineering colleges around 1900, he was full of admiration for their laboratories and workshops (König 1999). He was convinced that they contributed much to the success of American machine building. On the other hand, he spoke in an extremely negative manner about their design training. In his opinion, American college instruction in design was far below the level of German industrial schools, to say nothing of the *Technische Hochschulen*. The *Verein Deutscher Ingenieure* (VDI), the most important German engineering association, can be interpreted as a society of engineering designers. The majority of its members were designers, and design was the major theme in its journals. By contrast, in 1907 only 4 percent of the members of the American Society of Mechanical Engineers (ASME) classified themselves as "draftsmen and designers" (Sinclair 1980).

Design in Japanese industry resembled the American model in many respects (Moritz 1996). Mass production was more diffuse than custom production. Some firms trusted more to experimental work leading to prototypes than to design work on paper or with a computer. The product planning departments dominated small design offices. Product characteristics were effectively laid down by planning departments. Afterwards the design function had to elaborate the predetermined concepts for manufacture, trying in particular to cut costs. As a result of the more general university education in Japan, designers had less specialized knowledge. Firms tried to compensate for this by communicating exhaustively within the design group. Another Japanese approach to overcoming the separation of conception and execution was the development team. Development teams tried to solve problems collectively and undertake a process of continuous improvement.

In Britain and France, design was closer to the German model. Design variety was considered more important than standardization and mass production (Zeitlin 2000). However, it seems that the gap between design and manufacturing was not as wide as in the German industry. This could be explained mainly by the training of design engineers. The British possessed broad shop experience; the highly theoretically qualified Germans did not. French design engineers, often coming from the practice-oriented *Écoles des Arts et Métiers*, fell between the two poles. Thus within the general types of production and design culture, national variants existed which still influence design today even in the age of globalization.

REFERENCES

ARNOLD, E. (1984). *Computer-Aided Design in Europe*. Sussex European Paper 14. Sussex European Research Center.

BAYNES, K., and PUGH, F. (1981). *The Art of the Engineer*. Guildford: Lutterworth Press.

BELOFSKY, H. (1991). "Engineering Drawing: A Universal Language in Two Dialects". *Technology and Culture*, 32: 23–46.

BERNER, B. (2007). "Rationalising Technical Work: Visions and Realities of the Systematic Drawing Office in Sweden, 1890–1940". *Technology and Culture*, 48: 20–42.

BOOKER, P. J. (1963). *A History of Engineering Drawing*. London: Chatto & Windus.

BRINKLEY, D. (2003). *Wheels for the World: Henry Ford, his Company, and a Century of Progress*. New York: Viking.

BROWN, J. K. (1995). *The Baldwin Locomotive Works, 1831–1915: A Study in American Industrial Practice*. Studies in Industry and Society 8. Baltimore: Johns Hopkins University Press.

—— (1999). "When Machines became Gray and Drawings Black and White: William Sellers and the Rationalization of Mechanical Engineering". *Journal of the Society for Industrial Archaeology*, 25/2: 29–53.

—— (2000). "Design Plans, Working Drawings, National Styles: Engineering Practice in Great Britain and the United States, 1775–1945". *Technology and Culture*, 41: 195–238.

BUCHANAN, R. A. (1989). *The Engineers: A History of the Engineering Profession in Britain, 1750–1914*. London: Kingsley.

BUCHHEIM, G., and SONNEMANN, R. (eds.) (1990). *Geschichte der Technikwissenschaften.* Leipzig: Birkhäuser.

BUDRAß, L. (1998). *Flugzeugindustrie und Luftrüstung in Deutschland 1918–1945.* Schriften des Bundesarchivs 50. Düsseldorf: Droste.

CALVERT, M. A. (1967). *The Mechanical Engineer in America, 1830–1910: Professional Cultures in Conflict.* Baltimore: Johns Hopkins University Press.

CROWTHER, S. (1926). *John H. Patterson: Pioneer in Industrial Welfare.* New York: Garden City Publishing Company.

DEFORGE, Y. (1976). *Le graphisme technique.* Thesis presented at the University of Paris V, Sept. 23, 1975. Lille and Paris: Champion.

EDMONDSON, J. M. (1987). *From Mecanicien to Ingenieur: Technical Education and the Machine Building Industry in Nineteenth-Century France.* Modern European History: A Garland Series of Outstanding Dissertations. New York and London: Garland.

FEILDEN, GEOFFREY (1963). *Engineering Design: Report of a Committee Appointed by the Council for Scientific and Industrial Research to Consider the Present Standing of Mechanical Engineering Design.* London: HMSO.

FELDHAUS, F. M. (1959). *Geschichte des technischen Zeichnens,* 2nd edn. Wilhelmshaven: Kuhlmann.

FERGUSON, E. S. (1992). *Engineering and the Mind's Eye.* Cambridge, Mass.: MIT Press.

FORD, H., and CROWTHER, S. (1922). *My Life and Work.* New York: Heinemann.

GARNER, S. P. (1954). *Evolution of Cost Accounting to 1925.* Montgomery: University of Alabama Press.

HELLIGE, H. D. (1995). "Vom thermodynamischen Kreislaufprozeß zum recyclinggerechten Konstruieren: Leitbilder der Ressourcenschonung in der Geschichte der Konstruktion", in W. Müller (ed.), *Der ökologische Umbau der Industrie: Beiträge zur sozialwissenschaftlichen Umweltforschung.* Arbeitsgestaltung, Technikbewertung, Zukunft 3. Münster and Hamburg: LIT Verlag, 73–100.

HENDERSON, K. (1999). *On Line and On Paper: Visual Representations, Visual Culture, and Computer Graphics in Design Engineering (Inside Technology).* Cambridge, Mass.: MIT Press.

HERRIGEL, G., and SABEL, C. F. (1999). "Craft Production in Crisis: Industrial Restructuring in Germany during the 1990s", in P. D. Culpepper and D. Finegold (eds.), *The German Skills Machine: Sustaining Comparative Advantage in a Global Economy.* Policies and Institutions. Germany, Europe, and Transatlantic Relations 3. New York and Oxford: Berghahn, 77–114.

HINDLE, B. (1981). Emulation and Invention. New York: New York University Press.

HOUNSHELL, D. A. (1984). *From the American System to Mass Production 1800–1932: The Development of Manufacturing in the United States.* Studies in Industry and Society. Baltimore and London: Johns Hopkins University Press.

HUGHES, T. P. (1983). *Networks of Power: Electrification in Western Society, 1880–1930.* Baltimore and London: Johns Hopkins University Press.

—— (1998). *Rescuing Prometheus.* New York: Pantheon.

KALKOWSKI, P., MICKLER, O., and MANSKE, F. (1995). *Technologiestandort Deutschland: Produktinnovation im Maschinenbau: traditionelle Stärken—neue Herausforderungen.* Berlin: Edition Sigma.

KOCKA, J. (1969). *Unternehmensverwaltung und Angestelltenschaft am Beispiel Siemens 1847–1914. Zum Verhältnis von Kapitalismus und Bürokratie in der deutschen Industrialisierung.*

Industrielle Welt: Schriftenreihe des Arbeitskreises für moderne Sozialgeschichte 11. Stuttgart: Klett.

KÖNIG, W. (1993). "Technical Education and Industrial Performance in Germany: A Triumph of Heterogeneity", in R. Fox and A. Guagnini (eds.), *Education, Technology and Industrial Performance in Europe, 1850–1939*. Cambridge and Paris: Cambridge University Press, 65–87.

——— (1999). *Künstler und Strichezieher: Konstruktions- und Technikkulturen im deutschen, britischen, amerikanischen und französischen Maschinenbau zwischen 1850 und 1930* (suhrkamp taschenbuch wissenschaft 1287). Frankfurt am Main: Suhrkamp.

KRANAKIS, E. (2004). "Fixing the Blame: Organizational Culture and the Quebec Bridge Collapse". *Technology and Culture*, 45: 487–518.

LUBAR, S. (1995). "Representation and Power". *Technology and Culture*, 36, Supplement: S54–S81.

McGEE, D. (1999). "From Craftmanship to Draftmanship. Naval Architecture and the Three Traditions of Early Modern Design". *Technology and Culture*, 40: 209–36.

MACKENSEN, R. (ed.) (1997). *Konstruktionshandeln: Nicht-technische Determinanten des Konstruierens bei zunehmendem CAD-Einsatz*. Munich, and Vienna: Carl Hanser.

MEADOWS, D. L., ZAHN, E., and MILLING, P. (1972). *The Limits to Growth*. New York: Universe.

MORITZ, E. F. (1996). *Im Osten nichts Neues: Theorie und Praxis von Produktinnovation in Japan im Vergleich zu Deutschland*. Innovation: Einblicke, Perspektiven, Gestaltung. Sottrum: Artefact Verlag.

MOUTET, A. (1997). *Les logiques de l'entreprise: La rationalisation dans l'industre française de l'entre-deux-guerres*. Civilisation et Sociétés 93. Paris: École des Études en Sciences Sociale.

NEDOLUHA, A. (1960). *Kulturgeschichte des technischen Zeichnens*. Vienna: Springer.

NIEMITZ, H.-U. (1993). *Dampfturbinenkonstruktion bei der Brown Boveri AG & Cie nach dem Zweiten Weltkrieg*. Studien zur Technik-, Wirtschafts- und Sozialgeschichte 6. Frankfurt am Main: Peter Lang.

——— and PAULSEN, H. (1992). "Konstruktionspraxis im deutschen Maschinenbau von 1917 bis 1945". *LTR-Forschung: Reihe des Landesmuseums für Technik und Arbeit in Mannheim*, 9: 3–33.

PAHL, G., and BEITZ, W. (1996). *Engineering Design: A Systematic Approach*, 2nd edn. (1st pub. in German 1977). London and Berlin: Springer.

PFAFF, H., and BADURA, B. (1991). "Nutzung der CAD-Technik und Arbeitsbedingungen: Ergebnisse einer Umfrage bei Mitgliedern der VDI-Gesellschaft Entwicklung Konstruktion Vertrieb (VDI-EKV)". *Konstruktion*, 43: 323–9.

PFLIEGER-HAERTEL, H. (1929). "Friedrich v. Voith und sein Werk: Die Gründung und Entwicklung der Firma J. M. Voith, Heidenheim/Brenz (Wttb.) und St. Pölten (Niederösterr.)". *Beiträge zur Geschichte der Technik und Industrie: Jahrbuch des Vereines Deutscher Ingenieure*, 19: 61–70.

POITOU, J.-P. (1988). *Le cerveau de l'usine: Histoire des bureaux d'études Renault de l'origine à 1980: Recherche sur les conditions de l'innovation technique*. Aix-en-Provence: University of Provence.

——— (1989). *Trente ans de CAO en France*. Paris: Hermes.

REINTJES, J. F. (1991). *Numerical Control: Making a New Technology*. Oxford: Oxford University Press.

SAWAI, M. (1989). "The Development of Machine Industry and the Evolution of Production and Labor Management", in T. Yui and K. Nakagawa (eds.), *Japanese Management in Historical Perspective*. The International Conference on Business History 15. Proceedings of the Fuji Conference. Tokyo: University of Tokyo Press, 199–241.

SCRANTON, P. (1997). *Endless Novelty: Specialty Production and American Industrialization 1865–1925*. Princeton, NJ: Princeton University Press.

SINCLAIR, B., with HULL, J. B. (1980). *A Centennial History of the American Society of Mechanical Engineers 1880–1980*. Toronto: University of Toronto Press.

STAUDENMAIER S. J. J. M. (1985). *Technology's Storytellers: Reweaving the Human Fabric*. Cambridge, Mass.: MIT Press.

STRÖER, H. J. (1957). *Mehr Technik—mehr Ingenieure. Der Mangel an Maschinenbau-Ingenieuren. Ursache, Umfang, Abhilfe*. Frankfurt am Main: Maschinenbau Verlag.

WICKENDEN, W. E. (1929). *A Comparative Study of Engineering Education in the United States and in Europe*. Bulletin of the Investigation of Engineering Education 16.

WOLF, H., MICKLER, O., and MANSKE, F. (1992). *Eingriffe in Kopfarbeit: Die Computerisierung technischer Büros im Maschinenbau*. Berlin: Edition Sigma.

ZEITLIN, J. (1995). "Flexibility and Mass Production at War: Aircraft Manufacture in Britain, the United States, and Germany, 1939–1945". *Technology and Culture*, 36: 46–79.

—— (2000). "Americanizing British Engineering? Strategic Debate, Selective Adaptation, and Hybrid Innovation in Post-War Reconstruction, 1945–1960", in J. Zeitlin and G. Herrigel (eds.), *Americanization and its Limits: Reworking US Technology and Management in Post-War Europe and Japan*. Oxford: Oxford University Press, 123–52.

CHAPTER 17

MARKETING AND DISTRIBUTION

ROBERT FITZGERALD

17.1 MASS CONSUMPTION AND BUSINESS HISTORY

HISTORIANS drawn to the subject of mass marketing and distribution are impeded by its vast breadth and implications. There are macroeconomic issues of living standards, industrial change, output, trade, and infrastructure; there are also important legal, political, cultural, and even psychological dimensions. On the other hand, the enterprises that developed techniques of mass marketing and distribution did not respond passively to general trends in the economy and society. Success did not automatically follow the balancing of supply with available or rising demand, as economic theory might imply. The complexities of business entailed a proactive investment in consumer loyalty and in distribution networks; in other words, companies became concerned with the very creation and not just the "optimization" of consumer markets. The traditional interests of the business historian—product development, production methods, business organization, management, and competitive strategy—have to be considered alongside the macroeconomic and social aspects of mass consumption. To evaluate the vital role of marketing and distribution systems within modern economies and societies, their origins in practical solutions to business problems have to be understood. Schumpeter (1954) perceived consumer behavior as too heterogeneous to be easily explained, even by Keynes. Accordingly, the consumption function cannot account for the consumer's willingness to adopt new spending habits. It cannot consider fully the consumer's evaluation of value over price, and the attraction of quality and cachet over quantity. It cannot, furthermore, explain complex consumption decisions between the increasing numbers of substitute goods that drove inter-firm competition and brought structural and industrial change to national economies. Companies did not accept cultural attitudes or lifestyle inertia, but had to "educate" consumers on the advantages of manufactured soap, packaged foods, or electric appliances.

How effectively have business historians contributed to our understanding of marketing and distribution? Overall, those in the United States have proved themselves more willing than European counterparts to provide general explanations. They have achieved some consensus, for the period 1880–1920, on the arrival of large-scale companies, national markets, mass advertising, branding, department stores, and mail order, alongside critical improvements in distribution and storage. Most interpret these developments as the beginnings of "modern" marketing. Pope and Tedlow note the relationship between corporate policies, unitary mass markets, high volumes, low margins, and large profits. But they detect, after 1920, a further phase, with companies switching to greater market segmentation, more value-based pricing, and the use of emotive, associational advertising (Strasser 1995; Pope 1986; Laird 1998; Tedlow 1990). Other US historians have questioned the validity of distinct turning-points and periods, and stress instead earlier examples of segmentation and innovative advertising, the long-term diffusion of marketing approaches, and differences amongst firms and industries (Fullerton 1988; Hollander and Germain 1991; Fitzgerald 2005). Certainly, the alternative dating of market segmentation, in the United States, from the 1910s to the 1950s suggests that so diverse a concept and so varied a trend cannot yet be easily circumscribed. The challenges of international comparison are even more daunting.

Brands erected competitive entry-barriers and bestowed ownership rights that could be viewed as balance-sheet assets. To succeed at mass production and distribution, companies converted their products into brands with "personalities" that expressed what the consumer wished to be. Brands encouraged emotive, associational advertising that focused on the aspirations and social circumstances of the consumer rather than the product itself. Increases in disposable incomes favored brands and, ultimately, greater product diversification and market segmentation. In turn, the economic, social, and psychological aspects of consumer markets influenced and were influenced by business systems and techniques (Jones and Morgan 1994). Descriptions of production, product, sales, and marketing orientations that specify the aims of the firm are a workable heuristic device, revealing changes in corporate emphasis. Entrepreneurs concentrated, first, on improving production technology and factory operations, often seeking the twin objectives of better product quality and lower costs; second, they became more concerned with selling and distribution, as they coped with the effects of mass output; finally, the marketing-orientation gave priority to the wishes of consumers, ultimately guided by market research, and purchasing, product development, production, and finance were brought under the direction of the marketing department.

For specific industries or nations, orientations may become common or dominant. A concern for production and products may demonstrate businesses driven by supply-side challenges. At early stages of their growth, producers in the United States and in Britain could largely rely on mass manufacturing, new technologies, falling prices, and the quality of their products to achieve distribution and sales. Consideration of these "internal" exigencies was enough to generate success. As markets grew in size or became more competitive, companies had to divert more resources to advertising, transportation, and other sales activities, and adjust their mix of organizational skills. However, manufacturing was still seen as preceding the separate if increasingly important activity of sales, or "marketing" as it became called in the United States and Britain of the 1920s. In contrast, the marketing-orientated company aims to discover consumer wishes, which are depicted as "external" to the firm, and does so through market research, psychological understanding, and product development systems. To achieve its goals, it ends the segregation of business functions and integrates them in a manner best able to satisfy consumer desires. For the marketing-orientated company, it is the consideration of "external" exigencies that generates success. Instances of this approach can be found in leading US and British companies during the interwar period, but it was a managerial "philosophy" more commonly adopted during the consumer boom of the 1950s and 1960s. In assessing these ideas, we encounter a number of problems. There is, despite numerous corporate examples, a shortage of historical writing on marketing's development as a business function. "Marketing" remains, unhelpfully, both an elusive and all-embracing concept, and so presents a herculean and intimidating research agenda. As case studies concentrate on major firms, it is difficult to judge the impact of marketing approaches on less-studied companies or on whole industries. The importance of "advance" marketing to consumer goods firms, and later to providers of services, might be assumed, but the selling of industrial goods is rarely considered.

In Britain and the United States, "early" industrialization was followed towards the end of the nineteenth century by the emergence of consumer goods and service sectors, in which intensive advertising, branding, and product choice were characteristic. The systems honed by US and British companies responded positively to structural changes in the economy, expenditure patterns, and social trends. Overviews of marketing and distribution history are available for Japan, as they are in the United States, but reveal variations in the nature of economic and marketing development. The term "late industrialization" is used to describe the policies of governments and business groups that fostered capital goods. Moreover, rapid industrialization by a "follower" nation might lead to the polar co-existence of advanced and untransformed practice. In the Japan of the 1920s, new products and new means of distribution expanded alongside traditional goods and systems.

Japanese sales operations vitally assisted the solution of specific production and product-orientated problems, generated by speedy industrialization and urbanization, and became associated with distribution in particular. Other sales activities such as advertising had emerged as a greater part of the marketing mix in Britain and the United States. Before the Second World War, the strength and capabilities of the consumer product sectors in Germany, France, and Italy were also dissimilar, in comparison to the United States and Britain. Convergence in manufacturing, products, branding, and advertising would be more evident towards the end of the postwar boom.

17.2 The 'Emergence' of the Mass Market

17.2.1 The Invention of Consumers

Historians do not view mass consumption as "natural", but see it as a "cultural" or "social construction" fashioned over time. The social transformation that accompanied mass consumption was, in turn, built upon an economic base and formed by conscious business policies. While part of a modern human's upbringing is the process of consumer socialization, in the past a majority could not assume the availability of consumption choices and expanding consumption opportunities. Conceiving these circumstances is an act of historical imagination. At the beginning of "modern" marketing and distribution, rising real wages and falling prices were not sufficient causes. If the increasing rate of product innovation was to succeed, it was necessary to alter entrenched ideas, life habits, and customary product choices. Price became a diminishing component of the marketing mix, as manufacturers employed advertising and branding to forge a "psychological" or "emotional" connection between consumers and producers. Committed to strategies of output, quality, and branding, they could not remain weak links within a commodity chain dominated by wholesalers, and they used consumer advertising or vertical integration to enhance their competitive strength. Accordingly, historical insight into the origins of "modern" marketing and distribution presents a particularly valuable contribution to our understanding of an important business and social phenomenon.

17.2.2 Britain

In Britain, real wages increased by some 60 percent between 1860 and 1900, and, whereas 50 percent of the population in 1851 had dwelt in towns with 20,000 or more inhabitants, the percentage was 77 by 1901. Consumer industries and extensive distribution networks were formed to meet the needs of a larger, richer, and more concentrated population. Urban infrastructure, such as buildings and transportation, and mass newspapers provided greater opportunities for advertising, while packaging, labelling, and the promotion of "hidden" goods indicated long-distance deliveries to cities. For consumer goods manufacturers, the rapid growth of markets and the appropriation of new technologies had initially placed an emphasis on production processes and supply. Yet some companies safeguarded capital investments and consumer loyalty by focusing on quality, product identity, and branding. Many of the firms that evolved into leading advertisers of national products gained a long-lasting first mover advantage, such as pharmaceutical companies Thomas Holloway and Beecham; chocolate and confectionery makers Cadbury, Fry, Rowntree, and latterly Mackintosh; soap producer Lever Brothers; Wills, and its successor Imperial Tobacco (Fitzgerald 1995, 2000; Jeffreys 1954; Mathias 1967; Benson 1994; Wilson 1954; Corley 1987; Nevett 1982; Fraser 1981).

Overall expenditure was increasingly diverted to the fixed shop and multiples. Retailers began to embrace branded, packaged goods that carried claims of quality and purity, and, accordingly, attracted higher margins. Between 1915 and 1980, the market share of retailers with less than ten outlets was to decline from 80 to 30 percent, while that of more impersonal outlets grew from 10 to nearly 70 percent. National retailers were well-established by 1914, including Allied Suppliers, W. H. Smith, Marks and Spencer, Sainsbury, and the Cooperative movement. Department stores such as Harrod's, Selfridge's, and John Lewis were highly visible presences in city centers, and served a high-class market (Jeffreys 1954; Fraser 1981). Whereas geography and demographics favored smaller, more specialist wholesalers, and vertical integration amongst manufacturers and distributors was similarly uncommon, market mechanisms and established trading relationships thrived through low transaction costs and locational externalities, such as advanced transport systems and concentrated, urban populations.

17.2.3 United States

Were circumstances in Britain, the first industrial nation, especially suited to the development of mass marketing? Chandler lists the opportunities that concentrated, urbanized markets and highly evolved transport and distribution systems made available to British companies (Chandler 1990). These advantages explain the early emergence of numerous competitors, each making a diverse range of products and brands that rapidly won consumer recognition and loyalty. Economies of scale could be achieved by several competitors in pursuit of a national market that was, consequently, more segmented than the one that emerged in the United States. Tedlow asserts that, "[m]ore than any other nation in the history of the world", Americans constitute a "nation of consumers". Lebergott states that the size and homogeneity of the US home market were unmatched assets. The subsequent standardization of products improved both quality and price and required an innovation in distribution as well as production. To understand how Americans began to associate their needs with the new factory goods is to emphasize the central role of mass marketing in the economy and society. While Veblen (1924) had already identified the New York elite that could indulge in "conspicuous consumption", other commentators could aver by 1914 that a mass consumer consciousness was overtaking class loyalties (Tedlow 1990; Lebergott 1996; Glickman 1999).

In 1913, the US population reached 97.2 million, significantly larger than Britain's 45.6 million. Total GDP, roughly equivalent to Britain's in 1870, was 2.4 times larger in 1913. By 1903, GDP per capita in the United States had caught up with Britain's, and, from 1918, it assumed a permanent lead. The building of the railway and telegraph system underpinned an emerging national market: 46,800 miles of track in 1869 had been extended by 1913 to 240,000. Considering the vast distances of North America, frozen winter waterways, and population spread, railways had a bigger economic impact in the United States than in Britain. In 1870, 26 percent of Americans lived in towns of 2,500 plus, and, by 1910, the figure was still only 46 percent. It was not until 1960 that half of the US population resided in towns of 5,000 plus, whereas half the British 110 years earlier could be found in towns of at least 20,000 (Tedlow 1990; Norris 1990; Chandler 1990).

Geographic and demographic factors in the United States had three major marketing implications. First, in comparison to British companies, manufacturers placed greater emphasis on distribution and wholesaling, and vertical integration was more usual. Second, general rather than specialist shippers were more dominant, and economies of scope were needed to carry a variety of products over large distances. Changes in wholesaling were neither so extensive nor so necessary in Britain. Third, mail order was an important means of purchase in the United States compared to the British case. Mass production and product standardization assisted rising living standards and demand. Rural household and disposable income improved during this period, and the demand for foods was income elastic enough to benefit the sale of other consumables. The growing number of urban dwellers, who had to purchase all their requirements, was another spur to mass manufacturers and distributors, and to the replacement of regional by national markets. The local general store, not surprisingly, remained the focal point of small town communities and rural areas, and retailing was not as transformed as the manufacturing and wholesaling sectors. Exceptions were the emergence of department stores and chain stores in cities, most obviously in the highly populated northeast, and the mail order enterprises that reached the United States more scattered populations (Tedlow 1990; Norris 1990; Pope 1983; Laird 1998).

Manufacturers adopted production and product-orientated strategies based on new technologies, higher output, lower price, and better quality. Guarding their investments in manufacturing capacity, companies created distribution systems, secured access to consumers, and gained their repeated loyalty. They used branding as marks of quality, and advertised the characteristics of their brand to a mass and distant population. Packaging facilitated branding and transportation and offered assurances against adulteration. As in Britain, mass advertising urged consumers to demand manufactured brands, undermined the appeal of unpackaged goods, and lowered per unit distribution costs. By threatening retailers with withdrawal of popularized products, manufacturers could exercise greater control over final prices. In many cases, and in furtherance of product diversification and corporate growth, advertising convinced consumers into accepting products that had uses previously unknown to them.

There were numerous examples of food and household goods manufacturers that emerged as mass advertisers of packaged lines, including Sapolio soap and Royal Baking Powder. Coca-Cola was an intensively advertised national line by 1900. Originally designed as a nerve tonic and a stimulant, it ceased to be a medication and emerged as a beverage with an appeal for long boondoggle days. In 1905, Coca-Cola's travellers, attending their first sales convention, discussed the company's mission, advertising strategy, and sales schemes. It was the launch of Ivory Soap in 1879 that constituted Procter & Gamble's watershed. As well as slogans and illustrations showing happy, clean families, Ivory became, as the "soap that floats", a novelty product. By 1914, the advertising of soaps had moved from a product-orientated approach to a consumer-orientated emphasis on values, status, and cachet. While Ivory was a fortuitous product subsequently mass marketed, the company consciously tested and, in 1911, developed the cottonseed cooking oil Crisco. As well as food and soap, instances of nationally advertised lines could be found in tobacco, matches, detergents, and household products. Their success was rooted in distinctive brands, standardization, affordable price, national distribution, packaging, large sales teams, convenience purchasing, and advertising. In 1917, the US spent some $1 billion on advertising (Tedlow 1990; Sivulka 1998; Norris 1990; Pope 1983).

Manufacturers recognized the need to educate consumers about factory goods and unfamiliar products. Colgate, which introduced its Ribbon Dental Cream in 1905, had to prove the advantages of dental hygiene to skeptical consumers. For Gillette to promote the habit of daily shaving, it altered popular male fashion against those who wished to remain hirsute. While most advertising was filled with often prolix product information, many major brands had revealed a trend towards story-lines, emotional appeals, and an association with desirable lifestyles and values. From the 1890s, people became acquainted with personalities representing the integrity, reliability, or wholesomeness of brands. The American Cereal Company took a product formerly linked with invalids or expatriate Scotsmen and invented Quaker Oats as a breakfast cereal and as a symbolic personality. The firm provoked an instinctive reassurance amongst consumers, and yet the firm had no links with the Society of Friends. In many other cases, characters in advertisements relied on racial caricatures of African-Americans, and contemporaneous parallels can be found in Britain or France, where the popular appeal of Empire was reaching its height. Columbia Gramophone's picture of a dog listening to a phonograph and its caption, "His Master's Voice", created one of the world's most enduring and best-loved images (Strasser 1995; Sivulka 1998; Norris 1990; Pope 1983). Overall, corporate cases demonstrating the existence of planned marketing campaigns and "emotional" advertising undermine, to some extent, the argument for a definitive turning point in strategy and techniques after 1920.

As general wholesalers worked for a number of clients, producers of food and household products employed advertising and branding to influence the upstream requests of consumers and retailers, so pressuring distributors to stock better-known lines. The dangers of overstocking were an additional motivation for manufacturers of perishables. Food and household goods companies sought success through the "pull" marketing of advertising and branding rather than the "push" of distribution. They did, nevertheless, recruit teams of salesmen, and, by 1920, Scott Paper, Heinz, Colgate, Gillette, Procter & Gamble, and Sherwin-Williams' paints were amongst those manufacturers that had founded wholesaling networks. It was the manufacturers of durables that generally sought more direct access to consumers. Remington typewriters, Eastman Kodak cameras and film, the Victor Talking Machine, and Singer sewing machines influenced consumers through ownership of urban outlets. Vertical integration served several objectives: it provided an unequalled sales service and expert advice; eased the supply of interchangeable parts and credit facilities; seized market share and, ultimately, price leadership. Despite the initial inexperience of his dealers, Henry Ford was personally un-interested in sales issues. Advertising was minimal, and the company remained production-driven. Ford held that he could sell everything he made, and preferred the simplicity of cash orders (Strasser 1995; Tedlow 1990; Pope 1983; Sivulka 1998; Norris 1990).

Some urban retailers made gains in scale and scope economies. Chain stores, department stores, and mail-order companies operated in bulk and offered set, low prices. F. W. Woolworth had 774 outlets in 1914, and Atlantic and Pacific, the grocers, a highly impressive 3,782 in 1917. One other interesting fact is worth knowing: the Piggly Wiggly store, located in Memphis, is the first-known example of self-service. Macy's of New York evolved as a regional entity for urban customers, as did other department stores, such as John Wanamaker in Philadelphia, or Gimbel Brothers of Milwaukee. The cities offered a new, modern way of life. With their service, fashions, ornate furnishings, restaurants, and beauty salons, department stores consciously reflected the aspirations of the middle classes and the pursuit of shopping as an intrinsic pleasure. Montgomery Ward and Sears Roebuck, having combined mail with rail, advertised widely in newspapers, systemized ordering and delivery processes, built wholesaling networks, and, through money-back guarantees, instilled confidence in catalogue purchasing. Nevertheless, one survey, in 1923, records that mail orders accounted for only 4 percent of national sales, compared to 8 percent for multiples and 16 percent for department stores. Given the prevalence of homesteads and small towns, two thirds of purchases were still made at the general store (Norris 1990; Tedlow 1990; Strasser 1995; Pope 1983). When compared to Britain, the scale of mail-order and US retailing generally were major differences, explained by demographic characteristics. Yet it is the similarity in overall living standards, product development, branding, and advertising, and not British managerial "failure", that is striking.

17.2.4 Continental Europe and Japan

Between 1907 and 1912, 11 of the 93 British firms valued at £2 million or above were located in the food, drink, and tobacco sector; there were none in Germany or France with their respective totals of 45 and 21. Large-scale enterprise in Germany was associated with coal, steel, and engineering and the banks that financed these industries. Before the First World War, two lesser-sized German firms, the Schultheiss Brauerei and chocolate manufacturer Stollwerck, produced consumer goods. Despite Stollwerck's achievements overseas, Chandler exaggerates its marketing capabilities in advertising, packaging, and branding, notably in his comparison with the larger British firm, Cadbury. German GDP per head, in 1914, remained significantly less than the US or British figures (see Table 17.1). Between 1871 and 1910, the percentage of Germans living in towns of 2,000 or more rose from 36 to 60. Seven cities acquired in 1910 populations of over 250,000, Berlin having nearly 2 million, yet the total 65 million population was still more widely scattered than in Britain or even the United States (Cassis 1997; Chandler 1990; Wischermann and Shore 2000; Benson and Shaw 1992).

By the time of the First World War, Germany was, like France and Italy, less advanced in terms of consumption and corporate marketing capabilities than

Table 17.1 Levels of GDP per capita, 1870–1973 (1990 Geary–Khamis dollars)

Country	1870	1914	1929	1938	1950	1973
USA	2,457	4,805	6,220	6,134	9,573	16,607
Britain	3,263	5,038	5,195	5,983	6,847	11,992
Germany	1,913	3,227	4,335	5,126	4,281	13,152
France	1,858	3,206	4,666	4,424	5,221	12,940
Italy	1,467	2,487	3,026	3,244	3,425	10,409
Japan	741	1,276	1,949	2,356	1,873	11,017

Source: Maddison (1995: 180–97).

the United States or Britain. The speed of the transformation in Britain and the United States means that we can refer to the emergence of national products, and even to a single national market. But it is more difficult to characterize the position in Continental Europe, where change was more partial or patchy. Rising population levels and wealth, for example, were important to Dutch margarine makers Jurgens and Van den Bergh, which later merged with Lever Brother to form Unilever. By the late 1890s, the urban workers of Germany were, after their British peers, their most important market (Wilson 1954; Stuyvenberg 1969). In 1908, the famous sociologist Werner Sombart commented on the pervasiveness of advertising in German and Austrian cities, but Germany remained a collection of regional economies. Lack of scale and scope limited the growth of indigenous consumer goods manufacturers, and constrained policies rooted in output, price, distribution, packaging, branding, and mass advertising. The food and packaged products sector in Germany did not imitate the organizational and international successes of the electrical and chemicals industries. Amongst fixed retailers, some urban department stores had established themselves by the 1890s, notably Wertheim in Berlin. Others such as Tietz, later called Kaufhof, or Schocken & Sons became chains, and used the rail system to supply mail orders. The origins of chain stores Karstadt and Edeka can also be discovered in this period, and, by 1903, the Central Union of German Cooperative Societies had 1,597 affiliated shops (Cassis 1997; Chandler 1990; Wischermann and Shore 2000; Benson and Shaw 1992).

Financial institutions and trading companies, and not industry, were the dominant big business sectors in France. Amongst makers of consumer goods, Raffinerie et Sucrerie Say was large, at least by French standards. Without a national market, consumer goods firms did not transform their production, products, and marketing approaches in the manner of US and British contemporaries. France was, like Britain, a pioneer of the department store, and the existence of Bon Marché, one of oldest and biggest in the world, Louvre, Samaritaine, Printemps, and Galeries Lafayette in Paris were proof of an important metropolitan culture accustomed to high consumption levels. The visits of an aspiring bourgeois to the capital's many department stores inspired Zola to write *Au Bonheur des Dames*. Yet chain stores on the British or US model were unknown, with the exception of newsagent Hachette (Cassis 1997; Wischermann and Shore 2000; Williams 1982). The Michelin Man, promoting a successful brand of tires, first appeared in 1898. Recognized by his Latin name, Bibendum, he was frequently and fittingly portrayed as a good-time character. By the early 1900s, the company was already publishing its famous travel, hotel, and gastronomic guides (Harp 2001). Italy remained, despite its unification, a collection of regional and city identities, as well as divided between the north and the less developed south. An important commercialized city like Milan did become home to the department store Magazzini Bocconi, later Rinascente, and Mele was located in Naples. To reach beyond urban customers, both developed as regional mail-order companies. It is known, too, that the urban middle classes and affluent working classes were the targets of advertised brands made by Borsalino, Cinzano, and Campari. Real wages in Italy's northern industrial "triangle" were, by 1910, comparable to those of Germany or France (Morris 1993; Arvidsson 2003).

Although the demand for consumer goods was expanding, average Japanese consumption was in 1913 approximately seven times lower than in Britain. For a developing country, Japan was highly urbanized: in 1879, 11 percent of the population lived in cities with 10,000 or more people; in 1908, 25 percent. It required a complicated network of small-scale distributors to bring food and more durable items from the countryside or from production centers throughout Japan. The majority of goods were sold locally or regionally, yet the national trade in ceramics, rice, sake, soy sauce, silk, and cotton was important. Demand, population density, and urbanization led to extensive trading networks before the era of rapid economic development. These supply chains, moreover, formed an institutional inheritance that conditioned later trends in marketing and distribution, which were largely stimulated by the production of "modern" goods. In large population centers, general stores gradually gave way to specialist outlets and to department stores like Mitsukoshi, founded in 1904. Despite most distributors dealing only in undifferentiated consumer goods, there was a history of packaging and labelling by urban wholesalers and retailers. Before the First World War, several sake and soy sauce companies made use of advertising and brand identity, most famously Kikkoman, as did Noritake ceramics and Ajinomoto seasonings (Maeda 1981; Kawabe 1989, 1993).

17.3 THE "MATURING" OF THE MASS MARKET

17.3.1 The Culture of Consumption

In Britain, the advance of marketing and the domestically orientated consumer industries during the 1920s ran counter to the costs of the war, the loss of export markets, and the cycle of economic depression. While Britain's fortunes were mixed, but troubled, the United States benefited from a conjunction of favorable trends. It established itself as the world's leading economy, in terms of size, trade, and living standards, and, fundamentally, in terms of management and marketing practice. Between 1914 and 1929, total consumption rose in real terms by 71.1 percent, and per capita expenditure by 39.3 percent. In the same period, having peaked in 1919, total consumption in Britain grew by only 5.8 percent, and per capita expenditure, interestingly, by the greater sum of 6.9 percent. Following the good years of the 1920s in the United States, the Wall Street Crash brought an abrupt descent.

Table 17.2 Growth in consumer expenditure, 1914–1973 (real terms, percentages)

Country	1914–29	1929–38	1950–73
Total Consumer Expenditure			
USA	71.1	2.9	127.7
Britain	5.8	16.6	86
Germany			290.2
France			218.8
Italy			230.9
Japan			662.9
Per Capita Consumer Expenditure			
USA	39.3	8.9	63.6
Britain	6.9	12.5	67.2
Germany			99.8
France			155.7
Italy			186.7
Japan			482.5

Source: *The Economist* (1985: 13–117).

Total and per capita consumption fell respectively by 2.9 and 8.9 percent between 1929 and 1938; in Britain, the figures rose by 16.6 and 12.5 percent (Table 17.2). In the 1930s, Britain closed the gap in consumer expenditures and marketing approaches. As a result, GDP per capita in the United States and Britain, noticeably variant in 1929, were more equal in 1938. Significant if aggregate differentials, however, existed between these two nations and Germany, France, Italy, and Japan (see Table 17.1).

The interwar period as a whole was important to the development of marketing in the United States and Britain: their home markets became substantially bigger and richer; companies sought, as a result, to solve the pressing problem of "sales", alongside those of "production", by increasing the scale of their marketing operations and improving the sophistication of their techniques; and, certainly for foods, household products, and clothing, a consumer culture based on choice, cachet, and lifestyle rather than price and basic wants was widely "democratized". Admittedly, the social transformation was incomplete: such material gains evaded the legions of the unemployed, and the middle classes were disproportionate beneficiaries in durables as well as housing. In Continental Europe, overall living standards, the lack of large-scale consumer goods producers, or economic disorder hampered attempts to imitate the US culture of consumption. With its circumstances of "late" industrialization, the very specific requirements of consumer goods manufacturers and independent distributors in Japan did not induce direct imitation of US practice, but, as in Europe, created large intra-national variations in marketing.

While there are detectable similarities between the United States and Britain during the interwar years, the combination of growth and convergence in consumption was, internationally, a feature of the postwar boom. With the damage inflicted on Europe and Japan during the Second World War, GDP per capita was by 1950 markedly higher in the United States (see Table 17.1), where total and per capita consumption had grown, since 1938, by 88.6 and 37.7 percent respectively. The issue was the capacity of other countries to narrow this fissure between the high point achieved in the United States and the economic well-being of their own citizens. Between 1950 and 1973, the other major economies, with the exception of Britain, closed the gap in the size of national markets and total consumer expenditure levels, and all of them, spurred by postwar recovery, gained comparatively in consumption per head (see Table 17.2). By 1973, the United States still enjoyed the advantages of an early lead and continued growth in market size and personal wealth, but the material welfare of other nations had progressed comparatively and absolutely.

17.3.2 United States

During the 1920s, US firms increased the scale of their marketing operations, the number and size of advertising agencies spread, and a key business function was established as an identifiable profession. The use of demographics and statistical testing assisted the planning of distribution, and greater understanding of the consumer further supported the design of "emotional" advertising. These techniques originated from earlier decades. The founding of the Harvard Graduate School of Business in 1908 bore witness to the American tradition of pragmatism, and, by 1920, both Harvard and New York Universities hosted a Bureau of Business Research. Large-scale companies, undertaking or completing essential reforms in production management and business organization, responded to the booming consumer demand of the 1920s. Market research agencies, such as Nielsen and Gallup, burgeoned. Having founded a market research department, and departments in planning and statistics, J. Walter Thompson became the United States' most influential advertising agency. Its use of surveys to discover the cognizant and hidden wishes of consumers complemented the arrival of a bigger and richer market which emphasized quality and cachet over price, and facilitated greater product segmentation (Tedlow 1990; Schuwer 1966; Sivulka 1998; Morris 1993). Large-scale companies strove for the "scientific" organization and coordination of product development, branding, advertising, and distribution, and replaced the "entrepreneurial intuition" of small firms with the managerial objective of the marketing orientation.

Although electrical domestic appliances were available before the First World War, it was the 1920s that marked the era of the toaster, water and room heaters, and refrigerators, in addition to powered vacuum cleaners and washing machines. The vacuum cleaner was a sign of style and modernity, and the association of cleanliness with social status, family values, and guilt followed the success of soap and detergent producers. When domestic appliance makers promoted the saving of labor, they fortuitously tracked the declining numbers of servants. Manufacturers were supplying the means to transform the home-life of Americans. In the auto industry, it was General Motors that set trends in distribution, promotion, and product development. To surpass Ford, it extended the range of its products and price, and advertised intensively. It formed a credit company, and exclusive retailers with set locations enhanced its distribution network. In the 1920s, only food and beverages and then drugs and toiletries outdid autos in terms of promotional outlay. Between 1918 and 1928, consumer expenditure on consumer durables, including vehicles, grew in real terms by 75 percent. United States firms, in 1928, spent some $2 billion on all forms of advertising, with General Motors, American Tobacco, Coca-Cola, and Procter & Gamble determining the pace. In general, advertising volumes quadrupled between 1909 and 1929. One spur to this expenditure was the new medium of radio, which began selling products from 1923. Procter & Gamble was the first manufacturer to add the sponsorship of radio programs to its advertising armory, when, in 1927, it identified itself with an everyday drama called "Amos and Andy", and gave birth to the genre of "soap opera" (Norris 1990; Sivulka 1998; Tedlow 1990; Pope 1983 260–1; Schuwer 1966).

Department stores were still mainly located in the cities of the east and midwest, but chains had national prominence. A&P, Woolworth, and J. C. Penney were amongst those that continued to expand. As farm incomes declined as a proportion of national wealth, Sears and Montgomery Ward used the fame of their catalogues to open stores that could serve growing urban markets. With 23 million car owners in 1930, Sears also built near highways at sites where they could conveniently park. By 1935, its 428 stores were the United States' biggest supplier of furniture, fixtures, kitchen equipment, and electrical appliances, and multiples generally attracted 25.7 percent of consumer expenditure. With 13,314 stores in 1937, A&P was far bigger than its major rivals, but needed to respond urgently to the new source of competition, notably from large-scale supermarkets (Tedlow 1990; Pope 1983).

The United States maintained its international lead in marketing techniques during the postwar decades. While the depression years and wartime circumstances had restrained innovation, the period 1950–73 brought a consumer boom of unprecedented opportunity. Increases in market size and disposable incomes drew manufacturers to particular income levels or income groups. Marketers had from the 1920s already revealed their interest in the science of psychology, but, by the late 1940s, greater emphasis on psychological insight was beginning to replace a reliance on statistical planning techniques. Companies and agencies were attracted to "Motivational Research" as the era of affluence seemingly erased the concerns of "rational" economics. The instincts for Sex, Status, and Security were potentially contradictory, but a deepening understanding of basic human desires assisted the sale of numerous products. Studies disinterred the importance of the home and the conformity of the American housewife. They showed that "Mrs Middle Majority" belonged to the white collar, skilled, and semi-skilled classes that, in the 1950s, constituted 65 percent of the workforce. It seemed, too, to be the age of the suburbs and the automobile. Women in Maidenform bras were shown dreaming of material and sexual success, and Buick and Oldsmobile drivers were portrayed as would-be Cadillac owners. Motivational Research inspired Vance Packard, in 1957, to write *The Hidden Persuaders*, in which a quiescent people were unknowingly manipulated. If true, Americans were easily persuaded to consume more and more. Since networked television had reached 60 percent of homes by 1951, advertisers did, indeed, have access to a medium that was potent and suited to imagery. Following the traditions of United States radio, manufacturers sponsored television programs. Philip Morris introduced "I Love Lucy", and the luminary of the Dinah Shore Show sang the praises of the Chevrolet (Sivulka 1998).

By the 1960s, low cost chains and discount stores, such as Korvette, posed problems for the traditional multiples, although Woolworth and Kresge respectively founded Woolco and K-Mart. Moreover, in the United States, the shopping mall grew into a centerpiece of life outside the home: there were eight in 1945, and 3,840 by 1960 (Glickman 1999; Tedlow 1990). Wal-Mart, founded as late as 1962, was by 1990 the largest retailer in the United States, offering the proprietary brands of manufacturers at discount prices. By 2002, its worldwide sales were three times larger than its next biggest rival, France's Carrefour, and its 30 percent control of household staples expenditure in the United States had major implications for the supply-chain and consumer choice.

17.3.3 Britain

Between 1922 and 1938, British consumer expenditure grew in real terms by 32 percent. For many goods, unit costs fell dramatically, and the variety of products expanded. The composition of personal expenditure shifted towards consumer durables, but statistics conceal important trends towards more expensive, branded foods and clothing. Although improvements in management and business organization lagged behind those in the United States, they were far-reaching enough to transform living standards and consumption patterns. Despite the decline of the heavy industries, economic dynamism came from consumer goods and more domestically orientated concerns. For many producers and their consultants, the "manufacturing problem" was largely solved. Efforts could be focused, instead, on the selling or marketing "problem". Considering the advances in production technology, products and business organization, it was the state of the consumer market that demanded new managerial skills. Whether it was cigarettes, or confectionery, or canned goods, what for many had been, a generation before, an occasional indulgence or a considered choice was converted into frequent semi-luxuries and impulse purchases. In the 1920s, leading firms in the food industry became increasingly interested in the collection and use of statistics as a means of assessing future demand, estimating output, and organizing distribution. Some formally re-conceived "marketing" as an activity based on scientific planning, rather than intuition, and as a complement to the detailed and technical task of manufacturing and factory organization. Their activities strengthened sales efforts, but grew out of management's inherent production-orientation. Although the actual word "marketing" was clearly a US import, changes in technique and business organization were initially indigenous rather than transatlantic in origin. In the 1930s, a few leading firms, notably Rowntree and the soap and food conglomerate Unilever, consciously adopted intensive advertising approaches and what became labelled in the postwar boom the "marketing orientation" (Fitzgerald 1995, 2000, 2005; Corley 1987; Benson 1994; Jones and Morgan 1994).

The early development of British markets and capabilities meant that the decades following the Second World War did not bring substantial marketing change, in contrast to Continental Europe. Many companies were understandably concerned, after so many years of austerity, with simply re-establishing their well-known brands, although new products and especially electricals extended the horizons of the consumer. Per capita consumption grew by 1.9 percent per annum between 1946 and 1973, compared to the 1.6 percent achieved between 1922 and 1938. For many, the British had lost an empire, or looked enviously at United States or German growth rates; in truth, the average Briton had never lived better. The greater concentration of retailing outlets, especially supermarkets such as Tesco and Sainsbury, challenged the control that manufacturers had deliberately forged over distributors. As in the United States, market power had come through the ownership of proprietary brands, but the multiples' competitive advantages in logistics, bulk purchase, and price by the 1960s weighed against the manufacturers' emphasis on cachet and image. Producers were forced to invest in supply chain management, organization-to-organization relationships, and push marketing rather than the creative development of brands. The concentration and power of UK retailers increased in the 1980s and became internationally notable. In fashion goods, long production runs were not suited to greater market segmentation and rising youth sales, and new arrivals such as Next were beginning to exploit the vulnerability of clothing giant Marks and Spencer. Yet British consumers did not abandon their desire to buy from the national supermarkets, especially Tesco, which emerged as the country's largest retailer (Fitzgerald 1995, 2000; Corley 1987; Nevett 1982; Tedlow and Jones 1993; Jones and Morgan 1994).

17.3.4 Japan

By 1920, there were 16 Japanese cities with 100,000 or more residents, and, by 1940, urban areas of this size held 30 percent of the nation. Their very size required a response in distribution, marketing, and consumer goods. Total consumption increased by a remarkable 7.6 percent per annum over the long period of 1946–73, and by an equally remarkable 6.2 percent per capita. In 1960, Japan had the world's second largest domestic market after the United States. The origins of the country's "modern" marketing systems can be detected in the interwar period, but the scale of Japan's postwar consumer boom is apparent.

The arrival of station terminal shops linked rising incomes, consumption, and enlarging cities, as well as commuting: between 1929 and 1940, the Hankyu, Tokyo Yokohama Electric, and Seibu Railways all established shops. In 1931, "small" retailers still accounted for 98 percent of Tokyo establishments, although eight department stores had 33 percent of city-wide purchases. By 1933, Mitsukoshi consisted of ten branches. Department stores, like the railway outlets, largely competed for the custom of the urban middle class, but long-term trends had by the interwar period created new consumption opportunities in food, clothing, health, and education for regularly employed, urban workers and their families. In 1934, labor-intensive, indigenous products absorbed over half of consumer expenditure, but some firms utilized imported technologies and established large-scale enterprises. The duality of manufacturing techniques and organization was necessarily reflected in the duality of marketing systems. Innovative producers in Japan found the hierarchy of entrenched, traditional distributors unsuitable, and many of them established both wholesaling and retailing branches. In some cases, they decided on directly owned networks, but most did not have the capital and preferred to contract with tied distributors.

In a developing market, manufacturers used this contact with consumers to demonstrate the benefits of their new products. Needing quickly to build scale and scope distribution economies to balance growing manufacturing operations, they outflanked the protected, traditional wholesalers and shopkeepers and replaced them with outlets exhibiting sales commitment and product-knowledge. Leading producers of cosmetics, clothing, foods, footwear, furniture, and electricals implemented marketing innovations and the establishment of distribution *keiretsu*, including Shiseido Cosmetics, Morinaga confectionery, Pine Sewing Machine and subsequent maker of the famous Janome line, and Tokyo Electric, Toshiba's forerunner. In 1923, Matsushita Electrical Industries founded a central marketing department and a regional sales network. Pursuing rapid market penetration, it established a system of exclusive wholesalers in 1933, and, two years later, an association of registered retailers. Toyota in 1935 imitated the car dealerships created by General Motors and Ford in Japan (Kawabe 1989, 1993; Maeda 1981).

Rapid industrialization from a position of relative backwardness continued to have marketing consequences during the consumer revolution that followed the disaster of the Second World War. Larger-scale companies hurriedly materialized and needed marketing solutions suited to Japan's specific market conditions. Manufacturers did not seek to encourage consumption, since demand outstripped demand, and the efficacy of advertising was questioned. The key objective was distribution to potential consumers, growing in number and spending-power. Electrical, autos, synthetic fiber, pharmaceutical, cosmetic, camera, and processed food manufacturers opted in this period for directly controlled *keiretsu* wholesalers and retailers. Ultimately, consumers benefited from product and brand saturation, the prevalence of local stores, after-sales service, and product information, but were disadvantaged by controlled and non-competitive prices.

Changes in distribution moved in parallel to urbanization: in 1950, 26 percent of the population lived in cities with 100,000 or more inhabitants; the figure was 52 percent by 1970. In 1955, 33 percent of households owned a washing machine, and the level was 58 percent in 1962, by which point 79 percent possessed a television. It was companies such as Matsushita, having 33,000 federated retail stores in 1952, that pioneered the postwar boom. Between 1956 and 1960, Hitachi, Toshiba, Mitsubishi, Sanyo, and Sharp imitated MEI's policies. In avoiding price competition, electrical companies stressed instead technology, product quality, and advertising. By the late 1950s, Nissan and Toyota had re-established and expanded a system of franchised dealers, forcing a relative latecomer such as Honda to form a directly owned sales operation in the following decade (Maeda 1981; Shimotani 1995; Yoshino 1975; Okochi and Shimokawa 1981).

In Japan, the term "marketing" is contrasted with the supply-side challenges of "distribution", and implies a "managerial science" of statistical techniques, product testing, and psychological models, imported from the United States in the postwar years. With possible exaggeration, a 1959 survey detected no marketing function in Japanese manufacturing companies, in part because sales companies or agents assumed these responsibilities through *keiretsu* linkages, in part because general trading companies or *sogoshosha* maintained their key role in the national economy. At Matsushita, and other firms, the approach continued to be production or product-driven, and push marketing along a distribution chain supported this emphasis. Japanese economic conditions, growth rates, and federated business structures were less amenable to the marketing-orientated approach, which stressed creative product development and cachet and holistically combined marketing functions within one large, unified enterprise.

Nonetheless, advertising expenditures grew with the increasing importance of specific brands and labels, and television advertising was introduced in 1953. By 1965, the sums spent on promotions equalled 1.1 percent of GDP in Japan, compared to 1.4 percent in Britain. Challenges to the practice of resale price maintenance and the distribution *keiretsu* did gradually encourage "pull" marketing.

New and alternative forms of retailing—including supermarkets, installment plan department stores, chain stores, and greater numbers of railway station shops—joined the opposition lobby. By the 1970s, Daiei, Seibu-Seiyu, supermarkets such as Ito-Yokado, Futagi, and Shiro, and the forerunners of JUSCO and Nichii had already arrived as influential, independent multiples (Yonekawa 1990; Yonekawa and Yoshihara 1987; Yoshino 1971, 1975; Maeda 1981; Kawabe 1993; Yoshino and Lifson 1986).

17.3.5 Continental Europe

Despite Berlin and regional capitals providing numerous and important centers of consumption, and high levels of per capita GDP, economic disruption and inflation hindered marketing developments in interwar Germany. Yet the retailer Karstadt, the merged Schultheiss-Patzenhofer Brauerei, Ostwerke, Suddeutsche Zucker, and Stollwercks did enter the lower reaches of the largest enterprises (Cassis 1997). Siemens strove to develop and promote consumer appliances during the interwar period. But the firm could not shake off its corporate culture, which was rooted in earlier decades, when demand had outstripped supply, and also built on a composite of technology, product, and production-orientations. German rearmament soon curtailed Siemens' initiatives, and pulled the firm back to its well-recognized expertise in engineering (Feldenkirchen 1995). The dominance and corporate objectives of the heavy chemicals industries were unchanged. Prior to the political turmoil of the 1930s, foreign-owned brands such as Unilever's *Rama* or *Blauband* margarines or Coca-Cola could regard Germany as one of its most lucrative markets. Throughout Europe, including Britain, American products, brands, machinery, and cars were well-established by the interwar decades (Jones and Morgan 1994; Jones 2005).

Change was more evident in France than in Germany, partly because consumption expanded more quickly in the 1920s. Citroën was the first to imitate United States production methods, and copied, too, the appointment of sole dealers and the provision of hire purchase. It outdid its rivals Renault and Peugeot in the scale of its advertising, and all three joined Michelin in linking the motorcar with the cause of French modernity. Moreover, Say Raffinerie et Sucrerie and Grand Moulin de Paris did enter amongst France's largest companies. Advertising agencies had been active in British and United States commercial life before the First World War, and, as witnessed by the establishment of Agence Havas in 1920, they became more prominent in France during the interwar period. They furthered the use of slogans and illustrations, and devised concerted advertising plans, while Radio Normandie and Radio-Cite in the 1930s brought the names of products into French homes. Department stores began to operate on a national scale. Le Printemps opened its cheap, fixed-price stores Uniprix, and Galeries Lafayette founded Nouvelles Galeries and Prisunic (Cassis 1997; Harp 2001; Schuwer 1966). In so doing, they perceived the potential of new consumers and acknowledged the commercial attractions of a broadening market.

Personal consumption was increasingly allied to concepts of modernity, and, consequently, to a European desire to close the gap with America. As in France, United States practice had by the 1930s an influence on the role and function of advertising agencies in Holland, and J. Walter Thompson already operated from 22 overseas offices. Marketing in Europe was gradually re-conceived as a profession, and psychological understanding and the use of emotional appeals indicated the growing sophistication of promotions (Wischermann and Shore 2000). Italy in particular felt the stigma of backwardness and the desire for modernity. Fiat was known to imitate United States mass production, but the practice was not common in Italy. Nonetheless, Fiat's 509 Balilla, canned food maker Cirio, Pirelli beer, Motta's Panetonne, Gi.vi.enne's Erba toothpaste, and Olivetti typewriters were examples of products transformed in use or popularity by innovative approaches. The advertiser was concerned with fashion, individual consumption, and cosmopolitanism, and one notion of modernity inevitably clashed with Fascism's martial and nationalistic alternative (Arvidsson 2003; Sivulka 1998).

After the Second World War, reconstruction, economic growth, and the consumer boom were noted features of Western Europe, as well as Japan. In the early 1950s, Suddeutsche Zucker and Margarine-Unie, a Unilever subsidiary, were the only two food firms to be considered large German businesses, although Karstadt's success continued throughout the decade. In France, Astra, Say, and Georges Lesieur et ses fils could be counted amongst the corporate elite (Cassis 1997). Demographic surveys conducted in France during 1955 discovered a population still generally more concerned with acquiring life's basic necessities. Imminent economic transformation, therefore, brought unexpected benefits, and, by the late 1950s or early 1960s, most Italians were replacing the anticipations of the outsider with realistic consumer expectations (Arvidsson 2003). No country matched the economic well-being enjoyed by Americans. But, in the 1960s, the consumer culture and modern lifestyles were available to many West Europeans and had moved out of particular cities, regions, or income groups (see Tables 17.1 and 17.2), and Unilever identified the potential impact of rising expectations on product development and advertising (Jones 2005). In France, the return of a "democratized" Bibendum, this time without the cigar or the pince-nez, signified the different attitudes and purchasing power of the ordinary postwar consumer (Harp 2001).

Retailing in Western Europe remained less concentrated than in Britain, or even in the United States, and fostered a manufacturing base emphasizing quality, specialization, and differentiation. Multiples and department stores, in 1987, controlled over 70 percent of clothing sales in the UK, and the figure for Germany was approximately 34 and nearer to 15 in the cases of France and Italy. One indicative international success was the Italian fashion firm, Benetton, which linked the smaller-scale networks to be found in industrial districts and sold through marketing franchises. On the other hand, from the 1960s onwards, French supermarkets such as Carrefour, Casino, and the Auchan Groupe became dominant suppliers, and Carrefour in 1963 invented the hypermarket. Supermarket multiples Metro, Rewe-Zentral, Aldi, Edeka, and Schwarz, which owned Lidl, similarly gained domination within Germany, and the largest, Tengelmann, controlled supermarket and drugstores Kaiser and Plus, apparel and general outlet Kik, and, from 1979, the ultimate prize, the United States' Atlantic and Pacific. In Britain, Germany, and France, resale price maintenance had been legally enforceable during most of the postwar boom, and mass retailers responded with own-label brands that combined price with quality. Alongside its association with fashion and cosmetics, France has, in BSN, one of the world's largest multi-brand food companies (Jones and Morgan 1994; Tedlow 1990; Jones 2005).

17.4 Conclusions

The origins of "modern" marketing are connected to increases in real wages, the choices generated by disposable incomes, transport and communication systems, the building of national markets, and urbanization. If the economic and social opportunities were to be fulfilled, businesses needed to innovate products and systems, and they succeeded with the manufacturing and distribution of standardized goods. The continued growth in personal wealth and market size raised expectations and capabilities, and led to greater product segmentation. It stimulated competition, and the more complex product demands of consumers necessitated more complex business systems. Changes of emphasis within the marketing mix of large-scale companies reflected broader trends. Production and product-orientations were complemented by an interest in sales, distribution, and advertising. The assumption of the marketing orientation, which started with the wishes of consumers, was a response by many leading enterprises to the greater individual spending power of the consumer. In several important cases, it brought the increasing segmentation of formerly homogenous markets. Market research assisted the process of product development, and the use of psychological analysis challenged the simplicities of "narrow" economics.

The business history literature, at present, rarely links developments in corporate marketing with broader trends in consumption, industrial structure, or international competitiveness. Most corporate histories, indeed, fail to give marketing the importance allotted to technology, organizational forms, or even labor policies. In the analysis of industrial product makers and service industries, such as banking and insurance, this deficiency is even more striking, and marketing by non-profit organizations and governments will no doubt require the attention of future historians. Overviews of trends in the United States contain many useful insights, but they generally attend to the period before 1920. Our knowledge of the interwar years and particularly the postwar boom, when marketing "matured" in the United States, is significantly less. This gap applies to Britain and Europe, in addition to the United States. It also complicates the historian's assessment of earlier periods, the whole era of mass marketing, and the stages of its development. With few exceptions, the lessons of history have not been applied to contemporary marketing.

The shortage of information significantly limits our understanding of the far-reaching changes that followed the end of the postwar boom after 1973. Falling growth rates reduced possibilities for marketing initiatives; inflation and economic depression shifted the market emphasis to some degree from brand cachet to price, as did the rising power of large-scale retailers in relation to manufacturers; and leading producers, no longer gaining competitive advantage from marketing-orientation policies that had become widespread, switched to business strategies dominated by merger, acquisition, and corporate restructuring. During the 1980s and 1990s, the power of retailing chains continued to increase, and the internationalization of producers and advertising agencies and possibilities of "global" branding challenged the certainties and practices of an earlier period. By extending research into a greater number of industries and periods, business history has the means as well as the approach to contribute more effectively to our assessment of marketing as a phenomenon of modern economies and societies.

REFERENCES

ARVIDSSON, A. (2003). *Making Modernity: Italian Advertising from Fascism to Postmodernity*. London: Routledge.

BENSON, J. (1994). *The Rise of Consumer Society in Britain, 1880–1920*. London: Longman.

—— and SHAW, G. (1992). *The Evolution of Retail Systems, c.1800–1914*. Leicester: Leicester University Press.

CASSIS, Y. (1997). *Big Business: The European Experience in the Twentieth Century*. Oxford: Oxford University Press.

CHANDLER, A. D. (1990). *Scale and Scope: The Dynamics of Industrial Enterprise*. Cambridge, Mass.: Harvard University Press.

CORLEY, T. A. B. (1987). "Consumer Marketing in Britain, 1914–60". *Business History*, 29: 65–83.

FELDENKIRCHEN, W. (1995). *Siemens, 1918–1945*. Columbus, OH: Ohio University Press.

FITZGERALD, R. (1995). *Rowntree and the Marketing Revolution*. Cambridge: Cambridge University Press.

—— (2000). "Markets, Management, and Merger: John Mackintosh & Sons, 1890–1969". *Business History Review*, 74: 555–609.

FITZGERALD, R. (2005). "Products, Firms and Consumption: Cadbury and the Development of Marketing, 1900–39". *Business History*, 47: 511–3.

FRASER, W. H. (1981). *The Coming of the Mass Market, 1880–1914*. London: Macmillan.

FULLERTON, R. (1988). "How Modern is Modern Marketing? Marketing's Evolution and the Myth of the 'Production Era'". *Journal of Marketing*, 52: 108–25.

GLICKMAN, L. B. (1999). *Consumer Society in American History: A Reader*. New York: Cornell University Press.

HARP, S. (2001). *Marketing Michelin: Advertising and Cultural Identity in Twentieth-Century France*. Baltimore: Johns Hopkins University Press.

HOLLANDER, S. C., and GERMAIN, R. (1991). *Was there a Pepsi Generation before Pepsi Discovered It? Youth Segmentation in Marketing*. Lincolnwood, Ill: NTC Business Books.

JEFFREYS, J. B. (1954). *Retail Trading in Britain, 1850–1950*. Cambridge: Cambridge University Press.

JONES, G. (2005). *Renewing Unilever: Transformation and Tradition*. Oxford: Oxford University Press.

——and MORGAN, N. J. (eds.) (1994). *Adding Value: Brands and Marketing in Food and Drink*. London: Routledge.

KAWABE, N. (1989). "The Development of Distribution Systems in Japan before World War II". *Business and Economic History*, 18: 33–44.

—— (1993). "The Development of the Retailing Industry in Japan". *Entreprises et Histoire*, 4: 13–25.

LAIRD, P. (1998). *Advertising Progress: American Business and the Rise of Consumer Society*. Baltimore: Johns Hopkins University Press.

LEBERGOTT, S. (1996). *Consumer Expenditures: New Measures and Old Motives*. Princeton, NJ: Princeton University Press.

MAEDA, K. (1981). "The Evolution of Retailing Industries in Japan", in Okochi and Shimokawa (1981), 265–92.

MADDISON, A. (1995). *Dynamic Forces in Capatalist Development*. New York: Oxford University Press.

MATHIAS, P. (1967). *Retailing Revolution: A History of Multiple Retailing in the Food Trades, based on the Allied Suppliers Group*. London: Longman.

MORRIS, J. (1993). *The Political Economy of Shopkeeping in Milan*. Cambridge: Cambridge University Press.

NEVETT, T. R. (1982). *Advertising in Britain: A History*. London: Heinemann.

NORRIS, J. D. (1990). *Advertising and the Transformation of American Society, 1865–1920*. New York: Greenwood Press.

OKOCHI, A., and SHIMOKAWA, K. (eds.) (1981). *The Development of Mass Marketing: The Automobile and Retailing Industries*. Tokyo: Tokyo University Press.

POPE, D. (1983). *The Making of Modern Advertising*. New York: Basic Books.

SCHUMPETER, J. A. (1954). *History of Economic Analysis*. New York: Oxford University Press.

SCHUWER, P. (1966). *History of Advertising*. Geneva: Edito-Service S.A.

SHIMOTANI, M. (1995). "The Formation of Distribution *Keiretsu*", in E. Abe and R. Fitzgerald (eds.), *The Origins of Japanese Industrial Power*. London: Frank Cass: 54–69.

SIVULKA, J. (1998). *Soap, Sex and Cigarettes: A Cultural History of American Advertising*. Belmont, Calif.: Wadsworth Publishing Company.

STRASSER, S. (1995). *Satisfaction Guaranteed: The Making of the American Mass Market*. Washington, DC: Smithsonian Institution Press.

—— (ed.) (2003). *Commodifying Everything: Relationships of the Market*. New York: Routledge.

STUYVENBERG, J. H. VAN (ed.) (1969). *Margarine: An Economic, Social and Scientific History, 1869–1969*. Liverpool: Liverpool University Press.

TEDLOW, R. (1990). *New and Improved: The Story of Mass Marketing in America*. Oxford: Heinemann Professional.

—— and JONES, G. (eds.) (1993). *The Rise and Fall of Mass Marketing*. London: Routledge.

The Economist (1985). *Economic Statistics 1900–1983*. London: Economist Publications Unit.

VEBLEN, T. B. (1924). *The Theory of the Leisure Class: An Economic Study*. London: Allen & Unwin.

WILLIAMS, R. H. (1982). *Dream Worlds: The Middle Classes in Late 19th Century France*. Berkeley: University of California Press.

WILSON, C. H. (1954). *The History of Unilever: A Study in Economic Growth and Social Change*, vols. I and II. London: Cassell.

WISCHERMANN, C., and SHORE, E. (2000). *Advertising and the European City: Historical Perspectives*. Aldershot: Ashgate Publishing.

YONEKAWA, S. (ed.) (1990). *General Trading Companies: A Comparative and Historical Study*. Tokyo: United Nations University.

—— and YOSHIHARA, H. (eds.) (1987). *Business History of General Trading Companies*. Tokyo: University of Tokyo Press.

YOSHINO, Y. M. (1971). *The Japanese Marketing System: Adaptations and Innovations*. Cambridge, Mass.: MIT.

—— (1975). *Marketing in Japan: A Management Guide*. New York: Praeger.

—— and LIFSON, T. B. (1986). *The Invisible Link: Japan's Sogoshosha and the Organization of Trade*. Cambridge, Mass.: MIT.

CHAPTER 18

....

THE MANAGEMENT OF LABOR AND HUMAN RESOURCES

....

HOWARD GOSPEL

18.1 INTRODUCTION

....

How labor is managed is a central issue for all organizations and for all industrial societies. In this chapter, the management of labor is broadly defined to cover three broad interconnected areas—work relations, employment relations, and industrial relations. Work relations are taken to cover the way work is organized and the deployment of workers around technologies and production systems. Employment relations deal with the arrangements governing such aspects of employment as recruitment, training, job tenure, and reward systems. Industrial relations are taken to cover the voiced aspirations of workers and institutional arrangements which may arise to address them, such as joint consultation, works councils, trade unions, and collective bargaining (Gospel 1992).

I would like to thank the following for overall comments and for comments on countries and industries: Anthony Ferner, Robert Fitzgerald, Geoffrey Jones, Sanford Jacoby, Peter Howlett, Mary Rose, and Jonathan Zeitlin.

Throughout the chapter, the emphasis will be on major patterns in these three areas as they have developed, especially in large private-sector firms, over a long period of time from the early nineteenth century onwards. It draws mainly on the core economies of the twentieth century, especially the United States, UK, Germany, France, and Japan. The focus is primarily on the management of intermediate and lower classes of labor, which have constituted the majority of employees over time and which are best covered in the literature. Wherever possible an attempt will be made to deal with all three areas of labor management as defined above. However, training is covered in the chapter by Kathleen Thelen in this volume.

The chapter is organized as follows. The next section provides a broad overview of the contexts within which labor has been managed, including the market, technological, political, and business contexts. There then follow sections which present broad "stages" in the history of labor management, taking examples from leading sectors of the economy. However, throughout, the aim is to stress continuities over time between stages, the coexistence of systems at any one point in time, and how older sectors also adapt over time. In a penultimate section, caveats and areas for further research are outlined. In the final section, broad conclusions are drawn.

18.2 THE CHANGING CONTEXTS OF LABOR MANAGEMENT

There are a number of major contexts which shape the management of labor and which are outlined schematically here and used further in each section. These include the changing technological, market, political/legal, social, and business environments. Though these contexts shape the activities of employers, managers, and workers, the chapter also shows how the actors themselves have shaped the situations within which they operate (Dunlop 1958; Maurice et al. 1984).

The technological context shapes basic aspects of labor management. Some writers have suggested a broad movement over time from artisanal or craft production (with skilled workers having significant control over work), to mass production (often associated with Ford-type assembly-line systems in industries such as automobiles), and to more flexible and specialized production systems (sometimes referred to as post-Fordist) (see Tolliday 1998 for an overview of the literature). Of course, in practice, changes have been complex, with overlaps in types of production regimes over time and with older sectors adopting aspects of new arrangements. Thus, skilled, small-batch production was never superseded in many areas often typified as mass production, such as metalworking and light assembly industries. Similarly, many aspects of work in modern fast-food restaurants, call centers, and retail stores are very much of a mass-production kind. A constant theme in the history of labor management has been employers' introduction of new technologies, workers' counter-attempts to exert some control over these, and managers' further attempt to develop and refine management systems (Nelson 1975; Hounshell 1984; Piore and Sabel 1984; Lazonick 1990; Tolliday 1998; Scranton 1997).

In terms of the market context, labor management has been shaped by labor, product, and financial market circumstances. In the labor market, there are both longer-term and shorter-term influences. For example, longer-term factors include demographic changes, the broad balance of labor supply and demand, and the changing composition of the labor force. Thus, in various periods in different countries, labor shortages have induced firms to substitute capital for labor and to introduce new production systems, as was the case in the United States in the early/mid-nineteenth century (Lewis 1952; Habbakuk 1962). Shortages also induced firms to introduce systems to attract and retain labor and these have often become embedded and left continuing inheritances, as for example with skilled labor shortages in Japan in the early twentieth century (Jacoby 1979; Gordon 1985 and 1998). Shorter-term labor market influences include the fluctuating level of unemployment in the economy which has immediate direct effects on the balance of power between management and labor. In this respect, for example, sharp rises in unemployment in the UK in the early 1920s and early 1980s significantly affected the bargaining power of management and unions, strengthened managerial prerogatives, and led to major changes in labor management and industrial relations (Gospel 1992).

In terms of product markets, the boundaries of markets and the degree of competition in them have an effect on labor management, both directly and indirectly. Smith (1776), for example, in his celebrated examination of a pin factory, pointed out that the extent of the market shaped the division of labor. Similarly, Commons (1909) used the extension of markets to explain the organization of production, the emergence of distinct classes of masters and men, and the subsequent growth and organization of trade unions. Historically, a large and relatively homogeneous market in the United States facilitated mass production in that country, compared to the smaller and more fragmented markets of Europe (Habbakuk 1962; Rosenberg 1969; Hounshell 1984). The degree of competition within the product market also influences the constraints on management. Thus, over a long period from the interwar years onwards, high levels of product market protection and collusive behavior underpinned the position of trade unions and the development of internal labor market-type arrangements in many countries. Subsequently, the increasing opening-up of markets and the growth of international competition, especially since the 1970s, have reshaped the international division of labor and the extent to which labor can extract rents from management (Gospel 2005).

Financial markets and corporate governance also shape labor systems. Owner-financed and controlled firms historically often had a personal form of paternalism and such firms tended to oppose dealings with trade unions. The growth of equity financing and the separation of ownership and control in countries such as the United States and UK from the early twentieth century onwards allowed for a more bureaucratic approach to labor and lay behind the development of what some have described as "welfare capitalism", with strong internal labor market-type arrangements (Brandes 1976; Jacoby 1985 and 1997). In recent years, new financial pressures from institutional owners and private equity capital have put pressures on firms to adjust employment more directly to market forces. By contrast, up until recently, the continuation of private and more concentrated ownership and greater reliance on insider finance has meant that such pressures have been less strong in Germany and Japan (Gospel and Pendleton 2004).

The political and legal contexts have profoundly shaped labor management systems. In countries such as the United States and UK, liberal states have overall been less interventionist in labor management than in some other countries, and so-called "voluntarism" has been a strong tradition. Even in these countries, however, there have been major exceptions, especially during two world wars, the New Deal in the United States, and arguably in the 1980s under the Reagan and Thatcher administrations. By contrast, in more coordinated economies, such as Germany, Japan, and France, there has long been a tradition of state intervention in labor matters (Crouch 1993; Friedman 1999; Yamamura and Streeck 2003). Nevertheless, it is probably true to say that over time, in most countries, there has been a gradual build-up in intervention in terms of rights off-the-job (state welfare and pension systems), rights on-the-job (workmen's compensation, health and safety, racial and sexual equality legislation), and regulation of collective employment matters (the law on trade unions, collective bargaining, and information and consultation at work). In Europe, the European Union (EU) has in recent decades taken these tendencies further (Supiot 2001).

The social context is in many ways the most difficult to categorize and summarize. Over the decades, the position of children and women at work has changed profoundly, at least in advanced market economies. The starting age of employment has slowly risen and the proportion of women in paid employment has increased. Major changes have also come with rising living standards and a greater awareness of social and human rights. Over time, social identities have also changed, with notions of "class" playing a significant part in worker mentalities through much of the twentieth century, but becoming less powerful in more recent decades. Other social identities at work which have long existed, on the basis of gender, race, and religion, and immigrant status have been successively reshaped and added to with new identities in terms of age, sexual orientation, and disability (Noiriel 1989; Magraw 1992; Piore and Safford 2005). On the other hand, traditional divides between works and staff or between hourly/weekly and monthly-paid, have slowly eroded. Managements have had to take account of these changing social contexts. The so-called "management of diversity" in the workplace is now stressed in modern management discourse; however, history shows that this has always been a concern of management (Kossek and Lobel 1996).

Finally, and more specifically, there is the business context. This is the subject of other chapters and here only the following broad points are made. First, in all the economies under consideration, most firms have been small and medium-sized—though in practice least is known about labor management in such firms. Over time, big firms have come to constitute a larger proportion of total output and of total employment, though this is larger in the United States and UK than countries such as Germany, Italy, and Japan, which have more employment in medium-sized firms. Second, there have been major compositional shifts. With slight differences between countries, the typical large employer in the early to mid-nineteenth century was a textile company; by the mid to late nineteenth century, the biggest single group of major firms in most economies were railway companies; by the mid-twentieth century, the main groupings were manufacturers (steel, chemicals, automobiles, electrical); and by the end of the twentieth century, the biggest single group of large firms was to be found in retailing and financial services (Gospel and Fiedler 2005). This predominance of certain industries played an important part in laying down patterns of labor management. Third, as other chapters describe, over time, big firms in particular have developed more sophisticated hierarchies, not least in the labor area, with the growth of "welfare" or "labor" managers, later "personnel" managers, and now "human resource" managers (Niven 1967; Jacoby 1985; Morikawa and Kobayashi 1986; Kocha 1991; Tsutsui 1998; Fombonne 2003). However, it should be remembered that in some countries, especially those of northern continental Europe, firms still rely significantly on outside employers' organizations and their staff for the management of industrial relations. Fourth, big firms have also changed in structure from being historically either loosely organized holding companies or centralized, functionally organized firms at the beginning of the twentieth century, to being more coordinated multidivisional structures and sometimes decentralized networks of firms by the end of the century (Chandler 1962, 1977, and 1990; Cassis 1997; Whittington and Mayer 2000). As will be analyzed below, this has also had implications for labor management. Finally, as already stated, ownership and governance has changed, though differentially between countries, with personal and family ownership declining over the course of the twentieth century and outsider ownership increasing in the big firm sector, especially in the United States and UK.

18.3 EARLY FORMS OF LABOR MANAGEMENT IN THE "FIRST" INDUSTRIAL REVOLUTION: THE CASE OF TEXTILES

Textile industries were at the forefront of industrialization in many countries. Classic problems for employers emerged in these industries—in terms of work relations (how to organize production and the division of labor), employment relations (how to attract, retain, and motivate labor), and industrial relations (how authority was to be maintained and whether or not to concede employees a voice at work).

In practice, nineteenth century textile and allied industries in Europe and the United States always had elements of both older artisanal and newer factory production. In artisanal sectors, production was on a small scale, work was often organized on a putting-out to households basis or small workshops, and family involvement was important. In these circumstances, masters relied on key (usually male) workers to organize their own work and controlled and paid them by piecework where this was possible. Problems for the masters were uncertainties about the quality of production and the wage–effort relationship (Mendels 1972; Berg 1985). As technologies developed and markets expanded, masters increasingly built their own factories, in both rural and urban areas, and installed machinery. In turn, this meant they had the problem of attracting larger labor forces, especially where factories were located in less populated areas near water power sources. In cotton spinning, large numbers of women and children were employed, usually under tight and often coercive systems of direct control and often paid by time. However, even within the new factories, there persisted forms of inside contracting to key workers and the possibility of drawing on pools of specialized craft labor from local industrial districts (Lazonick 1990; Rose 2000). The motivation to develop the factory system came from market and technological opportunities, but it also gave employers a means for better control over their labor forces (Marglin 1974; Landes 1986).

Pollard (1965) classically describes the emergence of this system in the UK, with its heavy reliance on child and female labor, extensive use of piecework, and devices such as factory housing. At the same time, there was in most textile districts a reliance on external economies of scale, for example in terms of apprentice-type training and piecework price lists. The more vertically integrated US cotton industry moved more quickly to introduce new technologies, to build larger factories, and to develop a greater internal division of labor within the workplace under management control. Later, in Japan, during industrialization in the late nineteenth and early twentieth centuries, some similar problems for management and some similar responses are discernible. For example, in the Japanese textile industries, factory and artisanal production also coexisted, though the latter was much smaller; in the large factory sector, employers used predominantly female workforces; they built factory dormitories and provided various forms of paternalistic benefits; and used tight supervision and simple pay and benefit systems to control workers (Nakagawa 1979; Hunter 2003). Many of these forms of work organization and employment relations have later appeared and are still to be found in textile industries in India, China, and other fast developing countries today.

Industrial relations systems were diverse under early forms of labor management. As suggested, the management of labor was often a mixture of both hard, direct control and also of paternalistic oversight of a personal ad hoc kind (Joyce 1980). Nevertheless, some key male workers could exert control over their work and employers depended on them to organize production. In the UK, by the final half of the twentieth century, unions of male textile workers had grown to become the largest in the country, along with unions for other artisan and craft trades, engineering workers, and coalminers. Those with skills or a strong position in the production process were able to force recognition from employers of their trade societies and to establish regional or national collective bargaining where firms joined together in employers' organizations to deal with trade unions (Jowitt and McIvor 1989; McIvor 1996). In the United States and continental Europe, by the First World War, collective bargaining had also developed in certain craft sectors, such as small metalworking, printing, and footwear, but on the whole it was less extensive than in the UK (Mommsen and Husung 1985; Montgomery 1987).

This section has stressed the slow and uneven development of new forms of management in the factory sectors of the textile and related industries in the late eighteenth and early nineteenth century. It has also been pointed out that artisanal forms of organization coexisted and were not superseded. Hence, craft forms of working survived alongside and within factory production in industries such as textiles, footwear, clothing, and small metalworking (Sabel and Zeitlin 1997; Scranton 1997).

18.4 RAILWAYS AND THE RISE OF THE "MODERN" BUSINESS ENTERPRISE

Developing from the mid-nineteenth century onwards, the railways represented a further stage in the growth of the large modern business enterprises in most countries (Chandler 1977, 1990). In terms of labor management, railway companies encountered both a traditional and a new set of problems. The traditional problems were in terms of recruiting, training, and controlling staff, albeit on a very large scale. The new problems included the complexity of scheduling, the safety of goods and passengers, and the geographical dispersion of work. Under managements from various backgrounds (technical, governmental, military, and accounting), the railway companies were the first to put in place some of the largest bureaucratic systems of employment: more systematic recruitment, the creation of job and promotion hierarchies, and related pay systems based on fixed rates of pay. They also introduced welfare arrangements, of a less personal and more bureaucratic kind, such as housing, basic sick care, and later pension benefits for some workers, usually dependent on length of service with the firm.

In terms of industrial relations, the large railway companies of the United States, UK, and continental Europe were run according to a "unitarist" rather than a "pluralist" model of management (see Fox 1985 for the concepts). Management was the sole source of authority, issued commands, and expected workers to obey. A plurality of sources of authority, with legitimate worker voice and checks and balances, was not permitted. Discipline was based on the notion of a "uniformed" service. In keeping with this and in contrast with the sectors described above, trade unions were not recognized and collective bargaining was rare, until just before or after the First World War.

This pattern of bureaucratic labor management later grew in other sectors, such as the emerging gas, electricity, and water utilities (Melling 1979; Berlanstein 1991). It also provided something of a model for areas of industry such as steel, chemicals, and later oil refining. Developed in the late nineteenth and early twentieth centuries, the model has in many respects persisted up to the present day in both state and private railways and utility systems, albeit often with extensive unionization and collective bargaining.

In this description of bureaucratic employment, three further, significant points should be noted about the railways. The first complements what has already been said in terms of bureaucratic employment; the next two bring out the coexistence within railway operations of older and different types of arrangements.

First, the railways were some of the first companies to develop extensive hierarchies of managerial and white-collar staff. These were necessary to organize and coordinate diverse and dispersed operations. Such employees were offered something like "careers" within the company and moved up wage and benefit hierarchies. Though they learnt on the job, there were books, magazines, and courses which they could attend. Second, however, the railways were constructed and to some extent maintained in more traditional ways, by gangs of laborers, who were apart from this bureaucratic system and did not partake of the benefits of others who worked on the railways. Third, the workshops owned by the railway companies, where engines and rolling stock were built and maintained, were also different. Here workers had more control over production, belonged to occupational craft communities, were paid wages which related more to those in craft labor markets, and were more likely to belong to trade unions. Within them, craft forms of production and management existed and unions were more likely to be recognized. However, it should also be noted that the railway workshops included some of the more sophisticated engineering shops of their days, especially in terms of work organization (Coleman 1981; Drummond 1995).

18.5 THE DEVELOPMENT OF LABOR MANAGEMENT IN THE "SECOND" INDUSTRIAL REVOLUTION: THE CASE OF HEAVY PROCESS AND ASSEMBLY-LINE INDUSTRIES

In the late nineteenth and early twentieth centuries, major industries were transformed or created entirely anew with the advent of the new general purpose technology of electricity and with new production processes (steel, chemicals, and later electrical products and automobiles). Employers in these sectors used some old methods and developed other newer forms of labor management.

In steel and chemicals, for example, for a time, systems of internal contracting under skilled workers and gang masters continued to exist. Much of the work involved these arrangements and some more skilled and strategically placed workers had considerable control over work organization. Employment was often short-term and wage and benefit systems simple. Slowly, however, different arrangements developed. Large firms, such as Carnegie and US Steel in the United States, Krupp in Germany, and Schneider in France, substituted their own foremen for internal contractors, began to recruit more systematically, trained workers internally on the job but usually not through apprenticeship systems, and developed employment hierarchies and some of the welfare arrangements described above (notably housing, workmen's compensation, sick pay, and pensions) (McCreary 1968; Stone 1975; Jacoby 1985; Fitzgerald 1988; Vishniac 1990; Gospel 1992; Welskopp 1994).

In these sectors and in large-scale metalworking, there was a desire on the part of employers to gain information on worker effort and to organize work more systematically under managerial control. This developed rapidly in the United States, where fast-growing and large national markets and a shortage of skilled labor gave managers an incentive to invest in the development of skill-displacing technologies. In metalworking and engineering, as early as the mid to late nineteenth century, there emerged a distinctive "American system of manufactures", based on standardized and interchangeable parts. This in turn came more and more to use semiskilled or unskilled workers who tended high throughput machinery or worked on what came to be assembly lines (Rosenberg 1969; Hounshell 1984).

From the early twentieth century onwards, in various forms, this led to the development of so-called systematic and scientific management (Litterer 1963; Nelson

1975; Littler 1982; Merkle 1980; Fridenson 1986; Tsutsui 1998). The latter is usually associated with Frederick Taylor (Taylor 1911; Nelson 1980), but there were other writers and practitioners at the time advocating new systems of labor management. These involved elements of the following: a study of the organization of work by specialist time-and-work-study experts; the reorganization of work, often leading to a greater subdivision of jobs; and the fixing of wages by new types of bonus systems related to performance. In practice, such arrangements developed only slowly, but with some acceleration after the First World War, especially in lighter areas of manufacturing (Nelson 1992). The most significant technological and organizational development was the spread of the assembly line and mass production from the early twentieth century onwards (Ford 1926; Fridenson 1978; Hounshell 1984; Nelson 1975; Meyer 1981; Schatz 1983; Lewchuk 1987).

However, these developments also met with worker resistance, especially where unions had a presence in these sectors. In part to counter unions, there was some development of new welfare and personnel policies, though these grew as much in sectors of light industry such as food and light assembly work (Nelson 1970; Nelson and Campbell 1972; Jacoby 1985; Gospel 1992). There was also some interest in human relations as a less collectivist approach to the management of labor (Gillespie 1991).

18.6 Coming to Terms with Organized Labor from the 1930s onwards: The Case of the Automobile Industry

As already suggested, in all countries, employer recognition of trade unions and collective bargaining was a minority phenomenon up to the First World War. Union membership and recognition by employers was most extensive in the UK, followed by Germany and the United States. Overall, union membership was much lower in countries such as France, Italy, and Japan, in part reflecting larger agricultural sectors and smaller scale industry in those countries. Even where unions were recognized in the UK in craft industries such as metalworking and printing, in parts of cotton spinning, and in coalmining, collective bargaining was underdeveloped and often informal and spasmodic.

The First World War significantly strengthened the position of trade unions: labor markets were tight, product market competition was curtailed, and both employers and the state were crucially dependent on workers to achieve production. In these circumstances, employers were constrained to recognize unions, not least at government prompting, and collective bargaining developed, in many cases on a multi-employer basis, covering a whole industry either regionally or nationally. After the war and especially where there was economic depression in the 1920s, employers launched counter-offensives and curtailed the scope of, or withdrew entirely from, collective bargaining, as in the UK, the US, and Germany. The depression which affected all countries from 1929 onwards further reduced union presence and collective bargaining declined in coverage and content (Brody 1980; Clegg 1985; Schneider 1991).

From the mid-1930s onwards, however, this situation changed, especially in automobiles, electricals, and other growing industries. In the UK, unions slowly increased their membership and managements had increasingly to deal with them (Tolliday and Zeitlin 1986; Lewchuk 1987). For the most part they chose to do this on a multi-employer basis. In France, in the late 1930s, a combination of economic and political factors led French employers to enter into new dealings with unions, especially in metalworking, albeit temporarily (Vinen 1991; Chapman 1991). Employer opposition was particularly strong in the United States. But, even there, the large automobile firms recognized unions, in significant part in the context of a change in the stance of government and legal requirements introduced in the New Deal from the mid-1930s onwards and during the Second World War and its aftermath (Dubofsky 1994). Thus, General Motors recognized the United Auto Workers in 1937 and Ford in 1941. In the United States, in contrast to Britain, employers chose to deal with unions more at a company level and negotiated formal legally binding contracts which regulated wide aspects of wages and conditions, employment, and work organization. There were elements of pattern-setting and following within industries, but, for the most part, dealings were at the level of the firm (Slichter *et al.* 1960; Brody 1980; Harris 1985; Jefferys 1986; Tolliday and Zeitlin 1986). By contrast, in the UK, bargaining was often at multiple levels, including informal bargaining with shop stewards at the workplace (Edwards and Terry 1988).

In Germany, France, Italy, and Japan, the settlement with organized labor came after the war. Under Fascist and military regimes and foreign occupation, independent unions were outlawed, state- and employer-dominated labor bodies were imposed, and most aspects of work and employment were unilaterally determined by management or government.

After the war, in Germany, in a situation of turmoil, unions were recognized by employers and a system of regional and industry-wide collective bargaining emerged which has largely persisted up to the present day. Reverting to an earlier German tradition, with origins in the nineteenth century mining industry and in legislation after the First World War, there was also established by law a system of works councils at company and workplace level and worker representation on the boards of German companies. In part this was at the prompting of the British occupation authorities and met with some resistance from German business. However, over time, German employers came to live with these arrangements and accommodated them into their systems of labor management (Teuteberg 1961; Streeck

1992; Dartmann 1996). It should be noted that works councils and board-level representation are to be found in other continental European countries, but not usually on the scale or with the powers of those in Germany (Rogers and Streeck 1995).

In Japan, employers also came to terms with unions, though along different lines. At first, again in a situation of considerable turmoil, they confronted demands from militant general and industrial unions. With support from the American occupation authorities and the Japanese government, in the late 1940s and early 1950s, employers confronted and defeated these unions in major lockouts and strikes and replaced them with a system of enterprise-based unions. Collective bargaining was subsequently conducted mainly at enterprise level, with some industry coordination by employers' organizations and federations of unions. This settlement with enterprise unions interacted with traditional and emerging Japanese management practices and led during the subsequent years of economic growth in the 1950s and 1960s to key aspects of the Japanese employment system: the provision of job security for core male (but not usually female) workers, the use of complex wage and benefit hierarchies often related to seniority, systems of management-led consultation within the firm, and a strong ideological encouragement of the notion of the company as an enterprise community. By the mid to late 1950s, such a system was largely in place in firms such as Toyota, Nissan, Toshiba, Hitachi, and other large manufacturing companies. In the 1970s, this came to be recognized as the "Japanese system of management" and attracted considerable foreign attention (Dore 1973; Taira 1970; Gordon 1985 and 1998; Koike 1988; Cusomano 1985; Shiomi and Wada 1995; Hazama 1997; Inagami and Whittaker 2005). However, in the slowdown in the 1990s, as will be seen below, the system has come under growing pressure, with some reduction of "lifetime employment", an increase in pay based more on merit and performance, and less of a role for enterprise unions especially in bargaining about work organization and wage levels.

In France and Italy, the postwar industrial relations settlements were rather less clear and in some ways more akin to the British situation. After the war, employers increasingly had to recognize unions and enter into collective bargaining. However, they were less able to contain a system of multi-unionism (including in these two continental countries Communist-dominated unionism) and multi-level collective bargaining. Large firms such as Renault, Citroen, Peugeot, and Fiat made varying compromises depending on the economic and political contexts at particular times (Fridenson 1986; Durand and Hatzfeld 2003). In some respects, it was only in the 1980s and 1990s, when union power was on the wane, that French and Italian companies reached a more effective settlement of their industrial relations.

In all these countries, over the first three decades after the war, with full employment and union bargaining, there developed systems of relative job security, possibilities for internal promotion to higher paying jobs, and wages based on seniority and hierarchical grading systems. However, there were differences between countries. In Japan, the United States, and Germany, management maintained more control over the production system than in the UK or Italy. In Germany and Japan, workers received more training than in most of the other countries and were more involved in improvements in processes and products. This was to lead to what in Germany has been called the "diversified quality production" system and in Japan to what came to be called the Toyota or "lean production" system, with more consultation and discretion given to better trained workers (Ohno 1982; Dohse *et al.* 1985: Streeck 1992; Shimokawa 1993; Wada 1995; Tolliday 1998).

The union-based system of industrial relations and labor management has declined differentially across these countries. In the United States, union membership fell from the mid-1960s onwards, and the coverage of collective bargaining contracted (Kochan *et al.* 1986; Jacoby 1997). It is now restricted to a few areas of the private sector, such as parts of the steel, automobile, and metalworking industries. In France, union membership never attained very high levels; it has fallen since the 1970s, and collective bargaining is much constrained (Howell 1992). In the UK, a change in the economic and political climate in the 1980s led to a hollowing out of the collective bargaining-based system of labor management and the development of new forms of human resource management such as will be discussed below. Along with this, union membership has fallen (Millward *et al.* 2000; Gospel 2005). In Germany and Japan, changes have been slower, but in recent years employers have come to have less recourse to collective bargaining with trade unions and more to consultation with their workers, either via work councils in Germany or more informal joint committees in Japan (Inagami and Whittaker 2005).

18.7 DEALING WITH DIVERSITY AND FLEXIBILITY: THE DEVELOPMENT OF HUMAN RESOURCE MANAGEMENT—THE CASE OF THE FAST-MOVING CONSUMER GOODS SECTOR

Alongside the developments described above, other trends may be distinguished from the 1960s and 1970s onwards. In the postwar years, sectors which grew rapidly included electrical goods, food and drink, and household and personal consumer products. In the United States and UK, large firms, which had often grown by merger and acquisition and which had increasingly diversified into new lines of business, developed multidivisional forms of organization to manage their diverse activities (Chandler 1962, 1977, and 1990; Whittington and Mayer 2000). Increasingly, such firms faced "new" labor forces, enjoying higher standards of living, with less commitment to trade unions, and more heterogeneous in terms of interests.

In this situation, firms began to develop new policies to deal with growing product market competition and changes in labor market composition. Here examples are taken from the fast-moving consumer goods sector where firms came to adapt and transform a set of centralized and often paternalistic policies which they had first developed in the late nineteenth and early twentieth centuries. Some of these approaches have since come to be collectively described as human resource management. This account is based on the following sources (Foulkes 1980; Jacoby 1997; Gospel 2006).

Procter & Gamble (P&G) had begun as a soap and detergent maker. After the Second World War, it organized its labor management centrally, though with some plants unionized and others remaining non-union. Employment systems were rather bureaucratic; use was made of scientific management, and dealings with the labor force had elements of paternalism. Through the 1950s to 1970s, the company grew, in part organically and in part through merger and acquisition, and diversified into new areas such as food and drink, paper goods, and personal care products. These it came to manage with central direction in some key areas (the development of managerial staff and the non-recognition of unions in new plants). In most other areas, labor management was increasingly left to the level of the constituent divisions or companies, where a degree of differentiation and controlled experimentation was allowed. On the basis of this, the company introduced new forms of job flexibility, management-directed team working, and pay for skills and performance, wherever possible maintaining a non-union environment and often with the use of contingent labor.

The development of similar flexible and decentralized strategies can also be seen in Unilever in the UK, though with a time lag of a decade or more. Unilever had a tradition of rather centralized, somewhat paternalistic employment practices which it had developed in the interwar years. In the UK context, it was less able or inclined to escape from a collective bargaining based system than P&G. Nevertheless, through the 1970s and 1980s, it transformed its practices into a more differentiated and flexible set of arrangements, based on its divisions and subsidiaries (Jones 2005b). In France, a comparable example is Danone, that country's largest food company. Over the 1970s, BSN-Danone moved from being a glass producer to a glass bottle, drinks, and diversified food producer and then later restructured around a range of food products. It developed a rhetoric and practice of social partnership with its employees, including unions, but essentially ran its various parts in a decentralized, flexible manner. This enabled experimentation in labor management and facilitated the acquisition and disposal of companies. In many instances, these and similar firms increased their flexibility by employing a core labor force, supplemented by part-time and temporary workers (Dyer et al. 2004).

Reference should also be made to the German and Japanese equivalents of these companies. Henkel and Kao both began as soap and detergent makers. Both had a rather centralized and paternalistic system of labor management through to the

1970s. More slowly than their counterparts referred to above, they nevertheless introduced different arrangements—less reliance on union bargaining, more reliance on joint consultation and direct employee involvement, greater use of flexible pay and conditions, and more resort to contingent employment for different parts of their companies (Feldenkirchen and Hilger 2001; Gospel 2006). However, to date, they have not proceeded as far as their US, UK, and French counterparts in terms of developing a variegated and flexible employment system. In part this reflects the fact that they have grown organically and are less diversified and divisionalized companies—a broader characteristic of both countries. In part, it also reflects the fact that they have been subject to rather more legal and union constraints (in Germany) and ideological and customary constraints (in Japan). Nevertheless, cumulatively these developments constitute major changes in the labor management systems in these countries.

This section has described the development of decentralized and flexible systems of labor management which have spread across the large firm sector. However, again we stress continuities and diversities. We have already noted national differences. In addition, some firms still remain relatively centralized (automobiles) and bureaucratic (utilities). Also, in the medium and small firm sectors, firms have not had to confront the issues of diversity of operations in the same way. Here labor management is usually less purposely decentralized and less professionalized. In some localities, medium and small firms have also maintained external economies of scale in terms of skills training and innovative working in industrial districts such as have been identified especially in Germany and Italy (Crouch *et al.* 2001). There is also a considerable spread, with some firms pursuing "high road" practices of good pay and conditions, high training, and employee involvement, while others pursue "low road" practices of minimal benefits and cost minimization (Foulkes 1980; Guest and Hoque 1996; Osterman 1999).

18.8 LABOR MANAGEMENT IN THE SERVICE ECONOMY OF THE "THIRD" INDUSTRIAL REVOLUTION

The most marked change in employment composition in the final quarter of the twentieth century has been the decline of manufacturing and the rise of services. Service companies and service work cover a wide spread. They cover the financial sector, information and communications services, hotels and catering, health and personal care, and retailing. They also cover a spread in terms of company size, from small start-up firms in the so-called "new economy" to some of the largest companies in the world. They also cover a wide spread of occupational levels from graduate managerial, technical, and professional employees to low-level mundane work in call centers, fast food restaurants, and retail stores. Recent changes in this sector have been very much driven by the application of new general purpose technologies, of information and communications.

In financial services, there are some patterns which have long existed, as in banks and insurance companies—relative job security, gendered and educationally segmented hierarchies, and salaries and benefits which rise with age. In recent years, some of these have been subject to change, especially the notion of lifetime careers and incremental salary scales. There are also new aspects, within both old and new firms in these sectors—the reliance on self-investment in training and development, greater mobility and more flexible careers, more project working, and, especially for higher-level employees, the spread of share- and stock-based pay. However, in many telephone call centers, connected with the new service economy, work is organized along different lines—with elements of mass production, tight computer monitoring, and limited pay and benefit systems. In recent years, in these areas, there has been a growth in so-called "outsourcing" and "off-shoring" of jobs (Marchington *et al.* 2005).

Here reference is also made to the retailing sector with its large number of lower-level employees. As already stated, by the end of the twentieth century the biggest single grouping of large employers were retailers such as Wal-Mart, Target, and Home Depot in the United States, Carrefour and Auchan in France, Tesco and Kingfisher in the UK, and Metro and Karstadt in Germany. Such firms have developed further some aspects of systematic and scientific management. They make extensive use of information and communication technology to match the flow of goods, customer demand, and the deployment of labor. In turn, extensive use is made of part-time employment, often young, female, and immigrant workers, to facilitate flexible scheduling. Jobs are narrowly defined, with little scope for training and development, but employees may be expected to work flexibly across jobs, such as unloading, stacking, and checkout. Wage hierarchies are flat and non-wage benefits limited. In the United States, Wal-Mart and other large retailers make efforts to promote individual identification with the company and are strongly anti-union (Lichtenstein 2006). In Europe, unions have a limited presence and play little part in management calculations.

Management systems such as operate in call centers and supermarkets have elements of mass production such as have existed from the early twentieth century onwards. However, there are a number of important differences with earlier systems. First, computer control facilitates a more exact synchronization of production and work. Second, there would seem to be more mixed identities on the part of workers and less solidarity and opposition to management. Third, union membership shows little sign of developing as it once did in earlier mass-production systems and more sophisticated managements seem more likely to prevent its growth.

In recent years some commentators have referred to a growing diversity within national systems; this may in turn maintain diversities between national systems (Katz and Darbishire 2000). A historical perspective suggests there has always been diversity. Certainly many arrangements described in the sections above are to be found side by side within national systems such as the provision of discretion for more skilled and higher-level employees versus mass-production-type systems for many workers as well as elements of bureaucratic forms of management versus more differentiated and flexible systems. This same diversity may increasingly be found in manufacturing where, among other factors, unions are less able to impose uniformity. Hence in manufacturing, some firms are pursuing so-called "high-performance" and "high-involvement" policies while many others have not developed sophisticated human resource strategies and provide little employee voice (Foulkes 1980; Guest and Hoque 1996; Osterman 1999).

18.9 SOME CAVEATS AND UNFINISHED BUSINESS

This chapter has concentrated on major stages in the development of labor management in advanced capitalist economies, while stressing continuities and diversities across stages. However, a number of major gaps have been left.

First, the chapter has concentrated on the history of labor management in the United States, Western Europe, and Japan. It has left out other countries. Not least it has excluded the following: smaller countries of the developed world; Russia and the Soviet Union, China, and other former Communist states; and labor management in developing countries. For some of these countries, there is an extensive literature on management and labor; for others, there are still gaps to be covered in terms of research and the writing of integrated business and labor histories. These countries posed questions about similarities in the growth trajectories of labor management and about forces making for convergence and divergence.

Second, the chapter has focused mainly on large firms at particular stages of history. There has been some coverage of smaller firms, especially with reference to textiles at the beginning of the period and start-up high-tech companies at the end. On the whole, however, less is known about labor management in the medium and small firm sector, with the exception of what can be derived from industry studies, such as those of textiles, clothing, leather and footwear, printing, pottery, light metals, and construction. More recently, however, there has been the development of a large literature on industrial districts and external economies of scale, again drawing attention to the long-term continuities which have existed in forms of labor management (Marshall 1890; Pyke and Sengenberger 1990 and 1992; Sabel and Zeitlin 1997; Crouch *et al.* 2001; Farnie *et al.* 1999; Wilson and Popp 2003).

Third, the chapter has largely left out the public sector, in central and local government and in organizations such as national post offices, utility companies, and public health service organizations. Such public sector organizations are important, not only because of their size, but also because they were often considered to be "good" employers and historically at times acted as trend-setters for the private sector. Studies of such firms do exist, for example, of gas and electricity companies (Frost 1983; Hannah 1979 and 1982; Berlanstein 1991). They show the extensive use of bureaucratic management methods, the presence of a certain paternalism, and the strength of trade unions and collective relations with the labor force, especially through the post-Second World War period. More recently, in these sectors, there are new political and market pressures which are leading to management practices emphasizing more flexibility and decentralization of operations, not least as parts of the public sector have been privatized and opened to more outside market competition.

Fourth, labor has been treated as a rather homogeneous entity. For example, little has been said specifically about the management of female labor. There are, however, some excellent studies of women's employment which might be drawn on, in both manufacturing and service industries (Glucksmann 1990; Fourcaut 1982; Hunter 2003; Milkman 1987; Cobble, 1991; Omnes 1997; Wightman 1999). These pose questions as to whether the management of female labor has been largely the same as that of men or to what extent there are different patterns of gender segregation. In so far as the latter is the case, there is then the further question as to whether such differences have increased or reduced over time and how.

Fifth, the chapter has concentrated mainly on lower- and middle-level, especially blue-collar-type, workers, on the basis that these have been the main group of employees over most of the time period under consideration. However, in most national economies, these are now a declining part of employment. We have touched on white-collar and managerial labor forces in several of the industry sectors, for example, in discussing railways and financial services. A wide literature exists on white-collar, professional, technical, supervisory, and managerial workers (Lockwood 1958; Kocha 1977 and 1991; Melling 1980; Hyman and Price 1983; Morikawa and Kobayashi 1986; Morikawa 1991; Prendergast 1999), but it has not been possible to consider it here in any detail.

Finally, the chapter has dealt with employment within the firm largely within one country, namely the country of origin. Since the early twentieth century, a growing number of large firms have had multinational activities and this has accelerated in the post-Second World War period. Further work needs to be done on the historical development of labor management in such multinationals, where some of the essential decisions concern whether firms take practices from their home country, adopt those of the host country, or develop distinct global patterns of labor management (Perlmutter 1969; Enderwick 1985; Knox and McKinlay 1999; 2002; Ferner and Varul 2000; Rosenweig and Nohria 1994: Kristensen and Zeitlin 2005; Jones 2005*b*).

18.10 CONCLUSIONS

Bearing in mind the gaps and caveats referred to above, a number of conclusions may be drawn from the above survey.

First, broad stages in the development of labor management can be discerned. Thus, from the early nineteenth century, there coexisted artisanal and factory models in sectors such as textiles. The railways, heavy industry, and assembly-type industries brought the development of newer more bureaucratic systems of labor management, especially from the late nineteenth century onwards. Subsequently, in the mid-twentieth century, in the golden age of manufacturing, union-based systems of labor management were strong, especially in the big firm sector. More recently there has been a growth of more differentiated and flexible systems of human resource management within firms, in both manufacturing and services. However, it was also stressed that much work in the modern service sector and in retailing still has elements of mass-production-type systems. It was suggested that different stages have coexisted side-by-side and older industries have adapted to new developments. Overall, the tendency may be towards growing diversity within firms and within countries.

Second, some movement may be discerned over time from direct systems of management (based on personal supervision, simple piecework systems, and traditional paternalism), to technical or mechanical systems of management (based on scientific management principles with an attempt to build control into production processes), to bureaucratic forms of working and employment, with internal labor markets and complicated administrative hierarchies (Edwards 1979). However, in recent years, there has been some reconfiguration of bureaucratic employment systems and of internal labor markets and there have been complex backward and forward movements between direct control and more autonomy and responsibility on the job. The examples of modern retailing and work in call centers show how direct systems of supervision and computer control continue. Thus, motivation and control based on mixes of coercive, remunerative, and normative policies have always existed. There is no linear movement in these forms of labor management.

Third, in terms of industrial relations, there have been significant shifts over time. In the nineteenth and early twentieth centuries, most employers were what might be termed "unitarist" and believed that they had a right unilaterally to dictate aspects of work and employment. The period from the 1930s and 1940s saw a shift in a more "pluralist" direction and a greater preparedness to admit employee representation in the form of trade unions and collective bargaining (Fox 1985). Such systems grew and even predominated through the early post-Second World War years in many industries, especially in manufacturing. However, beginning in the 1970s, there has been a shift away from such managerial ideologies and their replacement by new forms of direct employee voice, joint consultation, and employee involvement of various kinds, such as participation in small groups and team working. To date, these shifts have been greater in countries such as the United States, France, and the UK, where union membership in the private sector is weakest, and least in countries such as Germany and the Scandinavian countries, where union membership remains stronger.

Fourth, some of the changes analyzed above can be captured by the notion of externalizing and internalizing decisions (Coase 1937). Firms can externalize decisions in the following ways: they can make use of external subcontracting forms of production; recruit as much as possible from the external labor market and lay off workers into the market; fix wages and benefits according to market signals; and, where they have to recognize trade unions, deal with them through outside employers' organizations. By contrast, firms can internalize decisions in various ways: they can bring production in-house and develop more elaborate internal divisions of labor; rely less on the external labor market and institute stronger internal labor markets, with more in-house training and greater job security; fix wages and benefits by internal administrative rules such as seniority or job rank; and provide employee voice via company-based consultation and bargaining (Gospel 1992). In practice, different firms in different countries have pursued mixed strategies. However, in a long-term perspective, the following might be argued. In the nineteenth century much use was made of externalizing strategies, subject to paternalistic constraints and with exceptions such as the railways where companies internalized. Over the course of the twentieth century, there was some tendency towards greater internalization of work and employment relations, with Fordist mass production and internal labor markets, but not necessarily internalization of industrial relations, since in Europe considerable reliance was placed on outside employers' organizations. The tendency to internalize employment relations was particularly strong in continental European countries and in Japan. Over the last quarter century, there may be some movement towards an externalization of work and employment relations, but with a greater internalization of industrial relations within the firm. However, strategies depend not only on their relative cost, but also on the capacity of the firm to pursue them and the micro- and macro-political context within which they are implemented.

As stated at the outset, the management of people at work has always been a central problem and challenge for employers. It is a universal problem, but it has been tackled in different ways, in different industries and countries, at different periods of time.

References

BERG, MAXINE (1985). *The Age of Manufactures*. Oxford: Oxford University Press.

BERLANSTEIN, LENARD (1991). *Big Business and Industrial Conflict in Nineteenth Century France: A Social History of the Parisian Gas Company*. Berkeley: University of California Press.

BRANDES, STUART D. (1976). *American Welfare Capitalism, 1880–1940*. Chicago: Chicago University Press.

BRODY, DAVID (1980). *Workers in Industrial America: Essays on the Twentieth Century Struggle*. Oxford: Oxford University Press.

CASSIS, YOUSSEF (1997). *Big Business: The European Experience in the Twentieth Century*. Oxford: Oxford University Press.

CHANDLER, ALFRED (1962). *Strategy and Structure: Chapters in the History of the American Industrial Enterprise*. Cambridge, Mass.: MIT Press.

—— (1977). *The Visible Hand: The Managerial Revolution in American Business*. Cambridge, Mass.: Harvard University Press.

—— (1990). *Scale and Scope: The Dynamics of Industrial Capitalism*. Cambridge, Mass.: Harvard University Press.

CHAPMAN, HERRICK (1991). *State Capitalism and Working Class Radicalism in the French Aircraft Industry*. Berkeley: University of California Press.

CLEGG, HUGH (1985). *A History of British Trade Unions since 1889: Volume 2, 1910–1933*. Oxford: Clarendon Press.

COASE, RONALD (1937). "The Nature of the Firm". *Economica*, 4: 386–405.

COBBLE, DOROTHY SUE (1991). *Dishing It Out: Utilities and their Unions in the Twentieth Century*. Urbana, Ill.: University of Illinois.

COLEMAN, TERRY (1981). *The Railway Navvies*. Ebury: Vintage.

COMMONS, JOHN (1909). "American Shoemakers 1648–1895: A Sketch of Industrial Evolution". *Quarterly Journal of Economics*, 24: 39–84.

CROUCH, COLIN (1993). *Industrial Relations and European State Traditions*. Oxford: Oxford University Press.

—— LE GALES, PATRICK, TRIGILLIA, CARLO, and VOELZKOW, HELMUT (eds.) (2001). *Local Production Systems in Europe: Rise or Demise?* Oxford: Oxford University Press.

CUSOMANO, MICHAEL (1985). *The Japanese Automobile Industry: Technology and Management in Nissan and Toyota*. Cambridge, Mass.: Harvard University Press.

DARTMANN, CHRISTOPH (1996). *Redistribution of Power: Joint Consultation or Productivity Coaltions? Labor and Postwar Reconstruction in Germany and Britain 1945–1953*. Bochum: Brockmeyer.

DOHSE, KNUTH, JÜRGENS, ULRICH, and MALSH, THOMAS (1985). "From 'Fordism' to 'Toyotaism'? The Social Organization of the Labor Process in the Japanese Automobile Industry". *Politics and Society*, 14/2: 115–46.

DORE, RONALD (1973). British Factory—Japanese Factory. Berkeley: University of California Press.

DRUMMOND, DIANE K. (1995). *Crewe: Railway Town, Company, and People, 1840–1914*. Aldershot: Scolar Press.

DUBOFSKY, MELVYN (1994). *State and Labor in Modern America*. Chapel Hill, NC: University of North Carolina Press.

DUNLOP, JOHN (1958). *Industrial Relations Systems*. New York: Henry Holt.

DURAND, JEAN-PIERRE, and HATZFELD, NICHOLAS (2003). *Living Labor: Life on the Line at Peugeot France*. London: Palgrave Macmillan.

DYER, DAVIS, DAZELL, FREDERICK, and OLEGARIO, ROWENO (2004). *Rising Tide*. Cambridge, Mass.: Harvard Business School Press.

EDWARDS, RICHARD (1979). *Contested Terrain*. New York: Basic Books.

EDWARDS, PAUL, and TERRY, MIKE (1988). *Shopfloor Politics and Job Control*. Oxford: Blackwells.

ENDERWICK, PETER (1985). *Multinational Business and Labor*. London: Macmillan.

FARNIE, DOUGLAS, JEREMY, DAVID, WILSON, JOHN, NAKAOKA, TETSURO, and ABE, TAKESHI (1999). *Region and Strategy in Britain and Japan: Business in Lancashire and Kansai 1890–1990*. London: Routledge.

FELDENKIRCHEN, WILFRIED, and HILGER, SUSANNE (2001). *Menschen und Marken*. Dusseldorf: Henkel.

FERNER, ANTHONY, and VARUL, MATTHIAS (2000). "Internationalisation and Personnel Management in German Multinationals". *Human Resource Management Journal*, 10/3: 79–96.

FITZGERALD, ROBERT (1988). *British Labor Management and Industrial Welfare 1846–1939*. London: Croom Helm.

FOMBONNE, JEAN (2003). *Personnel et DRH*. Paris: Vuibert.

FORD, HENRY (1926). "Mass Production", in *Encyclopedia Britannica*, 23rd edn., suppl. vol. 2. London and New York: Encyclopedia Britannica, 821–3.

FOULKES, FRED K. (1980). *Personnel Policies in Large Nonunion Companies*, Englewood Cliffs, NJ: Prentice Hall.

FOX, ALAN (1985). *History and Heritage*. London: Allen & Unwin.

FOURCAUT, ANNIE (1982). *Femmes a l'usine en France dans l'entre-deux-guerres*. Paris: Maspero.

FRIEDMAN, GERALD (1999). *State-Making and Labor Movements: France and the United States, 1876–1914*. Ithaca, NY: Cornell University Press.

FRIDENSON, PATRICK (1978). "The Coming of the Assembly Line in Europe", in W. Krohn (ed.), *The Dynamics of Science and Technology*. Dordrecht: W. Krohn.

—— (1986). "Automobile Workers in France and their Work, 1914–1983", in S. L. Kaplan and C. J. Koepp (eds.), *Work in France: Representation, Meaning, Organization, and Practice*. Ithaca, NY: Cornell University Press.

FROST, ROBERT (1983). *Alternating Currents*. Ithaca, NY: Cornell University Press.

GILLESPIE, RICHARD (1991). *Manufacturing Knowledge*. Cambridge: Cambridge University Press.

GLUCKSMANN, MIRIAM (1990). *Women Assemble: Women Workers in the New Industries in Interwar Britain*. London: Routledge.

GORDON, ANDREW (1985). *The Evolution of Labor Relations in Japan: Heavy Industry 1853–1955*. Cambridge, Mass.: Harvard University Press.

—— (1998). *The Wages of Affluence: Labor and Management in Postwar Japan*. Cambridge, Mass.: Harvard University Press.

GOSPEL, HOWARD (1992). *Markets, Firms, and the Management of Labor in Modern Britain*. Cambridge: Cambridge University Press.

—— (2005) "Markets, Firms, and Unions: Historical and Institutionalist Perspectives on the Future of Unions", in Sue Fernie and David Metcalf (eds.), *Unions and Performance*. London: Routledge.

GOSPEL, HOWARD (2006). "The Development of Labor Management in Divisionalised Companies". Mimeo, London, King's College.

—— and FIEDLER, MARTIN (2005). "The Long-Run Dynamics of Big Firms: The 100 Largest Employers in Global Perspective". Mimeo, London, King's College.

—— and PENDLETON, ANDREW (2004). "Corporate Governance and Labor Management: An International Comparison", in Howard Gospel and Andrew Pendleton, *Corporate Governance and Labor Management: An International Comparison*. Oxford: Oxford University Press, 1–32.

GUEST, DAVID, and HOQUE, KIM (1996). "The Good, the Bad, and the Ugly: Employment Relations in New Non-Union Workplaces". *Human Resource Management*, 5/1: 1–14.

HABBAKUK, JOHN (1962). *American and British Technology in the Nineteenth Century: The Search for Labor-Saving Inventions*. Cambridge: Cambridge University Press.

HANNAH, LESLIE (1979). *Electricity before Nationalisation*. Baltimore: John Hopkins University Press.

—— (1982). *Engineers, Managers, and Politicians*. Baltimore: John Hopkins University Press.

HARRIS, HOWELL (1985). *The Right to Manage: Industrial Relations Policies of American Business in the 1940s*. Madison: University of Wisconsin Press.

HAZAMA, H. (1997). *History of Labor Management in Japan*. London: Macmillan.

HOUNSHELL, DAVID A. (1984). *From the American System to Mass Production, 1800–1932: The Development of Manufacturing Technology in the United States*. Baltimore: John Hopkins University Press.

HOWELL, CHRISTOPHER (1992). *Regulating Labor*. Princeton, NJ: Princeton University Press.

HUNTER, JANET (2003). *Women and the Labor Market in Japan's Industrialising Economy*. London: Routledge.

HYMAN, RICHARD, and PRICE, ROBERT (eds.) (1983). *The New Working Class? White Collar Workers and their Organisations*. London: Macmillan.

INAGAMI, TAKESHI, and WHITTAKER, D. HUGH (2005). *The New Community Firm: Employment, Governance and Management Reform in Japan*. Cambridge: Cambridge University Press.

JACOBY, SANFORD (1979). "The Origins of Internal Labor Markets in Japan". *Industrial Relations*, 18: 184–96.

—— (1985). *Employing Bureaucracy: Managers, Unions and the Transformation of Work in American Industry 1900–1945*. New York: Columbia University Press.

—— (1997). *Modern Manors: Welfare Capitalism since the New Deal*. Princeton, NJ: Princeton University Press.

JEFFERYS, STEPHEN (1986). *Management and Managed*. Cambridge: Cambridge University Press.

JONES, GEOFFREY (2005a). *Multinationals and Global Capitalism: From the Nineteenth Century to the Twenty-First Century*. Oxford: Oxford University Press.

—— (2005b). *Renewing Unilever: Transformation and Tradition*. Oxford: Oxford University Press.

JOWITT, J. A., and McIVOR, ARTHUR, J. (eds.) (1989). *Employers and Labor in the English Textile Industries, 1850–1939*. London: Routledge.

JOYCE, PATRICK (1980). *The Culture of the Factory in Later Victorian England*. London: Methuen.

KATZ, HARRY, and DARBISHIRE, OWEN (2000). *Converging Divergencies: World-Wide Changes in Employment Systems*. Ithaca, NY: Cornell University Press.

KNOX, WILLIAM, and MCKINLAY, ALAN (1999). "Working for the Yankee Dollar". *Historical Studies in Industrial Relations*, 7: 1–26.

——— (2002). "Organising the Unorganised: Union Recruitment Strategies in American Transnationals", in Gregor Gall (ed.), *Union Organising*. London: Routledge.

KOCHA, JÜRGEN (1977) *White-Collar Workers in America 1900–1940*. London: Sage.

——— (1991). *Industrial Culture and Bourgeois Society: Business, Labor, and Bureaucracy in Modern Germany*. New York: Berghahn.

KOCHAN, TOM, KATZ, HARRY, and MCKERSIE, ROBERT (1986). *The Transformation of American Industrial Relations*. New York: Basic Books.

KOIKE, KAZUO (1988). *Understanding Industrial Relations in Modern Japan*. London: Macmillan.

KOSSEK, ELLEN, and LOBEL, SHARON (1996). *Managing Diversity*. Oxford: Blackwell.

KRISTENSEN, PEER HULL, and ZEITLIN, JONATHAN (2005). *Local Players in Global Games: Strategic Constitution of a Multinational Corporation*. Oxford: Oxford University Press.

LANDES, DAVID (1986). "What Do Bosses Really Do?" *Journal of Economic History*, 46/3: 585–623.

LAZONICK, WILLIAM (1990). *Competitive Advantage on the Shopfloor*. Cambridge, Mass.: Harvard University Press.

LEWCHUK, WAYNE (1987). *American Technology and the British Vehicle Industry*. Cambridge: Cambridge University Press.

LEWIS, W ARTHUR (1952). "Economic Development with Unlimited Supplies of Labor". *The Manchester School*, 22/2: 139–91.

LICHTENSTEIN, NELSON (ed.) (2006). *Wal-Mart: Template for 21st Century Capitalism*. New Press: New Press.

LITTERER, JOSEPH A. (1963). "Systematic Management: Design for Organizational Recoupling in American Manufacturing Firms". *Business History Review*, 27/4: 369–91.

LITTLER, CRAIG (1982). *The Development of the Labor Process in Capitalist Societies*. London: Ashgate.

LOCKWOOD, DAVID (1958). *The Black Coated Worker*. London: Allen & Unwin.

MCCREARY, EUGENE C. (1968). "Social Welfare and Business: The Krupp Welfare Programme, 1860–1914". *Business History Review*, 42, spring: 24–49.

MCIVOR, ARTHUR, J. (1996). *Organised Capital: Employers' Associations and Industrial Relations in Northern England, c. 1880–1939*. Cambridge: Cambridge University Press.

MAGRAW, ROGER (1992). *A History of the French Working Class*, vols. 1 and 2. Oxford: Blackwell.

MARCHINGTON, MICK, GRIMSHAW, DAMIAN, RUBERY, GILL, and WILLMOTT, HUGH (2005). *Fragmenting Work, Blurring Organisational Boundaries, and Disordering Hierarchies*. Oxford: Oxford University Press.

MARGLIN, STEPHEN (1974). "What Do Bosses Do? The Origins and Functions of Hierarchy in Capitalist Production". *Review of Radical Political Economics*, 6/2, summer: 60–112.

MARSHALL, ALFRED (1890). *Industry and Trade*. London: Macmillan.

MAURICE, MARC, SELLIER, FRANCOIS, and SILVESTRE, JEAN-JACQUES (1984). "Rules, Contexts, and Actors: Observations based on a Comparison between France and West Germany". *British Journal of Industrial Relations*, 22: 346–63.

MELLING, JOSEPH (1979). "Industrial Strife and Business Welfare Philosophy: The South Metropolitan Gas Company from the 1880s to the First World War". *Business History*, 21: 183–221.

MELLING, JOSEPH (1980). " 'Non-Commissioned Officers': British Employers and their Supervisory Workers, 1880–1920". *Business History*, 21.

MENDELS, FRANKLIN (1972). "Proto-industrialisation: The First Phase of the Industrialisation Process". *Journal of Economic History*, 32/1: 241–61.

MILKMAN, RUTH (1987). *The Dynamics of Job Segregation by Sex during World War II*. Urbana, Ill.: University of Illinois Press.

MEYER, STEPHEN (1981). *The Five Dollar Day: Labor Management and Social Control in the Ford Motor Company, 1908–1921*. New York: Charles Scribner.

MERKLE, JUDITH (1980). *Management and Ideology: The International Scientific Management Movement*. Berkeley: University of California Press.

MILLWARD, ALAN, BRYSON, ALEX, and FORTH, JOHN (2000). *All Change at Work*. London: Routledge.

MOMMSEN, WOLFGANG J. and HUSUNG, HANS-GERHARD (eds.) (1985). *The Development of Trade Unionism in Great Britain and Germany, 1880–1914*. London: Allen & Unwin.

MONTGOMERY, DAVID (1987). *The Fall of the House of Labor*. New York and Cambridge: Cambridge University Press.

MORIKAWA, HIDEMASA (1991). "The Education of Engineers in Modern Japan: An Historical Perspective", in H. F. Gospel (ed.), *Industrial Training and Technological Innovation: A Comparative and Historical Study*. London: 1991, 136–47.

—— and KOBAYASHI, K. (eds.) (1986). *Development of Managerial Enterprise*. Tokyo: Tokyo University Press.

NAKAGAWA, KEIICHIRO (1979). *Labor and Management*. Tokyo: Tokyo University Press.

NELSON, DANIEL (1970). " 'A Newly Appreciated Art': The Development of Personnel Work at Leeds & Northrup, 1915–23". *Business History Review*, 44, winter: 520–35.

—— (1975). *Managers and Workers: Origins of the New Factory System in the United States, 1880–1920*. Madison: University of Wisconsin Press.

—— (1980). *Frederick W. Taylor and the Rise of Scientific Management*. Madison: University of Wisconsin.

—— (1992). "Scientific Management in Retrospect", in Daniel Nelson (ed.), *A Mental Revolution*. Columbus: Ohio State University Press.

—— and CAMPBELL, STUART (1972). "Taylorism versus Welfare Work in American Industry: H. L. Gantt and the Bancrofts". *Business History Review*, 56, spring: 1–16.

NIVEN, MARY (1967). *Personnel Management 1913–63*. London: Institute for Personnel Management.

NOIRIEL, GERARD (1989). *Workers in French Society in the Nineteenth and Twentieth Centuries*. London: Berg.

OHNO, TAIICHI (1982). "How the Toyota Production System was Created". *Japanese Economic Studies*, 10/4, summer: 83–101.

OMNES, CATHERINE (1997). *Ouvrières Parisiennes*. Paris: École des Hautes Études en Sciences Sociales.

OSTERMAN, PAUL (1999). *Securing Prosperity: How the American Labor Market has Changed and What to do about It*. Princeton, NJ: Princeton University Press.

PERLMUTTER, HOWARD (1969). "The Tortuous Evolution of the Multinational Enterprise". *The Columbia Journal of World Business*, 4/1: 9–18.

PIORE, MICHAEL, and SABEL, CHARLES (1984). *The Second Industrial Divide: Possibilities for Prosperity*. New York: Basic Books.

——and Safford, Sean (2005). "Changing Regimes of Workplace Governance: Shifting Axes of Social Mobilisation". Mimeo, Cambridge, Mass.: MIT Press.

Pollard, Sidney (1965). *The Genesis of Modern Management.* London: Edward Arnold.

Prendergast, Canice (1999). "The Provision of Incentives in Firms". *Journal of Economic Literature,* 37/1: 7–63.

Pyke, Frank, and Sengenberger, Werner (1990). *Industrial Districts and Inter-firm Co-operation in Italy.* Geneva: International Institute for Labor Studies.

————(1992). *Industrial Districts and Local Economic Regeneration.* Geneva: International Institute for Labor Studies.

Rogers, Joel, and Streeck, Wolfgang (eds.) (1995). *Works Councils: Consultation, Representation, and Participation.* Chicago: Chicago University Press.

Rose, Mary (2000). *Firms, Networks, and Business Values: The British and American Cotton Industries.* Cambridge: Cambridge University Press.

Rosenberg, Natan (ed.) (1969). *The American System of Manufactures.* Edinburgh: Edinburgh University Press.

Rosenweig, Philip, and Nohria, Nitin (1994). "Influences on Human Resource Management Practices in Multinational Companies". *Journal of International Business Studies,* 25/2: 229–51.

Sabel, Charles, and Zeitlin, Jonathan (eds.) (1997). *World of Possibilities: Flexibility and Mass Production in Western Industrialisation.* Cambridge: Cambridge University Press.

Schatz, Ronald W. (1983). *The Electrical Workers: A History of Labor at General Electric and Westinghouse 1923–1960.* Urbana, Ill.: University of Illinois Press.

Schneider, Michael (1991). *A Brief History of the German Trade Unions.* Bonn: Dietz.

Scranton, Phillip (1997). *Endless Novelty: Speciality Production and American Industrialisation 1865–1925.* Princeton, NJ: Princeton University Press.

Shimokawa, Koichi (1993). "From the Ford System to the Just-in-Time Production System: A Historical Study of International Shifts in Automobile Production Systems". *Japanese Yearbook of Business History,* 10: 83–105.

Shiomi, Haruhito, and Wada, Kazuo (eds.) (1995). *Fordism Transformed.* Oxford: Oxford University Press.

Slichter, Sumner H., Healy, James J., and Livernash, Robert E. (1960). *The Impact of Collective Bargaining on Management.* Washington, DC: Brookings.

Smith, Adam (1776). *An Enquiry into the Nature and Causes of the Wealth of Nations,* 1904 edn. London: Methuen.

Stone, Katherine (1975). "The Origins of Job Structures in the Steel Industry", in Richard C. Edwards, Michael Reich, and David M. Gordon (eds.), *Labor Market Segmentation.* Lexington, Mass.: D. C. Heath & Co., 27–84.

Streeck, Wolfgang (1992). *Social Institutions and Economic Performance: Studies of Industrial Relations in Advanced Capitalist economies.* London: Sage.

Supiot, Alain (2001). *Beyond Employment: Changes in Work and the Future of Labor Law in Europe.* Oxford: Oxford University Press.

Taira, Koji (1970). *Economic Development and the Labor Market in Japan.* New York: Columbia University Press.

Taylor, Frederick W. (1911). *The Principles of Scientific Management.* New York: Harper.

Teuteberg, Hans Jürgen. (1961). *Geschichte der industriellen Mitbestimmung in Deutschland.* Tübingen: J. C. B. Mohr.

Tolliday, Steven (ed.) (1998). *The Rise and Fall of Mass Production*, vols. 1 and 2. Elgar Reference Collection: International Library of Critical Writings in Business History, Cheltenham: Edward Elgar.

——and Zeitlin, Jonathan (eds.) (1986). *The Automobile Industry and its Workers: Between Fordism and Flexibility*. Cambridge: Polity Press.

Tsutsui, William (1998). *Manufacturing Ideology: Scientific Management in Twentieth-Century Japan*. Princeton: Princeton University Press.

Vinen, Richard (1991). *The Politics of French Business 1936–45*. Cambridge: Cambridge University Press.

Vishniac, Judith, E. (1990). *The Management of Labor: The British and French Iron and Steel Industries, 1860–1918*. Greenwich, Conn.: JAI Press.

Wada, Kazuo (1995). "The Emergence of the 'Flow Production' Method in Japan", in Shiomi and Wada (1995).

Welskopp, Thomas (1994). *Arbeit und Macht im Hüttenwerk: Arbeits- und industrielle Beziehungen in der deutschen und amerikanischen Eisen- und Stahlindustrie von den 1860er bis den 1930er Jahren*. Bonn: Dietz.

Whittington, Richard, and Mayer, Michael, (2000). *The European Corporation: Strategy, Structure, and Social Science*. Oxford: Oxford University Press.

Wightman, Clare (1999). *More than Munitions: Women, Work, and the Engineering Industries 1900–1950*. London: Longmans.

Wilson, J. F., and Popp, A. (eds.) (2003). *Industrial Clusters and Regional Business Networks in England, 1750–1970*. Ashgate: Aldershot.

Yamamura, Kozo, and Streeck, Wolfgang (eds.) (2003). *The End of Diversity? Prospects of German and Japanese Capitalism*. Ithaca, NY: Cornell University Press.

CHAPTER 19

ACCOUNTING, INFORMATION, AND COMMUNICATION SYSTEMS

TREVOR BOYNS

19.1 INTRODUCTION

MODERN businesses need to generate and communicate information for two purposes: satisfying the needs of those external to the business, for example, shareholders, both actual and potential; and for internal, managerial purposes. Accounting plays a key role in both these respects: "Accounting has always concerned itself with information production, processing and reporting while management accounting has sought to provide managers with information-based intelligence" (Bhimani and Roberts 2004: 1). Moreover, "Accounting information enables different organizational activities to be classified uniformly and to be altered so that they become economically functional and managerially controllable" (Bhimani and Roberts 2004: 2). The purpose of this chapter is to examine the relationship between the

I would like to express my thanks to my colleagues in the Accounting and Business History Research Unit at Cardiff University and to the editors for comments on an earlier draft of this chapter.

historical development of accounting, information, and communication systems (AICS) and that of business organizations since the late eighteenth century. Its findings are based largely on research conducted by accounting and business historians during the last quarter of the century, a period in which accounting history, once a niche area of research heavily focused on the development of double-entry book-keeping, has been brought more firmly into the business history fold. This reflects the work of those historians who have focused their attention on the development of cost/management accounting[1] practices within firms, and the "new" accounting historians who have examined the wider relationship between accounting and the organizations and society within which it is embedded.

19.2 AN OVERVIEW OF KEY DEVELOPMENTS

The information needs of those running businesses are many and varied, foremost amongst them being: What type of information? How is it to be collected and by whom? By what means is it to be conveyed, when, and to whom? In basic terms, information comes in two forms, financial and non-financial, and can be collected centrally within the organization, e.g. at headquarters by an accounting office, or within the various operating units of the business. Such information then has to be communicated to those who require it, and traditionally this was done through reports, either verbal or written. With the advent of modern information and communication technology (ICT), such reports are today often produced and communicated electronically.

Technological changes in communication methods since the second half of the nineteenth century, commencing with the telegraph and the telephone, have enabled the speedier communication of information. At the end of the nineteenth century, the development of typewriters and calculating and tabulating machines revolutionized the preparation and presentation of data and written reports, while single leaf sheets and carbon copies enabled their wider dissemination (Yates 1989). Since the Second World War, developments in ICT have radically altered the nature of AICS. The advent of the computer, in particular modern real-time computing, together with bar code technology, e-mail, and electronic data interchange, has resulted in faster data collection and communication and compressed the time frame for feedback, control, and decision making, within both the production and accounting spheres (Tyson 1996).

---

[1] The difference in meaning, as between different countries and even the same country at different points in time, of terms such as costing, cost accounting, and management accounting, the last of which appeared in the Anglo-Saxon world *c*.1950, is a complex subject which is only just being investigated by historians. To avoid problems as to meaning, we will often use cost/management accounting as a catch-all term.

While technological change relating to office and, in particular, accounting procedures, has revolutionized the preparation and dissemination of information within an organization, in the production sphere technological change has altered the nature of the information required. In the late nineteenth century, the move towards ever more capital-intensive methods of production encouraged a move away from a concern with prime costs, i.e. the cost of direct labor and materials, to a concern with the total, or full, costs of the business. The development of full-costing systems in the late nineteenth and early twentieth centuries represents the first of six major phases in the development of cost/management accounting identified by Schweitzer (2000). It was followed, between the two world wars by, first, a move from an approach based on historical cost information to a standard costing approach, focusing on what costs should be, coupled with budgeting and, second, a concern with the issue of what costs were relevant for decision making (the variable costing approach[2]). After the Second World War, Schweitzer (2000) identifies three major developments: relative contribution costing (1959), target costing (1963), and activity-based costing (ABC) (1988).

These developments in cost/management accounting during the twentieth century have occurred against the background of certain ongoing debates about fundamental, underlying issues in accounting such as the relationship between financial reporting and cost/management accounting, the relevance of full costs or variable costs to managerial decision making, and the role of financial information vis-à-vis non-financial information. The remainder of this chapter will seek to examine these underlying issues by bringing together historical evidence relating to the development of theory and practice within three major regions: the United States, Europe,[3] and Japan.

19.3 The Nature of Accounting and the Relationship between Financial Reporting and Cost/Management Accounting

Traditionally, accounting has been seen as a neutral, value-free, technical reporting instrument and while some still view it in this way, others see it differently. "New

---

[2] The term "variable costing" is used throughout to describe a group of closely related, though not identical, concepts, namely, direct costing, marginal costing, and contribution margin accounting.

[3] It should be noted that although Britain resides geographically within Europe, much of its accounting history has been different from that of countries within mainland, Continental Europe.

accounting historians" recognize that, since there are different ways of constructing accounts, what Miller and Napier (1993) have described as "genealogies of calculation", accounting is a discursive device, i.e. it is an analytical, interpretative, communicative, and symbolic practice. As Fear (2005: 35) has put it, accounting is a "communicative process which shapes managerial perceptions and actions", but it should not be forgotten that, since managerial actions determine the accounting system, the process is not simply unidirectional. Accounting, being a managerial device, is distinguishable from the merely bureaucratic procedure of bookkeeping. Whereas the nature of the latter has often been rooted in commercial codes which required the following of specific bookkeeping methods, accounting has been a matter of choice for each business. Different firms, however, utilize different *conceptions of control* (Fear 2005), i.e. differing relationships between strategy, organization, information, and accountability.

The development of AICS during the last two centuries has been closely tied to the rise of the corporate economy and, in particular, of large-scale business enterprise. Yamey has noted that this development has been accompanied by the growth of the

accounting profession and its organization; the use of auditors by business enterprises; the provision of financial statements to absentee shareholders; the development of stock markets; management accounting as a separate discipline; accounting theory; accounting standards; external regulation and self-regulation . . . (Yamey 1994: 380)

In the American context, Chandler (1977) has argued that it was the advent of big business from the late nineteenth century, and especially the rise of the multidivisional form (MDF) of business enterprise in the 1920s, which called forth developments in AICS, while Johnson and Kaplan (1987) expressed the view that it was prior developments in AICS which were vital in enabling the development of big business. The advent of the MDF increased "the volume of financial information and control . . . [and placed] it more firmly in the province of the accounting profession" (Armstrong 1987: 430).

The advent of legal status for companies, which in many countries began in the middle of the nineteenth century, together with the globalization of business and the growth of external financing of businesses and stock markets, has stimulated the development of financial reporting standards across the world. For modern global businesses, financial reporting is important because it "is a means of communicating financial information from the directors of companies to users of such information who are external to the management process of the company and who therefore do not have access to the internal management information system" (Thorell and Whittington 1994: 215). However, national accounting standards differ, sometimes substantially, with Nobes and Parker (2004) attributing this to differences in the external environment, culture, legal systems, providers of finance, the accounting profession, inflation, and theory, and to accidents.

Two distinct strands are observable in national standard setting: that of "codification", i.e. establishing a Commercial Code, whereby rules are set entirely in prescriptive law or statutory regulation, and which tend to favor the provision of information for creditors over that for shareholders; and that of common law, which tends to favor shareholders, where the legal framework establishes no mandatory rules and is essentially permissive, until legal rulings are made regarding actions that cannot be taken, such as those proscribing fraudulent financial reporting. In the Anglo-Saxon world, the common law approach has prevailed, while the former, or Continental model, became widespread throughout mainland Europe during the nineteenth and twentieth centuries, not least due to the impact throughout much of the region of the Napoleonic Commercial Code of 1807 (Walton 1993). Approaches can, and do, change; in the 1880s and 1890s, Japan developed a commercial code based on the Continental model but, after the Second World War, under Allied control, adopted a more Anglo-Saxon approach (Cooke 1991).

Despite national differences in approach, businesses are normally required, by law, to produce two audited statements on at least an annual basis: a balance sheet showing the assets and liabilities at the end of the accounting period and a profit and loss account showing the performance of the business during the accounting period. Different standards in financial reporting make comparisons of firms' results problematic, so attempts have been made to try to improve standardization. In Anglo-Saxon countries the main role in developing principles and practices to eliminate inconsistencies and actions which have led to financial crises has been played by professional accounting bodies. In the United States, Generally Agreed Accounting Principles (GAAP) were developed during the twentieth century and are now the responsibility of the Financial Accounting Standards Board, established in 1973, whose activities are overseen by the Securities and Exchange Commission (SEC).[4] In Great Britain, a similar role is played by the Accounting Standards Board.[5]

Attempts were also made during the late twentieth century to harmonize accounting rules on an international basis. Thus, on June 29, 1973, the International Accounting Standards Committee (IASC) was founded by the leading accounting bodies of Australia, Canada, France, Germany, Japan, Mexico, the Netherlands, Great Britain, Ireland, and the United States. The major objectives of the IASC were "to formulate and publish, in the public interest, accounting standards to be observed in the presentation of financial statements and to promote their world-wide acceptance and observance and, second, to work generally for the improvement and harmonisation of regulations, accounting standards and procedures relating to

[4] Although they have Commercial Codes, both France and Italy have established bodies to control their securities' markets, modelled to some extent on the American SEC.

[5] In 1970, the British profession established an Accounting Standards Steering Committee to issue Statements of Standard Accounting Practice. This body was renamed the Accounting Standards Committee in 1976, and its functions were taken over in 1990 by the Accounting Standards Board.

the presentation of financial statements" (Kikuya 2001: 351). Within the member countries of the European Union (EU), attempts were similarly made to encourage harmonization of financial reporting through the Fourth (July 1978) and Seventh (June 1983) accounting directives of the EU's Council of Ministers. Despite such developments, countries have often shown a high level of inertia, with different economic, social, and cultural environments militating against change.

At the beginning of the twenty-first century, however, new moves are taking place. In 2001, the IASC was replaced by the International Accounting Standards Board (IASB), and the IASs have been replaced by International Financial Reporting Standards (IFRSs). The European Union (EU) has passed legislation which requires the financial reports of all EU listed companies to comply with IFRSs beginning January 1, 2005, and there is a greater spirit of cooperation between the SEC and the IASB. Indeed, there are signs that more and more companies are moving towards adopting either the United States GAAP or IFRSs for consolidated reporting (Nobes and Parker 2004). The recent financial scandals surrounding Enron, WorldCom, Parmalat, etc., however, indicate that the development of national and international accounting standards is not, of itself, guaranteed to eliminate fraudulent or any other activity.

In Europe, many countries achieved some degree of internal uniformity in accounting through the development of charts of accounts, which specified the accounts to be kept, their relationship to one another, and the bookkeeping methods to be used. In their modern guise, charts appeared at the end of the nineteenth century, stimulated by the development of financial markets, an accelerating concentration of businesses, and a sharp increase in scientific thinking about standardization (Richard 1995*a*). Between 1900 and 1918, the concern was with "formal monism", that is, a single chart for both financial and cost/management accounting purposes, but between 1918 and 1937, a new type of chart emerged aimed "at organizing and standardizing cost, and more generally management accounting" (Richard 1995*a*: 88). Between 1937 and 1945, the emphasis was on developing charts in which financial accounting was more independent, as with Goering's chart under the German Reich in 1937, used also in France from 1942 following the German occupation. Although statutory charts of accounts were no longer a legal requirement in Germany after the war, their use has been enshrined in France since 1947 by the issuance of a series of *Plans Comptables Généraux*. Charts of accounts were also widely used in Soviet Russia and Eastern Europe prior to the fall of Communism. The marketization of former Eastern bloc countries, however, has led to significant divergences in practices. In Russia, the "old method, derived from Schmalenbach's chart of accounts, has been preserved and adapted to the new market economy by being brought closer to American practices", whereas in Romania, "for essentially political and cultural (not technical) reasons", there was a break with the old Russian-inspired system and they have copied the French model (Richard 1995*b*: 320).

The nature of charts of accounts adopted has varied markedly from country to country, and Bechtel (1995) noted that the German chart allowed firms much more flexibility than the French one. The closest that the Anglo-Saxon countries have come to the use of charts of accounts has been the adoption, at certain times, of uniform costing systems (UCS) in some industries and sectors. UCS can help prevent "ruinous competition" by making manufacturers aware of their costs, thereby helping to prevent them setting prices at below cost and, by making cost information more widely available in a trade, help spread best practice. The adoption of UCS has often been aided by trade bodies, with Berk and Schneiberg (2005) finding that UCS provided a means to collaborative learning within American associations in intermediate or producer goods sectors such as lumber/timber and printing between c.1900 and c.1925. An added boost to the development of UCS was provided by the enactment of the National Industrial Recovery Act of 1933 (Fleischman and Tyson 1999). In Great Britain, similar schemes were developed in various sectors from the late nineteenth century (Boyns 1998b), but their take-up was not always especially high (Edwards et al. 2003). Examples can also be found in Scandinavia where, during the 1930s, we find an emphasis on standardizing recording systems and calculation principles in Denmark (Israelsen et al. 1996), while in Sweden, "Uniform principles of full costing" were established in 1937. This was followed by the establishment of standard charts of accounts to support the costing procedures, the first being that of the trade association representing the Swedish mechanical and electrical engineering industries in 1943 (Ask et al. 1996).

That this event in Sweden occurred during the Second World War may be no coincidence. Several historians have highlighted the impact of war on cost accounting, not least because governments in many countries, concerned to control the prices that they paid for their war materials and to prevent profiteering, introduced cost-based controls. Loft (1986, 1990), for example, has claimed that controls introduced during the First World War in Great Britain had a significant impact, leading to costing "coming into the light", though she possibly underestimates the nature and extent of cost calculation practices before 1914 (Boyns 2003b). In Germany, the introduction of the Goering chart in 1937 was designed to establish administered prices to be applied when supplying the state, while in 1939 and 1940 respectively, the Japanese Army and Navy set up their own cost accounting rules to control the price of munitions (Yoshikawa 2001). These rules were replaced in April 1942 by the Manufacturing Industry Cost Accounting Guideline, designed to control commodity prices and to increase the efficiency of management. Twenty years later, in November 1962, the Cost Accounting Standard was established, and though not legally binding on Japanese companies, social pressures ensured that it has become "the foundation for every company" (Yoshikawa 2001: 279).

While in many Continental European countries and Japan, cost accounting standards have often been imposed by the state, in Anglo-Saxon countries such an occurrence is rare, except in wartime. However, during the 1970s, and again from the late 1980s, regulations were introduced in the United States determining the methods of costing to be used by companies engaged on government contracts, with a Cost Accounting Standards Board being established to oversee and monitor their implementation (Previts and Merino 1998).

The existence of charts of accounts or standards, whether imposed by law or adopted on a voluntary basis, does not, however, mean that companies are forced to use a specific costing system. Under the Japanese Cost Accounting Standard, for example, companies are free to implement their own cost accounting practices, since it does not "define or describe the practical methods" to be used (Yoshikawa 2001: 271).

19.4 COSTING THEORY AND PRACTICE

The link between costing theory, as espoused in accounting texts, and business practice is not well understood. Texts on costing were rare in the Anglo-Saxon world before the 1880s, though they were more prevalent in France from early in the nineteenth century (Boyns *et al.* 1997). In Germany, texts discussing cost behavior and the use of costing for forward looking management decisions appear from the late 1870s, with the first description of a German costing system coming in Lilenthal's 1907 book (Coenenberg and Schoenfeld 1990: 96–7). In Great Britain, the key development was the publication of *Factory Accounts* by Garcke and Fells in 1887, an act which stimulated the writing of other British costing texts. However, it was the United States which, before the First World War, came to dominate the production of English-language costing texts. In Japan, where the term cost accounting was not recognized before 1914, ten books on the topic of industrial bookkeeping appeared before the First World War, the first being Arisawa's *Bookkeeping for Manufacturers*, published in 1887 (Kimizuka 1991). Since 1914, and more especially since 1945, the literature on cost and, subsequently, management accounting has burgeoned in all countries.

Knowledge of actual practices used by businesses prior to the late twentieth century, and even then, however, is limited due to the lack of systematic and comprehensive evidence, whether on a national or international basis. Even in the United States, where contemporary surveys have a longer pedigree, they were often limited in their scope and heavily biased in their coverage. Thus, traditional historians such as Solomons (1952), Garner (1954), and Chatfield (1977), largely based their studies of accounting developments in the Anglo-Saxon world on costing texts, while more recent historians have placed a greater reliance on archive-based research. Such research was initially focused on cost calculation practices in the Anglo-Saxon world, but is now being supplemented by work relating to other countries. Our understanding of developments in practice, however, remains piecemeal, reliant as it is on the patchy and limited survival of business archives and, within them, of accounting records. Nevertheless, certain of the generalizations made by traditional historians have been found wanting, not least that of the link between theory and practice.

19.4.1 Pre-1850

Despite the dearth of a relevant English-language literature on costing prior to the 1870s and 1880s, cost calculation in Great Britain has a long pedigree, stretching back, as in other countries, before the Industrial Revolution. Thus, industrial accounting, i.e. costing conducted within the financial books kept on the double entry system, was being conducted at the Staveley ironworks by the end of the seventeenth century (Edwards and Boyns 1992). During the second half of the eighteenth century, evidence of costing exists for the pottery manufacturer, Wedgwood (McKendrick 1970), the Scottish ironmaker, Carron (Fleischman and Parker 1990), as well as at the Mona Mine Company and the Cyfarthfa ironworks (Jones 1985), in addition to Staveley. Such evidence, together with that on Charlton Mills (Stone 1973), and the Dowlais and Consett ironworks (Boyns and Edwards 1997) during the first half of the nineteenth century, undermines Pollard's claim that entrepreneurs of the British industrial revolution "did not develop to any significant extent the use of accounts in guiding management decisions"(1968: 289).

Despite industrialization proceeding at a much slower pace, similar developments in costing can be found in other countries. Thus, in France, the Baccarat Crystalworks, the ironworks of Decazeville, Allevard, and Le Creusot, and the glass manufacturer Saint-Gobain began to utilize industrial accounting during the first half of the nineteenth century (Nikitin 1992; Boyns *et al.* 1997). In Japan, Kimizuka (1991) reports costs being calculated at the Nakai Ichizo soy sauce plant in Tokyo between 1788 and 1799 and, in the first half of the nineteenth century, at the Ohtaya Kazo sake brewery at Ohta between 1835 and 1850 and the Tanabe family's iron and steel operations. In the United States, Porter (1980) noted a move from mercantile to industrial accounting at the textile mills of the Boston Manufacturing Company in the 1810s, while Tyson (1992) found evidence of the use of costs for stimulating cost reduction and enhancing productivity at the Lyman Mills in the 1830s.

19.4.2 1850–c.1920

While signs of systematic costing can be found in many countries before 1850, it is from that time that costing became more and more widespread. Thus, in Great Britain after 1850, costing became much more common (Boyns 2003*b*), not only in sectors such as iron and steel and engineering but also in chemicals, where practice continued to lead theory up until the Second World War (Boyns *et al.* 2004). A similar situation can be found in Germany where the system of "dynamic accounting" developed by the iron and steel manufacturer, Thyssen, during the late nineteenth and early twentieth centuries predated Schmalenbach's writings on this topic (Fear 2005). In Japan, cost calculation also seems to have become more widespread after 1850, examples including the Yokosuka shipyard *c.*1865, the Tomioka spinning factory from 1870, the Onoda Cement Manufacturing Co. in the early 1880s, and the Sado Gold Mine of Mitsubishi & Co. Ltd. in 1897 (Kimizuka 1991).

Conventional wisdom, however, has it that it was the United States which became the frontrunner, at least in the Anglo-Saxon world, in relation to the development of both theory and practice after 1850. Chandler (1977) links the development of accounting to that of organizational forms, which he sees as beginning with single unit management, developed at the Springfield Armory and in textile mills before 1850, moving through multi-unit management at the American railroads and telegraph companies between 1850 and the 1880s, to the MDF developed at Du Pont and General Motors between the 1890s and the early 1920s. Chandler notes that the railroads developed new methods of financial, capital, and cost accounting, but their systems, which focused on the calculation of prime costs and the use of renewal accounting, were inappropriate for firms like General Electric, which wanted to know the profits made on different product lines or the rate of return generated on invested capital (ROI). It was Du Pont which first developed an integrated system of modern industrial asset accounting during the early years of the twentieth century utilizing ROI as a basic management tool for both evaluation and planning (Chandler 1977). By 1910, Du Pont was employing nearly all the basic methods that became commonplace later in the twentieth century for managing big business.

While Chandler sees modern management as a rupture in economic history, Hoskin and Macve (2000: 97) see the invention of administrative coordination not in economic terms but as a "combination of writing, examining, and grading, a means to inventing a new kind of economic world". In a Foucauldian manner, this new grammatocentric method of "writing the world" provided managers with the knowledge and, therefore, power by which to control workers. Hoskin and Macve see the development of managerialism, i.e. the process by which accounting values could be placed on individuals as well as objects, as being developed initially at the American Military Academy at West Point during the early decades of the nineteenth century. It then spread via West Point's engineering graduates to the Springfield Armory in the middle of the nineteenth century, to the American railroads in the latter decades of the nineteenth century, and to big business during the twentieth century.

Recent research by American business historians has also begun to question the extent to which the development of American capitalism should be seen purely in terms of the development of Chandler's MDF. Berk and Schneiberg (2005: 74), in their study of developmental associations, and echoing the findings of Scranton (1997) in relation to specialty producers, have suggested that American capitalism was "a loosely coupled system composed of multiple—sometimes linked, sometimes autonomous, and sometimes conflicting—institutional projects, logics, or paths". Not surprisingly then, the role of accounting generally, and cost/management accounting specifically, differed between the various types of institutions, as well as between firms within the same institutional form. Scranton (1997) notes that specialty manufacturers, producing small batches of a large number of different products, faced different costing problems from mass producers; therefore, generalizations as to the nature of costing systems used, whether for firms in a particular country, within a specific institutional framework, or even within a specific industry, will often be misleading.

19.4.3   c.1920–c.1988

19.4.3.1   *Costing, Financial Reporting, and Strategic Management Accounting*

The fundamental distinction in cost analysis is between full, or absorption, cost on the one hand, and variable cost on the other, and although accountants and economists did not make any substantial pronouncements on such issues until the period between the two world wars, recent historical research has revealed that some businessmen of the nineteenth century were aware of such distinctions. Nevertheless, the emphasis of many businessmen in the late nineteenth century was on keeping track of prime costs. However, as the size and capital-intensity of businesses increased, engineers became concerned with the issue of general business expenses, particularly those concerned with management, the depreciation of capital equipment, and the opportunity cost of the capital invested in the business. This concern led to attention being turned towards full, or absorption, cost, which brought with it concerns over the appropriate method by which to allocate overheads, or general expenses, to products and/or processes. Amongst the allocation bases utilized were labour, prime costs, machines, and machine hours, the most sophisticated method suggested in the early twentieth century being that of Alexander Hamilton Church, whose scientific machine rate method was employed by Hans Renold Ltd. in Great Britain, but failed due to inherent problems with the system and its requirement for the processing of large amounts of data (Boyns 2003a).

The growing influence of accountants from the early twentieth century meant that even in those countries where they were initially distinct, especially the United States,[6] costing and financial accounting increasingly became integrated within

---

[6] A by-product of engineers being responsible for costing and accountants for the financial books.

a single accounting system, with the result that the key role of cost accounting came to be the provision of full-cost figures by which inventories could be valued for financial reporting purposes. Together with the failure to develop new ideas over the next fifty years, this subservience to financial reporting led Johnson and Kaplan (1987: 1) to claim that cost/management accounting had lost its relevance for managerial purposes: "Today's management accounting information, driven by the procedures and cycle of the organization's financial reporting system, is too late, too aggregated, and too distorted to be relevant for manager's planning and control decisions". Johnson and Kaplan advocated a return to the full-costing approaches adopted by engineers such as Church which led Kaplan and Norton, in the late 1980s, to promote ABC as the savior for American business.

Wells (1978), however, considered that engineers' full-cost systems had never been relevant for management decision-making purposes: "The average cost of production never could, and never will, be relevant for those classes of decisions where only the change in total costs and revenues are relevant" (Gormly and Wells 1992: 599). The advent of modern ICT, therefore, is irrelevant to the issue of trying to relate two things, i.e. overhead costs and individual units of production, that are not related. Wells argued that overhead allocation can only serve as a rough guide to rate-fixing and the pricing of unique goods or specific services, so the engineers of the late nineteenth and early twentieth century were wrong because their systems were at odds with economic theory. Johnson, the co-author, with Kaplan, of *Relevance Lost*, also subsequently came to be of the view that modern ICT was not the solution. Indeed, he came to "doubt the idea that companies can improve their cost performance by compiling better cost information", going on to suggest that "Cost accounting should always be viewed as an aspect of financial accounting, reporting and planning—never a tool for managing operations" (both quotes, Johnson 2002: 17). For Johnson (2002: 18), cost management "must be viewed as an aspect of enterprise system design, not an accounting exercise", and hence the need is to "manage the means", not "manage the results". This view reflects the Japanese approach developed since the Second World War where management accounting is not, as it is in the West, viewed as the provider of objective financial information, but rather used to service the strategic objectives of the organization, being viewed "primarily as a means of encouraging economically desirable behavior" (Yoshikawa *et al.* 1994: 3).

The Japanese emphasis on the use of management accounting within a long-term, strategic approach to business, rather than the American approach in which the concern was with short-term financial accounting ratios such as ROI, was suggested as a possible explanation for the relative success of Japanese firms compared with their American counterparts in the late twentieth century. The debate about the efficacy of the different approaches also affected Europe where the American approach has had an ever greater impact on local accounting practices since 1945. Some commentators advocated the adoption in the United States and the West more generally of Japanese accounting techniques, including target costing, which is not a costing system as such, but a process that turns on its head the conventional Western process, in oligopolistic markets, of using costs to determine prices. Under target costing, developed by some Japanese firms in the 1960s, a firm determines the price, which will enable it to obtain a predetermined market share, and then sets the target cost appropriately. Costs are then monitored through a conventional costing system to ensure that the target is not exceeded. Simultaneously, in the 1960s and 1970s, the development of automated manufacturing techniques, together with just-in-time (JIT) organizational structures led to a redefining of inventory valuation, cost control, and product costing (Tyson 1996). In response to the 1973–4 oil crisis, the motor car manufacturer, Toyota, developed the JIT management system, where cost reduction in the manufacturing process was supported by the use of Kaizen costing (Monden and Hamada 2000). As more was learned in the West about Japanese techniques, there developed a new approach to cost/management accounting, namely that of strategic management accounting, a technique which utilizes both financial and non-financial information.

19.4.3.2 *Full Costing versus Variable Costing*

Concern with the issue of which costs were relevant for decision making initially developed in the late nineteenth and early twentieth centuries as certain economists, such as Jevons and Marshall in Great Britain and Clark in the United States, and accounting theorists, such as Schmalenbach in Germany, became increasingly interested in the relationship between economic theory and cost. Schmalenbach formalized the distinction between fixed, semi-fixed, and variable costs in 1899 (Coenenberg and Schoenfeld 1990), but it is Clark who is usually credited with developing the concept that there are different costs for different purposes. The key point of his work was that, in making a decision, only those costs which would change, i.e. were variable, should be taken into consideration.

Which of a firm's costs are fixed and which are variable, however, depends on a number of factors, including the issue being considered, the nature of the business, the technology being used, and the time horizon (short-run or long-run) being considered. Clark's work led to a switch of attention in the literature away from traditional full-costing systems towards what economists call marginal costing, but which attracted different descriptions in different countries, including direct costing (America) and contribution margin costing[7] (e.g. Germany; Denmark). In Great Britain, marginal costing began to gain ground after the Second World War, theoretical developments flourishing there because of the positive emphasis on its use for planning and control, as opposed to the more negative stance of opposition to full-costing found in the United States (Marple 1965). In Europe in the 1950s,

---

[7] Strictly speaking, the contribution margin for a product is what one gets when one considers the difference between its sales price and direct cost.

we find the development of relative contribution costing, as attention increasingly focused on attempting to find determinants for costs traditionally considered to be fixed, certain components of fixed costs therefore acquiring the character of "relative direct costs".

Despite the theoretical developments surrounding variable costing since the 1930s, it is full-costing that has played, and continues to play, the dominant role in the practices of firms in most countries. It has been the norm since the 1920s in American and British companies, not to mention in France, where Rimailho's *sections homogènes* method, developed between the wars, was enshrined in the *Plan Comptable Général* of 1947. Berliet and Renault (motor vehicles), Pechiney (aluminium), and Saint-Gobain (glass and chemicals) used full-costing systems between the wars, and it was not until the 1950s that marginal costing made some headway in the French literature, though the impact on practice was small. In Germany, the Goering chart of 1937 led to the promotion of full-cost pricing (Busse von Colbe 1996) and despite no longer being a legal requirement after the Second World War, over 50 percent of German companies in the 1980s and early 1990s continued to use full-cost methods which had been standardized and applied in the 1930s, though this was often supplemented by indirect costing and contribution margin accounting (Scherrer 1996).

German attitudes influenced the development of Sweden's "Uniform principles of full-costing" in 1937, where mass producers, such as Volvo (cars and trucks) and SKF (ball bearings), "argued for standard costing and for keeping cost calculation and cost accounting separate", while ASEA (heavy manufacturing) and Ericsson, producers of large ranges of differentiated products, "wanted to integrate cost calculation into the cost accounting system in the German tradition" (both quotes, Ask *et al.* 1996: 204). The standards subsequently adopted enshrined Clark's concept of different costs for different purposes. As for marginal costing, this was discussed in Sweden after 1949, but there was little change in practice, though some industries, e.g. steel, did take up marginal costing in the early 1950s. The costing standards implemented in the 1930s, however, as in Germany, have continued to hold a strong influence on Swedish costing practices.

19.4.3.3 *Standard Costing and Budgeting*

Standard costing and budgeting are techniques which can be used in conjunction with either full or variable costing methods. Whereas traditional (historic) costing determined the costs experienced in the previous accounting period, the essence of standard costing is to determine, in advance, what costs should be, thereby facilitating not only price setting but, more importantly, the efficient control of costs through a system of management by exception. Standard costing, however, is not a system of accounting for costs as such, but rather a system whereby standard cost figures are determined a priori, and then the variance between actual cost, as determined by the cost accounting system, and the standard cost are computed and reported to management. Managers can then immediately see where problems exist in the production process and take remedial action, quickly and efficiently.

Standard costing is generally considered to have emerged amongst mass producers in the United States during the scientific management era of the early decades of the twentieth century (Sowell 1973), though evidence of the use of "standard" or predetermined costs can be found in a number of businesses located in various countries before this. Although Harrison (1930: 26) claimed that, during the 1920s, "the standard cost plan has made immense headway", Fleischman has recently cast doubt on the rapidity of its take-up by American businesses, arguing that the development of scientific management theory, of which standard costing and variance analysis were major innovations, was probably far in advance of practice in the United States, and that a "vast schism between theory and practice may have existed, perhaps extending until the decade of the 1920s and probably until the 1940s" (2000: 600). Likewise, while the use of budgeting and ROI systems to plan and control the use of capital may have been pioneered by the Du Pont Powder Company between 1903 and 1915, it was only in the 1920s that their use began to develop at companies such as General Electric, United States Rubber, General Motors, and Sears Roebuck, which responded to the inventory crisis of 1920–1 by developing techniques that set and adjusted their production flows to carefully forecasted future demand (Chandler 1977).

The use of budgeting and standard costing in the United States was still only partial in the early 1930s (NICB 1931) but, according to Chandler, became adopted much more widely as a result of the Second World War which put the "capstone on the institutional developments of the interwar years" (1977: 476). The war brought small firms, usually as subcontractors for the larger concerns, into contact with modern methods of forecasting, accounting, and inventory control. However, the first comprehensive survey of costing practices in American business, carried out in 1946, suggested that only 4,050 out of the 187,370 companies surveyed, that is, just 2.2 percent, used a standard costing system (Black and Eversole 1946).[8] Furthermore, even by the mid-1960s, the use of standard costing was not comprehensive either within or across industrial sectors in the United States, reflecting in part the different circumstances pertaining to each firm and sector (PHES 1965).

Development of the use of standard costing and budgeting between the two world wars, however, was not confined merely to the United States. British firms such as Hans Renold Ltd., Austin Motors, BSA, and Dunlop, to mention just a few, have been found to have introduced them in the 1920s and 1930s (Boyns 1998a, 1998b, 2003a). In France, though no cases have as yet been found of the use of

---

[8] It is also of interest to note that only 22 percent of the total number of companies maintained any form of costing records.

standard costing before 1939 (Zimnovitch 1997), the use of budgeting was quite wide spread, with important pioneers in the 1920s being Commentry-Fourchambault and Les Imprimeries Delmas (Berland 1999; Berland and Boyns 2002). The traditional view that the United States developed these techniques in the 1910s and 1920s, and that they then spread rapidly in that country but only somewhat belatedly to Europe during the 1950s and 1960s, is clearly no longer tenable, at least in the cases of France and Great Britain (Berland *et al.* 2002). Despite some instances of early adoption in Europe, however, the utilization of budgeting and standard costing did grow dramatically after 1950, coinciding in part with the growth in business size and the accompanying adoption of the MDF organizational form experienced in many countries at this time, though archival research has shown that it was not always the largest firms which were at the forefront of early developments in the use of budgeting and standard costing (Boyns *et al.* 2000).

Despite archival revelations of the earlier usage of cost information for managerial purposes in many countries, stretching back to the British Industrial Revolution and before, the developments of the 1950s and 1960s are seen in the Anglo-Saxon world as marking a shift from cost accounting to management accounting, reflecting the "impact of a growing body of work in organisational theory and economics" (Previts and Merino 1998: 325). It was followed in the 1960s by a move away from a concern with product costing to one with the activities over which individuals had control, or responsibility accounting (Scapens 1991), in which standard costing and budgetary control played an important, but not always a straightforward, role. Responsibility accounting[9] represents a top-down "control over" philosophy of management, and increasingly became questioned as realization dawned that processes aimed at achieving efficiency could be manipulated by employees to achieve the desired accounting results in a way that was not necessarily beneficial to the business. Attention thus tended to be turned towards an approach more akin to that of the Japanese, where the philosophy was one of "control with", encouraging teamwork and group decision making.

19.4.4 Since 1988

As already noted, determining full cost is problematic, and despite the development of more sophisticated overhead allocation methods, in practice, simple methods, most notably, direct labor, tended to hold sway throughout the twentieth century. By 1991, however, direct labor contributed only about 10 percent of operating expenses for most industrial companies in the United States (Previts and Merino 1998). Accurate determination of costs, therefore, required the use of more sophisticated allocation methods than the volume-driven allocation bases then in

---

[9] Responsibility accounting has now reached even China, being used at the Han Dan Iron and Steel Company (Jun Lin and Yu 2002).

use. Hence, Cooper and Kaplan (1988) developed ABC, a modern variant of earlier full-costing methods which utilizes multiple "cost drivers", some volume-based, others not.

The concepts underlying ABC were not new, even in the United States, where "activity costing" had previously been suggested by Staubus (1971). The Dane, Madsen, had developed similar ideas in the 1960s, with his variability accounting approach, which was "built on the argument that arbitrary [overhead] allocations should be avoided and cost drivers identified so that accounting information could be made more relevant to the user situation" (Jönsson 1996: 445). Madsen's views were taken on board by Swedish researchers and, alongside the development of computers, began to influence the design of accounting information systems in that country. While the focus of changes before the mid-1990s in Sweden was on improving "traditional" methods and techniques, rather than adopting new ones, some firms began to examine ABC and "new" accounting techniques (Ask *et al.* 1996). However, as in many other countries, including the United States itself, ABC had its opponents. Many have viewed it as a fad, rather than as a useful technique with decision-making relevance, and one whose implementation is both problematic and costly (Innes *et al.* 2000). Thus, perhaps not surprisingly, ABC has not enjoyed as widespread acceptance within companies as it has in certain academic circles (see Bhimani 1996).

19.4.4.1 *The Utilization of Non-financial Measures*

One element in the early debates between Kaplan and his supporters on the one hand, and his detractors on the other, was the relevance of accounting numbers, especially those produced by full-costing methods such as ABC. Implicit in the Johnson and Kaplan critique of traditional management accounting systems in the United States is the view that businessmen rely solely on accounting numbers to run their businesses. Thirty years previously, however, Simon *et al.* (1954) had shown that this was not the case, leading Tyson (1996) to argue that to blame traditional systems for irrelevance and inadequacy because they generated the wrong accounting numbers was to judge them inappropriately.

Kaplan seems to have recognized some validity in such arguments, developing, in conjunction with Norton, the concept of the Balanced Scorecard, an approach to managerial control which incorporates four perspectives: financial, customer, internal business, and innovation and learning. In many respects the Balanced Scorecard approach mirrors that of the *Tableau de Bord* (TdB) in France, which emerged spontaneously in the 1960s and subsequently evolved from a "loosely defined tool into a formally structured instrument with well-defined purpose, content and form" (Lebas 1994: 471). While both approaches utilize the monitoring of physical and financial indicators to assess and anticipate performance, thereby facilitating both strategic and operational management, they differ in key respects:

the underlying strategic concepts, causal performance models, modes of deploying objectives and indicators within the organization, and the relationship between performance measures and rewards in terms of tightness (Bourguignon *et al.* 2004). The explanation for such differences lies in the different ideological underpinnings of society and the resulting different ways of managing: in France, "social hierarchy, obedience, legitimacy and security are mainly questions of education and honour", whereas in the United States they are largely determined by management instruments (Bourguignon *et al.* 2004: 129). As a result of these differences, the Balanced Scorecard approach has not received a particularly favorable response in France.

In Japan, the attitude towards accounting numbers has traditionally been more flexible than in the West, there being less concern with data precision, and a greater willingness of managers to take a longer view and to base their decisions on "hunch, tradition, common sense, judgement and experience" (Yoshikawa *et al.* 1994: 4). Furthermore, Japanese cost accountants are responsible for calculating not only expected and actual costs, but also actual and expected *kousuu*, the working hours required for manufacturing one unit of a product or needed to carry out one job. Techniques which do not help to reduce the number or level of *kousuu* do not retain, for long, their credibility for cost management purposes (Yoshikawa 2001).

19.5 CONVERGENCE?

Earlier, we noted that there has been a tendency towards convergence in respect of financial reporting. Commentators like Shields (1998) see a similar tendency in respect of management accounting, with recent developments in different parts of the world suggesting a significant degree of convergence, not towards a single "American" method of management accounting but rather a set of global management accounting practices, in which practices will become similar in all firms within a particular industry, but will vary across industries. For Shields it is increased levels of competition, the availability of similar operating technologies, cheap and fast communication and transportation, increasing global homogenization of management accounting education, the rise of global consulting firms, and the development of global corporations which are the key factors explaining such convergence. However, not all observers see things in the same way. Reviewing a survey of the experiences of European countries during the twentieth century, Macintosh (1998) was more struck by the similarities than the differences, while Birkett (1998) considers that the differences far outweigh any commonalities.

19.6 Conclusions

The discussion in this chapter has revealed that recent research by accounting and business historians has provided us with a clearer understanding of the importance of AICS in the development of business organizations over the last 250 years. While information always has been, and no doubt always will be, fundamental to the smooth running of businesses and capitalist economies, over time, the nature, type, and amount of information utilized, and the method of its collection and dissemination, have changed. National practices have been found to reflect social and cultural factors as well as differences in legal and political systems. Despite this, and due in part to the globalization of business, some convergence has been discerned, especially in respect to financial reporting but also in cost/management accounting. Most recently, there have been clear indications amongst Western companies of a shift from financial methods of business control, which had grown in importance since the early decades of the twentieth century, towards the use of methods which incorporate physical measures and adopt a more strategic focus, in the manner of Japanese corporations since the Second World War. However, while some businessmen at times may have been susceptible to new academic fads or fashions, many today continue to utilize full, rather than variable, costing methods, just as did their predecessors at the beginning of the twentieth century.

There is still much, however, that we do not know about the nature and exact timing of the development of AICS in individual countries, or the factors and historical processes involved. Establishing the extent of any historical convergence in practices will require further archive-based research, both within countries and of a comparative nature. Comparative international accounting history, currently in its infancy (Carnegie and Napier 2002), will be vital to developing further our knowledge of the impact, on the dissemination of ideas and the diffusion of practices, of such factors as colonization, trading links, and the sharing of common languages and cultures. Further research will hopefully help us to better understand the links, if any, between advances in accounting theory and accounting practice. With accounting history becoming a respected research discipline for academics in many countries, with the possible exception of the United States, the omens are generally good, but for historians to be successful in these quests, it is imperative that archivists the world over are prepared to preserve bulky accounting records.

References

Armstrong, P. (1987). "The Rise of Accounting Controls in British Capitalist Enterprises". *Accounting, Organizations and Society*, 12/5: 415–36.

Ask, U., Ax, C., and Jönsson, S. (1996). "Cost Management in Sweden: From Modern to Post-modern", in Bhimani (1996), 199–217.

BECHTEL, W. (1995). "Charts of Accounts in Germany". *European Accounting Review*, 4/2: 283–304.

BERK, G., and SCHNEIBERG, M. (2005). "Varieties *in* Capitalism, Varieties *of* Association: Collaborative Learning in American Industry, 1900 to 1925". *Politics and Society*, 33/1: 46–87.

BERLAND, N. (1999). "L'histoire du contrôle budgetaire en France", doctoral thesis. Paris-Dauphine University.

——and BOYNS, T. (2002). "The Development of Budgetary Control in France and Britain from the 1920s to the 1960s: A Comparison". *European Accounting Review*, 11/2: 329–56.

————and ZIMNOVITCH, H. (2002). "The Influence of the USA on the Development of Standard Costing and Budgeting in the UK and France", in M. Kipping and N. Tiratsoo (eds.), *Americanisation in 20th Century Europe: Business, Culture, Politics*. Lille: University Charles de Gaulle, 129–44.

BHIMANI, A. (ed.) (1996). *Management Accounting: European Perspectives*. Oxford: Oxford University Press.

——and ROBERTS, H. (2004). "(Editorial) Management Accounting and Knowledge Management: In Search of Intelligibility". *Management Accounting Research*, 15: 1–4.

BIRKETT, W. P. (1998). "Management Accounting in Europe: A View from Down-Under". *Management Accounting Research*, 9: 485–94.

BLACK, M. L., and EVERSOLE, H. B. (1946). *A Report on Cost Accounting in Industry*. Washington, DC: Government Printing Office.

BOURGUIGNON, A., MALLERET, V., and NORREKLIT, H. (2004). "The American Balanced Scorecard versus the French Tableau De Bord: The Ideological Dimension". *Management Accounting Research*, 15: 107–34.

BOYNS, T. (1998a). "Budgets and Budgetary Control in British Businesses to c.1945". *Accounting, Business and Financial History*, 8/3: 261–301.

——(1998b). "The Development of Costing in Britain, c.1900–c.1960". *Entreprises et Histoire*, 20: 33–66.

——(2003a). "In Memoriam: Alexander Hamilton Church's System of 'Scientific Machine Rates' at Hans Renold Ltd., c.1901–c.1920". *Accounting Historians Journal*, 30/1: 3–44.

——(2003b). "Illuminating the Darkness: The Impact of the First World War on Cost Calculation Practices in British Firms". Paper presented at the 15th Accounting, Business and Financial History Conference, Cardiff, 10–11 Sept.

——and EDWARDS, J. R. (1997). "The Construction of Cost Accounting Systems in Britain to 1900: The Case of the Coal, Iron and Steel Industries". *Business History*, 39/3: 1–29.

————and MATTHEWS, M. (2000). "A Study of the Interrelationship between Business, Management Organisation and Accounting Developments: Budgets and Budgetary Control in Britain between the Wars", in *Accounting and History*. Madrid: AECA, 71–90.

————and NIKITIN, M. (1997). *The Birth of Industrial Accounting in France and Britain*. New York and London: Garland Publishing.

——MATTHEWS, M., and EDWARDS, J. R. (2004). "The Development of Costing in the British Chemical Industry, c.1870–c.1940". *Accounting and Business Research*, 34/1: 3–24.

BUSSE VON COLBE, W. (1996). "Accounting and the Business Economics Tradition in Germany". *European Accounting Review*, 5/3: 413–34.

CARNEGIE, G. D., and NAPIER, C. J. (2002). "Exploring Comparative International Accounting History". *Accounting, Audit and Accountability Journal*, 15/5: 689–718.

CHANDLER, A. D., JR. (1977). *The Visible Hand: The Managerial Revolution in American Business*. Cambridge, Mass.: Belknap Press.

CHATFIELD, M. (1977). *A History of Accounting Thought*. Huntington, NY: Robert E. Krieger Publishing Co.

COENENBERG, A. G., and SCHOENFELD, H. M. W. (1990). "The Development of Managerial Accounting in Germany". *Accounting Historians Journal*, 17/2: 95–112.

COOKE, T. E. (1991). "The Evolution of Financial Reporting in Japan". *Accounting, Business and Financial History*, 1/3: 251–77.

COOPER, R., and KAPLAN, R. S. (1988). "How Cost Accounting Distorts Product Costs". *Management Accounting*, Apr.: 20–7.

EDWARDS, J. R., and BOYNS, T. (1992). "Industrial Organization and Accounting Innovation: Charcoal Ironmaking in England 1690–1783". *Management Accounting Review*, 3: 151–69.

————— and MATTHEWS, M. (2003). "Costing, Pricing and Politics in the British Steel Industry, 1918–1967". *Management Accounting Review*, 14: 25–49.

FEAR, J. (2005). *Organizing Control: From August Thyssen to Heinrich Dinkelbach*. Harvard: Harvard University Press.

FLEISCHMAN, R. K. (2000). "Completing the Triangle: Taylorism and the Paradigms". *Accounting, Audit and Accountability Journal*, 13/5: 597–623.

——— and PARKER, L. D. (1990). "Managerial Accounting Early in the British Industrial Revolution: The Carron Company, A Case Study". *Accounting and Business Research*, summer: 211–21.

——— and TYSON, T. N. (1999). "Opportunity Lost? Chances for Cost Accountants' Professionalization under the National Industrial Recovery Act of 1933". *Accounting, Business and Financial History*, 9/1: 51–75.

GARNER, S. P. (1954). *Evolution of Cost Accounting to 1925*. Alabama: University of Alabama Press.

GORMLY, C., and WELLS, M. C. (1992). "Costing Activities: Alternative Views of History", in A. Tsuji (ed.), *Collected Papers of the Sixth World Congress of Accounting Historians*. Tokyo: Japan Accounting History Association, 590–606.

HARRISON, G. C. (1930). *Standard Costs: Installation, Operation and Use*. New York: Ronald Press.

HOSKIN, K. W., and MACVE, R. H. (2000). "Knowing More as Knowing Less? Alternative Histories of Cost and Management Accounting in the U.S. and the U.K.". *Accounting Historians Journal*, 27/1: 91–149.

INNES, J., MITCHELL, F., and SINCLAIR, D. (2000). "Activity-Based Costing in the U.K.'s Largest Companies: A Comparison of 1994 and 1999 Survey Results". *Management Accounting Research*, 11: 349–62.

ISRAELSEN, P., ANDERSEN, M, ROHDE, C., and SORENSEN, P. E. (1996). "Management Accounting in Denmark: Theory and Practice", in Bhimani (1996), 31–53.

JOHNSON, H. T. (2002). "A Former Management Accountant Reflects on his Journey through the World of Cost Management". *Accounting History*, new series, 7/1: 9–21.

——— and KAPLAN, R. S. (1987). *Relevance Lost: The Rise and Fall of Management Accounting*. Boston: Harvard Business School Press.

JONES, H. (1985). *Accounting, Costing and Cost Estimation*. Cardiff: University of Wales Press.

JÖNSSON, S. (1996). "Accounting and Business Economics Traditions in Sweden". *European Accounting Review*, 5/3: 435–48.

JUN LIN, Z., and YU, Z. (2002). "Responsibility Cost Control System in China: A Case of Management Accounting Application". *Management Accounting Research*, 13: 447–67.

KIKUYA, M. (2001). "International Harmonization of Japanese Accounting Standards". *Accounting, Business and Financial History*, 11/3: 349–68.

KIMIZUKA, Y. (1991). "The Evolution of Japanese Cost Accounting to 1945", in O. F. Graves (ed.), *The Costing Heritage: Studies in Honor of S. Paul Garner*. Harrisonburg, Va.: The Academy of Accounting Historians.

LEBAS, M. (1994). "Managerial Accounting in France: Overview of Past Tradition and Current Practice". *European Accounting Review*, 3/3: 471–87.

LOFT, A. (1986). "Towards a Critical Understanding of Accounting: The Case of Cost Accounting in the UK, 1914–1925". *Accounting, Organizations and Society*, 11/2: 137–69.

——— (1990). *Coming into the Light: A Study of the Development of a Professional Association for Cost Accountants in Britain in the Wake of the First World War*. London: Chartered Institute of Management Accountants.

MACINTOSH, N. B. (1998). "Management Accounting in Europe: A View from Canada". *Management Accounting Review*, 9: 495–500.

MCKENDRICK, N. (1970). 'Josiah Wedgwood and Cost Accounting in the Industrial Revolution". *Economic History Review*, 2nd series, 23: 45–67.

MARPLE, R. P. (ed.) (1965). *National Association of Accountants on Direct Costing*. New York: Ronald Press.

MILLER, P., and NAPIER, C. J. (1993). "Genealogies of Calculation". *Accounting, Organizations and Society*, 18/7–8: 631–47.

MONDEN, Y., and HAMADA, K. (2000). "Target Costing and Kaizen Costing in Japanese Automobile Companies", in Y. Monden (ed.), *Japanese Cost Management*. London: Imperial College Press, 99–122.

NICB (1931). *Budgetary Control in Manufacturing Industry*. New York: National Industrial Conference Board.

NIKITIN, M. (1992). "La naissance de la comptabilité industrielle en France". Doctoral thesis. Paris Dauphine University.

NOBES, C. and PARKER, R. H. (2004). *Comparative International Accounting*, 8th edn. Harlow: FT Prentice Hall.

PHES (1965). *Encyclopedia of Cost Accounting Systems*. Englewood Cliffs, NJ: Prentice Hall.

POLLARD, S. (1968). *The Genesis of Modern Management*. Harmondsworth: Penguin.

PORTER, D. M. (1980). "The Waltham System and Early American Textile Cost Accounting 1813–1848". *Accounting Historians Journal*, spring: 1–15.

PREVITS, G. J., and MERINO, B. D. (1998). *A History of Accountancy in the United States. The Cultural Significance of Accounting*. Columbus, Oh.: Ohio State University Press.

RICHARD, J. (1995a). "The Evolution of Accounting Chart Models in Europe from 1900 to 1945: Some Historical Elements". *European Accounting Review*, 4/1: 87–124.

——— (1995b). "The Evolution of the Romanian and Russian Accounting Charts after the Collapse of the Communist System". *European Accounting Review*, 4/2: 305–22.

SCAPENS, R. W. (1991). *Management Accounting: A Review of Recent Developments*. London: Macmillan.

SCHERRER, G. (1996). "Management Accounting: A German Perspective", in Bhimani (1996), 100–22.

SCHWEITZER, M. (2000). "The Significance of Production and Cost Theory for Costing Systems in the 19th and 20th Centuries", in *Accounting and History*. Madrid: AECA, 285–95.

SCRANTON, P. (1997). *Endless Novelty: Specialty Production and American Industrialization, 1865–1925*. Princeton, NJ: Princeton University Press.

SHIELDS, M. D. (1998). "Management Accounting Practices in Europe: A Perspective from the States". *Management Accounting Research*, 9: 501–13.

SIMON, H. A., GUETZKOW, H., KOZMETSKY, G., and TYNDALL, G. (1954). *Centralisation vs Decentralisation in Organising the Controller's Department*. New York: Controllership Foundation.

SOLOMONS, D. (1952). *Studies in Costing*. London: Sweet and Maxwell.

SOWELL, E. M. (1973). *The Evolution of Theories and Techniques of Standard Costs*. Tuscaloosa: University of Alabama Press.

STAUBUS, G. J. (1971). *Activity Costing and Input-Output Accounting*. Homewood, Ill.: Irwin.

STONE, W. E. (1973). "An Early English Cotton Mill Cost Accounting System: Charlton Mills, 1810–1889". *Accounting and Business Research*, winter: 71–8.

THORELL, P., and WHITTINGTON, G. (1994). "The Harmonization of Accounting within the EU: Problems, Perspectives and Strategies". *European Accounting Review*, 3/2: 215–39.

TYSON, T. (1992). "The Nature and Environment of Cost Management among Early Nineteenth Century US Textile Manufacturers". *Accounting Historians Journal*, fall: 1–24.

—— (1996). "The Impact of Advancements in Manufacturing and Information Technology on Management Accounting Systems", in T. A. Lee, A. Bishop, and R. H. Parker (eds.), *Accounting History from the Renaissance to the Present*. London: Garland Publishing, 143–65.

WALTON, P. (1993). "Company Law and Accounting in Nineteenth Century Europe: Introduction". *European Accounting Review*, 2: 286–91.

WELLS, M. C. (1978). *Accounting for Common Costs*. Urbana, Ill.: University of Illinois.

YAMEY, B. S. (1994). "Accounting in History". *European Accounting Review*, 3/2: 375–80.

YATES, J. (1989). *Control through Communication: The Rise of System in American Management*. Baltimore: Johns Hopkins University Press.

YOSHIKAWA, T. (2001). "Cost Accounting Standard and Cost Accounting Systems in Japan: Lessons from the Past—Recovering Lost Traditions". *Accounting, Business and Financial History*, 11/3: 269–81.

—— MITCHELL, F., and MOYES, J. (1994). *A Review of Japanese Management Accounting Literature and Bibliography*. London: CIMA.

ZIMNOVITCH, H. (1997). "Les calculs du prix de revient dans la seconde industrialisation en France". Doctoral thesis, Poitiers University.

CHAPTER 20

....

CORPORATE GOVERNANCE

....

GARY HERRIGEL

20.1 INTRODUCTION

....

THE history of corporate governance arrangements, understood as the constitutive processes shaping the relationship between ownership and management of enterprises, is a relatively new field of inquiry for business historians.[1] Indeed, most of the recent historiography has been written by non-historians (especially economists and legal scholars) concerned with tracing the roots of contemporary corporate governance regimes. The historical core of this literature focuses on the origins of dispersed (Anglo-American) and concentrated ownership systems, together with the financial and political factors that shaped different development paths. The arguments advanced by these scholars and the debates they have generated are highly stimulating—if, as we shall see, largely unresolved. They underscore the centrality of corporate governance not only for understanding the historical dynamics of firm performance and economic development, but also for understanding the co-evolution of the corporation with modern ideas of political and legal order.

What follows is a survey of historical arguments about the origins of corporate governance regimes ranging across several disciplines, in particular economics, legal studies, sociology, political science, and, in a few cases, business history.

---

[1] Notable exceptions include Fohlin (1997, 2000, 2005), Lamoreaux (1995, 2004), Lamoreaux and Rosenthal (2004), Lipartito (2004), and Dunlavy (2004).

The chapter begins by outlining the historical evolution of corporate governance systems in five major countries: the United States, Britain, Germany, France, and Japan. Section 20.3 then examines the major causal arguments advanced to account for diachronic variations within the country cases as well as synchronic variations between them. It will become clear that the debate is largely unresolved. In particular, problems emerge in attempting to account for the emergence and evolution of the different systems over time.

The chapter concludes with a discussion of what the current literature on the history of corporate governance does not tell us. By this I mean not only those issues that remain open or are raised by the existing work. I will also highlight some empirically significant phenomena obscured by the framework of the current debate and suggest some ways in which their reintegration may provide greater purchase on the problems of transformation and recomposition thrown up by the debate itself. Here, some insights of an older historical literature on corporate governance will be discussed. A central conclusion is that the entire contemporary debate could benefit from more careful archival scholarship on the development of corporate governance regimes across the major countries.

20.2 FIVE CORPORATE GOVERNANCE REGIMES

Contemporary discussions of corporate governance focus on relations between ownership and management within joint-stock, limited-liability, publicly held, predominantly large-scale enterprises. This focus centers attention on the balance of power between share owners and managers, together with the consequences of that balance for enterprise performance. The literature has generated two ideal-typical property systems, based on concentrated and dispersed ownership respectively. The "concentrated ownership system" is "characterized by controlling blockholders, weak securities markets, high private benefits of control, and low disclosure and market transparency standards, with only a modest role played by the market for corporate control, but with a possibly substitutionary monitoring role played by large banks". The "dispersed ownership system" is characterized "by strong securities markets, rigorous disclosure standards, and high market transparency, in which the market for corporate control constitutes the ultimate disciplinary mechanism" (Coffee 2000: 2).

Countries can be organized around the concentrated versus dispersed ownership distinction. But most of the literature also argues that the system of corporate property relations in each country is embedded in a broader set of social, institutional, and power arrangements. In particular, three institutional domains and groups of actors are held to shape the nature of corporate property relations: financial systems (e.g. bank- versus market-driven[2]); the governance role of stakeholders versus stockholders;[3] and the political governance of the economy (e.g. state-directed, associational, or market-driven[4]).

As we shall see in Section 20.3, different authors place varying emphases on the degree of integration between the levels of corporate governance, the financial system, stakeholder rights, and political authority. But most use each of these as empirical components in constructing contrasting national models of corporate governance. The following portraits of the United States, UK, France, Germany, and Japan, therefore, will be structured by their location in relation to these four dimensions.

The United States is typically portrayed in contemporary corporate governance debates as the paradigmatic liberal economy where financing is based on well-developed and highly liquid securities markets, enterprise stock is widely dispersed, managers seek to maximize shareholder value, and the government allows market relations to drive the economy by strongly defending the rules of contract and the rights of property—in particular of minority interests within joint-stock companies. But this system did not always exist in its present form. When unrestricted incorporation and limited liability became available in the mid-nineteenth century, closely held family firms dominated the corporate form (Roy 1997; Horwitz 1977; Hovenkamp 1991). This gradually gave way to dispersed ownership during the first half of the twentieth century, as the securities markets grew more robust and managerial control of enterprises solidified (Chandler 1977; O'Sullivan 2000; Navin and Sears 1955).

American banking was very regionally decentralized and fragmented. Many of its activities originally revolved around the financing of trade. Banks played a very small and never more than short-term role in industrial finance in the nineteenth century. To the extent that they utilized external finance, young American corporations relied on bond issues (Calomiris 1995). There were efforts to construct universal banking arrangements (involving both commercial and investment roles), allowing financial institutions to take equity stakes and intervene more directly in the internal governance of firms (DeLong 1991). But these experiments co-existed with increasingly liquid securities markets and were, finally, legally constrained in the 1930s by the Glass–Steagall Act institutionalizing specialized banking (Kroszner and Rajan 1994).

---

[2] Other relevant distinctions in financial systems are those between specialized and universal banking and arm's-length and relational banking. For general discussions see Rajan (1992), Boot (2000), Mayer (1988), Verdier (2002), and Lescure (this volume).

[3] For overviews of this enormous debate, and a defense of stockholder over stakeholder systems, see Hansmann (1996) and Blair (1995).

[4] See Hansmann (1996); Hall and Soskice (2001); Whitley (1999); Rajan and Zingales (2003*a* and 2003*b*).

Stakeholder views, especially in the guise of movements for manager autonomy, competed with stockholder views for much of the mid-twentieth century. Collective bargaining also regulated labor markets in important industrial sectors for much of this period, but stopped well short of union involvement in corporate governance. The government experimented with stronger forms of interventionism and collaboration with corporations and business associations during much of the Progressive and, especially, New Deal eras. But these mechanisms of intervention have been receding since the 1980s (Kaufman and Zacharias 1992; O'Sullivan 2000; Hansmann 1996; Kochan *et al.* 1986; Jacoby 1997).

Britain's corporate governance regime is portrayed in contemporary accounts as resembling that of the United States. But the history of British corporate governance is actually quite divergent from that in the United States. Indeed, unlike Americans, Britons were very skeptical about limited liability for much of the nineteenth century. Once adopted, moreover, closely held family firms dominated the joint-stock company form for a much longer period of time than in the United States. Not until the 1930s and a subsequent succession of merger waves, did dispersed ownership begin to predominate (Cheffins 2001, 2002, 2004; Toms and Wright 2002; Franks *et al.* 2004*a* and 2004*b*; Hannah 1982).

Corporate finance in Britain has always been characterized by specialized banking, with a clear distinction between commercial and investment roles. The absence of universal banks, however, does not mean that bank–industry relations were purely arm's-length. On the contrary, long-term and often quite intimate relations frequently prevailed between commercial bankers and their clients. Close, performance-monitoring ties were produced and reproduced through cooperatively constructed short-term contracts—loans, overdrafts, etc. But this "relationality" in British banking stopped short of the strong form engaged in by continental universal banks: British banks did not become involved in the transfer of property and never strategically sought ownership stakes in their clients (though stock was sometimes accepted as collateral for loans). Securities markets were significant but often little utilized by domestic firms for much of the early period of industrialization. The London capital market grew significantly in both depth and liquidity over the course of the twentieth century (Ross 1996; Collins 1998; Capie and Collins 1999; Fohlin 1997).

There is ambivalence in British corporate history about stakeholder rights. Labour governments supported unionization and worker rights relative to corporate actors for much of the twentieth century. Moreover, during the mid-twentieth century there were numerous nationalizations after which companies were run in stakeholders' interests, rather than according to strict market criteria (Cheffins 2001, 2002). This stakeholderism has declined since the 1980s, as privatization and merger were accompanied by the dispersal of stock ownership and political struggles weakened the labor movement.

France presents in many ways the greatest contrast with the US and British cases, due to the strong role of the state. During the nineteenth and early twentieth centuries, there were very few large corporations in France. Those that did exist were closely held. In large part, these firms financed investment from earnings and engaged with banks only for short-term loans. Relational banking (in the sense of banks holding equity stakes in firms) was rare. Like the British, French banks maintained a specialized divide between commercial and investment functions. Similarly, the securities market was used, particularly in the 1920s, but it was not a significant factor in corporate finance (Fridenson 1997; Lévy-Leboyer 1978; Fohlen 1978; Murphy 2004).

But the most distinctive aspect of French development is the state's extremely strong role in enterprise governance, especially after 1945. Beginning around World War I, the French state began to encourage the development of "national champions" in strategic industries—channeling capital to firms and acting as their major customers. After World War II, this role increased as national plans were developed, banks and firms were nationalized, and public influence was exercised both directly and indirectly on the composition of boards and corporate investment strategies. The stock market atrophied and firms became dependent on state-underwritten bank debt (Berger 1981; Zysman 1983; Cohen 1969; Hall 1986). In this context, however, the number of public corporate enterprises proliferated. Given the state's prominent influence, corporate managers directed their enterprises towards stakeholder rather than stockholder interests. Despite the proliferation of large corporations in the postwar period, ownership remained concentrated, not only because of the importance of public enterprises, but also because managers engaged in significant cross-shareholding. The rights of minority holders were not well protected in French corporate law. Since the mid-1980s, following important financial system reforms, a series of major self-dealing scandals involving prominent managers and state officials, and pressures from the European Union to reduce the economic role of the state, French corporations have become more exposed to market pressures. The size and role of the stock market has increased and shareholding has gradually become more dispersed (Hancke 2002; MacClean 1999; Fanto 1995; O'Sullivan 2003).

Even earlier than in the United States, large-scale corporate enterprises played a prominent role in *Germany*'s industrialization (Kocka 1978; Dornseifer and Kocka 1993). Liberalization of incorporation law occurred in 1870 and was then reformed in 1884. Germans enthusiastically took to limited liability and the joint-stock company form—though the former principle was much more broadly embraced than the latter (Jackson 2001; Fohlin 2005). German enthusiasm for the joint-stock form was significant even though German law was ambivalent with respect to minority shareholder protections (Schubert and Hommelhoff 1985; Cheffins 2003; Fohlin 2005). In any case, there was space in the German economy, at least prior to World War II, for a variety of corporate governance forms. Closely held family enterprises

have predominated in the German political economy since the beginning of industrialization. But their share of all joint-stock companies gradually declined
between 1884 and 1933, restabilized after 1945, and began to decline again only in
the 1990s. The decline of family ownership before 1933 was also accompanied by
a gradual dispersal of shareholdings. But this trend was radically reversed after
1945, as concentrated holdings came to dominate the ownership structures of the
100 largest firms. Cross-shareholding, especially after 1945, became an important
form of concentrated ownership (Fohlin 2005; Jackson 2001; Franks and Mayer
2001; Faccio and Lang 2002).

From the beginning of industrialization, German finance was bank-driven and
universal banking was the norm (Gerschenkron 1962). Banks extended loans and
credits, provided bridging finance, facilitated the transfer of ownership (securities
underwriting) and participated in corporate governance through both the exercise
of shareholders' proxy votes and direct equity holdings. Despite the existence of
these broad capacities, strong bank participation in corporate governance was
a dominant feature of the German landscape only during the first few decades
after World War II and began to weaken in the 1990s. This is not to say that
there was no strong relationality between banks and industry in Germany before
World War II. But it was less common than is often believed. Indeed, nineteenth
and early twentieth-century firms seldom relied on bank debt for financing and
banks seldom took significant equity stakes in their clients (Fohlin 2005; Vitols
2001; Collins 1998). Indeed, recent research suggests that securities comprised a
lower percentage of German than British banks' assets prior to World War I—
though unlike their British counterparts, German banks tended to take strategic
advantage of ownership stakes when they had them (Fohlin 2005). Strikingly, given
the breadth of bank capacities, financial institutions lived in apparent harmony with
relatively, deep, active, and efficient securities markets prior to 1914 (Gehrig and
Fohlin 2004). Political turbulence and shifts in the power of universal banks led
to reduced significance for securities markets in the twentieth century, particularly
after 1945 (Fohlin 2005; Rajan and Zingales 2003b).

Stakeholders have traditionally played an important role in German corporate
governance. When banks held positions of internal influence within German firms,
they constituted a stakeholder interest that shaped the character of management
calculation. This was always the case among widely held firms and it became more
generally true during the first few decades after World War II (Fohlin 2005). Even
broader attention to stakeholders was written into the obligations of enterprise
management after 1945 by co-determination legislation requiring labor representation on the supervisory boards of all corporations employing a minimum number
of people (Jackson 2001; Streeck 1984). Enterprise managers' obligation to conduct
business in the interest of stakeholders not otherwise defined was also written into
the postwar West German Constitution (Article 14, Paragraph 2 of the Basic Law—
see Jackson 2001).

Except for the twelve-year interlude of centralized National Socialist dictatorship, the German state has been federally organized with highly fragmented authority and a small central bureaucracy oriented toward the protection of market order (as opposed to free markets) and the coordination of public associational debate (Katzenstein 1987). Prior to 1918, this was done quasi-democratically with a systematic bias toward organized property groups (including joint-stock enterprises). During the Weimar Republic, liberal and democratic norms governed the state's relations with associations, but without formally conceding to them any public authority. The liberal democratic Federal Republic formalized many of those concessions of public authority and relied more comfortably on associational governance. Associations representing property owners, employers, and employees play a significant governance role within the German economy, organizing wage determination, the development of training curricula, standards setting, and the organization of political debates regarding industrial and economic policies (Streeck and Yamamura 2001; Jackson 2001; Thelen 2004).

As in France, Britain, and the United States, there has been a movement, beginning in Germany in the 1990s, toward greater dispersal of holdings, less relationality in banking, more liquidity in securities markets, greater attention to shareholder value, and more emphasis on market solutions to public problems. The full implications of current changes, however, remain ambiguous and uncertain (Streeck and Höpner 2003; Höpner 2001). Intriguingly, Fohlin (2005) points out that current trends suggest a return to the pre-1933 (or even pre-1913) norm in corporate governance.

Corporate governance in *Japan* has a distinctive history, with a caesura in the mid-twentieth century caused by the experiences of imperialism, war, defeat, and occupation. Prior to the militarization of Japan in the 1930s, there were three different patterns of corporate governance. The dominant pattern involved broadly held joint-stock companies, supported by highly liquid securities markets, headed by professional management directing their companies in the interest of shareholders (Hoshi and Kashyap 2001). Another pattern involved state ownership of enterprise where professional bureaucratic managers pursued public economic development goals (Samuels 1994). A third involved a limited partnership holding company structure where family owners controlled diversified networks of publicly quoted enterprises, run by professional management known as *zaibatsu* (Morikawa 1992). Interestingly, Japanese corporate law reflected this fragmentation of development paths in that it was both protective of and hostile to minority property interests (Morck and Nakamura 2003).

The financial sector remained very diversified and securities far outweighed bank lending as a source for industrial finance until the 1930s. Banks engaged in specialized arm's-length, mostly short-term lending. Relational banking did not exist, though there were some *zaibatsu* banks with very close relationships to *zaibatsu* holdings. But these relationships were not monitoring ones; nor were *zaibatsu* banks the primary sources of finance for the *zaibatsu*. In prewar Japan, professional managers directed enterprises in shareholders' rather than stakeholders' interests— with the exception of state-owned enterprises, which pursued national economic development goals. Thus the state was a significant presence in the prewar Japanese corporate economy, but it did not dominate or even remotely direct vast reaches of the private sector. Beyond its (significant) direct holdings, the state governed the economy by establishing framework rules for private actors (in many cases adopting and adapting foreign models for public education, limited liability, stock ownership, law, etc.) (Morikawa 1986; Samuels 1994; Hoshi and Kashyap 2001; Morck and Nakamura 2003).

This system was completely transformed in the mid-twentieth century by the turbulent course of military government, war, occupation, and then economic recovery. Key changes occurred on each of the four dimensions relevant to corporate governance. First, the robust securities markets of the prewar era were destroyed by a military government hostile to private economic interests. A variety of laws taxing private stockholdings and outlawing dividends, combined with efforts by the state to use banks to direct investment shifted enterprise finance away from securities toward banks. This bank centrality was reproduced in the postwar economy, though the state's role in directing bank lending and corporate investment became more indirect (Hoshi and Kashyap 2001; Vitols 2001; Morck and Nakamura 2003).

The second change was the growth of inter-corporate shareholding. After Japan's defeat, the occupation authorities forced the titular new Japanese government to pass a series of laws disbanding the *zaibatsu*, expropriating their family owners, outlawing holding companies, protecting minority stockholders, and establishing guidelines for accounting transparency, auditing, and depreciation (Hoshi and Kashyap 2001; Morck and Nakamura 2003). Such measures, followed by an inflation that devalued the price of existing stock, produced an active market for corporate control, which in turn led managers to purchase substantial shares in related and friendly companies in order to stave off takeovers. Over the course of the 1950s and 1960s, this produced loosely interconnected *keiretsu* in which related firms owned small amounts of shares in one another. Such holdings were often small, but they summed up to a majority stake in the group by its own members—making it difficult for outsiders to gain a foothold (Okazaki 1995; Sheard 1994).

Banks were crucial players in the governance of these interconnected enterprise groups. Though each group borrowed from a variety of banks, they ultimately relied on a "main bank" to coordinate their financing. Main banks in many ways made the inter-corporate shareholding strategy work as a defense against takeovers, since the new *keiretsu* were not formally directed by a central administration. Main banks could coordinate the strategic development of member firms and mobilize disparate stakes in the event of an outside challenge. They also used their central position as credit-givers to monitor *keiretsu* firms and took responsibility for directing restructuring efforts within member enterprises in the event of a crisis (Aoki and Patrick 1994).

The third significant change in the postwar corporate governance regime was the growth of employees as acknowledged stakeholders in Japanese enterprises. The crucial mechanism for this was the "institution" of permanent lifetime employment. Although employment contracts were formally "at will", Japanese courts nonetheless developed case-law decisions penalizing large enterprises when they attempted to lay off "regular" employees. As a result, enterprise managers were practically compelled to manage their firms in the interest of shareholders, bankers, and employees (Jackson 2001; Aoki 1988).

The final significant mid-century transformation in the Japanese corporate governance regime concerned the role of the state. The 1930s military government centrally directed corporate investment through the destruction of the securities market and control of the banks. In the postwar period, government control over banks became more indirect, but nonetheless remained significant. The Ministry of Finance rewarded banks which fostered investment in directions favored by state economic development policies and penalized bank measures that contravened them. This linkage between the public and private sector was reinforced through the effective abolition of the national corporate bond market. With their stock bound up in highly complicated cross-shareholdings, postwar Japanese enterprises— unlike their prewar predecessors—were overwhelmingly dependent on the banking system for finance. And the Japanese state was in a very strong position to direct the flow of investment funds from banks (Hoshi and Kashyap 2001).

As in the other cases, this system came under pressure in the 1990s, due to the globalization of financial markets and internal distress in the Japanese economy. As in the other cases, too, the future direction of change is both ambiguous and uncertain (Hoshi and Kashyap 2001).

The preceding narratives organize the history of corporate governance in all five countries in terms of the categories that have shaped contemporary scholarly discussion. These narratives show how difficult it is to identify countries consistently as stable "dispersed shareholder" or "concentrated shareholder" systems. There is enormous variation and change over time in the way in which the analytical categories of corporate governance studies fit the cases. At best, the United States and the UK can be coded as dispersed ownership, or outsider, systems for the post-1980s period, while France, Germany, and Japan plausibly approximate concentrated ownership, or insider, systems during the postwar period. Germany differs from France and Japan in that the latter two have a stronger role for the state, while Germany (excepting the Nazi interlude) has an associational regime. The non-Anglo-American countries were substantially stable from the late 1950s through the early 1990s, but before and after that period, the range of variation within each model is considerable.

20.3 Explaining Variation within and across Cases

The corporate governance literature has generated a number of competing arguments to account for the different regime patterns identified in the previous section. All the explanations have strengths and weaknesses and nearly all involve some sort of historical argument. None, however, completely succeeds in developing an explanation that can account for both the full variation within the national cases as well as the differences in contemporary regime types.

Alfred Chandler is the most prominent business historian in current debates on national variations in corporate governance (Chandler 1977, 1988a, 1988b, 1990). Ironically, Chandler's many writings do not focus primarily on corporate governance. Rather he makes claims about the evolution of governance arrangements as part of his larger explanatory project about the development of the modern corporate enterprise in the United States, Britain, and Germany. For Chandler, governance forms change with the endogenous development of the corporation as an organizational response to the expansion of markets. Specifically, he claims that increasing capital requirements (associated with growth in scale and scope of enterprise) lead to the separation of ownership and control and to the dispersal of ownership.

Chandler presents an ideal-typical development trajectory, driven by technology, management complexity, and market expansion, in which corporate organization evolves through three stages: from personal or family, through financial or entrepreneurial, to managerial enterprises. The nature of corporate governance differs at each stage: families both own and manage enterprises in the first stage, while in the second stage, in response to growing scale and complexity, they begin to cede control to professional managers. Family owners also bring in outside investors, especially bankers, to governing board positions in the firm to cover the costs of expansion. Here management and ownership still remain linked—family owners and their bankers can participate in strategic decision-making as well as monitoring operational management. In the final stage, however, the scale and scope of enterprise become so immense, expensive, and complex that owners (and creditors) become fully detached from any realistic internal monitoring role. Owners become a kind of "rentier" (Chandler 1988a). Ownership thus became progressively dispersed within individual enterprises as managers sought to raise funds from broad sources to sustain expansion and owners diversified their investments. Ultimately for Chandler, the capital requirements generated by increasing enterprise scale led to the dispersal of ownership in securities markets.

Chandler accounts for national differences in corporate governance arrangements by suggesting that open markets and political support for competition allow his ideal model to "naturally" unfold, while smaller, politically limited markets blocked the natural process of corporate development. For him, the fact that the United States had already achieved the modern corporate form by the beginning of the twentieth century was a reflection of the size and openness of US markets and America's political commitment to competition. Similarly, the fact that Britain remained mired in the initial "personal" capitalism phase of corporate development, while Germany managed to attain only the intermediate "financial" phase, also reflected the limited size and political and cultural commitments to competition in those domestic markets. Once the barriers to openness and competition were lifted in the post-1945 period, Chandler argues that corporations in both societies began to abandon commitments to family and inter-firm cooperation and move toward the (American) ideal. "The historical story suggests that the modern business enterprise was the more 'natural' response to the technological and marketing imperatives of modern mass urban and industrial societies and that interagency agreements were more of a transitional form" (Chandler 1988*b*).

Whatever the many strengths of the broader Chandlerian view of corporate development, his specific argument about the evolution of governance forms is very weak. Chandler repeatedly assumes that large-scale capital needs led to the dispersion of ownership through the securities markets. But most evidence on corporate expansion in the late nineteenth and early twentieth centuries emphasizes that growth in both the United States and Europe was typically financed by retained earnings rather than through bank lending or the issuing of securities (O'Sullivan 2000; Fohlin 2005; Feldenkirchen 1991). Moreover, Britain, Germany, and Japan had much higher market capitalizations than the Unites States, even as late as 1913 (Rajan and Zingales 2003*b*). Owners in other words were not forced to dilute their interests in American firms *because* they could not otherwise expand their enterprises. Likewise, British and German (and French and Japanese) owners did not retain controlling stakes in their firms simply *because* their capital needs were not as deep as those of their American competitors. Something else is required to account for the observed differences in governance patterns.

The literature outside business history on corporate governance has supplied a broad array of alternative explanations for why a dispersed ownership system emerged in the United States, and then later in Britain, while more concentrated systems prevailed in France, Germany, and Japan. Three types of explanation dominate the current literature: those emphasizing political differences among countries, those emphasizing differences in legal structure, and those emphasizing the power of class or social factions in shaping corporate governance regimes.

Mark Roe (1994, 2002, 2003) argues most prominently for the importance of political factors in the emergence of distinctive corporate governance regimes. He contends that strong political forces favoring stakeholders over private property rights produce concentrated holding systems, while weak political support for stakeholders allows for dispersion. The logic of the argument emphasizes managerial agency costs. When states support stakeholder interests, managers are forced to act against the interests of stock owners. In order to limit the extent to which private stock owner interests are compromised in this way, owners seek large controlling stakes and resist the separation of ownership and control. Such strategies, in turn, strengthen the hand of banks and weaken securities markets. Thus, in countries where stakeholders have political power, owners strategically keep their holdings very concentrated and dispersion is blocked. In societies in which there has been no significant political movement for the defense of stakeholders over private stock owner interests, Roe claims, indirect mechanisms for the control of managerial agency costs can develop—minority protections, transparency rules, independent fiduciary systems for monitoring, active securities markets, and markets for corporate control. Under such conditions, owners can diversify their holdings with less fear that dispersion will allow management to neglect their interests. Corporate growth under such political circumstances can follow the path Chandler suggested, where increasing capital needs are satisfied through the dispersion of ownership in the securities market.

Roe uses this general theory to construct particular historical stories to account for dispersed or concentrated ownership in each of the five countries. For the US case, he suggests that political concern to limit concentrated economic power— particularly that of financial institutions and labor—created a political and economic terrain where there were neither banking interests that could shepherd the development of closely held large corporations, nor socialist interests that might have sought to place limits on managerial decision-making. In Germany, Japan, and France, neither of these two conditions held. Large banks could shepherd the growth of the corporate sector, while labor (in Germany and Japan) and the state (in France) were able to achieve significant stakeholder rights. Responding to different managerial agency costs, Roe argues that US owners allowed shareholdings to become dispersed while political power focused on legal and competitive mechanisms for the indirect control of managerial agency. By contrast, in Germany, France, and Japan owners sought to keep their holdings as concentrated as possible in order to control managers. This kept securities markets in those countries weak and improved the position of banks.

There are a number of problems with this elegant argument. First, the German economy between 1884 and 1914 had concentrated ownership and strong banks— but the latter were neither significant holders of corporate equity nor important lenders. They engaged in a broadly diversified array of financial activities, including underwriting new issues in what were at the time comparatively strong securities markets (Rajan and Zingales 2003b; Fohlin 2005). Moreover, legal protection for stock owners was also comparatively strong (Cheffins 2003). Thus, relations between concentrated ownership and strong banks existed long before significant labor stakeholder legislation was imposed on corporations. Indeed, during the first twenty years of joint-stock enterprise in Germany, there was a state-imposed ban on socialism and trade unions. The lifting of that law seems neither to have encouraged nor discouraged owners from changing the concentration of their holdings. The number of corporations in the economy steadily increased up to 1914, most remained closely held and relied on retained earnings for expansion, while an ever increasing minority grew to be more widely held (Fohlin 2005). The lack of stakeholder threat and the presence of functioning securities markets did not induce closely held German firms to expand by diluting ownership (or by increasing debt). Roe's explanation of increased concentration under such conditions relies on the assumption that dispersion is the preferred outcome for property owners and will naturally occur with growth, if not constrained. Pre-1914 Germany does not provide anything like unambiguous confirmation of this argument.

Roe's argument about the United States makes a similar assumption—in the absence of political constraints on dispersion, owners will cash out and diversify in the securities market. For Roe, there is an attractive securities market in the United States because the possibility of relational banking was eliminated by political concerns to limit financial power. Roe does not view the relatively modest size of the late nineteenth-century securities market and the absence of effective minority holder rights as an obstacle to dispersion. Yet if German owners did not (significantly) exercise the option to cash out when they were constrained neither by banks nor strong limits on the securities market, why did those factors induce American owners to act in the opposite way? Roe can't help us here—at least not without finer-grained historical evidence.

Finally, many have pointed out that Roe has a very difficult time accounting for the British case (Cheffins 2002; Franks *et al.* 2004*a*, 2004*b*). Britain, like the United States, never developed a tradition of strong (equity-based) relational banking, though there were no legal or political barriers to such practices. During the early twentieth century, despite a functional securities market, and the absence of relational banks and legal protections for stakeholders, British family owners kept their enterprise stakes and did not try to cash out and diversify their holdings. But when they did (gradually) begin to do so, Britain was ruled by a Labour government that energetically nationalized capital and imposed strong welfare measures on private firms. Thus, in Roe's terms, when the potential for the creation of indirect mechanisms to regulate managerial agency costs were perhaps even greater than they were in the United States, British owners did not take advantage. And when stakeholder threats to their interests became most acute, owners increasingly cashed out and allowed holdings to become dispersed. Clearly something other than Roe's argument about politics and managerial agency costs must be deployed to account for the historical emergence of dispersed and concentrated holding systems in many of these cases.

An alternative line of argument has emphasized legal differences among countries in explaining the propensity for either concentrated or dispersed ownership. The most prominent argument that "law matters" has been made by La Porta *et al.* (1997, 1998, 1999, 2000). These economists attribute differences in corporate governance regimes, in particular the dispersion or concentration in holdings and the robustness of markets for external finance, to the extent of legal protection for minority shareholders and creditors. They argue that common-law countries, such as the United States and Britain, have very strong protections for minority shareholders and creditors, while civil-law countries, such as Germany, France, and Japan, provide far fewer protections to minority shareholders or to creditors. The strength of these protections, and their enforcement, is the mechanism that accounts for the relative dispersion or concentration of holdings—and, indeed, the strength and depth of external finance possibilities more generally.

Because minority protection is very weak in Germany, Japan, and especially France, owners have many options for exercising control over minority holders. A market for securities does not develop and deepen in these countries because there is little incentive to take non-controlling stakes in companies, while there is great incentive for owners to protect themselves against unwanted takeover attempts. Similarly, because legal protections for creditors are weak, bond markets do not develop and banks seek close relations with their clients in order to monitor their investments effectively. The logic works in the opposite direction in common-law countries, where minority holdings and creditors have stronger protection and hence there is little penalty for taking smaller equity stakes and less reason for bankers to involve themselves directly in enterprise monitoring.

La Porta *et al.*'s argument does a good job of establishing a correlation between legal traditions and corporate governance regimes in the late twentieth century. But the explanatory mechanism they offer becomes questionable in light of the historical evolution of corporate governance in the five major cases considered above. Each of these countries had the same legal traditions throughout its industrial history, yet as we saw, the character of corporate governance (and the density of stockholdings) varied considerably within them over that period. Britain and Japan, in particular, experienced radical shifts in corporate governance arrangements without any significant change in their legal systems—at least not at the level of reliance on common versus civil law. Indeed, there are many empirical problems with the strong La Porta *et al.* claim. For example, in the United States and the UK dispersion of ownership significantly preceded the passage of strong minority rights protection statutes (Coffee 2001). The lack of legal minority protection seems, therefore, to have been an obstacle to the emergence of neither robust securities markets nor dispersed ownership. Something else must be at work in the evolution of corporate governance regimes than a simple difference in legal tradition and, specifically, the existence of strong legal protections of minority shareholders.

Brian Cheffins (2001, 2002, 2003, 2004) offers an alternative argument to account for the emergence of concentrated versus dispersed holdings systems that also emphasizes legal differences among countries. Cheffins notices the weaknesses in both Roe's political argument and the "law matters" thesis regarding minority protections. He argues that even in the absence of minority protections, dispersion can emerge if antitrust law favors horizontal merger over cooperation and investor sentiment is favorable toward securities, as can be seen from the cases of the early twentieth-century United States and late twentieth-century Britain. In the late nineteenth-century United States many industries were characterized by excessive competition and instability. Personal benefits of control were, as a result, very low for owners and they sought to reduce the level of competition (and instability). Since cooperation was legally difficult to achieve, firms thus sought to create market stability through horizontal merger.

In itself, Cheffins points out, such mergers did not require the dispersion of ownership. Block-holding by owners could still have been possible if after the merger the private benefits of control were high enough to divert owners from cashing out their holdings.[5] But in the US case, owners cashed out, Cheffins claims, because there was an enthusiastic market for corporate securities where a multitude of investors competed for stock. By selling into the market, investors could diversify their own investment risks. Cheffins notes that traditional securities markets in the nineteenth-century United States were very small and regarded as inappropriate for all but the most specialized investors. The new investor enthusiasm for securities at the end of the century, he suggests, was caused by a general contemporary optimism in the United States about the economy's future growth prospects. Such optimism had to do largely with the success of mergers themselves and with the public endorsement of them by prominent intermediaries, such as the Morgan Bank.

In the British case, mergers and investor sentiment took much longer to come together. During the early twentieth century, British mergers created holding companies rather than integrated new enterprises. This, Cheffins claims, allowed owners to retain their private control benefits. Moreover, even though there was investor interest in corporate securities, the market proved to be too unstable and as a result, unattractive to owners as an alternative location for their investments. Only in the 1960s, after laws stabilizing stock issues had quieted owner concerns and renewed equity enthusiasm emerged among investors, did stock begin to disperse in the merger wave that broke over the British economy between 1960 and the late 1980s (see also Franks *et al.* 2004a).

The difficulty in the argument concerns the moment when owners judge, after a merger, that cashing out is preferable to continued enjoyment of private control benefits. Cheffins introduces empirical examples in both the US and British cases showing that owners were interested in cashing out and that the happy existence of an enthusiastic market of investors afforded them that possibility. But it is not clear what caused those owners to prefer cashing out over continued private control. Cheffins suggests, logically enough, that continued holding increased owners' investment risk, while cashing out allowed them to spread that risk across the

---

[5] He also notes that merger was unnecessary for the dispersion of holdings in the United States. Ultimately, for Cheffins, merger is neither necessary nor sufficient as a cause of dispersal. It is an "agent of change" that creates the possibility for owners to cash out.

market. But this is only one of a number of ways that owners' investment risk can be diversified—others involve diversification and risk-spreading at the level of the firm and its products. Diversification at that level—which was occurring—could in principle reduce investor risk while affording a higher return than would be possible in a diversified securities portfolio. Why did owners choose cashing out over this alternative option?

Cheffins attempts to meet these questions by looking at the German case, but the (relative) failure of German owners to cash out only deepens the puzzle (Cheffins 2003). Germany did not experience merger waves of the order of those in either the early twentieth-century United States or the late twentieth-century Britain. Instead, around the same time as the great merger movement in the United States, German owners solved the market instability problems that produced merger elsewhere by entering into cartel and syndicate (*Konzern*) arrangements. Such arrangements, which stabilized producer markets, also consolidated owners' private control benefits. Corporate growth could in this way take place without eroding private control benefits relative to diversified securities portfolios.

Cheffins notices that his argument does not sufficiently resolve the puzzle. German owners in syndicates were exposed to the same problem of undiversified investment as owners within newly merged companies in the United States and Britain. Why didn't they also cash out? Cheffins notes that it can't be because there were no potential investors in the securities market. The German market for securities was both deep and active—there were continuous new listings throughout the period up to World War I, and, indeed, a significant jump in listings occurred during the period of cartelization. Moreover, he points out that investor protections in Germany were as strong as anywhere at the time. Why, then, did private benefits of control continue to be more attractive to owners than cashing out? Ultimately, Cheffins (following Schumpeter 1939) suggests that there was a cultural norm in Germany, particularly after the passage of the 1896 securities market law, discouraging gambling in the stock market. This norm, he suggests, kept investor enthusiasm for the stock market low and hence restricted owner opportunity to cash out.

But this claim (based on no other historical authority than a passing remark by Schumpeter) has all the hallmarks of an answer advanced because the question would otherwise remain open. It is easy to provide counter-examples of late nineteenth and early twentieth-century Germans who, unlike Schumpeter, discerned no norm discouraging speculative trading in the stock market. Georg Simmel's *Philosophie des Geldes* (1900), for example, argued that the modern capitalist economy in Germany was so depersonalized and objectified that it made decisions that ignored human ties and cultural norms not only possible, but increasingly the norm. The point, here, is not to suggest that Simmel is a better authority than Schumpeter, but rather to point out that in the existing state of research, the available evidence to support such a cultural argument is very contradictory. For all we know, German holdings stayed concentrated in the pre-1914 period not because there was no potentially enthusiastic market for their holdings, but rather because owners could make satisfactory profits and diversify their risks without selling off their assets. Until we know what was actually happening among German owners, Cheffins's argument linking dispersal to mergers and investor sentiment must be considered unproven.

A final set of arguments seeking to account for cross-national variations in the evolution of corporate governance arrangements, and particularly for the dispersal or non-dispersal of holdings, emphasizes the positive or negative role of well-positioned interest groups or classes. Here there are two prominent arguments in the literature, one by Raghuram Rajan and Luigi Zingales and the other by Mary O'Sullivan.

Like Chandler, Rajan and Zingales' (2003a, 2003b) argument about variation in corporate governance practices forms part of a larger argument—in their case, about the historical evolution of financial systems. They claim that openness to trade and cross-border capital flows creates pressure for financial market development: better law (e.g. minority protections, clear property rights, reliable enforcement), more transparency, more active and deeper securities markets. Under such conditions, competition from new entrants in domestic industrial and financial markets makes it difficult for large players to protect monopoly rents. Control in many directions—by large banks over credit markets, by large firms over product markets, by banks over firms, or even by owners over corporations—is undermined, and competitive and dynamic arm's-length market relations appear. On the other hand, when openness to trade and capital flows is compromised, then competition is lessened and "incumbent" players—large industrial firms and banks—can exploit their position to restrict the possibilities for new entrants into their markets and keep rents politically inflated. According to Rajan and Zingales, concentrated holdings, relational banking, bank-driven financial systems, etc. all result from structural conditions in which exposure to trade and mobile capital are limited and incumbent self-dealing is therefore successful.

The two economists apply this "political economy of financial development" to the history of twentieth-century financial systems and find that it accounts for many cases. In Japan, the decay of the securities market, the concentration of the banking system, the emergence of the "main bank system" and large-firm cross-shareholding all emerged between the 1930s and 1950s from efforts by the Japanese state and strong incumbent banking and industrial firms to limit domestic competition and centralize capital allocation and investment decisions in the context of restricted capital and trade flows. In a similar way, their structural argument offers a plausible if not always explicit explanation for the significant shift in bank control and shrinkage in the number of firms participating in the German securities market, as well as the capacity of the French state and industrial elites after 1945 to control both the capital market and large firms. In each case, incumbent actors exploited the absence of foreign competition in trade and capital markets to establish control and protect excessive rents. Similarly, as Japan, Germany, and France became more exposed to both capital and trade flows during the late twentieth century, incumbent groups' ability to protect their arrangements from the acid of competition declined. In particular, industrial firms, long hostage to financial control by domestic banks, eagerly exploited new financial openness to raise capital in international markets. As a result, all three economies became more open, and their corporate governance structures became more dispersed and arm's-length.

Suggestive as this argument is in accounting for the evolution of late twentieth-century financial systems, there are empirical problems in linking financial system development to variations in corporate governance. In particular, Rajan and Zingales' argument has great difficulty accounting for variations in corporate governance structures during the first half of the twentieth century. The authors present data for 1913 showing how surprisingly (from a twenty-first century perspective) financially developed and relatively economically open were both France and Germany. For example, they show that Germany and France had higher ratios of bank deposits to GDP, higher stock market capitalization as a percentage of GDP, and higher equity financing to fixed investment ratios in 1913 than did the United States (Rajan and Zingales 2003*b*). Such financial and legal "development", however, did not translate in those cases, as it did in the United States (and as Rajan and Zingales suggest it should) to dispersed holdings and an outside, arm's-length system of corporate governance. The persistence of concentrated holdings, despite structural conditions favoring competition and the free flow of capital, apparently has to be explained by something else. Dispersion of ownership, active securities markets and market-based financial systems are the result of more than simply the existence of free movement in goods and money across borders.

Mary O'Sullivan (2000) seeks to explain the dispersion of holdings in the United States by linking possibilities latent within the securities markets to power consolidation strategies on the part of managers. O'Sullivan points out, contra Chandler, that the modern business enterprise in the United States emerged prior to a market for industrial securities. In large part, the market for securities was created to negotiate managerial continuity within such enterprises as original owners retired and also to accommodate the fusion of property rights during the great late nineteenth-century merger wave. In both cases, stock was distributed within a very elite circle of investors. "Of the $6.2 billion of industrial common and preferred stock issued during the peak of the merger movement between 1898 and 1902" she writes, "only six percent . . . was sold to the general public" (O'Sullivan 2000: 75).

O'Sullivan suggests that the elite circle of stockholders, generally holders of preferred stock, behaved more like creditors than arm's-length investors. They also carefully monitored enterprises and, significantly, had the power to challenge management if dividend payments were missed. In reaction to this kind of relational dominance, O'Sullivan claims that managers of these newly public enterprises sought to dilute owners' power and insulate their own organizational authority by issuing common stock to the public, often without any voting rights. Ultimately, such practices were outlawed and replaced with clear rules regarding stock voting rights. Yet by that time stock had diffused so broadly that the effect of the new regulations simply legitimized stockholding and fostered even greater diffusion.

On this view, then, the diffusion of ownership in the United States did not emerge out of owner/investor diversification strategies to minimize risk—that is, from the structural condition of market openness. Rather, it resulted from systematic management efforts to dilute the power of stock owners through the creation of greater liquidity in the securities market. Dispersion emerged not out of a market logic, but out of an organizational power logic.

O'Sullivan's argument is empirically very powerful for the US case, yet it begs at least as many questions as it answers when placed in comparative perspective. Why were American mangers able to exploit the structural potential of the nascent securities market against relational owners, while German and Japanese managers seem rather to have worked together with major owners to enhance enterprise competitiveness in the context of comparably liquid markets? O'Sullivan's argument does a nice job of showing that the structural condition of market liquidity does not determine owners' investment strategies. But it does not account for (or appear even to notice)[6] the possibility that managerial interests are equally contingent and unconstrained by structure.

This survey demonstrates not only the creativity but also the deep irresolution of the contemporary debate on the historical development of cross-national variations in corporate governance. It remains unclear how to explain the observed patterns of dispersion and concentration in holdings, both across cases and within cases over time. Strikingly, the cases contain far greater heterogeneity in the pattern of holdings, the character of finance, and the role of stakeholders and government than the explanatory theories seem to be able to handle. It's a bit like a boy frantically using all his arms and legs in a fruitless effort to plug holes in a leaking dike. Seeming success in one area is contradicted by anomalous development in another.

20.4 CONCLUSIONS

The above analysis suggests that the key problem in trying to explain the origins of cross-national divergence in corporate governance is that the major national cases do not fall neatly into dispersed/outsider and concentrated/insider systems, either

---

[6] In her treatment of Germany, O'Sullivan (2000) attributes ownership concentration in Germany to relational bank control over enterprises—a position more recent literature has shown to be inaccurate.

over time or cross-sectionally. The five countries surveyed all include examples of dispersion and concentration, arm's-length and relational finance, and stockholder and stakeholder governance. The periods when the actual cases resemble pure system types are extremely fleeting—the last fifteen years in the United States and Britain resemble the outsider/dispersed holding model, while France, Germany, and Japan (in different ways) resembled the concentrated holding/insider model between 1945 and 1990. Otherwise, the cases display remarkable heterogeneity—stakeholderism and relationality in the United States, robust securities markets in pre-1914 Germany, Japan, and France. Moreover, improbable combinations abound—such as the particularly intimate role of German banks within corporations with dispersed ownership and more arm's-length ties to closely held corporations in the pre-1914 period, or the strong stakeholder commitments of diffusely held American corporations after 1945.

One reason the debate has trouble coping with this heterogeneity is that it is far too wedded to the unitary evolutionary sequence of organizational forms that is postulated in the Chandlerian model of corporate development: family firm, entrepreneurial firm, modern managerial enterprise. Virtually all the historical explanations discussed above cite Chandler for historical authority in their analysis. Even where they reject Chandler's specific causal arguments, they accept his postulated range of organizational possibilities as accurate descriptions of the economic-historical landscape. Within this unitary developmental trajectory, heterogeneity appears either as transitional or as an example of blockage.

But much recent work in business history, economic sociology, political economy, and business economics calls into question this reliance on the Chandlerian paradigm. The alternative literature argues that Chandler's typological framework blends out a broad range of organizational possibilities that are less hierarchical, more cooperative, and driven by bottom-up impulses. On this alternative account, the Chandlerian large-scale joint-stock enterprise is viewed as an historically specific entity that emerged at a specific historical moment (the late nineteenth and early twentieth century) under specific historical conditions, and largely in the United States. The conditions that sustained that corporate form were not present in nineteenth-century America; nor were they completely hegemonic even within the twentieth-century US economy (Berk 1994; Scranton 1997; Lamoreaux *et al.* 2004). Finally, they were very weakly present during much of European or Japanese industrialization (Sabel and Zeitlin 1997; Zeitlin, Chapter 10 this volume; Herrigel 1996; Fridenson 1997; Jones 1997); and they no longer seem to pertain in the contemporary global environment (Sabel 2005; Roberts 2004).

This alternative literature shows that where the conditions conducive to the emergence of the Chandlerian corporation were absent (or not hegemonic), alternative organizational forms emerged with different boundaries, value-generation processes, management structures, labor relations, contests for control, and possibilities for opportunism, etc. In short, alternative conditions produced very different governance dilemmas and structures within and across organizations. Moreover, the alternative literature argues that the evolution of governance practices within the large-scale Chandlerian enterprise, where and when it emerges, should be seen as co-evolving through encounters, discussions, and processes of experimentation with many other enterprise forms. Exchange, borrowing, and imitation across fields and nations expands the range of possibilities available to all actors and provides the material for innovation in governance practice (Zeitlin and Herrigel 2000). From this perspective, heterogeneity in governance forms within a given national economy is not a problem. It is an expression of a basic economic process—indeed, it is something that is constantly reproduced by that process itself.

Unfortunately, much like the Chandlerian tradition that it criticizes, this literature tends to focus on a broad array of organizational and relational problems of industrial order rather than on the internal problems of enterprise governance at the heart of the debates discussed above. An alternative literature specifically devoted to the analysis of historical heterogeneity in corporate governance has yet to emerge. The only historical literature that has an explicit concern for the heterogeneity of governance forms in the industrializing economy is nearly a century old. Not surprisingly, the German Historical School and British historical economists are most prominent in this older literature, but even American writers a century ago were concerned to systematically catalogue alternative governance arrangements.[7]

One prominent example of this older concern for heterogeneity can be found in a series of articles by Gustav Schmoller on the historical emergence of the corporation (Schmoller 1890*a*, 1890*b*, and 1890*c*). Schmoller surveyed a broad array of arrangements governing relations between owners, managers, and stakeholders ranging from manorial and household production systems (*oikos*) and producer cooperatives (*Genossenschaften*, *artels*), to the governance structures in early trading houses and shipping enterprises, guilds, and domestic putting-out systems. Schmoller focused on the ways power was allocated and value generation was controlled in these organizations. In the household economy, power was centralized and hierarchical. Efforts were made from the top of the hierarchy to direct and capture the value generated by the disparate production processes in the household. By contrast, cooperative arrangements avoided hierarchy, coordinated the flow of production collaboratively, and distributed rents across all participants (normally according to an agreed-upon formula).

Schmoller explored a wide array of possible variations on each of these governance forms: partnerships, profit-sharing arrangements, collective ownership, etc. In his view, this historical variety served as resources for governance experiments in the industrial economy emerging around him. Schmoller was fascinated by

---

[7]   Relevant texts include Scott (1910–12), Bauer (1936), Streider (1914), Balderston (1937), and Gilman (1889).

organizational plasticity and the range of possibilities for constituting relations among owners, workers, and managers in his own time. And he was acutely aware of the conceptual and practical interchange among organizational fields in the economy, society, and politics, as well as the constitution and continuous recomposition of organizational practices in economic life.[8]

One contemporary example of how consideration of alternative governance forms can illuminate peculiarities in the development of large corporate enterprises is a recent book by Koberg (1992) on the emergence of the "society with limited liability" in Germany and France (the GmbH and the SARL) during the late nineteenth and early twentieth centuries. This organizational form was conceived as a mechanism for achieving limited liability without the creation of a joint-stock enterprise. It required a contract and insisted on a very generally specified governance structure. But the intention was to facilitate a broad array of specific forms of governance—cooperative-egalitarian, family-autocratic, profit-sharing, passive participations etc.—under a limited-liability rubric without requiring the specific governance structures legally mandated of joint-stock companies.

Indeed, Koberg points out that calls for the creation of such a legal form of incorporation came strongly from cooperative enterprises and small and medium-sized family firms (SMEs). Both required additional capital to grow, but they were not attracted to the specific framework for governance imposed by German joint-stock enterprise law—cooperatives because they resisted hierarchy, and SMEs because they did not want to distribute authority away from the family. Passage of the new law allowed such firms to expand while avoiding becoming joint-stock enterprises. This alternative legal enterprise form was a notable success both in Germany and, later, in France. The GmbH and SARL forms quickly proliferated and soon massively outnumbered the joint-stock company and the simple partnership as a percentage of total enterprises in both economies. One implication of this study, of course, is that a major factor accounting for the comparatively low numbers of joint-stock enterprises in Germany and France, in both the past and the present, is that there were very attractive alternatives available to expanding companies which allowed them to govern themselves in a more congenial manner.

More of this kind of close historical work on the variety of legal and organizational mechanisms for the governance of industrial enterprise is plainly needed.[9] The existing corporate governance literature, even in its irresolution, has done a great deal to open questions about the range of organizational possibilities in

---

[8] Some of this spirit, though limited by a preoccupation with the Chandlerian paradigm, made its way into the work of Jürgen Kocka, who has repeatedly shown how the pre-existence of a robust bureaucracy in the Prussian state influenced the development of late nineteenth-century German large enterprises (Kocka 1978; Dornseifer and Kocka 1993). Lipartito (2004) is an interesting genealogical effort on the American side.

[9] See Lamoreaux (1995, 2004) and Lamoreaux and Rosenthal (2004) for interesting efforts in this direction in the United States.

industrial economies both past and present. But it will only be possible to advance
the debate if stereotyped national models are put to one side and researchers seek
to explore the range of viable possible governance forms through careful, archivally
based historical studies of specific governance practices, across all the major industrial economies.

REFERENCES

AOKI, MASAHIKO (1988). *Information, Incentives and Bargaining in the Japanese Economy.*
New York: Cambridge University Press.
—— and PATRICK, HUGH (eds.) (1994). *The Japanese Main Bank System.* New York: Oxford
University Press.
BALDERSTON, C. CANBY (1937). *Profit Sharing for Wage Earners.* New York: Industrial Rela-
tions Counselors.
BAUER, CLEMENS (1936). *Unternehmung und Unternehmungsformen im Spätmittelalter und
in der beginnenden Neuzeit.* Jena: Gustav Fischer.
BERGER, SUZANNE (1981). "Lame Ducks and National Champions: Industrial Policy in the
Fifth Republic", in William G. Andrews and Stanley Hoffman (eds.), *The Impact of the
Fifth Republic on France.* Albany: State University of New York Press.
BERK, GERALD (1994). *Alternative Tracks.* Baltimore: Johns Hopkins University Press.
BLAIR, MARGARET (1995). *Ownership and Control: Rethinking Corporate Governance for the
Twenty-First Century.* Washington, DC: Brookings Institute.
BOOT, ARNOUD W. A. (2000). "Relationship Banking: What Do We Know?". *Journal of
Financial Intermediation,* 9: 7–25.
CALOMIRIS, CHARLES W. (1995). "The Costs of Rejecting Universal Banking: American
Finance in the German Mirror, 1870–1914", in Naomi R. Lamoreaux and Daniel M.G.
Raff (eds.), *Coordination and Information: Historical Perspectives on the Organization of
Enterprise.* Chicago: University of Chicago Press.
CAPIE, FORREST, and COLLINS, MICHAEL (1999). "Banks, Industry, Finance, 1880–1914."
Business History, 41/1, January: 37–62.
CHANDLER, ALFRED (1977). *The Visible Hand: The Managerial Revolution in American Busi-
ness.* Cambridge, Mass.: Harvard University Press.
—— (1988a). "The Development of Modern Management Structure in the US and UK",
in Thomas K. McGraw (ed.), *The Essential Alfred Chandler: Essays toward an Historical
Theory of Big Business.* Cambridge, Mass.: Harvard University Press, 356–81.
—— (1988b). "Administrative Coordination, Allocation and Monitoring: Concepts and
Comparisons", in Thomas K. McGraw (ed.), *The Essential Alfred Chandler: Essays
toward an Historical Theory of Big Business.* Cambridge, Mass.: Harvard University Press,
398–424.
—— (1990). *Scale and Scope: The Dynamics of Industrial Capitalism.* Cambridge, Mass.:
Harvard University Press.
CHEFFINS, BRIAN R. (2001). "History and the Global Corporate Governance Revolution:
The UK Perspective". *Business History,* 43/4, Oct.: 87–118.
—— (2002). "Putting Britain on the Roe Map: The Emergence of the Berle-Means
Corporation in the United Kingdom", in Joseph A. McCahery, Piet Moerland, Theo

Raaijmakers, and Luc Renneboog (eds.), *Corporate Governance Regimes: Convergence and Diversity*. New York: Oxford University Press, 147–74.

—— (2003). "Mergers and Corporate Ownership Structure: The United States and Germany at the Turn of the 20th Century". *American Journal of Comparative Law*, 51: 473–504

—— (2004). "Mergers and the Evolution of Patterns of Corporate Ownership and Control: The British Experience". *Business History*, 46/2, Apr.: 256–84.

COFFEE, JOHN C., JR. (2000). "The Rise of Dispersed Ownership: The Role of Law in the Separation of Ownership and Control". Columbia Law and Economics Working Paper No. 182, Dec.

COHEN, STEPHEN S. (1969). *Modern Capitalist Planning: The French Model*. Cambridge, Mass.: Harvard University Press.

COLLINS, MICHAEL (1998). "English Bank Development within a European Context, 1870–1939". *Economic History Review*, 51/1: 1–24

DeLONG, J. BRADFORD (1991). "Did J. P. Morgan's Men Add Value?: An Economist's Perspective on Financial Capitalism", in Peter Temin (ed.), *Inside the Business Enterprise: Historical Perspectives on the Use of Information*. Chicago, Ill.: University of Chicago Press, 205–36.

DORNSEIFER, BERND, and KOCKA, JÜRGEN (1993). "The Impact of the Preindustrial Heritage: Reconsiderations on the German Pattern of Corporate Development in the Late 19th and Early 20th Centuries". *Industrial and Corporate Change*, 2/2: 233–48.

DUNLAVY, COLLEEN A. (2004). "From Citizens to Plutocrats: Nineteenth-Century Shareholder Voting Rights and Theories of the Corporation", in Kenneth Lipartito and David B. Sicilia (eds.), *Constructing Corporate America: History, Politics, Culture*. New York: Oxford University Press, 66–93.

FACCIO, MARA, and LANG, LARRY H. P. (2002). "The Ultimate Ownership of West European Corporations". *Journal of Financial Economics*, 65: 365–95.

FANTO, JAMES A. (1995). "The Transformation of French Corporate Governance and United States Institutional Investors". *Brookings Journal of International Law*, 21/1: 1–77.

—— (1998). "The Role of Corporate Law in French Corporate Governance". *Cornell International Law Journal*, 31: 31–91.

FELDENKIRCHEN, WILFRIED (1991). "Banking and Economic Growth: Banks and Industry in the Nineteenth Century and their Changing Relationship during Industrialization", in W. R. Lee (ed.), *German Industry and German Industrialization*. London: Routledge.

FOHLEN, CLAUDE (1978). "Entrepreneurship and Management in France in the Nineteenth Century", in Peter Mathias and M. M. Postan (eds.), *The Cambridge Economic History of Europe, Volume VII*. Cambridge: Cambridge University Press, 347–81.

FOHLIN, CAROLINE (1997). "Bank Securities Holdings and Industrial Finance before World War I: Britain and Germany Compared". *Business and Economic History*, 26/2, winter: 463–75.

—— (2000). "Economic, Political, and Legal Factors in Financial System Development: International Patterns in Historical Perspective". California Institute of Technology, Social Science Working Paper, No. 1089, May.

—— (2005). "The History of Corporate Ownership and Control in Germany", in Randall Morck (ed.), *A History of Corporate Governance around the World: Family Business Groups to Professional Managers*. National Bureau of Economic Research Conference Report. Chicago: University of Chicago Press.

FRANKS, JULIAN, and MAYER, COLIN (2001). "Ownership and Control of German Corporations". *Review of Financial Studies*, 14/4, Winter: 943–77.

FRANKS, JULIAN, MAYER, COLIN, and ROSSI, STEFANO (2004*a*). "Spending Less Time with the Family: The Decline of Family Ownership in the UK". ECGI Working Paper Series in Finance, Working Paper No. 35/2004, Jan.

———————(2004*b*). "Ownership: Evolution and Regulation". ECGI Working Paper Series in Finance, Working Paper No. 9/2003, Dec.

FRIDENSON, PATRICK (1997). "France: The Relatively Slow Development of Big Business in the Twentieth Century", in Alfred Chandler, Franco Amatori, and Takashi Hikino (eds.), *Big Business and the Wealth of Nations*. New York: Cambridge University Press, 207–45.

GEHRIG, THOMAS, and FOHLIN, CAROLINE (2004). "Price Discovery in Early Securities Markets: The Case of the Berlin Stock Exchange, 1880–1910". Manuscript, Johns Hopkins University, Department of Economics.

GERSCHENKRON, ALEXANDER (1962). "Economic Backwardness in Historical Perspective", in Gerschenkron, *Economic Backwardness in Historical Perspective*. Cambridge, Mass.: Harvard University Press.

GILMAN, NICHOLAS PAINE (1889). *Profit Sharing between Employer and Employee. A Study in the Evolution of the Wages System*. New York: Houghton Mifflin.

HALL, PETER (1986). *Governing the Economy. The Politics of State Intervention in Britain and France*. New York: Oxford University Press.

——and SOSKICE, DAVID (eds.) (2001). *Varieties of Capitalism: The Institutional Foundations of Comparative Advantage*. New York: Oxford University Press.

HANCKE, BOB (2002). *Large Firms and Institutional Change: Industrial Renewal and Economic Restructuring in France*. Oxford: Oxford University Press.

HANNAH, LESLIE (1982). *The Rise of the Corporate Economy*. London: Methuen.

HANSMANN, HENRY (1996). *The Ownership of Enterprise*. Cambridge, Mass.: Harvard University Press.

HERRIGEL, GARY (1996). *Industrial Constructions: The Sources of German Industrial Power*. New York: Cambridge University Press.

HÖPNER, MARTIN (2001). "Corporate Governance in Transition: Ten Empirical Findings on Shareholder Value and Industrial Relations in Germany". MPIfG Working Paper No. 01/5.

HORWITZ, MORTON J. (1977). *The Transformation of American Law, 1780–1860*. Cambridge, Mass.: Harvard University Press.

HOSHI, TAKEO, and KASHYAP, ANIL K. (2001). *Corporate Financing and Governance in Japan: The Road to the Future*. Cambridge, Mass.: MIT Press.

HOVENKAMP, HERBERT (1991). *Enterprise and American Law, 1836–1937*. Cambridge, Mass.: Harvard University Press.

JACKSON, GREGORY (2001). "The Origins of Nonliberal Corporate Governance in Japan and Germany", in Streeck and Yamamura (2001), 121–70.

JACOBY, SANFORD (1997). *Modern Manors: Welfare Capitalism since the New Deal*. Princeton, NJ: Princeton University Press.

JONES, GEOFFREY (1997). "Great Britain: Big Business, Management, and Competitiveness in Twentieth-Century Britain", in Alfred Chandler, Franco Amatori, and Takashi Hikino (eds.), *Big Business and the Wealth of Nations*. New York: Cambridge University Press, 102–38.

KATZENSTEIN, PETER (1987). *Policy and Politics in West Germany: The Growth of a Semi-Sovereign State*. Philadelphia, Pa.: Temple University Press.

KAUFMAN, ALLEN, and ZACHARIAS, LAWRENCE (1992). "From Trust to Contract: The Legal Language of Managerial Ideology, 1920–1980". *Business History Review*, 66/3, autumn: 523–72.

KOBERG, PETER (1992). *Die Entstehung der GmbH in Deutschland und Frankreich unter Berücksichtigung der Entwicklung des deutschen und französischen Gesellschaftsrechts.* Cologne: Dr Otto Schmidt KG.

KOCHAN, THOMAS A., KATZ, HARRY C., and MCKERSIE, ROBERT B. (1986). *The Transformation of American Industrial Relations.* New York: Basic Books.

KOCKA, JÜRGEN (1978). "Entrepreneurs and Managers in German Industrialization", in Peter Mathias and M. M. Postan (eds.), *The Cambridge Economic History of Europe: Volume VII.* Cambridge: Cambridge University Press, 492–589.

KROSZNER, RANDALL S., and RAGHURAM, G. RAJAN (1994). "Is the Glass-Steagall Act Justified? A Study of the US Experience with Universal Banking before 1933". *American Economic Review*, 84/4, Sept.: 810–32.

LAMOREAUX, NAOMI R. (1995). "Constructing Firms: Partnerships and Alternative Contractual Arrangements in Early Nineteenth-Century American Business". *Business and Economic History*, 24/2, Winter: 43–71.

——(2004). "Partnerships, Corporations, and the Limits on Contractual Freedom in US History: An Essay in Economics Law, and Culture", in Kenneth Lipartito and David B. Sicilia (eds.), *Constructing Corporate America: History, Politics, Culture.* New York: Oxford University Press, 29–65.

——and ROSENTHAL, JEAN-LAURENT (2004). "Corporate Governance and the Plight of Minority Shareholders in the United States before the Great Depression". NBER Working Paper No. 10900.

——RAFF, DANIEL M. G., and TEMIN, PETER (2004). "Beyond Markets and Hierarchies: Toward a New Synthesis of American Business History". *American Historical Review*, 108/2: 404–33.

LA PORTA, RAFAEL, LOPEZ-DE-SILANES, FLORENCIO, SHLEIFER, ANDREI, and VISHNY, ROBERT W. (1997). "Legal Determinants of External Finance". *Journal of Finance*, 52/3, July: 1131–50.

————————(1998). "Law and Finance". *Journal of Political Economy*, 106/6, Dec.: 1113–55.

————————(1999). "Corporate Ownership around the World". *Journal of Finance*, 54/2, Apr.: 471–517.

————————(2000). "Agency Problems and Dividend Policies around the World". *Journal of Finance*, 55/1, Feb.: 1–33.

LÉVY-LEBOYER, MAURICE (1978). "Capital Investment and Economic Growth in France, 1820–1930", in Peter Mathias and M. M. Postan (eds.), *The Cambridge Economic History of Europe: Volume VII.* Cambridge: Cambridge University Press, 231–95.

LIPARTITO, KENNETH (2004). "The Utopian Corporation", in Kenneth Lipartito and David B. Sicilia (eds.), *Constructing Corporate America: History, Politics, Culture.* New York: Oxford University Press, 94–119.

MACCLEAN, MAIRI (1999). "Corporate Governance in France and the UK: Long-Term Perspectives on Contemporary Institutional Arrangements". *Business History*, 41/1, Jan.: 88–116.

MAYER, COLIN (1988). "New Issues in Corporate Finance". *European Economic Review*, 32: 1167–89.

Morck, Randall, and Nakamura, Masao (2003). "Been There, Done That: The History of Corporate Ownership in Japan". ECGI Working Paper Series in Finance, Working Paper No. 20/2003.

Morikawa, Hidemasa (1986). "Prerequisites for the Development of Managerial Capitalism: Cases in Prewar Japan", in Kesaji Kobayashi and Hidemasa Morikawa (eds.), *The Development of Managerial Enterprise*. Tokyo: University of Tokyo Press, 1–27.

——(1992). *Zaibatsu: The Rise and Fall of Family Enterprise Groups in Japan*. Tokyo: University of Tokyo Press.

Murphy, Antoin E. (2004). "Corporate Ownership in France: The Importance of History". NBER Working Paper Series, Working Paper No. 10716, Aug.

Navin, Thomas R., and Sears, Marian V. (1955). "The Rise of the Market for Industrial Securities, 1887–1902". *Business History Review*, 29/2, June: 105–38.

Okazaki, Tetsuji (1995). "Evolution of the Financial System in Post-War Japan." *Business History*, 37/2, Apr.: 89–106.

O'Sullivan, Mary A. (2000). *Contests for Corporate Control: Corporate Governance and Economic Performance in the United States and Germany*. New York: Oxford University Press.

——(2003). "The Political Economy of Comparative Corporate Governance". *Review of International Political Economy*, 10: 23–72.

Rajan, Raghuram G. (1992). "Insiders and Outsiders: The Choice between Informed and Arm's Length Debt". *Journal of Finance*, 47/4, Sept.: 1367–400.

——and Zingales, Luigi (2003a). *Saving Capitalism from the Capitalists*. Princeton, NJ: Princeton University Press.

————(2003b). "The Great Reversals: The Politics of Financial Development in the Twentieth Century". *Journal of Financial Economics*, 69/1, July: 5–50.

Roberts, John (2004). *The Modern Firm: Organizational Design for Performance and Growth*. New York: Oxford University Press.

Roe, Mark J. (1994). *Strong Managers, Weak Owners: The Political Roots of American Corporate Finance*. Princeton, NJ: Princeton University Press.

——(2002). "The Political Foundations for Separating Ownership from Control", in Joseph A. McCahery, Piet Moerland, Theo Raaijmakers, and Luc Renneboog (eds.), *Corporate Governance Regimes: Convergence and Diversity*. New York: Oxford University Press, 113–46.

——(2003). *Political Determinants of Corporate Governance: Political Context, Corporate Impact*. New York: Oxford University Press.

Ross, Duncan M. (1996). "Commercial Banking in a Market Oriented Financial System: Britain between the Wars". *Economic History Review*, 49/2: 314–35.

Roy, William G. (1997). *Socializing Capital: The Rise of the Large Industrial Corporation in America*. Princeton, NJ: Princeton University Press.

Sabel, Charles F., (2005). "Theory of a Real Time Revolution", in Charles Heckscher and Paul Adler (eds.), *Collaborative Community*. Oxford: Oxford University Press.

——and Zeitlin, Jonathan (eds.) (1997). *Worlds of Possibility: Flexibility and Mass Production in Western Industrialization*. New York: Cambridge University Press.

Samuels, Richard J. (1994). *"Rich Nation, Strong Army": National Security and the Technological Transformation of Japan*. Ithaca, NY: Cornell University Press.

Schmoller, Gustav (1890a). "Die geschichtliche Entwicklung der Unternehmung, I und II: Die älteren Arbeitsgenossenschaften und die altere agrarische Familienwirtschaft".

Jahrbuch für Gesetzgebung, Verwaltung und Volkswirtschaft im Deutschen Reich, 14/3: 735–83.

—— (1890*b*). "Die geschichtliche Entwicklung der Unternehmung, III und IV: Handel, Handwerk und Hausindustrie". *Jahrbuch für Gesetzgebung, Verwaltung und Volkswirtschaft im Deutschen Reich*, 14/4: 1035–76.

—— (1890*c*). "Über Wesen und Verfassung der grossen Unternehmungen", in Schmoller, *Zur Social-und Gewerbepolitik der Gegenwart: Reden und Aufsätze*. Leipzig: Duncker & Humblot, 372–440.

SCHUBERT, WERNER, and HOMMELHOFF, PETER (eds.) (1985). *Hundert Jahre modernes Aktienrecht*. Berlin: Walter de Gruyter.

SCHUMPETER, JOSEPH (1939). *Business Cycles*. New York: McGraw-Hill.

SCOTT, WILLIAM ROBERT (1910–12). *The Constitution and Finance of English, Scottish and Irish Joint-Stock Companies to 1720*, 3 vols. Cambridge: Cambridge University Press.

SCRANTON, PHILIP (1997). *Endless Novelty: Specialty Production and American Industrialization, 1865–1925*. Princeton, NJ: Princeton University Press.

SHEARD, PAUL (1994). "Interlocking Shareholdings and Corporate Governance in Japan", in Masahiko Aoki and Ronald Dore (eds.), *The Japanese Firm: Sources of Competitive Strength*. New York: Oxford University Press, 311–49.

SIMMEL, GEORG (1900). *Philosophie des Geldes*. Leipzig: Duncker & Humblot.

STREECK, WOLFGANG (1984). "Co-determination: The Fourth Decade", in B Wilpert and Arndt Sorge (eds.), *International Perspectives on Organizational Democracy*. London: John Wiley, 391–422.

—— and HÖPNER, MARTIN (eds.) (2003). *Alle macht dem Markt? Fallstudien zur Abwicklung der Deutschland AG*. Frankfurt: Campus Verlag.

—— and YAMAMURA, KOZO (eds.) (2001). *The Origins of Nonliberal Capitalism: Germany and Japan in Comparison*. Ithaca, NY: Cornell University Press.

STREIDER, JAKOB (1914). *Studien zur Geschichte kapitalistischer Organisationsformen*. Leipzig: Duncker & Humblot.

THELEN, KATHLEEN (2004). *How Institutions Evolve: The Political Economy of Skills in Germany, Britain, the United States and Japan*. New York: Cambridge University Press.

TOMS, STEVE, and WRIGHT, MIKE (2002). "Corporate Governance, Strategy and Structure in British Business History, 1950–2000". *Business History*, 44/3, July: 91–124.

VERDIER, DANIEL (2002). *Moving Money: Banking and Finance in the Industrialized World*. New York: Cambridge University Press.

VITOLS, SIGURT (2001). "The Origins of Bank-Based and Market-Based Financial Systems: Germany, Japan and the United States", in Streeck and Yamamura (2001), 171–99.

WHITLEY, RICHARD (1999). *Divergent Capitalisms: The Social Structuring and Change of Business Systems*. New York: Oxford University Press.

ZEITLIN, JONATHAN, and HERRIGEL, GARY (eds.) (2000). *Americanization and its Limits: Reworking American Technology and Management in Post-War Europe and Japan*. New York: Oxford University Press.

ZYSMAN, JOHN (1983). *Governments, Markets, and Growth: Financial Systems and the Politics of Industrial Change*. Ithaca, NY: Cornell University Press.

PART IV

ENTERPRISE AND SOCIETY

CHAPTER 21

....

ENTREPRENEURSHIP

....

GEOFFREY JONES
R. DANIEL WADHWANI

21.1 INTRODUCTION

....

SINCE the 1980s, entrepreneurship has emerged as a topic of growing interest among management scholars and social scientists. The subject has grown in legitimacy, particularly in business schools (Cooper 2003). This scholarly interest has been spurred by a set of recent developments in the United States: the vitality of start-up firms in high-technology industries, the expansion of venture capital financing, and the successes of regional clusters, notably Silicon Valley. Motivated by the goal of understanding these developments, management scholars and social scientists interested in entrepreneurship have tended to focus their attention on studying new business formation, which provides a consistent and easily delimited basis for quantitative empirical work (Thornton 1999; Aldrich 1999, 2005; Gartner and Carter 2005). These studies commonly use large datasets of founders or firms and employ rigorous social science methodologies, but give little analytical attention to the temporal or geographical context for entrepreneurial behavior.

In contrast, historical research on entrepreneurship started much earlier, and traces its roots to different motivations and theoretical concerns. The historical study of entrepreneurship has been particularly concerned with understanding the process of structural change and development within economies. Business

The authors would like to thank Walter Friedman, Andrew Godley, Tom Nicholas, and Jonathan Zeitlin for their incisive comments on earlier drafts of this chapter.

historians have focused on understanding the underlying character and causes of the historical transformation of businesses, industries, and economies. This historical research has typically employed a Schumpeterian definition of entrepreneurship. Unlike the recent management scholarship, it has not focused primarily on new firm formation, but rather on the varying forms that innovative activity has taken and on the role of innovative entrepreneurship in driving changes in the historical context of business, industry, and the economy.

The role of entrepreneurship is identified in many streams of business history research. Several chapters in this Handbook consider aspects of the subject and as a result are not discussed here. The literature on the role of culture, gender, and regional agglomeration in shaping entrepreneurial activity is reviewed in the chapters by Lipartito, Zeitlin, and Lescure. Family business and international entrepreneurship are discussed in the chapters by Rose and Colli and Jones respectively.

This chapter begins by providing a brief introduction to the origins and evolution of historical research on entrepreneurship. It then turns to explore a series of different streams of business history research that deal with issues of entrepreneurship and historical change. These sections highlight the ways in which historical context shaped the structure of entrepreneurial activity and reveal the wide variation in organizational form and entrepreneurial behavior that historians have found. The chapter concludes by discussing the main contributions of business history to the study of entrepreneurship, and proposes a renewed research agenda.

21.2 ORIGINS AND MOTIVATION

The concept of entrepreneurship played a formative role in the emergence of business history as a distinct academic field. Since the middle of the nineteenth century, economic historians had critiqued the static theories of classical and neoclassical economic thought by documenting the ways in which the structure of economies had changed over historical time. This early historicism emphasized the ways in which the institutions of capitalism and industrialism evolved (Hodgson 2001).

By the early twentieth century, however, a number of historians and historical sociologists had moved beyond the institutional perspective to emphasize the mentality and agency of entrepreneurs in the process of economic change. German historical sociologists explored the role of religion and social relations in the development of modern capitalist attitudes toward economic gain and economic opportunity (Weber 1904; Simmel 1908; Sombart 1911). By the middle decades of the century economic and business historians were engaged in researching the careers of influential eighteenth-century entrepreneurs as a way of understanding the causes of the Industrial Revolution (Ashton 1939; Wilson 1955; McKendrik 1959, 1964). These studies focused attention on the creative agency and subjectivity of individuals in the process of economic change.

This growing attention to entrepreneurs as agents of historical change was bolstered by the theoretical work of Joseph Schumpeter. The Austrian economist's ideas helped establish entrepreneurship as a substantive area of historical research and deepened the significance of the business historians' endeavors by linking entrepreneurship to a theory of economic change. Schumpeter argued that the essence of entrepreneurial activity lay in the creation of "new combinations" that disrupted the competitive equilibrium of existing markets, products, processes, and organizations (Schumpeter 1947). The creation of such new combinations, he elaborated, was a constant source of change within markets, industries, and national economies. It underlay the "creative destruction" that replaced old forms of economic transaction with new forms in capitalist economies (Schumpeter 1942). In the decade leading up to his death in 1950, Schumpeter repeatedly stressed that the empirical study of entrepreneurship was an inherently historical endeavor because the phenomenon was best understood in retrospect as a critical element in the process of industrial and economic change. Social scientific investigation of entrepreneurship needed to focus not only on entrepreneurs and their firms but also on temporal changes in the industries, markets, societies, economies, and political systems in which they operated, an eclectic approach that history could provide (McCraw 2006).

By the 1940s, a number of historians, inspired in large part by the Schumpeterian concept of entrepreneurship as an agent of change in the economy, began to push empirical business history beyond the earlier biographical studies of entrepreneurs to higher levels of conceptualization. The group was led in the United States by the economic historian Arthur Cole. In 1948, he organized the Center for Research on Entrepreneurial History, based at Harvard. Affiliates of the Center included economists and sociologists as well as historians and Cole encouraged a wide range of approaches to "entrepreneurial history", including socio-cultural studies of entrepreneurial origins, neoclassical economic approaches, and work that focused on the evolution of industries and organizations. While research in entrepreneurial history took an eclectic set of directions, the Center and its journal, *Explorations in Entrepreneurial History*, provided the institutional mechanisms for bringing this wide-ranging empiricism together in ways that informed common concepts and theories of entrepreneurship (Sass 1978). Cole (1959, 1968) also published several articles and books that attempted to synthesize the empirical research and use it to address theories of entrepreneurship (Hughes 1983).

By the 1960s, however, a distinctive shift among American business and economic historians led them away from "entrepreneurial history" and its eclecticism.

In part, this was due to declining financial and institutional support for the Center, which closed its doors in 1958. Moreover, younger business historians were increasingly drawn to the more focused organizational and managerial studies that Chandler (1962) had pioneered. Chandler was ambivalent about the autonomous role of entrepreneurs in shaping the trajectory of business development. By 1970 a clear shift had taken place in American business history research toward building an "organizational synthesis" of the emergence of the modern, multidivisional corporation (Galambos 1970). At the same time, American economic historians increasingly adopted orthodox neoclassical economic theory and quantitative methods in their research, rejecting the eclecticism of "entrepreneurial history" and adopting neoclassicism's traditional skepticism of entrepreneurship as a concept. Emblematic of this change, the defunct *Explorations in Entrepreneurial History* was revived as *Explorations in Economic History*, a publication devoted to the new quantitative, neoclassical studies (Livesay 1995).

The Chandlerian shift of the research agenda toward the corporation did not entirely displace entrepreneurial history research, but it became marginal to the main research agenda of business history. Entrepreneurship and innovation continued to be explored, but entrepreneurship rarely occupied center stage in such studies. There was little traction behind using historical research to seek broader theoretical conceptualizations of entrepreneurship. Hence, entrepreneurship research in business history today is rarely considered a single coherent field, but rather is dealt with as part of many different subtopics.

Meanwhile the older tradition of writing historical biographies of leading entrepreneurs has continued. Although most such biographies are hagiographical, this genre continues to provide well-researched and deeply contextualized studies of major entrepreneurial figures such as Andrew Carnegie (Nasaw 2006), Walt Disney (Gabler 2006), Dudley Docker (Davenport-Hines 1984), Sir William Mackinnon (Munro 2003), Werner von Siemens (Feldenkirchen 1994), August Thyssen (Fear 2005), Kiichiro Toyoda (Wada and Yui 2002), Marcus Wallenberg (Olsson 2001), and Joe Wilson (Ellis 2006). Such studies offer compelling insights into how entrepreneurial opportunities were identified and exploited. For example, the biography of Robert Noyce, co-founder of Fairchild Semiconductor and Intel, explores the networks of information and financing which permitted the growth of the Silicon Valley technology cluster after World War II (Berlin 2005). From a methodological perspective, the primary drawback of business biographies arises from deriving meaningful generalizations about entrepreneurship from individual cases.

The growing research on entrepreneurial cognition in the management literature may provide an opportunity to revisit the research in these biographies from that perspective (Mitchell *et al.* 2002; Tripsas and Gavetti 2000). This literature is based on the notion that entrepreneurial opportunities are not immediately apparent but rather need to be perceived and enacted by individuals. Cognitive approaches assume that entrepreneurs understand reality not directly but rather through multiple perceptual lenses (Krueger 2003). The study of why and how some individuals and not others identify and pursue new economic opportunities, therefore, is seen as requiring an understanding of what influences and biases this process of perception. Biographies, and the business history literature in particular, has the potential to make a major contribution to understanding long-term patterns of information search and processing by entrepreneurs in different contexts.

Research on the cognitive psychology of entrepreneurship offers more precise ways in which to explain how cognition affects entrepreneurship without repeating many of the problems of casual empiricism and loose causality of the earlier historical scholarship.

21.3 Culture and Values

As the historical scholarship on entrepreneurship emerged in 1940s and 1950s, much of the early work in the field attempted to frame the research around a particular historical question: why, over the previous three centuries, had some countries grown extraordinarily rich and productive while others remained relatively poor? Schumpeter had theorized that entrepreneurial innovation was the source of productivity growth in capitalist societies. By the 1950s, historians were actively engaged in studying variations in the character and supply of entrepreneurship in the historical record of various countries and attempting to link their findings to the long-run economic performance of nations.

These national studies of entrepreneurial character were pioneered in the United States by Cochran, Jenks, and a few other historians associated with Cole's Research Center. Jenks and Cochran adapted the "structural functionalism" of Parsonian sociology in order to push historical research on entrepreneurship beyond the heroic Schumpeterian entrepreneur of individual case studies and to embed the study of entrepreneurs within particular historical and social contexts. "The theory of innovations is neither a 'great man' nor a 'better mousetrap' theory of history", Jenks explained in a landmark study of the railroad entrepreneurs in nineteenth-century America. "The innovator is a person whose traits are in some part a function of his socio-cultural environment. His innovation is a new combination of factors and elements already accessible" (Jenks 1944, 1949; Cochran 1950, 1960). The approach led to multiple "national studies" of how social roles and sanctions had conditioned the emergence of entrepreneurship in particular countries.

The approach was extended, most notably by Landes, by linking the socio-cultural examination of entrepreneurship to the long-term economic performance of particular countries. Landes (1953) made the case that culture was a consistent determinant of the supply of entrepreneurship and hence of long-term economic growth. In a classic study, he argued that France's allegedly poor economic performance in the nineteenth century could be attributed to the conservativeness and timidity of French entrepreneurs, who saw business as an integral part of family status rather than as an end in itself (Landes 1949). In a series of studies over half a century, Landes has continued to make the case for the importance of national cultural factors, values, and social attitudes in explaining the development of entrepreneurial activity, and in turn the economic performance of nations (1969, 1998, 2003).

Similar arguments about the role of national culture in determining the supply of entrepreneurship and long-run growth were used to try to explain a remarkably diverse set of historical conditions and outcomes. Sawyer (1954) pointed to the persistence of Puritan values and the frontier spirit in American society to explain the relatively high level of encouragement for entrepreneurship in the United States. There was a lengthy debate concerning whether the remarkable modernization of Meiji Japan in the late nineteenth century could be ascribed to "community-centered" entrepreneurs who put the interests of national development before all else (Ranis 1955; Hirschmeier 1964). Cultural factors, particularly the "gentrification" and complacency of British entrepreneurs in the Victorian Era, became a favorite subject for those interested in explaining the perceived relative economic decline in that era and later (Wiener 1981; Hannah 1984).

The national culture approach has been widely critiqued. Subsequent research suggested that the "community-centered" Meiji entrepreneurs were rather similar to entrepreneurs elsewhere (Yamamura 1968, 1978). In several cases, the underlying premise of the research agenda has proven questionable. Landes launched French economic historians on a four-decade-long search for the causes of France's slow economic growth and the failure of French entrepreneurship before it was established that the initial premise of failure was at least partly misleading, and based on the preconceived expectation that big business was equated with entrepreneurial success. Recent business history research has shown that French industry was more technologically advanced than had been imagined (Smith 2006).

Similarly, the premise of a Britain blighted by anti-entrepreneurial culture, at least until rescued by the Thatcher government of the 1980s, has been widely critiqued. On the one hand, while British firms lagged behind American and German firms in the mass-production industries of the Second Industrial Revolution, McCloskey and Sandberg (1971) provided the celebrated riposte that the technological choices of Victorian entrepreneurs were rational responses to resource endowments and exogenous technological possibilities from the perspective of neoclassical theory. On the other hand, the arguments that there was a significant "anti-industrial" spirit in Britain, and that the British situation differed from that in the United States or Germany, have been challenged on several grounds (Berghoff and Möller 1994; Coleman and Macleod 1986; Collins and Robbins 1990; Thompson 2001).

The overall argument that national culture and norms determine a national supply of entrepreneurial activity was strongly criticized by Gerschenkron (1962b, 1966). He noted that the notion of "national culture" envisioned in such studies was essentially static and rigidly functionalist, making it difficult for it to truly account for the dynamic nature of entrepreneurial activity. If such studies conceptualized entrepreneurs purely as products of their national cultural environment, they were inherently limited in their ability to understand how these entrepreneurs could act as agents of change in that environment. Gerschenkron also pointed out that there were many examples of historical settings in which entrepreneurial activity had flourished outside or even against prevailing national social norms. The socio-cultural perspective, he insisted, had missed Schumpeter's basic premise that entrepreneurs often acted as agents of change rather than as captives of their environment. As Nicholas (2004) has discussed in the case of alleged British entrepreneurial failure, the function of entrepreneurs is to upset status quos by unlocking predetermined paths of development.

Nevertheless, the persistent patterns of wealth and poverty in the world has in recent years led to a renewed interest in identifying variations in entrepreneurial performance caused by culture. The economist Mark Casson has suggested that countries vary in their entrepreneurial cultures. In particular, Casson (1991, 1995) points to variations in trust levels within cultures, which in turn affects the level of transactions costs on which overall economic performance depends. The impact of national culture on entrepreneurship has recently been tested historically by Godley (2001) in a comparative study of Eastern European Jews who emigrated to London and New York in the late nineteenth century. Godley argues that the Jewish immigrants to New York were much more likely to move into entrepreneurial occupations than those in London, despite coming from similar backgrounds. He suggests that in both countries the Jews assimilated some host country values. The novel methodology of using Jewish immigrants as the control group seems to provide robust evidence that American and British cultures varied in how they valued entrepreneurship. Godley suggests that entrepreneurs in Britain faced additional costs arising from conservative craft values among the working class, which erected hurdles not faced elsewhere to introducing new technologies and working practices. For the more recent period, Tsang (2006) provides a comparative study of the impact of national cultural heritage on entrepreneurship on Chinese and Irish software firms.

The role of religious values in the supply of entrepreneurship has attracted research since Weber (1904) famously argued that certain types of Protestantism favored rational pursuit of economic gain and gave worldly activities a positive spiritual and moral meaning. The link between religion and entrepreneurship has continued to be debated ever since. R. H. Tawney (1926) rejected a link between Protestantism and economic growth in sixteenth-century England. Many other scholars have since questioned a meaningful connection between Protestantism and modern capitalism. However, this has not prevented Landes (1998) from reasserting the case that Protestantism explains "the triumph of the West".

The correlation between Protestant sects and entrepreneurship during the initial and later stages of modern economic growth in Britain has attracted much research (Jeremy 1988, 1998). There has been a long tradition of research on the apparent overrepresentation of Protestant Dissenters among the successful entrepreneurs of that era (Hagen 1962). Although there is evidence that this overrepresentation may have been exaggerated (Howe 1984), it would seem that this group did foster many first-generation entrepreneurs, although this was probably explained by social constraints on alternative career paths rather than their religious values (Berghoff 1995). There were also powerful advantages of belonging to networked groups. The large number of successful Quaker entrepreneurs seems to be explained by access to mutual systems of support which provided access to information and capital (Kirby 1993). Minority status alone was certainly insufficient to stimulate entrepreneurship. Foreman-Peck and Boccaletti (2002) identified a disproportionate lack of minority Roman Catholics among entrepreneurs in nineteenth-century Scotland.

Protestantism is not alone in its alleged influence on entrepreneurship. Morris, for instance, helped popularize the notion that the Indian subcontinent suffered from a perpetual "Hindu rate of growth"—reflecting Indians' "other worldly" concerns stemming from mystical religious values that ostensibly made them less interested in material gain (Morris 1967).

The Weberian "values" approach to understanding the influence of religion and culture on entrepreneurial activity has clearly suffered from casual empiricism, unclear causal relationships, and excessively broad generalizations about the influence of formal values on the behavior of subjects. However, the literature has the merit that it addresses an issue that is critical for understanding the entrepreneurial process—the subjectivity of the entrepreneur.

Historians have increasingly sought to ground the study of how culture and nationality affect entrepreneurship by examining how specific social structures and relationships shape the influence of entrepreneurial culture. They have examined how social group affiliation—whether ethnicity, race, gender, family, or class—mediates entrepreneurial culture by constraining or providing specialized access to entrepreneurial opportunities and resources. Walker, for instance, has documented the influence of race relations in the United States in shaping the particular ways in which entrepreneurship came to be expressed among African-Americans. She shows how slavery and institutionalized racism severely limited entrepreneurial opportunities for blacks, but also how they fostered certain types of entrepreneurial responses among African-Americans designed to undermine the legitimacy of these institutions (Walker 1986). Others have emphasized the ways in which certain social group affiliations and relationships have been important sources of entrepreneurial information and resources. Studies of Jewish immigrant entrepreneurs in the United States by historical sociologists (Morawska 1996; Tenenbaum 1993), for instance, substantiate this finding, which has now become a common conclusion in many "ethnic entrepreneurship" studies in the social sciences (Aldrich and Waldinger 1990).

Historians have also found ethnic group affiliation and identity to be critical for understanding certain forms for international entrepreneurship. Research on the history of international business has identified the role of diaspora networks in enhancing trust levels and creating conduits for information and resources among its members, in turn reducing barriers to trade over long distances. Diasporic links facilitated the flow of information and credit and helped guarantee the enforcement of contracts among members. A large portion of new international market development over the last two centuries has been created by networks of entrepreneurs within such diasporas, including Jews, Greeks, Indians, Arabs, Chinese, and others (McCabe *et al.* 2005; Dobbin 1996).

In recent years, historians have used biographical and firm-level data to examine the influence of religion, nationality, and social group affiliation on entrepreneurship. In the United States, historians have used a range of sources, most notably the Dun and Bradstreet records, to examine patterns of entrepreneurship and access to resources by race, ethnicity, and gender (Kenzer 1989; Olegario 1999). In Great Britain, Nicholas (1999, 2000) used the multi-volume *Dictionary of Business Biography* (Jeremy 1984–6), which provides biographical data on a large number of businessmen active in England and Wales after 1860, to test the drivers of entrepreneurial success and failure. Using lifetime rates of wealth accumulation as a proxy for entrepreneurial success, he found that religion (along with region and industry) could not explain performance differences, but other social indicators (such as inheriting a family firm or attending a "public" school) negatively affected accumulation. Likewise, Foreman-Peck (2005) has outlined a series of quantitative methods for teasing out the relative importance of various cultural influences on propensity to become an entrepreneur and on an entrepreneur's social mobility.

Although recent quantitative studies might be criticized for certain methodological limitations, including the incompleteness of their data and the indicators they use to measure entrepreneurship (such as new firm creation or wealth accumulation), they represent an advance in research on the validity of cultural explanations that have traditionally lacked careful empiricism and tended toward broad generalizations about national values. Consequently, they provide one avenue for business historians to deepen their insights on the contribution of entrepreneurship to explaining patterns of wealth and poverty.

21.4 THE POLITICAL ECONOMY
OF ENTREPRENEURSHIP

The importance of political-legal institutions in explaining patterns of economic growth has re-emerged as a topic of interest among business historians. Where research by economists has done much to substantiate the assertion that inherited institutions matter for long-term economic growth, historical research has sought to identify the mechanisms and processes that help explain at a more nuanced level how and why institutions have mattered, particularly to entrepreneurial processes.

The economic historian Douglass North played a pivotal role in the emergence of the "new institutionalism". North's work emphasized the role of property rights, patent laws, and power-sharing political arrangements in the West to account for the development of a political framework that stimulated and supported the development of entrepreneurial activity (North 1990; Davis and North 1971; North and Weingast 1989). North and others helped once again place inherited institutions at the center of economic reasoning by arguing that institutions create the incentive structure for private enterprise.

The new institutionalism in economics posits that societies that provide incentives and opportunities for investment will be richer than those that fail to do so. By reducing transactions costs and facilitating potential gains from exchange, institutions can fuel productivity and growth. A particularly influential approach comes from the law and finance literature associated with LaPorta *et al.* (1997). Broadly this camp argues that the legal tradition a country inherited or adopted in the distant past has a long-term effect on financial development and in turn on long-term growth. Countries that had a common law legal system had on average better investor protections than most civil law countries, and French civil law countries were worse than German or Scandinavian civil law traditions. They suggest this had a major effect on financial development, which in turn can be assumed to have impacted entrepreneurial activity. There has been much criticism from historians of this hypothesis (see Herrigel, this volume).

Baumol (1988, 1990) has provided a causal explanation for how institutions affect entrepreneurship and, through that, long-term growth. He argues that inherited institutions matter because they create incentives that allocate entrepreneurship between productive activities such as innovation and unproductive activities such as rent-seeking or organized crime. This allocation is in turn influenced by the relative pay-offs offered by a society to such activities.

Recent historical research has explored the precise mechanisms by which institutions affected productivity and long-term growth. Maurer (2002), for instance, explores how the existence of an undemocratic political system and selective enforcement of property rights shaped the financial system and constrained entrepreneurial opportunities in late nineteenth-century Mexico. Limited in its ability to raise taxes to finance infrastructure projects as well as fend off political opponents, the Mexican government relied on banks to provide it with credit, while the banks relied on the government to enforce property rights. A select few bankers were given extensive privileges producing a highly concentrated banking system. Each bank grew fat in its own protected niche. To overcome the problems associated with information asymmetry, banks lent to their own shareholders and other insiders. In the case of the textile industry, banks did not lend to the best firms, but the best-connected firms. Poorly defined property rights prevented those excluded from the insider networks from pledging collateral and finding another financial route for their entrepreneurial endeavors.

Historical studies have also looked more closely at the influence of patent rights and the law of business organizations to examine their influence on entrepreneurial activity. Khan (2005) found that antebellum US courts consistently supported inventors' patent rights based on the premise that the patent system fostered economic growth. She found that the structure of the American patenting system in early industrialization fostered widespread patenting by ordinary people. Access to patent protection (or lack of it) seems to have been important in determining not only technological development, but also the adoption and diffusion of technology. Aspiring late nineteenth-century Dutch and Scandinavian entrepreneurs were able to build businesses in more technologically advanced industries precisely because of the lack of patent protection afforded to foreign companies in those countries (Ruigrok and Tulder 1995).

Likewise, legal historians have long emphasized the importance of the development of the rights of private corporations for entrepreneurship that involved economies of scale and scope. Hovencamp (1991) suggests that the American law of corporations evolved functionally to meet these economic needs over the nineteenth and early twentieth centuries. Lamoreaux and Rosenthal (2005), however, caution against such broadly functionalist definitions and particularly against the sweeping claims of LaPorta *et al.* that civil law countries offered inferior economic rules to common law ones. In comparing nineteenth-century French and American law, they found little difference between the two countries in the legal system's responsiveness to business's organizational needs. In fact, US law offered entrepreneurs fewer options on how to organize their businesses and more limited adaptability.

Historians doing research at the nexus of law and business caution that the new institutionalism too often paints a picture of political development that is overly rigid, functionalist, and highly stylized. In particular, they point out that the historical evidence on economic rule-making suggests that the assumption of a division between inherited economic rules and entrepreneurial activity is artificial, especially when applied outside the sphere of the recent Anglo-American political economy (Novak 1996; Freyer forthcoming). In developing countries, political rule making is often part of the entrepreneurial process, not exogenous to it (Kilby 1971). Even in the Anglo-American world, the sharp divide between public rules and private enterprise implied in the new institutionalism is problematic as a framework for modeling political economic development (Novak 2001). In fact, Freyer (forthcoming) and others have argued that such an "instrumental" view of economic lawmaking fundamentally misinterprets what is actually a "constitutive" process, in which entrepreneurial actors are often re-negotiating or pushing the boundaries of legal rules in the process of innovation and where political actors fundamentally shape the private economy through innovations in the categories and rules they create. Certainly, many historical studies of the state as an entrepreneurial actor and regulator, especially in the United States, indicate that the state's role as rule maker is only one of a broad set of ways in which governments have been influential in shaping entrepreneurship (Hurst 1967; Scheiber 1973; Hughes 1991).

The growing economics literature on the role of colonialism in explaining the slow growth of Latin America, Africa, and Asia has direct relevance to the relationship between political institution development and entrepreneurship, although it is not typically framed within that debate. Engerman and Sokoloff (2005) stress the negative impact of colonization in altering the composition of populations. Soil and climate gave Latin America and the Caribbean a comparative advantage in growing crops that used slaves or natives. The resulting extreme inequality in distribution of wealth, they suggest, gave them institutions which contributed to persistence of substantial inequality. Acemoglu *et al.* (2002) distinguish between institutions of "private property" and "extractive institutions". The former provide secure property rights and are embedded in a broad cross-section of society. Extractive institutions concentrate power in the hands of a small elite and create a high risk of expropriation. In prosperous and densely settled areas, Europeans introduced or maintained extractive institutions to force people to work in mines and plantations. In sparsely settled areas, Europeans settled and created institutions of private property. The spread of industrial technology in the nineteenth century, it is suggested, required a broad mass of society to participate, so they won out.

With some exceptions (Banerjee and Iyer 2005), the economics literature on colonialism and institutions tends to be ahistorical. Business historians are well-placed to explore the issues in a more nuanced fashion. Colonialism changed greatly over time. The British colonial regime in late nineteenth-century India, for example, differed radically from that of its exploitative predecessor a hundred years previously. While traditional Indian handicraft industries were forced to compete with Lancashire textiles because of British free trade policies in the nineteenth century, by the interwar decades, British India was protectionist, including against British imports. Moreover, the impact of colonialism was multifaceted. It provided a channel for entrepreneurs in colonies to acquire international knowledge and access international markets, although within a context of institutional racism (Tripathi 2004). This may have been important in affecting entrepreneurial cognition. In crude terms, entrepreneurs who were not white men from the rich Western European and North American countries may have felt less qualified to pursue opportunities, even if they were not.

In general, the thrust of recent research suggests that although colonialism provided opportunities for Western entrepreneurs, colonial governments in Africa and elsewhere were rarely agents of expatriate enterprise or metropolitan industries (Hopkins 1987). Their general impact was to improve the business environment for all entrepreneurs, because of both improved institutions and investment in infrastructure. Goswami (1985) found that the rise of Marwari businessmen in Eastern India began well before Independence and that the political history of late colonialism was only loosely connected to the business history on the Subcontinent. Entrepreneurship also flourished among so-called "middlemen" ethnic minorities which forged special links with colonial authorities, such as the Parsees in nineteenth-century India or the Chinese in Southeast Asia (Dobbin 1996; Jones, this volume). However, the importance of such minorities remains contested. As Oonk (2006) has shown in the case of ethnic Asian entrepreneurs in late nineteenth-century Zanzibar, membership of such a minority was no guarantor of entrepreneurial success. Moreover, while in regions such as the Middle East, historians have focused their attention on non-Muslim and foreign merchants (Tignor 1980), recent research has identified the importance of "mainstream" Muslim entrepreneurs in late nineteenth-century Iran, the Ottoman Empire and elsewhere (Gilbrar 2003).

Business history research has made a particular contribution in showing how entrepreneurial performance takes place within a wider political economy environment. With perhaps the single exception of Britain in the eighteenth century, governments have contributed to entrepreneurship and firm growth not only by providing (or not providing) institutional rules of the game, but through a wide range of policy measures. The role of the state in catching up economic backwardness has been well-recognized since Gerschenkron (1962a), even if the ways in which governments facilitated entrepreneurial perception and exploitation of opportunities has not been the primary emphasis of this research. Recent work has extended the study of "state entrepreneurship" to the development of firms and industries in Singapore (Brown 2006), Taiwan, Israel, and Ireland (Breznitz 2006). Certainly it is difficult to account for the rapid economic growth of the United States in the nineteenth century without mentioning government policy. The US government purchased or else annexed much of the territory of the present-day country, and then largely gave it away to budding entrepreneurs. State governments were active promoters of infrastructure investment. During the late nineteenth century, tariff protection widened the market opportunities for US entrepreneurs and firms by shutting out cheaper imports from Europe (Scheiber 1973, 1997).

The impact of the wider political economy on entrepreneurship is evident in many settings. Explanations for why ethnic Chinese business has been disproportionately important in Southeast Asia typically stress cultural influences including the role of family, dialect groups, and the Confucian value system. With respect to the latter, it is often argued that social trust, the social obligations that bind family and lineage, is strengthened by the Confucian belief, and that has provided the bedrock of commercial networking (Hefner 1998). Yet business historians have shown that the strength of Chinese entrepreneurship in Southeast Asia has to be placed within a longer political economic context. From the fourteenth century, the region's rulers favored foreign over local merchants because the latter might pose a political threat. Through the seventeenth century, local trading communities—whether Malay or Filipino—continued to flourish, but the Chinese role was strengthened by the arrival of Western merchants, for the Chinese positioned themselves as intermediaries. By the late nineteenth century, the Chinese had secured the position of revenue farmers across the region, in both colonial and non-colonial areas. This made them indispensable for local governments, while providing a source of funds for their business interests (Brown 2000).

On the whole, political-economic approaches that focus on national institutions, policies, and political boundaries may provide the environmental settings for entrepreneurial activity, but often reveal little about either the extent of state involvement in entrepreneurship or the ways in which new economic opportunities have historically been created and exploited. The historical record suggests that state–entrepreneur interactions have been extensive and taken on a diverse array of forms, rarely limiting themselves to arm's-length economic rule making. Likewise, entrepreneurial opportunity structures have rarely, if ever, materialized as truly *national* constructs but rather have appeared and been exploited at the level of individuals, firms, industries, and regions.

As a result, a significant conclusion of historical research in recent years is that entrepreneurship is often better studied at a regional level rather than that of the nation state. In nineteenth-century Mexico (Cerutti 1996) and Colombia (Dávila 2003), there were significant regional differences in entrepreneurship. In colonial India, expatriate Scotsmen developed the modern industries of Calcutta during the second half of the nineteenth century, but the industries on the west coast were developed by Indians of various ethnicities (Tripathi 2004). Similarly, recent research on the emergence of modern entrepreneurship in late nineteenth and early twentieth-century China has focused on the growth of regional enterprises as local business empires (Köll 2003). Although institutions matter for entrepreneurship, they have often not been national ones.

21.5 CORPORATE ENTREPRENEURSHIP

As discussed earlier, Chandler's compelling framework for understanding the rise of big business displaced the earlier interest in Schumpeterian entrepreneurship as the center stage of the business history research agenda. From another perspective, there was a refocus of the discipline's research agenda on the entrepreneurial function within the firm, reframing the research to address a different historical context: the rise of big business.

An interest in organizational (as opposed to individual) entrepreneurship predated Chandler. It was an integral part of the research that Schumpeter had spurred in the 1940s and 1950s. Though overshadowed by the dominant socio-cultural approach to entrepreneurship, the notion of organizational entrepreneurship was explored in the 1950s in the work of, among others scholars, Arthur Cole and Edith Penrose, who framed ideas about the evolutionary development of firms using an explicitly Schumpeterian approach. Cole, for instance, developed an eclectic model of entrepreneurially driven evolution in business systems that included roles for organizational factors, industry-based linkages, and national cultural norms (Cole 1959).

Chandler focused research on one element of Cole's eclectic framework for entrepreneurial evolution—the innovative firm (Cuff 2002). The modern industrial enterprise, Chandler observed, was "entrepreneurial and innovative in the Schumpeterian sense" (Chandler 1990). Moreover, while emphasizing the importance of large firms, Chandler and other business historians in his tradition never argued that size and managerial control alone were sufficient to make a firm entrepreneurial and innovative. Chandler's studies repeatedly deal with failure as well as success, and provide ample empirical evidence to support the extensive management literature that large established corporations face major challenges in innovation arising from technological and resource lock-ins, and routine and cultural rigidities (Brown and Eisenhardt 1995; Teece 1998).

The business history literature on corporate entrepreneurship evolved in parallel and with minimal interaction with a burgeoning managerial literature on the subject (Zahra *et al.* 1999). The lack of interaction was unfortunate, as the historical literature provided valuable longitudinal insights into the significance of routines and culture in encouraging or retarding entrepreneurship and innovation within large firms. Graham and Schuldiner (2001) provided an historical study of innovation at US-based Corning which demonstrated that managerial hierarchies and economies of scale were less important in promoting technological innovation within firms than certain firm-specific cultural characteristics. Corning was a medium-sized, family-owned company which was able to progressively "re-invent" itself from a specialty glass manufacturer in the nineteenth century into a leading producer of television tubes after World War II, and then into one of the world's largest fiber-optics manufacturers.

The creation of internal venture units has provided one means to escape the inertia of existing organizations. In the decades after World War II, many large corporations began to respond to the perceived maturity of their traditional markets and their own declining levels of innovation by seeking new organizational means to facilitate new business creation within their own boundaries. It was too daunting to contemplate a transformation of the entire organization, and instead attention turned to trying to make or create more entrepreneurial components within it. During the 1960s, as Hounshell and Kenly Smith (1988) show in an authoritative study of innovation, the US chemical company DuPont utilized both its existing divisions and a development department to create new ventures. During the same period internal venture divisions were created within many large US corporations. The key problems faced by such internal venture units often arose from their relationship with the larger organization (Fast 1978). Venture managers were often "orphaned" and not effective in the parent firm's internal politics (Jones and Kraft 2004; Jones 2005).

Historical research has exercised an important influence on theories of firm-level entrepreneurship and industry evolution. While static neoclassical theories of the firm still predominate, evolutionary theories based on path-dependent firm innovations and capability development have been developed, in part based on the now-extensive historical record on Chandlerian firms (Nelson and Winter 1982; Aldrich 1999). Such evolutionary approaches to industry change through firm innovation have now become common among management scholars doing longitudinal studies (McKelvey 2000; Murmann 2003). More recently, and extensively, Lazonick (2003) has sought to synthesize the historical scholarship in this area into a theory of the innovative firm that incorporates variation over time. More extensively than the research on the contributions of individual entrepreneurship to the wealth of nations, the focus on firm-level entrepreneurship has made significant contributions to our understanding of innovation within large enterprises and how historical environments affect the entrepreneurial processes of firms.

21.6 FINANCING ENTREPRENEURSHIP

In the social scientific literature, entrepreneurial finance is practically synonymous with the study of venture capital firms (VCs). Venture capital, the reasoning goes, occupies a unique place in the financial system by specializing in relatively risky long-term financing of entrepreneurs with little in the way of assets to collateralize. Most entrepreneurial firms with high growth potential need external financing, but few intermediaries and individuals are in a position to extend such financing given the significant problems inherent in monitoring investments in new firms with no track record and tremendous uncertainties. VCs place themselves in a unique position to make such investments in two ways. First, they specialize in effectively understanding and monitoring such new firms and their managers in ways that reduce the chances of opportunistic behavior by entrepreneurs. And second, they transfer a critical bundle of knowledge, skills, and contacts to entrepreneurial firms that reduce the uncertainties they face and increase the likelihood of success (Gompers and Lerner 2000, 2005).

Because the venture capital industry is relatively new, few social scientists consider "entrepreneurial finance" an historical topic. Yet the problem that entrepreneurial finance addresses—the challenges of raising long-term risk capital to finance uncertain new businesses—is in fact central to understanding entrepreneurship in a wide range of historical settings. As historical research has highlighted, the problems of entrepreneurial finance have been addressed in a wide range of organizational and institutional ways in different historical contexts, each with implications for the nature of entrepreneurial activity in the period.

In the 1960s, Gerschenkron developed and popularized the idea that Germany's big universal banks played a critical innovative role in helping that country "catch up" with early industrializers. Gerschenkron's thesis was that German banks did not simply allocate capital to German industry but also helped it innovate by transferring knowledge from Western economies and concentrating managerial skills in key firms. They also monitored their investments closely, often sitting on the boards of the corporations in which they invested. German industrial firms grew big in part with the aid of banks that were willing to engage in long-term investments in such firms but also in aiding the development of economies of scope and managerial hierarchies needed for the success of these "champions" (Gerschenkron 1962*a*).

While aspects of Gerschenkron's thesis have been contested, his argument that banks did not simply invest in German firms, but were critical to the entrepreneurial processes and industry development, has, in interesting ways, been picked up by historians working in other national settings. Studies of banks in the early industrial period have revealed close relationships with entrepreneurs. Brunt (2005), in a study of the financing of the adoption by late eighteenth-century Cornish copper mines of the risky new technology represented by Watt steam engines, demonstrates that some English country banks resembled proto-venture capital firms.

A common theme of much recent research is that bank lending often favored "insiders", and that—contrary to modern beliefs—this was a sound business strategy when it was hard to find reliable information on prospective borrowers. Lamoreaux (1994) argues that this was the case in nineteenth-century New England. Similar conclusions have been drawn about the promotional and developmental role of banks in recent research on the financial system in industrializing Britain

(Collins 1991). Far from maintaining divisions between commercial banking, investment banking, and entrepreneurship, early banks in Great Britain and the United States seem to have provided a range of services, including long-term risk capital, knowledge, and inter-firm linkages, that were critical to innovation and the entrepreneurial process. In the United States and Great Britain, the separation of commercial and investment finance often associated with those financial systems did not develop until the early twentieth century.

Even as commercial banks became increasingly divorced from new venture financing in the early twentieth-century Anglo-American world, banks continued to play a significant role in entrepreneurial finance in other parts of the world. Japanese banks within larger Japanese business groups, for instance, played a critical role in coordinating capital and talent toward new venture development. Moreover, the role of banks was not limited to financing entrepreneurial innovation within large, established firms or groups. Through much of continental Europe, including France, Germany, and Italy, banks played a crucial role in financing the development of small and medium-sized enterprises that have proven to be a particularly dynamic and competitive segment of these economies (Carnevali 2005).

Banks and other formal financial institutions, however, represented only one way of raising entrepreneurial finance in the past. A very large portion of early stage innovation and entrepreneurship was financed through the personal networks of the entrepreneur—that is, through angel investors. Social networks—particularly kinship and ethnic networks—seem to have played an important role throughout much of the historical record, particularly in extending trade financing. Hamilton (1998) describes the importance of extensive family networks around Chinese entrepreneurs in pooling capital for new ventures. In the United States, immigrant Jews in the early twentieth century formed informal and formal credit organizations to finance small business and trade when access to bank credit was not a possibility. Likewise, Lamoreaux et al. (2004) have shown that certain innovative firms and former entrepreneurs served as hubs in entrepreneurial financing networks in turn-of-the-century Cleveland. Such informal credit networks were also important in the pursuit of international entrepreneurial opportunities. Diaspora networks were often an important source of credit in the nineteenth-century global economy, as were the personal contacts developed over the course of an international business career. Liu (1954), for instance, described how one nineteenth-century American entrepreneur in China was able to pull together financing for a new steamship company largely through the Chinese and ex-pat associates he had met while working for his employer.

In the United States and Great Britain, where banks did increasingly back away from entrepreneurial finance in the twentieth century, government policymakers stepped in to finance entrepreneurship through grants and subsidized loans. In the United States, much of the high-technology sector benefited from government research expenditures and the small business administration played a crucial role in extending low-cost lending to small and medium-sized businesses. Similar developments took place in Great Britain as bank lending to small business dwindled and as the banking sector became more concentrated. In particular, concerns over the lack of finance for small business in the interwar years led to the formation in 1945 of the Industrial and Commercial Finance Corporation (ICFC) and the Finance Corporation for Industry (FCI). As Coopey has shown, though both firms "were capitalized and owned by private sector banks and financial institutions, [they] were seen to have a sense of public duty". ICFC laid the foundations for the emergence of the modern British VC industry (Coopey 2005; Coopey and Clarke 1995).

Venture capital firms first emerged in the United States within this milieu in no small part because the formal institutional intermediaries in the country had largely given up on entrepreneurial finance. In the decades after World War II, a handful of VC firms concentrated in the northeastern United States and later in California developed in order to focus on new venture finance in a limited set of industries and regions. Until very recently, the rise of venture capital can only be described as having had a potentially important but narrow impact on entrepreneurship. To the extent that an historical record exists of VC's ability to spur entrepreneurship and innovation, this record is largely limited to the United States (Gompers 1994).

Nevertheless, recent scholarship on venture capital by social scientists has the potential to reinvigorate the ways in which historians examine and consider the historical development and contribution of entrepreneurial finance. Scholarship on the ways in which VC firms create contractual terms with entrepreneurs, for instance, suggests a model for similar studies of contracting and the relationships between the sources of entrepreneurial finance and its users across time. There is similar potential to understand the extent to which financial intermediaries played a role in shaping entrepreneurial firm strategy and the structure of emergent industries. The history of entrepreneurial finance hence remains an area in which research is likely to reveal important insights in the future.

21.7 CONCLUSIONS

Although the business history literature on entrepreneurship extends over six decades, few would regard it as the strongest area of research in the discipline. After its initial vitality during the postwar decades, the study of entrepreneurship ran into formidable methodological roadblocks. A number of lengthy debates, such as that over the role of entrepreneurship in the relative decline of late nineteenth-century Britain, became virtual symbols of the methodological challenges encountered in studying the topic. Decades of biographical studies of leading entrepreneurs failed to produce the "valid generalizations" which Schumpeter (1947) called for so long ago. Entrepreneurial research lost traction as attention focused on the corporation. This did not entirely displace research on entrepreneurship, but it left it fragmented and usually marginal to mainstream research agendas.

Nevertheless, business history has made important, and frequently overlooked, contributions to the study of entrepreneurship. By embedding entrepreneurship within the broader process of historical change in industries and economies, historical research provides insights for other social scientists into how contemporary entrepreneurial activity may be better contextualized in time and place. Management research on entrepreneurship over the last two decades has been narrowly clustered in its empiricism, often making broad generalizations based on high-technology start-up firms in a few locations. As Shane and Venkataraman (2000) have pointed out, the lack of attention to the context for the existence of entrepreneurial opportunities can be regarded as a major weakness of social scientific research today. In contrast, business history has made important contributions to the study of entrepreneurship through its diverse coverage of countries, regions, and industries, even if the literature has been heavily oriented towards large corporations. It has provided compelling evidence for how context—the economic, social, organizational, or institutional setting in and upon which entrepreneurs act—is ultimately as important to assessing and evaluating entrepreneurship as the characteristics and behavior of entrepreneurs themselves.

Business historians, in turn, can learn from the other social sciences about the study of entrepreneurial behavior and cognition. While historians have put considerable effort into understanding who became entrepreneurs and how context mattered, they have only occasionally focused on how entrepreneurs pursued opportunities (Stevenson and Jarillo 1990). Social scientific research provides significant insights into how to investigate such questions as how entrepreneurs perceive opportunities, how they assemble resources now on the promise of delivering uncertain future goods and services, and how they create governance and contracting relationships. These questions and approaches can be effectively adapted for historical research in ways that can offer historians a more fine-grained understanding of how entrepreneurs in a particular setting operated. Such careful behavioral studies can also help historians better understand the causal mechanisms by which particular institutions or events affected modes of entrepreneurial behavior over time.

Finally, historians can also advance their research on entrepreneurship by re-engaging central concepts and theories of entrepreneurship, and by drawing together the many different streams of research that now touch on the subject (Cassis and Minoglou 2005). Unlike other disciplines (and unlike the entrepreneurship research of the postwar era), entrepreneurship research in business history today can hardly be called a coherent field: no institutional mechanism exists to hold it together, few historians would consider themselves primarily entrepreneurship scholars, and little effort is made to tie together the various streams of work or to consider broader theoretical contentions about the nature of entrepreneurship in history.

There are now major opportunities to reassert entrepreneurship as a central research issue, and to build on the strong roots which are already in place. There is much work to be done on the historical impact of culture and values on entre-preneurial behavior, using more careful methodologies than in the past, and seeking to specify more exactly how important culture is relative to other variables. There are major research opportunities to complement existing research on the role of institutions in economic growth by exploring the relationship between institutions and entrepreneurs. Business historians are in a unique position to complement other social science contributions so as to enhance our understanding of what Baumol (1988) has described as the "inherently subtle and elusive character" of entrepreneurship.

References

ACEMOGLU, DARON, JOHNSON, SIMON, and ROBINSON, JAMES (2001). "The Colonial Origins of Comparative Development: An Empirical Investigation". *American Economic Review*, 91: 1369–401.

ACS, ZOLTAN J., and AUDRETSCH, DAVID B. (eds.) (2003). *Handbook of Entrepreneurship Research*. Boston: Kluwer.

ALDRICH, HOWARD (1999). *Organizations Evolving*. New York: Sage.

—— (2005). "Entrepreneurship", in Neil Smelser and Richard Swedberg (eds.), *Handbook of Economic Sociology*. Princeton, NJ: Princeton University Press.

—— and WALDINGER, R. (1990) "Ethnicity and Entrepreneurship". *Annual Review of Sociology*, 16: 111–35.

ASHTON, T. S. (1939). *An Eighteenth Century Industrialist: Peter Stubs of Warrington 1756–1806*. Manchester: A. M. Kelley.

BANERJEE, ABHIJIT, and IYER, LAKSHMI (2005). "History, Institutions and Economic Performance: The Legacy of Colonial Land Tenure Systems in India". *American Economic Review*, 95/4: 1190–213.

BAUMOL, WILLIAM J. (1988). *Entrepreneurship, Management, and the Structure of Payoffs*. Cambridge, Mass.: MIT Press.

—— (1990). "Entrepreneurship: Productive, Unproductive, and Destructive". *Journal of Political Economy*, 98/5: 893–921.

BERGHOFF, H. (1995). "Regional Variations in Provincial Business Biography: The Case of Birmingham, Bristol and Manchester, 1870–1914". *Business History*, 37: 64–85.

—— and MÖLLER, R. (1994). "Tired Pioneers and Dynamic Newcomers? A Comparative Essay on English and German Entrepreneurial History, 1870–1914". *Economic History Review*, 47: 262–87.

BERLIN, LESLIE (2005). *The Man behind the Microchip: Robert Noyce and the Invention of Silicon Valley*. Oxford: Oxford University Press.

BREZNITZ, DAN (2006). *Innovation and the State: Political Choice and Strategies for Growth in Israel, Taiwan and Ireland*. New Haven: Yale.

BROWN, RAJ (2000). *Chinese Big Business and the Weath of Nations*. London: Palgrave.

——(2006). "State Entrepreneurship in Singapore: Prospects for Regional Economic Power?" in Youssef Cassis and Ioanna Pepelasis Minoglou (eds.), *Country Studies in Entrepreneurship: A Historical Perspective*. New York: Palgrave.

BROWN, SHONA L., and EISENHARDT, KATHLEEN M. (1995). "Product Development: Past Research, Present Findings, and Future Directions". *Academy of Management Review*, 20/2, Apr.: 343–78.

BRUNT, LIAM (2005). "Rediscovering Risk: Country Banks as Venture Capital Firms in the First Industrial Revolution". *Journal of Economic History*, 66/1: 74–102.

CARNEVALI, FRANCESCA (2005). *Europe's Advantage: Banks and Small Firms in Britain, France, Germany and Italy since 1918*. Oxford: Oxford University Press.

CASSIS, YOUSSEF, and MINOGLOU, IOANNA PEPELASIS (eds.) (2005). *Entrepreneurship in Theory and History*. New York: Palgrave.

CASSON, MARK (1991). *The Economics of Business Culture*. Oxford: Clarendon Press.

——(1995). *Entrepreneurship and Business Culture: Studies in the Economics of Trust*, vol. 1. Aldershot: Edward Elgar.

CERUTTI, MARIO (1996). "Estudios regionales e historia empresarial en Mexico (1840–1920): Una revisión de lo producido desde 1975", in C. Dávila L. de Guevara (ed.), *Empresa e historia en América Latina*. Bogotá: Tercer Mundo Editores/Colciencias.

CHANDLER, ALFRED D., JR. (1960). "Cultural Factors in Economic Growth". *Journal of Economic History*, 20: 515–30.

——(1962). *Strategy and Structure*. Cambridge, Mass.: Harvard University Press.

——(1990). *Scale and Scope*. Cambridge, Mass.: Harvard University Press.

COCHRAN, THOMAS (1950). "Entrepreneurial Behavior and Motivation". *Explorations in Entrepreneurial History*, 2/5: 304–7.

COLE, ARTHUR H. (1959). *Business Enterprise in its Social Setting*. Cambridge, Mass.: Harvard University Press.

——(1968). "Introductory Remarks". *American Economic Review*, 58/2: 60–3.

COLEMAN, D. C, and MACLEOD, C. (1986). "Attitudes to New Techniques: British Businessmen 1800–1950". *Economic History Review*, 39/4: 588–611.

COLLINS, B., and ROBBINS, K. (eds.) (1990). *British Culture and Economic Decline*. London: Palgrave Macmillan.

COLLINS, MICHAEL (1991). *Banks and Industrial Finance in Britain 1800–1939*. London: Macmillan.

COOPER, ARNOLD (2003). "Entrepreneurship: The Past, the Present, the Future", in Acs and Audretsch (2003).

COOPEY, RICHARD (2005). "Venture Capital and Enterprise", in Cassis and Minoglou (2005).

——and CLARKE, DONALD (1995). *3i: Fifty Years Investing in Industry*. Oxford: Oxford University Press.

CUFF, ROBERT D. (2002). "Notes for a Panel on Entrepreneurship in Business History". *Business History Review*, 76: 123–32.

DAVENPORT-HINES, RICHARD P. T. (1984). *Dudley Docker: The Life and Times of a Trade Warrior*. Cambridge: Cambridge University Press.

Dávila L. de Guevara, Carlos (ed.) (2003). *Empresas y empresarios en la historia de Colombia: Siglos XIX y XX*. Bogotá: Norma/Uniandes.

Davis, Lance, and North, Douglass (1971). *Institutional Change and American Economic Growth*. New York: Cambridge University Press.

Dobbin, Christine (1996). *Asian Entrepreneurial Minorities: Conjoint Communities in the Marking of the World-Economy 1570–1940*. Richmond: Curzon.

Ellis, Charles D. (2006). *Joe Wilson and the Creation of Xerox*. Hoboken, NJ: John Wiley & Sons.

Engerman, Stanley L., and Sokoloff, Kenneth (2005). "Colonialism, Inequality and Long-Run Paths of Development". NBER Working Paper Series No. W11057.

Fast, Norman D. (1978). *The Rise and Fall of Corporate New Venture Divisions*. Ann Arbor, Mich.: UMI Research Press.

Fear, Jeffrey (2005). *Organizing Control: August Thyssen and the Construction of German Corporate Management*. Cambridge, Mass.: Harvard University Press.

Feldenkirchen, Wilfried (1994). *Werner von Siemens*. Columbus: Ohio State University Press.

Foreman-Peck, James (2005). "Measuring Historical Entrepreneurship", in Cassis and Minoglou (2005).

—— and Boccaletti, E. (2002). "French and British Businessmen in the Nineteenth Century", in P. Chassaigne and M. Dockrill (eds.), *Anglo-French Relations 1898–1998*. Basingstoke: Palgrave Macmillan.

Freyer, Tony A. (forthcoming). "Legal Innovation & Market Capitalism, 1790–1920", in Christopher Tomlins and Michael Grossberg (eds.), *The Cambridge History of Law in America*. New York: Cambridge University Press.

Gabler, Neal (2006). *Walt Disney: The Triumph of the American Imagination*. New York: Alfred A. Knopf.

Galambos, Louis (1970). "The Emerging Organizational Synthesis in Modern American History". *Business History Review*, 44/3: 279–90.

Gartner, William, and Carter, Nancy (2003). "Entrepreneurial Behavior and Firm Organizing Processes", in Acs and Audretsch (2003).

Gerschenkron, Alexander (1962a). *Economic Backwardness in Historical Perspective*. Cambridge, Mass.: Belknap Press.

—— (1962b). "Social Attitudes, Entrepreneurship, and Economic Development: A Comment". *Explorations in Entrepreneurial History*, 6: 245–72.

—— (1966). "The Modernization of Entrepreneurship", in Myron Weiner (ed.), *Modernization: The Dynamics of Growth*. New York: Basic Books.

Gilbrar, Gad G. (2003). "The Muslim Big Merchant-Entrepreneurs of the Middle East, 1860–1914". *Die Welt des Islams*, 43/1: 1–36.

Godley, Andrew (2001). *Jewish Immigrant Entrepreneurship in New York and London*. Basingstoke: Palgrave.

Gompers, Paul (1994). "The Rise and Fall of Venture Capital", *Business and Economic History*, 3: 1–26.

—— and Lerner, Josh (2000). *The Venture Capital Cycle*. Cambridge, Mass.: MIT Press.

—— —— (2003). "Equity Financing", in Acs and Audretsch (2003).

Goswami, Omkar (1985). "Then Came the Marwaris: Some Aspects of the Changes in the Pattern of Industrial Control in Eastern India". *The Indian Economic and Social History Review*, 22: 225–249.

GRAHAM, MARGARET B. W., and SHULDINER, ALEC T. (2001). *Corning and the Craft of Innovation*. Oxford: Oxford University Press.

HAGEN, EVERETT (1962). *On the Theory of Social Change*. Homewood, Ill: Dorsey Press.

HAMILTON, GARY. (1998). "Culture and Organization in Taiwan's Market Economy", in Hefner (1998).

HANNAH, LESLIE (1984). "Entrepreneurs and the Social Sciences". *Economica*, 51: 219–34.

HEFNER, ROBERT (ed.) (1998). *Market and Cultures: Society and Morality in the New Asian Capitalisms*. Boulder, Colo: Westview.

HIRSCHMEIER, JOHANNES (1964). *The Origins of Entrepreneurship in Meiji Japan*. Cambridge, Mass.: Harvard University Press.

HODGSON, GEOFFREY (2001). *How Economics Forgot History: The Problem of Historical Specificity in Social Science*. London: Routledge.

HOPKINS, ANTHONY G. (1987). "Big Business in African Studies". *Journal of African History*, 28: 119–40.

HOUNSHELL, DAVID A., and KENLY SMITH, JOHN (1988). *Science and Corporate Strategy: DuPont R & D, 1902–1980*. Cambridge: Cambridge University Press.

HOVENKAMP, HERBERT (1991). *Enterprise and American Law 1836–1937*. Cambridge, Mass.: Harvard University Press.

HOWE, A. C. (1984). *Cotton Masters 1830–1860*. Oxford: Oxford University Press.

HUGHES, JONATHAN R. T. (1983). "Arthur Cole and Entrepreneurial History". *Business and Economic History*, 12: 133–44.

——(1991). *The Government Habit Redux: Economic Controls from Colonial Times to the Present*. Princeton, NJ: Princeton University Press.

HURST, JAMES WILLARD (1967). *Law and the Conditions of Freedom in Nineteenth-Century America*. Madison: University of Wisconsin Press.

JENKS, LELAND H. (1944). "Railroads as an Economic Force in American Development". *Journal of Economic History*, 4: 18–20.

——(1949). "Role Structure of Entrepreneurial Personality", in *Change and the Entrepreneur: Postulates and the Patterns for Entrepreneurial History*. Harvard University Research Center in Entrepreneurial History. Cambridge, Mass.: Harvard University Press.

JEREMY, DAVID (ed.) (1984–6). *Dictionary of Business Biography: A Biographical Dictionary of Business Leaders Active in Britain in the Period 1860–1980*, 5 vols. London: Butterworth.

——(ed.) (1988). *Business and Religion in Britain*. Aldershot: Gower.

——(1998). *Religion, Business and Wealth in Modern Britain*. New York: Routledge.

JONES, GEOFFREY (2005). *Renewing Unilever: Transformation and Tradition*. Oxford: Oxford University Press.

——and KRAFT, ALISON (2004). "Corporate Venturing: The Origins of Unilever's Pregnancy Test". *Business History*, 46/1: 100–22.

KENZER, ROBERT (1989). "The Black Businessman in the Postwar South: North Carolina, 1865–1880". *Business History Review*, 63: 61–87.

KHAN, ZORINA (2005). *The Democratization of Invention: Patents and Copyrights in American Economic Development*. New York: Cambridge University Press.

KILBY, PETER (ed.) (1971). *Entrepreneurship and Economic Development*. New York: Free Press.

KIRBY, MAURICE (1993). "Quakerism, Entrepreneurship and the Family Firm in North-East England, 1780–1860", in Jonathan Brown and Mary B. Rose (eds.), *Entrepreneurship, Networks and Modern Business*. Manchester: Manchester University Press.

KöLL, ELISABETH (2003). *From Cotton Mill to Business Empire: The Emergence of Regional Enterprises in Modern China*. Cambridge, Mass.: Harvard University Press.

KRUEGER, NORRIS (2003). "The Cognitive Psychology of Entrepreneurship", in Acs and Audretsch (2003).

LAMOREAUX, NAOMI (1994). *Insider Lending: Banks, Personal Connections, and Economic Development in Industrial New England*. New York: Cambridge University Press.

——— and ROSENTHAL, JEAN-LAURENT (2005). "Legal Regime and Contractual Flexibility: A Comparison of Business's Organizational Choices in France and the United States during the Era of Industrialization". *American Law and Economics Review*, 7: 28–61.

——— LEVENSTEIN, MARGARET, and SOKOLOFF, KENNETH (2004). "Financing Invention during the Second Industrial Revolution: Cleveland, Ohio 1870–1920". NBER Working Paper Series No. 10923.

LANDES, DAVID (1949). "French Entrepreneurship and Industrial Growth in the Nineteenth Century". *Journal of Economic History*, 9: 45–61.

——— (1953). "Social Attitudes, Entrepreneurship, and Economic Development: A Comment". *Explorations in Entrepreneurial History*, 6: 245–72.

——— (1969, 2003). *The Unbound Prometheus: Technological Change and Industrial Development in Western Europe from 1750 to the Present*. New York: Cambridge University Press.

——— (1998). *The Wealth and Poverty of Nations*. New York: W. W. Norton.

LAPORTA, RAFAEL, LOPEZ-DE-SILANES, FLORENCIO, SCHLEIFER, ANDREI, AND VISHNY, ROBERT (1997). "Legal Determinants of External Finance". *Journal of Finance*, 52: 1131–50.

LAZONICK, WILLIAM (2003). "Understanding Innovative Enterprise: Toward the Integration of Economic Theory and Business History", in Franco Amatori and Geoffrey Jones (eds.), *Business History around the World*. Cambridge: Cambridge University Press.

LIU, KWANG-CHING LIU (1954). "Financing a Steam-Navigation Company in China, 1861–62". *Business History Review*, 28: 154–81.

LIVESAY, HAROLD (1995). "Introduction", in Livesay (ed.), *Entrepreneurship and the Growth of Firms*. Aldershot: Edward Elgar.

MAURER, NOEL (2002). *The Power and the Money: The Mexican Financial System, 1876–1932*. Stanford, Calif: Stanford University Press.

McCABE, INA B., HARLAFTIS, GELINA, and MINOGLOU, IOANNA P. (2005). *Diaspora Entrepreneurial Networks: Four Centuries of History*. New York: Berg.

McCLOSKEY, DONALD N., and SANDBERG, LARS G. (1971). "From Damnation to Redemption: Judgments on the Late Victorian Entrepreneur". *Explorations in Economic History*, 9: 89–108.

McCRAW, THOMAS K. (2006). "Schumpeter's Business Cycles as Business History". *Business History Review*, 80, summer: 231–61.

McKELVEY, MAUREEN D. (2000). *Evolutionary Innovations: The Business of Biotechnology*. Oxford: Oxford University Press.

McKENDRICK, N. (1959). "Josiah Wedgwood: An Eighteenth-Century Entrepreneur in Salesmanship and Marketing Techniques". *Economic History Review*, 12: 408–33.

——— (1964). "Josiah Wedgwood and Thomas Bentley: An Inventor-Entrepreneur Partnership in the Industrial Revolution". *Transactions of the Royal Historical Society*, 14: 1–33.

MITCHELL, RONALD K., BUSENITZ, LOWELL, LANT, THERESA, McDOUGALL, PATRICIA P., MORSE, ERIC A., and SMITH, J. BROCK (2002). "Towards a Theory of Entrepreneurial

Cognition: Rethinking the People Side of Entrepreneurship Research". *Entrepreneurship Theory and Practice*, winter: 93–104.

MORAWSKA, EWA (1996). *Insecure Prosperity: Jews in Small-Town Industrial America, 1880–1940*. Princeton, NJ: Princeton University Press.

MORRIS, MORRIS DAVID (1967). "Values as an Obstacle to Economic Growth in South Asia: An Historical Survey". *Journal of Economic History*, 27: 588–607.

MUNRO, J. FORBES (2003). *Maritime Enterprise and Empire: Sir William Mackinnon and his Business Network, 1823–1893*. Woodbridge: Boydell Press.

MURMANN, JOHANN PETER (2003). *Knowledge and Competitive Advantage: The Coevolution of Firms, Technology and National Institutions*. New York: Cambridge.

NASAW, DAVID (2006). *Andrew Carnegie*. New York: Penguin Press.

NELSON, RICHARD, and WINTER, SIDNEY (1982). *An Evolutionary Theory of Economic Change*. Cambridge, Mass.: Harvard University Press.

NICHOLAS, TOM (1999). "Wealth-Making in Nineteenth and Early Twentieth Century Britain: Industry v. Commerce and Finance". *Business History*, 41/1, Jan.: 16–36.

—— (2000). "Wealth Making in the Nineteenth- and Early Twentieth Century: The Rubinstein Hypothesis Revisited". *Business History*, 42/2, Apr.: 155–68.

—— (2004) "Enterprise and Management", in Paul Johnson and Roderick Floud (eds.), *The Cambridge Economic History of Modern Britain*. Cambridge: Cambridge University Press.

NORTH, DOUGLASS (1990). *Institutions, Institutional Change, and Economic Performance*. Cambridge: Cambridge University Press.

—— and WEINGAST, BARRY (1989). "Constitutions and Commitment: The Evolution of Institutions Governing Public Choice in Eighteenth-Century England". *Journal of Economic History*, 49, Dec.: 803–32.

NOVAK, WILLIAM (1996). *The People's Welfare: Law and Regulation in Nineteenth Century America*. Chapel Hill, NC: University of North Carolina Press.

—— (2001). "The American Law of Association: The Legal-Political Construction of Civil Society". *Studies in American Political Development*, 15: 163–88.

OLEGARIO, ROWENA (1999). " 'The Mysterious People:' Jewish Merchants, Transparency, and Community in Mid-Nineteenth Century America". *Business History Review*, 73: 161–89.

OLSSON, ULF (2001). *Furthering a Fortune: Marcus Wallenberg*. Stockholm: Ekerlids Forlag.

OONK, G. (2006). "South Asians in East Africa (1880–1920) with a particular focus on Zanzibar: Toward a Historical Explanation of Economic Success of a Middleman Minority". *African and Asian Studies*, 5/1: 1–32.

RANIS, GUSTAV (1955). "The Community-Centered Entrepreneur in Japanese Development". *Explorations in Entrepreneurial History*, 7: 80–98.

RUIGROK, WINFRIED, and VAN TULDER, ROB (1995). *The Logic of Internationals Restructuring*. London: Routledge.

SASS, STEVEN (1978). "Entrepreneurial Historians and History: An Essay in Organized Intellect". Ph.D. dissertation, Johns Hopkins University.

SAWYER, JOHN (1954). "The Social Basis of the American System of Manufacturing". *Journal of Economic History*, 14: 361–79.

SCHEIBER, HARRY N. (1973) "Property Law, Expropriation, and Resource Allocation by Government, 1789–1910". *Journal of Economic History*, 33/1: 232–51.

—— (1997) "Private Rights and Public Power: American Law, Capitalism, and the Republican Polity in Nineteenth-Century America". *Yale Law Journal*, 107, Dec.: 823–61.

SCHUMPETER, JOSEPH (1942). *Capitalism, Socialism, and Democracy*. New York: Harper and Brothers.

—— (1947). "The Creative Response in Economic History". *The Journal of Economic History*, 7: 149–59.

SHANE, SCOTT, and VENKATARAMAN, SANKARAN (2000). "The Promise of Entrepreneurship as a Field of Research". *Academy of Management Review*, 25: 217–26.

SIMMEL, GEORG (1908) "The Stranger", in K. H. Wolff (ed.), *The Sociology of Georg Simmel*, English trans. New York: Free Press, 1950.

SMITH, MICHAEL S. (2006). *The Emergence of Modern Business Enterprise in France, 1800–1930*. Cambridge, Mass.: Harvard University Press.

SOMBART, WERNER (1911). *The Jews and Modern Capitalism*. English trans. New Brunswick, NJ: Transaction Books, 1982.

STEVENSON, HOWARD, and JARILLO, J. CARLOS (1990). "A Paradigm of Entrepreneurship: Entrepreneurial Management". *Strategic Management Journal*, 11, summer: 17–27.

TAWNEY, R. H. (1926). *Religion and the Rise of Capitalism*. New York: Harcourt, Brace.

TEECE, DAVID J. (1998). "Design Issues for Innovative Firms: Bureaucracy, Incentives and Industrial Structure", in Alfred. D. Chandler Jr., Peter Hagstrom, and Orjan Sölvell (eds.), *The Dynamic Firm*. Oxford: Oxford University Press.

TENENBAUM, SHELLY (1993). *Credit to their Community: Jewish Loan Societies in the United States, 1880–1945*. Detroit: Wayne State University Press.

THOMPSON, F. M. L. (2001). *Gentrification and the Enterprise Culture: Britain 1780–1980*. Oxford: Oxford University Press.

THORNTON, PATRICIA (1999). "The Sociology of Entrepreneurship". *Annual Review of Sociology*. 25: 19–46.

TIGNOR, ROBERT (1980). "The Economic Activities of Foreigners in Egypt, 1920–1950: From Millet to Haute Bourgeoisie". *Comparative Studies in Society and History*, 22/3: 416–49.

TRIPATHI, DWIJENDRA (2004). *The Oxford History of Indian Business*. New Delhi: Oxford University Press.

TRIPSAS, MARY, and GAVETTI, GIOVANNI (2000). "Capabilities, Cognition and Inertia: Evidence from Digital Imaging". *Strategic Management Journal*, 21: 1147–61.

TSANG, DENISE (2006). *The Entrepreneurial Culture: Network Advantage within Chinese and Irish Software Firms*. Cheltenham: Edward Elgar.

WADA, KAZUO, and YUI, TSUNEHIKO (2002). *Courage and Change: The Life of Kiichiro Toyoda*. Toyota City: Toyota Motor Corporation.

WALKER, JULIET (1986). "Racism, Slavery, Free Enterprise: Black Entrepreneurship in the United States before the Civil War". *Business History Review*, 60/3: 343–82.

WEBER, MAX (1904). *The Protestant Ethic and the Spirit of Capitalism*, English edn. New York: Scribner, 1930.

WIENER, MARTIN (ed.) (1966). *Modernization: The Dynamics of Growth*. New York: Basic Books.

—— (1981). *English Culture and the Decline of the Industrial Spirit: 1850–1980*. New York: Cambridge University Press.

WILSON, C. H. (1955). "The Entrepreneur in the Industrial Revolution". *Explorations in Entrepreneurial History*, 7/3: 129–45.

YAMAMURA, KOZO (1968). "A Re-examination of Entrepreneurship in Meiji Japan". *Economic History Review*, 21: 144–58.

YAMAMURA, KOZO (1978). "Entrepreneurship, Ownership and Management in Japan", in Peter Mathias and M. M. Postan (eds.), *The Cambridge Economic History of Europe*, vol. VII, part 2. Cambridge: Cambridge University Press.

ZAHRA, SHAKER A., JENNINGS, DANIEL F., and KURATKO, DONALD F. (1999). "The Antecedents and Consequences of Firm-Level Entrepreneurship: The State of the Field". *Entrepreneurship Theory and Practice*, 24/2, winter: 45–65.

CHAPTER 22

....

BUSINESS AND THE STATE

....

ROBERT MILLWARD

22.1 INTRODUCTION

....

ALTHOUGH there is a huge literature relevant to the history of relations between the state and business, the emphasis here on international comparisons (Western Europe, Japan, and the United States) allows a distinct focus to be given to the analysis. It draws our attention to business as an instrument of the geopolitical strategy of governments and of internal social and political unification as well as to more traditional ideological differences between countries. It also embraces histories of particular business firms like AT&T and British Airways, whole industries such as steel and transport in Japan and Germany, electricity in Sweden and Italy, and issues like privatization and deregulation. Unfortunately much research has related to one country only. Even when published in edited collections covering several countries, the heart of the research output has been the country stories—true even of some excellent recent publications such as Anderson-Skog and Kranz (1999) on transport and telecommunications, Foreman-Peck on European industrial policy (with Federico 1999), and his earlier book on European telecommunications (with Mueller 1988).

The more general literature on business and the state includes competition policies and the role of multinationals (see Chapters 7 and 12, this volume). Government promotion of economic development has been an important element in the context of developing countries (the current Third World, manufacturing in

19th-century Japan) and in the role of science, R&D, and education in all modern economies. The regulation and ownership of natural monopolies, like railroads and natural gas distribution, featured strongly in the traditional literature and very much in recent discussions of the history of privatization and nationalization. The impact of taxes on firms spreads the net ever wider. Moving away from these narrow economic topics, the relations between business and the law and the government's role in providing that legal framework were deemed sufficiently important in the United States for a whole chapter to be devoted to it in the second (19th century) volume of Engerman and Gallman's recent edited authoritative economic history of that country (cf. Freyer 2000). Finally, and quite important for what is to follow, is the role of business as a tool of military strategy and national unification, features that had a big influence on the fortunes of nineteenth-century telecommunications companies and twentieth-century defense contractors.

22.2 A FRAMEWORK FOR INTERNATIONAL COMPARISONS OF BUSINESS–STATE RELATIONS

A focus on international comparisons makes certain elements stand out from that long list. Comparing countries means comparing specific geographic entities with particular political structures. While this seems to direct attention to the different political ideologies of different countries, and this has certainly colored more traditional approaches, it does also make us focus first on the particular geopolitical settings in which a business operates. Japan's efforts to control its raw material sources in the Far East, from Manchuria to Indonesia, and hence the importance of its shipbuilding industry and the development of indigenous shipping lines, may be compared with the French government's attempts to reduce the strategic weakness arising from its rather modest coal supplies by investing in nuclear and oil. Secondly, there are the various socio-political objectives of governments, such as the new Italian state's desire, from 1860, to strengthen the links between north and south. Such issues are often quite separate from commitments to broad ideological stances about economic performance under socialism, fascism, and capitalism—and Dowd and Dobbin (2001) have argued that such stances (including neo-liberalism) have not been constant over time, illustrating this with the fortunes of American railroad companies in the nineteenth and twentieth centuries.

Reliance on the strength of such different dogmas across countries has indeed colored quite a lot of the traditional literature. In the first half of the twentieth century, business firms in the manufacturing sector of Germany, Italy, and Spain operated at times under fascist regimes which, while often ambivalent about private and public ownership, were clear about the importance of self–sufficiency, promoting indigenous entrepreneurs and autarky (Overy 2003; Lyth 2003; Cabrera and del Rey 2003; Hayes 2002; Toninelli 2004). Debate about the scale of business complicity with the Nazis continues strongly in the literature (cf. review by T. Ferguson in EH.Net, April 3, 2006 of Kobrak and Hansen 2004 and Nicosia and Huener 2004). In its control of natural monopolies, the central government in the UK in the 20th century has been seen to be more prone to use public ownership than have the state and federal layers of government in the United States where arm's-length regulation has been more common, reflecting, it is argued, a stronger commitment to *laissez-faire* and private ownership (Keller 1990).

To some extent the reaction of the central governments of the Western World to the decline of traditional manufacturing industries like steel, cotton, shipbuilding, and heavy engineering has also reflected the degree to which intervention was politically acceptable in each country. Big structural changes were left, at one extreme, to the market and in other cases to subsidies and state takeovers. Sometimes the reaction appeared to be market-orientated while the reality was tariff protection. There is a large literature for every country and well beyond the scope of this chapter. Britain's position is worth singling out, for illustrative purposes, since it demonstrates the problems of both diagnosis and industrial policy recommendations.

British manufacturing was very successful in the 19th century and was heavily export orientated whereas its production base was highly concentrated by region. The blossoming of new industrial producing countries in the twentieth century faced it with immense economic and social problems of adaptation (Lazonick 1983; Elbaum 1986; Tolliday 1986). Large-scale structural unemployment could not be ignored by politicians and civil servants who, however, in the mid-twentieth century, had little experience (in contrast to the utilities and railroads) of dealing with oligopolistic industries like steel, which was nationalized and de-nationalized twice in the post-1945 period. In many cases, the problems were complex, generating strongly divergent views amongst business historians. In the case of cotton, for example, UK cloth exports accounted for 30 percent of world exports as late as 1930, a figure which had fallen to 3 percent by 1968, in the face of fierce competition from Japan and other low-wage Asian producers. The diagnosis by Lazonick was that British industry failed to develop mass production in large business units and to keep pace with modern technology, a product of conservative family firms and intransigent trade unions. The industry failed to switch from (skilled labor-intensive) mule spinning to the American-favored ring spinning and integrated businesses engaged in both spinning and weaving. The state's response, by way of re-equipment subsidies legislated for in the 1948 and 1959 Cotton Acts, was deemed to be small scale and weak in not providing enough incentives for organizational change and integration along the lines of the large American firms. Of course, the latter were never so export orientated as British industry and Rose's devastating demonstration (1997) that American industry survived at home mainly because of tariff protection undermines the conclusions drown from the comparison with the United States. Moreover, many small firms can exist efficiently when there are lots of them together—external economies of scale go back to Alfred Marshall and have recently been revived to explain the British case (Broadberry and Marrison 2002; Leunig 2003, and, more generally, Sabel and Zeitlin 1985). Ring spinning was never profitable in Britain before 1945, though, thereafter, it did expand as the demand for a rougher cotton cloth temporarily increased in the austere post-1945 years. When large companies did emerge it was in man-made fibers but the results here for Courtaulds and ICI were "appalling" (Singleton 1991; Higgins 1993).

The equation of international differences solely with differing ideologies about economic performance under capitalism, socialism, and fascism has carried the implication that big changes in business organization involving the state are strongly associated with a change in political ideology. The literature on privatization and nationalization has often picked up this theme and in the case of Portugal's rapid shifts from one to the other in the 1970–90 period and Britain's ideological lead on privatization, such a role cannot be denied (Nunes *et al.* 2004; Stephens 2004). Yet it has also been argued recently that the emergence of privatized business and deregulation in the last quarter of the 20th century was due in no small way to technological changes in sectors like telecommunications and electricity which altered market opportunities and the relative strengths of different interest groups (Koebel 1990; Chick 2002; Millward 2005). Even the incidence of privatization across European countries seems to have been due as much to pressures from the European Union's drive to a single market and to public sector financial crises as to any ideological lead set by Britain (Clifton *et al.* 2003). Indeed heavy reliance on conventional distinctions between socialism, fascism, and capitalism in the analysis of business–state relations runs into problems with countries like Japan which do not fit readily into the standard ideological boxes. Whether Japan in the twentieth century has had a "developmental state" prompting and directing the manufacturing sector or has historically determined special labor relations, with employees strongly committed to particular companies, or has simply witnessed a central government continuously involved in "facilitating communications" between business leaders and others, is still a matter of keen debate (Noble 1989; Hashimoto 1996; Kosai 1995).

Similarly, the Italian state holding company, Istituto per la Ricostruzione Industriale (IRI), was set up in 1933 with the rather pragmatic aim of easing the financial problems of some key sectors of the Italian economy. It provided multilayered support and access to finance. Like Ente Nazionale Idrocaruri (ENI, the state-owned oil and gas company established in 1953) it was a joint-stock company but 100 percent state owned and both of them held majority shares in subsidiaries like STET (telephones) and Azienda Generale Italia Petroli (AGIP). Even that layer was not directly involved in operations but exercised part ownership of telephone companies and others in methane gas products and piping. The Instituto Nacional de Industria (INI) in Spain was similarly constituted but its objectives can perhaps more easily be linked to the autarkic policies of the fascist regime of the Franco dictatorship in its drive for Spanish self-sufficiency. It was 100 percent state owned and gave financial and other general support to its subsidiaries in electricity, coal, oil distribution, to the airline Iberia, and to manufacturing, often in competition with private firms in these sectors (Acena and Comin 1991; Amatori 2000; Gomez-Mendoza 1997; Galvez and Comin 2004; Toninelli 2004).

Looking beyond questions of economic performance draws our attention to the behavior of business in relation to government aims with respect to military strategy and social and political unification. Here an historical perspective brings out clearly how central these are to comparisons of business–state relations across countries. This is for two reasons. The first is that different geographic settings generate different geopolitical strategies. In nineteenth-century continental Europe, every nation state seemed to have hostile neighbors on its borders. In the case of France, its prime concern from the 1860s was the burgeoning giant about to appear from the motley collection of German states. Thereafter, its railroads and rather modest coal deposits came to have great strategic significance. Germany was better blessed with coal but had also the growing threat of Russia on its eastern flank. Others, like Sweden and Norway, with populations spread thinly over huge areas, were keen to use the telegraph and telephone companies as well as the railroads to promote social and political unification. So also Italy after 1860, Belgium after 1830, and Portugal in the 20th century, in all of which the state took significant operational and ownership rights over the railroad companies (Anderson-Skog 2000; Fremdling 1999; Hentenryk 1986; Espeli 2002; Nunes *et al.* 2004). Given its dominance of the seas and island setting, the British government had few of these security worries and left its coal and railroads in the private sector, electricity, gas, and water to local determination and brought only telegraph and telephone under its direct control, perhaps reflecting concerns about Ireland, and about Britain's pervasive interests in imperial and other international business matters (Perry 1977; Foreman-Peck 1989*a* and 1989*b*; Lipartito 2000).

Europe's land mass was politically fragmented by nation states and the form of their strategic concerns contrasts strongly with Japan and the United States. Japan has been heavily dependent on the Asian mainland and islands for raw materials including oil. It has often felt geographically isolated and economically vulnerable. The fact that, by the 1960s, the development of synthetic products reduced some its import needs and was such a relief is testimony to the relevance of this factor (Lockwood 1965). The size of state subsidies to Japanese shipping and shipbuilding, from the late nineteenth century, has no parallel in Europe or North America. By the late 1880s two major indigenous shipping companies (Nihon Yusen Kaisha and Osaka Shōsen Kaisha) had emerged under government protection and they developed shipping lines to China, Korea, and Russia (Mitsuhaya 1958). The United

States had no hostile neighbors on its borders (certainly from the late 19th century), foreign trade was important but much less so than for many European countries, and businesses could develop over a huge geographic area with a common language. McCraw's authoritative (1975) survey of the history of business regulation is noticeably empty of any discussion of socio-political strategic matters. The internal battle with foreign interests in the south and west in the late eighteenth and early nineteenth centuries, as well as throughout the nineteenth century with Native Americans, was reflected in the Federal government's land grant policy. A rapid development of the West with low prices per acre and small allotments helped the armed forces establish strategic outposts. Once that had been accomplished, the "internal" strategic concerns which bedeviled Europe were largely absent.

However, the ability of businesses to expand had to reckon with the Constitution of the United States, and in particular with the rights of the constituent states, and the fear, in some quarters, of federal intervention. This brings us to the second reason why socio-political strategic issues are at the heart of international comparisons of business–state relations. Business operations are obviously affected by each country's political structure, which, for our purposes, may be taken as an historical datum, notwithstanding that it may have been determined to some extent by the geopolitical setting and by ideologies. The powers of the Federal government, on some interpretations, were significantly circumscribed by the Constitution. The constituent states had rights and autonomous powers quite different from the constituent regions in the UK, France, Japan, Spain, and even Germany. Business operations across state boundaries, such as railroads and telecommunications, were relatively untouched by regulatory bodies until the 1887 Interstate Commerce Act. Indeed, many of the regulatory disputes were bound up with the power of the states vis-à-vis the Federal government, and provide a nice historical counterpart, as Dunlavy (2001) has argued, to modern globalization problems of matching the rights of nations with global governance.

In France, the central government was traditionally more powerful, and circumscribed the power of municipalities in economic matters, a factor which largely explains the fact that much of the electricity, gas, and water supplies in the period 1800–1920 was run by private enterprise under concession systems designed by the Conseil d'État (Fernandez 1996). Regulation of business in Germany and Italy by the late 19th century was very much an administrative rather than a legal matter (as in the United States). In Canada, the strong element of decentralized government has often generated competition between the provinces. In electricity supply, the growth of state-owned enterprises, which came to be called the Provincial Hydros, reflected a desire to promote the economic development of the provinces in part as an attempt to emulate and catch up with Ontario Hydro, which had set the pace after 1945 with a massive investment in hydro-electricity. For Quebec, state enterprise was seen as part of the struggle to wrest control from Anglo-Canadian financial elites (Nelles 2003).

In the rest of this chapter, the links between business, geopolitical strategies, and political structures will be developed in the context of Western Europe, Japan, and the United States over the period *c.*1800–1990, focusing on particular industrial sectors, taken to be illustrative rather than comprehensive. We will be examining how international differences in business–state relations have been affected by socio-political strategies and how technological change has altered the role of businesses in that context. The significance of these themes will, at the same time, be assessed relative to the histories of the regulation of natural monopolies, of government promotion of business performance, and the more traditional reliance, in international comparisons, on the varying ideological stances of different governments. Areas for further development will be identified at the end. We will present the issues chronologically and this will tend to move the coverage broadly from surface transport to the energy companies, airlines, telecommunications, and ending with privatization and the European Union (EU).

22.3 Business, the State, and Transport 1800–1920

Surface transport, the telegraph, and coal supplies had potentially strategic significance for the nation states of the 19th century. Some were newly formed, such as Italy, Belgium, the United States, Germany, and others like Japan emerged into the modern world after a major social transformation. Cross-country differences in political structures and in the socio-political objectives of government were manifest in the way that businesses were organized and owned as well as in their financial dealings with the state. In transport and communications, some of the vested interests of state and business arose from these sectors' basic economic characteristics—high fixed costs, natural monopoly conditions, ability to discriminate in pricing. But since these were common to all countries, they cannot, on their own, account for differences across countries. Business and the state were reluctant partners in the nineteenth century and what drew them together initially was that rights of way were needed for canal companies, telegraph undertakings, turnpike trusts, and railroad enterprises and the rights to compulsorily expropriate land were granted by governments. Such rights gave a temporary monopoly position which was often sustained because of the costs of duplication (reflecting the natural monopoly conditions). Hence, we get state legislation for ceilings on tolls, rates, and fares for track usage and, in the case of railroads, where free competition by carriers on the track was not feasible, regulation of conveyancing. That would have left the type of business–state relations found in Britain in the nineteenth century, but how then to account for the very different positions for transport undertakings in continental Europe, the United States, and Japan?

Within Europe, relations between business and the state varied from the fairly loose arm's-length regulation in Britain, through the extensive use of subsidies and capital guarantees in France and Spain and state ownership of trunk lines in Scandinavia, to virtually complete public ownership in Prussia and Italy (Millward 2004). The nation states were concerned to enhance social and political unification, ensure key routes were kept open, and in some cases to directly control operations—as all countries did for the telegraph as we shall see later. The French state was noted for its "orchestration" of the rail network and relieved critical shortages of capital in the 1830s and 1840s by providing guarantees to private investors (Dormois 1999). Later in the century and especially after the Franco–Prussian War of 1870–1, it became clear that railroads were of vital military importance. Following the establishment of the 1883 "conventions", the government was committed to financing the sub-structure of new track and no lines could be closed without the permission of the Ministry of War. The Paris–Orleans line was taken into public ownership and then in 1906 the whole of the Western Network and by 1913, 90 percent of company capital was in the form of bonds and 9,000 kilometers of track were in state ownership.

Belgium was a new state in 1830, Italy in 1860, Norway and Sweden had scattered communities and fragile political structures. In all cases the state stepped in and, rather than subsidies, it was state ownership which dominated the form of intervention. This stemmed primarily from the urgency attached to the construction of trunk networks with state operation (as in wartime) effectively bypassing normal market forces. In Sweden, the first railroad did not appear until the 1850s and, in that difficult terrain, even with subsidies the system would not have been built in the time required by the government. By the end of the century one-third of the lines were in state ownership, 85 percent in Norway, 57 percent in Denmark, 88 percent in Belgium (Anderson-Skog 2000; Foreman-Peck 1987), and relative to population the Scandinavian countries had bigger networks than the rest of Europe. There are doubts whether, in this period, the trunk lines built in Italy generated any significant economic benefits (Schram 1997; Fenoaltea 1972). The demands of unification were urgent and subsidies were never a sufficiently strong instrument. Lines were brought into public ownership in Piedmont, Calabria, Liguria, and Campania, and in some cases sold back during fiscal crises. Then from 1885 the state took over complete responsibility for all the national lines and by 1906 the system had been effectively nationalized. The rail network was organized not as a company under private law with government shares (like SNCF in France from 1937) nor as a public corporation (like British Rail in the post-1945 period) but rather as an "azienda autonoma", an administrative unit under the direction of a government minister. The desire of the state to exercise direct control was so strong, in other words, that in Italy the railroads took the form of the Azienda Autonoma delle Ferrovie dell Stato.

Similar considerations explain the economic organization of the railroad undertakings in Prussia following the unification of Germany in 1870. Faced with France and Russia as neighbors, Prussia not only nationalized its railroads in 1879 but through routes from east to west were sedulously developed in the period 1880–1913. High profits were not initially expected though they did blossom into an important element of state revenues. Regulation was by administrative means (not by law as in the United States). The Deutsche Reichsbahn which was established by the Federal Constitution of 1919 was supposedly an autonomous enterprise but remained strictly under ministerial control (Fremdling 1980; Fremdling and Knieps 1993; Keller 1979, 1990; Mierzejewski 1995, 1999).

The fortunes of business in Japan in the second half of the nineteenth century were vitally shaped by its geopolitical setting and also by the fact that in many key sectors there were few indigenous entrepreneurs and businesses. There is a strand in the never-ending debate about the state which stresses that a key role of the central government was not so much to aid manufacturing as to build up the infrastructure (Yamamura 1978: 235). The geopolitical setting wherein Japan relied on the Asian mainland for many raw materials and viewed it as territory to be developed and controlled meant that shipping and the shipbuilding industry would be of central importance. They were important in Europe and of course Britain was another island economy but, whereas Japan had only 210 sailing, steam, and motor merchant ships in 1880, Italy, for example, had nearly 8,000 and the UK 25,000. Support for shipbuilding and subsidies to shipping were modest in Europe, apart from Spain which is a better analogy and where central government support for shipping and the navy program saw its merchant fleet tonnage climb to equal by 1913, relative to population, those of France and Germany.

For two centuries, Japan had effectively been isolated from the world outside and shipping was restricted to coastal waters. At the start of the Meija era, the only vessels of Western design were owned by local notables or the government so they had to be leased off if local entrepreneurship was to be encouraged. The rail network was in no better shape. Only 283 miles had been built by 1883. So if Japan was to expand and dominate economically and militarily, speed in adjustment was essential and this put an onus on the state to push the private sector and/or activate state enterprises. The Sino–Japanese War of 1894–5 and the Russo–Japanese War of 1904–5 vividly drew attention to the need for development in these infrastructure areas. The Mitsubishi company was the first to benefit from government support. Its Shanghai line was the only overseas route serviced by Japanese ships and the first diesel-powered ship was built under its auspices in 1923. Its shipping interests were merged into NYK in the 1880s and formed part of the big expansion of the merchant fleet to 1913 (Wray 1984). Massive government subsidies effectively allowed risks to be shared between business and the state and the fleet grew from 45,000 tons in

1883 to 1.5 million tons in 1913. Per thousand head of population, this works out at 29 tons, only slightly less than Italy at 33, Spain (45), and Germany (49). In these terms, Japan was well ahead of those countries by 1938 and had become the third largest shipowner in the world by as early as 1919 (Crawour 1997; Harada 1993; Masuda 1993; Millward 2005; Mitchell 1995, table 3.1; Vandaliso 1996).

The first railroad in Japan was not opened until 1872—from Tokyo to Yokohama. There was much private capital, including foreign capital, involved initially, albeit with government subsidies. By the 1880s the strategic significance of railroads for binding the country socially and politically and providing rapid means of troop movements on the long island chain had become apparent. In the 1880s there were pressures for the development of a planned network and after the Russo–Japanese War of 1904–5 there were strong demands for a linked system embracing Manchuria and Korea. One-third of all central government subsidies went to railroads, a portion exceeded only by the allocations to shipping and shipbuilding. The speed of development and the faltering profitability of many private railroad companies meant that reliance on subsidies would never be enough. Pressure for nationaliza-tion from the military as well as business users, from the 1880s, was reinforced by the Diet stressing its urgency on military and economic grounds in 1906 at which point 17 private companies were taken over. The railroads were subsequently a key element in all Japanese strategies as the state share of lines rose. Symptomatic of the driving force was that the state undertaking, Japanese Railways was, from 1908, under the control of the Railway Agency, which reported direct to the Prime Minister's office—and included railroads in Korea and Manchuria. It became a Railway Ministry in 1920 and took all motorized transport under its wing in 1928 (Harada 1993; Aoki 1993; Macpherson 1987; Yamamoto 1993a; Lockwood 1965).

By the late nineteenth century, the United States had, unlike Japan, already ex-perienced sustained economic growth and needed no dramatic hasty development of its infrastructure to further military ambitions. In contrast to the nation states of Europe, it had no hostile neighbors on its borders. The main analogy to the strategic concerns of France and Germany was the Federal government's land grant policy in confronting the Native Americans as the frontier spread west. Here it was important for military purposes to provide a chain of outposts and rapid settlement of the land. Land was abundant, but much of it in the early nineteenth century was still in Federal hands. Policy was to sell off the land cheaply, which was initially $2 per acre in 1796 and lowered later, and to set smaller and smaller minimum sized holdings. By the time of the Homestead Act of 1862, settlers with five years' residence could obtain 160 acres free. Although it does not look like it, this was a massive set of business–state transactions. For much of the nineteenth century, fear of Federal power constrained federal activities but, as Galambos has recently reminded us, in the context of agricultural business, "managing US federal public lands was the single largest SOE [state owned enterprise] in any of the capitalist countries of the West" (2000: 284).

Otherwise, in the nineteenth century, business dealings with government were linked more to sub-federal levels. The early nineteenth-century activity of the constituent states and municipalities in the construction of roads, canals, and railroads is now a standard in the literature reflected in the early work of Goodrich (1960) and in the reviews by McCraw (1975) and Lively (1955), who argued that it was part of a longer-term involvement of government, not a simple story of rise, corruption, and fall. The municipalities were not inhibited by notions of *laissez-faire*. The freedom to act in economic matters extended to a freedom to act collectively. Much mixed business ensued with the states also active in grants, licenses, charters, loans, stock purchases, land grants, and public bonds. Dowd and Dobbin (2001) view these activities as indicative of policy adapting to circumstances—there was no continuous neo-liberal consensus in the United States in the 19th or 20th centuries. When New York State could fund the $6 million Erie Canal and provoke competition from other states and protests from towns within the state that they be able to enjoy state-financed projects like that benefiting the city of New York, we are truly in a world of "urban centered mercantilism" (Galambos 2000: 277).

One recent estimate is that by 1871, the states and municipalities owned at least one half of the US railroad capital, notwithstanding that private investment dominated thereafter (Dowd and Dobbin 2001). The driving force here then was the competition between political entities for a share of the spoils and the injection of public funds to speed up the process. It was not necessarily a matter of trying to anticipate demand and several writers continue to argue that most railroad companies simply followed rather than preceded the settlement lines (Fishlow 2000). The development of long east–west routes heralded competition on a grand scale. Such competition was rarer in Europe. Parallel routes were for a time encouraged in the Netherlands and Germany (Fremdling 1999; Fremdling and Knieps 1993) and duplication was allowed in Britain, but by the end of the century competition was limited to multiple bidding for contracts. "Opening up" the territory was not the game in Britain which, by the early 19th century, already had a transport network and population that was dense by contemporary standards. In other European countries, strategic factors intervened, as we have seen, to generate more route planning and state support.

As long then as fear, in the United States, of the concentration of power inhibited Federal action, the need for regulation fell initially on the states and municipalities. This created no problems as long as the main businesses were canal companies or the enterprises involved in constructing turnpike roads or railroad businesses operating over short distances. It would suffice to regulate tolls for the track and let competition between carriers secure the public interest with respect to conveyance, at least for canals and roads. Once, however, the railroad companies started catering for long-distance shippers, problems emerged. Competition between carriers on the track was unsafe so some regulation of conveyance rates was required. But that had to involve interstate traffic yet the regulatory bodies were at state not federal level. The economics of rail operations (low variable costs, high fixed costs, scope for rate discrimination) meant that companies would charge low rates where competition from other routes or modes existed and high rates for routes where they had some monopoly power (often short distance). Then there were the volume discounts which the companies wanted to offer to the likes of Standard Oil. The state authorities were in a pickle because their traditional brief had been to set maximum rates and yet many of the complaints were about low rates.

In the 1840s, when competition between routes heated up, shippers turned to the courts but they could do little because the legislation referred only to high rates. For a large part of the nineteenth century (1830s to 1880s), the railroad companies argued amongst themselves and with state courts and legislators about rate regulation (Dunlavy 2001). In the 1870s, four states passed the Granger Laws facilitating more intervention in interstate rates but the railroad companies challenged this in the Federal courts. It was not until 1886 that the Supreme Court ruled explicitly that states could not regulate interstate traffic and this prompted Congress to pass the Interstate Commerce Act in 1887. While this outlawed rate discrimination and company pooling, the wording was loose and the Commission (ICC) had no rate-setting powers until the passing of the Hepburn Act of 1906 (Keller 1990).

In fact the main driving force behind that Act and the 1890 Sherman Anti-Trust Act was the curtailment of the power of big business, perceived in some quarters to be bloated and corrupt. The Acts outlawed the cooperation on routes which many railroad companies sought but had few teeth initially when it came to rate regulation. Over the following 40 years, straddling the Progressive Era, much of this regulation was tightened up and was supplemented at lower levels by the establishment of Public Utility Commissions. Government in the United States has often been seen to regulate and restrict business with semi-autonomous bureaucracies, formal procedures, and judicial oversight, in contrast to Europe where business was promoted and encouraged or taken into public ownership and/or administered directly (the last in Germany and Italy, telegraph and telephone everywhere). Views still vary on how to explain the US pattern. McCraw (1984) has argued that, alone of all the market economies, the rise of big business in the United States preceded the rise of big government. The US government was the only one to enact legislation against big business at an early stage. Big business was seen as the first threat to "liberty". Hence, an adversarial relationship between business and the state was established and when the state grew in the twentieth century, it was challenged; suspicion and mistrust of government followed. Berk (1994) puts less emphasis on the role of the gilded-age Robber Barons. "Corporate liberalism"—huge capitalist enterprises, many small city markets with the state brokering the claims of the non-corporate classes—is his characterization of systems which reflected political choices and which changed over time (cf. also Dowd and Dobbin 2001).

22.4 ENERGY COMPANIES AND THE STATE
C.1900–1980

The strategic role of energy was different from transport and communications. It lay essentially in the key economic role of coal, electricity, gas, and oil as sources of heat and power where short-run substitution was difficult. Business–state relations were also affected by the economics and technology of these sectors. Coal was a classic constant returns to scale industry which readily took the form in the nineteenth and early twentieth centuries of competition amongst the many; oil was not too dissimilar although tending to a more oligopolistic form (a sector which was dominated by multinationals, also discussed elsewhere in this book). The "utilities" in contrast were classic natural monopolies. In the nineteenth century, the networks were spatially limited so that the main interface for business undertakings in electricity, gas, and water was with the municipalities. As transmission lines extended in the twentieth century, the shift to larger, sometimes national, grid networks came to depend on how well local interests were subdued.

Coal did not generate security problems. The issue was, rather, how well endowed was each country and how far they could adapt during war and crises. Germany, the United States, Britain, and Belgium were well endowed with coal deposits, Japan less so. Others like Italy, Spain, and the Scandinavian countries relied on British exports but took quickly to hydro-electricity as this emerged at the end of the nineteenth century (Kaijser and Hedin 1995; Giannetti 1987; Antolin 1992, 1999; Aubanell-Jubany 2004). Portugal's precarious position was exposed during the Second World War when it was blockaded from British exports; the drive to hydro took off (Nunes *et al.* 2004). France's problems have been shown to be continuously at the heart of business–state relations. Output in 1913 was 41 million tons, no more than 15 percent of Germany's or Britain's. Although French private companies dominated the industry in the nineteenth century, this was under a concession system designed by the central government, which could exercise direct control in emergencies.

After 1945 the government was determined to reduce its reliance on the modest deposits located near the north-east frontier and hence exposed in the three German invasions since 1870. There was not only a large commitment to nuclear plants for electricity generation but coal prices were allowed to approach world levels and the coal industry to be run down faster than anywhere else in Europe. Chick (2002, 2006) has shown how that determination explains why the principles of marginal cost pricing (including the "tarif vert" of Électricité de France) were more readily absorbed into energy policy in France than in the UK. Otherwise, in Europe generally, the problems of coal companies surrounded their dealings with the workforce and these took center stage in the middle of the twentieth century. The state's interest in the nineteenth century was largely restricted to safety issues, public ownership was limited, and some of the recent literature has shown how the economic performance of the mining companies, for example in Britain with an ageing set of deposits, was beyond the control of the mine owners (Supple 1987; Greasley 1990, 1995). Coalface work was dangerous and dirty and it is the history of labor relations that lies behind the nationalization of the coal companies in France and Britain in the 1940s.

The natural monopoly characteristics of electricity, gas, and water supply were governed by national legislation in many European countries but often by the constituent states and municipalities in the United States where again the interstate problem reared its head. All but three of the states had Public Utility Commissions by 1914. Some writers support an old argument that many of these were "captured" by the industry (Hausman 2004; Hausman and Neufeld 2002, for electricity), but Keller (1981, 1990) has argued that the outcomes often reflected a plurality of inter-est groups. Interstate regulation was limited until the Federal Power Commission (FPC) was established in 1920 but this covered only hydro. The courts had ruled that holding companies were not public utilities and it was not until the 1935 Public Utility Holding Company Act that the FPC could effectively regulate interstate transmission of electricity (Keller 1990; Young 2003). Many of the utilities were privately owned in the United States—94 percent of electricity power generation in 1932. Keller (1990) argues that the impetus for municipal ownership came from a desire to use utility profits to relieve local tax burdens. That seems the explanation in Europe where the more pervasive spread of operations by local government had traditionally been explained in ideological terms.

Recent writers have argued that the initial burst of municipal activity occurred between 1850 and 1880, well before the debates on municipal socialism and the electoral success of socialist and social democratic parties (Millward 2001, 2004; Schott 2005). The pattern of private and public local utilities was quite complex and does seem best understood in terms of the pressure on growing industrial towns to finance public health programs and to use utility profits for finance; in more stagnant towns and rural areas private enterprise remained. That argument does not carry over to water supply where municipal ownership was over 50 percent in the United States and Europe, noticeably higher than the shares of electricity and gas. The municipal water undertakings were never run for profit and it seems that, faced with the transactions costs of meeting the rising quality standards demanded by ever more public health-conscious municipalities and the rising costs of storage and distribution, private companies struggled financially and gave way to municipal ownership in both the United States and Europe (Jacobson 2000; Millward 2007).

In gas and electricity, the more extensive spread of municipal ownership in Europe (about one-third) than in the United States created its own problems when it came to the development of national grids. Many towns were reluctant to give up local electricity generation so the large companies that were emerging for generation and transmission in the 1919–39 period often had difficulties in forging new networks. Central government intervened and that proved successful in the UK (with the establishment of the publicly owned Central Electricity Board in 1926) and to some extent in Sweden. The recent literature for Italy, France, and Spain brings out how well entrenched and stubborn were some of the local interest groups and indeed some of the large companies when it came to connecting up regional groupings (Fernandez 1996, 1999; Morsel 1987, 1994; Giannetti 1987; Aubanell-Jubany 2004; Antolin 1992, 1999).

The economics of oil and natural gas is such as to facilitate competitive conditions across world markets, albeit with natural monopoly elements in the pipelines. The state has however intervened strongly in these sectors, essentially because these commodities are key intermediate inputs in modern economies, difficult to replace in the short run, and because of the attractive taxability of the rents and royalties associated with accessing and using the reserves. In the first half of the twentieth century, only the United States, of the countries covered in this chapter, had significant deposits. The poor endowments of coal in Italy, Spain, Portugal, and Scandinavia found no domestic relief from oil and natural gas. The second half of the century saw discoveries in Europe but they were heavily concentrated in the UK and Norway and in the Netherlands for natural gas. Germany continued to benefit from its good coal supplies but France and Italy remained, with other European countries, heavily reliant on external sources. Japan's location and resources made it extremely vulnerable throughout the twentieth century. When coal was king, the annual output of Japan was only some 20 million tons (in 1912), less than 4 tons per head of population—more than Spain but significantly less than France. In 1973, Japan produced 0.7 million tons of oil and 3,198 million cubic meters of natural gas—again significantly less than even France, Italy, and Germany (Mitchell 1995, 1998).

Some of the decisive interventions occurred in the early decades of the century as governments took share ownership of oil companies to exert leverage effects in Middle East oilfields. The Anglo-Persian Oil Company and Compagnie Française des Petroles were partly owned by their British and French governments respectively, and these companies had major shares in the Turkish Petroleum Company. In the 1920s, the successors to the Standard Oil Company dominated the American consortium (Near East Development Company), but the US government was actively involved in negotiations, with Anglo-Persian and Royal Dutch Shell, to put an end to market struggles and they divided up the world market into the shares then held—the "as if" agreement of 1928. Domestically the central governments of countries like France and Japan legislated for control of oil imports and provision of refinery capacity while mixed owned enterprises like Campsa in Spain were given dominant positions in local storage and distribution (Nowell 1994; Melby 1981; Jones 1981; Bamberg 1994).

After 1945 all countries were engaged in exploration but some were luckier than others. Mattei promoted the development of hydrocarbons in the Padua Plain which led to the establishment of the state-owned ENI in 1953 and its various subsidiaries, including AGIP. France's interests in the politically volatile North Africa proved fragile and hastened its shift to nuclear and to Middle East oil. Germany's position as belligerent in two world wars circumscribed the activities of its central governments, after 1945, and a fairly free market was allowed to operate (Frankel 1966; Lucas 1985; Noreng 1981). In contrast, the state intervened strongly where large indigenous deposits were found. In 1955 the Nederland Aardolie Maalschappij was established to explore the large gas field in the north of the Netherlands and this was joint owned by Shell, Esso, and the state mining company Staatsmijnen. The state enterprise Statoil came to dominate matters in Norway while in Britain the British National Oil Corporation had only a short life in the 1970s. The general aim of governments was to secure national sovereignty and property rights in such a way as not to prejudice tax income from successful businesses (Bamberg 1994; Whiteman 1985; Corley 1991). The UK used its licensing powers as a physical control over development rather than as a means of generating revenue. Neither the strategic or tax dimensions required control in the form of state ownership—arm's-length regulation and licensing was enough—so that privatization in these sectors came as no surprise.

22.5 TELECOMMUNICATIONS, AIRLINES, AND PRIVATIZATION

The 1980s and 1990s witnessed a pervasive pattern of deregulation and privatization. The first sectors to change were airlines and telecommunications and the first countries were the UK and the United States with the 1978 Airline Deregulation Act, followed in the mid-1980s by the privatization of British Telecom and British Airways and the break-up of AT&T. Both these sectors experienced great technological changes and there is a case for seeing that as more important than ideological shifts in accounting for the occurrence of the institutional changes in the last quarter of the 20th century. Technology change from the 1980s in the generation of electricity also offered opportunities for different market structures (Koebel 1990; Chick 2004; Millward 2005).

Given the economics of aviation, we might expect a competitive industry to emerge over large land masses and oceanic routes. Elements of such a picture can be seen within the United States in the 1919–39 period though it was largely dominated by the embryonic nature of the industry and the reliance on government mail contracts (Vander Meulen 1991; van der Linden 2002). It was disputes over the award of such contracts that triggered off federal interest leading to the establishment in 1938 of the Civil Aviation Board to regulate fares and entry conditions. Although the US industry was dogged, in the 1940s and 1950s, by financial problems, excess capacity and never-ending mergers, it was carrying more passengers than the rest of the world combined. This was because the economic organization of airlines in Europe was very different and stemmed from some key geopolitical factors. Europe was a large land mass but it was spotted with nation states. Since airspace has a strategic value, sovereignty over it was established by each state, whether large or small. Since air transport also had socio-political dimensions, at a minimum from servicing the colonies in Africa, Asia, and South America and more generally in times of war, each nation state, in the 1919–39 period, protected its airlines by subsidy. Operating in many cases on fairly short domestic routes, these airlines struggled financially so that in the end one airline was allowed to dominate each country and it was publicly owned (see the histories of Air France, KLM, Lufthansa, Lot, and British Airways in Dienel and Lyth 1998). Unable to reap large economies of scale they were likely to be out-competed by the American airlines. These issues lay at the heart of the inauguration of the fare-fixing body, the International Air Transport Association (IATA), in 1945. The American airlines were given fairly free rein on the Atlantic crossings in exchange for fares fixed elsewhere at levels that would allow the small national carriers to survive.

Many opportunities for air travel opened up after the war, especially when the jets came on stream, and the high cost national carriers were under constant pressure. The emergence of inclusive tours, packaging flight and hotel, eventually, in the 1960s, proved too attractive to resist and the independent operators with charter flights were allowed to blossom (Lyth and Dierikx 1994). The logic of having one scheduled carrier for each country, from the early strategic concerns, lost some force by the 1980s and paved the way for privatization and deregulation. The industry was constantly plagued by cycles of boom and depression, often exacerbated by technology advances which generated much excess capacity which, as Vietor has pointedly remarked "was just the most perverse consequence of a hybrid regulation that prevented price competition but not service rivalry" (1990). A bigger market share had to be achieved by more frequent departures, better services and "lounge wars"—not by prices which were generally insensitive to cost variations across different service packages. In the United States the year 1978 saw not only the passing of the Deregulation Act but also the withdrawal by the CAB of anti-trust immunity from IATA though that body managed to keep much of its traditional role for two more decades (Dobson 1994; Lyth 1996).

Telecommunications were a different kettle of fish, for in Europe they had not only been in public ownership since the late nineteenth century but had been deeply embedded in sections or agencies of government departments, with the employees effectively civil servants. The early Chappe flag-waving telegraph which originated in the eighteenth century was deemed to be secure unlike the electric which fright-ened rulers and officials. Thus, telegraph development was often financed by the armed forces or other state sources and closely monitored as was the telephone when it came on the scene in the late nineteenth century (and note the absence of these worries in the United States). Local networks gave way to national and the desire to have a universal service prompted subsidies, reinforced in the case of countries like Sweden by aims for social and political unification. The basic technology had natural monopoly characteristics but the potential mixture of private monopoly and subsidies proved sufficient for arm's-length regulation to be rejected and by 1913 all the trunk networks in Europe were publicly owned—Televerket in Sweden, Telegrafslyret in Norway, with Spain rather late in nationalizing the ITT company in 1940 (Little 1979; Calvo 1998). Indeed security considerations were important enough to ensure that telecommunications were rarely allowed to develop in autonomous state enterprises. Instead they were, by the 1920s, often integral parts of Ministries of Post, Telegraph, and Telephone (in the form of the Reichpost in Germany, the Azienda di Stato per i Servizi Telefonici in Italy and PTT in France, the Low Countries, and Denmark). Britain had some special strategic concerns arising from its empire and large overseas investments in which both telegraph and telephone links had a vital part to play. In addition to the Post Office, the government supported the establishment of Cable and Wireless in 1928 to develop overseas networks (Lipartito 2000).

In the meantime, unencumbered by these security worries, the US saw AT&T emerge in the late nineteenth century as a dominant player. Large economies of scale and scope plus the advantages of standardized equipment provided strong incentives for the takeover of local telephone companies, tying others to contracts for access to the "long lines" and vertically integrating Western Electric in 1882 as its equipment-supplying subsidiary (Vietor 1989, 2000). The interstate issue again loomed large. A dual system of regulation emerged eventually but it was not until 1910 that ICC was given authority over interstate services. As AT&T's market share rose to 80 percent in the 1920s, pressure grew for closer federal supervision leading in 1934 to the creation of the Federal Communications Commission with a brief to promote "reasonable rates and an efficient service" (Vietor 2000; Keller 1990).

In both Europe and the United States, the technology available up to the 1970s made for a fairly simple system; a long-distance network with natural monopoly features plus one type of terminal equipment, the telephone. Hence, the telecommunications business had strong monopoly power, regulated at a distance in the United States, less concerned at it was by security issues than the European countries where the business was ensconced in government departments. The large element of fixed costs and the low variable costs provided an opportunity for universal service. This meant standard tariffs largely undifferentiated across users but implicitly high (relative to costs) for large business users and urban areas and low for residential customers and rural areas. This appealed to municipalities and central governments in Europe as well as the Public Utility Commissioners (PUC) in the United States where, in addition, there was a constant battle about the attribution of fixed costs as between local and interstate charges. Since changes in the volume of interstate traffic had little impact on local fixed costs, this was effectively an attempt to get the interstate business to subsidize local telephone exchanges.

The PUC welcomed the benefits to residential users, the simplified administration involved in uniform rates, and that fact that it seemed to be "fair" (Vietor 1989).

This conflict between business customers and households was one of the underlying problems which prompted deregulation and privatization in the last quarter of the twentieth century. From the 1960s, technological advances lowered the costs of long-distance inter-exchange services but local exchange costs continued to rise so the subsidy element in the rates approved by the FCC only exacerbated matters, while in Europe there was much grumbling about the large costs arising from local traffic relative to the revenue it generated (Nguyen 1988; Vietor 1989). The distinction between communications and data processing was becoming blurred and once the possibilities for alternative long-distance networks arose and the simple handset came to be replaced by a complex terminal equipment market of computers, fax, email, etc., the case for dominant monopolies was undermined. Hence, the 1980s saw the divestiture by AT&T of its 22 telephone companies which were reorganized into seven new regional Bell companies, the regulation of which required a review of the PUC's regulatory procedures (Temin 1987). In Japan, the state-owned Nippon Telephone and Telegraph was privatized in 1985, albeit with 51 percent of shares still in government hands and universal service retained. In Europe new telecommunications companies emerged as part of a threefold process: disentanglement of operations from being a section of a government department since the telegraph and telephone were no longer regarded as key sources of security concern; privatization of the new undertakings (Telecom Denmark, British Telecom, etc.); deregulation of the markets. This was a complex process where ideological passions certainly affected the pace, while in other cases (Deutsche Bundespost) several Parliamentary hurdles had to be jumped.

A growing interest within history in these processes is therefore of considerable relevance to privatization and its historical precedents (Davids 2005; Nunes *et al.* 2004; Toninelli 2004; Jenkins 2004; Chick 2004; Florio 2004). It is clear that an important element of the privatization process was the disappearance, by the 1990s, of any major hangovers from the interwar depression years 1919–39 in arm's-length regulation of private natural monopolies. By the 1940s, that kind of solution was shunned but it became an acceptable alternative in the 1990s in Europe and Japan, manifest clearly in the privatization of natural gas and electricity transmission grids and of Japanese National Railways in 1987 and of British Rail (much less successfully) in the 1990s. The Japanese case is of interest because privatization and deregulation did not go hand in hand (Mizutani and Nakamura 2004; Yamamoto 1993a; Kosai 1995; Gourvish 2002). Technological advances in electricity supply, especially in the use of combined cycle gas turbines, facilitated the break-up of the generation market, which was enhanced by the promotion of competition in the retail market, by for example the 1992 Energy Policy Act in the United States and the break-up of Ontario Hydro in 1998 (Hirsch 2004; Nelles 2003).

Questions about security and about social and political unification were still important but a wider range of instruments were available and railroads, telephone, and airlines no longer seen as essential tools. The tension for state enterprises in the period 1945–90 between their public service obligations, on the one hand, and the requirement, on the other hand, to balance revenues and expenditures, is well documented. An important thread from that issue is that state enterprise financial losses were an important part of public sector deficits, which plagued many countries in the Western world after the macroeconomic disturbances of the 1970s. The incidence of privatization can often be traced to specific financial crises in each country. Nonetheless, the great technological changes of the last quarter of the twentieth century, the changing priorities in geopolitical strategies, and the changing array of policy instruments have each played an important part in the whole deregulation and privatization process.

They are especially important in explaining the onset of privatization and deregulation in Europe, Japan, and the United States in the last quarter of the century, rather than sooner or later. However, there were, within Europe, for example, very large differences in the precise timing and scope within the 1980–2005 period and here it seems the EU may well have played a decisive role. That is, the pattern cannot be explained simply in terms of a British (or American) ideological lead followed slavishly in the rest of Europe. To start with, in the 1980s, Britain was largely alone in Europe. Also the cumulative government revenues from privatization (by 2000) varied from 2 percent of GDP in Belgium to 4 percent in France and Germany, 11 percent in the UK, and 23 percent in Portugal, so it cannot be said that a radical UK-type privatization process was being imitated. Revenues per annum shot up from $20,000 million in 1990 (mainly UK) to over $30,000 million in 1993 (with little by now from the UK), rising to $70,000 million in 2000.

The major Continental spurt in the early 1990s coincided with the consolidation of the Single Market and the 1992 Treaty of Maastricht (Clifton *et al.* 2003, 2004, 2006). In the face of European market liberalization of telecommunications, and later energy, many countries, and especially smaller countries like Denmark, moved to privatization as well as seeking alliances with American and Asian companies. Finnish and Swedish telecom firms sought joint ventures in Denmark, Norway, and new EU states like Estonia, Latvia, and Lithuania. Privatization of manufacturing firms followed closely on competition policy and deregulation from the single European Market Programme. The early and pervasive privatizations in airlines were largely a response to the Single European Act, which called for an end to pools and fixed prices as well as making specific demands for the opening up of cabotage rights. EU energy market liberalization has been subject to delays and revisions and privatization of energy has been patchy. In electricity, gas, and water supply, the wholesale shift to private enterprise in the UK and Spain, by 2000, looked very different from the rest of Western Europe. Thus the EU has played a significant role in the privatization process. It has not, however, managed to enforce a common pattern of governance for the sectors in question. Certainly it has encouraged the establishment of independent regulatory agencies, but their precise powers have varied considerably, reflecting the role of political interest groups as much as any objective functional aims (Thatcher 2002; Chari and Cavatorta 2002).

22.6 CONCLUSIONS

As a framework for analysis, geopolitical settings and political structures, as a supplement to ideological issues, do therefore shed considerable light on international differences in business–state relations. We have been looking at two large land masses, the United States and continental Europe, plus two high income island economies, Japan and Britain. The fragmentation of nineteenth-century continental Europe into nation states made their central governments very aware of the importance of railroads and telecommunications as instruments of military strategy and social and political unification; in the twentieth century it led to one dominant airline in each country, endowed with monopoly power as the chosen instrument of national policy. These interfaces between business and the state contrasted starkly with the United States where transport and communications were allowed to develop in a much more uninhibited way, not simply because of ideological commitment but because of the geopolitical setting. Here the issue was the fragmented nature of power as between different layers of government such that, prior to the 1880s, interstate transactions escaped firm regulatory oversight. For Britain and Japan, access to raw materials and control of sea transport were of central concern but whereas, by the 1880s, Britain already had a large merchant and naval fleet, Japan was virtually starting from scratch. *Laissez-faire* was acceptable for Britain but the Japanese state had to support a new shipbuilding industry and develop indigenous shipping of modern design, capable of doing rather more than catering for the coastal trade. Haste was of the essence and the intervention of the state here, and also in railroads, was an echo of the young nation states of Belgium, Italy, and Germany.

Another factor which competes with the traditional invocation of ideological differences is technological advance. Business historians have taken a keen interest in the historical background to the privatization and deregulation of industry which occurred in the last quarter of the twentieth century. While the pace and timing have often been affected by strong ideological surges in some countries (Portugal and Britain), the underlying economics of electricity supply, telecommunications, and airlines has been altered by technological changes which invited new market structures. In fact the history of the economic organization of electricity supply companies and other local utilities in the late nineteenth and early twentieth centuries is also not a story about (municipal socialist) ideologies but much more about the fiscal requirements of local government (using utilities as cash cows). In the interwar years, pressures to facilitate the spread of national networks in electricity and telephones together with a growing reluctance, especially after the depression of the 1930s, to regulate private monopolies at arm's length, made for a significant state presence. By the late 1940s, many European countries had much of their infrastructure business in public ownership, whether their governments of the previous 30 years had been fascist, socialist, or capitalist in orientation.

The need for further light to be shed on these issues points to research which embraces more than one company/country simultaneously. Several scholars are showing the way: Dunlavy (1992), Chick (2004, 2006), Anderson-Skog (2000) on American and German railroads, French and British electricity companies, Swedish and Danish telephone enterprises. It is, moreover, not enough to have edited collections of country studies; we need editors to devise collections where the chapters are about comparisons of specific features of business–state relations rather than on individual countries. Many enterprises (private and publicly owned) in the nineteenth and twentieth centuries had public-service obligations, sometimes related to state objectives for social and political unification, in other cases to questions of security and military strategy. How were they to be financed? Was it simply a cross-subsidization within the enterprise; did managers lobby Ministers for subsidies? Why was it often forgotten that many state enterprises were basically providing public services, like the police and education, under a budget constraint, and that the injunction to break even did not solve the matter? Business historians have a lot to say to economists in this area. Whereas economists for the last 50 years have spent most of their time devising pricing (at marginal cost) schemes and regulatory constraints for profit and price levels, many of these enterprises had been founded with the precise aim of providing services which were not only non-commercial but often non-economic. The real story of such enterprises has been mainly about such policy programs—whether or not they make "economic sense". More is also needed from business historians about the history of security and how it affected managerial behavior in telecommunications, more on business dealings with Ministers (like Little's 1979 study of ITT and the Spanish and US governments 1924–44), more on the military-industrial complex which space has precluded covering here but which needs to be drawn into a general history of business–state relations.

References

ACENA, M. A., and COMIN, F. (eds.) (1991). *INI: 150 años de industrializacin en España*. Madrid: Espase Calpe.

AMATORI, F. (2000). "Beyond State and Market: Italy's Futile Search for a Third Way", in Toninelli (2000).

ANDERSON-SKOG, L. (2000). "National Patterns in the Regulation of Railways and Telephony in the Nordic Countries to 1950". *Scandinavian Economic History Review*, 47/2: 30–46.

——and KRANTZ, O. (eds.) (1999). *Institutions and the Transport and Communications Industries*. Canton, Mass.: Science History Publications, Watson.

ANTOLIN, F. (1992). "Public Policy in the Development of the Spanish Electric Utility Industry". Paper presented at the European Historical Economics Society Conference on A Century of Industrial Policy in Europe, Worcester College, Oxford.

——(1999). "Iniciativa Privada y Politica en el Desarrollo de la Industria Electrica en Espana: La Hegemonia de la Gestion Privada, 1875–1950". *Revista de Historia Economica*, 17/2: 411–45.

AOKI, E. (1993). "Policy: Developing an Independent Transportation Technology (1910–1921)", and "Policy: Consolidating the Transportation System (1922–1937)", in Yamamoto (1993b), *Technological Innovation and the Development of Transportation in Japan*. Tokyo: United Nations Press, 72–83 and 114–23.

AUBANELL-JUBANY, A. M. (2004). "Cartel Stability in the Electricity Industry: The Case of Electricity Distribution in Madrid in the Inter-War Period". Paper presented at the European Business History Conference, Barcelona, Sept.

BAMBERG, J. H. (1994). *The History of the British Petroleum Company: Vol. 2, The Anglo-Iranian Years, 1920–1954*. Cambridge: Cambridge University Press.

BERK, G. (1994). *Alternative Tracks: The Constitution of the American Industrial Order 1965–1917*. Baltimore: Johns Hopkins Press.

BROADBERRY, S., and MARRISON, A. (2002). "External Economies of Scale in the Lancashire Cotton Industry". *Economic History Review*, 55/1: 51–77.

CABRERA, M., and DEL REY, F. (2002). "Spanish Entrepreneurs in the Era of Fascism: From the Primo de Rivera Dictatorship to the Franco Dictatorship, 1923–1945", in James and Tanner (2002).

CALVO, A. (1998). "El telefono en Espana antes de Telefonica (1877–1921)". *Revista de Historia Industria*, 13: 59–80.

CARDOT, F. (ed.) (1987). *1880–1980: Une Siècle de l'Électricité dans le Monde*. Paris: Presses Universitaires de France.

CHARI, RAJ S., and CAVATORTA, F. (2002). "Economic Actors' Political Activity in 'Overlap Issues': Privatization and EU State Aid Control". *West European Politics*, 25/4: 119–42.

CHICK, M. (2002). "Le Tarif Vert Retrouvé: The Marginal Cost Concept and the Pricing of Electricity in Britain and France 1945–73". *Energy Journal*, 23/1: 97–116.

——(2004). "The Power of Networks: Defining the Boundaries of the Natural Monopoly Network and the Implications for the Restructuring of Electricity Supply Industries". *Annales historiques de l'électricité*, 2, June: 89–106.

——(2006). "The Marginalist Approach and the Making of Fuel Policy in France and Britain, 1945–72". *Economic History Review*, 59/1: 143–67.

CLIFTON, J., COMIN, F., and FUENTES, D. D. (2003). *Privatization in the European Union: Public Enterprises and Integration*. London: Kluwer.

————(2004). "Nationalization, Denationalisation and European Integration: Changing Contexts, Unfinished Debates". *Entreprises et Histoire*, 37, Dec.: 9–23.

————(2006). "Privatising Public Enterprises in the European Union 1960–2002". *Journal of European Public Policy*, 13/5.

CORLEY, T. (1991). "Oil Companies and the Role of Government: The Case of Britain, 1900–75", in G. Jones and M. Kirby (eds.), *Competitiveness and the State: Government and Business in Twentieth Century Britain*. Manchester: Manchester University Press.

CRAWOUR, E. S. (1997). "Industrialisation and Technological Change 1885–1920", in K. Yamamura (ed.), *The Economic Emergence of Modern Japan*. Cambridge: Cambridge University Press.

DAVIDS, M. (2005). "The Dutch Way: The Privatization and Liberalisation of PTT". *Business History*, 47/2: 219–43.

DIENEL, H.-L., and LYTH, P. J. (eds.) (1998). *Flying the Flag: European Commercial Air Transport since 1945*. Basingstoke: Macmillan.

DOBSON, A. (1994). "Regulation or Competition?: Negotiating the Anglo-American Air Services Agreement of 1977". *Journal of Transport History*, 15/2: 144–64.

DORMOIS, J.-P. (1999). "France: The Idiosyncracies of *Voluntarisme*", in Foreman-Peck and Federico (1999).

DOWD, T., and DOBBIN, F. (2001). "Origins of the Myth of Neo-liberalism: Regulation in the First Century of US Railroading", in Magnusson and Ottosson (2001).

DUNLAVY, C. A. (1992). *Politics and Industrialisation: Early Railroads in the United States and Prussia*. Princeton: Princeton University Press.

—— (2001). "Bursting through State Limits: Lessons from American Railroad History", in Magnussson and Ottosson (2001).

ELBAUM, B. (1986). "The Steel Industry before World War I", in Elbaum and Lazonick (1986).

ESPELI, H. (2002). "From Dual Structure to State Monopoly in Norwegian Telephones, 1880–1924". Working Paper 2002, Norwegian School of Management, Scandvika, Norway.

FENOALTEA, S. (1972). "Railroads and Italian Industrial Growth 1861–1913". *Explorations in Economic History*, 9: 323–51.

FERNANDEZ, A. (1996). "Production and Distribution of Electricity in Bordeaux, 1887–1956: Private and Public Operation". *Contemporary European History*, 5/2: 159–70.

—— (1999). "Les Lumières de la Ville: L'Administration Municipale à l'Épreuve de l'Électrification". *Vingtième Siècle Revues d'Histoire*, 62: 107–22.

FISHLOW, A. (2000). "Internal Transportation in the 19th and 20th Centuries", in S. Engerman and R. Gallman (eds.), *The Cambridge Economic History of the USA: Vol. II: The Long Nineteenth Century*. Cambridge: Cambridge University Press.

FLORIO, M. (2004). *The Great Divestiture: The Welfare Effects of British Privalisation*. Cambridge, Mass.: MIT Press.

FOREMAN-PECK, J. (1987). "Natural Monopoly and Railway Policy in the 19th Century". *Oxford Economic Papers*, 39: 699–718.

—— (1989a). "L'État et le développement du Réseau de Telecommunications en Europe à ses Débuts". *Histoire, Économie et Société*, 4: 383–402.

—— (1989b). "Competition, Cooperation and Nationalization in the Early Telegraph Network". *Business History*, 31/3: 81–102.

—— and FEDERICO, G. (eds.) (1999). *European Industrial Policy: The Twentieth Century Experience*. Oxford: Oxford University Press.

—— and MUELLER, J. (eds.) (1988). *European Telecommunications Organization*. Baden-Baden: Nomosverlagsgellschaft.

FRANKEL, P. H. (1966). *Mattei: Oil and Politics*. London: Faber and Faber.

FREMDLING, R. (1980). "Freight Rates and the State Budget: The Role of the Nationalized Prussian Railways 1880–1913". *Journal of European Economic History*, 9/1: 21–39.

—— (1999). "The Prussian and Dutch Railway Regulation in the 19th Century", in Andersson-Skog and Krantz (1999).

—— and KNIEPS, G. (1993). "Competition, Regulation and Nationalization: The Prussian Railway System in the 19th Century". *Scandinavian Economic History Review*, 41/1: 129–54.

FREYER, T. A. (2000). "Business Law and American Economic History", in S. Engerman and R. Gallman (eds.), *The Cambridge Economic History of the USA: Vol. II: The Long Nineteenth Century*. Cambridge: Cambridge University Press.

GALAMBOS, L. (2000). "State-Owned Enterprise in a Hostile Environment: The US Experience", in Toninelli (2000).

GALVEZ, L. G., and COMIN, F. (2004). "Enterprises publiques et multinationals sous l'autarcie franquiste". *Entreprises et Histoire*, 37: 88–103.

GIANNETTI, R. (1987). "Resources, Firms and Public Policy in the Growth of the Italian Electrical Industry from the Beginnings to the 1930s", in Cardot (1978).

GOMEZ-MENDOZA, A. (1997). "Competition between Private and Public Enterprise in Spain, 1939–59: An Alternative View". *Business and Economic History*, 26/2: 696–708.

GOODRICH, C. (1960). *Government Promotion of American Canals and Railroads 1800–1890*. New York: Columbia University Press.

GOURVISH, T. (2002). *British Railways: 1974–97: From Integration to Privatization*. Oxford: Oxford University Press.

GREASLEY, D. (1990). "Fifty Years of Coal Mining Productivity: The Record of the British Coal Industry before 1939". *Journal of Economic History*, 50/4: 877–902.

—— (1995). "The Coal Industry: Images and Realities on the Road to Nationalization", in R. Millward and J. Singleton (eds.), *The Political Economy of Nationalization in Britain 1920–50*. Cambridge: Cambridge University Press.

HARADA, K. (1993). "Policy and Railroads: Transportation in the Period of Railroad Priority (1892–1909)", in Yamamoto (1993*b*).

HASHIMOTO, J. (1996). "How and When Japanese Ecpnomic and Enterprise Systems were Formed". *Japanese Yearbook on Business History*, 13: 5–26.

HAUSMAN, W. J. (2004). "Webs of Influence and Control: Personal and Financial Networks in the Formative Years of the US Electric Power Industry". *Annales historiques de l'électricité*, 2, June: 53–68.

—— and NEUFELD, J. L. (2002). "The Market for Capital and the Origins of State Regulation of Electric Utilities in the United States". *Journal of Economic History*, 62, Dec.: 1050–73.

HAYES, P. (2002). "Industry under the Swastika", in James and Tanner (2002).

HENTENRYK, G. KURGEN-VAN (1986). "Les Chemins de Fer Belges ou les Ambiguïtes de l'Entreprise Publique en Economie Capitaliste au XIX Siècle", in V. Zamagni (ed.), *Origins and Development of Publicly Owned Enterprises*, University of Florence, Ninth International Economic History Conference, Section B111.

HIGGINS, D. M. (1993). "Rings, Mules and Structural Constraints in the Lancashire Textile Industry, c.1945–c.1965". *Economic History Review*, 46/2: 342–62.

HIRSCH, R. F. (2004). "Power Struggle: Changing Momentum in the Restructured American Electric Utility System". *Annales historiques de l'électricité*, 2, June: 125–38.

JACOBSON, C. D. (2000). *Ties that Bind: Economic and Political Dilemmas of Urban Utility Networks 1800–1990*. Pittsburgh, Pa.: University of Pittsburgh Press.

JAMES, H., and TANNER, J. (eds.) (2002). *Enterprise in the Period of Fascism*. Aldershot: Ashgate.

JENKINS, A. (2004), "Government Intervention in the British Gas Industry, 1948–1970". *Business History*, 46/1: 57–78.

JONES, G. (1981). *The State and the Emergence of the British Oil Industry*. London: Macmillan.

KAIJSER, A. (1987). "From Local Networks to National Systems: A Comparison of the Emergence of Electricity and Telephony in Sweden", in Cardot (1987).

——and HEDIN, M. (eds.) (1995). *Nordic Energy Systems: Historical Perspectives and Current Issues*. Canton, Mass.: Science History Publications.

KELLER, M. (1979). "Public Policy and Large Enterprises: Comparative Historical Perspective", in N. Horn and K. Kocka (eds.), *Recht und Entwicklung der Gros Unternehmen im 19 und fruhen 20. Jahrhundert*. Gottingen: Vandenhoeck & Ruprecht.

——(1981). "The Pluralist State: American Economic Regulation in Comparative Perspective", in T. K. McCraw (ed.), *Regulation in Perspective: Historical Essays*. Cambridge, Mass.: Harvard University Press, 56–94.

——(1990). *Regulation and the New Economy: Public Policy and Economic Change in America 1900–1933*. Cambridge, Mass.: Harvard University Press.

KOBRAK, C., and HANSEN, PER H. (eds.) (2004). *European Business Dictatorship and Political Risk, 1920–1945*. New York: Berghahn Books.

KOEBEL, P. (1990). "Deregulation in the Telecommunications Sector: A Movement in Line with Recent Technological Advances", in G. Majone (ed.), *Deregulation or Re-regulation?: regulation in Europe and the United States*. London: Pinter.

KOSAI, Y. (1995). "Government-Business Relations and Competitiveness: The Japanese Case", in M. Hyung-Ki, M. Muramatsu, T. J. Pempel, and K. Yamamura (eds.), *The Japanese Civil Service and Economic Development: Catalysts of Change*. Oxford: Clarendon Press.

LAZONICK, W. (1983). "Industrial Organization and Technological Change: The Decline of the British Cotton Industry". *Business History Review*, 57/2: 195–236.

LEUNIG, T. (2003). "A British Industrial Success: Productivity in the Lancashire and New England Cotton-Spinning Industries a Century Ago". *Economic History Review*, 56/1: 90–117.

LIPARTITO, K. (2000). "Failure to Communicate: British Telecommunications and the American Model", in J. Zeitlin and G. Herrigel (eds.), *Americanisation and its Limits: Reworking US Technology and Management in Post-war Europe and Japan*. Oxford: Oxford University Press.

LITTLE, D. J. (1979). "Twenty Years of Turmoil: ITT, The State Department and Spain, 1924–1944". *Business History Review*, 53/4: 449–72.

LIVELY, R. A. (1955). "The American System". *Business History Review*, 29/1: 81–96.

LOCKWOOD, W. W. (ed.) (1965). *The State and Economic Enterprise in Japan*. Princeton, NJ: Princeton University Press.

LUCAS, N. (1985). *Western European Energy Politicies*. Oxford: Clarendon Press.

LYTH, P. J. (1996). "Institutional Change and European Air Transport 1910–85", in L. Magnusson and J. Ottosson (eds.), *Evolutionary Economics and Path Dependence*. Cheltenham: Edward Elgar.

——(2003). "Deutsche Lufthansa and the German State 1926–1941", in T. Gourvish (ed.), *Business and Politics in Europe, 1900–1970*. Cambridge: Cambridge University Press.

——and DIERIKX, M. L. (1994). "From Privilege to Popularity: The Growth of Leisure Air Travel". *Journal of Transport History*, 15/2: 97–116.

McCraw, T. K. (1975). "Regulation in America: A Review Article". *Business History Review*, 49/2: 159–83.

——(1984). "Business and Government: The Origins of the Adversary Relationship". *California Management Review*, 26/2: 33–52.

Macpherson, W. J. (1987). *The Economic Development of Japan, 1868–1941*. London: Macmillan.

Magnusson, L., and Ottosson, J. (eds.) (2001). *The State, Regulation and the Economy: An Historical Perspective*. Cheltenham: Edward Elgar.

Masuda, H. (1993). "Policy and Coastal and River Transport: Transportation in Transition (1868–1891)", "Coastal Transport: Transportation in the Period of Railroad Priority (1892–1909)", and "Inland Shipping: Transport in the Postwar Recovery Period (1946–1954)", in Yamamoto (1993*b*), 32–44, 64–71, and 214–21.

Melby, E. D. K. (1981). *Oil and the International System: The Case of France, 1919–69*. New York: Arno Press.

Mierzejewski, A. C. (1995). "Payment and Profits: The German National Railway Company and Reparations 1924–32". *German Studies Review*, 18: 65–85.

——(1999). *The Most Valuable Asset of the Reich: A History of the German National Railway Company*. Chapel Hill, NC: University of North Carolina Press.

Millward, R. (2001). "The Political Economy of Urban Utilities in Britain 1840–1950", in M. Daunton (ed.), *Cambridge Urban History of Britain: Vol. III, 1850–1950*. Cambridge: Cambridge University Press, 315–49.

——(2004). "European Governments and the Infrastructure Industries c.1840–1914". *European Review of Economic History*, 8/1: 3–28.

——(2005). *Private and Public Enterprise in Europe: Energy, Telecommunications and Transport c.1830–1990*. Cambridge: Cambridge University Press.

——(2007). "Urban Water Supplies c.1820–1950: The Dilemma of the Private Companies", *Histoire, Economie et Société*, 26/1: 111–28.

Mitchell, B. R. (1995). *International Historical Statistics: Africa, Asia and Oceania 1750–1988*, 2nd rev. edn. New York: Stockton.

——(1998). *International Historical Statistics: Europe 1750–1993*, 3rd edn. London: Macmillan.

Mitsuhaya, K. (1958). "Development of Transportation and Communication Systems", in S. Keizo (ed.), *Japanese Society in the Meija Era*. Tokyo: Obunsha.

Mizutani, F., and Nakamura, K. (2004). "The Japanese Experience with Railway Restructuring", in T. Ito and A. O. Krueger (eds.), *Governance, Regulation and Privatization in the Asia-Pacific Region*. Chicago: University of Chicago Press.

Morsel, H. (1987). "L'hydro-électicité en France: du patronal disperase a la dorection nationale (1902–46)", in P. Fridensen and A. Strauss (eds.), *Le Capitalisme Francaise*. Paris: Librairie Arthème, Fayard.

——(1994). "Reflexions sur le nationalisation de l'éléctricité", in M. Levy-Leboyer and H. Morsel (eds.), *Histoire de l'Électricité en France: Vol. II L'interconnection et le Marché, 1919–46*. Paris: L'Association pour l'Histoire de l'Electricité en France, Fayard.

Nelles, H. V. (2003). "Hydro and After: The Canadian experience with the Organization, Nationalization and Deregulation of Electrical Utilities". *Annales historiques de l'électricité*, 1, June: 117–32.

Nguyen, G. D. (1988). "Telecommunications in France", in Foreman-Peck and Mueller (1988).

NICOSIA, F. R., and HUENER, J. (eds.) (2004). *Business and Industry in Nazi Germany*. New York: Berghahn Books.

NOBEL, G. W. (1989). "The Japanese Industrial Policy Debate", in S. Haggard and chung-in Moon (eds.), *Pacific Dynamics: The International Politics of Industrial Change*. Boulder, Colo.: Wastview Press, 53–95.

NORENG, Ø. (1981). "State-Owned Oil Companies: Western Europe", in R. Vernon and Y. Aharoni (eds.), *State-Owned Enterprise in Western Economies*. London: Croom Helm.

NOWELL, G. P. (1994). *Mercantile States and the World Oil Cartel, 1900–1939*. Ithaca, NY: Cornell University Press.

NUNES, A. B., BASTIEN, C., and VALERIO, N. (2004). "Nationalisations et dénationalisations au Portugal (XIXᵉ–XXᵉ siècles): une evaluation historique". *Entreprises et Histoire*, 37: 104–19.

OVERY, R. J. (2003). "German Business and the Nazi New Order", in T. Gourvish (ed.), *Business and Politics in Europe, 1900–1970*. Cambridge: Cambridge University Press, 171–86.

PERRY, C. R. (1977). "The British Experience 1876–1912: The Impact of the Telephone during the Years of Delay", in I. de Sola Pool (ed.), *The Social Impact of the Telephone*. Cambridge, Mass.: MIT Press.

ROSE, M. (1997). "The Politics of Protection: An Institutional Approach to Government-Industry Relations in the British and United States Cotton Industries, 1945–73". *Business History*, 39/4: 128–51.

SABEL, C., and ZEITLIN, J. (1985). "Historical Alternatives to Mass Production: Politics, Markets and Technology in Nineteenth Century Industrialisation". *Past and Present*, 108: 133–76.

SCHOTT, D. (2005). "From Gas Light to Comprehensive Energy Supply: The Evolution of Gas Industry in Three German Cities: Darmstadt—Mannheim—Mainz 1850–1970", and "The significance of Gas for Urban Enterprises in late 19th century German Cities", in S. Paquier and J.-P. Williot (eds.) (2005). *L'industrie du gaz en Europe aux XIXᵉ–XXᵉ siècles*. Brussels: Peter Lang.

SCHRAM, A. (1997). *Railways and the State in the 19th Century*. Cambridge: Cambridge University Press.

SINGLETON, J. (1991). *Lancashire on the Scrap-Heap: The Cotton Industry 1950–1970*. Oxford: Oxford University Press.

STEPHENS, R. (2004). "The Evolution of Privatization as an Electoral Policy, c.1970–1990". *Contemporary British History*, 18/2: 47–75.

TEMIN, P., with GALAMBOS, L. (1987). *The Fall of the Bell System*. New York: Cambridge University Press.

THATCHER, M. (2002). "Delegation to Independent Regulatory Agencies: Pressures, Functions and Contextual Mediation". *West European Politics*, 25/1: 125–47.

TOLLIDAY, S. (1986). "Steel and Rationalisaion Policies, 1918–1965", in Elbaum and Lazonick (1986).

TONINELLI, P. A. (ed.) (2000). *The Rise and Fall of State Owned Enterprise in the Western World*. Cambridge: Cambridge University Press.

—— (2004). "Between State and Market: The Parabola of Italian Public Enterprise in the 20th Century". *Entreprises et Histoire*, 37: 53–74.

VANDALISO, J. M. (1996). "The Diffusion of Technological Change in the Spanish Merchant Fleet during the Twentieth Century: Available Alternatives and Conditioning Factors". *Journal of Transport History*, 12/2: 1–17.

VAN DER LINDEN, F. R. (2002). *Airlines and Airmail: The Post Office and the Birth of the Commercial Aviation Industry*. Lexington: University Press of Kentucky.

VANDER MEULEN, J. A. (1991). *The Politics of Aircraft: Building an American Military Industry*. Lawrence: University Press of Kansas.

VIETOR, R. H. K. (1989). "AT&T and the Public Good: Regulation and Competition in Telecommunications, 1910–1987", in S. Bradley and J. Hausman (eds.), *Future Competition in Telecommunications*. Boston, Mass.: Harvard Business School Press.

—— (1990). "Contrived Competition: Airline Regulation and Deregulation, 1935–88". *Business History Review*, 64: 61–108.

WHITEMAN, T. (1985). "North Sea Oil", in D. Morris (ed.), *The Economic System in the UK*. Oxford: Oxford University Press.

WRAY, W. D. (1984). *Mitsubishi and the N.Y.K., 1870–1914: Business Strategy in the Japanese Shipping Industry*. Cambridge, Mass.: Harvard University Press.

YAMAMOTO, H. (1993a). "An Analysis of the Privatization of the Japanese Railway Corporation", in T. Clarke and C. Pitelis (eds.), *The Political Economy of Privatization*. London and New York: Routledge.

—— (ed.) (1993b). *Technological Innovation and the Development of Transportation in Japan*. Tokyo: United Nations University Press.

YAMAMURA, K. (1978). "Enterpreneurship, Ownership and Management in Japan", in P. Mathias and M. M. Postan (eds.), *Cambridge Economic History of Europe: Vol. VII: The Industrial Economies: Capital, Labour and Enterprise*. Cambridge: Cambridge University Press, part 2.

YOUNG, W. (2003). "Atomic Energy: From 'Public' to 'Private' Power in the US, UK and Japan in Comparative Perspective". *Annales historiques de l'électricité*, 1, June: 117–32.

CHAPTER 23

SKILL FORMATION AND TRAINING

KATHLEEN THELEN

23.1 INTRODUCTION

THIS chapter surveys the literature on skill formation and training, presenting arguments about the significance of skills and the historical sources of variation in training regimes.[1] It is divided into three main parts. Section 23.2 considers briefly a range of arguments by economists and political scientists on the implications of different, nationally specific models of skill formation. It presents an overview of the various typologies that have been devised to characterize cross-national differences in training systems, and links these to recent claims about how vocational education and training (VET) systems fit into broader national political-economic models. Different production regimes, characterized by distinctive institutional constellations in which training institutions are a central component, it is argued, have important implications for a range of economic, social, and political outcomes.

Section 23.3 turns to the question of the origins of cross-national differences in training and skill formation systems. Most of the historical literature is organized around the analysis of single country cases, and only a few works are explicitly comparative. However, drawing on a larger historical literature I argue

[1] Sections of this chapter draw on material from my book, *How Institutions Evolve: The Political Economy of Skills in Germany, Britain, the United States and Japan* (New York: Cambridge University Press, 2004). The relevant paragraphs are reprinted with permission from Cambridge University Press.

that cross-national differences in training regimes are intimately connected to the history of working-class formation and, especially, to the fate of the traditional artisanal sector. This argument is elaborated on the basis of a comparison of the development of skill formation in four countries, Germany, Great Britain, the United States, and Japan. The final section lays out an agenda for further research that builds on existing studies of the origins and development of training and links this to theoretical developments in the literature on comparative politics, comparative-historical sociology, and political economy.

23.2 ROLE AND IMPORTANCE OF TRAINING AND SKILL FORMATION

Vocational training institutions occupy a central role in the contemporary literature on the political economies of the advanced democracies. Current research suggests that skills are associated with a variety of outcomes of interest to political economists.[2] Economists have documented a highly robust and unambiguously positive relationship between education and wages at the level of the individual worker (Ashton and Green 1996). At the intermediate level of firms or industries, several studies point to a strong link between skills and productivity and adaptation to new technologies (Acemoglu 1996; Black and Lynch 1996; Bishop 1994; Lynch 1994; Haskel and Martin 1996; see also Weiss 1994; Gospel 1991*b*).[3] At the level of whole economies, some economists argue that skills and investment in human capital are important as "an engine of growth" (Acemoglu and Pischke 1999; see also Booth and Snower 1996). While some studies have linked cross-national differences in education to persistent disparities in per capita income across national economies (Romer 1990), others have detected a connection between skills and overall export performance and national competitiveness (Oulton 1996; Mason *et al.* 1996).

Political scientists and sociologists are as interested in the social consequences of various skill development systems as they are in the economic impact (e.g. Brown *et al.* 2001). Wolfgang Streeck's pioneering work was important in drawing attention to the importance of skill formation systems within the context of broader political-economic models (Streeck 1992). In particular, Streeck showed how strong private

---

[2] See e.g. Ashton and Green (1996) for an overview of the empirical evidence generated by economists. They usefully distinguish among the findings of studies pitched at three levels—concerning outcomes at the individual level, the industry or firm level, and the national level. I follow their distinctions in this paragraph.

[3] Crouch *et al.* also discuss the impact of training on productivity and provide a nuanced account that differentiates outcomes by type of skill and by industry (1999).

sector training in Germany supported firm strategies based on what he called "diversified quality production". Vocational training institutions that required firms to train to uniform national standards, he argued, were a key element in "forcing and facilitating" a shift on the part of companies away from strategies based on cost competition toward higher valued-added, quality-based production (Streeck 1991). In Streeck's view, cultural or political constraints that bend the logic of individual market incentives—in this case encouraging firms to "over invest" in skills—turn out to impose "beneficial constraints" that improve economic performance even as they enhance equality (Streeck 1992; Streeck 1997).

A number of other sociological and/or political-economic studies fill out other aspects of the social and political impact of skill formation systems. For example, some studies document lower rates of unemployment among young workers in countries with well-developed apprenticeship programs (Lippman 2002). Hall and Soskice distinguish between training programs in so-called liberal versus coordinated market economies, and observe that training regimes in "liberal market economies" (the United States is an example) appear to be associated with wide gaps in the opportunities available to different types of workers (Hall and Soskice 2001; see also Soskice and Hancké 1996; Culpepper 2003; see also Crouch *et al.* 1999). Less skilled workers in the so-called coordinated market economies (e.g. Germany) have greater chances to advance through skill development, which is one reason such countries are characterized by greater income and wage equality than liberal market economies (see also Acemoglu and Pischke 1999).

Other analysts have pointed to the consequences of different skill formation regimes for broad social and institutional outcomes, including gender inequality and divergent social policy regimes (Estevez-Abe *et al.* 2001; Mares 2000; Iversen and Soskice 2001; Lauder 2001). Lauder, for example, explores the gender biases of different occupational labor markets, as well as the dynamics of internal labor markets. He notes a longstanding problem of "gender stereotyping" in the German apprenticeship system that has been a "major barrier to skill diffusion" (Lauder 2001: 173), and suggests that "while the system has been extremely successful in diffusing skills in the intermediate, mainly male-dominated sector, the major question confronting the [German system] now is to what extent it can be successfully applied to a service sector comprising a significant proportion of women" (ibid.). Similarly, he notes a strong gender bias (toward a male breadwinner model) in countries like Japan that are characterized by strong internal labor markets and company-based training (ibid.; see also Estevez-Abe 2005). More flexible labor markets (as in Britain and the United States), he notes, have higher numbers of women in managerial and professional occupations (also greater participation of women in higher education), but also exhibit a chronic gap between men's and women's pay.

Until recently, the political economy literature was heavily focused on manufacturing industries. In that context, Germany was widely considered a model of successful vocational training and skill formation, and comparisons to other countries were mostly invidious (see e.g. Berg 1994; Oulton and Steedman 1994; Finegold 1993). In one important contribution, for example, David Finegold and David Soskice examined the institutional bases of Germany's "high skill" and the UK's "low skill" equilibria (Finegold and Soskice 1988).[4] In particular, they argued that Britain's chronic undersupply of training went back to public good or free-rider problems, and the resulting dearth of skills in the economy encouraged firms to pursue product strategies premised on low skills—which in turn discouraged investment in skills, which reinforced product strategies based on unskilled labor, and so on in a vicious cycle.

In the meantime, the literature has begun to paint a more differentiated picture of strengths and weaknesses of different national training systems (see e.g. Crouch et al. 1999; Culpepper 2003; Culpepper and Finegold 1999; Hall and Soskice 2001; Green and Sakamoto 2001). Thus, for example, Finegold's more recent work highlights Germany's continued high investment in initial manufacturing skills (apprenticeship) but notes deficits in firms' commitment to further training—now arguably more important than ever in the context of rapidly changing production technology—as well as the overall scarcity of certain high-end skills (e.g. in information technology and engineering) (Crouch et al. 1999; Atkins 2000; see also Pichler 1993). Conversely, the United States—long viewed as a skills "laggard"—is now getting more credit for producing an abundance of high-end skills—having become a net exporter of skills in information technologies for example—despite continued worries about the country's under-investment in traditional manufacturing skills (Hall and Soskice 2001; Smith 2000; Lauder 2001). Similarly, Green and Sakamoto note that while the UK does not fare well in international comparisons focusing on vocational training in traditional manufacturing, much of the literature overlooks the service sector, which in Britain "includes many highly successful industries competing primarily on skills" (Green and Sakamoto 2001). They argue that the characterization of Britain as a "low skill" economy is oversimplified, and speak instead of skill polarization and an uneven or "patchy" high skills economy. In general, however, it is clear that the emphasis in the political economy literature has shifted from an effort to identify overall differences in the *quantity* of training cross-nationally,[5] toward a more fine-grained analysis of cross-national differences in the particular *mix of jobs and qualifications* that characterize different political economies (Estevez-Abe et al. 2001; Crouch et al. 1999; Lauder 2001; Green and Sakamoto 2001).

[4] See also Snower (1996), who employs the parallel language of a "low-skill, bad-job trap".
[5] The available, mostly OECD, data are anyway notorious for their lack of comparability (e.g. OECD 1998b). For a discussion see Lynch (1994).

23.2.1 Classifying Skills and Training Systems

Economists, sociologists, and political scientists have attempted to capture the relevant distinctions—for economists across types of *individual-level* skills, for sociologists and political scientists, across types of skill formation *systems*. The typologies and categorizations they have generated serve as a cornerstone for an examination of the origins of cross-national differences in vocational education and training systems.

Within the economics literature, the standard point of reference is Gary Becker's now-classic distinction between general skills and specific skills (Becker 1993). Becker defined *general skills* as those skills that are fully transportable and hold value to many employers, whereas specific skills are completely non-transportable and hold no value except for the present employer. Becker was responding to longstanding claims that societies would under-produce skills because of market failures going back to poaching externalities and collective action problems (see e.g. Pigou 1912; Stevens 1996).

Becker called into question the posing of the problem (1993). For *general skills*, it is quite true that firms have no incentive to invest in training. But even if firms do not invest, workers will, or in Becker's words, "it is the trainees, not the firms who would bear the cost of general training and profit from the return" (1993). Poaching is not a problem and in fact competition for skilled workers (and its impact on wages) provides the incentive for workers to acquire skills. Poaching is not a problem for employers imparting only *specific skills*, either, for these by definition have value only to the particular firm in which the worker is employed (Becker 1993). Here the equilibrium outcome is for the firm and the worker to share the costs of training. Facing no external competitors for the skills they are imparting, firms can pay workers a wage below marginal product in order to realize a return on the training investment. Workers will be willing to share the costs since the resulting wage will lie above the external market wage but below marginal productivity wage after training (Becker 1993).

Other classification schemes point less to individual-level skills and more to national education and training *systems*. Perhaps the most common distinction is that drawn by the OECD, between countries whose education systems favor academic over vocational training in the upper secondary levels. This distinction "leads to a clear division . . . into two groups: those of the British Commonwealth—Australia, Canada, and the United Kingdom—where the academic pathway is very much in the majority, and those of continental Europe where it is VOTEC [vocational education and training] which dominates: Austria (about 80 percent), Switzerland (75 percent), Germany and the Netherlands (about 70 percent), Denmark, France and Italy (about 60 percent)" (OECD 1998*b*: 11–12). This broad distinction corresponds to that mentioned above, between liberal market economies (LMEs) and coordinated market economies (CMEs).

Where academic pathways predominate (LMEs), there is significant state sponsorship of general education, but company-based training is rarer, and mostly accomplished on the job and without special certification (OECD 1998*a*). CMEs, by contrast, tend to feature better developed systems for vocational tracks, including apprenticeship training and certification of specific occupations. Further distinctions can be drawn among continental European countries based on the relative importance of formal apprenticeship within companies and school-based vocational training (OECD 1998*b*). Switzerland, Germany, and Austria, for example, all have "dual systems" that combine formal apprenticeship within companies with part-time classroom-based vocational training. In France and Italy, by contrast, training is more dominantly school based, and "apprenticeship is mainly limited to the craft trades" (France) or aimed at "those who have left school early" (Italy) (OECD 1998*b*: 12; on France, see also Bouyx 1996).

Such considerations and comparisons form the basis for Soskice and Hancké to develop a somewhat less dichotomous categorization. They draw a three-way distinction between (1) systems (such as the United States) where training and certification are coordinated through the market, (2) systems (e.g. Germany, Japan) where they are coordinated by employers (either employer organizations or "groups"), and (3) systems (e.g. France) where the state is directly involved in setting norms, certifying skills, and facilitating coordination among employers (the so-called "state-business-elite coordinated market economy") (Soskice and Hancké 1996; see also Culpepper 2003; also Lane 1989, which is broadly compatible). Moreover, and as many of these studies have noted, the numbers of workers possessing some kind of vocational certification is much lower overall in both "market-based" systems such as the United States and more "centralized, state-based" systems such as France than in countries like Germany where organized employer groups play a larger role.[6]

One of the most careful recent studies, providing both quantitative and qualitative evidence and data on the vocational education and training systems of the seven leading industrial countries is by Crouch *et al.* (1999).[7] This study shows that no case can be unambiguously classified in a single "box", since most countries

---

[6] A now-classic study of work organization and stratification in France and Germany by Maurice *et al.*, for example, notes that at the time of their survey, "a relatively large number of workers [in Germany] hold some form of professional certification" and "almost all skilled workers in Germany possess some kind of basic apprenticeship certificate; indeed only 10 percent of German skilled workers are without such certification", whereas in France, "more than half of skilled workers have no professional certification" (1986).

[7] The seven countries that figure most prominently in the study are: the UK, United States, Germany, Italy, France, Sweden, and Japan. See also the excellent study by Green (Green and Sakamoto 2001) which discusses several different "variants" of a high skill economy, including notably the UK, which as Green points out exhibits a pattern of high skills (and competitiveness) in some service sector industries, even if vocational training in traditional manufacturing does not compare well to other countries.

in fact blend together different elements (state-sponsored vocational schooling, company-based training, training organized through local firm networks). However, the authors nonetheless identify "dominant" forms that can be observed in particular national contexts (for an overview, see Crouch *et al.* 1999). They distinguish those cases in which there is strong direct state involvement in the provision of vocational education and training (or significant state subsidization in some cases), with France and Sweden providing the more successful examples of this (and Italy a less successful example) (ibid.). Crouch *et al.*'s framework codes Germany, by contrast, as the premier example of a training system that *combines* elements of state-sponsored VET (the schooling part of the country's "dual" system) with strong in-plant apprenticeships, overseen nationally by corporatist organizations.[8] More purely market-based or firm-led training systems, they argue, come in two models. One features what they call "institutional firms" that combine plant-based training with long-term employment commitments—i.e. the Japanese model. The other is a more "pure market" model, where relations among firms and between firms and their employees are based on shorter-term contracting (and also therefore associated with less firm-sponsored training)—i.e. the US model. Thus, whereas both Japan and the United States provide for high quality general education, in Japan this is combined as well with an overall higher level of in-plant, employer-sponsored training (Crouch *et al.* 1999).

In general, Crouch *et al.* avoid sweeping claims about the absolute superiority of one model over others, though they do suggest that heavy reliance on state-sponsored training often results in problems of "fit" between the skills being generated and the evolving needs of companies (ibid.). This finding holds both for France, which the authors see as caught in a "low skill equilibrium", but also for Sweden, which overall provides better training, especially general education (ibid.). They argue that "France and Sweden demonstrate how even states with strong historical records of skill provision encounter severe difficulties under competitive conditions", among other things because of the chronic gap between school curricula and company needs in the context of ongoing rapid changes in technology and markets (ibid.).

23.2.2 The Embeddedness of Training Systems in National Political-Economic Models

Most authors writing in this field view training regimes as closely linked to other institutional features of national political economies, and seek to understand skill formation as part of a broader set of interconnected and complementary institutions

---

[8] Some parts of Italy have systems that operate through informal community networks, resembling some aspects of the German system in terms of employer coordination (Crouch *et al.* 1999: ch. 5).

that define distinctive "varieties of capitalism" (see, especially, Hall and Soskice 2001). In this literature, in other words, vocational training systems are a central component of differing national political-economic models generally (Boyer and Hollingsworth 1997; Streeck 1992; Albert 1993).

As mentioned above, one of the most influential frameworks, introduced by David Soskice but elaborated and extended in collaboration with Peter Hall, distinguishes between "coordinated" versus "liberal" market economies, and where the crucial difference between the two concerns the capacity of employers to coordinate among themselves (Hall and Soskice 2001; Soskice 1991). The Hall and Soskice framework pays particular attention to the link between institutional structures and individual-level incentives, both for firms and for young people. The coordinated market economies are associated with institutions providing incentives for firms to train, but also, and equally important, for workers to acquire particular, *specific*, skills (specific either to the firm or the industry).[9] The institutions associated with liberal market economies, by contrast, encourage workers to acquire *general* (broadly portable) skills.

The mutual interactions of vocational training with other, "complementary" political-economic institutions are the subject of a vibrant and growing literature (Aoki 1994; Estevez-Abe *et al.* 2001; Soskice 1994; Iversen 2003; Culpepper 2003).[10] Thus, for example, short-term financing arrangements and the (associated) tendency for firms in liberal market economies to respond to economic downturns by laying off workers encourages young people to acquire skills that are generally marketable rather than firm- or even industry-specific. Companies may upgrade this education with some company training but they would typically attempt to add only non-transferable (firm-specific) skills whose full benefit they and only they could recoup (Hall and Soskice 2001). The US training regime thus does not favor strong firm-based investment in private sector vocational training. However, it appears to support very well the production of a plentiful supply of "high end" skills—for example, engineering and programming—that thrive in a context that rewards strong general (especially university) education and where demand for training on the part of young people is driven by intense competition among firms.

In the coordinated market economies, by contrast, firms are more likely to invest in training workers because other institutions exist that introduce labor market imperfections that reduce labor turnover or compress wages, and/or that reduce poaching and free riding (see especially Acemoglu and Pischke 1998; and Acemoglu

---

[9] This categorization can be criticized for collapsing firm-specific skills and occupational skills into the same broad category, "specific". Wolfgang Streeck's work, discussed above, distinguishes the two and lays out the distinct logics, and elsewhere I have explored the historical sources and important differences in the dynamics and operation of regimes based on firm-specific skills versus those based on occupational skills (Thelen 2004).

[10] See also Ashton and Green (1996) who emphasize "how the institutional context can influence the salience of skill formation systems".

and Pischke 1999; also Thelen 2004). In Japan, for instance, long job tenure and seniority wages allow employers and employees to share the gains from their joint investment in human capital development. In Germany, in a different way, encompassing industry-level bargaining compresses the wages of skilled and unskilled workers (allowing firms to earn rents from training). But labor market imperfections also dampen the demand for training among youth, especially training that involves high investments of their own time and money, since these workers will not be able to capture the full rents on their training investment. This would be consistent with the observation of skill shortages at the high end (e.g. information technology (IT) industries) in some "coordinated" market economies (Smith 2000).

The causal links run not just from complementary institutions to skills but rather, also, from skill systems to other institutions and policies. Iversen and Soskice have recently developed a theory that links different educational systems to different levels of social protection (Iversen and Soskice 2001). They argue that workers who have invested in firm- or industry-specific skills (associated with CMEs) will generally support social policies that insure them against income losses due to unemployment, whereas workers who possess general (portable) skills will not be as supportive of social insurance (Iversen and Soskice 2001). Conversely, and as also argued in another piece by the same authors (plus Estevez-Abe), in countries in which social policy does not "safeguard returns on specific skills" (e.g. LMEs like the United States and UK), workers face strong incentives to invest in transferable skills instead (Estevez-Abe *et al.* 2001).

23.3 ORIGINS OF CROSS-NATIONAL DIFFERENCES IN TRAINING REGIMES

The overall lesson of the literature just discussed is that the structure and operation of skilled labor markets can be significantly influenced by the interaction of vocational training regimes and other, adjacent political-economic institutions. Such arguments that situate the economic logic of training in a broader political-institutional context provide the basis for important insights into the historical origins of cross-national differences in training. Training regimes developed in tandem with the development of other key labor-market institutions and organizations, in particular, employer associations, unions, collective bargaining institutions, and in some cases artisanal associations. The interactions among these institutional arenas had a profound effect on *what kind of skilled labor market* employers (and trainees) faced, as well as the kinds of solutions available for redressing the particular (different) market failures that emerged in different contexts. The problems (and solutions) that emerged historically are what lie behind some of the striking contemporary national differences in training regimes.

In this section I address the question of where cross-national differences in training regimes originate. As Gospel has noted, training and skill formation have in the past gotten rather short shrift in the business history literature (Gospel 1991*b*). To the extent that it comes up, the emphasis has often been more on managerial training than blue-collar skill formation—partly no doubt because the latter is, in many key cases, organized informally.[11] The same is true for treatments of the subject by historians of education, who tend to focus on formal schooling systems rather than skill formation in industry. Apprenticeship has received some attention in the work of labor historians, but mostly in its connections with the structure and strategies of craft unions (Gospel 1991*b*). In general, and as Streeck *et al.* have pointed out, while much has been written about how industrial relations institutions affect training (e.g. the way that craft unions have tried to regulate the content and amount of training as part of their strategies) "less is known . . . about the inverse effect of training on industrial relations" (Streeck *et al.* 1987: 1).

Moreover, the comparative literature dealing specifically with skills, as the foregoing discussion has already implied, is based mostly on observed contemporary differences (and their consequences); few scholars have explicitly explored the *sources* of such differences in comparative perspective. There are a number of excellent single country studies that focus on key cases such as Germany, whose system of industrial training has long been a model for other nations.[12] While many of these works provide excellent accounts of the origins and evolution of Germany's "dual" system of training, they are by and large not comparative, certainly not explicitly so. Moreover, and with a few key exceptions (notably, Kocka 1984; Welskopp 2000), the literature on Germany does not probe the connections between skill formation and other complementary (labor and industrial relations) institutions.

The same cannot be said for Britain, where there is also a significant literature on the co-evolution of training and collective bargaining institutions (see, especially, the excellent works by Knox 1980; Zeitlin 1996, 2001; More 1980; Perry 1976; Kelly 1920). The work of Zeitlin and Knox in particular explore the connections between the development of skill formation in Britain and the evolution of industrial and labor relations, extending on a rich tradition first pioneered by the Webbs (Webb *et al.* 1911). Zeitlin tracks the interplay between the development of vocational training and labor relations in the engineering industry, and traces the failure of training

---

[11] There is also a large literature on training for engineers. A survey of that literature would go beyond the bounds of this chapter, but see the discussion (with further references) in Zeitlin (1996).

[12] The historical literature on Germany's dual system is quite extensive. Among the most important works are Pätzold (1989, 1991); Hoffmann (1962); Abel (1962, 1968). On the Imperial and Weimar periods, see especially von Behr (1981); Tollkühn (1926); Muth (1985); Schütte (1992). On the development of the system under national socialism, see Wolsing (1977); Stratmann (1994); Seubert (1977). For post-World War II developments, see Baethge (1970) among others.

in Britain back to crucial developments in the 1920s that aborted experiments and collective arrangements for strengthening apprenticeship that might otherwise have succeeded and thrived (Zeitlin 1996, 2001).

A few works have drawn out explicit comparisons of the origins and development of training systems across a larger number of cases, in some instances linking these also to the evolution of other institutional arrangements and/or to some of the overarching theoretical frameworks discussed above. Ashton and Green present a broad though cursory historical treatment of several prominent cases that distinguishes sharply between Germany and Japan on the one hand (as countries pursuing a "high-skill route to accumulation") and the UK (and, to a lesser extent, the United States) on the other hand (as "low-skill route" countries). They argue that these differences go back to the character of state formation and industrialization, with late industrialization being a key variable in their account. In the United States and UK, the government did not play a strong role in actively promoting industrial development, and industrialization proceeded without a commitment on the part of the state elite to technical education. Late industrializers like Germany and Japan, by contrast, featured modernizing political elites who played a crucial role in developing the infrastructure for industrial "take off", including an infrastructure for skill development: "at the time of industrialization the ruling elites saw particular merit in developing the education, including the technical skills, of the working classes" (Ashton and Green 1996: 7). Although the Ashton and Green volume does not provide a fully developed and deep historical treatment, the book is unique in the way it incorporates and blends together insights from highly diverse literatures ranging from econometric analyses to detailed historical accounts.

Another important contribution is the unusually coherent volume edited by Howard Gospel (Gospel 1991a), which pursues some of these same ideas in more historical depth for a slightly narrower range of cases—Britain, the United States, and Japan. Although the contributors to the volume each emphasize different aspects of training and focus on different countries, Gospel's framing introductory essay draws the various strands of argument together into a synthetic treatment that emphasizes differences in the timing of industrialization and associated variation in industrial structures and strategies (especially on the part of large firms) as the crucial factors that set these countries on different trajectories when it came to industrial training. The British educational system was deeply affected by the timing and character of industrialization. Since the UK was the leading industrial power of the nineteenth century, and endowed with a relatively plentiful supply of skilled manual workers, "technical manpower could often be acquired in a piecemeal fashion by upgrading or it could be imported from abroad to meet the modest demands of British industry" (Gospel 1991b: 5). The United States, by contrast, grew extremely rapidly at the turn of the nineteenth century, and did not command the same stock of skills as Britain. In this context, managers turned to mass production to minimize their reliance on blue-collar skills, and the educational system (based on high quality colleges and universities) catered to the needs of industry, educating highly skilled managers and engineers who could manage these huge new enterprises.

Finally, Japan was also a late industrializer, but one that was much more reliant on foreign rather than indigenous technologies. Borrowing ideas (also with respect to education and training) from abroad, the Japanese developed a hybrid system that combined colleges and universities (for training managerial and technical staff) with internal training within large firms (for blue-collar workers) (ibid.). Gospel summarizes the overall comparative results: "Britain stressing the practical and training for traditional industries; with the United States emphasising more formal education and training; and Japan stressing applied engineering, but being weaker in basic scientific education and research" (ibid. 7). As in the accounts discussed above, a key part of the explanation, especially of the different trajectories of the British and Japanese cases, goes back to the very different policies pursued by the national government. Britain's strong voluntarist tradition contrasts most sharply with the more direct involvement of Japan's "developmentalist" state (ibid. 6).

Among economic historians, the work of Bernard Elbaum should also be mentioned. In a widely cited contribution, Elbaum compared Britain with the United States to answer the question of why apprenticeship persisted in the former and declined in the latter (Elbaum 1989, 1991).[13] His answer, resonating with arguments made also by Charles More (1980), is that British apprenticeship survived both "because it was customary and because it contributed in several ways to economic efficiency" (Elbaum 1991: 195). Apprenticeship might not have been the optimally efficient solution; however, given the government's *laissez-faire* orientation, it had the advantage that it did not require significant infrastructure for collective regulation of skill formation, and it functioned in ways that benefited all parties. In Elbaum's words, "Left to their own devices, employers, youths, and parents judged that the mutual benefits gained from apprenticeship and indenture exceeded the costs" (ibid. 204). The United States, by contrast, lacked a similar tradition of apprenticeship, and, given intense skill shortages and high labor mobility (both internal mobility and large-scale immigration), "firms were unable to establish collective, market wide standards regulating employment and training in the skilled trades" (ibid. 208).[14]

Another important contribution to the literature is the work by Hal Hansen comparing the trajectory of education and training in Germany and the United

---

[13] See also the work of Jeffrey Haydu, who analyzes divergent industrial relations outcomes in the same two cases (Haydu 1988). His current work deals broadly with employer class formation and ideology, but along the way there is a discussion of businessmen's views and activities in the area of industrial training, particularly in the United States (Haydu in progress).

[14] An exceptionally interesting volume by Colin Crouch (1993) similarly places a good deal of emphasis on the survival or not of a guild tradition, although the outcome that he is explaining is less strictly vocational training regimes than it is different industrial relations systems (corporatism).

States (Hansen 1997). Hansen analyzes over a long historical sweep how it came to be that the United States and Germany embarked on such different trajectories when it came to education and training for work. He examines the survival and upgrading of apprentice training in Germany, not as a sticky relic of the past, but as a result of its explicit and active adaptation to changes in the market environment in the context of industrialization. In Germany a vibrant "dual" system flourished that combined high-quality in-plant training with accompanying school-based vocational instruction sponsored by the state. This pattern contrasts sharply with developments in the United States where public schools became focused on providing education for upwardly mobile middle-class children, while the institutions supporting vocational training (of all varieties) languished and indeed became stigmatized as routes for less gifted youths. Whereas in Germany, vocational training remained strongly connected to firms and industry (indeed, in large measure, sponsored by them), in the United States the link between schools (including vocational schools) and industry was weak and tenuous.

My own research on the origins of cross-national differences in training regimes in Germany, Britain, the United States, and Japan builds on the insights of some of these other works (see Thelen 2004, on which the following treatment draws). Briefly, the argument developed there is a political-coalitional one. Cross-national differences in vocational training regimes can be traced back to differences in the political settlement achieved in the early industrial period between three critical groups: independent artisans, skilled industrial workers, and employers in skill-intensive industries. The kinds of settlements that were possible in individual countries were heavily mediated by state action (or inaction), which frequently tipped the balance in ways that either facilitated coordination—both among firms and between unions and employers—and supported non-liberal (or coordinated) training regimes, or aggravated the conflicts of interest among them in ways that proved fatal to the institutionalization of a stable system of firm-based training.

One broad and consequential divergence among these countries goes back to the fate of the traditional artisanate in the early industrial period. In the United States and Britain, industrialization occurred in a context in which traditional artisanal organizations (the guilds) had either been destroyed (Britain) or never developed (United States) and where early labor organizations faced a less overtly repressive political regime. In both countries, status distinctions between masters and journeymen were more attenuated than in Germany and Japan, and political and market conditions encouraged skilled workers to band together to defend their interests by attempting to control the market in their skills. But union-administered craft labor markets could be stabilized only with substantial support from employers, a rare though not impossible occurrence, as the case of Denmark (discussed below) demonstrates. More often, the emergence of craft unions in the early industrial period led to a situation in which skill formation was contested across the class divide, as unions sought to use apprenticeship to maintain the value of their scarce skills and employers sought to defeat union attempts to control training to get the upper hand in labor conflicts.

Where unions of skilled workers sought to manipulate the supply of skills by imposing restrictions on apprenticeship training, especially on the numbers of workers being trained, employers fought tenaciously (also generally successfully) against these measures. Conflicts between unions and employers over skills and apprenticeship intensified rather than mitigated the kind of credible commitment problems on which in-plant training often founders,[15] resulting in an overall decline in apprenticeship and firm-based training. Recurring skill shortages, generated in part by the failure of firms to sponsor training, redounded to the advantage of skilled unions in the short run. However, this dynamic intensified competition for (and poaching of) skilled labor among firms, which further reduced firm incentives to train and pushed them instead toward strategies that minimized their dependence on skill (see also Finegold and Soskice 1988). Skilled unions responded to these developments by attempting to claim the right to perform particular jobs as their exclusive domain (job control unionism), such that, ironically, craft unions frequently evolved over time into hodge-podge organizations whose membership was increasingly defined more by the jobs they did rather than by the skills they commanded (Piore and Sabel 1984).

In Germany and Japan, by contrast, industrialization occurred under authoritarian auspices, and the traditional artisanal sectors survived as important corporate actors in apprenticeship training. In these cases, unions of industrial workers developed in a context in which strategies based on controlling craft-labor markets were not an option, among other reasons because master artisans (i.e. self-employed or small employers) monopolized these functions. Here, skill formation was not contested between labor and capital in industry, but rather, between the artisanal sector and the modern industrial sector. This competition proved constructive rather than destructive to the preservation of firm-sponsored training since firms that relied on skills were forced to adopt strategies of skill formation that either emulated (Germany) or encapsulated and absorbed (Japan) elements of the artisanal model of training. Unions were not the constitutive or driving force in the creation of these systems in either case, but in both Germany and Japan alliances between skill-intensive industrial firms and emerging unions—forged in large part against independent artisanal craftsmen—shaped and consolidated divergent patterns of training in the two countries.[16]

---

[15] For apprenticeship to "pay off" for firms, apprentices must commit to stay until the end of their training term and possibly beyond, thus allowing firms to amortize their training investment; but for such an arrangement to attract youth, firms for their part must commit to providing high-quality training, thus forgoing opportunities to simply exploit trainees as a source of cheap labor (there is a good discussion of this logic in Hansen 1997).

[16] The argument is fully developed in Thelen (2004).

The German and Japanese systems are similar to the extent that both support high levels of investment in private sector training, but the two systems are based on very different principles and sustained by quite different institutional arrangements. An early divergence between the two lies in differences in the treatment by the state of the artisanal sector in the early industrial period, which in turn affected the strategies of firms that depended heavily on skills and also powerfully shaped their relations with emerging unions. In Germany, government policy in the late nineteenth century actively organized and modernized the artisanal sector, in the process also endowing it with parapublic authority in the area of skill formation. Industries that relied heavily on skills were pushed toward a more coordinated approach to skill formation through their competition with the artisanal sector whose power to certify skills they coveted. After their incorporation in the early Weimar years, German unions—which organized significant numbers of workers in these skill-intensive sectors—emerged as allies for industry against the artisanal monopoly on skill formation and in support of a solidaristic skill formation regime for industry.

By contrast, government policy in Japan in the late nineteenth century contributed to the destruction and political disorganization of the corporate artisanal sector, which was viewed as an impediment to modernization and industrialization. Facing severe skilled labor shortages, the state took a more direct hand in promoting skill formation through the importation of foreign workers and the establishment of training programs in state-owned enterprises—in both cases, however, bringing indigenous independent artisans in as important intermediaries in training. Private firms followed the lead of public sector companies in embarking on a more "segmentalist" path, dealing with the problem of skill formation by incorporating traditional craftsmen (*oyakata*) into a system of direct employment and company-based training. Early labor unions reinforced such autarkic tendencies in the 1920s because they defined their goals and strategies within the context of these internal labor markets.

Summarizing the overall argument in its most skeletal version: In the United States and Britain, the alliance in the early industrial period of unions and independent artisans on the one hand (or the absorption and dominance of the latter into the former), against skill-intensive firms on the other hand, was destructive of apprenticeship because it meant that conflicts over skills were played out across the class divide. By contrast, by the 1920s the political alignment in Germany and Japan pitted skill-intensive industries *and their unions* against artisans but in support of firm-based training. Differences in the training regimes that emerged in these two countries were a consequence above all of differences in the level at which these alliances were forged—in Germany at the national level (supporting the development of a collectivist system for skill formation), in Japan at the plant level (promoting the development of internal labor markets and associated firm-based training).

A complete treatment of additional cases is not possible, though an important research agenda for the future would be to probe the extent to which the explanations reviewed above, based on particular subsets of countries, "travel" to new cases. One obvious fruitful extension would be to Denmark, a case that (unlike Germany and Japan) combined, historically, the survival of craft-based unions with strong apprenticeship. Kristensen and Sabel's analysis suggests that the framework developed for the countries just discussed could be fruitfully applied to the Danish case as well (see Kristensen and Sabel 1997, on which this paragraph draws). As in Germany, relatively strong artisanal associations survived the onset of industrialization in Denmark despite legislation that formally abolished the guilds. These associations (again, similar to Germany) were specifically assigned a significant "parapublic" role in administering and organizing training, in this case through an elaborate network of technical schools that were originally founded by artisans but later (late nineteenth century) increasingly financed and sponsored by the state. Kristensen's description of the role of Danish artisans in the period of industrialization parallels developments in Germany in which organized artisans, through their craft chambers, oversaw, monitored, and "policed" firm-based apprentice training:

By codifying skills in a nation-wide system of vocations and creating a technological institute to modernize education to match the emerging new technologies following in the wake of industrialization, the artisan sector and skilled workers had created an effective institutionalization ... of the nation-wide criterion for "good workmanship" and had institutionalized pressure on individuals to observe their craft sense of honour. (Kristensen 1997: 22–3)

Where Danish developments differed from the German case was in the role of organized labor, for in Denmark, unions of journeymen organized themselves into craft unions rather than industrial unions. What prevented skills in Denmark from being contested across class lines—as they were in Britain, where craft unions also prevailed—is that the master craftsmen who employed these workers (and who administered the training system) relied on craft unions to achieve the co-ordination among themselves on which their individual competitive strategies were premised. Joint regulation of wages with craft unions prevented individual firms from gaining advantage in product markets through cut-throat competition, while joint regulation of apprenticeship (institutionalized in the Apprenticeship Law of 1889 that was supported both by associations of independent artisans and by craft unions) prevented individual firms from engaging in competition based on reduction in quality—a strategy that would have diminished the reputation of all Danish producers in international markets. Thus, as in the cases discussed earlier, so too in Denmark, the survival of an independent and vibrant artisanal class was crucial to the persistence of plant-based apprenticeship training, though the political alignment that supported this outcome over time (skilled unions plus master craftsmen) differed in some specifics from that in Japan and Germany.

Further extensions of the argument to more school-based systems such as France and Sweden would also be valuable. More research is needed here, but for Sweden at least, a few stylized facts seem to indicate that lines of argument developed for other countries could be extended to this case as well. In the nineteenth century, Sweden was characterized by a "pattern of 'company schools,' in which children might, if their parents so chose, take their secondary education at a school controlled by a firm rather than by the local authority" (Crouch *et al.* 1999: 123). This situation closely parallels the one in Germany in the pre-World War I period, when corporation schools co-existed alongside the collectivist system of training organized by the artisanal (handicraft) associations. In Sweden, however, artisans did not survive as corporate actors (let alone enjoy parapublic authority to certify skills); these tasks were taken over directly by large industrial firms, who would have trained for their own needs. Such a firm-based system (of the sort that prevailed in Japan) was however likely to have foundered on the resistance of Sweden's stronger unions, which can be expected to have opposed a system of training (and associated socialization of youth) that was dominated and unilaterally administered by employers. Certainly in the post-World War II period, the social democratic strategy was "to bring vocational education out of the workplace and into the schools. This was not an attack on vocationalism as such, only on the role of firms as its lead providers" (Crouch *et al.* 1999: 119). Historians such as Olofsson and Ohlsson (1993) have shown how the Swedish and German systems diverged in the 1930s, a period in which social democracy was on the advance in the former, and when social democrats would been in a position to act on longstanding skepticism about the more employer-dominated German model (Crouch *et al.* 1999), and impose a more democratically accountable (school-based, subject to government oversight) alternative.

23.4 Conclusions

Beyond extending existing comparative work to new country cases, two further lines of investigation suggest themselves as particularly promising. The first of these would explore the interactions between the development of training institutions and other, "adjacent" and interrelated institutional arenas. As indicated above, a thriving debate in the literature on the political economy revolves around recent work that characterizes distinctive "varieties of capitalism" as more or less integrated systems in which various institutional arenas (industrial relations systems, financial systems, vocational education and training systems, and systems of corporate governance) cohere in important ways, characterized as they are by what political economists call "institutional complementarities". A growing body of research provides compelling evidence of such complementarities among a number of realms based on quantitative data drawn from across the developed democracies (Hall and Gingerich 2004). Another, overlapping literature documents synergies and "elective affinities" between specific institutional realms, for example, industrial relations institutions and financial arrangements, or particular training systems and social policy outcomes (Hall 1994; Iversen and Soskice 2001).

The existence of these kinds of complementarities must be seen as an historic achievement of considerable significance, since it is clear that the various institutional arrangements that comprise any national polity or political economy were not created in a single "big bang". Rather, individual components were forged at different historical junctures and often brought into being through the actions of different political actors and coalitions. Many prominent theories of political and political-economic development predict, if anything, *discord* and *conflict* across institutional realms with different temporal underpinnings (Orren and Skowronek 1994). Thus, to the extent that institutional realms do "fit together" in a functionally coherent way, it is well worth investigating how it is that specific national institutional arrangements originate and evolve over time, and how observed complementarities across institutional arenas were forged historically and continue to develop today. While some works have explored the co-evolution of other realms, for example, social policy and industrial relations (e.g. Manow 2001), the history of vocational training has not typically been folded into this type of analysis in any systematic way.[17]

A second promising line of inquiry concerns ongoing institutional change in specific (historically evolved) arrangements. The historical research surveyed above has given us valuable insights into the origins of different national trajectories and yet each and every national "model" is undergoing constant revision and change. Some of the work to date on the sources of observed cross-national variation suggests a slightly static view (asking: what were the historic causes of observed cross-national differences—or in other words, how did the countries come to be "sorted" into their respective boxes in a typology?). An important agenda for further work is to track the continuing evolution of diverse systems of training through subsequent (and ongoing) significant changes in the market and political context.

Among the trends that would appear to have a significant impact on training in the contemporary period, the rise of the service sector and the decline of traditional manufacturing deserve special attention. The training systems around which most existing analyses have been organized were forged in the context of industrialization and in response to the demands of manufacturing. It is an open question whether and how these systems will continue to be adapted to contemporary changes in

---

[17] A partial exception is Iversen (2005), which explores complementarities between skill formation systems and electoral systems.

markets and politics. It is entirely possible, and indeed recent research strongly suggests, that the German system of training that has proved so important in sustaining a certain kind of high quality production in manufacturing in the past is overall less well suited to the requirements of an economy that increasingly relies on the service sector to generate new employment (Culpepper 1999; Culpepper and Thelen 2007). As mentioned above, the various typologies have noted some of the (previously latent) weaknesses of the German system in this new context, while at the same time underscoring the strengths of other, previously maligned, training systems (e.g. the United States), in important emerging areas such as information technologies, biotechnology, and other high technology sectors. Tracking how different systems are adapted (or not) to new challenges thus constitutes another important research frontier in the study of skills and training.

References

ABEL, HEINRICH (1962). "Zur Entwicklung und Problematik der Berufserziehung: Ein Bericht über die Zentralstelle zur Erforschung und Förderung der Berufserziehung", in K. Stratmann (ed.), *Berufserziehung und Beruflicher Bildungsweg.* Brunswick: Georg Westermann Verlag.

—— (1968). *Berufserziehung und Beruflicher Bildungsweg*, ed. by K. Stratmann. Brunswick: Georg Westermann Verlag.

ACEMOGLU, DARON (1996). "Credit Constraints, Investment Externalities and Growth", in Booth and Snower (1996).

—— and PISCHKE, JÖRN-STEFFEN (1998). "Why Do Firms Train? Theory and Evidence". *Quarterly Journal of Economics*, 113/1: 79–119.

—— —— (1999). "Beyond Becker: Training in Imperfect Labour Markets". *Economic Journal*, 109: F112–F142.

ALBERT, MICHEL (1993). *Capitalism versus Capitalism.* New York: Four Wall Eight Windows.

AOKI, MASAHIKO (1994). "The Japanese Firm as a System of Attributes: A Survey and Research Agenda", in M. Aoki and R. Dore (eds.), *The Japanese Firm: Sources of Competitive Strength.* Oxford: Clarendon Press.

ASHTON, DAVID, and GREEN, FRANCIS (1996). *Education, Training, and the Global Economy.* Cheltenham: Edward Elgar.

ATKINS, RALPH (2000). "Germany's Greens Watch as their Support Withers". *Financial Times*, 17/2, Mar.

BAETHGE, MARTIN (1970). *Ausbildung und Herrschaft: Unternehmerinteressen in der Bildungspolitik.* Frankfurt am Main: Europäische Verlagsanstalt.

BECKER, GARY S. (1993). *Human Capital*, 3rd edn. Chicago: University of Chicago Press.

BERG, PETER B. (1994). "Strategic Adjustments in Training: A Comparative Analysis of the U.S. and German Automobile Industries", in Lynch (1994).

BISHOP, JOHN (1994). "The Impact of Previous Training on Productivity and Wages", in Lynch (ed.), *Training and the Private Sector: International Comparisons.* Chicago: University of Chicago Press.

BLACK, SANDRA E., and LYNCH, LISA M. (1996). "Human Capital Investments and Productivity". *American Economic Review: Papers and Proceedings*, 86/2: 263–7.

BOOTH, ALISON L., and SNOWER, DENNIS J. (eds.) (1996). *Acquiring Skills: Market Failures, their Symptoms and Policy Responses*. London: Center for Economic Policy Research.

BOUYX, BENOIT (1996). "Examinations in a Centralised, School-Based Training System", in OECD (ed.), *Assessing and Certifying Occupational Skills and Competences in Vocational Education and Training*. Paris: OECD.

BOYER, ROBERT, and HOLLINGSWORTH, J. ROGERS (eds.) (1997). *Contemporary Capitalism: The Embeddedness of Institutions*. New York: Cambridge University Press.

BROWN, PHILLIP, GREEN, ANDY, and LAUDER, HUGH (2001). *High Skills: Globalization, Comptetitiveness, and Skill Formation*. Oxford: Oxford University Press.

CROUCH, COLIN (1993). *Industrial Relations and European State Traditions*. Oxford: Clarendon Press.

——FINEGOLD, DAVID, and SAKO, MARI (1999). *Are Skills the Answer?* Oxford: Oxford University Press.

CULPEPPER, PEPPER D. (1999). "The Future of the High-Skill Equilibrium in Germany". *Oxford Review of Economic Policy*, 15/1: 43–59.

——(2003). *Creating Cooperation: How States Develop Human Capital in Europe*. Ithaca, NY: Cornell University Press.

——and FINEGOLD, DAVID (eds.) (1999). *The German Skills Machine: Sustaining Comparative Advantage in a Global Economy*. New York: Berghahn.

——and THELEN, KATHLEEN (2007). "Institutions and Collective Actors in the Provision of Training: Historical and Cross-National Comparisons", in Karl Ulrich Mayer and Heike Solga (eds.), *Skill Formation: Interdisciplinary and Cross-National Perspectives*. New York: Cambridge University Press.

ELBAUM, BERNARD (1989). "Why Apprenticeship Persisted in Britain but Not in the United States". *Journal of Economic History*, 49/2: 337–49.

——(1991). "The Persistence of Apprenticeship in Britain and its Decline in the United States", in Gospel (1991*a*).

ESTEVEZ-ABE, MARGARITA (2005). "Gender Bias in Skills and Social Policies: The Varieties of Capitalism Perspective on Sex Segregation". *Social Politics*, 12, summer: 180–215.

——IVERSEN, TORBEN, and SOSKICE, DAVID (2001). "Social Protection and the Formation of Skills: A Reinterpretation of the Welfare State", in Hall and Soskice (2001).

FINEGOLD, DAVID (1993). "Making Apprenticeships Work". *Rand Issue Papers*, 1, Mar.: 6.

——and SOSKICE, DAVID (1988). "The Failure of Training in Britain: Analysis and Prescription". *Oxford Review of Economic Policy*, 4/3: 21–53.

GOSPEL, HOWARD F. (ed.) (1991*a*). *Industrial Training and Technological Innovation: A Comparative and Historical Study*. London: Routledge.

——(1991*b*). "Industrial Training and Technological Innovation: An Introduction", in Gospel (1991*a*).

GREEN, ANDY, and SAKAMOTO, AKIKO (2001). "Models of High Skills in National Competition Strategies", in P. Brown, A. Green, and H. Lauder (eds.), *High Skills*. Oxford: Oxford University Press.

HALL, PETER A. (1994). "Central Bank Independence and Coordinated Wage Bargaining: Their Interaction in Germany and Europe". *German Politics and Society*: 1–23.

HALL, PETER A., and GINGERICH, DANIEL (2004). "Spielarten des Kapitalismus und institutionelle Komplementaritäten in der Makrooekonomie: Eine empirische Analyse". *Berliner Journal für Soziologie*, Winter.

HALL, PETER A., and SOSKICE, DAVID (eds.) (2001). *Varieties of Capitalism: The Institutional Foundations of Comparative Advantage*. New York: Oxford University Press.

HANSEN, HAL (1997). "Caps and Gowns". Ph.D. dissertation, Department of History, University of Wisconsin-Madison, Madison.

HASKEL, JONATHAN, and MARTIN, CHRISTOPHER (1996). "Skill Shortages, Productivity Growth, and Wage Inflation", in A. L. Booth and D. J. Snower (eds.), *Acquiring Skills*. Cambridge: Cambridge University Press.

HAYDU, JEFFREY (1988). *Between Craft and Class: Skilled Workers and Factory Politics in the United States and Britain, 1890–1922*. Berkeley: University of California Press.

HOFFMANN, ERNST (1962). *Zur Geschichte der Berufsausbildung in Deutschland*. Bielefeld: W. Bertelsmann.

IVERSEN, TORBEN (2003). "Capitalism, Democracy and Welfare: The Changing Nature of Production, Elections, and Social Protection in Modern Capitalism". Cambridge, Mass.: Harvard University Manuscript.

——(2005). *Capitalism, Democracy and Welfare*. New York: Cambridge University Press.

—— and SOSKICE, DAVID (2001). "An Asset Theory of Social Policy Preferences". *American Political Science Review*, 95/4: 875–93.

KELLY, ROY WILLMARTH (1920). *Training Industrial Workers*. New York: Ronald Press Company.

KNOX, WILLIAM (1980). "British Apprenticeship, 1800–1914". Ph.D. dissertation, Edinburgh University.

KOCKA, JÜRGEN (1984). "Craft Traditions and the Labor Movement in Nineteenth Century Germany", in P. Thane, G. Crossick, and R. Floud (eds.), *The Power of the Past: Essays for Eric Hobsbawm*. Cambridge: Cambridge University Press.

KRISTENSEN, PEER HULL (1997). "National Systems of Governance and Managerial Prerogatives in the Evolution of Work Systems: England, Germany and Denmark Compared", in R. Whitley and P. H. Kristensen (eds.), *Governance at Work: The Social Regulation of Economic Relations*. Oxford: Oxford University Press.

—— and SABEL, CHARLES F. (1997). "The Small-Holder Economy in Denmark: The Exception as Variation", in C. F. Sabel and J. Zeitlin (eds.), *World of Possibilities: Flexibility and Mass Production in Western Industrialization*. New York: Cambridge University Press.

LANE, CHRISTEL (1989). *Management and Labour in Europe*. Aldershot: Edward Elgar.

LAUDER, HUGH (2001). *Innovation, Skill Diffusion, and Social Exclusion*. Oxford: Oxford University Press.

LIPPMAN, LAURA (2002). "Cross-National Variation in Educational Preparation for Adulthood: From Early Adolescence to Young Adulthood". *Annals AAPSS*, 589: 70–102.

LYNCH, LISA M. (ed.) (1994). *Training and the Private Sector: International Comparisons*. Chicago: University of Chicago Press.

MANOW, PHILIP (2001). "Social Protection, Capitalist Production: The Bismarckian Welfare State and the German Political Economy from the 1880s to the 1990s". Habilitation text, University of Konstanz, Konstanz.

MARES, ISABELA (2000). "Strategic Alliances and Social Policy Reform: Unemployment Insurance in Comparative Perspective". *Politics & Society*, 28/2: 223–44.

MASON, GEOFF, VAN ARK, BARK, and WAGNER, KARIN (1996). "Workforce Skills, Product Quality and Economic Performance", in Booth and Snower (1996).

MAURICE, MARC, SELLIER, FRANÇOIS, and SILVESTRE, JEAN-JACQUES (1986). *The Social Foundations of Industrial Power*, transl. by A. Goldhammer. Cambridge, Mass.: MIT Press.

MORE, CHARLES (1980). *Skill and the English Working Class, 1870–1914*. New York: St. Martin's Press.

MUTH, WOLFGANG (1985). *Berufsausbildung in der Weimarer Republik*, ed. by H. Pohl and W. Treue. Vol. 41, *Zeitschrift für Unternehmensgeschichte*. Stuttgart: Franz Steiner.

OECD (1998a). *Human Capital Investments: An International Comparison*. Paris: OECD.

OECD (1998b). *Pathways and Participation in Vocational and Technical Education and Training*. Paris: OECD.

OLOFSSON, JONAS, and OHLSSON, ROLF (1993). "Labour Market Policies in the Interwar Years: Passive and Active Actions". *Lund Papers in Economic History*, No. 22.

ORREN, K., and SKOWRONEK, S. (1994). "Beyond the Iconography of Order: Notes for a 'New' Institutionalism", in L. C. Dodd and C. Jillson (eds.), *The Dynamics of American Politics*. Boulder, Colo.: Westview.

OULTON, NICHOLAS (1996). "Workforce Skills and Export Competitiveness", in Booth and Snower (1996).

——and STEEDMAN, HILARY (1994). "The British System of Youth Training: A Comparison with Germany", in L. M. Lynch (ed.), *Training and the Private Sector: International Comparisons*. Chicago: University of Chicago Press.

PÄTZOLD, GÜNTER (1989). "Berufsbildung: handwerkliche, industrielle und schulische Berufserziehung", in D. Langewiesche and H.-E. Tenorth (eds.) *Handbuch der deutschen Bildungsgeschichte: Die Weimarer Republik und die nationalsozialistische Diktatur*. Munich: C. H. Beck.

——(ed.) (1991). *Quellen und Dokumente zur Betrieblichen Berufsbildung*. Cologne: Böhlau Verlag.

PERRY, P. J. C. (1976). *The Evolution of British Manpower Policy*. Portsmouth: British Associations for Commercial and Industrial Education.

PICHLER, EVA (1993). "Cost-Sharing of General and Specific Training with Depreciation of Human Capital". *Economics of Education Review*, 12/2: 117–24.

PIGOU, A. C. (1912). *Wealth and Welfare*. London: Macmillan.

PIORE, MICHAEL J., and SABEL, CHARLES F. (1984). *The Second Industrial Divide*. New York: Basic Books.

ROMER, PAUL M. (1990). "Endogenous Technological Change". *Journal of Political Economy*, 98/5: S71–S102.

SCHÜTTE, FRIEDHELM (1992). *Berufserziehung zwischen Revolution und Nationalsozialismus*. Weinheim: Deutscher Studien.

SEUBERT, ROLF (1977). *Berufserziehung und Nationalsozialismus*. Weinheim: Beltz.

SMITH, MICHAEL (2000). "Warning over IT skills gap". *Financial Times*, 7/3, Mar.

SNOWER, DENNIS J. (1996). "The Low-Skill, Bad-Job Trap", in Booth and Snower (1996).

SOSKICE, DAVID (1991). "The Institutional Infrastructure for International Competitiveness: A Comparative Analysis of the UK and Germany", in A. B. Atkinson and R. Brunetta (eds.), *The Economics of the New Europe*. London: Macmillan.

——(1994). "Reconciling Markets and Institutions: The German Apprenticeship System", in Lynch (1994).

——and HANCKÉ, BOB (1996). "Von der Konstruktion von Industrienormen zur Organisation der Berufsausbildung", in *Working Paper, Wissenschaftszentrum Berlin für Sozialforschung*. Berlin.

Stevens, Margaret (1996). "Transferable Training and Poaching Externalities", in Booth and Snower (1996).

Stratmann, Karlwilhelm (1994). "Das duale System der Berufsbildung: Eine historisch-systematische Analyse", in G. Pätzold and G. Walden, *Lernorte im dualen System der Berufsbilder*. Berlin und Bonn: Bundesinstitut für Berufsbildung.

Streeck, Wolfgang (1991). "On the Institutional Conditions of Diversified Quality Production", in E. Matzner and W. Streeck (eds.), *Beyond Keynesianism*. Aldershot: Edward Elgar.

—— (1992). *Social Institutions and Economic Performance: Studies of Industrial Relations in Advanced Capitalist Economies*. London: Sage.

—— (1997). "Beneficial Constraints: On the Economic Limits of Rational Voluntarism", in J. R. Hollingsworth and R. Boyer (eds.), *Contemporary Capitalism: The Embeddedness of Institutions*. New York: Cambridge University Press.

—— Hilbert, Josef, van Kevelaer, Karl-Heinz, Maier, Frederike, and Weber, Hajo (1987). *The Role of the Social Partners in Vocational Training and Further Training in the Federal Republic of Germany*. Berlin: CEDEFOP.

Thelen, Kathleen (2004). *How Institutions Evolve: The Political Economy of Skills in Germany, Britain, the United States and Japan*. New York: Cambridge University Press.

Tollkühn, Gertrud (1926). *Die planmäßige Ausbildung des gewerblichen Fabriklehrlings in der metall- und holzverarbeitenden Industrien*. Jena: Gustav Fischer.

von Behr, Marhild (1981). *Die Entstehung der industriellen Lehrwerkstatt*. Frankfurt am Main: Campus.

Webb, Sidney, Webb, Beatrice, and Peddie, Robert Alexander (1911). *The History of Trade Unionism*. London and New York: Longmans, Green and Co.

Weiss, Andrew (1994). "Productivity Changes without Formal Training", in Lynch (1994).

Welskopp, Thomas (2000). *Das Banner der Brüderlichkeit*. Bonn: Dietz.

Wolsing, Theo (1977). *Untersuchungen zur Berufsausbildung im Dritten Reich*. Kastellaun: A. Henn.

Zeitlin, Jonathan (1996). "Re-forming Skills in British Metalworking, 1900–1940: A Contingent Failure". Paper presented at 21st meeting of the Social Science History Association, October 10–13 (panel on "Skill Formation in Comparative-Historical Perspective"), at New Orleans.

—— (2001). "Re-Forming Skills in British Metalworking, 1900–1940: A Contingent Failure", in G. Gayot and P. Minard (eds.), *Les ouvriers qualifiés de l'industrie (XVIe–XXe siècle): Formation, emploi, migrations*. Lille: Revue du Nord.

CHAPTER 24

....

BUSINESS EDUCATION

....

ROLV PETTER AMDAM

24.1 INTRODUCTION

....

IN recent years there has been a steady expansion in the literature on the history of business education. This expansion reflects the fact both that business historians have paid more attention to the formation of human capital in business and also that business education in most countries has been a major success story in universities in the last quarter of the twentieth century (Starkey *et al.* 2004). After presenting the main contributions to the existing knowledge of the development of business education internationally, this chapter will discuss the developmental path of business education around the world.

The chapter is organized into four sections that reflect different chronological phases within the international development of business education. First, the emergence of higher business education will be discussed as a phenomenon that occurred in different forms in parallel within major economies. Second, the chapter will characterize the first decades after the Second World War as a period of Americanization. Third, during the 1970s, Americanization is seen as overshadowed by tendencies towards regionalization and the strengthening of national systems for higher business education. Finally, international business education over the last two decades is seen as characterized by globalization and regionalization.

24.2 CONTOURS OF AN EMERGING LITERATURE

While several industrialized countries offered commercial education at secondary level from the beginning of the 19th century, it was not until the 1880s that parallel systems of higher business education emerged in a number of countries, including the United States (Sass 1992), Germany (Meyer 1998), France (Takagi and de Carlo 2003), and Japan (Ikema *et al.* 2000). The emergence of these systems has been described in anniversary monographs at different business schools (e.g. Amdam 1993; Barnes 1989; Barsoux 2000; Cruikshank 1987; Ikema *et al.* 2000; Meuleau 1981; Sass 1982; Sedlak and Williamson 1983; Wilson 1992) and in different national studies (e.g. Austin 2000; Engwall 1992; Genell 1997; Keeble 1992). Since the publication of Robert R. Locke's study in 1984 of the formation of the business education system in Germany, France, and Great Britain, *The End of the Practical Man*, there has been an emerging interest in comparative research on national systems for business education. Locke himself has followed up his study in his comparative volume on business education in the United States, Germany, France, and the UK, *Management and Higher Education since 1940* (1989) as have others in several comparative studies on management and business education in Europe (Amdam *et al.* 2003; Engwall and Zamagni 1998; Gourvish and Tiratsoo 1998) and across continents (Amdam 1996; Byrt 1989*a*; Engwall and Gunnarsson 1994; Kawabe and Daitō 1993). Other studies have examined comparatively the development of business education in two or more countries, including the Nordic region (Engwall 1998), Norway and France (Larsen 2003; Larsen 2005), and Germany, Denmark, and Turkey (Üsdiken *et al.* 2004).

The development of business education has not only attracted business historians, but also a substantial number of organization scholars (e.g. Engwall 1992; Engwall and Gunnarsson 1994; Engwall and Zamagni 1998; Genell 1997; Hedmo 2004; Kieser 2004; Wedlin 2004). Within the organizational tradition, new institutional theory has had a strong influence on this new field of research. According to the new institutional theory, organizations that work within the same organizational field have a tendency to become more similar due to coercion, norms, and imitation (DiMaggio and Powell 1983). This view fits well with observations from historians that the United States had a very strong influence on European business education after the Second World War. Consequently, historians and organizational theorists have converged on the use of the concept Americanization as a concept used to characterize the postwar development of international business education.

Since the development of business education has been closely linked to national systems of higher education, the systemic character of business education has been strongly emphasized. However, recently there has also been an emerging interest in studying the content of business education (e.g. Amdam *et al.* 2003; Austin 2000;

Engwall 1992; Üsdiken and Cetin 2001; Üsdiken *et al.* 2004). Other topics that have been examined include gender and business education (Larsen 2003; Larsen 2005) and the symbolic function of management degrees (Boutaiba and Strandgaard Pedersen 2003; Byrkjeflot 2003). In the Anglo-Saxon tradition, business education has been closely linked to management education. In other countries, such as Japan and Germany, management education has primarily taken place within firms or organized by institutions outside the formal educational system. These phenomena are studied by, for example, Kipping (1998) and Nishizawa (1998).

The above studies illustrate the fact that graduating from a business school represents only one way to reach management positions. Several researchers have therefore been concerned with the question of how business schools fit into the broader qualification system for management positions and for recruitment to the business elite (e.g. Amdam 1999; Bourdieu 1989; Byrkjeflot 2001; Engwall *et al.* 1996; Fellmann 2001; Hartmann 1996; Larson 2003; Marceau 1989). While business schools in the United States established themselves early in the 20th century as the main provider of graduates for managerial positions, business schools in most part of the world played a minor role within qualification systems until the last decades of the century. In the UK, the main route to management positions has historically been characterized not by higher educational criteria but by a combination of social background and exam scores from some of the best private boarding schools. Graduation from a technical university in Germany and graduation from a "grande école" of technology in France have performed this role.

24.3 THE FORMATION OF NATIONAL SYSTEMS OF HIGHER BUSINESS EDUCATION

During the last decades of the nineteenth century, different national systems of higher business education developed simultaneously in the United States, Europe, and Japan. The emergence of higher business education reflected, to some extent, the Second Industrial Revolution's need for better qualified managers and administrative staff (Locke 1989). The differences among higher business education systems reflected variations between different national business systems (Whitley 1999). The country that experienced the most significant relative decline in this period, Great Britain, lagged behind in establishing this kind of higher education (Keeble 1992; Larson 2003; Wilson 1992). As the industrialization process moved forward, business schools emerged in countries including Sweden (1909), Finland (1911), The Netherlands (1913), and Denmark (1919). When this era of rapid economic growth ended, the first formative period in the history of business education was also over (Engwall and Zamagni 1998).

The different national systems of business education can be grouped into two categories. First, there were the first movers—United States, Germany, and France—where parallel systems that reflected general patterns within the national systems of higher education emerged. Second, there were the followers—other European countries and Japan—where the new systems of business education were strongly influenced by at least one of the first movers.

24.3.1 The United States of America

As Sass (1992) has shown, Wharton School of Finance and Economy was established as the first American business school in 1881. Being a successful industrialist, Joseph Wharton felt the need to recruit business leaders who were trained to become more than clerks, as those from the commercial colleges were. His initiative to establish a business school at the University of Pennsylvania expressed not only the entrepreneurial spirit of the Second Industrial Revolution, but also the American university system's positive attitude toward including new vocational programs. When Dartmouth College created its Amos Tuck Business School at the turn of the century, the first exclusive graduate business school was established (Daniel 1998). During the twentieth century, the Master of Business Administration program (MBA) became the foremost symbol of American business education. In 1908 Harvard Business School was established (Cruickshark 1987), giving strength to a new wave of graduate business education in the United States. In 1922 the number of American business schools exceeded 140. The fact that 10 percent of all undergraduates at American universities and colleges in 1939 were studying business (Locke 1989) illustrates the popularity of the new subject.

American business schools offered the students several different functional subjects, such as accounting, auditing, marketing, and announcing in addition to economics and topics within public administration, which to some extent was inspired by research in economics and political sciences in Germany (Daniel 1998; Sass 1992). However, the development of management as a separate discipline being the core of the curricula made the American business schools unique. This focus on management reflected a period of managerial revolution in the United States, during which businessmen were recruited and promoted due to their ability to manage. Consequently, graduate business education developed through the first part of the 20th century into the dominant feature of the American qualification system for managerial positions (Byrkjeflot 2001).

24.3.2 Germany

In Europe, Germany and France took a leading role in developing national systems of higher business education. With regard to both structure and content, the systems for business education were strongly influenced by the dominant forces within the national higher educational system. Rather than reflecting concrete industrial demands, such as in the United States, the German *Handelshochschulen* expressed the state's active role as a modernizer of society (Locke 1984). The first *Handelshochschulen* were established in Aachen and Leipzig in 1898, followed by, among others, Cologne (1901) and Berlin (1906). The schools were modeled on the technical universities, and their primary aim was to offer a structured diploma program where the students attended the same class throughout each year.

Concerning the content, the German business schools developed two characteristics. First, they served as an arena for the movement led by Eugen Schmallenbach to create a new business economics discipline (*Betriebwirtschaftslehre*) based on accounting as the core, and they developed a strong focus on functional disciplines (Locke 1984; Meyer 1998). Second, the *Handelshochschulen* also reflected a strong scientific tradition in German higher education. Within the business schools, there was a strong academic drift to develop business economics in a scientific way so that the academic community would recognize it as an academic discipline. One result of this attempt was that the business school in Berlin in 1926 was awarded the right to offer a Ph.D. degree. Another consequence was the fact that business schools in the 1930s no longer remained independent, but were included in faculties of economics or business economics at universities with business economics and political economy as the basic disciplines (Locke 1984; Meyer 1998).

The German *Handelshochschulen* graduated students to a labor market where engineers were preferred for top management positions. The preference for engineers reflected a strong belief within the German labor market that authority was based on relevant technical skills, more than leadership as in the United States. The focus on functional disciplines may be regarded as an attempt to adjust the *Handelshochschulen* to this tradition. Like the engineers, who were trained as experts on technical issues, business school graduates became experts on administrative functional issues, like accounting and budgeting (Locke 1984; Byrkjeflot 2001).

24.3.3 France

In France, business education dated back to the creation of the Ecole Supérieure de Commerce (ESCP) in Paris in 1819, which in 1854 became a school of higher education (Grelon 1997; Engwall and Zamagni 1998). Another milestone was the establishment of the Ecole des Hautes Etudes Commerciales (HEC) by the chamber of commerce in Paris in 1881 with the ambition to select and develop future members of the French business elite (Larsen 2005; Meuleau 1981). These two institutions were the first of many *grandes écoles de commerce* in France. Structurally, these and subsequent *grandes écoles de commerce* were modeled after the technical *grandes écoles*, the *polytechniques*, which during the nineteenth century had achieved the position as the main providers of members of the French elite. Thus, the business schools strengthened the basic structures of the French educational system, and they contributed to the segmentation of the dual structure in French higher education. The two foundations of this dual system were the universities, which were owned by the state, and the more prestigious system of *grandes écoles*, which were primarily owned by the local chambers of commerce (Larsen 2005; Takagi and de Carlos 2003).

Concerning content, the French business schools were originally oriented toward the practical. The chambers of commerce owned the schools, and from the very beginning the business community and the *grandes écoles* cooperated closely. The chambers also provided the schools with practicing managers as part-time teachers. Consequently, the business schools offered a professional education with the focus on practical topics like accounting and on general disciplines like geography, economic history, and law. Also, it is important to note that the business schools adopted the practice from the *polytechniques* of setting tough entrance exams in order to be accepted as institutions whose graduates would join the French business elite (Meuleau 1981). This aspect of the school reflected the strong elitism as well as the importance of tight networks based on exams from top schools within the elite of French business and civil servants.

24.3.4 Diffusion

During the 19th and the first decade of the 20th century, several other European countries established higher institutions of business education. Among these were Belgium, Austria, Italy, Switzerland, Hungary, and Great Britain (Engwall and Zamagni 1998). Some of these were less successful, as in Great Britain, where accounting and other business subjects were offered at the universities of Birmingham and Manchester and the London School of Economics from 1901 (Tribe 2003). Developments in Britain were characterized by skepticism toward business education within both the academic and the business community. While formal higher education became more and more important for top management positions in the United States, Germany, and France, Great Britain remained characterized until the 1960s by what some scholars describe as a non-educational system reflecting a tendency to promote managers based on social class rather than education (Keeble 1992; Locke 1984, 1989; Wilson 1992). Others, however, have emphasized that the system for training accountants and engineers, which basically took place outside the university system, made a strong contribution to the British qualification system for management positions (Matthews *et al.* 1998; Sanderson 1972). During the interwar period some of the largest British firms also began to offer middle managers in-house management training programs (Larson 2003).

Among academic institutions in the Western world, the period from the 1880s to the Second World War was a period of international exchange of knowledge. European academic institutions and traditions influenced the United States in the natural sciences and social sciences (Sass 1992). With regard to business education, although United States influence on France and Germany and influence between France and Germany was minimal, both European nations served as role models within Europe as others developed their national business education systems.

The German system of business education not only influenced other German-speaking countries like Austria, but also the Nordic countries. When the first Nordic business school was established in 1909 in Stockholm, Sweden, it was like a blueprint of the German business school with German professors as lecturers, German textbooks, and German business economics as the core discipline. Structurally, the diploma model fit well into the Scandinavian countries because the university system in general was strongly influenced by the German system (Amdam 1999; Engwall 1992). The German influence was also strong in the Netherlands (Man 1996; Man and Karsten 1994).

The establishment of a system of business education in Turkey provides an interesting case of how different role models may interplay in creating a national system (Üsdiken 2003; Üsdiken and Cetin 2001; Üsdiken *et al.* 2004). In 1883 the first commercial school in Istanbul was created as a replica of the French HEC. This new school became a role model for similar schools in Turkey. Later during this formative period, two universities began to offer courses in business economics based on German textbooks. These two streams of education developed in parallel. The mixture of different role models became more complex in the late 1950s when a new university was opened in Ankara and offered programs modeled after American business schools.

In Japan new institutions that were heavily influenced by foreign role models also emerged during this period. After the Meiji Restoration in 1868, Japan focused on developing institutions to promote modernization based on the transfer of knowledge and technology from the Western world. This wave of modernization also included the establishment of new educational institutions, such as the Imperial University in 1877, which became the main provider of graduates to the privileged elites of modernization (Nishizawa 1998). Business education mainly developed outside the universities. In 1875 Arinori Mori founded the Commercial Training School in Tokyo after visits to the UK and the United States. In 1887 this institution became the Tokyo Higher Commercial School at Hitotsubashi and in 1918 the Tokyo University of Commerce. Following the Hitotsubashi model, Osaka City University of Commerce came into being in 1928 as well as Kobe University of Commerce—originally Kobe Higher Commercial School from 1902—in the following year (Ikema *et al.* 2000). In addition to strong British and American influence from the very beginning, these business schools were also influenced by Germany and Belgium. For instance, at the Higher Commercial School in Tokyo, which in

1885 merged with Tokyo Higher Commercial School, the program was originally modeled after the Institut Supérieur de Commerce d'Anvers in Belgium, and students and teachers visited Belgium regularly. However, the result of this diffusion process was not a blueprint of any one system, especially since the Japanese also began to develop systems of internal management training, which later emerged as a typical feature of the Japanese system (Daitō 1993).

Outside Europe, German business education strongly influenced the first attempts to establish institutions for higher business education in South America (Locke 1996) and South Africa (Ahwireng-Obeng 1999). In Canada institutions for higher business education emerged based on the American model (Austin 2000). An exception was HEC in Montreal that was modeled after French and Belgian business schools (Boothman 2000; Harvey 2000).

24.4 AMERICANIZATION, 1945 TO THE 1960S

American business education had a major impact on changes in business education, especially in Western Europe and Japan, after the Second World War. This influence has remained strong until the contemporary period, but it was exceptionally strong during the first two postwar decades. The Americanization of business education has been explained by several factors, including the changes that took place within American business schools, the existence of new channels for transferring knowledge from the United States, and the search for new business knowledge in the industrialized world.

24.4.1 The New Look and Transfer of Knowledge from the United States

After the war, American business education underwent a process of self-criticism and criticism from outside. Programs were criticized for the absence of a coherent business study curriculum. In 1959 two different reports on management education funded by the Ford Foundation (Gordon and Howell 1959) and the Carnegie Foundation (Pierson 1959) were published. The reports, which had a great impact on American business education, suggested that business education schools should become more academic, making greater use of the application of science to the solution of management problems (Aaronson 1992; Daniel 1998; Gemelli 1998a, 1998b; Gleeson 1997; Locke 1989). Within this process, a new scientific paradigm contributed to moving the business schools closer to academia and further from practice. The New Look evolved, differing from previous practice in its analytical, conceptual, and methodological approach and by including statistical, operational research, and behavioral science in management teaching and research. At the same time the MBA programs were expanding to become the flagship of American business schools (Daniel 1998).

This move toward a more academic approach is one reason why the American business education system became the most important international role model for business education (Locke 1989). Another reason is that management education became a strategic weapon for the United States in the battle against communism during the Cold War (Gemelli 1998a; Daniel 1998). A third reason was the existence of new channels for transferring knowledge.

The first major channel for transferring business knowledge to Europe was set up within the framework of the Marshall Plan in 1948. As part of the Technical Assistance program, several study-trips were arranged across the Atlantic in both directions in order to introduce American business practice and knowledge to Europe (Gourvish and Tiratsoo 1998; Kipping and Bjarnar 1998; Djelic 1998; McGlade 1998a, 1998b). This channel was replaced in 1953 with the creation of the European Productivity Agency (EPA) by the Organisation of European Economic Cooperation (OEEC) (Boel 1998; Gourvish and Tiratsoo 1998). In addition to creating national productivity centers, the EPA diffused business knowledge through sending hundreds of American professors and consultants to European industries and educational institutions during the 1950s and by organizing study-trips for thousands of managers, consultants, and business academics to the United States (Amdam and Yttri 1998; Boel 1998; Gourvish and Tiratsoo 1998; Kipping and Nioche 1998). A third process of transferring knowledge took place within the framework of the Ford Foundation (Gemelli 1998a), which cooperated closely with the EPA, and which became a major source of finance for transferring business knowledge beginning in 1960 when the EPA was dissolved. In addition to creating programs for the exchange of professors, the Foundation contributed to the establishment of European business schools, including INSEAD in France in 1959 (Barsoux 2000), the London Business School in 1964 (Barnes 1989), and the Manchester Business School (Wilson 1992) in 1965. It also contributed to the establishment of the European Institute for Advanced Studies in Management (EIASM) in Brussels (Gemelli 1998a). In Japan, American influence also made a strong impact on business education through the American education mission (Nishizawa 1998).

24.4.2 National Responses

The process of transferring knowledge internationally from American business schools has been characterized by Byrt (1989b) as "educational imperialism". Locke (1996) follows up this view by emphasizing that Americans perceived their knowledge on business as superior, and he regarded this attitude as an attempt to impose knowledge on the rest of the world. However, this position has been challenged by several scholars who have emphasized that other industrialized countries were not only passive receivers of knowledge, but were actively searching for new knowledge. More than passively adopting American models of business education, they translated new ideas into their own context (Amdam and Bjarnar 1998).

Based on a study of the structural aspects of European business education, Engwall and Zamagni (1998) have categorized the European countries into four groups according to their reaction to the American model of business education. The first category consisted of countries that were *resistant toward the American model*, i.e. Germany and France. One of the consequences of this resistance in Germany was that executive management training developed as in-house training (Kieser 2004; Kipping 1998). The second category grouped countries where *the American model was a challenge to the university system*, meaning that business schools of an American type were established, but that they did not fit into the system. One of these countries was Spain, where the creation of several business schools in the 1950s led to the successful development of a business school system outside the traditional university structure (Puig 2003). The third category was comprised of countries where *the American model altered a German model*. Examples of this group were the Nordic countries. The last category included *the late adopters of the American model*, especially Great Britain, which adopted the American idea of a business school with an MBA program in the 1960s. When the American model was adopted, it also developed closely along American lines (Wilson 1992), as the Henley Management College did. In 1946 the Administrative Staff College at Henley was established as a private executive management institution modeled after the executive programs at Harvard Business School (Larson 2003).

In Japan the American model contributed to the strengthening of national practices already established in business education. Also, the American education mission contributed to the introduction of a new university structure with a distinction between junior colleges and "new" universities. Within this system business education focused on arts and general studies rather than on practical and functional subjects, leaving business and management training and development to the companies themselves or to courses offered by the Japanese Productivity Center and other business organizations (Nishizawa 1998).

Concerning Europe, it has been claimed that one of the American aims was to restructure business education (Engwall and Zamagni 1998). However, one could argue that in general the Americans did not see existing institutions as constraints on change. Their main task was not to revamp the national systems of business education that had emerged in both the higher education system in general and in the concrete national business systems, but rather to convince business schools to introduce the key elements found within the content of American business schools, especially management as a discipline. In this perspective the transfer of ideas was basically successful. The traditional European business school that offered a diploma program very often responded positively to the idea of including new American disciplines like management, work studies, psychology, operational research, and statistics (OECD 1964). In Germany, American organizational behavior and marketing were included in their *Betriebwirtschaftslehre* in this period (Kieser 2004). France, which was one of the countries which experienced the least structural change, was also one with whose openness to new knowledge the Americans were most satisfied. In the 1960s, several French universities developed their programs in *gestions* so that it became more in line with the American concept of management (Chessel and Pavis 2001; OECD 1964). When experts from the United States and the OECD countries met in Paris in 1964 to summarize ten years' work on the diffusion of management education ideas, they all agreed that the success should be measured according to whether the idea was "integrated into national systems of higher education". They concluded that it had been most successful in countries where "the formal education system has traditionally provided a large proportion of managerial groups" (OECD 1964: 20).

However, in countries where business education was weakly developed, or where existing institutions declined to cooperate with the Americans, efforts were made to support local initiatives to promote business education. In Spain, Italy, and Turkey, close personal networks with scholars at Harvard Business School, which were very active in the 1950s, were of great importance (Gemelli 1998*a*, 1998*b*). Another example was Finland, where the Ford Foundation in the late 1950s supported a Finnish initiative to establish a new management training center with a grant that led to the opening of the Finnish Institute of Management in 1964 (Amdam 1998). A third example was the Ford Foundation's decision in the 1960s to support initiatives to establish business schools offering MBA degrees in Manchester and London (Wilson 1992). In Japan, the emergence of the productivity movement also secured the transfer of American management knowledge to businesses through different courses at executive and middle management levels (Nishizawa 1998). Regardless of the form or degree of Americanization in international business education, there is, however, no support in the research literature for the claim that American influence had any substantial impact on the different national qualification systems for management positions in this period.

24.5 REGIONAL AND NATIONAL VISIONS, 1960S TO 1980S

The period from the mid-1960s to the beginning of the 1980s was a period of rapid growth of MBA programs and undergraduate business studies in the United States (Daniel 1998; Locke 1996; Sass 1992). The creation of new business schools resulted in a strong movement to develop these institutions into academic institutions which would be accepted in the academic community. One expression of this academic trend was that more effort was placed on improving academic standards than on developing relationships with practice, which resulted in a growing gap between academia and practice (Aaronsen 1996; Locke 1996). At the same time, the new management consulting industry was expanding, providing some of the services previously provided by the business schools (Kipping and Engwall 2003; McKenna 1997).

The American influence on European business education was also strong after the 1960s. One could, however, argue that it weakened during the late 1960s and 1970s, especially in its influence on structural changes in business education. In general the American period was replaced by a period where two visions were competing: a vision of developing a European approach to business education and a vision of strengthening national systems of business education. Also, beginning in 1960, Japan's management education was in transition from what Nishizawa (1998: 92) describes as "the laborious assimilation of American management techniques to a more systematic and Japanese approach".

Already in the 1950s, voices were heard that wanted to develop a European cross-national approach in business education. The establishment of INSEAD outside Paris in 1959 can, as Barsoux (2000) has shown, be understood in this perspective. During the 1960s this European dimension gained strength as demonstrated by the foundation of European organizations like the European Foundation for Management Development (EFMD) and the European Institute for Advanced Studies in Management (EIASM) in 1971. These organizations shared the goal of developing new institutions at the European level. "At that time", the president of EFMD says in the organization's 25th anniversary book (Hubert 1996), "Europe slowly became aware that there was a need to keep what was good in the American model, but also to develop its own approach".

In this case it is important to notice that American institutions supported the establishment of these organizations, especially through grants from the Ford Foundation. Overall, however, the Americans reduced their support for business education in Europe during this period. The EPA programs ended in 1963, and the Ford Foundation also wanted to go into new geographical areas outside Europe. In the case of EIASM, it was explicitly said by its supporter the Ford Foundation that it was better to develop European institutions for training professors in business administration than to support their stay in the United States after they had completed their Ph.Ds. (Naert n.d.).

Gemelli (1998a) has shown that EFMD was established as a member organization for institutions and individuals with three main purposes: first, to serve as a bridge between management practice and management learning; second, to dedicate itself to the exchange of experience and ideas; and third, to represent management development to third parties. Thus, EFMD focused strongly on bridging practice and academia, and it carried further the work done by a Dutch organization, International University Contact, and a Latin organization, European Association of Management Training Centres (Hubert 1996). The aim of EIASM was to develop a center for advanced studies in management to graduate Ph.D. candidates and train professors in management, and it was based on active cooperation with existing national business schools in Europe (Gemelli 1998a). By serving as a center to graduate European Ph.D. candidates and trained professors in business administration, EIASM aimed at influencing the content of the participating schools. Concerning the structure, however, EIASM had no intention of interfering with how each country organized their business education.

During the 1970s the European vision faded. There is no research literature on the results of the EIASM's attempt to become a center of expertise for European business schools. Archival findings, however, show that the program in general was successful during the first years, but that its activities declined over time (Naert n.d.). The number of total activities (seminars, etc.) at EIASM declined from 32 with 1,306 participants in 1976–7 to 21 with 796 participants three years later. Also, the number of Ph.D. candidates declined after some years of strong growth.

One reason for this decline of the European vision was a general tendency to focus less on Europe as a unit, coupled with a certain revitalization of nationalistic attitudes following the economic crisis that began in 1973. Another reason was that the launch of the European vision took place at the same time as several nations were taking big steps toward strengthening their national systems of higher education. Considering the scale of these nationalistic efforts, it might have been difficult to pay the necessary attention to developing parallel plans at the European level. The big step was no less than an attempt to transform the university system into a mass education system. Rather than creating new national systems of higher education, countries aimed at extending those that were already established. This process increased the number of students at existing universities and contributed to the creation of new undergraduate colleges. In most countries this movement resulted in the strengthening of business studies, especially at undergraduate level. In Italy, where attempts to create new business schools of an American type in the 1950s failed, and where changes in the majority of existing institutions were slow, other institutions, like the Bocconi University in Milan, experienced an upgrade in terms of faculty and students during this period (Gemelli 1998b).

In the mid-1980s this development reached its peak. In European higher education in general, the strong belief in investment and expansion in higher education was replaced by an emerging concern that the expansion had been so expensive that it was necessary to revise the notion that the state alone could cover all costs (Williams 1991). However, European nations had used these years to strengthen their educational system based on each country's specific characteristics. This was also the case for the national systems for business education.

24.6 GLOBALIZATION AND REGIONALIZATION, 1980S–

Since the 1980s there has been a booming interest in business education worldwide. In the United States, more than 100,000 MBA degrees are awarded annually, with business representing one-quarter of all bachelor degrees at American universities and one-quarter of all masters degrees (Rukstad and Collins 2001). At the same time, MBA programs during this period have been strongly criticized for being too academic (Aaronsen 1996; Locke 1996; Mintzberg 2004), and this critique has been seen as one reason for the strong expansion of corporate universities (Locke 1996; Meister 1998), as well as for the introduction of management consulting companies as providers of programs for executive management training (Kipping and Amorin 2003).

Worldwide, the number of MBA programs increased from at least 1,600 in September 1998 to at least 2,200 in 126 countries in February 2000. During this time, while the number of programs increased by 14 percent in the United States and 52 percent in Europe, they expanded from 272 to 535 in the rest of the world, an increase of 97 percent (Byrkjeflot 2003). According to Mintzberg (2004), the MBA degree has emerged as the only global degree in the sense that it is relatively homogenous worldwide, although there are certainly nuances between regions.

24.6.1 Europe

There have been some clear similarities between developments in business education in the United States and Europe. The increasing success of the MBA programs at European business schools reveals that the US influence was an important factor in the transformation of business education in Europe. Especially in the UK, the number of MBA programs expanded rapidly from the mid-1980s, and in the mid-1990s there were more than 100 different MBA programs at British universities (Brown *et al.* 1996; Larson 2003). In Europe as a whole, one MBA program on average was established annually between 1959 and 1987. From 1987 to 1993, however, more than seven were established a year, and the annual numbers expanded dramatically after 1993 (Boutaiba and Strandgaard Pedersen 2003). There was also a noteworthy expansion of business education in Eastern Europe after 1989 (e.g. Genell 1997; Lee *et al.* 1996; Pieper 1994).

However, there is also evidence that the European dimension was of increasing importance in this period. In the 1990s, there was "a new wave" that pushed forward the idea of a European standard in business education (Crawshaw 1995). First, European business schools continued to develop elements that gave them a strong European flavor. They had a stronger international profile than the Americans, and it was primarily the one-year European version of the MBA program that expanded rather than the two-year American model. At the end of the period, four of them (IMD in Lausanne, INSEAD in France, London Business School, and IESE in Barcelona) were regularly ranked among the top 25 schools in the world by different ranking institutions (Hedmo 2004; Wedlin 2004).

Second, although there was a general trend in Europe for more MBA graduates to be recruited to top management position (Byrkjeflot 2001), the recruitment patterns at the end of the period were still strongly dominated by nation-specific recruitment patterns to top business positions (Mayer and Whittington 1999). In some countries, such as the Scandinavian countries, the business schools had strengthened their positions so that they had replaced the technical universities as the main provider of new members of the business elite (Amdam 1999; Engwall 1992). In others, however, the qualification system for management positions has not been so radically transformed. In France, for instance, 75 percent of the CEOs of the 1,000 largest firms in 1996 were graduates from the *grandes écoles* (Nioche 1996).

Third, the 1990s was the decade of the emergence and revitalization of European professional associations in accounting, organizational studies, international business, etc. that had been created in the 1970s (*Organization Studies* 2000). These associations were of great importance for the development of a European understanding of concepts like organization and management. Parallel to the institutional development, there was also a strong interest in developing the concept of European management, expressed for instance in books like *Euro Management: A New Style for the Global Market* by Bloom *et al.* (1994).

Another change in the 1990s occurred within the system of the accreditation of business schools. The organization EFMD was strengthened from the mid-1980s through an increase in membership. When it was founded, the organization had 92 members, and this number increased slowly to 193 in 1981 and 400 in 1998. EFMD was also strengthened through its development into a European accreditation association for business schools. The traditions for accreditation were long established in the United States. However, when the American accreditation association, AASCB, tried to establish itself as an accreditation institution in Europe in 1996, some of the EFMD members reacted. EFMD quickly established a European accreditation system for business schools called EQUIS, which soon became a competitor to AASCB in accrediting business schools outside Europe and the United States (Hedmo 2003, 2004).

24.6.2 Rest of the World

There has been limited research on the growth of business education outside Europe and the United States. In all continents the first business schools were established before this period. However, their numbers and impact were quite limited until the end of the 20th century. One of the countries outside North America and Europe with the strongest traditions in business education is Australia. In this country higher commercial education emerged in the 1920s due to its strong links to Europe. After the Second World War, the American influence was very strong, and the universities of Melbourne and New South Wales offered MBA programs beginning in 1963 (Byrt 1989*b*). From the 1980s business education expanded strongly. In 2003, 33 percent of all students in higher education were studying for a business degree, and Australian business schools have been very successful in attracting foreign students making it one of the country's most important export industries (Starkey *et al.* 2004).

In Latin America the Adolfo Ibáñes University (UAI) was established as the first business school in Chile in 1953. During recent decades some Latin American business schools have developed strongly, and in 2003 three business schools from Latin America were on the *Financial Times* top 100 list of business schools (nos. 83, 88, and 99). In Africa there has recently been strong growth in business schools since the establishment of the Ghana Institute of Management and Public Administration in 1961 and Lagos Business School in 1973. While South Africa offered five MBA programs in 1990, the country offered 46 programs in 2000 (Byrkjeflot 2001).

In Asia, several business schools were established from the 1960s, including the Asian Institute of Management (AIM) in the Philippines (1969) and NUS Business School, Singapore (1961). China is an interesting case since the Fudan University in Shanghai introduced business administration courses in 1917 and established a Department of Business Administration as early as 1920. In the 1960s, however, Chinese programs in business administration at Fudan and other universities were closed down for political reasons. A new era in the history of business education began in the 1980s. In 1984 Dalian Institute of Technology and SUNY Buffalo Management School offered the first joint MBA program in China, initiated by a discussion between Chairman Deng and the former Secretary of State, Henry Kissinger. Expansion began in 1991 when nine institutions offered MBA programs. This number increased to 67 in 2003 (Alon and Lu 2004).

Some Chinese business schools are joint ventures between Chinese universities, local governments, and business schools from other countries, like CEIBS established in Shanghai in 1994 by the European Union, the state, and local government (Alon and Lu 2004). The formation of joint ventures in business education reflects not only a general tendency within Chinese businesses, but also a global tendency to develop networks, strategic alliances, and joint ventures in business education (Green and Gerber 1996). Some of these agreements date back to the 1960s and 1970s, such as the partnership between Adolfo Ibáñes University in Chile and Harvard Business School and also between IESE in Barcelona and Lagos Business School through the Catholic organization Opus Dei. From the mid-1990s there has been tremendous growth in cross-national partnership agreements between business schools. Some schools have also invested in their own campuses abroad, examples being INSEAD in Singapore and the BI Norwegian School of Management in Lithuania. Others, like the French HEC, the American NYU Stern School of Business, and the British London School of Economics, have cooperated on joint global executive MBA programs.

24.7 CONCLUSIONS

In the twentieth century the business school developed into the most dynamic institution within the higher education system, with the power, especially during the last two decades, to reshape the systems of higher education. The business school has also been in a dual position between the academic world and the business world. In most countries the relationship to practice was originally very strong. However, critics claim that the academization process beginning in the 1950s has weakened the links to practice which have accompanied the expansion of the late 20th century.

It has been generally agreed that European business schools were strongly influenced by American role models after the Second World War. This chapter supports this view; however, it also emphasizes that the concept "Americanization" most suitably characterizes the relationship between American and Western European business education during the first two decades after the war. In later decades there have been certain limitations regarding this influence, and in the 1990s a tendency toward regionalization of business education ran parallel to the process of globalization. The American influence has been especially strong concerning the content of European business education, but it has had a weaker impact on its structure. In general, the structure of business education in Europe still reflects strong national traditions in higher education, which have been slow to change. The new wave of European integration in business education from the 1990s is based on an understanding of national structural differences. One question for further research should be to investigate to what extent the expansion of MBA programs within business schools from the mid-1980s has transformed the different national qualification systems for management positions. Our knowledge on this issue is still very fragmented.

Concerning the recent expansion of business education outside North America and Europe, the rapid growth of MBA programs indicates a strong tendency toward global homogenization, concerning both structure and content. In most of these countries, the system for higher education has in general been more weakly developed than in Europe, meaning that the institutional conditions for adopting outside educational models and ideas have also been weak compared to Europe, where longstanding educational traditions have remained intact. Research on this process is one of the most interesting topics for further study on the international development of business education.

More research should also be done on the consequences of the recent global expansion of business education on the qualification system for management positions. Historically, there have been strong national variations concerning the business schools' position within the qualification system for management positions. While American business schools achieved a status as the main provider of graduates for those positions, business schools in other parts of the world have played a minor role compared to technical universities (e.g. Scandinavia, Germany, France), executive training centers outside the educational system (e.g. Germany), in-house training (e.g. Japan), and promotions based on social class (e.g. the UK) or family or other networks (e.g. South-East Asia). Recent research has shown that in some areas like the Scandinavian countries, business schools have been able to change their status to become the main suppliers of future managers since the 1970s. In most parts of the world, however, the changing role of the business schools within national qualification systems for management positions is still under-researched.

References

Aaronsen, S. (1996). "Dinosaurs in the Global Economy? American Graduate Business Schools in the 1980s and 1990s", in Amdam (1996).

Ahwireng-Obeng, F. (1999). "Internationalizing Economics Education in South Africa". *CR Special Issue*, 9: 30–9.

Alon, I., and Lu, L. (2004). "The State of Marketing and Business Education in China". *Marketing Education Review*, 14/1: 1–10.

Amdam, R. P. (1993). *For egen regning: BI og den økonomisk-administrative utdanningen 1943–1993*. Oslo: Universitetsforlaget.

—— (ed.) (1996). *Management Education and Competitiveness: Europe, Japan and the United States*. London and New York: Routledge.

—— (1998). "Productivity and Management Education: The Nordic Countries", in Gemelli (1998a).

—— (1999). *Utdanning, økonomi og ledelse: Fremveksten av den økonomisk-administrative utdanningen 1936–1986*. Oslo: Unipub.

—— and Bjarnar, O. (1998). "The Regional Dissemination of US Productivity Models in Norway in the 1950s and 1960s", in Kipping and Bjarnar (1998).

—— Kvålshaugen, R., and Larsen, E. (eds.) (2003). *Inside the Business Schools: The Content of European Business Schools*. Copenhagen: Copenhagen Business School Press.

—— and Yttri, G. (1998). "The European Productivity Agency, the Norwegian Productivity Institute and Management Education", in Gourvish and Tiratsoo (1998).

Austin, B. (ed.) (2000). *Capitalizing Knowledge: Essays on the History of Business Education in Canada*. Toronto: University of Toronto Press.

BARNES, W. (1989). *Managerial Catalyst: The Story of London Business School, 1964–1989*. London: Paul Chapman.

BARSOUX, J.-L. (2000). *INSEAD: From Intuition to Institution*. Houndsmill: Macmillan.

BLOOM, H., CALORI, R., and DE WOOT, P. (1994). *Euro Management: A New Style for the Global Market*. London: Kogan Page.

BOEL, B. (1998). "The European Productivity Agency and the Develoment of Management Education in Western Europe in the 1950s", in Gourvish and Tiratsoo (1998).

BOOTHMAN, B. E. C. (2000). "Culture of Utility: The Development of Business Education in Canada", in Austin (2000).

BOURDIEU, P. (1989). *La noblesse d'état: grandes écoles et esprit de corps*. Paris: Minuit.

BOUTAIBA, S., and STRANDGAARD PEDERSEN, J. (2003). "Creating MBA Identity: Between Field and Organisation", in Amdam *et al.* (2003).

BROWN, R. B., MCCARTNEY, S., and CLOWES, J. (1996). "Do They Mean Business? An Investigation of the Purpose of the 'New University' Business Schools in Britain", in Amdam (1996).

BYRKJEFLOT, H. (2001). "Management Education and Selection of Top Managers in Europe and the United States". *LOS Senteret Rapport*, R0103.

——(2003). "To MBA or not to MBA? A Dilemma Accentuated by the Recent Boom in Business Education", in Amdam *et al.* (2003).

BYRT, W. (ed.) (1989a). *Management Education: An International Survey*. London and New York: Routledge.

——(1989b). "Management Education in Australia", in Byrt (1989a), 78–103.

CHESSEL, M.-E., and PAVIS, F. (2001). *Le technocrate, le patron et le professeur: Une histoire de l'enseignement supérieur de gestion*. Paris: Belin.

CRAWSHAW, R. (1995). "Management Education: The European Dimension and Beyond". *EFMD Forum*, 2.

CRUIKSHANK, J. L. (1987). *Delicate Experiment: The Harvard Business School 1908–1945*. Boston: Harvard Business School Press.

DAITŌ, E. (1993). "Business and Education in Historical Perspective: The Interwar Years in Japan", in Kawabe and Daitō (1993).

DANIEL, C. A. (1998). *MBA: The First Century*. Lewisburg, Pa.: Bucknell University Press.

DIMAGGIO, P. J., and POWELL, W. W. (1983). "The Iron Cage Revisited: Institutional Isomorphism and Collective Rationality in Organizational Fields". *American Sociological Review*, 48: 147–60.

DJELIC, M.-L. (1998). *Exporting the American Model: The Post-War Transformation of European Business*. Oxford: Oxford University Press.

ENGWALL, L. (1992). *Mercury Meets Minerva*. Oxford: Pergamon Press.

——(1998). "The Making of Viking Leaders: Perspectives on Nordic Management Education", in Engwall and Zamagni (1998).

——and GUNNARSSON, E. (eds.) (1994). *Management Education in an Academic Context*. Uppsala: Uppsala University.

————and WALLERSTEDT, E. (1996). "Mercury's Messengers: Swedish Business Graduates in Practice", in Amdam (1996).

——and ZAMAGNI, V. (eds.) (1998). *Management Education in an Historical Perspective*. Manchester: Manchester University Press.

FELLMANN, S. (2001). "Finnish Industrial Management in a Historical and Nordic Perspective", in H. Byrkjeflot, S. Myklebust, C. Myrvang, and F. Sejersted (eds.), *The Democratic*

Challenge to Capitalism: Management and Democracy in the Nordic Countries. Bergen: Fagbokforlaget.

GEMELLI, G. (ed.) (1998*a*). *The Ford Foundation and Europe (1950s–1970s): Cross-Fertilization of Learning in Social Science and Management.* Brussels: Europe Interuniversity Press.

—— (1998*b*). "The 'Enclosure' Effect: Innovation without Standardization in Italian Postwar Management Education", in Engwall and Zamagni (1998).

GENELL, K. (1997). *Transforming Management Education: A Polish Mixture.* Lund: Lund University Press.

GLEESON, R. E. (1997). "Stalemate at Stanford, 1945–1958: The Long Prelude to the New Look at Stanford Business School". *Selections,* summer.

GORDON, R. A., and HOWELL, J. E. (1959). *Higher Education in Business.* New York: Columbia University Press.

GOURVISH, T., and TIRATSOO, N. (eds.) (1998). *Missionaries and Managers: American Influence on European Management Education 1945–60.* Manchester: Manchester University Press.

GREEN, R. T., and GERBER, L. V. (1996). "Educator Insights: Strategic Partnership for Global Education—Linkages with Overseas Institutions". *Journal of International Marketing,* 4/3: 89–100.

GRELON, A. (1997). "Ecole de commerce et formations d'ingénieurs jusqu'en 1914". *Enterprise et histoire,* 14/15: 29–45.

HARTMANN, M. (1996). *Topmanager: Die Rekrutierung einer Elite.* Frankfurt and New York: Campus Verlag.

HARVEY, P. (2000). "The Founding of the École des Hautes Études Commerciales de Montréal", in Austin (2000).

HEDMO, T. (2003). "The Europeanisation of Business Education", in Amdam *et al.* (2003).

—— (2004). *Rule-Making in the Transnational Space: The Development of European Accreditation of Management Education.* Uppsala: Uppsala Universitet.

HUBERT, T. (1996). "Retracing the Roots: Twenty-Five Years of efmd Bridge-Building", in *Training the Fire Brigade.* Brussels: EFMD.

IKEMA, M., INOUE, Y., NISHIZAWA, T., and YAMAUCHI, S. (2000). *Hitotsubashi University, 1875–2000: A Hundred and Twenty-Five Years of Higher Education in Japan.* Houndmills: Macmillan.

KAWABE, N., and DAITŌ, E. (eds.) (1993). *Education and Training in the Development of Modern Corporations.* Tokyo: University of Tokyo Press.

KEEBLE, S. P. (1992). *The Ability to Manage: A Study of British Management, 1890–1990.* Manchester: Manchester University Press.

KIESER, A. (2004). "The Americanization of Academic Management Education in Germany". *Journal of Management Inquiry,* 13/2: 90–7.

KIPPING, M. (1998). "The Hidden Business Schools: Management Training in Germany since 1945", in Engwall and Zamagni (1998).

—— and AMORIM, C. (2003). "Consultancies as Management Schools", in Amdam *et al.* (2003).

—— and BJARNAR, O. (eds.) (1998). *The Americanisation of European Business: The Marshall Plan and the Transfer of United States Management Models.* London and New York: Routledge.

—— and ENGWALL, L. (eds.) (2003). *Management Consulting: Emergence and Dynamics of a Knowledge Industry.* Oxford: Oxford University Press.

—— and NIOCHE, J.-P. (1998). "Much Ado about Nothing? The United States Productivity Drive and Management Training in France, 1945–60", in Gourvish and Tiratsoo (1998).

LARSEN, E. (2003). "Cultures of Content: A Comparison of French and Norwegian Business Schools", in Amdam *et al.* (2003).

—— (2005). *Invisible Strategies: Gender in French and Norwegian Business Education, 1870–1980*. Bergen: Rokkansenteret.

LARSON, M. J. (2003). "Practically Academic: The Formation of the British Business School", Ph.D. thesis in History, University of Wisconsin, Madison.

LEE, M., LETICHE, H., CRAWSHAW, R., and THOMAS, M. (eds.) (1996). *Management Education in the New Europe*. London: International Thomson Business Press.

LOCKE, R. R. (1984). *The End of the Practical Man: Entrepreneurship and Higher Education in Germany, France, and Great Britain, 1880–1940*. Greenwich and London: Jai Press.

—— (1989). *Management and Higher Education since 1940: The Influence of America and Japan on West Germany, Great Britain, and France*. Cambridge: Cambridge University Press.

—— (1996). *The Collapse of the American Management Mystique*. Oxford: Oxford University Press.

McGLADE, J. (1998a). "The United States Technical Assistance and Productivity Program and the Education of Western European Managers, 1948–58", in Gourvish and Tiratsoo (1998).

—— (1998b). "The Big Push: The Export of American Business Education to Western Europe after the Second World War", in Engwall and Zamagni (1998).

McKENNA, C. D. (1997). "'The American Challenge': McKinsey & Company's Role in the Transfer of Decentralization to Europe, 1957–1975", *Academy of Management Proceedings*, 226–30.

MAN, H. DE (1996). "Continuities in Dutch Business Education: Engineering, Economics, and the Business School", in Amdam (1996).

—— and KARSTEN, L. (1994). "Academic Management Education in the Netherlands", in Engwall and Gunnarsson (1994).

MARCEAU, J. (1989). *A Family Business? The Creation of an International Elite*. Cambridge: Cambridge University Press.

MAYER, M., and WHITTINGTON, R. (1999). "Euro-elites: Top British, French and German Managers in the 1980s and 1990s", *European Management Journal*, 17/4: 403–8.

MATTHEWS, D., ANDERSON, M., and EDWARDS, J. R. (1998). *The Priesthood of Industry: The Rise of the Professional Accountant in British Management*. Oxford: Oxford University Press.

MEISTER, J. C. (1998). *Corporate Universities: Lessons in Building a World-Class Work Force*. New York: McGraw-Hill.

MEULEAU, M. (1981). *Histoire d'une grande école HEC 1881–1981*. Paris: Bordas-Dunod.

MEYER, H.-D. (1998). "The German Handelshochschulen, 1989–1933: A New Departure in Management Education and Why it Failed", in Engwall and Zamagni (1998).

MINTZBERG, H. (2004). *Developing Managers Not MBAs*. London: FT Prentice Hall.

NAERT, P. A. (ed.) (n.d.). "Ten Years European Institute for Advanced Studies in Management: Evaluation and Perspective". Ford Foundation Archive (FFA) 71.100, EIASM.

NIOCHE, J. P. (1996). "Management Education in France: Two Centuries of Development". Paper for the International Conference on Management Education in a Historical Perspective, Bologna, October 25–6.

NISHIZAWA, T. (1998). "The Development of Managerial Human Resources in Japan: A Comparative Perspective", in Engwall and Zamagni (1998).

OECD (1964). "International Conference on Management Education, Paris, 9th–12th December, 1964, Final Report".

Organization Studies (2000) 20th anniversary number.

PIEPER, R. (1994). "Division and Unification of German Business Administration and Management Education", in Engwall and Gunnarsson (1994).

PIERSON, F. C. (1959). *The Evolution of American Business: A Study of University-College Programs in Business Administration*. New York: McGraw-Hill.

PUIG, N. (2003). "Educating Spanish Managers: The United States, Entrepreneurial Networks, and Business Schools in Spain, 1950–1975", in Amdam *et al.* (2003).

RUKSTAD, M., and COLLINS, D. (2001). "Unext: Business Education and e-Learning". Boston, Mass.: Harvard Business School Case No. 9-701-014.

SANDERSON, M. (1972). *The Universities and British Industry, 1850–1970*. London: Routledge and Kegan Paul.

SASS, S. A. (1992). *The Pragmatic Imagination: A History of the Wharton School 1881–1981*. Philadelphia: University of Pennsylvania Press.

SEDLAK, M. W., and WILLIAMSON, H. F. (1983). *The Evolution of Management Education: A History of Northwestern University J. F. Kellogg Graduate School of Management, 1908–1983*. Urbana, Ill.: University of Illinois Press.

STARKEY, K., HATCHUEL, A., and TEMPEST, S. (2004). "Rethinking the Business School". *Journal of Management Studies*, 41/8: 1521–32.

TAKAGI, J., and DE CARLO, L. (2003). "The Ephemeral National Model of Management Education: A Comparative Study of Five Management Programmes in France", in Amdam *et al.* (2003).

TRIBE, K. (2003). "The Faculty of Commerce and Manchester Economics, 1903–44". *The Manchester School*, 71/6: 680–710.

ÜSDIKEN, B. (2003). "Plurality in Institutional Environments and Educational Content: The Undergraduate Business Degree in Turkey", in Amdam *et al.* (2003).

—— and CETIN, D. (2001). "From Betriebswirtschaftslehre to Human Relations: Turkish Management Literature before and after the Second World War". *Business History,* 43/2: 99–124.

—— KIESER, A., and KJAER, P. (2004). "Academy, Economy, and Polity: Betriebswirtschaftslehre in Germany, Denmark and Turkey before 1945". *Business History,* 43/3: 381–406.

WEDLIN, L. (2004). *Playing the Ranking Game: Field Formation and Boundary-Work in European Management Education*. Uppsala: Uppsala Universitet.

WHITLEY, R. (1999). *Divergent Capitalisms: The Social Structuring and Change of Business Systems*. Oxford: Oxford University Press.

WILLIAMS, G. (1991). "Markets and Higher Education". *Higher Education Management*, 3/3: 214–25.

WILSON, J. F. (1992). *The Manchester Experience: A History of Manchester Business School, 1965–1990*. London: Paul Chapman.

CHAPTER 25

....

BUSINESS CULTURE

....

KENNETH LIPARTITO

25.1 THEORY AND HISTORIOGRAPHY

....

IN the nineteenth century, social thinkers readily acknowledged that economic practices were deeply embedded in society. Max Weber, Werner Sombart, Thorstein Veblen, and R. H. Tawney, among others, explored the connection between status, religion, and values on the one hand, and economic change and practice on the other. Karl Marx looked for the determinants of ideas and ideology in the material forces of production and class struggle. In the twentieth century, Karl Polyani and members of the Frankfurt School continued to ponder the cultural dimensions of the market. In the 1950s and 1960s, non-Marxist modernization theory emphasized the replacement of traditional forms of authority, kinship ties, and religious values with secular rationality (Cronin 2000). All of these theoretical orientations, however, treated culture and economy as homologous. Culture followed material development in a predictable way. The historical arc moved from a premodern world, where economy and culture were deeply interconnected, to modern life, where the free market and the universal solvent of money dissolved cultural affinities. There was little role for chance or contingency here, little allowance that different cultures might travel their own unique economic paths, or that a variety of cultural forms might thrive even in the most advanced modern societies.

When business history emerged as a professional discipline, it followed the same theoretical bent. Influenced by structural-functionalism, with its division of society into distinct if interrelated systems, scholars such as Thomas Cochran treated culture in a largely instrumental fashion, as an adjunct to modern economic growth. Cochran considered how American values of freedom, democracy, and individualism encouraged entrepreneurship and innovation, in contrast to other, less successful nations (Sicilia 1995; Cochran 1967, 1985).[1] But as economics separated itself from society and culture, business historians influenced by economics paid less and less attention to the latter. Alfred Chandler gave culture almost no consideration, either at the level of the firm or, for the most part, at the level of the national economy. Works that followed the Chandlerian model rarely even had an entry for culture in their indexes.

Nonetheless, many firm histories continued to address culture, with chapters on firm traditions, values, and ways of life. These works generally looked at how culture supported (or contradicted) economic imperatives. Treatments of culture in management literature follow the same approach. Books such as Peters and Waterman's highly influential *In Search of Excellence* (1982) described firm culture as a set of traits that promoted competitive success. Following in this vein, recent works have argued that some firms have functional and others have dysfunctional cultures (Goffee and Jones 1998).

Only the most sophisticated thinkers held reductionism in check when discussing culture and the economy. In *The Protestant Ethic and the Spirit of Capitalism*, Max Weber found a counter-intuitive affinity between capitalism and Protestantism. Out of deep religious conviction came a secular motivation for material achievement. Raymond Williams argued strongly against reductionism in Marxian theory, seeking to make consciousness a part of production, rather than an effect of it (Williams 1977). Such works offered ways to integrate economic and cultural matters in the study of history and social change. Yet for the most part, neither economic and business historians nor scholars of culture pursued this opportunity.[2]

Modern cultural theory offers a way to rethink the relationship between business and culture (Lipartito 1995; Burke 2004). Rather than reducing culture to a function or effect of social structure, it starts from the position that all experience is mediated through some symbolic or linguistic system. Symbolic expression is necessary to social structure and action, because people can only coordinate behavior, gather information, make decisions, and react to their environment through some framework of meaning. Even when it is utilitarian and instrumental, action is also meaningful. Culture is thus not a separate system alongside economics or politics; it constitutes (in the sense of both representing and composing) the social order. Indeed, our identity, our very subjectivity and sense of self, is dependent on context. Rather than assuming that universal variables, such as self-interest or the pursuit of wealth, always drive people, historians are obligated to investigate the way actors

---

[1] Reflecting a largely static view of culture, Cochran also found in business firms a stable cultural substratum immune to dynamic changes in technology and organization.

[2] Cultural historians and theorists have not delved deeply into economic matters. Mary Douglas is perhaps the most notable exception (Douglas 1986).

in the past saw and understood matters, including how they defined self-interest (Bonnell *et al.* 1999; Ortner 1999).[3]

Treating culture as constitutive turns familiar business issues of strategy, structure, and technology into objects of meaning and interpretation, "artifacts" of values and practice, rather than hard, settled facts.[4] Such an approach argues for giving business ideas, practices, and expressions equal footing with material matters of production and profit. Indeed, it argues that the two classes of phenomena cannot be separated, since the expressive aspects of culture, operating on consciousness, often have material effects.

25.2 THE EMBEDDEDNESS OF BUSINESS

25.2.1 Culture and National Economic Performance

In mapping the relationship between economy and culture, historians have addressed issues of both causality and constitution. One set of studies in the first mode engages the relationship between culture and economic performance. Perhaps the strongest recent statement comes from David Landes, who claims that unique features of culture, society and politics led to the West's global economic dominance (Landes 1998). Other studies look at the question from the reverse angle of failure, most notably in the case of Great Britain. Martin Wiener's work has laid special stress on that nation's unfavorable cultural habits and educational system, which supposedly led to loss of industrial pre-eminence (Wiener 1981). Others have taken Wiener's thesis to its logical cultural conclusion by arguing that Britain's decline was not so much a matter of material reality as cultural representation. The fear of decline in Anglo-Saxon culture can be traced as far back as Adam Smith. Other nations have at times expressed similar fears of falling behind at a key moment of economic change (Clarke and Trebilcock 1997).

Linear models of the Landes and Wiener type suggest that a competitive global economy permits only one optimal business culture. Other works find a somewhat greater range of cultural options. When Asia challenged European and American economic pre-eminence in the 1970s and 1980s, studies emphasized the economic advantages of Asian values and religion (Abegglen 1958; Heine 2004). In a careful comparison of British and Japanese factories, Ronald Dore noted how notions of

---

[3] This is not to say cultural determinism replaces material or structural determinism. Semiotic systems are "minimally coherent" to use William Sewell's term, but symbols are ambiguous (Sewell 1999). Put into practice by actors, symbols can vary and migrate from their original context, providing opportunities for creative performance. But action always creates or recreates some system of meanings.

[4] For an informed discussion of this approach, see Fear (1999).

reciprocity grounded in Confucian values encouraged maximum productivity from labor (Dore 1973, 1987).

Scholars have questioned the contribution of unique Japanese cultural traditions to business. Some have placed more emphasis on the creative borrowing of western ideas by Japanese managers. Both Frederick Taylor and the American prophet of total quality management W. Edward Deming found a place in Japanese managerial thinking, though their ideas were used in ways perhaps different than the authors intended. Discursive constructions of management practices, as much or more than ancient traditions, may be responsible for the Japanese style of business (Tsutsui 1998).

Studies of Asian business culture resonate with scholarship on the varieties of capitalism within the West. Here too it has been noted that the American model was not adopted wholesale, but interpreted through the lens of local culture in European nations after World War II (Zeitlin and Herrigel 2000; Hall and Soskice 2001). Economic change may be seen as a cultural process, involving emulation, rhetoric about what is "advanced" and "successful", and linguistic struggles over notions of progress or the public good.

An alternative to models that posit either convergence or the functional value of difference are works suggesting that modern economic structures emerged out of earlier practices. Scholars of China argue that "western" economic institutions, including private firms and contracts, developed indigenously (rather than being emulated) in so-called "traditional" Chinese society (*Enterprise & Society* 2005). Such views call into question notions that western (or eastern) historical patterns developed unique forms of business. In fact, the same practices may well emerge out of distinctive cultural histories.

Refusal to accept western economic practices has also been interpreted as a form of cultural resistance, a resistance that reflects fundamental differences in notions of economic value. As anthropologist James Scott has argued, traditional cultures invaded by western imperial powers have often resisted economic subordination through notions of a moral economy. Prasannan Parthasarathi has examined the intrusion of British colonial policy into Indian caste-based weaving networks holding strong ideas of a moral economy (Parthasarathi 2001). With respect to multinational firms, Patrick Fridenson cautions that styles of management and practices can vary significantly depending on the home country of managers and chief stockholders. In the end, people are the irreducible element of business, and people have identities—local, national, perhaps even global, but identities that go beyond the firms for whom they work (Fridenson 1996).

25.2.2 Identity

Just as business structures and practices do not make a smooth transition from premodern to modern, neither do people. Even for the most powerful agents of the modern world, business people, the new and modern emerges out of, and in some cases preserves, the premodern and traditional, with plenty of local variation.

Joyce Chaplin's *An Anxious Pursuit* (1993), for example, notes how planters in the lower colonies of North America drew on Enlightenment notions of progress to refashion their natural environment for profit. They were modern and capitalist in outlook, but also deeply conservative and committed to slavery. Seeing the modern and traditional riding side by side in the same carriage of identity is typical of a number of studies of the growth of commerce in the eighteenth and nineteenth centuries. The assessment of personal creditworthiness, for example, has always contained an irreducible subjective element, variously encoded as character or morality. Older notions of reciprocity and mutuality carried over even into twentieth-century credit relations (Finn 2003). At the same time, borrowers sought to increase creditworthiness and mitigate risk through their personal and kinship networks (Matson 2004).

Even as credit became more widely available and transparent, there were still matters that could not be reduced to rational calculation (Smail 2003). Bankruptcy law has often been cited as an example of the shift from a traditional, morally inflected definition of risk to a modern, market-oriented one. But in Victorian America, Scott Sandage has argued, bankruptcy laws did not eliminate notions of character or personal responsibility, but reframed them in new, formal systems of credit reporting (Sandage 2005). Conversely, but in parallel fashion, studies of modernizing economies such as China have noted that although family business and kinship networks remained important, they did not conflict with or preclude the construction of more "modern" impersonal institutions of trust and credit (Sheehan 2003). Like anthropologist Claude Levi-Strauss' *bricolage*, the institutions of finance are assembled from materials at hand.

Such an approach argues for greater attention by business historians to discourses and rhetoric. Toby Ditz's study of eighteenth century merchants, for example, views business correspondence not just as a source of information, but as a literary device by which merchants fashioned themselves (Ditz 1994). Such self-fashioning could serve an instrumental purpose, such as gaining time against creditors, but it also created a moral and gendered identity for business people, with implications for other social relations. As Daniel Rabuzzi shows, the information contained in merchants' handbooks went well beyond the functional to outline a public persona for the would-be man of commerce (Rabuzzi 1995–6). Even in their private dealings, business people were taking on civic and public roles that had to be articulated in texts and public documents. Similarly, Natalie Davis argues against the long tradition in social theory of seeing Jewish business activities as representative of the modern spirit of rational calculation. Instead, she emphasizes the porous boundaries between commercial activities of Jewish merchants in the early modern period and their religious and family lives. Business account books, rather than being transparent, were actually deeply embedded in family lore, narratives, and ethnic identity (Davis 1999).

In business, as in all else, life does not divide neatly into separate realms. David Hancock's pioneering work on British merchants in the eighteenth century moves from their business ventures, family and kinship networks, to their values as expressed in art, architecture, and consumption (Hancock 1995). Peter Earle's *The Making of the English Middle Class* brings together the business practices, material culture, patterns of consumption, and family life of the artisans and commercial gentry of London (Earle 1989). Leonore Davidoff and Catherine Hall do likewise, with greater attention to gender, focusing on the commercial classes outside London (Davidoff and Hall 1987). They argue that business retained an evangelical sense of mission and religious values.

For industrializing Germany, Jürgen Kocka makes a Weberian case that "the spirit and practice of capitalism emerged from non-capitalist structures and nourished them for a long time" (Kocka 1999). Particularly important was the family, which nurtured entrepreneurship. Reversing the usual assumptions, however, Kocka argues that the pre-industrial, pre-bourgeois family was the key institution, in contrast to those who see family as antithetical to large-scale industrial capitalism. Studies of small business and the non-industrial sector have likewise found that pre-industrial family forms and values remain important well into the industrial era (Crossick and Haupt 1998; Harlaftis and Theotokas 2004). Studies have noted how differences in family background may be crucial in determining firm strategy and structure, or in providing opportunities for growth and profit (Arnoldus 2002; Buchenau 2004).

While much literature shows the complex, uncertain relationship between economic change and identity, another body of work looks at the processes whereby the capitalist class developed an awareness of itself as an agent of modernization. Sven Beckert argues, in Thompsonesque fashion, that through political discourse New York's various business interests coalesced into a ruling class in the wake of the Civil War and growth of an industrial labor force (Beckert 2001). In the era of the corporation, the same process of class formation can been seen taking place inside the firm. Olivier Zunz has argued that large corporations "made" America corporate by creating a new class of middle managers, dispersed across the nation in the many communities in which large corporations operated (Zunz 1990).

Studies of business functions, such as sales and marketing, also note the ways in which firms or entrepreneurs combined religion, morality, occult philosophies, and scientific principles to forge the modern corporate worker personality. Indeed, some of the most successful firms have instilled in their employees, sales personnel in particular, a powerful sense of mission. Part of the reason is that sales has long been an avenue of advancement for the middle class or a road to middle-class status for ambitious members of the working class. A strong sense of purposeful community characterizes the effective sales forces (Spears 1995; Friedman 2004). Sales has also had a strong gender dimension. Women were frequently relegated to special sales roles involving direct contact with the public, where supposedly female virtues were thought to create the proper selling personality (Porter Benson 1986; Hornstein 2002). Sales work often provided a point of entry for women otherwise excluded from the corporate world. For men, on the other hand, sales connoted a loss of status from that of the independent producer. Through self-help manuals, diaries, and other texts, men in business constructed new narratives for their lives that reconciled them to their new duties (Augst 2003; Hilkey 1997; Davis 2000).

Many studies of ethnic or immigrant entrepreneurs have emphasized their use of cultural resources to build enterprises (Fontaine 1996; Rath 1999). German immigrant guitar maker C. F. Martin, for example, brought a craft tradition of musical instrument making to the United States. Rather than adapting to an American impulse for mass production, he built up a high quality, exclusive brand reputation that emphasized old world craftsmanship (Gura 2003).

This functional and instrumental view of ethnicity, however, has been challenged by works that emphasize differences in education, access to capital, and other more traditional economic resources in explaining immigrant business ventures. Comparing Jewish entrepreneurs in London and New York who came out of the same Eastern European communities, Andrew Godley found that those who went to America soon exhibited greater entrepreneurial initiative than their London counterparts, something that presumably did not reflect cultural background so much as environment (Godley 2001).

Questions remain whether immigrant and minority business activity should be seen as a means of preserving an existing culture, or as the source of cultural change and transformation (Stolarik and Friedman 1986). Non-elite entrepreneurs may have seen their task as preserving their families, rather than as seeking great wealth and elite status. Juliet Walker's works on black business in America, for example, note that even under slavery African-Americans revealed a strong entrepreneurial spirit, one that originally may have reflected their African heritage of market activity and long-distance trade. But for African-Americans, profits and capital accumulation took second place to self and family liberation (Walker 1983, 1988; Winch 2001; Weare 1973). Work on women in business has challenged the very definition of business (Scott 1998). Women often perform economic activities in the home, or in contexts that at first appear not to be business activity at all—in philanthropic or religious institutions for example (Kwolek-Folland 1998; Goldman 1981). Studies incorporating gender, race, and ethnicity into business challenge notions of business as a universal, affective-neutral act quantified by some transparent measure of profitability.

Perhaps nowhere is the line between business and other activities less clear than with religion. The traditional view of modernization would suggest that with economic growth and rationalization, we move from religiously inspired to secular pursuits, presumably in business as in all else. In classical Weberian terms, religious authority is usually opposed to the legal rational structures that characterize the modern age. Weber and others following him, of course, also noted the ways in which religion could serve to introduce secular acquisitive values and promote rational, calculating practices. Recent studies tend to confirm this latter aspect of the Weberian paradigm. Dissenting or minority religious groups, such as Quakers and Huguenots, have often played a disproportionate role in business activity (Jeremy 1990). Moreover, some of the most powerful and successful entrepreneurs have often expressed a strong sense of religious duty and stewardship, seeing their business activities as God's work (Dellheim 1987; Kemp 2002; Hughes 1986).

Yet modernization has not produced the secular society Weber would have expected by now, not even in the sleek offices of the modern firm. Some businesses with purely secular purposes rely more on charismatic than rational forms of leadership (Biggart 1989). Indeed, the continued emphasis on "leadership" in large corporations can be seen as an attempt to infuse personality and charisma into soulless bureaucracy. Since the nineteenth century, moreover, religious institutions have availed themselves of the same organizational and marketing tools that business firms use, further blurring the line between secular and sacred pursuits (Giggie and Winston 2002; Nord 1996).

25.3 Organizational Culture

The concept of firm or organizational culture first appeared in the literature on labor management early in the twentieth century. In reaction to Frederick Winslow Taylor's mechanistic view of worker motivation, more psychologically and sociologically astute scholars revealed the hidden world of the shop floor (or office cubicle) beyond the control of top management, most famously in the Hawthorne studies of the 1920s (Cohen 2001; Rosenband 2000; Gillespie 1991). Later studies treated organizational culture more broadly, seeing in well-functioning organizations an alignment between strategy, structure, and culture (Schein 2004; Deal and Kennedy 1999). This approach often takes the pronouncements of top management as indicative of the values and perceptions of everyone in the organization. Indeed, management is sometimes seen as the clever manipulation of firm culture by the CEO. By changing values, leaders can bring employees in line with the firm's strategic goals (Casson 1991).

There is little doubt that firms have an official culture. David Nye explored the "image worlds" of General Electric's public presentation of itself. Stephan Harp has argued that Michelin used its famous anthropomorphic character to both humanize the firm and to create a sense of Frenchness for the company as it adopted what were perceived as suspiciously "foreign" managerial tools such as Taylorism. In his careful study of the Japanese firm Kikkoman, Mark Fruin paid attention to the philosophical dimensions of firm management based on Confucianism (Nye

1985; Harp 2001; Fruin 1983). But official culture is not always integrative. Critical assessments of the legacies of Taylorism and post-Taylorism, for example, note ways in which they served as foundations of management self-identity as the justification for managerial capitalism shifted from rights based on ownership to expertise and professionalism (Shenhav 1999).

One important implication of historical studies of firm culture is that culture is dynamic, and that firms are always drawing inspiration and ideas from the cultural materials at hand. Eric Guthey, for example, has noted how Ted Turner constructed a powerful identity for himself as an outsider that both helped to redefine what leadership in a large organization meant, and also served as an effective tool of entry into an industry, telecommunications, that was stable and regulated (Guthey 2001).

The best studies of organizational culture recognize that one must compare the official pronouncements of values with the acceptance or rejection of them at other levels of the organization (Dellheim 1986). There may be numerous subcultures striving for power within an organization. Nikki Mandell's history of welfare work inside large American corporations of the early twentieth century, for example, notes how the language of family was important, both as a way of asserting control over workers as company "dependents" but also as a way for the women who ran company welfare offices to carve out for themselves a space within the corporate hierarchy (Mandell 2002). Far from being an impediment to change, moreover, a complex and contested firm culture can also serve as a source of competitive advantage (Cheape 1985; Silcox 1994). Used in this manner, cultural diversity is enabling, not a problem to be managed.

This broader view of corporate culture argues against drawing a straight line from strategy to structure to culture, seeing instead that firms may take their own unique paths to success (Smith 2001). Local variations among firms in the same industry facing similar conditions suggest the creative ways in which actors use alternative readings of the market for innovative purposes. Within the firm, differences in values, orientation, and identity among members permit such creative and variable responses (Church 1994; Fear 2001).

This perspective is particularly useful when dealing with information. Erica Schoenberger argues that before managers can take action, they must place information in an interpretative framework that tells them what is important, relevant, and meaningful (Schoenberger 1997). In any system of knowledge, or discourse to use Foucault's term, what counts and who gets to say what counts are crucial questions. Power is the struggle over the right to interpret and assign meanings to things. Schoenberger suggests that managerial identity is crucial to strategy, for the framework of meaning and knowledge is congruent with the identity of the key decision makers. The danger firms face, therefore, is not resistance by subcultures but rather the opposite: a culture reduced to a single perspective or identity.

Jeffrey Fear shows in his study of Thyssen that culture permeates practices and is constituted through discourses and debates over strategy and structure taking place within the firm. By debate and discourse, firm members come to understand and constitute their way of doing things (Fear 2005). Robert Freeland has argued that the M-Form was determined by debate and discourse not function and technology. Alfred Sloan decentralized General Motors (GM), but then spent his career deliberately blurring the lines between the formal structure and the informal but vital relationships between headquarters and operating units (Freeland 2001). In this, Sloan was practicing the approach outlined by Bell Executive Chester Barnard, who came to his ideas at roughly the same time. Barnard's ideal executive was a consummate performer, slyly bending the formal rules of organization to cultivate human relationships and adapting abstract managerial schemata to complex reality (Barnard 1938). There was as much aesthetics as rationality in executive behavior.

It was, however an aesthetic sense of what was right, fitting, and proper that eventually impelled GM's directors to implement full decentralization, with negative consequences for performance. They had adopted the M-Form from DuPont, where executives had mingled informally in Delaware, but failed to notice that this crucial mitigating factor would be absent in the sprawling GM empire. These sorts of subtle cultural and social nuances were lost as the M-Form came to be seen as a pure, rational organizational structure appropriate to all large, diversified firms. The auto maker's executives could not escape the very structure and form of knowledge they themselves had created.

One might argue that GM was a victim of ideology—a blind commitment to a system of ideas that hid an underlying reality. Ideology has also been studied as a tool of managerial interest and self-creation. In a wide-ranging history of management compensation schemes, Ernest Englander and Allen Kaufman show how corporations have increased the power and compensation of top managers. These shifts they link to a new ideology of management, created by academic economists, business school faculty, and associations of CEOs through organizations such as the Conference Board. They argue for contingency rather than conspiracy in explaining these shifts, but they suggest that a powerful ideology was at work justifying the privileged position of the very top managers (Englander and Kaufman 2004).

25.4 BUSINESS MAKING CULTURE

Many authors have commented on business's cultural influence, mostly to condemn it as a corrupting force. There is much to be gained, as I will argue in this section, from abandoning traditional models of the business–culture nexus. Taking the insights of business historians together with the literature on consumption, leisure, and popular culture can provide a much fuller and more sophisticated understanding of how business makes culture.

25.4.1 Consumption

Three basic models mark the study of culture and consumption. One takes a Weberian approach, finding a growing rationalization of consumption in modern society, with the business firm an agent of this change (Lears 1994). A second finds an expanding market commodifying more and more areas of experience, to the detriment of authentic cultural expressions (Horowitz 1992; Daniel 2002). A third pits consumers against business, and sees in consumption an oppositional force to the power of producers (Bourdieu 1984; de Certeau 1984).[5]

While many authors admit that consumption has long been a part of human experience, works nonetheless seek to distinguish the moment that the ancient practice of consuming goods gave way to a consumer society. This shift is usually thought to have occurred, in the West at least, sometime between the seventeenth and nineteenth centuries (Stearns 2002). Some scholars locate it in England, others in the Netherlands, and still others France (McKendrick *et al.* 1982; Schama 1987; Williams 1982). Works on other parts of the world generally find a transition to a consumer society occurring apace with economic growth and industrialization, often led by multinational corporations (Bauer 2001).

In this regard, Timothy Burke notes the subtle interaction between sales, consumption, and self-definition that followed the penetration of Unilever personal care products into Africa. Unilever marketing created not just new desires, but new "needs" or standards of cleanliness. Corporate hegemony reworked existing cultural categories and exported western notions of uplift and civilization along with products (Burke 1996). But other works studying the penetration of corporations into foreign economies actually found that consumers were able to resist corporate designs by practicing consumption in unpredicted ways (Scarpellini 2004; Fox and Lears 1983).

Studies have likewise interpreted the advertising of products in diverse ways. Some have seen in advertising messages pervasive notions of modernity (Leach 1993; Marchand 1985). To others the modernity promised by marketers is an elaborate mechanism to discipline and regulate consumption in line with the needs of mass production (Laird 1998; Lears 1994). Still others have put a more positive spin on the regulation of desire. Advertising and marketing, they argue, supported wise choices by consumers and promoted economic growth by assuring a steady market for mass-produced goods (Pope 1983; Calder 1999).

---

[5] Business historians, on the other hand, have sometimes followed a fourth variant, seeing in consumption, and mass consumption in particular, a democratic tradition (Tedlow 1990).

A key issue is the nature of the consumer–producer relationship. Is it more like finance, where marketing institutions are simply intermediaries connecting two sides of a market? Or is it more dialectical, whereby the signal from consumer to producer must be interpreted, rather than simply passed on? Some works suggest that producers engage in a form of entrepreneurship as they seek out their consumers, drawing on their own cultural knowledge to understand their customers (Koehn 2001). Regina Blaszczyk's close study of this process identifies "fashion intermediaries" who must imagine consumers and engage in a creative process involving both design and discourse with the factory (Blaszczyk 2000). A recent article by Daniel Robinson addresses the simultaneous creation of goods and meanings (Robinson 2004). Marketing, he argues, is both a functional and representational process, with messages as much the "thing consumed" as the object itself. These works call into question both corporate hegemony and consumer resistance. Instead, they problematize production and place it in a dialectic with consumption. The act of consumption constructs mental categories ("needs"), to be sure, but these exist beyond the control or often the self-awareness of consumers and producers alike (Douglas and Isherwood 1979).

The means and practice of consumption also require close investigation from a cultural perspective. Department stores, for example, captivated consumers with their dream-world displays of opulence, their clever orchestration of modern materials, and their new, large-scale approach to sales. William Leach and Rosalind Williams emphasize the ways in which stores defined a new type of consumerism, giving rise to new cultural agents such as window dressers and lighting technicians and calling upon other institutions, such as universities and museums (Leach 1993; Williams 1982). Michael Miller, on the other hand, saw in the grand Parisian department store, the *Bon Marché*, a link between French traditions of family and household and a new bureaucratic world of regulated work and consumption (Miller 1981). Even revolutionary forms of consumption can, as Miller found, also be conservative forces, preserving and reinforcing the role of women as shoppers.

Shopping has been seen as a transformative experience, connected with the rise of consumer society, the growth of the city, and the expansion of individualism (Zukin 2004). It is often at the point of sale that consumers have the greatest agency (Benson and Ugolini 2003). Shopping has also been a highly gendered activity. To conservatives who feared incipient female liberation, the pleasures of shopping pointed to decline and decadence; to women seeking freedom and adventure in the city, it became one of the most important forms of licit public pleasure (Abelson 1989; Rappaport 2000). As much if not more than the purchase of goods, the shopping experience has raised debates about social order, political virtue, and moral decline in practically every economically advanced nation.

The reordering of urban space for profit itself has a long history. One of the best examples of creative destruction can be found in the building up and tearing down of urban landscapes (Page 1999; Rilling 2001). The building of the modern city is also one of the best examples of the intersection of profit and mentality. Nicholas Papayanis argues that it was the idea of circulation as a way to make the city clean and safe, and to control crowds, that spurred private and government capital to flow into Paris's urban transportation system in the nineteenth century (Papayanis 1996). Robert Fogelson has pointed out that while economics drives much of the contemporary urban landscape, even profit-oriented business interests have based their calculations on a presumed model of what space—in this case the classic urban downtown—should look like (Fogelson 2001). Rearrangement of space was a business activity to be sure, though creative entrepreneurs also carried notions of community into their plans (Hardwick 2003).

25.4.2 Material Culture and Design

If culture is seen as deriving from both the material and ideational, then the products that businesses make and sell are cultural forms as well as material objects. Certainly the term material culture seeks to capture this sense that as we make and use things, we also define ourselves. New materials have often started out as solutions to problems of production, but then captured the imagination of consumers, as with aluminum and plastics (Meikle 1995; Schatzberg 2003). In almost every society, electricity has quickly come to express values and beliefs about progress through technology (Nye 1990). Railroads, automobiles and telephones have all been held up as icons of modernism (Lipartito 2003; Tobey 1996). In postwar Japan, electrical goods were used in strategic fashion as part of a scheme for modernization of the countryside, to break down Japanese rural traditions (Partner 1999). In each case, the meaningful materials of the modern world have come about as business ventures and worked their way into consciousness through the interaction of producers and consumers.

Less certain is how well modern business and technology fit with aesthetic values. The machine age spurred members of the Arts and Crafts Movement to seek a return to joy in labor and to rediscover the aesthetics of earlier, simpler times. On the other hand, German architect Peter Behrens made his most important architectural statement right in the heart of the industrial world, in his design of the AEG turbine factory. In this and other commissions Behrens created a corporate identity for the giant German corporation (Anderson 2000). In the United States business patronage has supported major figures in design, who nonetheless took as their mission the taming of raw commerce with good taste (Meikle 1979; Adamson 2003). As Marina Moskowitz has shown, the concept of an American standard of living has done dual service. Technically, it referred to a system of efficient production, but culturally it expressed a moral imperative about a certain style of life (Moskowitz 2004).

In many cases, design could simultaneously investigate new, even revolutionary possibilities of industrial technology, while hewing closely to older cultural values.

Alison Clarke notes how Tupperware used a modern material (plastic) and innovative design to promote a very traditional virtue of frugality during the Great Depression. It succeeded not through the new marketing avenues of chain stores or by national advertising, but by drawing on female networks in the "Tupperware party", invented by saleswoman Brownie Wise (Clarke 1999).

Even where businesses have self consciously embraced modernism in design they have often done so as much for aesthetic as for pragmatic purposes. Corporate offices fashioned in the international style announced a firm's commitment to progress and modernity (Martin 2003). In fact, at times such expressions contradicted practical necessity. Firms that eagerly embraced modern architectural principles for their headquarters and research laboratories found that modernism served their functional requirements poorly (Knowles and Leslie 2001).

Important as design and material culture are in their own right, business history can also link such matters back to production. Studies of industrial districts and specialty goods industries note the close connection between products that are highly differentiated with respect to style and flexible production strategies. Such differentiation is rooted in national tastes and styles, as Whitney Walton notes in her study of France's rejection of British mass production methods at the Crystal Palace exhibition in 1851. Indeed, just as important as the actual products and designs on display was the discourse over their meaning, as French producers interpreted their opportunities and comparative advantage in distinction to the British emphasis on standardization and large-scale production (Walton 1992).

25.4.3 Business in Everyday Life

The number of ways in which business has penetrated aspects of what used to be private life has expanded enormously over the past century. The very idea of leisure stems from the transformation of work and family life in an urban age where most people earn their living working for others (Beder 2000). Businesses have seen in that transformation new opportunities for profit. In an urban society, the desire to reconnect with nature manifests itself in tamed commercial spaces where nature can be observed at a safe distance (Davis 1997). Even supposedly pristine national parks have had aspects of a "brand name" tourist attraction (Daniel 2002). No firm has better exploited this possibility than the giant Disney corporation, whose founder, Walt Disney, was a man given to straightening the chaos of nature with a vengeance (Foglesong 2001).

Even more than with the consumption of things, the consumption of experiences, packaged and marketed for profit has drawn the fire of social critics for undermining genuine experiences (Butsch 1990). The relationship between business and popular culture, however, may not be quite so one dimensional. In the highly ordered spaces of theme parks, trimmed wildernesses, and suburban living, one also has to ask, is anyone deceived? Perhaps some people actually prefer a rationalized nature to the real thing, and applaud the virtuoso performance of business organization and technology.

The practices of everyday life in fact have long had a business dimension. As Carole Frick shows for Renaissance Florence, for example, clothing was crucial to constructing an identity for the city's elite. Business enterprises in response constructed elaborate costumes to be worn for key ceremonial occasions. The expensive finery was then taken apart and reused, permitting producers to make profits and keeping prices low for consumers (Frick 2002). Business and culture, profit, consumption, display, power and identity all went hand in hand. The pursuit of profit did not disrupt or negate cultural meaning; indeed it contributed to it.

In other times as well, successful business enterprise became the institutional mechanism for cultural expression and the construction of identity. Studies of the French wine industry show a clear transition from local production to national or even international commodity as far back as the seventeenth century (Brennan 1997). The same is true of products such as Champagne and Camembert cheese, which made the shift from relatively obscure local goods to symbols of the French nation in the nineteenth century. The actors behind these transitions were business people, to be sure, but they were also the very same local producers and merchants who had run the industries for generations. National brands in this case were created not by outside corporate interests, but from within traditional systems of production and distribution (Guy 2003; Boisard 2003; Terrio 2000).

A different issue inheres in what has been the most closely studied cultural enterprise—film. On the one hand, film was a new form of entertainment, started as a business, and controlled by entrepreneurs who used corporate methods. Works on "the business" (as it is called by its participants) have addressed competition among studios, the expansion of Hollywood overseas, and the creation of the film star in the service of product differentiation (Trumpbour 2002; Kerr 1990; Gomery 1992). It remains uncertain whether film is to be understood through the lens of profit alone, or whether national cinemas express an ideology, or indeed if the two go hand-in-hand. Some works find a dovetailing of studio interest in profit with American interest in, literally, projecting itself to allies and non-aligned nations during the Cold War.

Certain classes of goods, such as food, exhibit an almost inseparable relationship between their lives as for-profit commodities and the meanings that they hold for those who consume them. Works on sugar show that though a desire for sweetness may be universal, the way that craving is expressed can vary tremendously. As Sidney Mintz argues, those variations can reflect sugar's level and mode of production and its place in the world market (Mintz 1985; Woloson 2002). Studies of fashion show a similarly intimate relationship between mental and material history. Carol Turbin has investigated the production, consumption, and cultural meaning of the "white collar", as a changing symbol of masculinity, a marker of the division of labor, and a product of household labor (Turbin 2000).

Personal goods such as these have a strong cultural valance, which makes it difficult depict their business side in any simple, one-dimensional way. As Nancy Troy demonstrates in her study of the fashion industry, early twentieth-century couturiers skillfully blended appeals to uniqueness and high art with production and marketing strategies that made their designs available to the middle class (Troy 2004). In her study of how clothing and style move across cultures Alexandra Palmer depicts the business of *haute couture* as a set of international relationships between designers, producers, and consumers. Fashion moved across cultural boundaries but was locally mediated and adapted (Palmer 2001). Rather than cultural forms becoming inexorably globalized and homogenized by multinational business, we see that the local and global, the elite and the mass produced continue to interact and co-exist.

Kathy Peiss uses the beauty business to interrogate one-dimensional models of the "growing commercialization" of modern life. How ideas of beauty are inscribed in different ways at different times is an institutional process, engaging not only multinational corporations, but local producers, often of non-elite and minority backgrounds, and prescriptive literature, literature that itself is a business. Unpacking the institutions that define "the market" and problematizing business in this way shows how enormously complex is the relationship between meaning and profit, identity and commerce, business and culture (Peiss 2000).

In fact, ambiguity about the line between commerce and culture can be seen even in those industries most focused on money and profit. Financial institutions and mutual insurance plans have since the eighteenth century served in many nations the purpose of social uplift and reform (Wright and Smith 2004; Zelizer 1983). Entrepreneurs devised new investment schemes as alternatives both to class conflict and to more radical restructurings of society (Lipartito and Peters 2001; Pohl 2001). Insurance began with a mixture of profit and social reform (Goodheart 1990). Pursuing the "business of benevolence", corporate executives started voluntary associations to achieve similar ends (Tone 1997).

More generally, business has been used as a powerful model of social order. At various times, business people have proposed managerialism to solve social problems, and surpass the limitations of local cultures and politics (Scott 1992; Farber 2002). Henry Ford, Frederick Winslow Taylor, Thomas Watson, Alfred P. Sloan, and other major figures of the Second Industrial Revolution became symbols and spokespersons for a new industrial order that expressed ideas far beyond the obvious ones of material abundance and productive efficiency (Nye 1979; Merkle 1980).

An error made by those who ascribe motivations to business actors without studying them up close is to assume everyone in business knows exactly what their self-interest is (and indeed that business has a unitary interest) and can easily and instrumentally serve it. If business people are treated like other agents—bound by their systems of ideas, conflicted about their wants and interests, subject to an array of social and cultural disciplines—then it is worth taking their ideas and expressions at their full depth, and not reducing them to narrow self-interest.

25.5 CONCLUSIONS

As this chapter has shown, scholarship has been moving toward the reintegration of business and cultural history, in ways that offer payoffs for both. The best of this work avoids much of the determinism and teleology of older approaches, finding that business can be practiced, quite successfully, in many different ways in different cultural settings. Authors have abandoned the assumption that western history was driven by the rationalization of economic activity and the disarticulation of production, organization, and exchange from the socio-cultural matrix. They have rediscovered the ways in which business practices in modern industrial societies are deeply embedded in cultural settings. Even in a global economy, firms and national economies continue to show much variation. Indeed, the more research is done on business, the more difficult it becomes to see business moving toward a single, universal model of efficiency.

The new scholarship challenges business historians to recognize the more expressive aspects of business culture, beyond what culture may contribute instrumentally to firm growth. At the same time, it challenges cultural historians to see the connections between business and culture as polyvalent. Too many cultural historians assume that the search for profit negates any genuine cultural expression and treat markets as abstract forces that always and everywhere operate in the same fashion. As Kathy Peiss cautions, in doing so they produce an inflexible vision of "business as a monolith", with "motives uniform . . . actions synchronized . . . effects transparent", exactly the opposite of what cultural history should do (Peiss 2000: 486).

Cultural theory also offers an alternative to economics for the study of business history. Recently, economics has moved strongly in an institutional direction. Even the market is now understood as an institution, with its characteristic rules, practices, and history. But any effort to build economic theory on an institutional base must fail if it offers no scope for the way that humans make meanings and construct knowledge (Suny 2002).

Where a cultural approach to business subsumes economics is in its much more sophisticated treatment of information and knowledge. Many economic models of business (and economic activity in general) proceed from the assumption that actors learn directly from experience, in an unmediated, almost instinctual way.

No thinking, figuring, or contextualizing of information through a framework of knowledge is needed here. Even more sophisticated models that take information into account presume that it flows, like a signal, within firms, between firms, or between the firm and the market (Lamoreaux *et al.* 2003). Cultural theory rejects this abstract view of communication as signals passing between fully constituted actors. Instead, it sees language as constitutive, with communicants making themselves and grasping reality through language. The issue is not simply the limits or imperfections of information, but the way in which knowledge is constructed, and in turn constructs its subjects.

This perspective contradicts some foundational beliefs of business history. The discipline still largely assumes that the market and profit arbitrate questions of culture, much as they are presumed to arbitrate strategy and structure. But there are many ways to make a profit, many ways that firms can organize and act and still be successful. The disciplinary problematic is to investigate how firms make these choices, if there are no unambiguous signals from the market dictating "one best way" of organizing and acting. How actors learn what counts, how they influence those with capital to lend, how they sort through information to make choices, and how they represent themselves and their firms to others are crucial aspects of business behavior.[6]

Such matters should be objects of study for business historians. They can get at them by paying more attention to image, display, and symbol, all of which firms spend abundant money on. They can look deeply inside the firm, at the discourses and debates over key decisions that constitute knowledge, enable action, and tell business people who they are and what they should be doing.

This new synthesis of business and culture will require a willingness to use old sources in new ways. The information and texts of business life can be read for the meanings and values they encode, the way of life they express, the arguments they make. Images and representations of business practices, protocols and rules for behavior, dramatizations of business life all become important to understanding the core economic functions of firms. The causal arrow runs two ways here. Culture as the semiotic system through which business actors understand their environment and themselves affects strategy, structure, and behavior. But as cultural actors, businesses shape cultural discourse and practice. Discovering the mutual constitution of culture and business offers a new means to understanding the multiple, non-deterministic ways in which economic activities have been and may be practiced in capitalist societies.

---

[6] One of the most important forms of knowledge used by business, accounting, is itself culturally constructed. The ways firms account for themselves can vary widely, with implications for their strategy and organizational designs. For an insightful introduction to "critical accounting theory" see Fear (2005, appendix B).

REFERENCES

ABEGGLEN, JAMES (1958). *The Japanese Factory: Aspects of its Social Organization*. Glencoe, Ill.: Free Press.

ABELSON, ELAINE S. (1989). *When Ladies Go A-Thieving: Middle-Class Shoplifters in the Victorian Department Store*. New York: Oxford University Press.

ADAMSON, GLENN (2003). *Industrial Strength Design: How Brooks Stevens Shaped Your World*. Cambridge, Mass.: MIT Press.

ANDERSON, STANFORD (2000). *Peter Behrens and a New Architecture for the Twentieth Century*. Cambridge, Mass.: MIT Press.

ARNOLDUS, DOREEN (2002). *Family, Family Firm and Strategy: Six Dutch Family Firms in the Food Industry 1880–1970*. Amsterdam: Aksant Academic Publishers.

AUGST, THOMAS (2003). *The Clerk's Tale: Young Men and Moral Life in Nineteenth-Century America*. Chicago: University of Chicago Press.

BARNARD, CHESTER (1938). *The Functions of the Executive*, 30th anniversary edn. Cambridge, Mass.: Harvard University Press, 1968 (1st edn., 1938).

BAUER, ARNOLD J. (2001). *Goods, Power, History: Latin America's Material Culture*. New York: Cambridge University Press.

BECKERT, SVEN (2001). *The Monied Metropolis: New York City and the Consolidation of the American Bourgeoisie 1850–1896*. New York: Cambridge University Press.

BEDER, SHARON (2000). *Selling the Work Ethic: From Puritan Pulpit to Corporate PR*. New York: Zed Books.

BENSON, JOHN, and UGOLINI, LAURA (2003). *A Nation of Shopkeepers: Five Centuries of British Retailing*. London: I. B. Tauris.

BENSON, SUSAN PORTER (1986). *Counter Cultures: Saleswomen, Managers, and Customers in American Department Stores, 1890–1940*. Urbana, Ill.: University of Illinois Press.

BIGGART, NICOLE WOOLSEY (1989). *Charismatic Capitalism: Direct Selling Organizations in America*. Chicago: University of Chicago Press.

BLASZCZYK, REGINA LEE (2000). *Imagining Consumers: Design and Innovation from Wedgwood to Corning*. Baltimore: Johns Hopkins University Press.

BOISARD, PIERRE (2003). *Camembert: A National Myth*, trans. Richard Miller. Berkeley: University of California Press.

BONNELL, VICTORIA, HUNT, LYNN, and BIERNACKI, RICHARD (eds.) (1999). *Beyond the Cultural Turn: New Directions in the Study of Society and Culture*. Berkeley: University of California Press.

BOURDIEU, PIERRE (1984). *Distinction: A Social Critique of the Judgment of Taste*. Cambridge, Mass.: Harvard University Press.

BRENNAN, THOMAS (1997). *Burgundy to Champagne: The Wine Trade in Early Modern France*. Baltimore: Johns Hopkins University Press.

BUCHENAU, JÜRGEN (2004). *Tools of Progress: A German Merchant Family in Mexico City 1865–Present*. Albuquerque: University of New Mexico Press.

BULL, ANNA CENTO, and CORNER, PAUL (1993). *From Peasant to Entrepreneur: The Survival of the Family Economy in Italy*. Providence, RI: Berg.

BURKE, PETER (2004). *What is Cultural History?* Cambridge: Polity Press.

BURKE, TIMOTHY (1996). *Lifebuoy Men and Lux Women: Commodification, Consumption and Cleanliness in Modern Zimbabwe*. Durham, NC: Duke University Press.

BUTSCH, RICHARD (ed.) (1990). *For Fun and Profit: The Transformation of Leisure into Consumption*. Philadelphia, Pa.: Temple University Press.

CALDER, LENDOL (1999). *Financing the American Dream: A Cultural History of Credit*. Princeton, NJ: Princeton University Press.

CASSON, MARK (1991). *The Economics of Business Culture: Game Theory, Transaction Costs, and Economic Performance*. New York: Oxford University Press.

CHAPLIN, JOYCE E. (1993). *An Anxious Pursuit: Agricultural Innovation and Modernity in the Lower South 1730–1815*. Chapel Hill, NC: University of North Carolina Press.

CHEAPE, CHARLES W. (1985). *Family Firm to Modern Multinational: Norton Company, a New England Enterprise*. Cambridge, Mass.: Harvard University Press.

CHURCH, ROY. (1994). "How did Business Think?" *Scottish Economic and Social History*, 14: 5–18.

CLARKE, ALISON J. (1999). *Tupperware: The Promise of Plastic in 1950s America*. Washington, DC: Smithsonian Institution Press.

CLARKE, PETER, and TREBILCOCK, CLIVE (eds.) (1997). *Understanding Decline: Perceptions and Realities of British Economic Performance*. New York: Cambridge University Press.

COCHRAN, THOMAS C. (1967). "The History of a Business Society". *Journal of American History*, 54/1: 5–18.

—— (1985). *Challenges to American Values: Society, Business, and Religion*. New York: Oxford University Press.

COHEN, YVES (2001). *Organiser á l'aube du taylorisme: La pratique d'Ernest Mattern chez Peugeot 1906–1919*. Besançon: Presses Universitaires Franche-Comtoises.

CRONIN, JAMES E. (2000). "Convergence by Conviction: Politics and Economics in the Emergence of the 'Anglo-American Model'". *Journal of Social History*, 33/4: 781–804.

CROSSICK, GEOFFREY, and HAUPT, HEINZ-GERHARD (1998). *The Petite Bourgeoisie in Europe 1780–1914: Enterprise, Family and Independence*. New York: Routledge.

DANIEL, MARK (2002). *Selling Yellowstone: Capitalism and the Construction of Nature*. Lawrence: University Press of Kansas.

DAVIDOFF, LEONORE, and HALL, CATHERINE (1987). *Family Fortunes: Men and Women of the English Middle Class 1780–1850*. Chicago: University of Chicago Press.

DAVIS, CLARK (2000). *Company Men: White-Collar Life and Corporate Cultures in Los Angeles 1892–1941*. Baltimore: Johns Hopkins University Press.

DAVIS, NATALIE ZEMON (1999). "Religion and Capitalism Once Again? Jewish Merchant Culture in the Seventeenth Century", in Ortner (1999), 56–84.

DAVIS, SUSAN G. (1997). *Spectacular Nature: Corporate Culture and the Sea World Experience*. Berkeley: University of California Press.

DEAL, TERRENCE E., and KENNEDY, ALLAN A. (1999). *The New Corporate Cultures: Revitalizing the Workplace after Downsizing, Mergers, and Reengineering*. Reading, Mass.: Perseus Books.

DE CERTEAU, MICHEL (1984). *The Practice of Everyday Life*. Berkeley: University of California Press.

DELLHEIM, CHARLES (1986). "Business in Time: The Historian and Corporate Culture". *Public Historian*, 8/2: 9–22.

—— (1987). "The Creation of a Company Culture: Cadburys 1861–1931". *American Historical Review*, 92/1: 13–44.

DITZ, TOBY L. (1994). "Shipwrecked; or, Masculinity Imperiled: Mercantile Representations of Failure and the Gendered Self in Eighteenth-Century Philadelphia". *Journal of American History*, 81/1: 51–80.

DORE, RONALD PHILIP (1973). *British Factory, Japanese Factory: The Origins of National Diversity in Industrial Relations*. Berkeley: University of California Press.

—— (1987). *Taking Japan Seriously: A Confucian Perspective on Leading Economic Issues*. Stanford, Calif.: Stanford University Press.

DOUGLAS, MARY (1986). *How Institutions Think*. Syracuse, NY: Syracuse University Press.

—— and ISHERWOOD, BARON (1979). *The World of Goods*. New York: Basic Books.

EARLE, PETER (1989). *The Making of the English Middle Class: Business, Society and Family Life in London 1660–1730*. Berkeley: University of California Press.

ENGLANDER, ERNIE, and KAUFMAN, ALLEN (2004). "The End of Managerial Ideology: From Corporate Social Responsibility to Corporate Social Indifference". *Enterprise & Society*, 5/3: 404–50.

Enterprise & Society: Special Issue: Business History in Modern China (2005). 6/3: 357–491.

FARBER, DAVID (2002). *Sloan Rules: Alfred P. Sloan and the Triumph of General Motors*. Chicago: University of Chicago.

FEAR, JEFFREY (1999). "Constructing Big Business: The Cultural Concept of the Firm", in Alfred D. Chandler, Jr., Franco Amatori, and Takashi Hinkino (eds.), *Big Business and the Wealth of Nations*. Cambridge: Cambridge University Press, 546–74.

—— (2001). "Thinking Historically about Organizational Learning", in Meinolf Dierkes, Ariane Berthoin Antal, John Child, and Ikujiro Nonaka (eds.), *Handbook of Organizational Learning and Knowledge*. Oxford: Oxford University Press, 162–91.

—— (2005). *Organizing Control: August Thyssen and the Construction of German Corporate Management*. Cambridge, Mass.: Harvard University Press.

FINN, MARGOT (2003). *The Character of Credit: Personal Debt in English Culture 1740–1914*. Cambridge: Cambridge University Press.

FOGELSON, ROBERT (2001). *Downtown: Its Rise and Fall, 1880–1950*. New Haven: Yale University Press.

FOGLESONG, RICHARD (2001). *Married to the Mouse: Walt Disney World and Orlando*. New Haven: Yale University Press.

FONTAINE, LAURENCE (1996). *History of Peddlers in Europe*. Durham, NC: Duke University Press.

FOX, RICHARD WIGHTMAN, and LEARS, T. J. JACKSON (eds.) (1983). *The Culture of Consumption: Critical Essays in American History 1880–1920*. New York: Pantheon Books.

FREELAND, ROBERT (2001). *The Struggle for Control of the Modern Corporation: Organizational Change at General Motors, 1924–1970*. Cambridge: Cambridge University Press.

FRICK, CAROLE COLLIER (2002). *Dressing Renaissance Florence: Families, Fortunes, and Fine Clothing*. Baltimore: Johns Hopkins University Press.

FRIDENSON, PATRICK (1996). "Multinationals: The Cultural Dimension". *Business and Economic History*, 25/2: 155–8, 162–5.

FRIEDMAN, WALTER (2004). *Birth of a Salesman: The Transformation of Selling in America*. Cambridge, Mass.: Harvard University Press.

FRUIN, MARK W. (1983). *Kikkoman: Company, Clan and Community*. Cambridge, Mass.: Harvard University Press.

GIGGIE, JOHN, and WINSTON, DIANE (eds.) (2002). *Faith in the Market: Religion and the Rise of Urban Commercial Culture.* New Brunswick, NJ: Rutgers University Press.

GILLESPIE, RICHARD (1991). *Manufacturing Knowledge: A History of the Hawthorne Experiments.* New York: Cambridge University Press.

GODLEY, ANDREW (2001). *Jewish Immigrant Entrepreneurship in New York and London 1880–1914: Enterprise and Culture.* New York: Palgrave.

GOFFEE, ROB, and JONES, GARTH (1998). *The Character of a Corporation: How Your Company's Culture can Make or Break Your Business.* New York: HarperCollins.

GOLDMAN, MARION S. (1981). *Gold Diggers and Silver Miners: Prostitution and Social Life on the Comstock Lode.* Ann Arbor: University of Michigan Press.

GOMERY, DOUGLAS (1992). *Shared Pleasures: A History of Movie Presentation in the United States.* Madison: University of Wisconsin Press.

GOODHEART, LAWRENCE B. (1990). *Abolitionist, Actuary, Atheist: Elizur Wright and the Reform Impulse.* Kent, Oh.: Kent State University Press.

GURA, PHILIP (2003). *C. F. Martin and his Guitars, 1796–1873.* Chapel Hill, NC: University of North Carolina Press.

GUTHEY, ERIC (2001). "Ted Turner's Corporate Cross-Dressing and the Shifting Images of American Business Leadership". *Enterprise and Society,* 2/1: 111–42.

GUY, KOLLEEN M. (2003). *When Champagne became French: Wine and the Making of a National Identity.* Baltimore: Johns Hopkins University Press.

HALL, PETER A., and SOSKICE, DAVID W. (2001). *Varieties of Capitalism: The Institutional Foundations of Comparative Advantage.* New York: Oxford University Press.

HANCOCK, DAVID (1995). *Citizens of the World: London Merchants and the Integration of the Atlantic Community, 1735–1785.* Cambridge: Cambridge University Press.

HARDWICK, JEFFREY (2003). *Mall Maker: Victor Gruen, Architect of an American Dream.* Philadelphia: University of Pennsylvania Press.

HARLAFTIS, GELINA, and THEOTOKAS, JOHN (2004). "European Family Firms in International Business: British and Greek Tramp-Shipping Firms". *Business History,* 46/2: 219–55.

HARP, STEPHEN (2001). *Marketing Michelin: Advertising and Cultural Identity in Twentieth-Century France.* Baltimore: Johns Hopkins University Press.

HEINE, STEVEN (2004). "Critical View of Discourses on the Relation between Japanese Business and Social Values". *Journal of Language for International Business,* 15/2: 35–48.

HILKEY, JUDY (1997). *Character is Capital: Success Manuals and Manhood in Gilded Age America.* Chapel Hill, NC: University of North Carolina Press.

HORNSTEIN, JEFFREY M. (2002). "A Nation of Realtors®: The Professionalization of Real Estate Brokerage and the Construction of a New American Middle Class". *Enterprise and Society,* 3/4: 613–19.

HOROWITZ, DANIEL (1992). *The Morality of Spending: Attitudes toward the Consumer Society in America 1875–1940.* Chicago: I. R. Dee.

HUGHES, JONATHAN (1986). *The Vital Few.* New York: Oxford University Press.

JEREMY, DAVID J. (1990). *Capitalists and Christians: Business Leaders and the Churches in Britain 1900–1960.* New York: Oxford University Press.

KEMP, KATHRYN W. (2002). *God's Capitalist: Asa Candler of Coca-Cola.* Macon, Ga. Mercer University Press.

KERR, CATHERINE E. (1990). "Incorporating the Star: The Intersection of Business and Aesthetic Strategies in Early American Film", *Business History Review,* 64/3: 383–410.

KNOWLES, SCOTT G., and LESLIE, STUART W. (2003). " 'Industrial Versailles': Eero Saarinen's Corporate Campuses for GM, IBM, and AT&T". *Isis*, 92/1: 1–33.

KOCKA, JÜRGEN (1999). *Industrial Culture and Bourgeois Society: Business, Labor, and Bureaucracy in Modern Germany*. Providence, RI: Berghahn.

KOEHN, NANCY F. (2001). *Brand New: How Entrepreneurs Earned Consumers' Trust from Wedgwood to Dell*. Boston, Mass.: Harvard Business School Press.

KWOLEK-FOLLAND, ANGEL (1998). *Incorporating Women: A History of Women and Business in the United States*. New York: Twayne Publishers.

LAIRD, PAMELA WALKER (1998). *Advertising Progress: American Business and the Rise of Consumer Society*. Baltimore: Johns Hopkins University Press.

LAMOREAUX, NAOMI R., RAFF, DANIEL M. G., and TEMIN, PETER (2003). "Beyond Markets and Hierarchies: Toward a New Synthesis of American Business History". *American Historical Review*, 108/2: 404–33.

LANDES, DAVID S. (1998). *The Wealth and Poverty of Nations: Why Some are So Rich and Some So Poor*. New York: W. W. Norton.

LEACH, WILLIAM (1993). *Land of Desire: Merchants, Power, and the Rise of a New American Culture*. New York: Pantheon Books.

LEARS, T. J. JACKSON (1994). *Fables of Abundance: A Cultural History of Advertising in America*. New York: Basic Books.

LIPARTITO, KENNETH (1995). "Culture and the Practice of Business History". *Business and Economic History*, 24/2: 1–42.

—— (2003). "The Social Construction of Failure: Picturephone and the Information Age", *Technology and Culture*, 44/1: 50–81.

—— and PETERS, CAROL HEHER (2001). *Investing for Middle America: John Elliott Tappan and the Origins of American Express Financial Advisors*. New York: St. Martin's Press.

MCKENDRICK, NEIL, BREWER, JOHN, and PLUMB, J. H. (1982). *The Birth of a Consumer Society: The Commercialization of Eighteenth-Century England*. Bloomington: Indiana University Press.

MANDELL, NIKKI (2002). *The Corporation as Family: The Gendering of Corporate Welfare 1890–1930*. Chapel Hill, NC: University of North Carolina Press.

MARCHAND, ROLAND (1985). *Advertising the American Dream: Making Way for Modernity 1920–1940*. Berkeley: University of California Press.

MARTIN, REINHOLD (2003). *The Organizational Complex: Architecture, Media and Corporate Space*. Cambridge, Mass.: MIT Press.

MATSON, CATHY (2004). "Introduction: The Ambiguities of Risk in the Early Republic," *Business History Review*, 78/4: 595–606.

MEIKLE, JEFFREY L. (1979). *Twentieth Century Limited: Industrial Design in America 1925–1939*. Philadelphia, Pa.: Temple University Press.

—— (1995). *American Plastic: A Cultural History*. New Brunswick, NJ: Rutgers University Press.

MERKLE, JUDITH A. (1980). *Management and Ideology: The Legacy of the International Scientific Management Movement*. Berkeley: University of California Press.

MILLER, MICHAEL B. (1981). *The Bon Marché: Bourgeois Culture and the Department Store 1869–1920*. Princeton, NJ: Princeton University Press.

MINTZ, SIDNEY (1985). *Sweetness and Power: The Place of Sugar in Modern History*. New York: Penguin Books.

Moskowitz, Marina (2004). *Standard of Living: The Measure of the Middle Class in Modern America*. Baltimore: Johns Hopkins University Press.

Nord, David Paul (1996). "Free Grace, Free Books, Free Riders: The Economics of Religious Publishing in Early Nineteenth-Century America". *Proceedings of the American Antiquarian Society,* 106/2: 241–72.

Nye, David E. (1979). *Henry Ford, Ignorant Idealist*. Port Washington, NY: Kennikat Press.

——(1985). *Image Worlds: Corporate Identities at General Electric 1890–1930*. Cambridge, Mass.: MIT Press.

——(1990). *Electrifying America: Social Meanings of a New Technology 1880–1940*. Cambridge, Mass.: MIT Press.

Ortner, Sherry B. (ed.) (1999). *The Fate of "Culture": Geertz and Beyond*. Berkeley: University of California Press.

Page, Max (1999). *The Creative Destruction of Manhattan, 1900–1940*. Chicago: University of Chicago Press.

Palmer, Alexandra (2001). *Couture and Commerce: The Transatlantic Fashion Trade in the 1950s*. Vancouver: University of British Columbia Press.

Papayanis, Nicholas (1996). *Horse-Drawn Cabs and Omnibuses in Paris: The Idea of Circulation and the Business of Public Transit*. Baton Rouge, La.: Louisiana State University Press.

Parthasarathi, Prasannan (2001). *The Transition to a Colonial Economy: Weavers, Merchants and Kings in South India, 1720–1800*. Cambridge: Cambridge University Press.

Partner, Simon (1999). *Assembled in Japan: Electrical Goods and the Making of the Japanese Consumer*. Berkeley: University of California Press.

Peiss, Kathy (2000). "On Beauty . . . and the History of Business". *Enterprise and Society,* 1/3: 485–506.

Peters, Thomas, and Waterman, Robert (1982). *In Search of Excellence: Lessons from America's Best-Run Companies*. New York: Harper & Row.

Pohl, Hans (2001). *Die rheinischen Sparkassen: Entwicklung und Bedeutung für Wirtschaft und Gesellschaft von den Anfängen bis 1990: Eine Veröffentlichung des Rheinischen Sparkassen- und Giroverbandes*. Stuttgart: F. Steiner.

Pope, Daniel (1983). *The Making of Modern Advertising*. New York: Basic Books.

Rabuzzi, Daniel A. (1995–6). "Eighteenth-Century Commercial Mentalities as Reflected and Projected in Business Hand Books". *Eighteenth-Century Studies,* 29/2: 169–89.

Rappaport, Erika (2000). *Shopping for Pleasure: Women and the Making of London's West End*. Princeton, NJ: Princeton University Press.

Rath, Jan (ed.) (1999). *Immigrant Business: The Economic, Political and Social Environment*. New York: St. Martin's Press.

Rilling, Donna J. (2001). *Making Houses, Crafting Capitalism: Builders in Philadelphia 1790–1850*. Philadelphia, Pa.: University of Pennsylvania Press.

Robinson, Daniel (2004). "Marketing Gum, Making Meanings: Wrigley in North America 1890–1930". *Enterprise & Society,* 5/1: 4–44.

Rosenband, Leonard N. (2000). *Papermaking in Eighteenth-Century France: Management, Labor, and Revolution at the Montgolfier Mill 1761–1805*. Baltimore: Johns Hopkins University Press.

Sandage, Scott A. (2005). *Born Losers: A History of Failure in America*. Cambridge, Mass.: Harvard University Press.

SCARPELLINI, EMANUELA (2004). "Shopping American-Style: The Arrival of the Supermarket in Postwar Italy". *Enterprise and Society,* 5/4: 625–68.

SCHAMA, SIMON (1987). *The Embarrassment of Riches: An Interpretation of Dutch Culture in the Golden Age.* New York: Knopf.

SCHATZBERG, ERIC (2003). "Symbolic Culture and Technological Change: The Cultural History of Aluminum as an Industrial Material". *Enterprise & Society,* 4/2: 226–71.

SCHEIN, EDGAR H. (2004). *Organizational Culture and Leadership,* 3rd edn. San Francisco: Jossey-Bass (1st edn., 1985).

SCHOENBERGER, ERICA J. (1997). *The Cultural Crisis of the Firm.* Cambridge, Mass.: Blackwell Publishers.

SCOTT, JOAN W. (1998). "Comment: Conceptualizing Gender in American Business History". *Business History Review,* 72/2: 242–9.

SCOTT, WILLIAM G. (1992). *Chester I. Barnard and the Guardians of the Managerial State.* Lawrence: University Press of Kansas.

SEWELL, WILLIAM (1991). "The Concepts of Culture", in Bonnell *et al.* (1999), 35–61.

SHEEHAN, BRETT (2003). *Trust in Troubled Times: Money, Banks and State-Society Relations in Republican Tianjin.* Cambridge, Mass.: Harvard University Press.

SHENHAV, YEHOUDA (1999). *Manufacturing Rationality: The Engineering Foundations of the Managerial Revolution.* Oxford: Oxford University Press.

SICILIA, DAVID (1995). "Cochran's Legacy: A Cultural Path Not Taken". *Business and Economic History,* 24/1: 27–40.

SILCOX, HARRY C. (1994). *A Place to Live and Work: The Henry Disston Saw Works and the Tacony Community of Philadelphia.* University Park: Pennsylvania State University Press.

SMAIL, JOHN (2003). "The Culture of Credit in Eighteenth-Century Commerce: The English Textile Industry". *Enterprise and Society,* 4/2: 299–325.

SMITH, ROBERT J. (2001). *The Bouchayers of Grenoble and French Industrial Enterprise 1850–1970.* Baltimore: John Hopkins University Press.

SPEARS, TIMOTHY B. (1995). *One Hundred Years on the Road: The Traveling Salesman in American Culture.* New Haven: Yale University Press.

STEARNS, PETER N. (2002). *Consumerism in World History: The Global Transformation of Desire.* New York: Routledge.

STOLARIK, MARK M., and FRIEDMAN, MURRAY (eds). (1986). *Making It in America: The Role of Ethnicity in Business Enterprise, Education and Work Choices.* Lewisburg, Pa.: Bucknell University Press.

SUNY, RONALD GRIGOR (2002). "Back and Beyond: Reversing the Cultural Turn". *American Historical Review,* 107/5: 1476–99.

TEDLOW, RICHARD (1990). *New and Improved: The Story of Mass Marketing in America.* New York: Basic Books.

TERRIO, SUSAN (2000). *Crafting the Culture and History of French Chocolate.* Berkeley: University of California Press.

TOBEY, RONALD C. (1996). *Technology as Freedom: The New Deal and the Electrical Modernization of the American Home.* Berkeley: University of California Press.

TONE, ANDREA (1997). *The Business of Benevolence: Industrial Paternalism in Progressive America,* Ithaca, NY: Cornell University Press.

TROY, NANCY J. (2004). *Couture Culture: A Study in Modern Art and Fashion.* Cambridge, Mass.: MIT Press.

TRUMPBOUR, JOHN (2002). *Selling Hollywood to the World: U.S. and European Struggles for Mastery of the Global Film Industry, 1920–1950*. New York: Cambridge University Press.

TSUTSUI, WILLIAM M. (1998). *Manufacturing Ideology: Scientific Management in Twentieth-Century Japan*. Princeton, NJ: Princeton University Press.

TURBIN, CAROL (2000). "Collars and Consumers: Changing Images of American Manliness and Business". *Enterprise & Society*, 1/3: 507–35.

WALKER, JULIET E. K. (1983). *Free Frank: A Black Pioneer on the Antebellum Frontier*. Lexington: University Press of Kentucky.

—— 1998). *The History of Black Business in America: Capitalism, Race, Entrepreneurship*. New York: Twayne.

WALTON, WHITNEY (1992). *France at the Crystal Palace: Bourgeois Taste and Artisan Manufacture in the Nineteenth Century*. Berkeley: University of California Press.

WEARE, WALTER B. (1973). *Black Business in the New South: A Social History of the North Carolina Mutual Life Insurance Company*. Urbana: University of Illinois Press.

WEBER, MAX (1958). *The Protestant Ethic and the Spirit of Capitalism*, trans. Talcott Parsons. New York: Charles Schribner's Sons.

WIENER, MARTIN J. (1981). *English Culture and the Decline of the Industrial Spirit 1850–1980*. New York: Cambridge University Press.

WILLIAMS, RAYMOND (1977). *Marxism and Literature*. Oxford: Oxford University Press.

WILLIAMS, ROSALIND, H. (1982). *Dream Worlds: Mass Consumption in Late Nineteenth-Century France*. Berkeley: University of California Press.

WINCH, JULIE (2001). "'A Person of Good Character and Considerable Property': James Forten and the Issue of Race in Philadelphia's Antebellum Business Community". *Business History Review*, 75/2: 261–96.

WOLOSON, WENDY (2002). *Refined Tastes: Sugar, Confectionery, and Consumers in Nineteenth Century America*. Baltimore: Johns Hopkins University Press.

WRIGHT, ROBERT E., and SMITH, GEORGE DAVID (2004). *Mutually Beneficial: The Guardian and Life Insurance in America*. New York: New York University Press.

ZEITLIN, JONATHAN, and HERRIGEL, GARY (eds.) (2000). *Americanization and its Limits: Reworking US Technology and Management in Post-War Europe and Japan*. Oxford: Oxford University Press.

ZELIZER, VIVIANA A. (1983). *Morals and Markets: The Development of Life Insurance in the United States*. New York; Columbia University Press.

ZUKIN, SHARON (2004). *Point of Purchase: How Shopping Changed American Culture*. New York: Routledge.

ZUNZ, OLIVIER (1990). *Making America Corporate, 1870–1920*. Chicago: University of Chicago.

INDEX

Harrod's 400
Hartmann, M. 583
Harvard Business Review 194–5
Harvard Graduate School of Business 75, 408
Harvard University 408
  Center for Research on Entrepreneurial History 69, 503–4, 505
  see also HBS
Harvey, Charles E. 44
haulage 251
Hausbanken 340
Hausman, William J. 39 n., 52 n.
haute couture 618
Hawker Siddeley 182
Hawthorne studies (1920s) 610
Haydu, Jeffrey 569 n.
HBS (Harvard Business School) 9, 97, 99, 596
  close personal networks with scholars at 591
  established (1908) 584
  executive programs 590
health 27
  history of 19
heavy industry 177, 181, 182, 282, 283, 340, 363, 428–9
  decline of 410
  meeting demand for large one-off products 389
HEC (*École des Hautes Etudes Commerciales*) 585, 587, 588, 597
hedging strategies 124, 127, 131
Hefner-Alteneck, Friedrich von 378, 379
Hegel, G. W. F. 131
hegemony 107, 310, 613, 614
Heineken 200
Heinrich, Thomas 225 n.
Heinz 403
heirs 203, 205
  strengthening of 304
Helper, Susan 51 n., 123 n., 127, 132 n., 234 n.
Henkel 433
Henley Management College 590
Hennart, Jean-François 49
Hepburn Act (US 1906) 540
Herrigel, G. 4, 107, 109, 121 n., 125 n., 221 n., 224 n., 227, 273, 510
Hertner, Peter 48
heterogeneity 488, 489, 490
Hewlett Packard 353, 358, 360
"hidden" goods 400
hierarchical position 81
hierarchical responsibilities 79

hierarchies 43, 74, 186, 244, 269, 377, 384
  borders between markets and 26
  command-and-control 263
  employment 428
  fully integrated enterprise 271
  gendered and educationally segmented 435
  imbalances 132
  intermediary 26
  job and promotion 427
  managerial 55, 174, 178, 183, 252, 331, 360, 427, 515, 517
  rules and 153
  social 464
  sophisticated 424
  wage and benefit 427, 431, 435
  white-collar 427
high-technology sectors 155
  benefit from government research expenditures 518
  contemporary regions 224
  districts 225 n.
  emergence of 307
  industrial collaboration 364
  producers 257
  qualified and experienced labor 82
  R&D in 357, 364
  start-ups 76, 501, 520
  war boost to industries 181
higher education 81
  big business active role in shaping form and content of 75
  European 593
  national systems of 591
  products of investments in 77
  strengthening national systems of 593
  strong belief in investment and expansion in 593
  transformation of 75, 82
Hikino, Takashi 130 n.
Hill, F. E. 10
hindsight abuse 129
Hindus 159
Hippel, Eric von 257, 264
hire purchase 414
hiring and firing 79, 80, 246, 260
  mid-career 84
  temporary blue-collar employees 85
Hirsch, Jean-Pierre 228
Hirst, Paul 121 n., 125 n., 129 n., 134 n., 220 n., 227 n.
"His Master's Voice" 403
Hishagi-Osaka 230
historical alternatives approach 120–40, 224